ASIAN INDUSTRIAL CLUSTERS, GLOBAL COMPETITIVENESS AND NEW POLICY INITIATIVES

ASIAN INDUSTRIAL CLUSTERS, GLOBAL COMPETITIVENESS AND NEW POLICY INITIATIVES

editors

Bernard Ganne

CNRS, University of Lyon, Institute of Human Sciences,
MODYS, France

Yveline Lecler

University of Lyon, Institute of Political Studies and
Institute of East Asian Studies, France

World Scientific

NEW JERSEY · LONDON · SINGAPORE · BEIJING · SHANGHAI · HONG KONG · TAIPEI · CHENNAI

Published by

World Scientific Publishing Co. Pte. Ltd.

5 Toh Tuck Link, Singapore 596224

USA office: 27 Warren Street, Suite 401-402, Hackensack, NJ 07601

UK office: 57 Shelton Street, Covent Garden, London WC2H 9HE

British Library Cataloguing-in-Publication Data
A catalogue record for this book is available from the British Library.

ISBN-13 978-981-4280-12-9
ISBN-10 981-4280-12-7

Typeset by Stallion Press
Email: enquiries@stallionpress.com

Printed in Singapore by Mainland Press Pte Ltd.

NA
(same as
back cover)

Foreword

This book provides the final findings of a research programme, "Industrial clusters in Asia: old forms, new forms", granted by the CPER (State/Region Contract Projects) within the framework of a contract with the French State and the Rhône-Alpes Region.

The programme was carried out under the direction of Bernard Ganne and Yveline Lecler by two research units of the University of Lyon and of the Centre National de la Recherche Scientifique/National Scientific Research Center (CNRS):

— The Glysi (Groupe Lyonnais de Sociologie Industrielle/Lyon Group of Industrial Sociology, which became MODYS: Mondes et Dynamiques des Sociétés/Worlds and Dynamics of Societies) of the ISH (Institut des Sciences de l'Homme/Institute of Social Sciences, Lyon), attached to the Lumière Lyon 2 University,
— and the IAO (Institut d'Asie Orientale/Institute of East Asian Studies), of the ENS LSH (Ecole Normale Supérieure Lettres et Sciences Humaines à Lyon), also attached to the Lumière Lyon 2 University.

The research which involved some 20 researchers and PhD students during four years, has led to surveys in China, Japan, Vietnam and Thailand. This work is the result of an international workshop held in Lyon at the end of 2006 entitled 'Industrial clusters in Asia'.

Contents

List of Figures

List of Tables

Contributors

Stephen J. APPOLD, *Professor of Sociology, University of North Carolina, USA.*

He is a *Senior Research Associate* at the Kenan Institute of Private Enterprises. His research interests include Economic Sociology, Sociology of Organization, Demography, Social Network, Southeast Asian Development, and Inter-group Relations.

Audrey BARON-GUTTY, *PhD student in Political Science, University of Lyon: Lyon 2 University and Institute of East Asian Studies (CNRS, ENS-LSH), France.*

She has done research on regional development, particularly in Thailand, and is currently involved in research on the impact of globalisation on national educational and training policies. Supported by a 2-years scholarship from IRASEC (Bangkok), she is conducting field research in Thailand.

Ke DING, *Research Fellow, Doctor of Economics, East Asian Studies Group, Area Studies Center of Institute of Developing Economies, Japan External Trade Organization (IDE-JETRO), Japan.*

His research interests concern issues in industrialization, industrial organization, SMEs, industrial clusters, and marketplaces. His study is inclined to clarify the China-specific factors of SME development through comparisons with the experiences of Japan and other developing countries.

Catherine FIGUIÈRE, *Associate Professor, Faculty Economics, University of Grenoble, and researcher at the LEPII (Laboratory of Production Economics and International Integration. CNRS Grenoble) France.*

Her work focuses on both the Japanese economy, particularly the role of industrial conglomerates before the WWII, and regional economic integration in East Asia. She has published a number of book chapters and papers in academic journal on these two issues. She also supervises PhD students in economics working on East-Asia.

Bernard GANNE, *Research Director, Sociology, CNRS and GLYSI/MODYS, University Lumière Lyon 2, France.*

He specialises in the sociology of firms and industrial systems of activity. He is a specialist in the development of industrial districts and clusters, first of all in Europe and more recently in Asia. In addition to writing articles and books, he is well-known for including film in his research.

Akira HATTORI, *PhD student in Political Science, University of Lyon: Lyon 2 University and Institute of East Asian Studies (CNRS, ENS-LSH), France.*

He wrote his Master thesis on Japanese Regional Revitalisation through Cluster Policy Measures. (2006). Since 2009 he is also associated doctoral student at the Research Institute of the French-Japanese House in Tokyo.

Patarapong INTARAKUMNERD, *Senior research Fellow, College of Innovation, Thammasat University, Thailand.*

He is a regional editor of International Journal of Technology and Globalisation and a member of international editorial boards of Science, Technology and Society Journal and Asian Journal of Technology Innovation. His research interest is on innovation systems in Thailand and newly-industrialising countries in Asia.

Elsa LAFAYE DE MICHEAUX, *Senior Lecturer in Economics, Centre d'Economie de la Sorbonne, Paris, and University of Angers, France.*

Her field of research is development studies from an institutional stand-point, focusing on Malaysia's economic growth in the twentieth century. She teaches Economics and Sustainable Development in Angers.

Her publications include *Institutions et développement,* (with Mulot, E., Ould-Ahmed P.) Rennes, Presses Universitaires de Rennes, 2007, and *Un tigre dans la mondialisation . La Malaisie,* un développement souverain?, 2009, forthcoming.

Yveline LECLER, Presently *Senior Research Fellow at the Research Institute of the French-Japanese House in Tokyo (CNRS IFRE 19). She is also permanent Research Fellow at the Institute of East Asian Studies (CNRS, ENS-LSH) and Associate Professor at the Institute of Political Studies, University of Lyon, France.*

She specialises in political economy and studied mostly Japan but also South East Asian economies, in particular Thailand. Her research interests include SMEs, industrial districts, subcontracting, inter-firms relationships as well as industrial or science and technology policy implementation on which she published several books or articles.

Tomoo MARUKAWA, *Professor of Economics, Institute of Social Science, University of Tokyo, Japan.*

His publications include Modern Chinese Industries (in Japanese, Chuo Koron Shinsha 2007), Tectonic Changes in China's Labour Market (in Japanese, Nagoya University Press, 2002), The Dynamics of Market Development in China (in Japanese, IDE-JETRO, 1999).

Mitsuharu MIYAMOTO, *Professor of Economics, Senshu University, Japan.*

His publications include 'A Theory of Corporate Systems' (in Japanese), Sineisha 2004, Korean edition, 2005); 'Japanese Firms and Employment' (co-edition JIL publisher, 2007), 'Toward the

Kawasaki Innovation Cluster' (Senshu Economic Journal N° 10, 2007). His major is a study of corporate system with a comparative view, and recently focused on the regional industrial policy for development of SMEs and start-ups.

Quy Nghi NGUYEN, *Doctor of Sociology, Social and Humanities Studies Group, Hanoi's Institute for Socio-Economic Development Studies (HISEDS), Hanoi, Vietnam.*

His research interests include craft village development, industrial agglomeration, SMEs development in Vietnam.

Quy Thanh NGUYEN, *Associate Professor of Sociology, College of Social Sciences and Humanities, Vietnam National University, Hanoi, Vietnam.*

His research areas are Sociology of mass communication and public opinion, Economic sociology and Methodology for social investigation.

Yoichi SEKIZAWA, *Analyst, Ministry of Economy, Trade and industry (METI), Japan.*

He is an analyst for Economic Partnership Agreements at METI. He worked for the Japan Regional Development Corporation from 1999 to 2001 and was an Associate Professor at the Institute of Social Science, University of Tokyo (2006–2007).

Lu SHI, *Assistant Professor of Chinese, Jean Moulin Lyon 3 University, France.*

She is a researcher at the Institute of East Asian Studies, Lyon, France. She studies the phenomenon of internal migration in China and social changes in SMEs, especially in the Zhejiang province.

Jean-Christophe SIMON, *Research Fellow, IRD, LEPII-CNRS, University of Marseille, France.*

He is Senior economist at the Institut de Recherche pour le Développement, Marseille, France. He has worked for twenty five years on development issues, particularly in Newly Industrialised/

Emerging Countries in Asia, currently as research fellow at LEPII-CNRS Grenoble. He has contributed to field research and public consultancy on overall planning, industrial development and entrepreneurship in African and East Asian countries. He teaches applied development economics at Grenoble and Paris universities.

Akira SUEHIRO, *Professor of Economics, and Director of Institute of Social Science, University of Tokyo, Japan.*

His work on Asian socio-economic development involves both archival and field research, and spans more than three decades. He has contributed to and edited twenty books, mostly in Japanese, in the last ten years, and has written Capital Accumulation in Thailand 1855–1985 (1989) and Catch-up Industrialisation: The Trajectory and Prospects of East Asian Economies (2008).

Jici WANG, *Professor of Economic Geography, Beijing University, China.*

Since 1985 she has been committed to studying Western theories of industrial geography. Much of her work has dealt with the development of science parks in China. During recent years she has been working on the geography of economic change, on the regional innovation system and on industrial clusters, especially in Zhejiang Province and the ZhongGuanCun area of Beijing.

Jun WANG, *Professor of Economics, Zhongshan University, Guangzhou, China.*

He was a Fulbright Scholar in the Sloan School of Management, MIT, USA (2005–2006). His research fields are Development Economics, Industrial Clusters and Regional Development and the Economics of Firms.

Jianniu XU, *Doctor of Sociology, Lecturer, Department of Sociology, Fudan University, Shanghai, China.*

His research areas are Economic Sociology; Sociology of Organisations; Industrial Clusters and Quantitative methods.

Takayuki YAMAGUCHI, *Professor of Economics, School of Business Administration, Kwansei Gakuin University, Japan.*

Among other works he has published recently (in Japanese), *A Study of SMEs: Theory and Policy*, Moriyamashoten, 2008, 'Challenges in Promoting Industrial Cluster Policy in France', in Nichi-futsu Keiei Gakkaishi, n° 25, 2008; 'The Present Condition and Problems of SMEs in Hyogo', in Nihon Keieishindangakkai (ed), Chusokigyo no Shomondai 2004; 'SMEs in the EU and the Challenges to their Policy', in MIYAMA, A. and KAIDO, N. (eds), 2004.

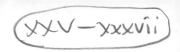

ydo

Book ti : Introduction

Bernard Ganne and Yveline Lecler

The research project, which outcomes are presented in this book, has started from the observation that definition and terminology used to classified industrial agglomeration had proliferated over time making the diverse concepts quite vague: industrial districts, localized specialization systems, village communities… and more recently overlapping all others, clusters.

The concept of cluster took its origin from the success of Silicon Valley that Saxenian (1994, 1998) has characterized as "decentralized regional network based on industrial system". This led Porter (1998) to review his diamond model (1990) to propose that of cluster-based competitiveness.

Governments using the concept as policy tool to promote competitiveness by innovation, clusters and poles of competitiveness, even if they develop on the basis of pre existing spontaneous industrial districts, appear as politico-economical constructs at the interface between sciences and technology on the one hand and production on the other hand. It is the reason why they are now at the core of National System of Innovation that they contribute to develop (case of emerging countries) or to restructure (case of advanced countries). But, these similar objectives do not preclude the form of organization which will remain as diversified, as this book will confirm.

The research main aim was therefore to question the theoretical approaches using three main models: industrial districts, industrial clusters, poles of knowledge or competitiveness through an overview of the case of Japan, China, Vietnam, Thailand and Malaysia.

What Can be Learned from Asian Industrial Clusters?

What can the industrial clusters of Asia teach us? At a time when the dynamics of the world's economy are leaning more and more towards Asia, the question takes on a particular relevance and deserves to be asked because of the explosion of clusters throughout Asia; and because of the different models which can be seen developing in the various countries:

— the emergence of new clusters in China and Thailand;
— the transformation of traditional systems of activity into new linkages ready for global production, as in Vietnam;
— the creation of agglomerations of specialised suppliers, as in Malaysia and Thailand;
— the development of new poles of competitiveness and the creation of scientific knowledge clusters as in Japan ...

The palette is varied, vast and certainly full of both theoretical and practical lessons for scientific analysts as well as practising of economy and policy makers.

Faced with this proliferation of models of organisation and dynamics of development, we may of course be tempted to reduce the varied phenomena we can observe in Asia to the models of the industrial districts and innovative clusters described by Porter, or the poles of competitiveness which are being developed in the advanced countries, and so on. However it is not at all certain that these classical approaches can account for the richness or the specificity of the developments observable during the last few years on the Asian continent. This is because, on the one hand, these analyses were constructed at an earlier era, when globalisation was not as widely developed and the competition it brought about less severe. On the other hand they emerged in specifically western socio-political contexts (the third Italy, Silicon Valley, etc.) which are not necessarily the most adequate to account for either the configurations we can observe in Asia, nor the vast upheavals, both quantitative and qualitative, we are faced with today.

While keeping in mind the approaches which have built up over time around the phenomena of the agglomeration of enterprises, our precise intention in this book is to carry out, with the help of the specialists of the various countries we have worked with (Japan, China, Thailand, Vietnam, Malaysia), a broad inventory of the modes of development and management of activities concentration which are emerging today, with the aim of gaining a renewed understanding of the phenomenon.

What phenomena of industrial concentration centred on a partic ular place and specialising in a particular activity can be observed in Asia? What role do these clusters play? What specific forms do they take? Finally, how do they put in question the appropriateness of the theoretical approaches which have developed over the last forty years around these questions? And what do they teach us about the policies and forms of intervention of the public sphere?

At a time when global economy is refocusing on the Asian side, it is all the more worth to learn from the observation of firms' agglomeration of this part of the world. Based on researches done by experts of and from some Asian countries significantly involved in such a dynamics, it is precisely the aim of this book which is the result from the international workshop held in Lyon and entitled: 'Industrial Clusters in Asia'.[1]

Based on this perspective we will start, in this presentation, by reviewing the various approaches which, over the last few decades — in the west and particularly in Europe — have centred around the localised concentration of enterprises and their impact on the economy and development. This will allow us later to emphasize more adequately the specificities observed in various Asian countries, the analysis of which remains at the core of this book.

Presentation of the Book

After the introduction presents the research aim and the book content, the first part will give a general overview of the theoretical framework (Part 1). Then, the book is divided into three other parts dealing with

---

[1] University of Lyon, November 29 to December 1, 2006; ENS–LSH (IAO) and ISH (MODYS).

Japan (Part 2), China (Part 3) and South-East Asia (Part 4), all from both empirical and theoretical points of view.

Part 1: Overview

In Chapter 1, Bernard Ganne and Yveline Lecler discuss first on the differentiated forms of conceptualisation: industrial districts, industrial clusters and poles of competitiveness. By summarising, the main findings of the research country by country, the authors then point out the lessons Europe may learn from the organisation and the implementation of clusters in Asia before tending to reconsider the theoretical approaches.

In Chapter 2, Akira Suehiro clarifies the two different policy frameworks for industrial development adopted by Japan and other East Asian countries in the past. The first framework deals with the industrial policy approach based on Japan's experience from the 1950s to the 1970s and which classifies industrial policy as being either industry-, issue- or area-specific. The second framework shows the industrial cluster approach which became more popular among East Asian countries after the 1990s. After the currency crisis in 1997, international financial institutions such as the World Bank tended to propose for the industrial cluster approach on the basis of the concept of 'innovation' in order to activate the industrial sector in crisis-hit countries. The Japanese government for its part was proposing for a more conventional approach, favouring industrial policy on the basis of the concept of 'international competitiveness', in order to restructure major manufacturing industries in general, and export-oriented industries in particular.

Using the experiences of Japan, South Korea, Taiwan and Thailand as examples the author discusses the difference between the two approaches in terms of targets, methodology, agents or players, sources of finance, economic environments, and finally attempts to analyse the results of these policies.

Comparing the two approaches in reference to past experiences he finally raises some theoretical implications concerning the possibilities and limitations of the cluster approach in East Asian countries.

Part 2: The Japanese Clustering Initiatives Approach — towards industrial poles of competitiveness and poles of knowledge.

This part is made up of four chapters which, taken together, gives an extensive view of what is at stake in a country which has developed a two-fold clustering approach on the basis of existing industrial or research potential. It shows how Japan uses cluster policies to rebuild competitiveness by developing new technologies and industries while at the same time revitalising through innovation regional areas and industrial districts that suffered from crisis and globalization. The first two chapters are more policy oriented while the following two centre on the groupings of small- and medium-sized enterprises, a major issue due to this sector's weight in the economy.

In Chapter 3, Akira Hattori focuses on Japanese government policies which led to or remained in association with cluster policies to address two issues: the revitalisation of industrial competitiveness (basically a regional issue) and the promotion of innovation. After outlining the legal framework he details the two types of cluster initiatives implemented in the 2000s, discussing their coordination and governance using case studies carried out on Kyushu Island.

In Chapter 4, Yoichi Sekizawa analyses the development of Industrial Parks through the mission of the Japan Regional Development Corporation in the 1990s. Japanese local government politicians from rural areas put pressure on central government to develop Industrial Parks which were regarded at the time as an effective policy for regional development. However, although some of them succeeded, many remained unsold or unused in many areas of Japan, leading to various problems such as financial crisis in certain local government areas, unnecessary destruction of the environment and an added burden on taxpayers. This policy, later recognised as a failure, shows that the theoretical assessment that clusters should not be developed by government policies but only strengthened and developed on the basis of pre-existing potential, is fully justified, but is however difficult to maintain in practice. All regions dream of becoming Silicon Valleys, and even some rural areas with no foundation of industry clusters want to get on the bandwagon.

In Chapter 5, Yveline Lecler and Takayuki Yamaguchi concentrate on small businesses and former industrial districts or *jibasangyô*. Based on a detailed analysis of the reasons why they are falling behind, they emphasise the need for innovation which led to the setting up of clusters, not only at national but also at regional and local levels. Although some of the initiatives concretely observed by the authors are not designated as clusters under the government policy framework, the case studies described show how the cluster concept, implying cooperation between industry, universities and government (*San-Gaku-Kan*), is used to address the difficulties that districts are facing. Comparing the new configurations which emerge from cluster policies with former industrial districts and from the point of view of the pattern of cooperation, they conclude that the shift from resource-based clusters or *jibasangyô* to knowledge-based clusters (innovative clusters of SMEs) might be interpreted as a necessary qualitative shift that agglomerations located in regional areas have to engage in to survive.

In Chapter 6, Mitsuharu Miyamoto discusses the results of a large survey carried out on Kawasaki just outside the city limits of Tokyo. Kawasaki is a typical Japanese industrial city with large manufacturing enterprises (electronics) around which a huge number of subcontracting SMEs have gathered. The numerous industrial districts they formed are facing difficulties, since large enterprises have relocated production to other regions in Japan or to China while occasionally transforming their Kawasaki plants into research centres. Kawasaki appears as a pioneer in promoting the city's industrial rebirth by creating a large scale innovative cluster. The issue addressed by the author is how SMEs can develop their businesses to become actors in this innovative cluster. Small businesses have to change their role from that of subcontractors to that of in-house product manufacturers, therefore they have to develop new products and improve profits by strengthening their bargaining power. Through regression analysis the author attempts to point out the determinants to achieve these goals by taking into account the importance of employing development and sales staff, of consulting with universities or with the Chamber of Commerce, suppliers, banks and so on. But finally the survey shows that what is needed is development-type SMEs.

Part 3: China. The Specificities of Chinese Industrial Clusters: their Importance and Weaknesses

This part is made up of six chapters which give an overview of the various types of development observed in industrial districts in China, describe the very particular specificities of some Chinese clusters and point out their problems and difficulties.

In Chapter 7, Jici Wang describes the new phenomena and the challenges of clusters in China and points out their main difficulties in the new era of globalisation.

She notes at the beginning how the theoretical underpinning of the deluge of cluster studies in the world is not clear to China and confutes the conventional wisdom that the location of the existing manufacturing capacities in China is mainly based on the low labour costs which is the sole source of manufacturing advantage. Based on a description of the Chinese cluster phenomenon she attempts to make four points. The first deals with the claim that Chinese clusters are the result of global-local tension. She observes on the one hand how the breathtaking speed of geographical dispersion has been combined with spatial concentration. On the other she points out how, in this context, the 'race to the bottom' that is observed between the clusters could be dangerous.

The second point concurs with the view that a value chain could thread through multiple clusters in different localities of a regional economy. The key task facing China should be to foster innovative clusters instead of building more 'low road' ones.

In her third point, Wang Jici concludes that a theory of clusters must do more than provide an account for the benefits of collocation and also explains the conditions that may lead to the progress, decline or extinction of the cluster.

Furthermore, in her fourth point, she explains that while cluster-based economic policy has a lot of potential, it is not a panacea for seeking to position local industries in the global value chain and in the global market.

In Chapter 8, Tomoo Marukawa analyses very precisely the emergence of industrial clusters in a region of China.

After an overview of the studies of the particular experiences of development in Wenzhou city since the economic reform, the author analyses the emergence of and later, the dominance of private enterprises in the city. He shows the effectiveness of 'the Wenzhou Model' and its specificities. In the first section, he describes how Wenzhou has a diverse array of industrial clusters ranging from leather shoes to electric parts, buttons, clothing, automobile parts, valves, cigarette lighters and many others. He describes the diversity of Wenzhou's industries and tries to understand why so many industrial clusters have emerged there.

In the second section, he develops a very precise methodology to describe the phenomenon. In the third section, he establishes a comprehensive map of Wenzhou's industrial clusters. In the fourth, he analyses the emergence of some typical industrial clusters.

In Chapter 9, Bernard Ganne and Lu Shi deal with the specificities of the development of the Zhejiang clusters.

In their first section, they show how industrial clusters play a particularly important role in the rapid industrial development that China is experiencing and how, among these, the Zhejiang clusters, characterised by the significant development of highly specialised production zones linked to both the national and global economies, present a unique form of dynamism. In the second section, they attempt to determine the unique features of these clusters in relation to traditional approaches. They show that, far from being based solely on the optimisation of production systems, it is the existence of wide-ranging commercial organisations at a local and regional level that makes the Zhejiang clusters so efficient. They suggest finally that the traditional approaches to the theory of clusters may require at least partial reconsideration.

In Chapter 10, Ke Ding analyses the distribution system of China's industrial clusters, describing very clearly the history and development of a merchant cluster. At first he shows how at the beginning of the 1980s a number of traditional marketplaces began to appear inside the industrial clusters in China. These markets within the clusters become connected to those in the cities due to interaction between traditional merchants and local government. He analyses how this has resulted in the formation of a powerful network based market distribution system which has played a crucial role for China's industrial clusters in responding to her exploding domestic demand. Using Yiwu China Commodity City as a case study he explains the features of this distribution system in detail, and the specificities of this kind of merchant cluster.

In Chapter 11, Jianniu Xu focuses on the local government's role in local economic development and rural industrialisation. From the perspective of sociology's new institutionalism he describes how local governments are engaged in the development of industrial districts. He shows through case study how, in the development of an industrial district in which the main economic actors are private companies, local government does not act as an entrepreneur inside the enterprise but as a broker outside the enterprise. He points out several reasons for this orientation in the government's role: fiscal decentralisation which stimulates the government to promote the development of the local economy, the rise of private businesses, the property rights of the corporation, the weakness of intermediary organisations and the size and capacity of the enterprises. From these observations, Jianniu Xu concludes that we are seeing in China the emergence of a 'new state local corporatism'.

In Chapter 12, Jun Wang deals with the question of interaction and innovation in cluster development. If local technological institutions can be regarded as the gateway of knowledge from outside in the clusters that lack both external resources and large firms, how can they be effective in supporting small businesses to innovate? Through observing two cases in Guandong he examines the processes of interaction for innovation between small businesses and TIC. Based on a model of supporting mechanism, he expounds the evolutional mechanism and determining factors, and draws some conclusions as the fundamental condition that an institutional context can be either necessary or effective for formal innovation. He points out further consequences and orientations.

Part 4: Clusters and the Building of Competitiveness in Emerging Countries: Some Evidence from South East Asia

This part is made up of five chapters, taking either Vietnam, Thailand or Malaysia as their fields of study to analyse the specificities of agglomerations that can be found (craft villages or industrial districts, industry-wide or geographically localised clusters). They take into account and focus on the level of industrialisation of the country, the development of the NSI, the skills of manpower, and of course policies implemented or even the strategies of the multinationals involved.

In Chapter 13, Quy Nghi Nguyen[2] explores the transition from craft villages to clusters in Vietnam: Transition through Globalisation.

He notes at the beginning how in Vietnam few research works treated craft villages as a form of agglomeration. Based on a deep quantitative and qualitative study of porcelain and ceramic craft work which is emerging today as an industrial district, he examines the rapid transition from an old district producing low quality products for a mainly domestic market to becoming one of the biggest suppliers of ceramic/porcelain products not only for the domestic but also for a large international market. He shows the reorganisation of the social actors involved in district development and how relations between these various actors need redefining in order to fit into the new rules of the game

---

[2] An earlier version of this paper was presented at the international conference 'Asian industrial clusters: new and old forms', Lyon, 29–30 November and 1 December 2006. The author would like to express his gratitude to Bernard Ganne, Research Director, Philippe Bernoux, Research director (MODYS, CNRS) for their comments.

better. He analyses the overlaps between traditional and modern industrial districts and the emergence of new institutions (public power, associations, enterprise clubs that shape district development). In conclusion he discusses the new stakes and new difficulties.

In Chapter 14, Stephen J. Appold and Nguyen Quy Thanh ask about the real role of social embedding in the success of Vietnamese industrial clusters, the need for reform and rapid economic growth, suggesting that the use of informal mechanisms of economic regulation such as social embeddedness are widespread. But the empirical enquiries carried out in small businesses in North and South Vietnam show that social embedding is in fact limited and that important exchanges and activities are undertaken without being socially embedded. Moreover, the need for performance monitoring does not appear to affect the level of interaction among business partners, and families (socially embedded actors) are not especially reliable sources of help, and when this help exists it appears to be expensive. In contrast they remark that a business provides a focus for family activities and thereby strengthens relationships. They conclude that there is not necessarily a causal link from social embeddedness through proximity benefits leading to financial success. They finally raise the question of extending the theory of industrial agglomeration by documenting the use of social embedding to regulate economic exchanges.

In Chapter 15, Audrey Baron-Gutty, Catherine Figuière and Jean-Christophe Simon suggest that several types of clusters have to be identified in Thailand in order to understand both their origins, specific dynamics and impact on the overall economy and national competitiveness. Matching some field observations (the cluster of Chaiyaphum, initiated by the Department of Industrial Promotion) and documented cases (in Chiang Mai Province) with cluster theory originating from advanced economies, they identified three categories of clusters, according to the sector linkages and to their economic and social embeddedness, namely 'tradi-clusters', 'neo-clusters' and 'plani-clusters'.

In Chapter 16, Patarapong Intarakumnerd focuses particularly on the Thai cluster policy initiative which aims at rectifying weaknesses and the fragmentation of the country's national system of innovation (NSI). He uses four case studies of clusters which are very different in terms of technological sophistication and business objectives (hard disk drives, bus body assembly, software, and chilli paste) to elucidate successful and unsuccessful aspects of clusters in Thailand. Pointing out the positive impacts on Thailand's NSI (selective industrial policy, more coherent policy implementation, more cooperation between firms and with other agents) the author also shows the problems which remain (misconception and confusion concerning the concept of clusters among policy makers and business leaders), while emphasising the importance of intermediaries in the process.

In Chapter 17, Elsa Lafaye de Micheaux studies the case of Penang, Malaysia's famous cluster. Chosen in 1970 as a location by major American semiconductor firms strongly supported by the local administration, then followed by Japanese and Taiwanese electronic companies, Penang has emerged as the 'Silicon Valley of South-East Asia'. Although Malaysia's national innovation system remains weak, due to a shortage of skilled manpower and a low level of research and development, Penang's territory seems to escape these constraints. From field surveys, monographs and local statistics, the author identifies what has been determinant in the choice of location and shows that human resources are playing an important role in the long-lasting success of the cluster. She explains how labour enrolment, turnover and training have contributed to Penang's industrialisation and development. These elements also foster the exchange of information as well as the creation of subcontractors and technical help within the cluster. The sustainability of Penang's competitiveness in the next decade is however under question due to the erosion of comparative advantages.

References

PORTER, Michael (1990). *The Competitive Advantage of Nations*, Macmillan and Basingstoke.

PORTER, Michael (1998). Clusters and the new economics of competition, *Harvard Business Review*, Novembre–December, pp. 77–90.

SAXENIAN, Anne Lee (1994). *Regional Advantage: Culture and Competition in Silicon Valley and Route 128*, Harvard University Press.

SAXENIAN, Anne Lee (1998). Regional system of innovation and the blurred firm, in de la Mothe, J., Paquet, G. (eds.), *Local and Regional Systems of Innovation*, Kluwer Academic Publishers.

Part One

Overview

Chapter 1

From Industrial Districts to Poles of Competitiveness

Bernard Ganne and Yveline Lecler

Behind the reflections concerning the concentration of enterprises and the enthusiasm for clusters lies the question of the efficiency of the forms of industrial activity, with the postulate that if companies are grouped or concentrated they will turn out to be more efficient than ones which are more dispersed or more thinly spread out. A. Miller had already located the problem but, with industrial reconstruction and more severe global competition in the last thirty years, thinking on this subject has become extremely diversified to the point of producing three major types of models for understanding these concentrations: industrial districts, clusters and poles of competitiveness.

We need to say a few words about these various approaches if only to clarify the terminology which is often very vague, using the word 'clusters' to cover agglomerations or concentrations of activity which used to be analysed using different terms ('industrial districts', 'localized production systems', but also 'village communities' and so on). The term clusters is also used to designate the policies covering the geographical agglomeration of enterprises or innovative poles. When these terms are put back into context they reveal themselves to be both specific and differentiated.

If we wish to locate the specificity of what can be observed in Asia it would be useful to start from these differences.

3

1.1 From Industrial Districts to Poles of Competitiveness via Industrial Clusters: Three Models of a Conceptual Approach

From industrial districts to poles of competitiveness via industrial clusters, analysis of the grouping of companies has grown and complexified constantly over the last forty years. One might think that by dint of widening its scope the concept has lost some of its strength or even led to confusion, mixing up realities of very different levels which need to be distinguished. It could also be considered that each of these approaches has chosen one of the three essential dynamics which characterise one form of development of the agglomeration of companies: endogenous local development for the districts; innovation for clusters as such; the central role of modes of governance for the poles of competitiveness. All of these are in fact so many complementary facets of a single dynamic at work, seeking to define itself.

The idea here is less to enclose ourselves in rigid definitions than to grasp in a dynamic way the history of the construction of these forms, the contexts and universes in which they can be seen, under the different definitions they have worn through time. We may then be in a better position to clarify the different interpretations which may be made of Asian clusters and their particularities.

Over forty years the perception of the agglomeration of enterprises has constantly broadened both in space (which country today has not got its clusters or poles of competitiveness to show off?), and through time; we have gone from 'industrial districts' to 'industrial clusters', and with the growth of global competition we have added to the panoply the development of 'poles of competitiveness' and so on. These notions, all of which are called upon to account for real or virtual forms of development, are very different from each other. One might even be tempted to think that bringing them together can only lead to confusion. After all, there is little in common between 'Italian industrial districts' and the gigantic poles of competitiveness which are being set up today in many developed or emerging countries.

This is in fact true, and it is important to distinguish the different levels of analysis, if only to understand how these notions formed a chronological chain which ended up producing (in precise economic contexts) specific configurations of activity, each of which, at its own level and in its own context maintains its own particular originality.

From districts to poles of competitiveness via clusters; we are making a wide sweep of the field of all the major forms of economic dialogue and local organisations which are still seeking to define themselves in order to continue to develop dynamic and competitive structures of production.

What kind of local economic structuring do these varied notions produce and what forms of relations between the local and the global do they produce?

1.1.1 *First of all 'Industrial Districts'*

They were born in the Italian context which is well known and first and foremost they showed us the pre-eminence of the local organisation of activities, the importance of inter-company cooperation, the strength of informal as much as formal links and the original dynamics produced by a system which combined cooperation and competition.

The industrial districts bore witness to the advantage of grouping small businesses together in terms of the local accumulation of skills, the great flexibility and adaptability of this system of small structures of specialised production working together, as well as the creative efficiency of these groups of entrepreneurs which developed autonomously, sometimes outside the system of public intervention.

They recalled the social basis, indissoluble and structural, of any economic action, the surprising efficiency of informal relations and *the importance of shared social capital as the very basis of endogenous development.*

It is true that the approach used to analyse industrial districts makes little mention of markets, marketing or outside competition; it remains focused on the company and looks mainly at the world of production.

To a certain extent it buries itself in the local situation, ignoring the fact that too many local links can, at a certain moment, lead a locality to close in on itself and perish, as was seen in many countries.

The social capital of a zone only remains efficient if the local organisation remains in active touch with the exterior, to organise itself, to handle difficulties, to link up with the adequate branches and so on. However that may be, the 'industrial districts approach' puts the emphasis on local links, both formal an informal, aiming above all to account for the phenomena of endogenous development through the interplay of essentially internal competition/cooperation among the economic players. It is true to say that markets at that time were not very concentrated and were rather noticeable by their rarity. Competition had not yet become as widespread or aggressive as in the 80s and 90s.

1.1.2 Industrial Clusters

It was in the 90s that the very successful reflection around 'industrial clusters' was developed, precisely to account for the challenges of external competition and markets, and to find solutions.

The emphasis was less on examining the essentially endogenous development of small entities which were coordinated informally, as was the case with the industrial district approach, and much more on groups of enterprises, small or big, developing more and more formalised links, both horizontally and vertically, in order to structure specialised and competitive entities, allowing them to face up to competition. In order to develop and stand out among its competitors, these groups of enterprises, which were strongly structured locally but connected to both internal and external networks, had to enter a dynamic of innovation, mobilising thus the economic actors and other institutional actors in research, training or administration. We are clearly a long way from the endogenous local districts of the Beccatini type.[1] The key words of Porter's[2] clusters thus become

---

[1] Cf. Giacomo Beccatini, one of the founding thinkers of the theory of Italian industrial districts.

[2] Cf. Michael Porter, theoretician of industrial cluster.

'enterprises', 'competition', 'specialisation', 'innovation', and 'high-tech network', with innovation occupying the central dynamic space. The centre of gravity remains the enterprise, but it is an enterprise faced with the competitive market, which mobilises all the resources of its environment, both economic (customers, subcontractors) and local (research and organisational resources) *to maintain its specificity and difference through innovation*. The 'local' level is considered less as creating its own dynamics than as a condition for these connections and synergies, the other institutional entities of research and local management being perceived as being subordinate to the primordial dynamic of innovation: another era, another universe, another concept.

1.1.3 *Poles of Competitiveness*

With the poles of competitiveness another change of register takes place. It is no longer enough for enterprises simply to organise themselves to innovate. At this stage the essential thing for enterprises, as for local and regional government is to coordinate with each other and reach agreement to set up, around specialised activities, powerful regional developments aiming to reach the world production chain of value, thus claiming global excellence by organising around a large local pole, all the various actors of a particular sector: firms, research organisations, teaching and training institutes, specialist management services and so on. In fact it means setting up powerful schemes and developments which are attractive and able to use multiple synergies which can decompartmentalise both sectors and actors (public/private, production/services, basic and applied research, economic management and management of innovation, etc.) so as to accumulate around a given sector strong potentialities and broad dynamics which allow the poles to present themselves as major benchmarks capable of holding their own not only nationally but globally.

The key words in this perspective are now competitiveness, global networks, attractiveness, and especially *governance*, the main problem of these new poles being to maintain the coordination of a large number of different actors at all levels.

Three great models for the agglomeration of enterprises, which refer thus to three distinct universes, determining three forms of understanding and three types of action and intervention, with the following key words:

— For districts: informal links, social capital, endogenous local development.
— For clusters: competition, specialisation, innovation.
— For poles of competitiveness: global competitiveness, attractiveness, governance.

With these three broad approaches in mind, what can we learn from the phenomena observed in Asia?

1.2 What Asian Clusters Teach Us

The agglomerations observed in Asia upset the apple cart. Their variety leads us to think about the great diversity of possible types of industrial organisation to achieve performance and competitiveness. Through their evolution, they also show us the fragility and limitations of each of these forms of organisation. They help us to question the theoretical approaches which have been accepted up till now.

What then is the situation of the agglomerations of enterprises in each of the countries studied: Vietnam, China, Japan and Thailand?

1.2.1 *Vietnam*

With more than a hundred clusters listed,[3] especially in clothing, textile and paper, Vietnam seems to have developed a very specific structuring of the agglomeration of its enterprises. The country is marked by the

---

[3] In 2004 there were 106 zones of all kinds in Vietnam, covering an area of 20233 hectares having attracted 1442 investment projects with a registered capital of $11.390 million of which 29% were from abroad (Tuan, 2005).

great vitality of craft villages and a greater grouping of its enterprises into poles of specialised activity than in other countries, giving rise today to a great variety of types of groupings of its enterprises.

1.2.1.1 *The Weight of Craft Activities and Craft Villages Clusters*

Craft activities sometimes go back a long way in Vietnam and are numerous today. In particular they are often organised on the basis of localised groupings especially in the Red River delta. These artisan (or craft) villages, some of which have lasted for several centuries in sectors such as ceramics, basketwork or textiles have modernised recently and have had a real boom which constitutes one of the great specificities of the country. With the *doi moi*,[4] the craft villages have taken on a new lease of life and are attempting to develop towards the national or even international markets.

It is a massive phenomenon and furnishes a solid basis of possibilities for going from the artisan phase to forms of enterprise or small businesses which are more organised and to more structured local dynamics. That in any case is the direction in which things are already going, in a context of greater division of labour and subcontracting, by most of the family businesses with little capacity to invest.

But contrary to Chinese industrial clusters, the craft village clusters in Vietnam work with totally national investment (mainly family, but some bank loans). There is no foreign investment as there is in China. This may explain the low level of production of the majority of the enterprises and their still informal character (80% are not declared). It is clear in any case that this craft structure constitutes a very specific social matrix for the economic development of the agglomeration of enterprises, and that the various implications of this model deserve to be studied with as much attention as that paid to the Italian industrial districts in Europe.

---

[4] In 1986 Vietnam liberalised all the sectors of the economy of the country under the policy of *doi moi* or 'renewal'.

1.2.1.2 *A Specific Mode of Allocation of the Clusters*

Clusters in Vietnam have developed greatly, but their distribution appears quite original. As recent studies carried out by Japanese researchers comparing Vietnam, China and Japan have shown (3and Tsuji, 2003), the grouping of enterprises by poles of activity turns out to be greater in Vietnam than elsewhere. This is due in particular to the influence exercised by the main urban poles, Hanoi and Haiphong in the north, Ho Chi Minh City in the south, which all in fact include, in a very wide sphere of influence, numerous clusters, notably in sectors like clothing, paper, fish factories, textiles, etc.[5] So the cluster phenomenon in Vietnam appears to be clearly influenced by the availability of access to land and the search for nearby infrastructure rather than employment or other variables. This produces a quite unique economico-spatial network.

1.2.1.3 *The Diversity of the Districts*

There are craft districts and also more urban small business districts, in different sectors of traditional or more recent industries. If we add to these the parks of suppliers and high technology zones, we can see that Vietnam today possesses a wide range of types of clusters, even if the term is a new one in the country.

A certain number of studies have attempted to classify this diversity. Whether it be the work of the IDE-JETRO 2002 programme (see above), or that completed in 2004 by Riedel and Ricord, we can state that researchers agree to recognise four different types of clusters in Vietnam:

— Local industrial districts organised and specialised locally around the production of a specific product.
— Districts or clusters characterised by a concentration of various firms subcontracting for a large enterprise (or 'industrial castle-town', which may be built up around a large state enterprise).

---

[5] The analysis is geographic, based on the GIS (Geographic Information System).

— Industrial clusters of small businesses made up of so many nuclei of specialised production; in large towns, centred around basic production.

— Industrial parks created and run by the government, very often with a high-tech connotation, notably in the spheres of information sciences and software. About twenty high-tech clusters are projected both in the north and the south.

— Craft villages refer to specific dynamics of agglomeration; particular forms of networks between specialised rural, peri-urban or urban zones; all these points refer to specific modes of embeddedness of the activities and agglomerations of enterprises which go well beyond the classical approaches and should allow us to enrich their comprehension.

The case of China provides us with other lessons.

1.2.2 *The Emergence of Clusters in China*

One of the keys to the industrial dynamics of China in the last few years comes without a doubt from the agglomeration of specialised enterprises which have sprung up over fifteen years in extremely varied forms, deeply affecting the development of certain regions. These agglomerations of enterprises make up an important part of the competitive power of the country both in traditional industries and the high technology sectors.

1.2.2.1 *Varied Forms of Clusters*

As we know the movement has been tremendously powerful. To take only a few examples, at the beginning of the twenty first century a quarter of the 404 administrative towns in the Pearl River delta in Guangdong made up as many clusters of specialised activity. The province of Zhejiang possesses for its part more than 300 zones of specialised activity which, in their production, enter what we might call the 'world top ten' in their category and more than a hundred others in second position, all of this of course without mentioning the impressive development of the high-tech zones.

The large body of research in China has tried to classify the different agglomerations of enterprises, by distinguishing for example[6]:

1. The agglomeration of traditional firms, the origins of which predate the reforms. They are highly integrated systems which can be fond in rural zones in the course of urbanisation or in small towns, mainly mono-industrial in consumer goods (Zhejian and Fujian provinces).
2. The agglomeration of foreign firms, mainly from Taiwan, Hong Kong and Singapore and which incorporate a certain number of other firms with whom they work (Guangdong and Shandong provinces). Some investors occasionally bring their own suppliers with them, so that a complete network moves to the Continent. This is notably the case of Taiwanese entrepreneurs.
3. High technology zones usually situated in the large cities and near university complexes (the Zhonguancun district in Beijing; the fibre optic cluster in Wuhan).
4. The agglomerations of small businesses grouped around big enterprises, as can be seen near the shipbuilding works in Shanghai and, more recently around the car industry in Wuhan, and so on.

But more even than the sheer size of the phenomenon, it is the expansion of these zones which is at the origin of the specific and original developments which classical perspectives of analysis have a certain difficulty to account for.

1.2.2.2 *Specific Operating Models*

If in fact the agglomerations of enterprises which can be observed in China seem in their form and appearance to be comparable to western industrial districts and clusters, if only from the simple fact of the concentration in a circumscribed territory of activities of the same

---

[6] Here we use the typology proposed by Professor Wang Jici in his work (2001): *Chuangxin de Kongjian* (Innovative Spaces: Enterprise Clusters and Regional Development).

type, they are in fact fundamentally different in many ways: weak links between the enterprises; major structuring role of commercial activity, which drags the productive activity along, so to speak, indirect and complex modes of socio-political regulation. We see at work here an entirely different universe than the one generally grasped by the classical approaches we have mentioned.

Brought up on the postulate of the efficiency of local dialogue between enterprises supposedly (in classical theory) bringing about an increase in efficiency due to the formal and informal links that have been forged, it is all the more astonishing to realise that what seems to prevail in a certain number of Chinese clusters (like those in Zhejiang for example) is not only the absence links of direct cooperation between enterprises, but downright mistrust. Moreover, it is much less the efficiency of production itself (dear to the classical theoreticians of districts) which seems to be the driving force of these zones, but rather their entry into the commercial networks which motivates them. But isn't that the role of merchant clusters — with their very specific role and organisation — to connect the agglomeration of enterprises to national opportunities and wider international networks?

And the question of the relationship to the territory and the endogenous/exogenous dynamics become even more complex in the case of technological clusters which, particularly with NTIC seem to point to the possibility to free themselves from the local, geographical dimension.

So, beyond the apparent similarities with hitherto known clusters, there is another configuration emerging in China which is not only economic but also social and political, for which only plural methodologies and broadened theoretical approaches can account. But there is an important paradox. Chinese social configurations do not have 'an easily usable equivalent'. If it is true that we can detect in the agglomeration of enterprises which are emerging analogies with proto-industrial forms or with the manufacturing model, the contemporary paradox is that it is the forms of economic organisation, which are apparently old fashioned or even regressive, which appear today to be efficient in an economy which is wide open to the global

economy: is it the paradox of the modular economy that we are seeing today (Berger, 2005) and the possible new spaces that are thus
opening up? We need to return to this later.

1.2.3 *Japan*

Japan offers us another spectrum of particularities due to the historic
roots of the phenomenon, thanks to the *jibasangyô*, and especially to
the recent important changes which have accompanied the setting up
of clusters up to the present poles of competitiveness.

1.2.3.1 *Historical Particularities: Industrial Districts and the Importance of Small Businesses*

Japan developed various craft agglomerations as far back as the Edo
era (1603–1868) which were extended after the restoration of Meiji
and especially after the WWII. These Japanese industrial districts
composed of numerous small businesses and known as *jibasangyô*, had
to restructure and improve their technological capacities in order not
to be left behind in the race for technical progress and keep in line
with the country's level of development. Thanks to the 'disappear-
ances/creations' of enterprises which worked very well until the 80s
and even constituting one of the factors of Japan's rapid adaptation,
whole districts were able to go from a 'traditional' specialisation
to a more modern industry without the number of small businesses
diminishing; quite the opposite. However from the 80s the mechanisms of restructuring no longer seemed to work. With the
globalisation of activities, and in particular the competition from
China and the countries of Southeast Asia, as well as the crisis of the
90s, small businesses found themselves in difficulty, even threatening
the survival of certain industrial districts. Japan's problem lies not so
much in the fact that the small businesses are finding it difficult to
keep up with globalisation or that certain industrial districts are dis-
appearing; that is the fate of many developed countries, particularly
in Europe (Galés *et al.*, 2002). It lies in the fact that, because the
small businesses make up 99% of Japan's manufacturing industry and

employ two thirds of the manpower in the sector, their problems have had a massive impact on employment and regional spaces' vitality. This has led government to pass, since the 70s, laws specifically aimed at the small businesses and industrial districts in order to revitalise regions which are falling behind. Integrating territorial management concerns the aim was to energise certain sectors of the economy[7] by setting up growth poles in the regions, establishing technopoles, or industrial research parks and so on.

These policies had mixed results though. They did come up against certain limits due to mismatches between central and local governments (prefectures, municipalities) often leading to a rather irrational choice of projects and localisations (the strength of lobbies…), and posing real problems of governance in the networking attempts of multiple actors.

1.2.3.2 *From Industrial Districts to Poles of Competitiveness and Knowledge*

While remaining in line with the former industrial policy, the cluster initiatives implemented at the beginning of the 2000s led to transforming it more and more into innovation policies.

To favour the spread of knowledge and therefore innovation the directive was to set up networks of all the actors and in particular to strengthen the links between public and private research and industry (*San Gaku Kan* or triple helix). Following simultaneously two objectives, two programmes have been independently set up.

In 2001 the METI (Ministry of Economy, Trade and Industry) launched the 'industrial cluster plan' to revitalise regional areas which were having problems, by fostering innovation. Well beyond the problems of small businesses, the objective was to guarantee the collaboration and networking of all the agents necessary for innovation, so as to create real poles of competitiveness on the basis of existing potential.

---

[7] High tech industries having to take over from heavy industry, badly damaged by the oil shock crisis.

In 2002 the MEXT (Ministry of Education, Culture, Sports, Science and Technology) launched the 'cluster initiative' aiming more directly at promoting the emergence of new clusters, known as 'knowledge clusters' in the industries of the future. The two initiatives were complementary, but going in reverse directions. The industries in the cluster were supposed to submit their needs to the research sector in the METI case, whereas in the MEXT, it was the research sector which offered its results (seeds) to entrepreneurs. To synchronise the whole, the Japanese government set up a unit to coordinate the two types of clusters in order to avoid duplication, risks of conflict, or too fierce competition.

The case of Japan is full of lessons for us. It shows that starting from its own pre-existing conditions which might be considered as path dependencies:

— the historical existence of a large number of industrial districts (not only of the Marshal or Becattini type) which have demonstrated over time their capacity to adapt and develop,
— the very great importance of the small businesses in the economy,
— the weakness of results in terms of spill over from basic research in spite of large budgets.

It is nevertheless possible to develop renewed policies towards international competitiveness while addressing both the regional difficulties and the new industries or technologies issues.

Although OECD[8] considers that following jointly two objectives, as different as promoting innovation and a balanced form of regional development constitute a weakness of the Japanese national system of innovation, Japan seems willing to continue in that past direction. But, through its strategy of clusters, which are today one of the essential instruments of the 'Science and Technology Basic Plan', the country intends to adjust by giving more and more space to research

---

[8] Cf. For example: Jones, R. and T. Yokoyama (2006). 'Upgrading Japan's Innovation System to Sustain Economic Growth', OECD, Economics Department Working Papers, No. 527

compared to production. This is doubtless one of the most novel aspects of Japan's strategy in the development of today's poles of competitiveness.

Considering the originality of the *jibasangyô* and their successive adaptations; the demonstration of the possible compatibility between small businesses and advanced structures of industrial development; the large range of policies and intervention to favour innovation as well as territorial planning; advanced experiments in forms of governance, Japan seems to offer us a lot of food for thought, in relation with existing theories.

1.2.4 *Thailand and the Cluster Policies*

Compared with existing interpretations of the agglomeration of enterprises Thailand presents another case, to the extent that in Thailand the concept of 'cluster' is used less to interpret existing situations than to promote policies, both concerning traditional agglomerations and modern and innovative ones.

The production economy of Thailand is characterised by a double structure: on the one hand, as in other countries, ancient traditional activities in the villages or in certain specialised urban districts; and on the other the concentration of enterprises in Industrial Estates (IE) which are the fruit of industrial policies and of the attraction of foreign investments since the 70s and 80s.

But it is not enough to pronounce the word 'agglomeration' to conjure up networks or cooperation between the various actors. Social relations did exist in the local communities and firms had common services and infrastructure at their disposal in the IEs, but the relations hardly ever went beyond the vertical relations between clients and sub-contractors. However, in the face of growing competition especially from its Asian neighbours (China and Vietnam), this very segmented system quickly revealed its limits. It was no longer possible to sustain the competition through prices so it was necessary for the country to improve the quality of its products, to rise in the value chain and develop goods with high added value. But the lack of interest in R&D on the part of multinational firms located in

Thailand and the total absence of R&D in Thai small businesses did not make the task of innovation easy, not to mention research, confined to the universities or public research centres with no connection with private firms or any real effect on the spread of knowledge. Having as its aims both[9] to reinforce the international competitiveness of the industries which were 'visible from the outside' (high-tech export industries and so forth) and to raise the capabilities of the 'interior economy' (domestic or rural industries) the Thai government, after the arrival in power of Thaksin, took the competitiveness of the country's economy as its main aim.

In order to carry out its policy, it invited Mr Porter and put the concept of clusters at the forefront, not without adapting, sometimes drastically, some of its tenets.

Clusters formed at the regional or local level are relatively classic whereas those concerned with high-tech industries sketch some new perspectives.

The former, which concern mainly traditional industries, use the 'one tambon (village), one product' programme and are **geographically very clearly defined**. These community-based clusters are no doubt fairly close, in their structure and dynamics, to the systems of localised production or industrial districts. Certainly, they advocate contact with the universities, but that often means improving the skills of the entrepreneurs (families, farmers, artisans, small businesses), and helping them to progress and improve the quality of the products rather than succeeding in setting up fundamental research projects. The objective of these community-based clusters also is to promote relations between the entrepreneurs so as to develop a local 'brand', the guarantee of wider recognition, either national or international.

Things are completely different as far as what is advocated for the high-tech export industries. For them, clusters, which are supposedly created to group activities together and exploit all the synergies, tend to free themselves from the purely local and geographic dimension (which is at the very heart of the definition of districts and traditional

---

[9] Hence the name 'Dual Track Policy'.

firms agglomeration theory), to take advantage of an enlarged network organisation. One of the recognised objectives is international competitiveness, so the clusters which have been formed tend to involve the whole of the target industry without worrying about any specific geographical dimension. So all the enterprises concerned with the given industry are invited, wherever they are located.[10] One organisation is entrusted with the coordination and acts as the geographical anchor of the activities of the cluster, and organises all the actors in a network: firms (the final assembler and suppliers or subcontractors; multinationals and pure Thai SMEs[11]), research centres and universities, professional organisations (if they exist), government representatives, etc. Whatever the results obtained, we can note that we go from a very local conception of the agglomeration of enterprises to a broad network-based conception of systems of cooperation. In terms of working out a real national system of innovation the impact of clusters is still limited. However, by putting this policy in place the Thai government has broken with the previous dynamics whether at the level of public policies, which form nowadays a more coherent whole, or at the level of fundamental attitudes. The concept of clusters, such as it is presented, is thus an instrument of public policy in the hands of the policy makers. The case of Thailand constitutes in any case an illustration of how one can evolve from an analytical concept of clusters to a practical one, the results of which, it is true, remain to be measured.

Beyond the accent put on the necessity to create links between the actors who previously had ignored each other and thus the attempt to make enterprises cooperate with each other and with universities and research centres, the cluster policy has first of all allowed changes to be injected into the previous public policies. The adoption of the concept of clusters thus seems to have played a role not only in the policies aimed at attracting foreign investment

---

[10] We should mention that in many cases the industries are relatively situated around Bangkok, with the exception of the textile industry which, although it is an export industry is considered as part of the traditional industries.

[11] Small- and medium-sized businesses.

(the link between obtaining privileges and investment in training and R&D in particular) but also in the technical and scientific policies which give much more importance to the working out of a real national system of innovation, based of course on clusters.

Despite numerous difficulties, little by little and through government action, clusters (sectorial or localised) seem to have become a reality in the Thai economy, not without going well beyond the classical approaches, as observed through the 'de-territorialisation' of the concept.

1.3 Reconsidering the Classic Approaches

After this short overview of the forms and developments taken by the agglomeration of enterprises in the four countries under discussion, we are bound to recognise that the cases observed lead us to seriously reconsider the approaches to districts, clusters and poles of competitiveness which were accepted until now, both in terms of their structures and their dynamics.

In relation to the approach in terms of 'industrial districts', from craft villages to *jibasangyô*, one can discover the importance and variety of proto-industrial forms of the concentration of activities which can serve as a matrix for some of the developments we have recently observed. We can also realise how the model of industrial districts which became prevalent in western thinking via the Italian situation, turns out to be narrow when trying to theorise the developments in China for example. In this country, it is less the organisation of production itself, optimised by internal inter-firm dialogue, both formal and informal, which seems to be at the heart of the dynamics we observed, but on the contrary it is the articulation around the commercial circuits. And it is these circuits which are the engine and produce today specialised merchant clusters at the heart of the national and global circuits. Internal cooperation, at the core of the theory of districts, is here supplanted by networks.

Concerning the approach in terms of clusters we can of course see, as in the case of Thailand, how the theory may be put into practice. But we can also see at the same time how the local framework of analysis, which is at the very heart of the analysis of clusters (since it is a question of setting up optimum dialogue between everyone concerned), simply explodes, once again to make way for networks, and by implication of all the enterprises or centres of resources around an activity or a product, wherever they are located.

Finally, as to the approach in terms of 'poles of competitiveness', it is interesting to note how contradictory the forms of governance can be in their attempts to reconcile the perspectives of territorial planning and innovation, as in Japan, or in the programmes which hesitate, in the choices to be done, between emphasizing the pre-eminence of research or enterprises.

The agglomeration of enterprises observed in Asia leads us therefore to seriously rethink the channels and paths of development observed by what are commonly called clusters, since the term itself as it is used today mixes up the different levels we have tried to differentiate, at the risk of creating confusion, by playing on all the registers which are touched on at once. In any case they force us to enlarge our frameworks of analysis and to re-think the new chances and advantages which are emerging in the framework of the global economy which is taking hold. For if the globalisation of the economy stiffens competition it also allows firms to play new and unusual cards, where the different types of agglomeration of enterprises can assume their complete role.

1.3.1 *The Openings Offered by the Modular Economy*

As S. Berger shows in 'How we compete: what companies around the world are doing to make it in today's global economy,'[12] in today's world there is not just one way to manufacture products, and from this point of view the channels have greatly diversified. Yes, competition is stiff, but multiple and the ways to respond to it are diversified too, as the variety of the models of production prove. Some firms can continue to choose to manufacture everything and integrate their

---

[12] Doubleday Broadway, 2005; French translation: *Made in Monde. Les nouvelles frontières de l'économie mondiale*, Seuil, Paris, Février 2006.

products totally (cf. Sony for Vaio for example); others can on the contrary externalise all these operations and keep only the assembling (Dell...), with of course all the models in between (closed modules, open modules, cf. Fujimoto Takahiro). The value production chain, when it is appropriate to join, is no longer as closed, unique and linear as before. It has fragmented and greatly diversified, with the appearance of firms which are positioned on intermediate markets like the Original Design Manufacturer enterprises (ODM) or the Original Equipment Manufacturer (OEM) and those occupying all other sorts of positions in the services. So it is possible for zones or firms to choose to specialise by positioning themselves on any point on the value chain either as parts manufacturers or as a designer, or even as a manufacturer without a brand or as being in charge of a specialised fragment, etc. The organisation of production obeys less and less a single predetermined model which would be a must for everyone, reducing the field of possible spaces. On the contrary it opens up this field.

The agglomerations of enterprises, districts, clusters or poles of competitiveness can perfectly benefit from the variety of their systems of organisation.

Fragmentation, specialisation and the greater opening of possibilities which the modular economy can allow gives renewed interest in the specific modes of organisation that these groupings will be able to find and in the specialised niches they will learn to construct and occupy. It is moreover in this framework that the forms of economic organisation which may appear outdated can quite easily, at a given time, find their place and specificity again, as the examples from Vietnam, China or Thailand illustrate. From a competitive model locked in closed systems of production in which competition can only operate on the reduction of costs resting on similar operations, a shift is occurring towards models in which it is the *different possible forms of organisation to be invented, which turn out to compete among themselves* and which represent the new challenges of developments to come.

In this context the environment of work, of research and wide reflection which clusters or poles of competitiveness are endowed with, doubtless constitute a real asset in the finding and exploiting of niches. In the prevalent globalisation, we may consider that the agglomerations of enterprises, at their different levels, not only find their total justification, but that by opening up the game, the latest developments of the modular economy provide a profound stimulus for them.

1.3.2 *Clustering and the Knowledge Impact*

True, this new context, more uncertain and multi-faceted, also takes us into a new era of economy or society based on knowledge. As Menkoff, Evers and Chay (2005) point out, the new element is that knowledge seems to have become the only significant and decisive factor of production, relegating other factors of production (natural resources, work, capital) to a secondary position. They are supposed to be easily accessible so long as knowledge is present (Drucker, 1993). Moreover, since knowledge becomes obsolete very quickly, what becomes important is not only knowledge itself, but the capacity, for an economy and a society, to learn, which is to say to create, spread and use new knowledge (Lundvall, 2002).That is why so much importance is given today to knowledge management and to new inflections and polarisations we can see today in the new forms of organisation which are being organised to respond to this 'Mega Competition of Knowledge'. It is this shift which is the heart and the challenge of the new groupings we can observe and particularly in the 'poles of knowledge', whether they take a local form or are organised as networks.

References

BECCATTINI, Giacomo. (a cura di), (1989). *Modelli locali di sviluppo*, Il Mulino, Bologna.

BECCATTINI, Giacomo. (1989). "Les districts industriels en Italie", in Maruani et alii, *La Flexibilité en Italie*, MIRE-TEN, Paris.

BECCATTINI, Giacomo. (1992). "Le district marshallien: une notion socio-économique", in Benko et Lipietz, *Les Régions qui gagnent*, PUF, Paris.

BERGER, Suzanne. (2006). *How We Compete: What Companies Around the World are Doing to Make It in Today's Global Economy*, Doubleday Broadway; French translation: *Made in Monde. Les nouvelles frontières de l'économie mondiale*, Seuil, Paris, Février, (2006).

DRUCKER, Peter. (1993). *Post Capitalist Society*, New York: Harper Collins.

FUJIMOTO, Takahiro. (2007). Architecture-based Comparative Advantage — A Design Information View of Manufacturing, in Evolutionary and Institutional Economics Review, 4(1), 55–112.

JONES, R., YOKOYAMA, T. (2006). 'Upgrading Japan's Innovation System to Sustain Economic Growth', OECD, Economics Department Working Papers, No. 527.

KAGAMI, Mitsuhiko, TSUJI, Masatsugu. (2003). *Industrial Agglomeration: Facts and Lessons for Developing Countries*, Chiba, Institute of Developing Economics (IDE) — Japan External Trade Organization (JETRO).

KUCHIKI, Akifumi, TSUJI, Masatsugu. (2004). *Industrial Clusters in Asia: Analyses of their Competition and Cooperation*, IDE-JETRO.

LE GALES, Patrick, TRIGILIA, Carlo, VOELZKOW, Helmut, CROUCH, Colin. (2001). *Local Production Systems in Europe: Rise or Demise?*, Oxford University Press.

LUNDVALL, Bengt-Ake. (2002). *Innovation, Growth and Social Cohesion: The Danish Model*, London: Elgar Publishers.

MENKHOFF, Thomas, EVERS, Hans-Dieter, CHAY, Yue-Wah. (2005). *Governing and Managing Knowledge in Asia*, Singapore: World Scientific.

PORTER, Michael. (1990). *The Competitive Advantage of Nations*, Macmillan and Basingstoke.

PORTER, Michael. (1998). Clusters and the new economics of competition, *Harvard Business Review*, novembre-décembre, pp. 77–90.

PORTER, Michael. (2001). Location, Competition and Economic Development: Local Clusters in *Global Economy in Economic Development Quarterly*, 14, pp. 15–34.

RIEDEL, J., RECORD, R. (2005). "Industrial clusters in Vietnam" in KUCHIKI Akifumi, TSUJI Masatsugu (eds.), (2004): *Industrial Clusters in Asia: Analyses of their Competition and Cooperation*, London, Macmillan.

TUAN, B. Q. (2005). *Vai trò của khu công nghiệp, khu chế xuất đối với tiến trình công nghiệp hóa ?. Việt Nam, (Industrial parks and local systems in the industrialisation process).*

Chapter 2

From an Industrial Policy Approach to an Industrial Cluster Approach: Japan, East Asia and Silicon Valley

Akira Suehiro

2.1 Introduction

This chapter aims to clarify the two different policy frameworks for industrial development in Japan and East Asian countries. The first framework is **an industrial policy approach**, which was adopted by Japan's Ministry of International Trade and Industry (MITI) from the 1950s to the 1980s, and was followed by the East Asian Newly Industrializing Countries or East Asian NICs such as South Korea and Taiwan since the latter part of 1960s. The key concept of this approach is 'international competitiveness' in terms of export performance of manufactured goods in the world market. Another framework is **an industrial cluster approach**, which became more important among East Asian countries including ASEAN members after the 1990s. When the currency crisis attacked East Asian countries in 1997, a group of economists from the World Bank principally proposed the industrial cluster approach based on the key concept of 'innovation' in order to activate and revitalise the industrial sector in the area. On the other hand, at the moment of the currency crisis, the Japanese government proposed to the crisis-hit countries the more conventional approach of improving and upgrading 'international competitiveness' of export-oriented industries.

What are the differences between the two approaches in terms of policy objectives, methodology, agents or players, the sources of financing and international economic environments? What are the differences between the two approaches in policy transferability and their policy effects? To answer these questions, the author of this chapter, at first, will make a comparison between the catch-up type industrialisation model on the basis of Japan's experience and Michael Porter's Diamond model on the basis of Silicon Valley in the United States. And then he will use the cases of Japan, South Korea, Taiwan and Thailand as examples to clarify the difference between two approaches.

The chapter consists of six parts including this introductory section. In Section 2 the author will try to provide a comparison of two major models as mentioned above. Section 3 is a major part of the paper and the author aims at providing an analytical framework to grasp the characteristics of the two approaches. More concretely, he will introduce two major models (industrial policy model and industrial cluster model) and three sub-models in industrial cluster approach (*sanchi*-type, export processing zone or EPZ-type, and Silicon Valley-type) in reference to major characteristics, principal promoters and players, type of business, and policy measurements.

In Section 4, the author will explain in more detail Japan's industrial policy by taking the case of the promotion of the tool machine industry between the 1950s and 1980s as an example. This policy seems to become the prototype of the industrial policy approach for the East Asian NICs in the sense that the government played an active role in formulating a master plan, providing policy loans (fiscal investment and loans), and coordinating relations between the government and the private sector. In Section 5, he will summarise the experiences of East Asian countries in relation to policies of promoting strategic industries in Korea, Taiwan and Thailand during the 1960s and the 1980s, together with *de facto* industrial cluster under the initiative of multinational corporations or MNCs in Thai automobile industry. In Section 6, or concluding part, the author will suggest both possibility and limitation of industrial cluster model in the context of the East Asian economies.

2.2 Catch-up Type Industrialisation Model and Diamond Model

2.2.1 *Late Comer Model in Industrialisation*

Generally speaking, the government in a developing country or a late comer in terms of the stage of economic development is required to play a more active role in industrial promotion than a front runner. The government formulates *national* economic development plans and promotes *particular* industries as strategic ones to accelerate the process of industrialisation.[1] As a consequence, the role of government inevitably becomes a prime promoter and a conductor of industrial promotion. Theoretical explanation can be done by employing the stage development model of industrialisation (see Figure 2.1, Suehiro 2008, 130).

When a developing country tackles industrialisation, three possible strategies present themselves: (1) export primary products and import industrial goods; (2) launch domestic production of industrial goods formerly imported (import substitution industrialisation); (3) export industrial goods manufactured domestically (outward-looking industrialisation; export-oriented industrialisation) (Chenery and Srinivasan 1989, volume 2, sections 29–31). Looking at the experiences of Japan and other East Asian NICs, most of the countries or region followed the process of starting with the export of primary products, then shifts from imports to domestic production to exports in labour-intensive industries, before moving to import and export substitution — first in labour-intensive industries, then in capital-intensive industries, and finally in technology-intensive industries (Suehiro, 2008). This of course is essentially the same process as that posited by Kaname Akamatsu in his theory of the so-called 'wild-geese-flying pattern' (Akamatsu, 1962).[2]

---

[1] This pattern is called a 'microscope type industrialisation' (Ohkawa and Kohama, 1989).

[2] For more detailed explanation of the wild-geese-flying pattern, see Kojima (1975 and 2000) and Suehiro (2008, Chapter 2).

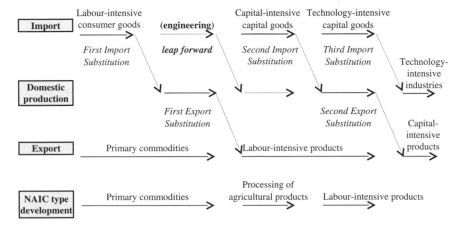

Figure 2.1:   Staged Development Model of Industrialisation: Import Substitution and Export Substitution.

Source: Made by the author.

In the process of stage development of industrialisation, the government is usually expected to undertake two major tasks: (1) promoting exports of manufactured goods to replace those of primary products (*export* substitution); and (2) promoting domestic production of the intermediate materials and capital goods needed in manufacturing processes (the second stage of import substitution). In addition to support of export promotion of labour-intensive type of industries, the promotion of tool machine industry (engineering) becomes a key element, as long as a developing country attempts to upgrade smoothly its industrial structure from the first stage of import substitution to its second stage.[3] This is the exact reason why the tool machine industry was frequently selected as a *strategic* industry to be promoted by the government not only in Japan but also in Korea and Taiwan. Tool machine industry was also chosen as a strategic industry with another two reasons, namely, a core of the supporting industries (SIs) for exportable finished goods and a typical

---

[3] Setting dual policy targets of export expansion and second-stage import substitution is called a strategy for 'dual-track growth' (Ohkawa and Kohama, 1989, lecture 2).

industry developed by a large number of small- and medium-sized enterprises (SMEs).

The stage development model of industrialisation also relates closely with the stage development model of late comer in late industrialisation as is illustrated in Figures 2.2A and 2.2B (Suehiro 2008, 44–45). In Figure 2.2A, black and white televisions (B&W TVs) are taken as examples of commodity and the USA is assumed as the first mover or a pioneer of developing a new product in any stage. The USA initiates production and export of B&W TVs, and later Japan catches up with the USA in production by introducing necessary technology from the outside. Facing with the challenge by Japan, the USA shifts its major products from B&W TVs to colour TVs, while Japan becomes a major exporter of B&W TVs. Likewise, in the process of development, Korea and Taiwan replace Japan in production and export of B&W TVs, while Japan shifts its major products to

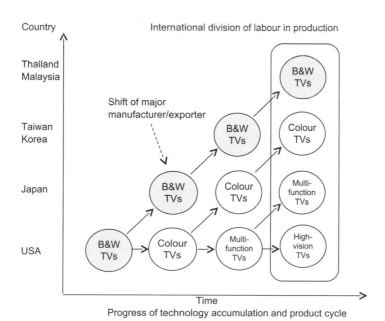

Figure 2.2A: Country and Product Cycle in Television Sets.
Source: Made by the author.

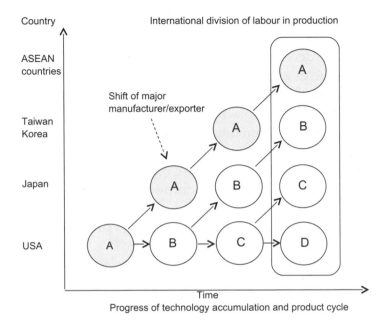

Figure 2.2B: International Product Cycle and Technological Innovation.
Source: Made by the author.

colour TVs. In brief, the stage development model of late comer or the 'catch-up type industrialisation model' may be depicted as in Figure 2.2B.

This model demonstrates concomitantly three different dimensions of industrial development of both front runners and late comers. Right-hand rising line of product <A> indicates the shift of leading country in production and export of <A>, while a vertical line of <A-B-C-D> shows an international division of labour in a particular industry like electronics industry in a particular period. Horizontal line of <A-B-C-D> in the USA shows the upgrading process of a particular industry from low-end commodity to high-end one in conjunction with the development of production technology. It is true that Figure 2.2B does not precisely represent the real world. But this model suggests how the East Asian NICs had successfully upgraded the stage of industrialisation one by one for the past shorter period.

What should be quickly noted here is the fact that a catch-up type industrialisation model presupposes two essential conditions: (1) A major player is a *country* and the focus is put on the competition among countries in a particular industry, being distinguished from the industrial cluster approach which tends to put stress on region wide production system and global value chain[4]; (2) A leading industry is supposed a *manufacturing* sector and the focus is put on the competitiveness of a particular industry in terms of country's market share in the world, being distinguished from industrial cluster approach which emphasises network of variety of industries including logistics, R&D and other business services.

2.2.2 *Michael Porter's Diamond Model*

Sharing basic interests with the hypothesis of the catch-up type industrialization, Porter also emphasises the competitiveness of manufacturing sector in his book *The Competitive Advantage of Nations* (1990). In this book, he addressed four major conditions as determinants for the competitive advantage of each country. They include: (1) factor conditions (infrastructure, human and natural resources); (2) demand conditions (market size, sophistication of home demand, segmented structure of demand); (3) firm strategy and rivalry relations among companies; and (4) the development of supporting industries (See Figure 2.3).

Comparing with the model of catch-up type industrialisation, we can find two major characteristics in his diamond model approach. First, he argued the role of government as an independent factor from four major conditions. He intentionally treated the government's role in the same way with the impact of 'chance' such as oil shocks and invention of new product. In this sense, he understood the government policy an external factor rather than an internal factor in determining the country-based competitive advantage. Second, at the

---

[4] For the hypothesis of global (international) value chain and production network, see Gereffi and Korzeniexicz eds. (1994), Gereffi (1999) and Sturgeon (2001).

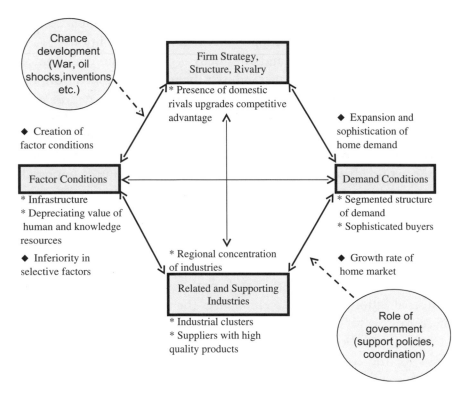

Figure 2.3:   Diamond Model of Competitive Advantage of Nations.
Source: Drafted by the author on the basis of Porter (1990, 131–143).

moment of 1990, he did pay less attention to the importance of industrial cluster, although he discussed it as a part of the fourth condition or the development of supporting industries. Rather, at that time, he stressed firm strategy much more than other three conditions.

Porter, however, changed his idea in a new article of 'Clusters and New Economic Competition' published in *Harvard Business Review* (Nov./Dec. 1998). Important movements affecting Porter's study are the impact of economic globalisation, the progress of IT revolution, and the diffusion of the concept of good corporate governance. In addition to these movements, the notable success of Silicon Valley in USA gave a great impact on the Porter's new article. As Saxenian (1994) characterised the development of Silicon Valley as the 'decentralised regional network-based industrial system', Porter also began to focus the space economy and networking system among various industries including non-manufacturing sector.

Figure 2.4 is made to illustrate the distribution of factories, offices and service centres locating in the Silicon Valley in order to examine this point. In around 1995, a total number of establishments in the area accounted for 8427 firms. Besides materials suppliers (326 firms), processing firms (899 firms), parts suppliers (458 firms), assemblers (190 firms) and finished goods producers (1052 firms), there were 1336 firms engaged in logistics services and 3207 firms in related services such as design, R&D, product development, software development and consulting services. Essential character of this industrial area is not only a vertical integration of suppliers of materials, parts suppliers and finished goods producers, but also a combination between manufacturing sector and non-manufacturing sector (logistics and services). This point is also emphasised frequently by academicians who analyse electronics and apparel industries by employing the global value chain approach (Sturgeon, 2001) and innovation-based development approach.

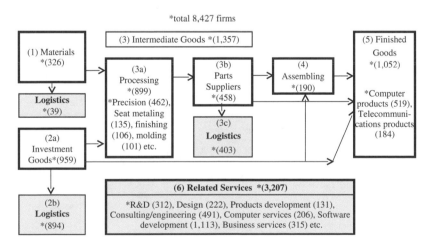

Figure 2.4: Industrial Networks in the Silicon Valley (1995).

Source: Kiyonari, Tadao *et al.* eds. *Nihon-gata Sangyo Shuseki no Miraizo*, (Perspective of the Japanese style Industrial Cluster), Nikkei Shimbun, 1997, p. 25.

Examining both emerging movements in the world market and the success of new production system (new business model) in the Silicon Valley, Porter revised his conventional Diamond Model into cluster-based new one. Figure 2.5 is a summary table of this revised model in reference to four major items: (1) decisive elements at the country level; (2) impact of economic liberalisation and globalisation; (3) development of information technology (IT); and (4) introduction of corporate governance into private firms.

In this revised model, he made a point of the space of business activities, the role of individual multinational corporations (MNCs), and the speed of economy and commodity cycle. He also emphasised

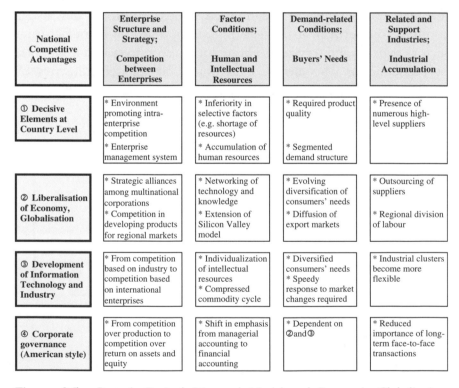

National Competitive Advantages	Enterprise Structure and Strategy; Competition between Enterprises	Factor Conditions; Human and Intellectual Resources	Demand-related Conditions; Buyers' Needs	Related and Support Industries; Industrial Accumulation
① Decisive Elements at Country Level	* Environment promoting intra-enterprise competition * Enterprise management system	* Inferiority in selective factors (e.g. shortage of resources) * Accumulation of human resources	* Required product quality * Segmented demand structure	* Presence of numerous high-level suppliers
② Liberalisation of Economy, Globalisation	* Strategic alliances among multinational corporations * Competition in developing products for regional markets	* Networking of technology and knowledge * Extension of Silicon Valley model	* Evolving diversification of consumers' needs * Diffusion of export markets	* Outsourcing of suppliers * Regional division of labour
③ Development of Information Technology and Industry	* From competition based on industry to competition based on international enterprises	* Individualization of intellectual resources * Compressed commodity cycle	* Diversified consumers' needs * Speedy response to market changes required	* Industrial clusters become more flexible
④ Corporate governance (American style)	* From competition over production to competition over return on assets and equity	* Shift in emphasis from managerial accounting to financial accounting	* Dependent on ②and③	* Reduced importance of long-term face-to-face transactions

Figure 2.5: Porter's Revised Diamond Model and Economic Globalisation, Progress of Information Technology and Corporate Governance.

Source: Made by the author on the basis of Porter (1990, 1998).

'strategic alliance', 'network of technology and knowledge', 'evolving diversification of consumer's goods', and 'outsourcing of suppliers' (see Figure 2.5). His revised model kicked around traditional approach of focusing production system of industries alone, and encouraged the rise of new business approach of focusing innovation, network and the speed of economy. Four years later after his publication of new article, he was invited to the Thai government to serve as a special advisor to formulate master plan of its National Competitiveness Plan (Porter, 2003).[5]

2.3 Analytical Framework: Industrial Policy and Industrial Cluster

2.3.1 *Four Types of Industrial Districts in Japan*

Now, let me introduce analytical frameworks to explore the two approaches, namely, industrial policy approach and industrial cluster one. Before explaining the idea of the present author, let me attempt to outline briefly the development of **industrial districts** (*sanchi*) or **industrial agglomeration area** (*sangyo shuseki-chi*) in Japan in order to help the understanding of readers on the topics.

In Japan, industrial districts and industrial agglomeration area are defined by the laws and temporary measurements for the government (MITI/METI and Small and Medium Enterprise Agency) to promote particular industries in a particular area (See Hattori, Chapter 3 in the present book). In these laws, the government specifies the

---

[5] Originally, the Ministry of Industry of Thailand formulated the Industrial Restructuring Plan (IPR) in close collaboration with JETRO Bangkok Office and Japan's MITI to overcome economic crisis in 1997, and submitted a detailed action plan targeting selected 13 industries (textiles, jewelry, garment, plastics, automobiles, etc.). But after Thaksin Shinawatra seized power in 2001, the Thai government and Finance Minister Somkhit (translator and promoter of Porter's theory) invited Porter, and ordered the NESDB and SASIN (business school at Chulalongkorn University) to produce a new plan of the National Competitiveness in accordance with Porter's advice. Finally, in October 2003, original IPR action plan was replaced by a new plan.

targets (SMEs), the type of business, and the area for the purpose of providing financial supports and other services.[6]

However, the definition of industrial districts in these laws is very practical and is less attractive to academic research. Rather conventional approach of Japanese scholars is more useful for our study when we aim to compare the Japanese traditional concept of industrial districts (*sanchi*) and western concept of industrial cluster. For instance, Kiyonari (1997) and Hashimoto (1997) categorised Japan's industrial district into four major types by using two criteria of the size of firms (large-sized firms vis-à-vis SMEs) and the location of firms (metropolitan cities vis-à-vis local cities). These four types include as in the following:

[A] Castle town centering in a core company (*kigyo-jyoka machi*) or Detroit-type town. Typical cases are seen in Toyoda-shi of Aichi prefecture with Toyota Motor Co. Ltd., Hitachi-shi of Ibaragi prefecture with Hitachi Ltd., Kamaishi-shi of Iwate prefecture with Nippon Steel Co., Ltd., and Hino-shi of Tokyo Metropolitan City with Hino Motor Co. Ltd. (see Figure 2.6 for a map of industrial districts). Castle town usually composes of a core firm, a large number of its related firms and majority of inhabitants belong to these firms.

[B] Industrial complex-type district (*konbinaato* in Japanese) locating in coastal areas. Typical cases are Chiba-complex with petrochemical and steel plants, Mizushima-complex (Okayama prefecture) and Niihama-complex (Ehime prefecture) with petrochemicals industry. Location of such type of industrial

---

[6] Before the Plaza Accord in 1985, MITI had given its policy priority on the SME modernisation plan as well as promotion of regional economy. Facing dramatic changes in international economic environments after the yen appreciation (Plaza Accord), MITI shifted its policy objectives to nation-wide industrial restructuring and, in 1998, they announced 'industrial cluster plan (Japan)' which was designed to create new businesses utilising the region's industry-academia-government network. Since this plan, 'industrial cluster' became an official concept widely accepted by government agencies. See METI (2006).

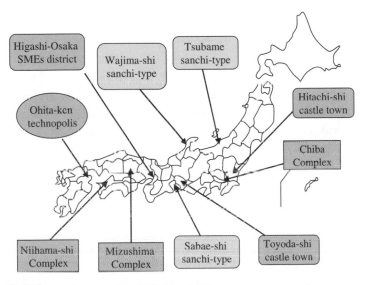

Figure 2.6: Map of Industrial Clusters in Japan: Castle Town, Complex, *sanchi*.
Source: Made by the author

complex is principally determined by the access both to large-sized container port facility and to a large sized hinterland for products.

[C] SMEs networking-type district. Famous areas are Ohta-ku in Tokyo Metropolitan City and Higashi-osaka-shi in Osaka City. A large number of small-sized and family-owned factories have concentrated in a specific area and they engage themselves in production of various types of parts and in provision of molding/dyeing services. Two areas are hinterlands of assemblers of automobiles and electronics products (Hino Motor, Nissan Motor, Matsushita Electrical Industrial etc.).

[D] Industrial district specialising in production of a particular consumer good, or is known as a *sanchi* and a district with community-based industry (*jiba sangyo*) in Japan.[7] According to

---

[7] For more detailed studies on *sanchi* or *jiba-sangyo*, see Yamazaki (1980) and Seki and Fukuda eds. (1998).

the survey by the SMEs Agency (2006), 54 areas are officially defined as the *sanchi* to be promoted according to the Law on Temporary Measure Concerning the Activation of Specific Small and Medium Enterprises of 2003. Typical cases are Tsubame-shi of Niigata prefecture specialising in production and export of forks and knives, Wajima-shi of Ishikawa prefecture specialising in production of Japanese lacquers products, and Sabae-shi of Aichi prefecture specialising in production of eye glass frame. Besides these *sanchi*-type area, the terminology of *jiba-sangyo* is used frequently to identify a kind of SMEs dominant industries such as weaving, knitting, wooden furniture, paper, printing, and toiletries in metropolitan and local cities.[8]

Figure 2.7 is a summary of these four types of industrial districts in references to location, the size of firms, the type of business and representative cases. What is important is that all three cases, excepting the case of [B], are not products of government policy but products of long-time autonomous development of local firms and local traders in the area. Supports of local governments for the development of firms and areas should not be overlooked. But more essential elements are long-time, face-to-face interactions between a giant assembler and part suppliers in the case of [A], networks formed among SMEs in the case of [C], and sophisticated social division of labour developed by local marketers in the case of [D].

Although Japanese industrial districts share characteristics in some aspects like networks with the Silicon Valley model, core players are manufactures rather than non-manufacturing sector such as universities, R&D centres and service offices. In the case of [D] or *sanchi*-type industrial district, a particular consumer's product has historically been developed in the process of utilising available resources

---

[8] According to the survey of Osaka-fu, 61 types of businesses are identified as *jiba sangyo* or SMEs dominant industries on the basis of production of traditional products, which accounts for 17,257 establishments (one third of the total) and produced 3,121 billion yen (one sixth of the total shipments) respectively in 2000 (http://www.pref.osaka.jp/kogyo/jiba/jiba2.html).

	Metropolis, Big Cities	Local Cities
Large-sized Companies	\<A\> **Castle town centering in a specific company,** (*Kigyo-jyokamachi*) *automobiles, electricals, steel, electronics, *Toyoda-shi (Aichi), Hitachi-shi (Ibaragi), Kamaishi-shi (Iwate), Hino-shi (Tokyo)	\<B\> **Industrial complex-type,** (*konbinaato*) *petrochemicals, steel *Mizushima-shi (Okayama), Chiba-shi (Chiba), Niihama-shi (Ehime)
Small- and Medium-sized Enterprises (SMEs)	\<C\> **SMEs networking district** *tool machine, casting, dyeing, molding, parts manufacturing *Ohta-ku (Tokyo, parts and molding for auto industry); HigashiOsaka-shi (Osaka, tools and machinery)	\<D\> **Industrial district centering in a specific consumer's good** (*sanchi*-type) *various type of consumers finished goods *Tsubame-shi (Niigata, knives and forks), Wajima-shi (Ishikawa, Japanese lacquers), Sabae-shi (Aichi, eye glass frames) etc.

Figure 2.7: Japan's Industrial Cluster: Complex, Castle Town, Sanchi, SMEs District.
Source: Drafted by the author on the basis of Hashimoto (1997) and Kiyonari (1997).

of location, natural resources, manpower and traditional human networks.

2.3.2 *Two Models and Three Sub-models in Industrial Cluster*

Keeping Japanese experiences into mind, let me compare the two approaches of industrial policy and industrial cluster. At the same time, industrial cluster approach is further breakdown here into three sub-models, namely, *sanchi*-type (Japan, or the case of [D]), export processing zone or EPZ-type (East Asia), and the Silicon Valley-type.

Table 2.1 is a summary of the two approaches and three sub-models in accordance with major six indicators: (1) what are key elements characterising each model; (2) who are major promoters in implementing policy or forming industrial districts; (3) who are locally important as organisers and coordinators; (4) who are major players; (5) what types of business are dominant in the area or are targeted in government policies; and (6) what kind of policy measurements are employed to support the area and the industry.

First approach is an industrial policy one. According to the classification of the Japan's MITI, industrial policies are classified into four types of industry-specific, item-specific, area-specific and other type. Industry-specific policy, as will be discussed in the next section of this paper, aims to promote particular industries in line with the national targets, while item-specific policy selects a specific task across the industry such as basic information services or an administrative measurement to escape exceeded competition in a particular industry. Area-specific policy aims at revitalising a particular area regardless of the type of industry. Typical cases are seen in government support for depopulated area in countryside and *sanchi*-area facing the hollowing of local industries (Japan Development Bank, 1993a).

In any type of industry or item, a special temporary law is enacted. At the same time, a particular council also is set up under the auspice of responsible ministry to serve as a core body of formulating main plans. Industrial council of MITI or *sangyo kouzo shingikai* is a typical one for the government to undertake industrial policy. So far as industry-specific policy is concerned, most important policy measurement is fiscal investment and loans (FILs), in which the government grants necessary funds with individual firms, mostly SMEs, through the Japan Development Bank (JDB) as we see in Section 4.

On the other hand, industrial cluster approach comprises of three sub-models. The author selects *sanchi*-type as a representative case among four major types of Japan's industrial districts. Such type of industrial district specialising in a particular industry or in production of a particular product can hardly be discovered in other East Asian countries except for Taiwan and China (town-based industry in southern China). Rather the governments of East Asian countries

Table 2.1:   Comparison of Industrial Policy and Industrial Policy Approach.

Item	Industrial Policy (Japan)	Industrial Cluster		
		District-based (Sanchi-type) Model (Japan)	Export Processing Zone (EPZ-type) Model (East Asia)	Silicon Valley (Network-type) Model (USA)
Key elements	*Industry-specific promotion *Information sharing between government and industrial base	*Area-specific promotion *Social division of labour in the area	*Export promotion *Provision of infrastructure	*Innovation *Networking-type industrial base
Promoter	*Government, government-sponsored banks	*Historical products, autonomous development	*Government	*Historical products, autonomous development
Organizer/ Coordinator	*Business associations	*Locally-based marketers, local government	*Parent company of MNC, foreign buyers	*University, research institutes, corporate associations
Players	*SMEs, large-sized manufacturing firms	*Local SMEs	*Foreign and local large-sized firms	*Large-sized firms, venture-type
Type of business	*Electronics, tool & machinery, supporting industries	*Consumer goods	*Labour-intensive, export-oriented industries	*Technology & knowledge-intensive industries
Finance, means of support	*Fiscal finance (loans), R&D	*Fiscal finance, tax-incentives	*Tax-incentives	*Stock market, seed money, R&D

Source: Made by the author.

have preferred Japan's style industrial policy for the purpose of promoting strategic industries such as electronics, tool machine, ship building, petrochemicals, automobiles, and semiconductors (Suehiro, 2008, Chapter 6). Besides industrial promotion of these strategic industries, they also constructed export processing zones (EPZ) to attract large-sized local firms as well as foreign ones to promote export-oriented industries (Fujimori ed., 1978). It is safe to say that EPZ may be the most typical type of industrial cluster in East Asia until the early times of 1990s.

For instance, in Taiwan the government set up EPZ mainly for the purpose of developing electronics and textile industries in Gaoxiong (1966) and Taizhong (1970), while in Korea they established Mazan Export Free Zone (1971) with the same purpose. In the Philippines, the Export Processing Area Act was introduced in 1970, while in Malaysia Special Incentive Act for Electronics Industry was formulated to construct EPZ in Penang Island in 1971.

In Thailand, there was no special act to set up EPZ. But the Industrial Estate Authority of Thailand or IEAT was established in 1972 to construct and manage both general industrial zones (GIZ) and export processing zones (EPZ). The total number of industrial estates constructed by both the government and the private firms amounted to as many as 49 places by the end of 1994. At the same time, since 1977, the Board of Investment (BOI) of Thailand divided the whole country into three zones, and granted different tax incentives in accordance with the stage of economic development in each zone (Poapongsakorn and Fuller, 1997).

Promotion of EPZ was frequently connected with welcome policy of foreign direct investment. Thanks to this policy, foreign firms in general, and multinationals in particular advanced into EPZ to become major players in the area, together with large-sized local firms. Governments were usually responsible for purchasing of land site and construction of infrastructure and fundamental facility such as electricity, water supply and telecommunications. They also provided firms in EPZ with couples of tax incentives. They included tax holidays of corporation tax for five to eight years, special exemption of both import duty and export duty, and tax refunding for export companies.

In addition to these tax incentives, more attractive factor for firms in EPZ is to enjoy efficient and speedy administrative services of the government such as proceedings of incorporation of company, application of work permits, and clearance of importing of machines and exporting of products (Fujimori ed., 1978).[9] In brief, key promoter of EPZ is the government, while major players are foreign and domestic large-sized firms. Local SMEs also advanced into EPZ to serve as parts suppliers and subcontractors for assemblers, but there was no development of organic interactions and effective networks among these SMEs. Subsidiaries of foreign firms were put under the direct control of headquarters outside EPZ, while large-sized local factories were also connected directly with parent companies in capital city. This is the limitation of EPZ. Unlike the *sanchi*-type industrial district, EPZ is not a historical product accompanying autonomous development of local firms, but is essentially a policy product.

In contrast to EPZ, the Silicon Valley-type shares the same characteristics with the *sanchi*-type in the sense that a government provides minimum physical and monetary services. Rather a government (or local government) supports R&D for firms locating in industrial districts. Another important element is a network or a social division of labour developed among members in the area, which includes not only inter-trade of products and services but also pooling of market information and sharing of technological knowledge.

However, looking at the type of business and major players, we can find sharp difference between the *sanchi*-type and the Silicon Valley model. More concretely, the *sanchi*-type mainly comprised of a group of SMEs under the coordination of local traders (*sanmoto shosha*), while the Silicon Valley had developed a network between SMEs and large-sized assemblers, and had effectively connected manufacturing sector with non-manufacturing sector including universities and

---

[9] EPZ usually has a centralised administrative service centre inside the compound, and various responsible government offices cooperate with each other to provide necessary services to support firms. From the view of firms advancing into EPZ, these services are very beneficial in economising waste time, curtailing delivery time, and reducing cost.

logistics centres. Leading industries are technology-based and knowledge-based industries, in which R&D, IT service, and product
development are essential. Consequently, when the concept of 'innovation' becomes more essential in industrial restructuring, governments
of East Asian countries began to turn their eyes to network-type
industrial district rather than EPZ-type industrial estates.

2.4 Industrial Policy in Japan: Mechanisms and Institutions

2.4.1 *Institutional Framework of Japan's Industrial Policy*

Now, let me return to Japan's industry-specific policy. Since the mid-
1950s, the government of Japan launched the promotion of tool
machine and electronics industries as targeted ones, and implemented
five-year promotion plan in every five year from 1956 to 1985 by
legislating special temporary measurement laws as is outlined in
Table 2.2.

The reason why the 'temporary measurement' law was selected
instead of permanent law is an effort of the government of adjusting
the promotion of particular industry with the legal framework of
Anti-Trust Law (Tsusho Sangyosho ed., 1990).[10] A core body to
formulate master plans is an industrial council (*sangyo kozo shingikai*),
which is formed one by one for each purpose. Industrial council's
members consist of four major groups: i) economic technocrats from
MITI, Ministry of Finance (MOF) and other related government
offices; ii) representatives of business associations related to targeted
industry; iii) specialists or experts from academic circle; and iv) representatives of other fields such as mass media, consumers associations,
NGOs and private think-tanks. After completing planning process

---

[10] Under the legal framework of the Anti-Trust Law, a preferential treatment in
favour of a particular industry or a particular firm was principally recognised unfair
trade. Therefore, the government fixed the period of validity of laws from three years
to five years.

Table 2.2: Temporary Measurement Law for Industrial Promotion in Japan, 1956–1985.

Period	Name of Temporary Law
1956–61	Temporary Measure for the Promotion of the Machinery Industry Law [A1]: machine tool, auto parts
1957–61	Temporary Measure for the Promotion of the Electronics Industry Law [B1].
1961–65	Extension of [A1] for next five years, [A2]
1966–71	Further extension of [A2] for next five years [A3]
1971–77	Temporary Measure for the Promotion of Electronics and Machinery Industries Law (integration of A3 with B1), [B2]
1978–85	Temporary Measure for the Promotion of the Information Machinery Industry Law (Extension of the scope of industrial category in B2).

Source: Made by the author on the basis of Friedman (1988) and Hashimoto (1994).

and legal arrangement, the work of implementing promotion schemes was transferred to the hands of responsible ministries, in particular MITI in charge of technology development and the Japan Development Bank (JDB) of MOF in charge of financing.

Structure of formulation and implementation of industry-specific policy is seen as depicted in Figure 2.8. Applicants, mostly SMEs, who hope to avail promotion scheme are requested to draft investment plans in detail as to how do they upgrade their production capacity and how do they modernise their management system. After that, they submit their plans to two offices of the Department of Heavy Industry (DHI) of MITI and the Japan Development Bank (JDB). DHI was responsible for examining investment plans from the view point of technological development (modernisation of production technology and equipment), while JDB was responsible for investigating the applicant's capacity in the fields of management, accounting and marketing. If the two offices agreed on the investment plan, JDB would grant policy loans or low-interest loans to the applicants. Such policy loans are called fiscal investment and loans (FILs, *zaisei touyushi*) because budgetary sources were mostly fiscal funds under the control of MOF.

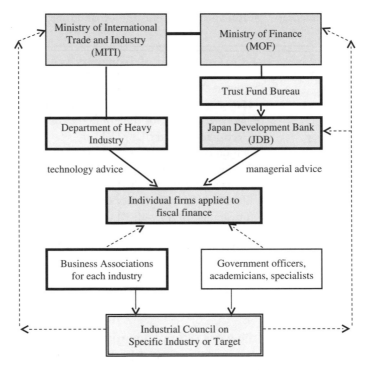

Figure 2.8:   Mechanism of FIL and Industrial Upgrading.

Source: Drafted by the author.

2.4.2 *Fiscal Investment and Loans and Budgetary Sources*

FILs are a kind of special account, being distinguished from ordinary budget. Apart from floatation of government bonds and borrowings, FILs mainly recruited necessary money funds from two major channels of the Trust Fund Bureau (TFB) of MOF and postal life insurance. Larger part of the TFB consisted of postal deposits and pension funds that the government absorbed through over 24,000 public postal offices in the whole country. On the other hand, the government gave preferential treatment in taxation to depositors at the public postal office. This important policy implies that a huge amount of savings at the households were intentionally mobilised as investment funds for national specific purposes (Japan Development Bank, 1993a). Percentage of TFB and postal life insurance combined together to account for 68% in 1955, 89% in 1965, and 95% in 1975 respectively (see Table 2.3).

On the other hand, purposes of FILs are classified into two major categories of supply of infrastructure for people's life (housing, transport, SMEs support, etc) and promotion of industry and trade. Industry-specific policy was included into the second category. According to Table 2.4, larger proportion of FILs was directed toward infrastructure rather than industrial promotion. FILs for industrial promotion accounted for 16% of the total outstanding loans in 1955, but its percentage dropped quickly to 8% in 1965 and further to 3% in 1975.

At the same time, looking at whole outstanding loans classified by type of financial institutions, we see that commercial banks had served as main suppliers of loans to private sector (48–62%), while FILs accounted for around 10 to 14% of the total. In particular, JDB which was responsible for promotion of strategic industries occupied 8% in 1955 and merely 2–3% between 1965 and 1985.

These figures immediately raise the question as to how we evaluate the result and the policy effects of industrial promotion policy. According to conventional arguments of academicians and government officers (MITI and JDB), they generally understood that FILs had contributed as important policy means to improve international

Table 2.3:   Distribution of the FIL by Monetary Sources, 1955–1990 (%).

	1955	1965	1975	1985	1990
Special account	14	4	1	0	0
Trust fund bureau*	52	66	84	78	78
Postal deposit	34	23	42	24	20
Pension funds	10	23	22	15	15
Postal life insurance	16	7	11	10	17
Government bonds, and borrowings	15	24	4	12	6
Total	100	100	100	100	100

Notes: Trust Fund Bureau of MOF was set up for the purpose of managing public funds and implementing the fiscal investment and loans. It was abolished in Jan. 2001.

competitiveness of supporting industries and to upgrade the quality of SMEs during the period of between the 1950s and the 1970s. Policy makers in East Asia also accepted positive evaluation. Indeed, after the 1960s, Korea and Taiwan employed Japan's policy measurements as a useful model to pursue their purposes of industrial promotion. However, figures in Tables 2.4 and 2.5 seem to provide strong counter evidence against conventional positive evaluation. The World Bank also doubted as to the policy effect of industrial promotion in Japan and other East Asian countries in its report of 'The East Asian Miracle' (1993).

The World Bank insisted that as in the following: 'Industrial policy narrowly defined — that is, attempts to achieve more rapid productivity growth by altering industrial structure — was generally not successful. In Japan, Korea, Singapore, Taiwan and China, promotion of specific industries had little apparent impact. Industrial growth tended to be market-conforming, and productivity change was not significantly higher in promoted sectors. Although governments in these four economies were undoubtedly trying to alter industrial structure to achieve more rapid productivity growth, with the exception of Singapore their industrial structures evolved largely

Table 2.4:   Distribution of the FIL by Purposes, 1955–1990 (%).

Purposes	1955	1965	1975	1985	1990
Infrastructure for people's life*	45	53	64	70	71
Housing	14	14	21	25	30
Small & Medium sized firms	8	13	16	18	16
Infrastructure for Industries	32	31	25	22	22
Transport	12	14	13	8	8
Regional development	9	7	3	2	3
Promotion of Industries, Trade	23	16	11	8	9
for Industries	16	8	3	3	3
for Trade	7	8	8	5	6
Total	100	100	100	100	100

Notes: Infrastructure for people's life include housing, environment improvement, public health, social security, education, supports for small and medium-sized firms, and agriculture/fisheries.
Source: Japan Development Bank ed. (1993b).

Table 2.5: Distribution of Outstanding Loans by Type of Financial Institutions 1955–1990.

En %	1955	1965	1975	1985	1990
Private financial institutions	87	90	89	86	88
Commercial banks	62	54	48	50	57
(1) City banks	36	30	27	26	27
(2) Local banks	17	15	11	15	15
Finance for SMEs	9	15	17	16	9
Fiscal Investment and Loans	13	10	11	14	12
JDB*	8	3	2	2	1
EIBJ*	1	1	2	1	1
Total	100	100	100	100	100

Notes. JDB: Japan Development Bank; EIBJ: Export-Import Bank of Japan.
Source: Japan Development Bank ed. (1993b).

in a manner consistent with market forces and factor-intensity-based comparative advantage.' (World Bank, 1993, 354–355).

2.4.3 *Information Sharing System and Return Match Game*

If so, how can we evaluate industry-specific policy in the context of Japan's high economic performance since the 1960s? We must consider not the *direct* effect but *indirect* effect of industrial policy. Key elements to be pointed here may be three.

Firstly, in the process of formulating master plan, there were exchange of a huge amount of information between the government and the private sector at the industrial council meetings as well as at other informal meetings. Through these intimated communications, the government in general, and MITI in particular could accumulate industrial knowledge and produced industrial experts on each industry. On the other hand, the private sector in general, and business associations in particular, successfully built a strong pipe with the government in exchange of information and data on targeted industry and individual firms. Such collaboration between the two sectors resulted in a system of information sharing, which in turn contributed to formulation of more realistic and rational policies for the two sides.

Secondly, applicants were given multiple chances to submit their investment plans. Even if applicants failed in getting funds from JDB, they had another chance of resubmitting revised investment plans the next time (examination was taken twice per year). They could obtain suggestions from DHI of MITI and JDB to revise their original plans without any political connections with the government or political party. Such *return-match game* gave learning effect to SMEs, and served as important channels for them to access to knowledge on advanced technology and modern management system. Strict investigation without political corruption and the return-match game apparently helped in upgrading the quality of SMEs at individual firm level (Hashimoto, 1994).

Thirdly, if comparing FILs with commercial banking loans, its amount was not so large (see Table 2.5). But if a certain company could obtain MITI-JDB approval in promotion scheme, large-sized city commercial banks were usually willing to provide additional loans to this company. This is because that the creditability of a company had already been confirmed by MITI and JDB, and commercial banks did not need any more to conduct its own costly research for new loans. In this sense, FILs scheme seemed to serve as a spark of fund-raising for SMEs rather than as a direct monetary source of new investment plan (Yonekura, 1993). Robert Wade, who studied the experience of Taiwanese industrialisation by using the key word of 'governing the market', calls such type effect with the 'announcement effect' of loans from the JDB (Wade, 1990, 30–31).

The Japan's experience of industrial policy suggests to us that three conditions are crucial for its effectiveness and rationality: (1) information sharing system between the government and the private sector or intimated communications between the two sectors; (2) the rule of return match game as a tool of educating and training SMEs in accordance with the government purpose of industrial upgrading; and (3) FILs as a spark of additional loans to connect with commercial banking loans. At the same time, effective industrial policy needs at least three important actors, namely, industrial experts in the government sector, business association which accumulated accurate information on their members, and entrepreneurial SMEs to challenge modernising their own business. If we cannot find such actors, it is difficult for the government to achieve its original targets. Poor result of industrial policy in Southeast Asia (the Philippines, Indonesia, and Thailand except automobile) may be attributable to this point.

2.5 Industrial Policy vis-à-vis Industrial Cluster in East Asia

2.5.1 *Recopy of the Japan's Industrial Policy in East Asia*

When East Asian NICs started industrialisation, all the countries/regions except Hong Kong adopted industrial promotion policies in similar style with that of Japan. Korea and Taiwan (ROC) in particular introduced directly Japanese methodology, in which the government selected strategic industries at first, and then promoted them by using subsidies, policy loans, tax incentives, and other services. Most typical case may be seen in the case of Korea (see Fukagawa, 1989; Amsden, 1989; Suehiro, 2008, 143–144).

In Korea, as early as in 1963, the government formulated a long-term plan to promote machine industry, and drafted the Machine Industry Promotion Act in 1968, and integrated it into a Five-Year Plan for Promoting Machine Industries in 1976. They also enacted the Electronic Industries Promotion Act in 1969. Entering the 1970s, they further expanded the scope of strategic industries to heavy and chemical industries (HCIs) to accelerate the second stage of import substitution. In line with the promotion of HCIs, in 1974, automobile industry became one of the most important targeted industries. Likewise, the semiconductor industry was chosen as the key industry since 1983. It is after the late 1980s when the Korean government switched its economic policies to liberalisation that they stopped actual support to particular industries.

Comparing with the Japanese experiences, we see that industrial policy in Korea shows some characteristics. Firstly, agents of developing strategic industries were mostly large-sized firms, especially companies belonging to the *chaebols* such as the Hyundai Group and the Samsung Group rather than SMEs (Amsden, 1989). It is the late 1970s that SMEs became policy objects in a real sense as agents of supporting industries in line with full promotion of automobile industry. Secondly, they principally employed public loans based on external debts rather than commercial banking loans. Unlike in Japan, private commercial banks in Korea were underdeveloped. Therefore, government-sponsored banks played a vital role as a main supplier of investment funds. Thirdly, the industrial policy of Korea inclined to cover the whole stage of a particular industry's development from its start-up through growth and expansion to the more advanced stage of industrial upgrading. Consequently, it took ten to twenty years for each industry.

As compared to the case of Korea, Taiwan employed a more moderate and flexible approach. Before the latter part of 1970s, the government had promoted several industries officially by appealing to various legal measurements such as the Investment Promotion Act, the EPZ Promotion Act and Joint-Venture Promotion Act. In November 1973, they decided to select ten important industries as targeted ones to be promoted. These ten industries included steel, ship building, petrochemical and other HICs. But since these heavy and chemical industries were put under the direct control of state enterprises, the private firms could hardly receive direct supports from the government in this field. Rather they must find niche industry and niche markets by applying to a general scheme of preferential treatment (Investment Promotion Act etc.).

However, in 1979, the government changed its policy and decided to adopt the similar approach to Korea. The Industry Development Bureau (IDB) of the Ministry of Economic Affairs (MOEA) established an executive committee to develop strategic industries, especially high-tech industries. IDB introduced matching fund programmes in 1982 to foster and promote these strategic industries. These programmes included the Targeted Leading Products (TLP) programme and the Development of Critical Component and Products (DCCP), all of which was aimed at upgrading of production technology and R&D capacity in targeted industries. It is reported that the government matched up to 50% of total R&D costs for IDB-approved projects. As of early 1994, 123 projects had applied for TLP subsidies. Among these 67 projects were awarded funds by IDB, with matching funds of about NT$1 billion and direct subsidies of about NT$0.9 billion (Wang, 1997, 77).

Prominent characteristics seen in Taiwan may be the dual-track policy, in which the government simultaneously pursued two targets of economic liberalisation and industrial upgrading. Concerning the former policy, they aimed at developing Taiwan into a regional operation centre in East Asia as we see in the development of electronics industry. As for the latter policy, in addition to IDB matching funds programmes, they also planned to promote transfer of high technology to the private sector by using the Industrial Technology Research Institute (ITRI, government) (Amsden and Chu, 2003). But under both the increasing pressure of liberalisation from the outside and the prevalence of outsourcing strategy (OEM/ODM) in high-tech industry, the latter is losing its validity. Instead, industrial cluster approach became dominant. At the same time, private firms began to depend on direct channels with foreign partners as we see in the case of the personal computer industry.[11]

Historically, network-type industrial cluster is not strange to local firms in Taiwan. Since major industries were put under the control of state enterprises, local SMEs tended to find their advantage in exports of labour-intensive products with low-technology. According to the survey of Kawakami (1999) on shoes making industries in Korea and Taiwan, a kind of industrial cluster was progressed in a particular area, in which a group of foreign buyers existed at the top with local trading companies at the middle, while small manufacturers supported at the bottom (see Figure 2.9). But such pyramid-type production team

---

[11] For the interesting case study of ICs industry and PC industry in Taiwan in reference to shift from partnership between the state and local engineers to more independent activity of private firms from the state, see Sato (2007).

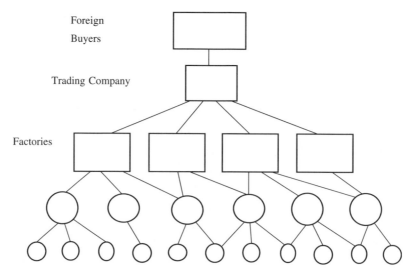

Figure 2.9: Production System under the Foreign Buyers in Taiwan.
Source: Drafted by the author on the basis of Kawakami (1999).

is not a vertical structure based on traditional sub-contracting system. Unlike in Korea (hierarchical structure), SMEs in Taiwan constructed more flexible network-type relationship among members. In this sense, an industrial cluster based on SMEs in Taiwan is categorised as autonomous development-type, being comparable to *sanchi*-type industrial district in Japan. Accordingly, when the concept of 'innovation' was introduced together with industrial cluster approach, both the government and local firms seemed to adjust to new circumstance more smoothly than in other East Asian countries.

2.5.2 *Arguments on Innovative East Asia and Industrial Cluster*

After the Asian currency crises erupted in 1997, many scholars at international financial organisations have attributed their major causes to the Asian way in economic management and proposed policies that could overcome the structural weakness that apparently led to the crises. Especially IMF and the World Bank pointed two major causes.

These two are instable corporate finance depending heavily on banking loans due to the underdevelopment of stock market and poor company management due to the lack of corporate governance. It is very natural for the World Bank to demand the governments in crisis-hit countries to implement institutional reforms both in local financial sector (financial institutional implement restructuring) and in local firms, mostly family-owned firms (corporate restructuring) (World Bank, 1998).

On the other hand, Yusuf and Evenett (2002), who were economists of the World Bank, argued that the major cause of the crises should be attributed to the conventional way of economic development in East Asia, or economic development depending on input of additional physical capital goods and labour force. According to their prospects, East Asian economies would face serious difficulty after exhausting additional capital goods and labour force as long as they did not take an effort of improving productivity. That is exactly the point that Paul Krugman emphasised in his article of 'The Myth of Asia's Miracle' before the crisis took place (Krugman, 1994). Yusuf and Evenett claimed that '...innovation will be the engine of growth for much of Asia now that the initial resource-intensive phase of industrialisation is ending. Innovation in a broad range of areas, from products to services and business organisation, will be the principal source of increases in productivity and in export competitiveness.' (Yusuf and Evenett, 2002, 3–4).

There are three areas of innovation for East Asian economies, they argued, to resume sustainable growth. The first area is an environment that stimulates innovation derives from spending on research and development (R&D) by public and private entities in a competitive milieu. In addition, they claim, 'product and process innovation is a function not just of investment in R&D, but also of the *clustering of networked firms* in an open and competitive policy environment'. The second area is a *closer interaction between services and manufacturing*. A strong services sector facilitates industrial development, and some of the commercially most successful innovation occurs when consulting, information management, and marketing services, for example, are combined with manufacturing in the biotechnology sector, automotive, engineering, and apparel industries as well as many others. A third area closely interconnected with the other two is *information and communication technologies* (*ICT*). ICT is so intrinsic to the innovation process by greatly facilitating communication, collaboration, and competition (Yusuf and Evenett, 2002, 4–5).

This argument is a declaration of rejecting the traditional East Asian development model including resources-based development strategy, state-led industrial promotion policy, and the EPZ-type industrial district approach. Rather they advised more flexible and decentralised regional network on the basis of combination between manufacturing and services, as the success of the Silicon Valley model suggests to us (Figure 2.4). The idea of *innovative East Asia* is not a peculiar policy agenda among economists of the World Bank. Booze-Allen and Hamilton, an international consulting firm, has already addressed the necessity of innovation-led development strategy as a key measurement to revitalise the Korean economy before it experienced the currency crisis (Booze-Allen and Hamilton, 1997; Suehiro, 2008, 310).

The words of innovation, clustering of networked firms, and ICT have now become key concepts for the governments in East Asian countries because they are commonly facing increasing pressure of economic liberalisation, enhanced competition with foreign firms in domestic market, unavoidable necessity of industrial upgrading, and the necessity of corporate restructuring on the global principle of good corporate governance. In this context, industrial cluster approach is sincerely considered by both the public and the private, instead of industrial promotion policy or the EPZ-type industrial parks. For instance, in Thailand, industrial cluster became an essential issue for the government as we typically see in the case of automobile industry. Therefore, let me move to the automobile industry in Thailand.

2.5.3 *Thailand's Automobile Industry: de Dacto Clustering of Firms Initiated by MNCs*

The development of Thai automobile industry can be dated from the year of 1961 when Ford Motor started its operation.[12] In 1969, the

---

[12] Ford Motor decided to close its plant in Thailand in 1966, and returned to Thailand in 1992.

Ministry of Industry (MOI) set up the special committee to formulate a master plan of automobile industry development in collaboration with American experts. As we see in Table 2.6, the government banned import of passenger cars, and raised import duties on auto parts in order to protect local suppliers. They also restricted the number of auto assemblers (license system), and fixed the number of car models to keep the some scale of production for existing assemblers.

Since 1978, the government started local contents programme or localisation of auto parts (the second stage of import substitution in Figure 2.2 of this paper). According to the programme, all the assemblers, mostly joint-ventures between local firms and foreign firms, were requested to use locally produced parts according to the government order. The percentage of locally produced parts was set from 25% in 1978, and was increased to 50% in 1983. In 1985, the government also raised the import duty on passenger cars with 2000cc and over from 150% to 200% (Siroros, 1997; Middlehurst and Nielsen eds., 2002; Suehiro, 2005).

Entering the 1990s, the government completely changed its policy on the automobile industry. In 1990, the Ministry of Commerce lifted import ban on passenger cars with less than 2300cc, following

Table 2.6: Promotion and Liberalisation of Automobile Industry in Thailand 1969–2000.

Period	Name of Temporary Law
1969	Ministry of Industry (MOI) established the Committee for the Development of Automobile Industry of Thailand.
1978	Ministry of Commerce banned import of large-sized cars with 2300cc
1978	MOI ordered assemblers to increase the ratio of usage of locally produced auto parts to 50% in next 5 years.
1984	MOI restricted the number of models of cars domestically assembled.
1986	MOI ordered assemblers to use locally manufactured engines.
1989	Prohibiting new factories / new investment in assembling.
1990	Lifting both ban of car imports and restriction on the number of models.
1994	Full-scale liberalisation of the automobile industry.
2000	Complete abolishing the localisation of auto parts scheme.

Source: Made by the author on the basis of *Bank of Thailand*, Suehiro and Higashi eds. (2000).

by the Ministry of Finance to reduce import duties on auto parts. Finally, in 1994, the government decided to abolish any protection policy, and to liberalise new entry of local and foreign firms into this sector. At the same time, the government also permitted existing assemblers to set up new plants or to expand production lines. Such liberalisation policy under the condition of growing domestic market gave golden chances for new MNCs to advance into Thailand (GM and Ford Motor), and otherwise for existing assemblers to set up new plants (Toyota and Honda).

New investments of both GM and Ford, in turn, attracted a large number of leading European and American parts suppliers. For instance, Dana (USA) advanced into Thailand in 1994, following by Robert Bosch (Germany, 1996), Visteon (USA, 1998, the second largest auto-parts maker in the world), TRF (USA, 1998), Johnson Controls (USA, 1999), and Delphi (USA, 2000, the largest one in the world). In line with the quick expansion of production capacity of Japanese assemblers, Japanese big parts suppliers also advanced into Thailand, and constructed a clustering of firms in eastern parts of Greater Bangkok (Bangpakorn Industrial Estate, Amata City Industrial Estate, Gateway Industrial Estate, etc.) (Suehiro, 2005, 62–64).

Crucial to the further development of the automobile industry in Thailand was *the timing* in switching policy from protection to liberalisation. At that moment, Malaysia still maintained the state policy of promoting a 'National Car Program' (Proton and Perodua),[13] while President Suharto of Indonesia announced a new programme of the 'National Car', granting monopolistic status to his third son and foreign partner (Kia Motor in Korea). In the Philippines, most of foreign assemblers divested or reduced their production after the collapse of the Marcos regime. It is very natural for the MNCs or global auto assemblers to turn their concerns to Thailand. In addition to the

---

[13] The Malaysian government shifted its automobile industry policy from protection to liberalisation since March 2006. In the same year, Perodua (Daihatsu of Japan) became the largest producer of passenger cars in Malaysia, exceeding Proton's cars in terms of production volume.

quick shift to liberalisation policy, industrial agglomeration of auto-parts makers is another important element to attract foreign investors. The comparative advantage of Thailand in accumulation of auto-parts makers (Japanese) is well demonstrated in Table 2.7.

Three different elements (economic liberalisation, agglomeration of auto-parts makers, and MNCs regional strategy) combined with each other to spark a new stage of Thai automobile industry development as illustrated in Figure 2.10. Owing to combination of the three elements and rapid expansion of exports (46% of the total production in 2006), the automobile industry in Thailand alone among the ASEAN 4 could enjoy the sharp V shape recovery after the crisis, and thereafter has achieved a rapid growth. Needless to say, such impressive growth since 2000 is a product of MNC's regional strategy to aim at making Thailand a *hub-centre* of the region.

For instance, Toyota Motor decided to select Thailand as one of four core countries in production and export of the world-wide strategic cars (Innovative International Multi-purpose Vehicle or IMV),[14] while Isuzu Motor also concentrated production and export of pickup-type commercial cars on Thailand. Other MNCs such as Nissan-Renault, Mitsubishi, Honda, Mazda-Ford, and GM also adopted a similar strategy to compete with rivalry companies in the world market. Furthermore, several Japanese MNCs newly set up their logistics service centres (Nissan, Isuzu) and R&D centres (Toyota and Honda) in order to response to the diversification of car models that they produced (Suehiro, 2005). In long run, severe competition among MNCs has contributed to the formation of industrial clusters in eastern part of Thailand.

What should be quickly noted here is the fact that the rise of industrial clusters centering in automobile industry is neither a product of autonomous development of local firms (*sanchi*-type or the Silicon Valley model in Figure 2.8) nor a product of well-designed government promotion policy (EPZ-type). Rather this type may be

---

[14] Toyota Motor decided to select four countries as strategic production and export base of IMV cars in the world: Thailand for Asia, Middle East and Europe; Indonesia for Oceania; South Africa for Africa; and Argentina for Latin America.

Table 2.7: Japanese Automobile Parts Manufacturers in East Asia (2000–2003).

Country	All Industries (Number of Firms) Nov. 2002	Manufacturing (Number of Firms) Nov. 2002	Non Manufacturing (Number of Firms) Nov. 2002	Outstanding Investment Value (100 Million Yen) 1998–2000	Automobiles Parts Makers (Number of Firms) 1998–2000	Japanese Parts Makers (Number of Firms) as of 2003
Thailand	1,381	833	548	11,719	938	164
Singapore	1,101	271	830	6,508	n.a.	28
Malaysia	850	496	354	7,299	295	34
Indonesia	690	480	210	10,523	246	79
Philippines	452	249	203	5,125	245	40
Vietnam	187	122	65	1,220	n.a.	16
India	180	123	57	2,059	2,810	56
China (excl. HK)	2,979	2,108	871	18,369	6,850	182

Source: Made by the author on the basis of Toyo Keizai Shinposha's survey and Minako Mori's own survey.

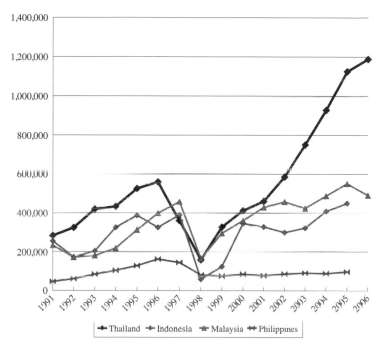

Figure 2.10: Production of Automobile in Southeast Asia 1991–2006.

Note: Production volume include both passenger cars and commercial vehicles.

Source: Drafted by the author on the basis of Fourin Data and Toyota Motor Company.

called *de facto* cluster under the initiative of MNCs because the main promoters are MNCs. Key members are also foreign auto-parts makers which are connected closely with MNCs in home country. Now, whether industrial cluster in a certain country can develop or not depends crucially on the region-wide MNCs strategy rather than the government policy.[15] In fact, there is no prominent development

---

[15] Thai government submitted a plan of 'Detroit in Asia' in 2004, while Thai Automotive Institute (TAI, semi-government) formulated the Second Master Plan of Automobile Industry Development in February 2006. In the two plans, the government stresses the importance of clustering, R&D centre, laboratory, industrial information centre, and human resources development programme in auto-parts manufacturing. But actual implementation of these ideas is expected to be undertaken by the private sector. The government is now expected to play a coordinator in facilitating these ideas.

of industrial cluster in Malaysia, although the government has strategically fostered local (*bumiputera*) auto-parts makers through vendor-development-scheme (VDS, 230 firms in 2003) among cooperation of the government, financial institutions, and assemblers. Rather they are facing with serious problems in quality of products and upgrading of production technology, which in turn discourages MNCs to do new investment in Malaysia.

2.6 Adaptability of Industrial Cluster Approach

Generally speaking, most of East Asian countries except the lower-income countries are facing two major tasks. First one is the *promotion of economic liberalisation*. Second one is *new industrial policy*, switching policy measurement from traditional-type promotion of strategic industries to upgrading of production technology and firm's management. Under the conditions of economic protectionism and government control over financial sector, the governments of East Asian countries could employ a variety of policy measurements including: government subsidies, quantitative control on import, import tariff, tax incentives, policy finance with lower interests (FILs through the Trust Fund Bureau and the JDB in Japan; public loans in Korea; and matching-fund scheme through the Industrial Development Bureau in Taiwan), and provision of infrastructure and facilities.

However, under the increasing pressure of economic liberalisation and globalisation, the governments can hardly use conventional-type policy means. Prevailing FTA negotiations in the region makes it difficult for the governments to maintain high import tariff for the purpose of protection of domestic market. Likewise, liberalisation of financial sector makes it difficult for them to employ policy loans to strategic industries. Liberalisation of foreign direct investment makes it difficult for local firms to utilise production technology, marketing know-how and capital funds through the form of joint-venture. Rather, foreign firm becomes a strong competitor, not a good partner for local firms as before.

On the other hand, for those who have successfully achieved industrialisation, the major task of the government is not a help in start-up of a particular strategic industry, but a further promotion of industrial upgrading. This type of industrial upgrading does imply not only upgrading of products, technology, and marketing, but also upgrading of *production system itself* in conjunction with new international circumstances like IT revolution. If local firms in East Asia hope to advance into high tech industries such as TFT LCD type televisions (not a Black & White TV), they need high technology, flexible management in response to quick-changing market, and R&D in collaboration with foreign pioneering companies. If they will survive in high tech industry, they need to employ a new production system or new business model combining manufacturing with R&D, logistics, and other services instead of conventional style of mass production system with cheap labour force. This is the important reason why industrial cluster model and East Asia on the basis of innovation and network becomes more and more popular among East Asian countries.

However, well-organised industrial cluster usually request autonomous development of local firms as the *sanchi*-type and the Silicon Valley model suggest to us. Even if the governments have strong intention to promote such type of industrial cluster, it is difficult to develop clustering of networked firms with no entrepreneurial promoters in private sector. Rather, as we see the case of Thailand, MNCs form industrial clusters in accordance with their own regional strategy. This type of *de facto* industrial cluster does not always contribute to upgrading of local firms. This is because that we can easily find similar pattern in the EPZ-type industrial cluster in the past. In order to overcome this dilemma, a government is expected to serve as a coordinator, not a conductor of industrial policy, while local firms are requested to find their core competence in clustering of networked firms as we see in Taiwanese ODM manufacturers in the personal computer industry. Referring to this point, we should retrace empirically the various cases in both Europe and East Asia to discuss the possibility and the adaptability of industrial cluster approach. That is precisely the task for us participating in the present workshop at Lyon.

References

AKAMATSU, Kaname. (1962). 'A Historical Pattern of Economic Growth in Developing Countries', *The Developing Economies* (Institute of Asian Economic Affairs), Preliminary Issue 1, March-August: 3–25.

AMSDEN, Alice H. (1989) *Asia's Next Giant: South Korea and Late Industrialisation.* New York: Oxford University Press.

AMSDEN, Alice H. and Wan-Wen CHU. (2003). *Beyond Late Development: Taiwan's Upgrading Policies.* Cambridge, Mass.: The MIT Press.

BALASSA, Bela. (1982). *Development Strategies in Semi-Industrialising Economies.* Baltimore, Md.: Johns Hopkins University Press.

BOOZ-ALLEN and HAMILTON. (1997). *Korean Report: Revitalizing the Korean Economy Toward the 21st Century.* Seoul: Booz-Allen and Hamilton.

CHENERY, Hollis and T.N. SRINIVASAN eds. (1989). *Handbook of Development Economics*, 2. North-Holland, Amsterdam: Elsevier Science Publisher.

DEYO, Frederic ed. (1987). *The Political Economy of the New Asian Industrialism.* Ithaca: Cornell University Press.

DONER, Richard. (1991). *Driving a Bargain: Automobile Industrialisation and Japanese Firms in Southeast Asia.* Berkeley: University of California Press.

FRIEDMAN, David. (1988). *The Misunderstood Miracle: Industrial Development and Political Change in Japan.* Ithaca: Cornell University Press.

FUJIMORI, Hideo ed. (1978). *Ajia Shokoku no Yushutu Kakoukichi* (Export Processing Zones in Asian Countries). Tokyo: IDE.

FUKAGAWA, Yukiko. (1989). *Kankoku: Aru Sangyo Hatten no Kiseki* (South Korea: A Trajectory of Industrial Development). Tokyo: Nihon Keizai Shimbunsha.

GERREFFI, Gary. (1999). 'International Trade and Industrial Upgrading in the Apparel Commodity Chain'. *Journal of International Economics*, 48.

GEREFFI, Gary and Miguel KORZENIEWICZ eds. (1994). *Commodity Chains and Global Capitalism.* Westport, CT: Praeger.

GERSCHENKRON, A. (1962). *Economic Backwardness in Historical Perspective.* Cambridge, Mass.: Harvard University Press.

HASHIMOTO, Jyuro. (1994). 'Koudo Seichoki niokeru Nihon Seifu, Gyokai Dantai, Kigyo: Kikai Kougyo Shinkou Rinji Sochi-hou no Jirei (Relationship among the Government, Business Associations and Firms in Japan: A Case Study of the Temporary Measure for the Promotion of the Machinery Industry Law). Institute of Social Science, University of Tokyo, *Shakai Kagaku Kenkyu*, 45(4), January: 235–256.

HASHIMOTO, Jyuro. (1997). 'Nihon-gata Sangyou Shuseki no Saisei no Hokosei (Synario of Revitalization of Japanese Style Industrial Agglomeration),' in Kiyonari *et al.* eds. (1997).

HOBDAY, Michael. (1995). *Innovation in East Asia: The Challenge to Japan.* Northampton, MA: Edward Elger.

HOBDAY, Michael and Howard RUSH. (2007). 'Upgrading the Technological Capabilities of Foreign Transnational Subsidiaries in Developing Countries: The Case of Electronics in Thailand'. *Research Policy,* 36: 1335–1356.

Japan Development Bank (Nihon Kaihatsu Ginko) ed. (1993a). *Zaisei Touyushi: Nihon no Keiken, Honbun-hen,* (Finance Investment and Loans: Japan's Experience, Full Text), Tokyo: JDB.

Japan Development Bank (Nihon Kaihatsu Ginko) ed. (1993b). *Zaisei Touyushi· Nihon no Keiken, Siryo-hen,* (Finance Investment and Loans: Japan's Experience, Supplemental Information and Statistics), Tokyo: JDB.

Japan Small Business Research Institute. (2005). *White Paper on Small and Medium Enterprises in Japan 2005: Structural Change in Japanese Society and the Dynamism of Small and Medium Enterprise.* Tokyo: JSBRI.

Japan Small Business Research Institute. (2006). *White Paper on Small and Medium Enterprises in Japan 2006: Small and Medium Enterprises at a Turning Point, Strengthening Ties with Overseas Economies and Population Decline in Japan.* Tokyo: JSBRI.

JOHNSON, Chalmers. (1982). *MITI and the Japanese Miracle.* Stanford: Stanford University Press.

KAWAKAMI, Momoko. (1999). 'Bijinesu Nettowaku to Sangyo Seicho: Taiwan, Kankoku Seika Kogyou no Jirei (Business Network and Industrial Growth: A Case Study of Shoes Making Industry in Korea and Taiwan), in Kayoko Kitamura ed., *Higashi Ajia no Chusho Kigyo Nettowaku no Genjyo to Kadai: Gurobarizeishon heno Sekkyokutekina Taiou,* (SMEs Network in East Asia: Active Response to the Globalisation), Chiba: IDE.

KENNEY, Martin and Richard FLORIDA eds. (2004). *Locating Global Advantage: Industry Dynamics in the International Economy.* Stanford: Stanford University Press.

KIMURA, Seishi. (2007). *The Challenge of Late Industrialisation: The Global Economy and the Japanese Commercial Aircraft Industry.* London: Palgrave Macmillan.

KIYONARI, Tadao. (1997). 'Sirikon Barei no Gendai-teki Igi' (Implication of the Silicon Valley's Development), in Kiyonari *et al.* eds. (1997).

KIYONARI, Tadao *et al.* eds. (1997). *Nihon-gata Sangyo Shuseki no Miraizo',* (Perspective of the Japanese Style Industrial Agglomeration), Nikkei Shimbun.

KOJIMA, Kiyoshi. (1975). 'Gankō Keitai-ron to Purodakuto Saikuru-ron: Akamatsu Keizaigaku no Ichitenkai (The Flying-geese Pattern and Product Cycle Model: Some Aspect of the Akamatsu's Economic Theory)' in Monkasei ed., *Gakumon Henro: Akamatsu Kaname Sensei Tuitō Ronshō* (Academic Trajectory: Memorial Essays for the Late Professor Kaname Akamatsu), Tokyo: Sekai Keizai Kenkyū-kai.

KOJIMA, Kiyoshi. (2000). 'The 'Flying Geese' Model of Asian Economic Development: Origin, Theoretical Extension, and Regional Policy Implications.' *Journal of Asian Economics*, 11(4), Winter: 375–401.

KRUGMAN, Paul. (1994). 'The Myth of Asia's Miracle'. *Foreign Affairs*, 73(6), November/December: 62–78.

MASUYAMA, Sei'ichi, Donna VANDENBRINK and Chia Siow YUE eds. (1997). *Industrial Policies in East Asia*. Singapore: Institute of Southeast Asian Studies.

MASUYAMA, Sei'ichi. (1997). 'The Evolving Nature of Industrial Policy in East Asia: Liberalisation, Upgrading, and Integration,' in Masuyama *et al.* eds. (1997).

MIDDLEHURST, Francis and Daniel NIELSEN eds. (2002). *Thailand's Automotive Industry*. Bangkok: The Brooker Group PLC.

Ministry of Economy, Trade and Industry (METI). (2007). *Accountability Report 2006*. Tokyo: METI.

Ministry of Economy, Trade and Industry (METI). Regional Economic and Industrial Policy Group (2006). *Second Term Medium-range Industrial Cluster Plan*. Tokyo: METI.

NABI, Ijaz and JAYASANKAR Shivakumar. (2001). *Back from the Brink: Thailand's Response to the 1997 Economic Crisis*. Bangkok: World Bank Office Bangkok.

NAUGHTON, Barry. ed. (1997). *The China Circle: Economics and Electronics in the PRC, Taiwan, and Hong Kong*. Washington D.C.: Brookings Institute Press.

OHKAWA, Kazushi and HIROHISA Kohama. (1989). *Lectures on Developing Economies: Japan's Experience and Its Relevance*. Tokyo: University of Tokyo Press.

POAPONGSAKORN, Nipon and Belinda FULLER. (1997). 'Industrial Location Policy in Thailand: Industrial Decentralisation or Industrial Sprawl?', in Masuyama *et al.* eds. (1997).

PORTER, Michael. (1990). *The Competitive Advantage of Nations*. New York: The Free Press.

PORTER, Michael. (1998). 'Clusters and the New Economic Competition.' *Harvard Business Review*, November–December: 77–90.

PORTER, Michael. (2003). *Thailand's Competitiveness: Creating the Foundations for Higher Productivity*. Bangkok: NESDB, May.

SATO, Yukihito. (2007). *Taiwan Haiteku Sangyo no Seisei to Hatten* (The Rise and Development of High-Tech Industries in Taiwan). Tokyo: Iwanami Publisher.

SAXENIAN, A. (1994). *Regional Advantage*. Cambridge, Mass.: Harvard University Press.

SAXENIAN, A. and J.Y. Hsu. (2001). 'The Silicon Valley-Hsinchu Connection: Technical Communities and Industrial Upgrading', *Industrial and Corporate Change*, 10(4): 893–920.

SEKI, Mitsuru and Jyunko FUKUDA eds. (1998). *Henbou suru Jibasangyou: Fukugo Kinzokuseihin Sanchi ni Mukau Tsubame*, (Changing Community-based Industries: Tsubame-shi Going Toward Integrated Production Area of Metal Products). Tokyo: Shin Hyoron.

SIROROS, Phatcharee. (1997). *Rat Thai kap Thurakit nai Utsahakam Rotyon* (State and Business in the Automobile Industry in Thailand). Bangkok: Thammasart University Press (in Thai).

STURGEON, Timothy. (2001). 'How Do We Define Value Chains and Production Networks?' *IDS Bulletin* [University of Sussex], 32(3): 9–19.

STURGEON, Timothy and Richard FLORIDA. (2004). 'Globalisation, Deverticalisation, and Employment in Motor Vehicle Industry,' in Martin Kenney and Richard Florida eds.

SUEHIRO, Akira. (2005). 'Tounan Ajia no Jidosha Sangyo to Nihon no Takokuseki Kigyo: Sangyo Seisaku, Kigyo-kan Kyoso, Chiiki Senryaku,' (Automobile Industry in Southeast Asia and Japanese MNCs: Industrial Policy, Competition among Firms, Regional Company Strategy), in Akira Kudo *et al.* eds., *Gendai Nihon Kigyo* (Contemporary Japanese Firms), II. Tokyo: Yuhikaku.

SUEHIRO, Akira. (2008). *Catch-up Industrialization: The Trajectory and Prospects of East Asian Economies*. Singapore: National University of Singapore Press

SUEHIRO, Akira and Shigeki HIGASHI eds. (2000). *Tai no Keizai Seisaku: Seido/ Soshiki/Akutā* (Economic Policy in Thailand: Institutions and Actors). Chiba: Institute of Developing Economies.

SUEHIRO, Akira and Toshiaki HAYASHI (1990). 'Electronics Industry' in Institute of Developing Economies ed. *Comparative Advantage of Manufacturing Industries in Asia*. Tokyo: IDE.

Tsusho Sangyosho Tsusho Sangyo Seisaku-shi Hensan I'inkai [MITI Editorial Board on the History of Trade and Industry Policy] ed. (1990). Tsūshō Sangyō Seisaku-shi 6 (The History of MITI Policies on Trade and Industry). Tokyo: Tsusho Sangyo Chosakai.

WADE, Robert. (1990). *Governing the Market: Economic Theory and the Role of Government in East Asian Industrialisation*. Princeton: Princeton University Press.

WANG, Jiann-Chyuan. (1997). 'The Industrial Policy of Taiwan, ROC', in Masuyama *et al.* eds. (1997).

World Bank. (1993). *The East Asian Miracle: Economic Growth and Public Policy*. New York: Oxford University Press.

World Bank. (1998). *East Asia: The Road to Recovery*. Washington D.C.: The World Bank.

YAMAZAKI, Mitsuru. (1980). *Japan's Community-based Industries: A Case Study of Small Industry*. Tokyo: Asian Productivity Organization.

YONEKURA, Sei'ichiro. (1993). 'Seifu to Kigyo no Dainamikusu: Sangyo Seisaku no Sofuto na Sokumen (The Dynamics of Government and Enterprises: Soft Aspects of Industrial Policy).' *Shogaku Kenkyu* (Hitotsubashi University), **33**: 249–292.

YUSUF, Shahid and Simon J. EVENETT eds. (2002). *Can East Asia Compete? Innovation for Global Markets.* Washington D.C.: The World Bank.

YUSUF, Shahid *et al.* (2003). *Innovative East Asia: The Future of Growth.* Washington D.C.: The World Bank.

Part Two: Japan

The Japanese Clustering
Initiatives Approach

Chapter 3

Public Policies in Japan: Industrial Revitalisation, Knowledge Creation and Clustering

Akira Hattori

Japan D83 R32 R58 L53 R38 L52 038

3.1 Introduction

As pointed out in the general introduction, the concept of cluster is very broad. Each cluster varies greatly in terms of key features such as geographic locations, products, functions, and patterns of inter-firmed linkages. Clusters differ from each other because of differences in historical circumstances, demand conditions, supporting industries, and competitive conditions that underlie their evolution. Each country, while keeping the idea of network, has its own conception of clusters' adding to the definition elements specific to the country. It is of course also the case for Japan.

This chapter will focus on the policy side of the story. The idea is that the way policies are implemented, their objectives and the measures taken to reach them will help in understanding what is really at stake when speaking of clusters. It therefore aims at analysing the evolution of Japanese industrial or innovation policies that finally led to cluster policies implementation in the early 2000s.

As Chapter 1 (Suehiro) explained, Japan has a long tradition of firms' agglomerations. Those are in the majority settled around cities, creating a certain unbalance between industrialised megalopolis and poor industry regions. As early as the 1960s, the government addressed this unbalance issue tending to support industrial spread all over the country. Considering after the oil shock in 1973 that heavy industry could no longer remain the country's economic base, priority was conscientiously given to the creation and development of new technologies, supported by the boundary regions' industry. To achieve this dynamism, Japanese government established in 1983 the 'Technopolis Act' which aims was to promote the implementation of technopolis at the local level. This project which might be considered as a preliminary cluster initiative did not really succeed in achieving territorial balance though.

The collapse of the bubble at the end of the 1980s dragged firms into a massive relocation trend, mostly to countries where production cost is lower, and particularly to ASEAN first, followed by China more recently. In response to this industry escape situation, also called 'Hollowing Out' (*Kûdôka* in Japan) a new set of public policies was needed to revitalise declining industrial agglomerations (see Chapter 4, Lecler and Yamaguchi).

Due to both the impact of the post-bubble crisis and the effect of globalisation, Japanese international competitiveness has been largely eroded in the past decade. Developing new technologies and industries for the future appeared as the only way to recover. This pushed the government to address more directly the innovation issue by enacting developmentalist laws and initiating programmes as early as the 90s. Indeed, in the context of globalisation, the role of science and technology as the engine for economic growth and international competitiveness has been increasingly recognised. International competition in the field of science and technology has greatly intensified in recent years and innovation has become the most important factor of production. Many countries all over the world are now considering 'innovation' as the most important issue to be addressed and have set up various initiatives to strengthen their National Innovation Systems (NIS). In Japan too, the efforts were further reinforced leading in the 2000s to the implementation of two clusters plan or initiative, clusters being considered as the best instrument to coordinate new and preexisting initiatives.

Clusters from METI and from MEXT are each addressing more precisely one of the issues on the agenda: the regional revitalisation for the former and the development of new technologies and industries for the latter. Both types of clusters: industrial clusters and intellectual or knowledge clusters, coming out from these policies focus on innovation though.

After having briefly described the different policies recently implemented by the Japanese government to address the issues of regional revitalisation and innovation, leading to the clusters plan (Section 2), the chapter will focus on the cluster policies and clusters implementation (Section 3). A special attention will be given to the respective role played by the State and local authorities in that new dynamics before analysing concretely the implications on the case of Fukuoka semiconductor cluster taken as an illustration (Section 4).

3.2 From Regional Revitalisation Policy Measures to Cluster Initiatives

The concept of clusters appeared in Japan during the 1990s with Michael Porter's Diamond Theory.[1] Nonetheless, national initiatives for creating clusters were only set a decade after. This new type of agglomeration would not exist though without having been settled on a solid legal base formed by the whole industrial policy measures implemented since the early 1970s. The different steps for achieving clusters policies implementation can be summarised in three periods.

3.2.1 *1970s to mid-1990s: Industrial Decentralisation and Development of Regional Core Cities*

This first period was for the government an opportunity to implement a geographical industry base. As already mentioned, activities were mainly concentrated around big cities' areas and in the opposite side boundary regions were abandoned. Therefore the challenge was to attract enterprises outside big cities' areas by decentralising growth industry fields and, at the end, by creating a driving force behind the regional economy and surrounding areas.

---

[1] Porter, *The Competitive Advantage of Nations* (1990).

This gave birth to the first policy measures for regional economy development.

— **The Industrial Relocation Promotion Law**[2] (1972–2006) is an introductive measure for the regional reactivation and development. The Law promotes the relocation of industry by dividing the nation into: relocation promotion regions (the three great metropolitan regions: Tokyo, Osaka and Nagoya), underdeveloped regions (regions with a low concentration of industry), and other regions. Incentives were provided to enterprises to promote industrial location primarily in underdeveloped regions.

— **The Law for Accelerating Regional Development based on High-Technology Industrial Complexes** (1983–1998), known as Technopolis Act, was one of the most important new technology creation measures. It presented some similarities with industrial clusters that developed later. The Technopolis programme was a national plan led by the MITI[3] to create science cities in peripheral areas. The 3 main objectives were (1) promotion of industrial development by raising the technological level of local businesses and establishing new high-technology industry, (2) sustained regional development through the encouraging of research and development at local level, and (3) creation of attractive living communities in which people can live and work (MITI, 1983; Itô, 1994; Yamasaki, 1992). Thus 26 Technopolis were created over the whole territory. This programme was finally ended in 1998. It is considered that it failed to resolve the problem of industry unbalance between city areas and regions due to a lack of coordination between the local and the national entities.[4]

— **The Knowledge-Intensive Industry Location Act or Brain Centre Site Act** (1988–1998) complemented the Technopolis Act by setting the 'Brain Centre Sites' of industries. The Law

---

[2] Law number 73 of 1972.

[3] Ministry of International Trade and Industry became the METI in 2001 with the administration reform.

[4] See for example, Pelletier (2007).

recognized that the 'brains' of industries, such as information processing and design, were crucial for the development of regional industries and more sophisticated local industrial structures around the country. But in 1998 the supplementary provision of the Law for Facilitating the Creation of New Business repealed the Technopolis Act and the Brain Centre Site Act.

— **The Law for Comprehensive Development of Regional Core Cities with Relocation of Office-Work Function or Regional Base Law**[5] (1992) was enacted to promote further relocation of industries, focusing on administrative facilities of firms. The law was dealing with the lack of vitality in regional areas and the unipolar concentration in Tokyo. By taking advantage of regional autonomy and by the creative and innovative abilities of regions it was aiming at improving urban areas that serve as regional bases. It also promoted the regional dispersion of administrative functions, a major cause of recent unipolar concentration, and encouraged appropriate distribution of these functions throughout Japan (MITI, 1992).

At the end of the 1980s, however, the collapse of the bubble, followed by the increase of the Yen, led the Japanese industry to relocate activities in countries where cost production is lower, and the government's new aim turned to the revitalisation of regional economy.

3.2.2 Mid-1990 to 2001: Prevention of the Hollowing-Out of Japanese Industry and Development of Next Generation Industries

Extended globalisation, difficulties of SMEs and industrial districts (see Chapter 4, Lecler and Yamaguchi), and limits of former period measures let the government to focus more on industrial criteria, and use them as new orientation framework, instead of giving priority to geographical criteria. Innovation became the new key concept of industrial development with measures in order

---

[5] Law number 76 of 1992.

to support linkages between intellectual domain (research) and business.

— **The Science and Technology Basic Plan**[6] (1996–2001) was enacted in 1995 by the national government to make Japan an advanced science and technology-oriented nation. This plan was set in order to promote the construction of a new R&D system by increasing competitive research fund, supporting 10,000 post doctoral fellows, promoting the industry-academia-government collaboration, etc. This law was introduced during a period of economic crisis, nevertheless the Japanese government tended to increase R&D expenditure to strengthen the potential,[7] and total budget exceeded 17.6 trillion yen for 5 years.

— **The Law on Temporary Measures for Activation of Specific Regional Industrial Agglomerations** (1997) stipulates measures to activate local area through diversification and adding value making use of techniques, etc. specific to the region and its local tradition for the purpose of spontaneous development of SMEs (METI, 1997).

— **The Law for Facilitating the Creation of New Business** (1998) was enacted due to the declining economic vitality and the worsening of employment situation. This Law brought (1) support for business starters by creating a special debt guarantee scheme and a special exception to the stock option system, (2) support for business activities by medium/small enterprises making use of new technology, and (3) improvement of the business environment using local industry resources. The Japan Association of New Business incubation Organisation (JANBO[8]) was created by the METI under this law in 1999 and capital

---

[6] Law number 130 of 1995.

[7] Statistic Bureau's data on http://www.stat.go.jp/english/data/kagaku/1534.htm

[8] The objective of JANBO that serve as coordinator is to promote networking between industry-assisting organisations, support-providers and entrepreneurs in a one-stop service according to its regional platforms. For more details, see Hattori-Lecler (2008).

were also provided for persons developing new business support facilities.[9]

— **The Law Promoting Technology Transfer from University to Industry or TLO Law** (1998) is used to facilitate the transfer of university technology to industries through an intermediary institution, the Technology License Organisation (TLO). It aims at upgrading industrial technology and at activating research activities within universities. TLO provides supporting services for faculty-owned patents in obtaining government subsidies, loan guarantee, and exemption of patent related fees. Entrepreneurs may benefit from advices from the National Centre for Industrial Property Information (NCPI), and from free access to national university facilities. Between 1998 and 2003, 32 TLOs were approved but some had been operating at university level before that. The development of new technologies by universities and the transfer to industries led to the commercialisation of new businesses supported by a credit guarantee system.

— **The Law to Strengthen Industrial Technology** (2000) reinforces the collaboration between industry and academia. It aims to give industries an opportunity to get advice from university professors, on a monetary reward basis, and to encourage them to hold management positions in companies that commercialise their inventions. This law also allowed TLOs to freely use national universities' infrastructure for the promotion of industrial development projects. Conditions have been laid down in order to more easily allow 'optional contracts' for the transfer of government-held patents to industries and the granting of exclusive licenses.

All these measures have not yet resolved the hollowing-out problem, but have encouraged industries to trust local resources' potential. Policies implemented during this period have reinforced on one hand the relations between some institutions and on the

---

[9] According to SMEs White Paper 2005 (p. 120), 181 facilities were created between 1998 and 2002 through the activation law (1997) and the JANBO.

other hand, created legal environments to facilitate cluster policy's implementation.

3.2.3 2001 to —: Developing a New Competitive Business in a Global Context

The Japanese industry, in terms of globalisation, had to strengthen the competitiveness and promote the independence of regional economies through their autonomous development in the international competition. At this point, countries like the United States, the United Kingdom, Germany or Finland were advancing industrial cluster formation at policy level and were reinforcing their international competitiveness with industrial concentration, increased employment, creation of venture companies and reactivation of regional economy. Follow this 'cluster wave' in the early 2000s the Japanese government decided to implement new measures to promote clusters that can allow to develop new industry based on R&D but also to revitalise declining regions using local potentials. Clustering projects were considered like the 'strongest card'[10] for Japanese economy, card that should be used to create between actors a 'network where each face is visible'. Complementary measures to facilitate clusters implementation and development were set by government.

— **The University-based Structural Reform Plan for Revitalising Japanese Economy** (2001) has a view to make universities more dynamic and internationally competitive. Based on the potential of American Universities to create new business the MEXT wants, through this measure to (1) pursue the realignment and consolidation of national universities, (2) introduce management methods of private sector into national universities, and (3) install a competitive mechanism with third party evaluation. The MEXT

---

[10] Clusters are qualified as *Kirifuda* for Japanese industry's revitalisation, in '*Nihon no Sangyô Kurasutâ Senryaku*' of Yôko ISHIKURA, a word which can also signify one's best card or joker.

also enacted the 'Top 30 Project',[11] to raise the standards of Japan's top 30 'research universities' to the world's highest levels and to generate venture businesses.

— **The Second Science and Technology Basic Plan** (2001–2005) was enacted as a 5-years extension of the first one (1996). But the new one focused on promoting basic research and giving priority to R&D on national and social issues.[12] The science and technology system was reformed with a doubling of competitive research funds and an enhancement of industry-academia-government collaboration. Therefore the total budget increased from 17.6 trillion yen to 21.1 trillion yen. Thanks to that the Japanese government is hoping to see 30 Nobel laureates within 50 years. This second phase was associated with the knowledge cluster initiative set up by the MEXT in 2002.

— **The Industrial Cluster Plan** (2001) elaborated by the METI defines an industrial cluster as an 'innovative business environment where new businesses sharing management assets with each other are created one after another through horizontal networks; such as industry-government-academia collaboration and collaboration between companies. And the resulting state in which industry with comparative advantage plays a central part in promoting industrial agglomerations' (METI, 2005). The objectives of this cluster policy are therefore (1) to form a network in order to encourage new cooperations between SMEs and with research institutes of universities and to develop an environment favouring innovation in a sustainable manner, (2) to develop and allow new industries to take root at regional level, and (3) to increase synergy effects in collaboration with regional industrial development.

— **The Knowledge Cluster Initiative** (2002) included in the Second Science and Technology Basic Plan established by the

---

[11] First called the 'Tôyama Plan' and after the controversy generated by the name 'Top 30 Plan' it changed to the 'Plan of Centres Of Excellence (COE) for the 21st Century of Japanese Higher Education'.

[12] Four domains of activity were selected: life science, IT, environment and nanotechnology.

Cabinet in March 2001, focuses on the formation of knowledge clusters as part of the regional science and technology promotion by Japanese government. The purpose of this initiative is to create internationally competitive knowledge-concentrated systems for technological innovation. Knowledge clusters are organised closely around the knowledge creation bases that consist of universities or public research institutions, which have unique R&D theme. Other related public research institutions and R&D firms are also expected to come in. Therefore a human network is naturally established in this clustering process and the interaction between technology seeds, joint research organisations and industry needs allow developing innovation.

— Through the **Basic Law on Intellectual Property**[13] (2003) and linked to the enactment of the knowledge cluster plan, the Japanese authorities intended to further enhance the central position of research institutions such as universities in the innovation process giving them more responsibilities and abilities. Under this law, 89 national universities were given a legal status allowing them to create competitive venture-businesses.

— **The New Cooperation Support System** (2005) or the **Small and Medium Entreprises' New Business Activity Promotion Law** was set up by the SMEs Agency to promote new partnership projects born into industrial clusters' networks. About 80 projects have been taken in charge by industrial cluster networked firms.

— **The Third Science and Technology Basic Plan** (2006–2010) was launched in 2006 and addresses the issue of a 'Mega-competition of knowledge' involving USA, Europe but also Asian countries (like China or Korea). Using the policy framework built during the previous programmes, it gives priority to the reinforcement of Japanese knowledge potentials and particularly the knowledge clusters' competitiveness. With a budget of 25 trillion yen, it aims at (1) increasing by 30% the amounts dedicated to the creation of sophisticated research area enhancing industry-academia-government collaborations through the promotion of joint research

---

[13] Law number 122 of 2002.

programmes, (2) strengthening emphasis on the role of 'wisdom' and increasing overseas research collaboration,[14] (3) reinforcing universities' competitiveness by upgrading 30 world-class universities[15] and by revitalising local area universities[16] in order to stimulate regional science and technology development, and (4) upgrading government-wide R&D data base thanks to efficient and appropriate budget allocation. The government has an important part of responsibility in this plan; it plays a role of regulator for raising a science and technology revolution, which could lead Japan to the top-industry nation.

Although the two clusters plans, considered as new and most achieved items for Japanese economic revitalisation and competitiveness, are now at the core of all initiatives, the short description above shows that they benefited from former laws and disposals and also led to new complementary supporting measures or laws enactment by concerned ministries (or related agencies and bureaus). All together these measures build around clusters a flexible framework whose aims is to adapt to all economic and social changes.

3.3 Cluster Implementation and Governance

So the Japanese government built a rather integrated policy environment to impulse revitalisation of the country competitiveness and innovation. But, as policies presented above have shown, the whole set of the legal framework, although bringing some flexibility, makes the situation rather complex. Also, Japan is the only country in the world to have established two types of cluster initiatives, managed by two different ministries. The way national government but also regional or local authorities deal with it but also regulate the different

---

[14] In 2005 only 51 projects over 13,020 were joint researches between Japanese universities and overseas firms (0.4%).

[15] Today about 10 universities are in the top 200.

[16] Local Brain Restart Programme, revitalising a region by revitalising the local brain university.

clusters activities have to be explained to better apprehend what clustering really means in Japan.

3.3.1 The Role of the State and Past Policies

In the literature, the role of State is largely debated around two distinct opinions:

State is considered as an important actor to enact policy measures targeting industrial competition or strategic industries and to create the right environment for innovation.

At the opposite side, upholders of the free market consider that the 'invisible hand' should conduct economy with State just accompanying or facilitating private initiatives.

According to Ketees (2006) and his regional typology,[17] Japanese clusters are considered as very specific in the world because of the government's high implication in their implementation and development process:

— Japan: two national cluster programmes enacted 100% by national government,
— Southern Europe: 60% by government, mostly local/regional initiatives,
— Western Europe: 50% by government, mostly local/regional initiatives,
— Australia, New-Zealand: 40% by government, mostly local/regional, high products branding,
— North America: 40% by government, mostly local/regional,
— Northern Europe: 40% by government mostly local/regional.

What this implication exactly means remains unclear though.

Michael Porter for example explains in *Clusters and the New Economics of Competition* (1998) that the Japanese case is special as it

---

[17] Ketels, presentation of preliminary findings from Greenbook II, World Clusters Forum in Lyon (October 2006).

is one of the rare cases where the government has assimilated the real role to play. According to him, the State should create a competition situation but should stay flexible to the economic changes. Japanese government having understood very early the importance of high technology innovation by (1) developing joint research projects and (2) creating price to reward high quality products, incentive measures have contributed to upgrade industrial innovation and to create new businesses.

In that sense, Japanese government's role in clustering policies could be qualified as 'developmentalist', because of its ability to redirect policy orientation in case of economic or social changes. But this characteristic may also lead to a great risk: Japanese government could overprotect the national market by modifying the industrial structure and then be submitted to a political pressure to protect small firms with poor capacities (agricultural or services sectors for example) or regions with less potential as it might have been the case under former programmes (see Chapter 3, Sekizawa).

Opponents to this opinion, Porter[18] at first, justify the differences existing with former policy measures such as the Technopolis Act, but also with policy packages that have been implemented since the 60s to support traditional form of Japanese industrial districts. Thus, 4 major differences have been defined (Kanoi, 2003):

— **Selection Criteria:** former policy like Technopolis Act was a Top-Down implemented system in which national government designated some regions or cities to revitalise, clusters process on the contrary is a Bottom-Up emergence initiative coming mostly from regions that self-estimate their capacities to be used as local resources to create competitive activities. Local autonomy is also given, considering that leaving actors to organise themselves in a dynamic geographical proximity, namely with research centres and universities located in the area, would ease local knowledge networks to emerge around innovation projects.

---

[18] Preface of Porter in *Nihon no Sangyô Kurasutâ Senryaku* (2003).

— **Extent of Action Field:** the action should not be limited to only one objective. For example the Technopolis Act was established to create knowledge network focusing on new technologies but without thinking about further commercialisation. Clusters tend to enlarge this field of action respecting steps, from innovation initiatives (starting point) to commercialisation and profits from created products (arrival point).

— **Continuity:** one of the clustering strategy's main objectives is the revitalisation of territory; nevertheless it is very difficult in practice to rebuild a declining region on a short period of time. Examples in the world show that the average period for a region to achieve competitive results is between 5 and 10 years. Clusters plans in Japan are seen as a long-lasting initiative (2001–2020 for Industrial Cluster Plan). But to continue being supported for such a long period of time, the real challenge is for projects to show their capacity of adaptability in terms of (1) social and economic changes, (2) human resources development such as changes of employees' numbers and functions, and (3) technology changes which evolution nowadays is fast. The Technopolis Act aimed to create innovative industrial agglomerations but could not address the social evolution specific to each concerned area, as clusters are supposed to do.

— **Special Characteristics:** the traditional industrial districts which emerged spontaneously used to upgrade the agglomeration's competitive level in general, emphasising their strongest points. Clusters structural base should be the existence of a competitive local resource which potential might be maximised, meaning that they are also supposed to emerge spontaneously although supported by policies. Ability to emancipate from 'fashionable activities' like IT or biotechnology and to find new domains to develop by using local resources is also important. Again, Technopolis created during the 1980s presented similar aspects with clusters such as the central position of innovation and therefore the importance given to relocation of research and academic institutions, firms concentration, competitiveness, etc. But while Technopolis remained anchored to improving former potential in terms of process innovation within the subcontracting value-chain, clusters are definitively emphasising product innovation taking into account the need for SMEs to free from subcontracting and innovate by themselves (see Chapter 4, Lecler and Yamaguchi; or Chapter 5, Miyamoto).

3.3.2　*The Industrial Revitalisation Issue: METI Industrial Clusters*

In the aim to reinforce Japanese industrial competitiveness in a globalisation context and to revitalise declining regional economies, the Industrial Cluster Plan aims, as already mentioned, at creating networks between industries, universities and public research institutions through which they are supposed to join their respective resources, materials and knowledge. Doing so, the national government intends to support the creation and promotion of new local industries. To reach these objectives METI has decided to promote innovation within such networks by developing an appropriate industrial environment. To do so, a solid collaboration between national and local levels is needed. National government cannot support all the regional characteristics though. Therefore, METI has spread part of its competence to Regional Bureaus (RBETI), more flexible and informed about local changes. RBETIs are not only the eyes and ears of central government in the regions; they have abilities to appreciate and to use in a rational way the public policies most adapted to local circumstances while following national priorities. The intermediary role played by the Bureaus not only gives a stronger autonomy toward national administration but also lead to consider the local level as an important actor in the clustering mechanism.

Industrial Cluster Plan is a long-term project divided into 3 periods and aiming to give progressively autonomy to industrial clusters. The first step or *The Industrial Cluster Start-Up* from 2001 to 2005 had as an objective to form a solid university-industry-government network that becomes the base of industrial clusters. More than 20 initial projects of industrial clusters were elaborated by the central government who worked in close cooperation with the concerned local governments to evaluate more easily the local policy needs and the industrial potential. The next step or *The Industrial Cluster Development* from 2006 to 2010, focus on continuing advanced networking and on developing specific businesses. At the same time, management reorganisation of companies and creation of venture companies are promoted. If necessary, projects are revised and new projects are prepared flexibly. The last period or *The Industrial Cluster Autonomous Growth* going from 2011 to 2020 is not still precisely defined but the government hopes it will be possible at that time to encourage the financial independence of industrial cluster activities and to further promote networking and development of specific businesses.

The plan follows industrial cluster's activities with attention, establishing at the end of every fiscal year, reports and review proposals to adapt development projects to contemporary situations and needs. But the ultimate targets for Industrial Cluster Plan are (1) to provoke a chain reaction of innovations using the synergy effect created through the linkages between different industries, combined with the close horizontal relations established in networks formed by industry, universities and government, (2) to optimise industries and strengthen their tolerance to changing environment, and (3) to stimulate brand-building for accelerating the emergence of international clusters, or for enhancing the quality of products created in national clusters with local resources in a way to promote their recognition as international brand.

In March 2006 the first period of Industrial Cluster Plan's ended. Its objectives were mainly completed with 19 clusters having established broad-area networks. Priority has been given to creation of networks in the regions. The METI and Regional Bureaus in cooperation with promotion companies from the private sector had managed to gather about 9800 regional SMEs to create new businesses with projects coming from more than 290 universities in Japan. About 81 organisations were designated as core organisations to provide assistance to the cluster's network members, and 105 clusters managers were designated to bring their experience in forming industrial clusters (industrial cluster study group, 2005).

Measures to support creation of new industries and businesses have been set up to help the university-business-government networks to conduct joint researches or other activities using technological seeds. Thus technology development was promoted through (1) partnership between local businesses and universities, (2) linkages with SMEs assistance policies and measures, and (3) support for universities in launching venture business.

In April 2006 the second phase of the Industrial Cluster Plan began with 17 industrial clusters[19] (see Figure 3.1) having new objectives: to develop technologies leading to practical applications in the regions and to reinforce the function of incubation to establish 40 000 new businesses by 2011. To promote industrial clusters for this new period, the Japanese Government decided to provide a budget of 20.8 billion yen[20] for 2007.[21]

3.3.3 *The Knowledge Creation Issue: MEXT Intellectual Clusters and City Area Programme*

In 2002 the MEXT established the Knowledge Cluster Initiative under the Second Science and Technology Basic Plan's S&T reform. These knowledge clusters, also called intellectual clusters, are considered as the complementary brain of the industrial clusters. Japan was the first, and for the moment, the only country to have set up a policy measure taking into consideration the fact that knowledge can be clustered. The MEXT define intellectual clusters as: 'a regional system of technological innovations in which a public research organisation

---

[19] The 19 initial clusters were reviewed after a first-term final evaluation of the METI (through RBETIs), five were eliminated, nine were modified, five others continued and three new ones were created.

[20] 6.5 billion for the formation and management of university-industry-government networks; 13.3 billion yen for the promotion of technology development incorporating the special characteristics of a region (including financial support for SMEs and venture business) and 1 billion yen to strengthen the functioning of incubation centres.

[21] In 2006 the national budget for industrial clusters was 30 billion yen for 19 projects, and only the fund for international development has increased between 2006 and 2007: 14.1 billion yen to 15.5 billion yen (Sakai, 2007).

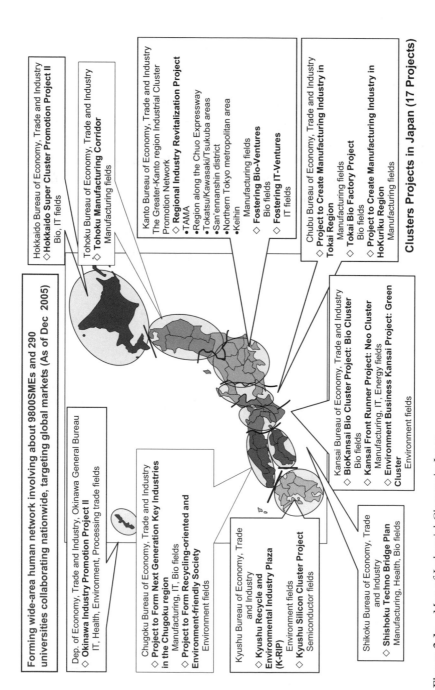

Figure 3.1:   Map of Industrial Clusters in Japan.

Source: From METI, http://www.meti.go.jp, viewed on December 2007.

uses its R&D potential and other unique abilities to lead companies in and around a particular region. More specifically, by utilizing a human resource network and systematic collaborative researches, the system fosters interaction between the original technological seeds of the public research organisation and the business needs of regional companies to create a chain of technological innovations and new industries'.

More precisely, a knowledge cluster is a system for technological innovation, organised by local initiative around universities and other public research institutions whose R&D focus is original and has potential. This system drives technological innovation and creates new industries by stimulating interaction between seeds and needs. In this process universities and public research institutions are considered as 'concentrations of knowledge and talent' and intend to create world-class technological innovation. In order to stimulate the centres of knowledge creation the Japanese government decided to put 500 million yen per year into each cluster, over five years, and also some grants for the core organisations (foundations or other organisations) designated by local governments.[22]

In 2002 the Knowledge Cluster Initiative started with 12 knowledge clusters but a year later 3 new ones were implemented and 3 more in 2004 (see Figure 3.2); but in 2007 the first term of this policy ended and the final evaluation showed that only 11 clusters out of 18 had the potential to survive in an open innovation competition.

The objective of the second term will be to focus on upgrading to world-class level clusters and to create international competitive businesses by patenting research results and conducting R&D leading to incubation projects.

In parallel to the Knowledge Cluster Initiative, in 2002, MEXT set up the City Area Programme that aims at 'developing small to medium-size clusters across Japan' with strengths that utilize unique regional resources to support the creation of new business

---

[22] The government budget for 2004 was about 9 billion yen and 10 billion yen for 2005.

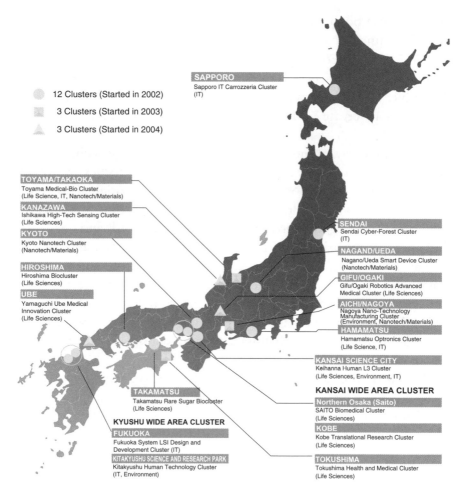

Figure 3.2:   Map of Knowledge Clusters in Japan.

Source: MEXT Knowledge Cluster Initiative Web Site, http://www.mext.go.jp/a_menu/kagaku/chiiki/cluster/index.htm, viewed on December 2007.

and R&D business through industry-academia-government collaborations.[23] This programme is a support to forming regional clusters under local initiatives and does not interfere with the knowledge clusters. 48 areas were selected and the Japanese government

---

[23] Kakizawa (2007).

decided to put 50 million yen for the starting stage, 100 million yen for the basic stage and 200 million yen for the development stage (selection from completed area of basic stage) per year for each stage area over a 3-year period.[24]

If knowledge cluster has to face a world-class competition, City Area Programme focuses on the promotion of regional R&D activities. Like industrial clusters, the aim is local revitalisation, but with research as starting point instead of industry.

3.3.4 *Governance and Coordination Between Industrial and Knowledge Clusters*

Both cluster initiatives represent together the core of industrial innovation and became the guideline for new businesses. Since their creation most of new policies implemented were adapted to them as we have seen before. Both cluster types are independent from each other and differ according to the objectives of their ministries of affiliation (METI or MEXT) and also in their governance. But a majority of industrial clusters and knowledge clusters are located in the same areas though. To favour the upgrading of the joint R&D level and increase the possibility of combined production or facilitate the using of local resources to create a regional brand product, collaboration between them is now on the agenda with as incentive the acquisition of additional subsidies from the government.

3.3.4.1 *Compared Governance of Industrial and Knowledge Clusters*

As already mentioned, METI has devolved part of its competence to Regional Bureaus (RBETI). Those have the ability to adapt national objectives to local needs according to their own appreciations. The governance structure, while regionalised to some extent thanks to a strong collaboration between national and local level, remains however rather centralised.

---

[24] The budget for the full year 2006 was 4 billion yen.

MEXT for its part does not have Regional Bureaus to delegate power as the METI has done and its role is limited to, on one hand, the selection of potentially competitive regions and, on the other hand, the support of projects' core institutions. This difference finally gave a larger autonomy to local governments to create and manage clusters. Core Organisations are designated by the local government concerned to set up a Knowledge Cluster Headquarters,[25] which acts in each region as a control body for project implementation.

Only a trust relation between local and central government allows the legitimacy of this acting power transfer. As already quoted, local government get the necessary knowledge of the field and is able to evaluate the risks and the advantage for building a strong intellectual network much better that national level. On another side, local actors, as well as population or firms, have much more faith in a closer government that can play the role of cluster's 'control tower' by setting up a science and technology coordination system adapted to the local context.

Despite the existence of two types of clusters, the idea was that regulation between them would come out from their complementary interdependence. The scheme is the following: METI's industrial cluster defines market needs while MEXT's intellectual cluster, in reverse, offers the adapted research seeds for new technology or product development. This ideal cooperation process is usually called seeds-needs relation. Very attractive as a concept, the relation is in fact not so easy to implement. A governmental entity constituted by different ministries and called 'Council for Science and Technology Policy' or CSTP is therefore in charge of regulating the interdependence between the two clusters initiatives.

3.3.4.2 *The Coordination Between Clusters: The CSTP*

The CSTP was established in January 2001 within the Cabinet Office as one of the governmental top councils based on the Second Basic

---

[25] Staffed by a President, a Project Director, a Chief Scientist and other members, and including S&T coordinators or advisers like patent attorneys.

Law. Its features are (1) strategic promotion with a comprehensive strategy of science and technology to respond to national and social issues in a timely and appropriate manner, (2) comprehensiveness in the policy making, considering social sciences and humanities to improve the relationship between science and society in areas such as ethics, and (3) discretion by expressing opinions to the Prime Minister or other Ministries on important issues of science and technology.

The CSTP consists of 14 members plus the Prime Minister, who chairs the council. Six Cabinet members, heading Ministries closely related to Science and Technology Policy, are included as regular members. Other Ministers may sit on the council as temporary member. One seat is designated for the President of the Science Council of Japan, and seven executive members, whose professional careers range from various natural sciences and technologies to social sciences, are drawn from industry and academia. Once a month, the Prime Minister convenes the CSTP Conference, which is presided over by the Minister for Science and Technology policy, to discuss various aspects of Science and Technology policy.

In theory CSTP plays a role of regulator and organiser, which watches over the collaboration between the two forms of clusters and verify that, staying in interaction, progressive initiatives come from each side. CSTP is a synergic regulation entity, and is better defined as 'place of ideas and wisdoms' focusing on the development or revitalisation of specific regions. In the reality CSTP's role is less important than initially planed by national authorities. At the beginning CSTP was created in order to be the coordinator of the METI and MEXT's cluster plans, but at the local level inter-minister cooperation became regular[26] and networks were spontaneously set up. By the way CSTP still exists for emphasising the synergy effect between ministries. For local level actors in the clustering process, a supraministerial entity like CSTP only adds another element in the administrative hierarchy and sometimes interfere with existing efficient regional network process.

---

[26] In some cases collaboration between miniterial entities existed locally before the creation of the CSTP.

Since 2004 CSTP has set up committees for regional cluster promotion, holding joint conferences to announce project results and encouraged cooperation and inter-clustered exchanges to reinforce the competitiveness.

Relevant ministries have to use a part of budget to this collaboration and extract all the potentials to serve the other ministries. Then in 2006, METI has spent 2.5 billion yen to allow Industrial Cluster Project to cooperate with two CSTP measures, which are the 'Regional Consortium Research and Development Project', and the 'Inter-ministerial Collaboration Framework', in order to bring new technology seeds from the Knowledge Cluster Initiative to practical use. In reverse, still in 2006, MEXT had used 0.9 billion yen for universities to carry out joint research with corporations taking part in the Industrial Cluster Project (see Figure 3.3).

National government took a very important decision by implicating itself in local level policy, but his role cannot be efficient without an entire collaboration between local actors and also without reducing the gap of competence between regional government and national entities.

In the next section based on case studies, we shall try to empirically illustrate the successful application of clustering public policies on the Kyûshû Island example, a former heavy industry region that managed to switch to a semiconductor's industry and to build an appreciated quality brand all over the world and particularly in Asia thanks to clusters implementation.

3.4 The Case of Kyushu Silicon Island: Kyushu Silicon Cluster

Kyushu, the southernmost Japan's four main islands, had a long tradition in the coal industry but the oil shock in 1973 announced its progressive decline. The semiconductor industry which started in the late 1960s with a few plants grew during this period, leading the island to be known as Silicon Island in the late 1980s. But, the Kyushu region which became home to a number of companies operating in this sector has been for a long time referred to as a 'brainless

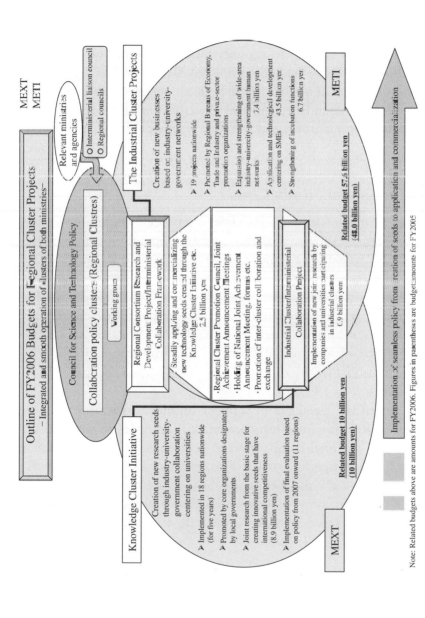

Figure 3.3: Coordination Between Clusters under the CSTP.

Source: Industrial Cluster Study Group, http://www.cluster.gr.jp/relation/data/pdf/gaiyou_eng200601.pdf, viewed on February 2008.

Note: Related budgets above are amounts for FY2006. Figures in parentheses are budget amounts for FY2005 silicon island' because of its relative scarcity of semiconductor design and development institutes. In the 1990s the island experimented a hollowing out phenomenon that strongly hurt the region. The heavy industry concentration around Kita Kyushu having led to high pollution levels, started to turn to ecology industry promotion while the semiconductor industry had to completely switch to LSI[27] semiconductor development (Fukuoka). The region now produces about 10% of the world's semiconductor devices. In 2001 and 2002 the Kyushu Silicon Cluster, in Fukuoka, and the Kita-Kyushu K-RIP Cluster were set up.

3.4.1 *The Kyushu Silicon Cluster*

The Kyushu Silicon Cluster[28] establishment process started in the late 90s, to address the scarcity of design and development institutes mentioned above. Based on a regional revitalisation plan the motivation was to create an innovative semiconductor industry. Some high performance industrial districts emerged in several Kyushu locations for that purpose. This prefigures the foundation of the future cluster and was characterised by a solid network lead by Aso Wataru, the charismatic governor of Fukuoka Prefecture. The implementation of the Industrial Cluster Plan by the METI in 2001 helped to upgrade the existing network (see Figure 3.4).

The aim of the cluster is to support business expansion, growth and progress for the semiconductor-related industries in the Kyushu region so that regional companies can acquire technologies, human resources, management etc. that are competitive and viable throughout the world and can independently develop active businesses.

The Kyushu Silicon Cluster is considered nowadays as one of the most competitive Japanese world-class industrial clusters because of

---

[27] Large Scale Integration, a new type of high integration chips used in computer main memories or second generation microprocessors and replacing standard DRAM system.

[28] Information based on interviews in February 2007, complemented by documentation provided (Kyushu Regional Bureau of Economy, Trade and Industry, 2007).

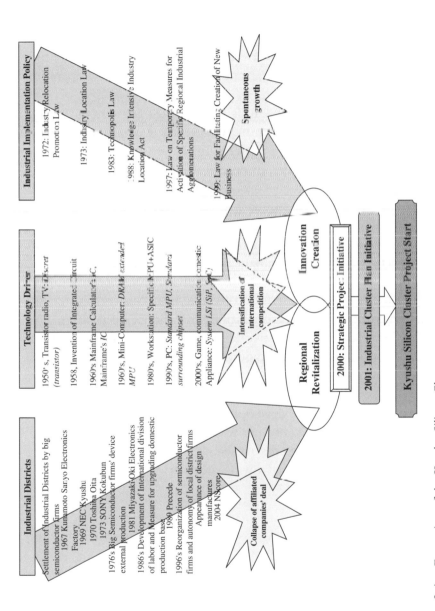

Figure 3.4: Formation of the Kyushu Silicon Cluster.

Source: Kyushu Regional Bureau of Economy, Trade and Industry.

its large potential and also its worldwide reputation.[29] The city's geographical proximity with other Asian countries (China, South Korea, Taiwan and Singapore) also constitutes an advantage: it makes it easier for the cluster to have linkages with the 'Silicon Sea Belt Project' whose goal is to create a real cross-border Asian semiconductor hub fostering a higher technological and human resource co-operation between the countries involved.

The Kyushu Regional Bureau is the nexus of the system and has a role as an intermediate institution between the Central Government and the local level. The appropriate funds are distributed to the RBETI on a Top-Down basis, in order to promote the cluster's projects. However management/coordination of the entire network is delegated to the Semiconductor Industries Technology Innovation Association which acts as a regional headquater. This association[30] which is a civilian agency was created in 2002, in order to promote the university-industry-government networks[31] within the cluster (see Figure 3.5).

Being the leading organisation of the Kyushu Silicon Cluster, the association works in close co-operation with the Regional Bureau of the METI to maximise the networks' potential. To realise the objective she has to follow established guidelines referring to some essential activities:

— **Network formation:** development of a collaborative aptitude between actors, using internet tools (newsletters, homepage,...), organising common events (research forum) or education programme, and formation of a wide-area network between industry and academia;

---

[29] In 2005 Kyushu Silicon Cluster produced 1.6 billion semiconductors, which represent 30% of the Japanese production and 10% the world production.

[30] 1020 members in 2006 mainly from companies and academic institutions.

[31] The network consists of about 150 companies, 42 universities, college of technology and public research institutes, 17 local governments and 5 financial institutions.

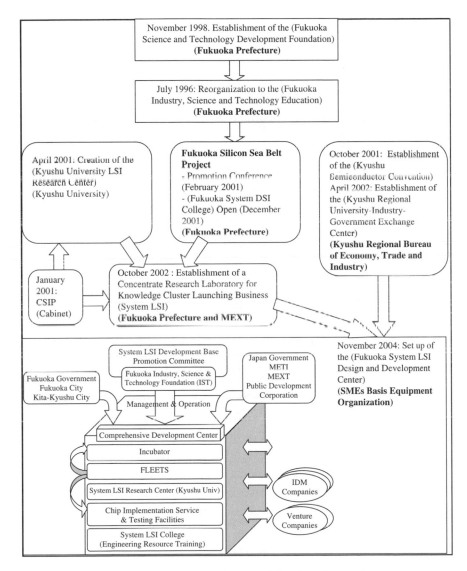

Figure 3.5:   Local Initiatives and Evolution of Kyushu Silicon Cluster.

Source: Created by the author, based on two untitled documents given by the Kyushu Regional Bureau of METI and Yasuura Hiroto, 2007: Silicon Sea Belt and CLUSS Project for SoC Design, System LSI Research Centre, Kyushu University: http://www.slrc.kyushu-u.ac.jp, viewed on November 2007.

— **R&D support:** organisation of seminars for the presentation of results, common technology workshops or the elaboration of new research projects;
— **New markets opening:** support for the finding of markets for new products created by the exploitation of project results, the creation of venture business for new marketable products manufacturing;
— **Encourage local talent:** support for the theoretical and practical study of the production device to improve management strategy;
— **Business support:** reinforcement of the management support through intellectual property seminars, strategic attraction of companies and construction of innovative regional models.

3.4.2 *Region-Wide Interrelation Between Clusters*

The Kyushu Silicon Cluster is collaborating with the 'Fukuoka LSI Design Development Cluster' which is a knowledge cluster under the MEXT cluster plan.[32] The idea behind such interdependence is to reinforce the seeds-needs relation between the two kinds of clusters, using their complementarities to enhance new businesses creation. By the way at the local level CSTP, which may play the role of link between industrial and knowledge clusters, has not a lot of influence, the core actors being often some local institutions.[33] In the case of Fukuoka for example it is the 'Fukuoka Industry, Science and Technology Foundation' (Fukuoka IST).[34] This Foundation is funded (and also politically supported) by public institutions including the Fukuoka Prefecture[35] and the MEXT.[36]

---

[32] Information based on interviews in February 2007 and documentation provided (Fukuoka IST, 2007).

[33] Mainly foundations, called *Zaidan* in Japanese.

[34] Representative from semi-conductor industries, alumnus (OB) of big firms like NEC or SONY and persons from administrative institution are the core members of this foundation.

[35] 6 million yen, 3 million yen from Fukuoka city and 3 other million yen from Kitakyushu city.

[36] 50 million yen for 5 years.

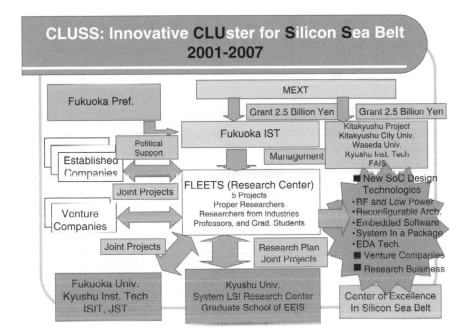

Figure 3.6:   Structure of Innovative Cluster for Silicon Sea Belt.

Source: http://www.slrc.kyushu-u.ac.jp/japanese/presentation/p_yasuura070515.pdf.

Its main activity is to set up innovative R&D projects through the Fukuoka Laboratory for Emerging and Enabling Technologies (FLEETS), an independent research laboratory supporting linkages between universities and industry by setting up core projects and by assigning expert researchers and staff to appropriate projects teams (see Figure 3.6).

The local government's aim was to gather all those entity in a same place in order to create a real 'Cluster' and to facilitate the coordination between MEXT and METI's institutions. Thus in 2004, in collaboration with the SMEs Basic Equipment Organisation, the METI (through the Fukuoka Regional Bureau) and the MEXT (represented by the Fukuoka Prefecture) set up a research centre, the Fukuoka System LSI Design and Development Centre, where each actor of the clustering process can work in close cooperation and where innovative projects can be established. Research laboratories settled by each ministry is represented inside, like the FLEETS (MEXT) which has the core function of creating new projects to develop the semiconductor business. Compared to the other regional clusters in Japan this model managed to link successfully the fundamental researches with a certain regional business model, based on local resource development, and aim to develop a Kyushu brand products. This concept of concentrating all the actors in a same infrastructure could be consider as one of the narrowest model of the cluster's initial theoretical definition.

Conclusion

The Kyushu Silicon Cluster showed that local initiatives can unify the actors towards the same goal. The originality of this cluster is the real autonomy of the local level actors for generating innovation initiatives because of the two charismatic 'Key Persons': Aso Wataru the former governor of Fukuoka Prefecture who has managed to unify and coordinate the different administrations and Yasuura Hiroto, a university professor recognised all over the world for his research on semiconductors, who has the natural credibility to be the technical leader of the researchers. The coordination between those two legitimate leaders has contributed to build a new type of relation between science and administration; a successful double-headed management. Cooperation between actors is not so easy in all the clusters though. There is often a gap between the needs as imagined by administration and what the researchers want to create, leading to opinions divergences. Conscious of the importance of intermediates such as the two charismatic leaders of the Fukuoka case, the Central Government tends to designate cluster managers, trained in the human coordination. By the way in many cases this cluster manager has not the authority toward the different actors who usually prefer trusting a credible local brain leader.

Thus looking at the success of the Kyushu Silicon Cluster the balance of power between the central Government and the regional level may be modified from the Top-Down system to a stronger and efficient Bottom-Up initiative; the decentralisation reform might facilitate such a change for creating worldwide competitive regions.

Presently, the 'mega competition of knowledge' experienced worldwide seems to lead to a new stage. Following the USA which enacted the US Competitiveness Initiatives in 2006 and America Competes Bill in 2007, or the European Union which used 53.2 billion euros for the 7th Research and Development Framework Project in 2006 to increase European technological competitiveness during the next 7 years,[37] Japan too decided in autumn 2006, under the Abe government, to launch a new long term innovation policy: the Innovation 25 Project. The objective is to develop by 2025 some essential innovation domains and push Japan which already has a world-class level in technology to an even higher level. A new organism will be set up to support projects and evaluate basic research. Also, local scientific talents, whose number is limited in Japan due to a decreasing interest of students for scientific fields, will be encouraged.[38] The priority is the development and implementation of an innovation strategy, based on objective assessment of the entity's strengths and weaknesses. It is too early though to determine what will be the concrete implication of this new programme.

As far as clusters are concerned, what is presently on the agenda as a new step to go forwards is international cooperation. Indeed, globalisation also makes it necessary to consider a 'competitive collaboration' with foreign industries or clusters. Not only top-level clusters which already start to establish cooperation with their European or American counterparts, but also some smaller ones coming out from declining industrial districts, with important number of SMEs, tend nowadays to develop cooperation with for example Asian regions in spite of the persisted existence of hollowing-out phenomenon.

---

[37] As examples for EU regional level, France set up the Pole of Competitiveness policy in 2004 and UK since 2006 has a programme to foster scientific researchers.
[38] USA and EU also aim at increasing the number of scientific professors, 70 000 for the USA in the next 5 years, principally in mathematics and biology, and 30 000 professors until 2014 in UK.

References

ARAI, Kôsuke. (August 2000). 'Technological Innovation, National Urban Policy and Local Development: Policy Implications of the Concept of Technopole and Japan's Technopolis Program for Developing Countries,' http://www.ucl.ac.uk.

ASANO, Tanemasa. (2004). 'Kyushu Silicon Cluster Formation Program, An Overview,' paper presented at RIETI Regional Cluster Seminar, June 25. RIETI: http://www.rieti.go.jp/users/cluster-seminar/pdf/011_a_e.pdf, viewed on January 2008.

Chusho Kigyo Cho, ed. (2007). 'Chusho Kigyo Hakusho 2006 nenpan' (White Paper on Small and Medium Enterprises 2006).

COLOVIC-LAMOTTE, Ana, TAYANAGI, Emiko. (2002). 'What Direction Should the Cluster Policy Take, Top-Down Implementation or Bottom-Up Emergence? The Case of Japan,' www.ne.jp/asahi/home/lemonade-studio/uddevallabook.pdf.

CSTP. (December, 2005). 'Outline for the 3rd Science & Technology Basic Plan (FY 2006–2010,' p. 11, www8.cao.go.jp/cstp/english/basic/3rd-BasicPlan_outline.pdf.

ETZKOWITZ, Henry. (November 2002). 'The Triple Helix of University-Industry-Government Implications for Policy and evaluation,' www.sister.nu/pdf/wp_11.pdf.

Fukuoka, IST. (2007). 'Silicon Sea Belt Fukuoka project and the Fukuoka System LSI Design and Research Center,' January, p. 42. (non published document provided by Fukuoka IST Executive, interview January 2007).

FURUKAWA, Yûji. (2004). 'Kurasutâ Seisaku wa chiiki saisei no kirifuda ni naruka?' in National Cluster Forum, www.cluster.gr.jp/event/forum/image/keynote_furukawa-yuji.pdf.

Hamamatsu Shinyô Kinko, Shinkin Chûokinko Sôgô Kenkyûjo. (2004). Sangyô kurasutâ to chiiki kasseika (Industrial Clusters and District Activation), Tokyo: Dôyûkan, p. 275.

HATTORI, Akira, LECLER, Yveline. (2008). 'Innovation and Clusters: The Japanese Government Policy Framework,' in Tokyo University, Institute of Social Science Research Series, March.

HATTORI, Akira. (2006). 'Public Policies in Japan: Revitalization, Technology Creation and Clustering,' paper presented at the International Workshop: Industrial Clusters in Asia: Old and New Forms, Lyon, November 29th–30th and December 1st.

ILLERIS, Sven. (2005). 'Districts industriels, clusters et politiques régionales: les réseaux du développement local,' http://fig-st-die.education.fr/actes/actes_2005/illeris/article.htm.

Industrial cluster study group. (2005). 'Industrial Cluster Study Report,' on line www.cluster.gr.jp/relation/d.ata/pdf/cluster_kenkyu_houkoku_english.pdf, viewed on June 2006.

Innovation 25 Strategy Council. (2007). 'Innovation 25, creating the future, challenging Unlimited possibilities,' interim report, October, Prime Minister's Official Residence Homepage: http://www.kantei.go.jp/foreign/innovation/interim_e.html, viewed on December 2007.

ISHIKURA, Yôko *et alii*. (2003). *Nihon no Sangyô Kurasutâ Senryaku, Chiiki ni okeru kyôsôyûi no kakuritsu* (Strategy for Cluster Initiatives in Japan), Tokyo: Yuhikaku, p. 301.

JANBO. (2006). 'Bijinesu inkyubeshyon shisetsu no genjo (situation of business incubation facilities),' October, JANBO home page: http://www.janbo.gr.jp/bidb/BIabstract.pdf, viewed on January 15, 2008.

JITEX. (2007). 'Les clusters au Japon et en Corée du Sud: enseignements, perspectives et opportunités,' April, MINEFI-DGE http://www.competitivite.gouv.fr/IMG/pdf/etude-cluster-japon-coree.pdf.

KAKIZAWA, Yuji. (2007). 'Knowledge Cluster Initiative and City Area Program — Present State and Issues,' MEXT: www.iar.ubc.ca/centres/cjr/seminars/locecondev/slides/kakizawa.pdf, viewed on January 2008.

KANAI, Kazuyori. (2003). 'Kurasuta riron no kentô to saihensei (experimentation and reorganization of the theory of cluster),' in ISHIKURA Yôko *et alii*, 2003. *Nihon no Sangyô Kurasutâ Senryaku, Chiiki ni okeru kyôsôyûi na kakuritsu* (Strategy for Cluster Initiatives in Japan), Tokyo: Yuhikaku, 43: 74.

KETELS, Christian. (2003). 'The development of the cluster concept — present experiences and further developments,' p. 25. www.planotecnologico.pt/fileviewer.php?file_id=73.

KETELS, Christian. (2004). 'European clusters,' http://www.isc.hbs.edu/pdf/Ketels_European_Clusters_2004.pdf, Knowledge Cluster Initiative Web Site http://www.mext.go.jp/a_menu/kagaku/chiiki/cluster/index.htm.

Kyushu Regional Bureau of Economy, Trade and Industry. (2007). 'Kyushu Silicon Cluster formation Program,' Kyushu RBETI Policy Information Section, p. 25. (non published document provided by Kyushu RBETI executive, interview February 2007).

LECLER, Yveline. (2006). 'The Revitalization of Regional Areas in Japan: Incubation and Clustering, paper presented at the International Workshop: *Industrial clusters in Asia: old and new forms*, Lyon, November 29–30th and December 1st.

MATSUSHITA, Keiichi. (1999). *Jichitai wa kawaruka?* (Will the Local Autonomy Change?), Tokyo: Iwanami Shinsho, p. 243.

METI. Ministry of Economy Trade and Industry. http://www.meti.go.jp.

MEXT. Ministry of Education, Culture, Sports, Science and Technology. http://www.mext.go.jp.

Ministry of Economy Trade and Industry. 'Regional Development Law,' http://www.meti.go.jp/english/aboutmeti/data/a506001e.html.

Ministry of Economy Trade and Industry. 'Small and Medium Enterprises Law,' http://www.meti.go.jp/english/aboutmeti/data/a510001e.html.

Ministry of International Trade and Industry White Paper, February (1999). 'Law for Facilitating Creation of New Business,' http://www.meti.go.jp/english/report/data/gIT1102e.html.

MITSUI, Itsumoto. (2003). 'Industrial Cluster Policies and Regional Development in the Age of Globalization. Eastern and Western Approaches and their Differences,' 30th ISBC in Singapore, p. 10. http://www.asahi-net.or.jp/~MQ7I-MTI/Regional03.pdf.

NISHIZAWA, Akio, FUKUSHIMA, Michi. (2005). *Daigaku hatsu benchâkigyô to kurasutâ senryaku* (University Initiated Ventures and Clusters Strategy), Tokyo: Gakubunsha, p. 275.

NOGUCHI, Tasuku. (1986). *Sentan gijutsu to jibasangyô* (Advanced Technology and Japanese Traditional Local Industry), Tokyo: Nihon Keizai Hyôronsha, p. 398.

NOGUCHI, Tasuku. (1988). *Sentan gijutsu to tekunoporisu* (Advanced Technology and Technopolis), Tokyo: Nihon Keizai Hyôronsha, p. 298.

OECD. (1999). 'Boosting Innovation: The Cluster Approach,' Paris.

PELLETIER Philippe. (2007). Le Japon, géographie, géopolitique et géohistoire, éd. Sedes

PORTER, Michael. (1990). *The Competitive Advantage of Nations.* New York: The Free Press.

PORTER, Michael. (1998). 'Clusters and the New Economics of Competition,' *Harvard Business Review.*

SAKAI, K. (2007). 'Sangyo Kurasuta Keikaku no Genjou to Kadai (Industrial Cluster Policy's Situation and Issues),' METI Industrial Cluster Project Promotion Section, Project leader, February 23, p. 53.

SAKAMURA, Ken. (2007). 'Kawareru Kuni Nihon e Inobeeto Nihon (To a Flexible Country, Innovate Japan),' Kabushiki Gaisha Ascii, March, p. 192.

Small and Medium Enterprise Agency, http://www.chuusho.meti.go.jp.

WHITTAKER, D. Hugh. (1997). *Small Firms in the Japanese Economy.* Cambridge University Press.

YAMASAKI, Akira. (2002). *Kurasutâ senryaku* (Strategy for Creating Industrial Clusters), Tokyo: Yûhikaku Sensho, p. 272.

YAMAWAKI, Hideki. (2001). 'The Evolution and Structure of Industrial Clusters in Japan,' *World Bank Institute no 37183*; on line pdf: http://siteresources.world-bank.org/wbi/resources/wbi37183.pdf, April 2005.

YASUURA, Hiroto. (2007). 'Silicon Sea Belt and CLUSS Project for SoC Design,' System LSI Research Centre, Kyushu University: http://www.slrc.kyushu-u.ac.jp, viewed on November 2007.

Chapter 4

Development of Industrial Parks by the Japan Regional Development Corporation in the 1990s: Is this a Failure of Regional Development Policy or Industrial Cluster Policy?

Yoichi Sekizawa

4.1 Introduction

Development of industrial parks or industrial sites is often regarded as a prerequisite for regional development, especially when the regions concerned do not possess appropriate sites for location of industries. Although this may be true at times, there is a danger that this way of thinking leads to the misunderstanding that if industrial parks are built, then successful regional development will follow. Such misunderstanding may have triggered the failure of Japan's regional development strategy in the 1990s. This paper examines this failure through a case study of the activities of the Japan Regional Development Corporation (JRDC), owned by the Japanese Government.[1]

In Japan, developing industrial parks was regarded as an effective method of regional development by both the central and local

---

[1] Missions of the JRDC comprised the development of industrial parks, development of building estates in urban areas, and several others. The development of industrial parks was under the jurisdiction of Ministry of International Trade and Industry (MITI). The development of building estates was under the jurisdiction of Ministry of Construction. In this paper, I will focus on the development of industrial parks.

governments. Thus, most industrial parks in Japan were developed by local governments and the JRDC. There are few industrial parks which have been developed by the private sector.

Many local governments were involved in developing industrial parks in their enthusiasm to create jobs, increase revenue from tax, and promote economic growth by attracting companies.

The central government had different expectations with regard to industrial parks. Their main concern was concentration of population and economic activities within urban areas, particularly in the Tokyo metropolitan area. In recognition of this, government officials as well as politicians representing rural areas thought it as important to transfer industries from urban to rural areas. The development of industrial parks was seen as a tool to realise this transfer. The JRDC was created by the central government with the intention of building and selling industrial parks in rural areas.

The developing and selling of the industrial parks was not a major problem until the end of the 1980s. However, in the 1990s, large amount of unsold industrial parks accumulated and remained vacant in many areas of Japan. This led to various problems such as financial crises for local governments, unnecessary destruction of the environment, and unnecessary burden on taxpayers in Japan.

Because of limited information on industrial parks developed by local governments, this paper focuses on a case study of industrial parks developed by the JRDC based on my first-hand experience as one of its employees.[2]

4.2 Mission of the JRDC

The JRDC was created in 1963. Its original goal was to assist in the revitalisation of areas that were forced to withdraw from the declining coal mining business. One of the major tools for revitalisation was the development of industrial parks.

A new mission was given to the JRDC in 1972: the development of 'Core Industrial Parks.' During a period of strong economic

---

[2] I worked for the JRDC during 1999–2001 on a job rotation of the MITI.

growth, the 'Industrial Relocation Promotion Law' was enacted with a view to realising the 'balanced development of national land.' The main goal of the law was to transfer factories from 'transfer promotion areas,' in which factories were concentrated to 'attraction-necessary areas,' in which factories were scarce. One measure taken to achieve this was to develop industrial parks in the 'attraction-necessary areas.' This task was allotted to the JRDC. The units in the first Core Industrial Park were put up for sale in 1978.

Despite central government's published policy of 'balanced development of national land,' the concentration of industries and people in the urban areas continued unabated. The accumulation of various urban functions in the Tokyo metropolitan area was particularly striking. During the 'bubble economy' of the 1980s, the central government began to recognise that not only factories but also 'brain' type industries such as research facilities and software industry should be transferred from urban to rural areas. With this recognition in mind, the 'Law to Promote the Group-Sitting of Designated Types of Business Contributing to More Sophisticated Local Industrial Structures' (known as the 'Brain Business Locating Law') was enacted in 1988. An idea similar to that of the 'industrial cluster' was incorporated into this law; it was intended that 16 types of industries including software and natural science research facilities were to be concentrated in designated areas. In other words, it was assumed that gathering industries together into these specific areas would lead to efficient and effective business activities through mutual stimulation and complementary activities (MITI, 1988). According to the law, it was stipulated that the JRDC should develop and sell industrial parks to be used for 16 types of industries. Although the names of these industrial parks varied, they typically became known as 'Brain Parks.'

Introduction of new types of industrial parks continued. The concentration of various functions in the Tokyo metropolitan area was deemed undesirable, and the relocation of core functions from urban to rural areas was regarded as necessary. In 1992, the 'Law for Comprehensive Development of Regional Core Cities with Relocation of Office-Work Function' was enacted. According to this law, measures to promote transfer of offices concentrated in urban areas to rural areas were stipulated. These measures included development and sale of industrial parks for offices by the JRDC. Those industrial parks were called 'Office Arcadia.'

A new version of the industrial parks was introduced in 1998. Policymakers were concerned about losing preexisting industrial clusters in Japan. Many Japanese manufacturers had relocated their factories overseas because of the appreciation of yen. With a view to maintaining the domestic industry clusters, the 'Law for Activation of Industrial Agglomerations' was enacted. Unlike the three laws mentioned above, this law did not aim at dealing with the disparity between urban and rural areas. Faced with a serious downturn in the economy and resistance from urban residents who were dissatisfied with the transfer of wealth to rural areas, the idea of the balanced development of the regions lost its impetus. Instead, the revitalisation of the Japanese economy as a whole became the priority. However, the development and sale of industrial parks became a legal device. This task was also allotted to the JRDC. These industrial parks were termed 'Frontier Parks.'

In 1998, the 'New Business Creation Promotion Law' was enacted. According to this law, the intention was that industrial clusters with advanced technology should be used as the incubators for creating new industry (MITI, 1999). In the law, the JRDC was given the new task of developing industrial parks which would contribute to development and utilisation of advanced technology. This type of industrial park was called a 'Creation Park.'

4.3 Concept of Industrial Parks

As described above, six types of industrial parks were developed by the JRDC (Table 4.1). The parks looked almost identical. The differences existed mostly in the intended purpose and scale.[3] Many industrial

---

[3] For example, sites of office arcadia were permitted to be used solely for the construction of offices, research facilities, and facilities assisting them. It was legally prohibited for those sites to be used as the sites for factories. Core Industrial Parks ranged from 52–384 ha. Brain Parks ranged from 7.9–20 ha. Office Arcadia ranged from 12.4–39 ha.

Table 4.1: Types of Industrial Parks Developed by the JRDC.

Type of Industrial Parks	Goal	Fiscal Year in which the First Project Started	Fiscal Year in which the Last Project Started	Number of Projects	
				Started until FY1990	Started after FY1990
Industrial parks for coal mining regions	Revitalising the coal-mining areas	1963	1994	132	8
Core industrial parks	Relocation of factories from urban areas to rural areas	1973	1998	24	7
Brain parks	Formation of clusters of 'brain industries' in rural areas	1989	1994	6	6
Office arcadia	Formation of offices and research facilities in rural areas	1993	2001	0	11
Frontier parks	Formation of industrial clusters	2000	2002	0	5
Creation parks	Contribution to development and utilisation of advanced technology	2002	2002	0	1

Source: METI, SMRJ.

parks had attractive names such as 'Research Park' and 'Office Park,' but these names reflected hope rather than reality.

The relationship between industrial parks developed by the JRDC and 'industrial cluster' is not clear. Regarding core industrial parks, there is no evidence that policy makers kept in mind the concept of industrial cluster. By contrast, in brain parks, they consciously aimed at making industrial clusters from the brain parks (MITI, 1988). In the frontier parks, this intention was clearer. The policy makers had the works of Alfred Marshal, Alfred Weber, Paul Krugman, and Michal Porter in mind when they drafted the law (MITI, 1998).

Even in the case of those industrial parks that were intended to form industrial clusters, most projects were trying to create the clusters from scratch. Many of the sites were transformed from farm lands and mountain forests and had no industrial foundation except for agriculture.

Each industrial park was built by the JRDC at the request of the local government in which the park was to be established. Prior approval of the central government was necessary for the JRDC to start work.

The finance necessary for the development of industrial parks was provided mostly through the Fiscal Investment and Loan Programme.[4] The central government collected money mainly through postal saving. The money collected was lent to public organisations including the JRDC. Although the interest rates were lower than those prevalent in the private sector owing to the guarantee of Japanese government, principal and interest had to be repaid, and it was assumed that the JRDC would recover its investment by selling the industrial parks. The expenditure for the development of industrial parks included not only the expenditure for purchasing land and the construction cost but also the salaries of the employees of the JRDC. In other words, what the JRDC did was almost the same as private real estate companies.

---

[4] On the Fiscal Investment and Loan Program, see, for example, Doi and Hoshi (2002).

4.4 What Happened in the 1990s?

The Japanese economy experienced extreme highs and lows because of the formation and collapse of the 'bubble.' In the late 1980s, firms competed in the purchase of real estates for fear that they will lose all available sites inside Japan. The number of newly locating factories radically increased (Figure 4.1). Land prices soared (Figure 4.2).

However, with the plunge of real estate prices, this trend changed its course. Japan entered 'the lost 1990s.' Firms refrained from

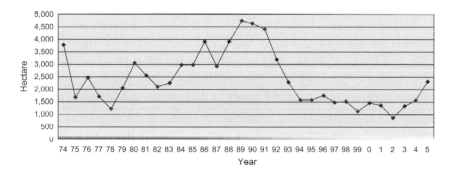

Figure 4.1:   Newly Locating Factories in Japan (area base).

Source: Japan Industrial Location Centre.

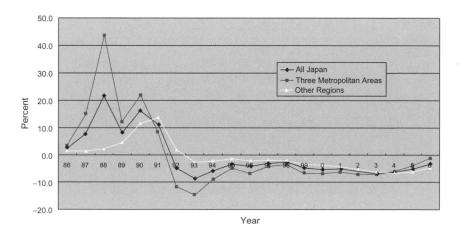

Figure 4.2:   Publicised Prices of Land in Japan.

Source: Ministry of Land, Infrastructure and Transport.

investing, in particular, investments accompanying purchase of real estate. As a result, the number of relocations, and the new establishment of factories, offices, and other industrial facilities plummeted.

This general trend was reflected in the sales figures of the JRDC. Core Industrial Park sales were at all time high in 1990. Three industrial parks of Brain Parks were sold out during this time. This trend did not continue for long. Sale of Core Industrial Parks dropped to a low (Figure 4.3) in the 1990s and early 2000s. Although the number of newly supplied sites was relatively low, the stock remained at a high level due to low sales.

Regarding Brain Parks and Office Arcadia, new supply of sites continued even after the collapse of the bubble economy (Figure 4.4). As a result of the new supply and low sales of the sites, stock accumulated.

Supply of new sites after the collapse of the bubble around 1990 is partly attributable to the length of the development period. From the start of construction of industrial parks, it took several years to start their sale resulting in a time lag. Industrial parks that had been planned during the bubble were on course of completion in the midst of a deep recession.

However, even after the collapse of the bubble economy, building of new industrial parks were planned and some were realised. The number

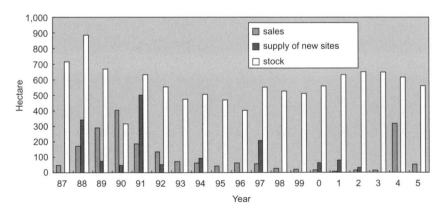

Figure 4.3:   Sales of Core Industrial Parks.

Source: SMRJ.

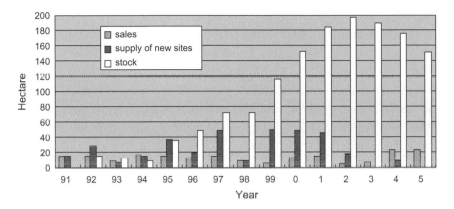

Figure 4.4: Sales of Brain Parks and Office Arcadias.
Source: SMRJ (1992).

of sites the JRDC acquired during 1992–1996 (on a fiscal year basis) in order to build industrial parks was 1.22 times greater than that during 1987–1991.[5] This increase contributed to the accumulation of unsold industrial parks.

It was in 2001 that the central government declared that it would desist from developing new industrial parks through the JRDC.[6] In 2004, the JRDC was merged with the Japan Small and Medium Enterprise Corporation (JASMEC) and became the 'Organisation for Small & Medium Enterprises and Regional Innovation, JAPAN' (SMRJ).

To summarise, in the 1990s, firms did not relocate to the industrial parks as was expected. Therefore, the transfer of industrial facilities such as factories and offices from urban to rural areas was not achieved. The formation of industrial conglomeration was not realised either. Even in the industrial parks to which firms did come, it is not clear whether or not the transfer of firms from urban to rural areas was actually achieved, because many of the firms who purchased the sites in these industrial parks were not from urban areas, but local ones.

---

[5] Management and Coordination Agency (2000).
[6] Tokushuhoujin Seirigourika Keikaku (Plan for Reshuffling and Rationalising Special Corporations) in December 19, 2001.

Although it had originally been expected that the JRDC's debt for the development of the industrial parks would be paid back within five years through sales, this expectation was not met. Due to the price reduction required to meet the slump in sales plus the interests that accumulated, and the JRDC employee salaries, the gap between the initial value of debt and the amount actually repayable by the JRDC has widened. Although the question of who will pay and how much the payment will be are not clear, it is clear that the burden will eventually fall onto the taxpayers of Japan.

4.5 Why has this happened?

How was such an undesirable situation brought about? Why did the government not stop the development of industrial parks earlier? Why could not the JRDC focus on regions with high potential? Answering these questions is not easy. But some possible arguments can be made.

First of all, the rise and collapse of the bubble economy distorted the perspective of those in charge of the JRDC, just as it did for many other Japanese people. With the collapse of the bubble, firms refrained from investment. In addition, the collapse of the bubble accompanied the plunge in real estate prices as a reaction against the extraordinary rise of the prices of real estate in the bubble era. Thus, firms were particularly reluctant to purchase real estate. But understanding this new trend on a real-time basis was difficult. Few people predicted that this recession, which was later named the 'lost 1990s,' would be deep and long. In the expectation of rapid recovery of the economy, there was a momentum for further development of industrial sites.

Second, local governments had a strong urge to escape from the stagnancy of the regional economy, and they saw a way of achieving this through attracting firms to their region. Therefore, despite the low demand for industrial sites, there was pressure from the local governments for development of industrial parks. As an organisation promoting regional development, it was hard for the JRDC to disregard such pressure.

Third, there was little, if any, discipline provided by the financial market. Had the projects of building industrial parks been planned by private companies who need finance (for the development of industrial parks) from private financial sectors such as banks, those financial sectors might have hesitated to lend the money, taking into account the risks generated by low demand for real estate and lack of potential of the regions. In reality, the JRDC as a government-owned corporation had access to the national fiscal investment and loan system. The Japanese government tried to stimulate the economy in order to surmount the acute recession, and the funds accumulated under the system were designated as ammunition for a package designed to stimulate the economy. Thus, there was no effective financial check for the projects by the JRDC.

Fourth, the executives of the JRDC lacked the expertise required to run the corporation. The structure of the JRDC was similar to that of private real estate companies. It had little budget support from the central government. The JRDC was compelled to stand on its own, which included reimbursing the money it had borrowed. To achieve success in this perspective, managerial expertise as in the case of private companies is inevitable. However, almost all the executives of the JRDC were retired government officials.[7] They had no experience of running a private company.

Fifth, there was the usual inertia to continue the business in a traditional manner. Developing the industrial parks had been the main business of the JRDC for a long time. It was predicted that ceasing that part of its business would generate the serious problem of how to relocate employees. In addition, the central government had another incentive to maintain the business. In Japan, the legal retirement age of government officials was 60, but most officials were recommended to retire prior to that age in return for jobs outside the government allotted for them by the ministries. The JRDC was one of the typical destinations of these retirees. In addition, about one third of the employees of the JRDC were government officials on temporary posting, partly due to the ceiling on the number of officials staying in the government. In these contexts, the government

---

[7] In Japan, this is called *amakudari*.

had a strong incentive to maintain the task of the JRDC regardless of the change of economic environment. Such potentially serious problems brought about procrastination.

4.6 Conclusion

Development of industrial parks, which turned out unnecessary in retrospect, were carried out in the 1990s. This caused a burden to taxpayers and unnecessarily damaged natural habitats in some areas. Whether or not this phenomenon was peculiar to Japan in the 1990s has yet to be explored.

Fujita (2003) argues, while quoting the presentation by Michael Porter that the government should not create brand new clusters but strengthen and develop preexisting ones.[8] Although this seems to be theoretically true, it is not feasible in practice. Most regions have the desire to develop. Those regions that have no foundation of industry clusters also want to develop. Extending this further, most regions dream of becoming another Silicon Valley. Such dreams encouraged many rural areas of Japan to build industrial parks as the first step, and the central government was involved in this move. However, in many of the regions there were no further steps.

Although the intervention of government for the formation of industrial clusters may be theoretically justifiable, actual intervention may not be carried out as assumed in theory due to the variegated pressures from local governments, bureaucrats, politicians representing rural areas, etc. In this context, it is not clear whether or not government intervention for industrial clusters would be better than no intervention. At least, industrial policies including the industrial cluster policy, should be carefully designed to take account of the possibility of government failure as well as market failure, and should be reviewed as objectively as possible.

---

[8] According to Fujita (2003), Michael Porter said, 'Clusters cannot be created without foundation' in December 4, 2003, at Ministry of Economy and Trade and Industry of Japan.

Many developing countries may be in a situation similar to that of the rural areas of Japan, in the sense that they lack the industrial foundation for forming an industrial cluster. If they don't build industrial parks at all, it will be difficult for firms to move in. On the other hand, if they create excess industrial parks or make them in unsuitable places, unused sites may accumulate and valuable natural habitats such as rainforests and mangroves will be meaninglessly lost. How to strike the correct balance is a difficult question. It seems that the projects tend to fail when the local communities' urge for development and the central government's will for balanced development of regions are the only motivators. Careful evaluations of the potential and profitability of the project are required.

References

DOI, Takero and Takeo HOSHI. (2002). 'Paying for the FILP.' NBER Working Paper 9385.

FUJITA, Masahisa. (2003). 'Kukankeizaigaku no Shiten kara Mita Sangyou Cluster Seisaku no Igi to Kadai (Significance and Challenge of Industrial Cluster Policy from the Perspective of Spatial Economics).' In Yoko Ishikura, Masahisa Fujita, Noboru Maeda, Kazuyori Kanai, and Akira Yamasaki, *Nihon no Cluster Seisaku* (*Strategy for Cluster Initiatives in Japan*). Tokyo: Yuhikaku.

Management and Coordination Agency. (2000). 'Tokushu Houjin ni Kansuru Chousa Kekka Houkokusho — Chiiki Shinkou Seibi Koudan — (Report on the Result of Research on Special Corporations. Japan Regional Development Corporation).'

MANO, Shuji. (1992). 'Chiiki Shinkou Seibi Koudan no Zunou Ricchi Jigyou no Tenkai (Outlook on Business of Brain Industry Location by the Japan Regional Development Corporation).' *Sangyou Ricchi*, February 1992.

MITI. (1988). *Zunou Ricchi Hou no Kaisetsu* (Explanation of 'Brain Business Locating Law'). Tokyo: Tsushou Sangyou Chousakai.

MITI. (1998). *Chiiki Sangyou Shuseki Kasseika Hou no Kaisetsu* (Explanation of 'Law for Activation of Industrial Agglomerations'). Tokyo: Tsushou Sangyou Chousakai.

MITI. (1999). 'Shinjigyou Soushutsu Hou ni Tsuite' (On 'New Business Creation Promotion Law').

Chapter 5

From *Jibasangyō* to Industrial Clusters in Japan: SMEs and Revitalisation Policies

Lecler Yveline and Yamaguchi Takayuki

Japan R.32 M13
L25 L11 L53
L60

5.1 Introduction

In general an industrial agglomeration may be defined as 'a situation in which many enterprises with close relations accumulate in a comparatively narrow zone' (Itami *et al.*, 1998). In Japan, as defined in Chapter 1, several industrial agglomeration or district types coexist since a more or less remote past.

Indeed, Japan's agglomerations have a long history, starting for some of them during the Edo period (1600–1868) around local handicraft activities (Yamawaki Hideki, 2001). The evolution after Meiji restoration (1868) and later on after the WWII, saw a large number of them shifting traditional activities to more industrial and modern ones, but this ensured the survival of firms concentrations in these local areas. So all along their history, industrial districts mostly based on SMEs concentration had to restructure and upgrade their technologies to be able to follow the technological progress level of the country and/or of their big clients. SMEs had to learn from principals, or through linkages with support institutions etc. (Lecler, 1982). The agglomeration impact is said as having played its part by helping such upgrading by the eased diffusion of information and cooperation within the districts etc. Different law dispositions or public programmes aiming at supporting SMEs, through loans and fund rising etc. were also implemented in the past by the

121

national government or prefectures (Afriat and Lecler, 1986). During the past period of accelerated technological progress, Japanese SMEs and districts already experienced large evolutions. A lot of firms could not survive during such period, while new ones developed eventually leading to new agglomerations to emerge and to a variety of situation to coexist. This chapter will concentrate on former industrial districts mainly type C and D (see definition in Chapter 1), that for simplicity we shall gather under the term of *jibasangyō*.

Typical SMEs in *jibasangyō* have depended on sales or marketing activities known as *sanchi donya* (home wholesale). Through this style of transaction, SMEs could have saved their limited quantitative/qualitative management resources and concentrated their managerial resources on production activities. For many SMEs, it was *sanchi donya* that decided what to produce. Under these conditions, SMEs in *jibasangyō* have long been devoted to the repetitive production of products that do not deviate from the home brand image. The situation does not differ for subcontractors agglomerations in which the main principal plays the same part that *sanchi donya*.

The influence of the long-term economic depression after the burst of the economic bubble, globalisation, and the further progress of IT changed the transactional structure that depended on *sanchi donya* and the home brand. As low-priced, alternative products flowed in as a result of globalisation, the competitiveness of labour-intensive SMEs in *jibasangyō*, declined and, as the amount of commodity handling was declining owing to the economic depression, the marketing and information-gathering ability of *sanchi donya* decreased. In addition, the further progress of IT led to the expansion of direct marketing. Also, to keep their international competitiveness, Japanese multinationals had to centre on their core business and to concentrate their activities in advanced economies around R&D, designing higher end products. They used to shift lower range product manufacturing to Asian emerging countries to benefit from lower production and labour costs. Subcontractors progressively lost part of their job when the big principals around which they are agglomerated shifted production abroad. SMEs concentrated in such industrial districts are mostly engaged in activities which competition with emerging Asian countries and especially China is severe.

Facing a decrease in order or sales opportunity and unable to compete through prices, SMEs absolutely need to upgrade their production, to engage in new product range or activities integrating more upgraded technologies, to free from subcontracting and develop new products or technologies by themselves... and foster their market expansion ability or find new markets. But SMEs currently lack product innovation, marketing, and business conversion abilities,[1] making it difficult for them to adapt to the new competition context, in which innovation is at the core of industrial restructuring.

As a result, firms' number is decreasing leading to a hollowing out of most of Japanese *jibasangyo* (Section 2). This situation conducted the Japanese government to take measures to support SMEs and promote firms creation (Section 3). The cluster policy, presented in Chapter 2, seems since its implementation considered as the best way to achieve such ends, but governmental cluster policy though targeting existing industrial agglomerations, are highly oriented towards the new economy and the creation of a knowledge society. The emphasis is therefore put, as far as SMEs are concerned, on preparing or incubating the institutional environment for start-ups to develop new high-tech industries for the next generation. This is of course positive, but might not be enough to mobilise the existing SMEs sufficiently and solve the problem most districts are facing. This situation is quite noticeable in the traditional or declining industrial agglomerations which tend to be relegated to the edges of the national or even regional cluster policy. But as case studies of two prefectures: Hyogo and Osaka will illustrate (Sections 4 and 5), numerous initiatives start at the local level without being recognised as cluster within the policy

---

[1] For many authors, the lack of product innovation is characteristic, not only of *Jibasangyō* but also of the Japanese industry in general. Fujimoto points out that the Japanese industries have developed deep-level competitiveness around process innovation. In the future, Japanese industry needs to reinforce deep- and surface-level competitiveness around product innovation (Fujimoto, 2001; Fujimoto and Yasumoto, 2001; Fujimoto, 2003).

framework. Some might be labelled and supported later on while other might not, but in most cases, the core elements of the cluster policies associated to former cooperation channels are used to foster restructuring through innovation (Section 6).

5.2 SMEs' Agglomerations and their Difficulties

Comparing the firms' closure and creation rates over time gives useful indications of what is at stake in Japan since the end of the 80s. Failures are increasing, as it did each time in the past that technological progress accelerated. The present period differs however from the past in that sense that for the first time in Japans' economic history, firms' closures are since the late 80s exceeding new creations, leading to a general decrease in firms' number that put into danger the survival of districts inherited from the past. Such an evolution is strongly hitting the vitality of their located territories which are not only loosing activities but also employment.

5.2.1 *The Lack of New Firms' Creation*

Since 1989, the rate of firms' closure exceeds the new firms' creation one. But as Figure 5.1 shows, although the exit rate increased a lot since 1989 with the post bubble crisis, the problem is mainly due to the new firms' creation which is declining in fact since the beginning of the 80s. If manufacturing industry is isolated, the situation is even worst with more than 1.5 points (1.68) closures more in the second half of the 90s (1994–2001) than in the 60s–70s and almost 3 points less creations (–2.94).

Several reasons might be pointed out to explain why closures are now exceeding creations or why Japan is lacking of new creations compared to the past.

The Japanese population is aging, and just began to decrease. Unlike older generation who generally started to work after graduating from secondary education before creating their own small firm, young generations who are in a great majority attending universities, are not very keen to work in SMEs and to succeed their father.

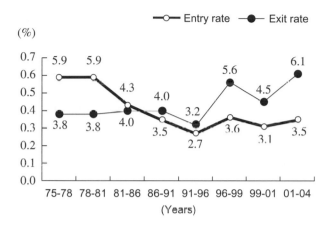

Figure 5.1: Trends in Entry and Exit ('annual' average for non-primary industry).
Source: Chūshōkigyōchō (2006).

Becoming a CEO even of a small production unit was seen as a dream to reach in the past while being an employee of a prestigious large MNE or a service sector establishment is largely favoured today. According to a survey of the Global Entrepreneurship Monitor (1999) quoted in a 2003 METI report,[2] the proportion of people saying that entrepreneurs are socially valuable was 91% in the USA compared to a low 8% in Japan. Young Japanese also seem to have more aversion to risk than their father. The difficult economic environment might at least partly explain this attitude as maintaining the family living standards while starting one's own business does not give the same guarantees than before. It seems however that this trend might be reversed in the future with university students having more difficulties to find employment because of stagnation and changes in the employment system (Chūshōkigyōchō, 2005).

With the aging of the Japanese population and its decreasing trend, the lack of highly experienced production workers is a new issue that firms will have to deal with.[3] Attracting high quality workers

---

[2] Data from the SME Agency: Survey on creative entrepreneurial activity, 1999.

[3] The baby boomers of the WWII are getting to 60 years old and are progressively retiring.

or technicians is becoming more difficult, even in industrial districts which are therefore loosing one of the agglomeration merits. This problem, mentioned by 41.3% of new enterprises (METI, 2003, p. 85) seems to also act as a break in new firms' creation.

But, getting funds appears as the main issue for new entrepreneurs with 62.3% of firms mentioning the difficulty (METI, 2003, p. 85). This has always been the case for SMEs but the after bubble time made it more difficult for risky projects to get the needed guarantee. As shown by Kawai and Urata (2001), around 70% of potential entrants of SMEs have an income of less than 5 million yen. Guarantors and collaterals are requested in Japan to borrow funds. In the past, a lot of SMEs started as spin-off from larger ones, to work as subcontractors. The large firm could serve as guarantor, but it became less the case since re-locations. Lack of market credibility and small scale of business were making it difficult to raise the necessary financial means to start. Recently the government addressed this question by implementing special scheme for business start-ups not requiring guarantors or collaterals. Personal savings of the entrepreneur but also of his family was often used as an initial mean, but the young generation hesitate more than their father's generations to take the risk of loss of personal property, may be also because the necessary funds to start with are higher today than it was before.[4]

Venture capital or angel funds are also available in Japan, but they are rather few compared to the USA for example: 1500 in Japan compared to 400,000 in the USA — with an average annual amount of investment of 3.94 and 7.08 million yen respectively (METI, 2003, p. 86). SMEs find it difficult to deal with these funds as they lack of knowledge on how to estimate the business, the targeted market, how to present the right information, etc.

---

[4] Even though since 2003, the establishment of a company with a capital smaller than the minimum required by the commercial code was allowed for example when locating in a Special Deregulated Zone; or since the new corporate law (2006) a capital of 1 yen only is possible to start (see later), investments are often more costly than in olden time where a single rather simple machine was enough to enter in business.

The diminution of subcontracting opportunities due to relocation and higher purchasing abroad by MNEs make it absolutely necessary for concerned SMEs not only to adapt their activities to the new needs of their client/principal, but to free from subcontracting and find new activities or products by themselves. Firms that have always been subcontractors, whatever their high level of technological know how, don't have the capability to design products by themselves nor marketing experience, making it more difficult than in the past to survive or re start in a new industrial activity

These problems are usually working together and for example, SMEs' CEO that have difficulties to secure workers will not fight to raise the necessary funds to start new activities, especially if they have no successor whom to leave the firm to after their retirement.

5.2.2 *The Agglomeration Situation in Numbers*

Following the national trend, the industrial establishments in districts is of course decreasing. But what is more significant to our purpose is that the deterioration rate is exceeding the national average. Table 5.1 shows this evolution according to the district's classification used by the revitalisation law that divided into 2 categories the industrial districts to be supported (Chūshōkigyō sōgōkenkyū kikō, 2003):

— agglomeration of fundamental technologies, including *monozukuri* (manufacturing) technologies (type A)
— agglomeration of SMEs, including the *sanchi* (production region type) and company castle town (type B).

Table 5.1: Evolution of Manufacturing Establishments in Japan: 1985–2000.

Year	All Japan	Type A	Type B
00/85	−22.1	−24.5	−25.7
90/85	−0.6	−0.7	−1.6
95/90	−11.1	−12.4	−12.1
00/95	−11.9	−13.1	−14.1

Source: Chūshōkigyōchō sōgōkenkyū kikō ed. (2003, p. 20).

Whatever the type, all districts experienced a decline in firms' number during the period, but the decreasing rate differs according to agglomerations and does not seem to be directly and/or exclusively correlated to the industry of specialisation of the agglomeration, or to the district types as Table 5.2 shows through several cases. For example, while the large concentration of the metal transformation and machine industries located in the metropolitan areas of Tokyo, Kanagawa and Osaka all exceed national average, some regional agglomerations (specialised in the same industries) stay below, with very few remaining positive though. Also, in the case of company castle town type of agglomerations, some like Hitachi

Table 5.2: Some Examples of the Evolution of Firms' Number in Agglomerations between 1985 and 2000 (based on establishments number).

Location	00/85
Metropolitan areas	
Tokyo: Ota district	−38.4
Kanagawa: Kawasaki city	−29.1
Osaka: Higashi-Osaka city	−23.3
Regional areas	
Iwate: Kitakami city	+2.7
Hiroshima: Fukuyama city	−11.7
Shizuoka: Hamamatsu city	−27.3
Kigyo jokamachi	
Ibaraki: Hitachinaka city	−13.4
Ibaraki: Hitachi city	−29.4
Hiroshima: Higashihiroshima city	+3.1
Hiroshima: Hiroshima city	−28.4
Sanchi	
Gunma: Kiryu city	−36.2
Niigata: Sanjo city	−23.0
Fukui: Sabae city	−15.2
News agglomerations	
Hokkaido: Sapporo city	+3.5
Shiga: Otsu city	−30.8
Chiba: Kashiwa city	−7.5

Source: Chūshōkigyōchō sōgōkenkyū kikō ed. (2003, p. 23).

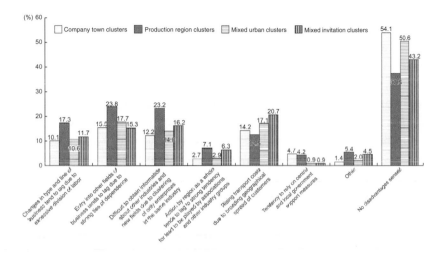

Figure 5.2: Disadvantages of Industrial Agglomerations.

Source: Chūshōkigyōchō (2006, Figure 2-4-17).

Notes:

1. Total exceeds 100 due to multiple responses.
2. In recent time, all types of agglomeration are called 'cluster' in the English version, but in the Japanese version, the term used is 'sangyōshūseki', namely, 'industrial agglomeration'.

city or Hiroshima city registered a very high rate of firms decrease while some others like Higashi-Hiroshima city experienced an increase. The analysis in terms of firms' number could be completed with data on the evolution of employment etc. It will however show the same trend.[5]

Although, it seems difficult to establish a strict correlation between decline and agglomeration types, Figure 5.2 indicates that even though roughly 50% of firms feel some disadvantages to be located in agglomerations, the percentage is differentiated according to types. In comparison with other forms, the production region type seems as having more difficulties in dealing with the management problems mentioned above. The former transaction structure appears as a path dependence constituting a bottleneck to the managerial reform.

---

[5] For data on employment, sales and value added, see Chūshōkigyō sōgōkenkyū kikō (2003).

5.3 New Policies: Favouring New Firms Creation

In such a context, local authorities are of course eager to support the existing SMEs located in their territories. They are also taking all kinds of measures to attract new firms, even foreign ones, to secure employment opportunities and keep their population. But all seem to be quite aware that revitalisation can only be achieved by developing new high-end products and industries based on technologies of the future. SMEs and firms agglomerations having the potential to move to that direction have a role to play, but some might not be able to do so whatever the support they could receive. The decrease in firms' number and, to some extent, a lesser concentration in (or even the disappearance of) existing districts might remain the trend for the coming years, but it could eventually be compensated by new firms and new districts (clusters) creation though.

But what is really at stake today is may be not a quantitative problem as population is decreasing, but much more the need for a qualitative shift to favour innovation and ensure competitiveness.

5.3.1 *The Change in the SMEs Policy*

Japanese policy on SMEs had been based on the previous Small and Medium Enterprise Basic Law enacted in 1963. The image of SMEs was that they represented the 'low point of dual structure' and the policy concept was to rectify the managerial and environmental gaps with respect to productivity and payments between SMEs and large enterprises.

However, with the new Small and Medium Enterprise Basic Law enacted in 1999, SME policy was revised completely (see Table 5.3). The previous policy of rectifying the gaps between SMEs and large enterprises was amended and the new concept — developing and growing a wide range of independent SMEs for greater economic vitality — was formulated. The main policy system consists of three strands: promotion of business innovation, support to start-ups, and promotion of venture. This change in SME policy requires an independent SME-sector and the image of SMEs changes into 'the source

Table 5.3: The Change of the Small and Medium Enterprise Basic Law.

The Previous Small and Medium Enterprise Basic Law (1963~)	The New Small and Medium Enterprise Basic Law (1999~)
[Policy concept]	**[Policy concept]**
Rectify the gap between LE & SMEs in terms of productivity	Developing and growing a wide range of independent SMEs for greater economic vitality (Expectation of SMEs)
	Creation of new business
	— Promotion of market competition
	— Increase of attractive job opportunities
	— Vitalisation of regional economy
[Policy system]	**[Policy system]**
Upgrading in structure of SMEs (Improving productivity)	Supporting self-help efforts for business innovation and start-ups (Support for ambitious enterprises)
— Modernisation of facilities Improvement of technology	— Promoting business innovation (Support for technology, equipment, intangible Management resources, etc.)
— Rationalisation of business management	
— Optimisation of corporate scale	— Promoting start-ups (Information services, training, programmes, Facilitating fund supply, etc.)
— Arrangement of joint operation for business	
— Commercial and services sectors	— Promotion of venture (R&D, supportive human resources, fund raising through stocks, bonds, etc.)
— Change of business	
— Labour related policies	

Source: Small and Medium Enterprise Agency, http://www.chusho.meti.go.jp/sme_english/outline/02/01.html (May, 2008).

of dynamism in Japanese Economy.' Indeed, Japanese SME policy changed its character from a social policy based on the disadvantages of SMEs to one oriented toward the new economy.

Given that the Japanese entry rate is declining and the exit rate is increasing as we have seen before, the Japanese government has set up a legal environment favourable to start-ups in the short term. The law for facilitating the creation of new business (*shinjigyō sōshutsu sokushinhō*) came into force in 1999 with as an objective to create new industries. In order to activate SMEs with technology development capability, and to support business activities with originality, platforms in regions were established and relevant ministries and agencies started to collaborate for the creation of new industries. In April 2005, the Temporary Law Concerning Measures for the Promotion of the Creative Business Activities of SMEs (*chūshōkigyō no sōzōteki jigyō-katsudō no sokushin ni kansuru rinji sochihō*), the Law on Supporting Management Modernization of Small and Medium Enterprises (*chūshō kigyō keieikakushin shienhō*), and the Law for Facilitating the Creation of New Business (*shinjigyō sōshutsu sokushinhō*), were all integrated in the latter.

The purpose of this integration was to simplify the support system and make it more consistent and secure for innovative and networking activities of SMEs. Furthermore, the corporate law (*kaishahō*) was revised in 2006, also with the aim to promote new business start-ups. In the revised law, publicly-traded company (*kabushiki gaisha*) and private limited company (*yūgen gaisha*) were integrated into a single form and the minimum capital requirements, 10 and 3 million yen respectively, were abolished. This revision made it easy for entrepreneurs to establish a company with small amounts of capital, even with as little as 1 yen.

5.3.2 *The Rapid Development of Incubation Facilities*

This emphasis on supporting new firms creation can also be seen through the acceleration of incubators development. Incubation started slowly in Japan. A first move in that direction occurred at the end of the 80s and throughout the 90s. But the increase became remarkable in the late 90s and early 2000s, when firms' reduction in number started to be addressed by national and local authorities. 181 facilities were created between 1998 and 2002 through the revitalisation law of 1997 and thanks to the creation of the Japan Association of New Business incubation Organisation (JANBO) by the METI in 1999 under the law for facilitating the creation of new business. The cluster plans including incubation in their disposition, new facilities creation was accelerated after their implementation, as the JANBO October 2006 survey shows (Table 5.4).

Table 5.4: Number of Incubation Facilities with Date of Creation (190 cases meeting JANBO definition).

Before 1989	1990–1999	2000	2001	2002	2003	2004	2005	2006	Total
4	26	9	30	27	41	24	12	12	185

N.B.: Among the 190 cases, 5 did not answer.
Source: JANBO Survey October 2006, http://www.janbo.gr.jp/bidb/BIabstract.pdf (January, 2008).

According to this survey, of the 345 responding Business Incubation structures, 323 are proposing offices and are centred on support and research activities. Among those, only 190 are meeting the 4 elements of the JANBO definition of Business Incubators though. These elements are the following:

— Providing an office to starting businesses
— Providing support through the appointment of incubation managers (people in charge of supervising the birth and growth of the business)
— Defining targets at entrance
— Having a differentiated graduation system for successful firms and others at the moment of their departure.

These drastic changes in legal and institutional circumstances form the background of the current cluster policy (see Chapter 2) oriented toward the new economy. Under the cluster policy supported by the idea of free competition, highly innovative SMEs are needed. But, SMEs in *jibasangyō* are clearly a long way from the image of independent and innovative leaders of the next generation. Even when regions are specified as 'pre-designated clusters',[6] few of them

---

[6] The authors view is that governmental clusters can be divided broadly into two types: 'pre-designated type' and 'ex post designated type.' The former means that the industrial cluster had already been formed by local actors' spontaneous activities prior to governmental cluster projects and afterward designated as an industrial cluster by the Japanese government. The latter means the zero-start industrial cluster designated by the Japanese government.

do not have the need of revitalising and restructuring the existing local industries as the following case studies will show.

5.4 Hyogo Cluster Projects and the Challenge of Local SMEs

Hyogo Prefecture is located in the centre of Japan, bordering on Osaka and Kyoto prefectures to the east. Population density is eighth out of the 47 Japanese administrative divisions. It is called 'the microcosm of Japan' because many industrial indexes indicate that it represents average for Japan. The weight of industry is high due to the presence of many large-scale industries in Kobe, Himeji, etc. In Hyogo, the so-called 'smokestack industries' of steel and shipbuilding contributed to the regional economy as leading industries until about 80s, but more recently, the electromechanical, general machine, and chemical industries have been increasing.

5.4.1 *Hyogo Industry and SMEs*

On the other hand, Hyogo has large number of *jibasangyō* based on local resources and has been called, 'the treasure house of *jibasangyō*.' The different geographical features, climate, and its historical difference as a region contributed to the creation of diverse enterprises.

Hyogo occupies the sixth position in Japan in the number of business establishments (11,300 offices, 4.2%), seventh in the numbers of employees (359,850, 4.4%), sixth in the amount of shipments (12,945.2 billion yen, 4.6%), and sixth in the amount of added value (4808.1 billion yen, 4.7%) (Hyogoken Kenminseisakubu Seisakukyokutōkeika, 2006).

Figure 5.3 shows the trends in number of business establishments, number of employees, amount of added value, and amount of product shipments of the Hyogo industry. Indexes increased at the end of 2004, but have taken a downtrend in the long term. The products included in the amount of shipments are margarine, sake, coffee, wax, footwear made of rubber, bags, incense sticks, abacuses, woodwork art goods, special steel cable, hand-craft saws, pearls, medical

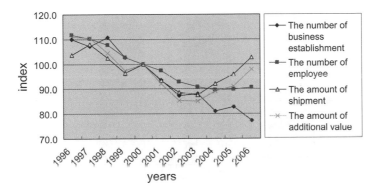

Figure 5.3:   Trends of Hyogo Industry.

N.B.: Results in 2000 = 100.0. Data does not contain the establishments with three employees or less.

Source: Hyogoken kikakukanribu kannrikyoku tōkeika (2006).

measurement equipment, trains, and nautical diesel motors. Most of these are from typical *jibasangyō* with a large number of SMEs. In addition, in the reports from Hyogo until 2002, more than 50 types of *jibasangyō* had been identified, in which small businesses formed the large majority of the companies. *Jibasangyō* represented 30.9% of enterprises, 11.0% of employees, and 9.7% of production in 2000 (Hyogo chūshōkigyō shinkōkōsha, 2002).[7]

Next, let us consider the position of SMEs in Hyogo industry. Along with the standard enterprise division of Japan (SMEs are enterprises with less than 300 employees), SMEs represent 98.7% of business establishments, 71.1% of employees, 52.4% of shipments, and 56.2% of added value. Judging from these figures, it can be said that SMEs have a large influence on the local economy (see Figure 5.4).[8]

To sum up, we can say that the Hyogo industry is characterised by the concomitance of agglomerations with SMEs around smoke-stack industries and *jibasangyō*. Most of these agglomerations are seen as declining industries. Since the Hyogo industry missed the shift to

---

[7] The data does not include the enterprises with three or less employees.

[8] The position of SMEs rises further if we consider the establishments with three employees or less which are not included in the data.

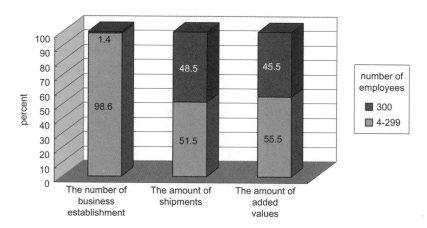

Figure 5.4:   The Proportion of SMEs in Hyogo Industry (based on the number of employees).

N.B.: Data does not contain the establishments with three employees or less.

Source: Hyogoken kikakukanribu kannrikyoku tōkeika (2006).

current industries, such as the car and electronics compared with other Japanese regions, it must now simultaneously consider next-generation industries and reactivate the existing industries.

5.4.2 *Cluster Projects in Hyogo*

The current governmental cluster projects in Hyogo are as follows:

- Bio five-star company and tissue-engineering project
- Kansai IT cluster promotion project
- Kansai energy and environment cluster promotion project
- Kinki energy and environmental upgrade promotion project (by METI)
- Kobe translational research cluster in Kansai wide area cluster (by MEXT).

Hyogo Prefecture has promoted the following programmes to reactivate the regional economy and to encourage employment.

- Economy and employment revitalisation programme
- Reinforcement of the SMEs support
- Corporate location and the international business exchange promotion
- Creation of work and employment.

In 2004, the 'Economy and employment revitalisation programme' was succeeded by the 'Economy and employment revitalisation acceleration programme,' which contains a three year programme, 'Hyogo cluster project,' devised by Hyogo Prefecture based on the governmental cluster projects.

In this project, four fields were selected: nanotechnology, next-generation robots (IT using mechatronics), health, and ecology (environment and energy). The Hyogo Prefecture aims to create clusters around these fields. Figure 5.5 shows the relationship between the selected four fields and existing industries.

As this diagram indicates, Hyogo intend to promote the entry of existing enterprises into high-technology fields. To develop each field

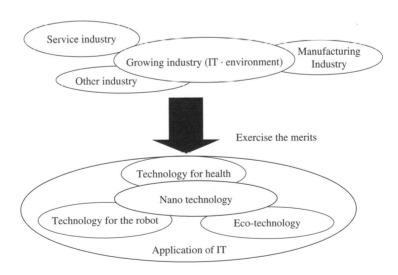

Figure 5.5:   Relationship Between the Fields and Existing Industries.
Source: Hyogoken, http://web.pref.hyogo.jp/contents/000036501.pdf (May, 2008).

as an industrial cluster, Hyogo Prefecture is trying to create networks with SMEs, manufacturers, and key industries that can play a role in integrating high-technology, business initiatives, commercialisation, universities that have intellectual resources, support industries, and support institutions around Kobe, Hanshin, and Harima areas, where 90% or more of shipments are concentrated.

For Hyogo Prefecture, the purpose of establishing an industrial cluster is to revitalise the local SME manufacturers, promote industrial transformation (switching from smokestack industries to next-generation industry), and activate intellectual institutions. Institutions and organisations around the Hyogo cluster project are shown in Figure 5.6.

However, interest in Hyogo cluster projects by local enterprises, especially SMEs is not high, therefore, the entry of the established companies into the four fields mentioned above is still limited, and will probably be limited in the future. The reason for this is the nature of the four fields and conditions of local SMEs. In general, these high-tech fields need a relatively long period from basic research to

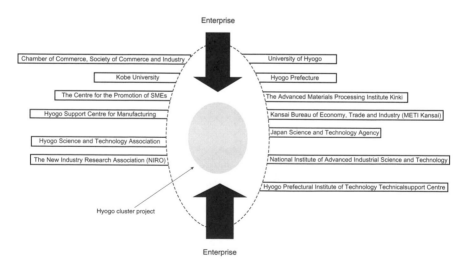

Figure 5.6:   Institutions and Organisations Around Hyogo Cluster Project.

Source: Hyogo Prefecture, http://www.kobe-liaison.net/Doc/205/20051115214217.pdf (May 2008).

commercialisation[9]; therefore, they impose a long-term commitment on SMEs. However, local SMEs, which have long been engaged in a declining industry, have short-term survival needs, and are characteristically risk-averse. As a result, a field with high-risk and difficulty in applying current management resources is not an attractive strategy for many SMEs in Hyogo. This type of mismatch between the local cluster policy menus and the needs of local SMEs are of course not limited to Hyogo Prefecture and led to some other initiatives to be locally launched.

5.4.3 *The Case of Hyogo Study Circle on New Welfare Industry*[10]

The Hyogo study circle on new welfare industry (*Hyogo fukushi sinsangyō kenkyūkai*) is a spontaneous, endogenous network aimed at product and sales development in the universal design field. It is linking SMEs located in *jibasangyō* (Miki city's hardware device tool, Ono city's woodwork) and support institutions such as welfare industries, universities, distributors, and retailers. In September 2006, the main members were 26 enterprises within and outside Hyogo Prefecture, including three support corporations, four institutions, and two universities.

Miki city has been known for its agglomeration of SMEs around hardware device tool manufacturing since the 16th century. After the WWII, it developed as *jibasangyō* for the production of tools for DIY (Do-It-Yourself), garden supplies, agricultural implements, and machinery. However, it has been declining since the second half of 1980s because of the changes in architectural industrial methods, the inflow of Chinese products, and the decline

---

[9] According to the survey of the Japan Society for the Promotion of Machine Industry carried on 1834 educational institutions, prefectures, Civil Services, biotechnology needs 7.82 years and nano-technology 7.75 years on average to become leading industries in the region (Kikaishinkōkyōkai Keizaikenkyūsho, 2005).

[10] Based on interview with the Miki Chamber of Commerce and the *Hyogo fukushi shinsangyō Kenkyūkai* in September 2006.

in housing demands. For SMEs in Miki, business recovery and business conversion are, therefore, major issues. Figure 5.7 shows the trends in the number of enterprises, employees, and the amount of production in Miki city's hardware device tools after 1985.

In 1997, a researcher from Hyogo Prefectural Institute of Industrial Research (Hyogoken Kōgyō Gijutsu Centre) in Miki city, who had a sense of crisis, worked with Miki city's hardware device tool manufacturers and Ono city's woodwork manufacturers in Hyogo aiming at new product development marketable with SMEs. The welfare industry was chosen because this field seemed likely to need product innovation and the best use of traditional craftsmanship (hardware-processing technology and woodwork-processing technology, etc.) that SMEs in the region have accumulated.

This network subsequently expanded with participation from the Co-op Kobe Welfare Tools Development Society, outside designers, ATC Ageless Centre, institutions for medical treatment and welfare, and universities. Figure 5.8 shows the product development system of *Hyogo fukushi shinsangyō kenkyūkukai* and the relationship with other exterior networks. The network is actually expanding with mini-clusters exceeding its geographical scope.

As a concrete result, the products created by *Hyogo fukushi shinsangyō kenkyūkai* received prizes for 5 consecutive years at the welfare device contest held by the Rehabilitation Engineering Society of Japan, which has been in operation for five years, and gained reputation through mass media coverage. This society stimulated voluntary cooperative activities with members, thus creating several new networks.

At an individual SME level, these networks have functioned as the means to overcome the managerial problems specific to SMEs in *jibasangyō*, such as lack of product innovation and marketing abilities. Some SMEs increased their chances of new product development orders from large enterprises, some of them got rid of their status as subcontractor by developing original products with the help of other members, and others increased business with enterprises outside of the region with the help of mass media, PR etc.

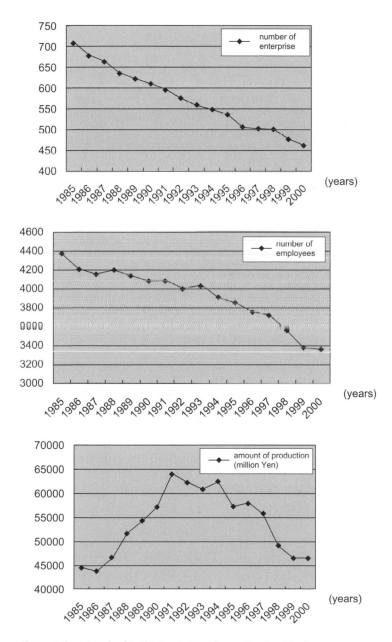

Figure 5.7: The Trend of Miki City's Hardware Device Tool.

Data: Hyogo Chūshōkigyō Shinkōkōsha (1992–2002).

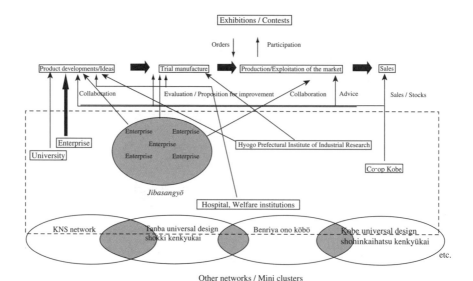

Figure 5.8:   Structure of *Hyogo fukushi shinsangyō Kenkyūkai* and Relationship with Other Networks.

Source: Interview with the Hyogo fukushi shinsangyō kenkyūkai, Shōkō Sōgō Kenkyūsho (2004, p. 38).

The key factor in the success of *Hyogo fukushi shinsangyō kenkyūkai* was the selection of a field in which local SMEs could apply abilities they have accumulated and a cluster in order to overcome their weaknesses. Although cluster formation is the key for revitalising local SMEs and the economy, clusters will not work well without objective and careful analysis of the managerial aspect of local actors, especially local SMEs.

5.5 Cluster Initiative as a Policy Tool to Promote Restructuring: Some Empirical Observations from Osaka Prefecture

With 7.7% for Osaka the prefecture is lagging far behind Tokyo (16.9%) in terms of contribution to National GDP while ranking at the 2nd position in Japan. Its GDP would put Osaka around Switzerland. The prefecture is however facing a difficult situation.

The decline in the manufacturing establishments' number of Osaka prefecture is rather severe with 24,812 in 2004 compared to 42,515 in 1991 (−41.6%) (Census of Manufactures, METI). As far as manufacturing employees are concerned, the numbers is 529,924 compared to 860,377 (−8.4%).

Due to historical conditions, the weight of SMEs in the regional economy is quite high in Osaka prefecture where manufacturing SMEs account for more than 60% (65.4%)[11] of total shipments. Osaka is historically a merchant and handicraft city giving to Osaka prefecture a very important historical weight in varied industries to start with manufacturing such as textile, metalwork and mechanics, electrical appliances, automotive, but also drugs, etc.

The prefecture recently implemented policy packages addressing the revitalisation of declining areas, the restructuring of SMEs districts, trough different programmes including clusters initiatives.

5.5.1 *The Osaka Industry Regeneration Programme and the Cluster Policy*

In 2000, to address the issue of its declining industries, the Prefectural Government implemented an action plan for the revitalisation of industrial activities. One of the major concerns of this 'Industry Regeneration Program' was 'rebuilding Osaka to the city of new business generation' by promoting 3 groups of actions:

— revitalisation of SMEs
— fostering business in new industry clusters
— enhancing attractiveness of the city.

During the first year of implementation, already nearly 140 programmes had been launched and financed. In 2003 the number was 164. The programme was rather successful although some critics were raised about its scope and implementation (see Hirai, 2004). A lack of analysis of the reasons of Osaka decline would have lead to

---

[11] Osaka keizai rodo hakusho (2005, p. 13), 2003 numbers.

implement too general policies; being industry-focussed, the programme left behind commerce which used to be the historical specialisation of the city; promoting new business creation and start-ups, existing SMEs felt to some extent excluded or disdained. Among the critics that were formulated the most important issue is probably the lack of cooperation with other level of governance to avoid redundancy and duplication of policies (Hirai, 2004). Nevertheless, Osaka prefecture now counts several cluster projects, often started at the regional level before becoming labelled under national plans such as the Nothern Osaka Life Science cluster project, Saito biomedical cluster (MEXT) or the Higashiosaka Monozukuri cluster project (METI). The prefecture is also part of broader projects such as the Keihanna cluster (Kansai Science city) including Kyoto and Nara prefectures and specialised in technologies to support sophisticated use of IT and genomics (MEXT). The Saito biomedical cluster is also integrated in a broader structure including Kobe bio five-star Company and Tissue Engineering project (METI), showing that progressively cooperation extend to larger geographical limits including the whole Kansai area. But those projects now recognised at the national (and even international) level are not the whole of the actions undertaken.

Osaka city for example intend to become the hub for new robotics industries based on its concentration of firms in this industry but also on the numerous universities having related departments. The local authorities and Osaka city have implemented the RooBO and Robo City CoRE[12] project with the aim to create one of the world's leading cluster in this field. Also, Osaka urban centre area is housing a high concentration of SMEs specialising in IT services, design and advertising, and video production, as well as large information and communications companies. This led to the ubiquitous IT project which should benefit from the newly created R&D hub in the Cosmosquare District where firms and universities engaged in IT industries or research are provided preferential measures if relocating in the special zone for IT industry development.

---

[12] Standing for core of next-generation robotics research and development.

Under its city revitalisation plan, Osaka is also rebuilding the northern district to serve as a 'knowledge capital' to house research institutions and venture activities. Intelligent robots of the next generation are focussed as well as ubiquitous IT, both being expected to join in the future.

These examples show that Osaka intends to regenerate its industrial competitiveness by specialising in 3 main domains of the future: biotechnologies (life science), robotics and IT technologies which are all priority industries under the science and technology basic plan of the country. But even though the prefecture houses several big firms in these industries and has a nationally high researching potential, competition is severe and the numerous SMEs that constitute the most part of industrial forces are not so easily able to shift from former activities to the newly needed ones, as the decline in firms number have shown. The following case studies will concretely illustrate the problem.

5.5.2 *The Ogimachi Creative Cluster, Mebic (Osaka)*

This northern Osaka industrial district has as existing potential a lot of SMEs specialised in information technologies (software, image and film making, etc.) which used to work as subcontractors to Matsushita, and a lot of firms specialised in printing as well as photograph or music studios etc. Most of these SMEs are accustomed to execute with a high quality and rapid delivery the work received by clients, but they have no specific knowledge in designing and are lacking creativity. This lack of creativity led firms like Matsushita to subcontract creativity related activities to firms in Tokyo even though Matsushita headquarter is located in Osaka. The type of work they were in charge is now subcontracted to Asian countries and China. So the Ogimachi's firms lost their former job but could not received new orders in relation with the work that remained done in Japan as they were lagging behind Tokyo SMEs in term of creative capabilities. The second weakness of these SMEs is also correlated to their origin. They don't have know-how in marketing as they never had to sell their production or services by themselves.

The Ogimachi incubator plaza (Mebic Ogimachi) was created by the city of Osaka and is managed by the Centre for the Promotion of Metropolitan Industries of Osaka City (*Osakashi toshigatasangyo shinko senta*). It aims at supporting firms by helping them to accumulate through the establishment of new business relations, the necessary creative and marketing forces in a way to evolve from their former subcontracting condition to new activities based on the different but connected technologies, represented in the area. It is supposed that putting these firms that have a real potential in relation with creators will allow them to develop completely new activities in high value-added products or services. For part of the firms, such an evolution means to move to service industry, but on segments that are directly derived from their present activity. Individuals who want to start business are of course welcomed. The main role of the staff is to boost the collaboration between involved firms and individuals.

The incubation plaza is housing firms to help them starting in such new activities and become competitive. The manager of Mebic incubation Plaza considers that it is often difficult to make communicate firms coming from different industrial domains. Therefore one of the goals of the plaza is to favour communication between firms. It already happened that two firms decide to joint their efforts and merge. Firms housed in the incubation plaza are also invited to participate to the Kansai Network System (KNS) which is a cross-industry regional network. Thanks to information exchange, KNS aims at supporting firms grouping to foster new ideas emergence. It proposes seminars 4 times a year. Each seminar is ending with a party which is said to favour mutual friendly relationships between members, creating informal linkages... and new business ideas.

The incubation activities started in 2003. Selected firms were granted a 3 year-contract, eventually renewable. They have to fix the goals to be achieved within these 3 years. After verification by the staff that these are realistic they are registered. Three times a year, a meeting is organised to check if the firm is going in the right direction and to measure the remaining efforts to be done. At the end of the 3rd year, another more exhaustive check occurs. If the firm has achieved its goals, it has to move outside the incubation centre. If the results are good, but the goals not yet achieved, the contract might be renewed. But if the firm is still far from being able to reach the goals, or if it is not doing what was registered, it has to leave the incubation centre.

Conditions are quite good for housed firms. They are granted a room with low renting price. Firms are generally first housed on the lower floors of the building where rather small office-rooms are available, then, when they progress, they move to the upper floors where office-space becomes larger and convenient, associated with meeting rooms, small bar, etc. and shared infrastructures like high standard computing room etc., but also more expensive in monthly rental fees. They benefit from the incubation centre's activities, mainly seminars, conferences, joint meeting, etc. aiming at exchanging information or learning from others.

In 2003, 41 firms were admitted to the incubation plaza. The number was then increased to 48. Since the beginning, 28 firms succeeded and left the centre after being 'graduated'. 13 firms failed before completing the 3 years. Eleven stayed the 3 years, but failed and had to leave without 'graduating'. The first selection which was may be more 'political' than rational, explaining the high rate of exits after only one year.

Now, the selection is more severe and for example, the 2006 selection resulted in 4 new admissions on 17 applicants bringing the total housed firms to 36. Another selection was under preparation at the survey time (May 2006), and the manager was expecting 3 new entries. The selection is based on a classification of firms in 3 categories:

— Those (a great number) who are facing difficulties but who don't have the potential to progress. Accepting them in the incubation centre would just be wasting money as they will not achieve the goal anyway.

— Those who are healthy and not facing any difficulties. Accepting them in the incubation centre would also be wasting money as they can achieve their goals by themselves without being aided.
— Those in between who cannot progress alone but have a good potential. These have to be targeted by the incubation centre.

The annual allocated budget is 33 million yen which do not include the infrastructure charges. The building belongs to Osaka city and is financed through another budget.

The Plaza staff is composed by 5 persons: 1 manager/director, 1 staff and 3 assistants. In 2005, there was also one person in charge of revitalisation, but according to the manager, this function was not clearly justified. If incubation is taking place at Ogimachi, it is because firms are agglomerated there. But if incubation is necessary, it is because the territory needs to be revitalised so the two functions were in fact similar.

Considering necessary to move a step forward and to favour communication with the outside of the incubation plaza, it was decided in 2005 to work to the creation of a cluster: Ogimachi Creative Cluster. A map was drawn to give geographical limits to the cluster. In the delimited area, there are several specialised schools (*senmon gakko*) but no university. However, not far away, around Umeda, some universities localised satellites research laboratories and doctoral schools. According to the manager, this means that there are a lot of students attracted by creation-type jobs who after graduating go to Tokyo because firms of the area are not creative enough. Promoting relations between these students and Mebic firms would be helpful to avoid students going to Tokyo and would bring creative ideas to firms. The cluster map was distributed to 2300 firms of the area. An internet homepage and data base was created and firms were proposed to register on the site with eventually a link to there own homepage. At the moment of survey, around 80 firms had accepted the proposition and were introduced in the data base. The activities were also enlarged to firms' visits outside the incubation plaza. All is done to create an image of the cluster and in that sense an Ogimachi Creative cluster logo was elaborated. The idea is also to create a brand, internationally known, in sectors around information technologies, images, design, advertising and publication.

5.5.3 *The Higashi-Osaka Monozukuri Cluster and Osaka East Urban Aria Project*

Higashiosaka and the closeby cities of Yao and part of Daito constitute a large and historical industrial district[13] in which numerous SMEs agglomerated. During the bubble period, around 12,000 firms were working in the district, but exceeding the national average reduction rate, the number felt at around 8000 in 2005. Some are small manufacturers of diversified goods but most of them used to be subcontractors for car and electronic industries. These SMEs lost their job due to relocation of big clients whose production bases were in Osaka. This trend was very high especially in electronic industry (Matsushita, Sharp). These SMEs, cannot find any new clients once the 'traditional' one cut orders because all Osaka big firms relocated their production abroad. They usually master a high level of technology, but have no development know-how, nor marketing and sales capabilities.

The Higashiosaka *Monozukuri* cluster, which creation was decided in 2002, aims at revitalising the existing district by supporting these manufacturing SMEs. Although centred on SMEs, the cluster is benefiting from the support of 13 universities and research institutions located in the area: Kinki University, Osaka Technology University, University of Commerce and Management of Osaka, Sanyo R&D multimedia research institute, Sharp electric development research centre, etc. The cluster aims at favouring relations between the high potential SMEs and the high level universities to create new business activities and/or new firms based on the development and commercialisation of research seeds.

---

[13] The agglomeration developed during Edo period with cotton work (Ueda, 2003).

Higashi-Osaka city opened in 2003 the Higashiosaka Creation Core that appears to be at the core of the cluster. Its missions and activities are as follow:

— advising on new technologies,
— searching new clients,
— supporting new firms creation: management advises, incubation facilities etc.,
— providing exhibition space (showroom) for innovative products of SMEs,
— providing research space and laboratories, allowing universities to localise their researches and attend meetings with firms and administration representatives.

The creation core staff gives advises on bilateral basis to requesting firms, but also organise joint conferences and seminars. The staff might also be sent to firms to help on technology, sales, patent, etc., issues. It is also housing some special activities, like the SME grouping engaged in satellite manufacturing (SOHLA) with the collaboration of JAXA (Japan Aerospace Agency) which opened an antenna inside the creation core too.

In 2005, the Higashiosaka Creation Core had already answered to 4631 advising requests, to 1409 requests by internet, of which 685 came from Japan and others from foreign countries. It has received 15,868 persons willing to present their products. 200 were at the survey time (May 2006) presenting some sample products in the exhibition showroom.

In the incubation centre, around 10 projects were housed at the survey time (May 2006) and 13 universities had localised research units.

The staff (coordinators, advisers and employees) is around 20 persons dispatched from the Osaka prefecture, the Higashiosaka chamber of commerce, the city of Higashiosaka. Several NPO also support the project. The building was funded by the national government, while management fees are at the Osaka prefecture charges.

The cluster also benefits from measures of the city of Osaka in terms of study/evaluation of incubation venture projects from universities, or of activities of the city of Yao in terms of firms' networking and upgrading of existing SMEs.

Since 2004, the creation core associated to firms and universities is also involved in the Osaka East Urban Area Industry-Academia-Government Collaboration Project sponsored by the MEXT under the policy for the promotion of science and technology in regional areas. The project based on the existence of one of the most important centres of the machining and metalworking industries in Japan having proved that previous collaboration between industry, government and academia exists to a certain extent aims at conducting research and development into next-generation welding of light metal alloys. The actions are centred on joint research and industrial application of results. It was attributed an approximate budget of 100 million yen during 3 years. The core organisation is Osaka Industrial Promotion Organisation Technology Licensing Organisation (TLO) division while the core research organisation is Higashiosaka Creation Core where as mentioned above 13 universities have open facilities. The structure of this project can be seen in Figure 5.9.

5.6 Towards New Configuration of *Jibasangyō*

As mentioned in Chapter 1, Japanese *jibasangyō* share some characteristics with clusters: cooperation versus competition, firms networking, etc. The strong embedment in local community (or territory) and the cooperation pattern involving firms and government agencies (national and regional) played its part in Japan as elsewhere, in the evolution and usually high performing of districts. But since the end of the 80s and for the reasons explained in Section 2, this cooperation seems as having reached its limits. To support innovation and/or new managerial capabilities acquisition by SMEs, new cooperation channels are needed as case studies have shown.

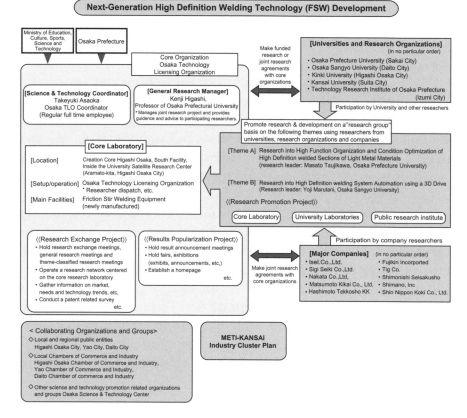

Figure 5.9: Structure of the Osaka East Urban Area Industry-Academia-Government Collaboration Project.

Source: http://www.m-osaka.com/fsw/en/project/oea_system.html (February 2008).

5.6.1 *The Former Cooperation Pattern in Jibasangyō*

Cooperation between firms qualified as 'friendly rivalry and confrere trading'[14] by Whittaker (1997) has always been important in Japanese districts.

Such cooperation might have been less developed in company castle town type's districts (*kigyō jō kamachi*, type A in Chapter 1) but they did exist too. In such districts dominated by a large company

---

[14] Sessa takuma and nakama torihiki (Whittaker, 1997).

subcontracting parts, manufacturing or production processes, to smaller specialised firms located close to their assembly plants, the numerous SMEs generally gained through inter-firm learning excellent capabilities on their specific technologies as well as in terms of flexible production and fast delivery (Lecler, 1993). The main characteristic of these districts which proved their efficiency over time thanks to positive externalities led to the high degree of cooperation between parent firms and suppliers/subcontractors. While horizontal cooperation between SMEs and/or with public agencies etc. were not excluded, it is clear though that vertical cooperation was the main stream of interrelation between firms in such districts that have played an important role in the competitiveness of Japanese assembling industries like machinery, automotive and electronics.

Horizontal cooperation was however the main characteristic of Marshall-type districts of SMEs, strongly embedded in local territories, specialised in one specific traditional industry or product (type D) like food, textile, furniture, etc. that can historically be considered as cottage-industry-type districts.[15] It was also the case of large concentrations of SMEs in urban areas (type C). Historically formed around big firms,[16] a high level of horizontal cooperation emerged like in type D, when due to high land prices, expensive labour force and also government incentives in the 70s these big firms relocated their main plants in the periphery or on the country side. Thanks to that horizontal cooperation these districts finally gained a great vitality. Composed of very small but highly specialised and flexible firms, they used to work as niche manufacturers or subcontractors for big clients located outside the district in a very well established division of labour.[17]

---

[15] Examples: Tsubame Sanjo region in the Niigata Prefecture-cutlery and blades, Asahikawa City in Hokkaido-furniture, etc.

[16] Pre-war production bases, ammunitions plants, or wartime factories, examples of so called mixed urban type: Ota-ku in Tokyo, Ōta area in Gunma Prefecture, Suwa area in Nagano Prefecture, Hamamatsu area in Shizuoka Prefecture, Higashi-osaka area in Osaka Prefecture, etc.

[17] See for example in the machine industry (Watanabe, 1997).

Japan has a long history of industrial policy which led in the past to consider the METI (at that time MITI) to be the orchestra conductor of Japan incorporated. Through this industrial policy aiming at establishing the priority towards industries to be promoted, and in turn because of the importance of the industrial policy, information exchange between business and government officers also took place to a large scale. Industrial associations etc. used to play an important part in these exchanges while also being very active in favouring the horizontal cooperation between firms as already mentioned. So information sharing between firms and with government's officers is a well established routine in Japan.

The positive externalities arising from such cooperation is not easy to measure though. It was mostly taking place through informal channels like industrial associations, cooperatives or different kind of clubs, strongly embedded in the local community, which were (and still are) quite numerous in Japan (around 45,000 according to Whittaker). These associations, clubs etc. organised frequent meeting (even diners, party), where firms representatives exchanged information or point of view on any topics which were not necessarily related to each ones job. More than the nature of the information exchanged, these meetings allowed face to face relationships making all the actors of the community directly and personally knowing each other. The friendly rivalry probably came out from these association or club activities which fostered a strong community spirit which in return favoured horizontal cooperation or confrere trading. From time to time, in the framework of their activities, and therefore with attendance of most members, these associations, clubs etc. were organising conferences or workshops on important issues for business improvement, inviting representatives of public organisations for example. They might also have proposed visit of factories where new technologies have been implemented etc., contributing to the diffusion of knowledge within the local community. To promote industries and help them grow to an international standard also meant that SMEs which were important in number but also in employment and in shipments had to be supported to continuously upgrade their technologies. Big principals were the main stream of this technology transfer, especially in the castle town company type districts, but again industrial associations cooperating with government played their part namely in other districts type. Test and experimentation laboratories, vocational training institutes, etc., were established in different regions with public funds to help SMEs to cope with the technological challenge they were facing. Also, public financial institutions had as main mission to support SMEs in providing loans or rising funds by serving de facto as guarantors etc.

5.6.2 Changes in Cooperation Pattern and Jibasangyō Reconfiguration

Thanks to such cooperation, *jibasangyō* restructured over time to survive although some eventually declined. Indeed, the high performing of most of them in the past prove that they were able to adapt to changes of their environment. The scale on which the cooperation among agglomerated actors occurred might be considered as depending on the needs that these actors had. Since the 90s, as innovation became the key word, what seems finally on the agenda is to involve new actors such as universities in the cooperating networks. Linkages between universities or research institutions and firms, especially small ones that don't have the capabilities to engage in R&D or to develop by their own new products or technologies from research seeds, are seen as the only way to address the problem districts are facing. But while cooperation between firms or with government agencies are a well established routine as mentioned above, cooperation with universities are not that easy to implement or at least does not occur spontaneously. The reform of national universities that took place at the beginning of the 2000s can be considered as one of the measures to facilitate the transfer from research to manufacturers of research results, the development of joint research projects or the creation of new firms by researchers. The establishment of TLO (Technology Licensing Offices) often located within university campus address the same goal helping to solve the problem of intellectual property, pattern registration, etc. But although these measures constitute a favourable legal framework for cooperation to emerge, the channels of that cooperation remain to be built.

The cluster policy and moreover the triple helix (*San-Gaku-Kan*) that is at its core appears as having become the keyword of all the initiatives whatever labelled as cluster like in Higashiosaka, or not like in Ogimachi and Hyogo study circle on new welfare industry. These 3 cases and a lot of others not related here share together the promotion of new linkages with universities or in other words the integration of universities and/or research institutions whether private or public ones, within the cooperation network of the past. This does not mean however that former cooperation channels became obsolete as for example the role given to KNS in the Ogimachi case. It does not mean either that spontaneous or informal cooperation does not work anymore like the SOHLA project within Higashiosaka which start from SMEs grouping, or the role played by a researcher of Hyogo Prefectoral Institute of Industrial Research show. But, as mentioned above, cooperation is now extended to involve new actors necessary for transforming SMEs into innovative independent firms.

Through this process that increases and mixes cooperation channels, complexity is growing. Formerly assumed by manufacturers or manufacturers' association on a rather informal basis, coordination of the network tends to change hands, while becoming more formalised. It is now generally managed by a special structure such as the creation core in Higashiosaka or the incubation plaza in Ogimachi for example, structure created to that end thanks to policy support.

So, the main measures or way of doing praised by cluster plans (*san-gaku-kan* linkages) seems to have spread to all restructuring initiatives whether supported by national, regional or local revitalisation policies. Therefore, although cases labelled as industrial clusters under the METI plan (see Chapter 2, Hattori) are rather few the impact of that policy might be broader. In other words, although numerous *jibasangyō* remain out of the scope of the industrial cluster plan which emphasises new technologies or industries start-ups, it is possible to assume that, as other policy in the past, it constitutes a new step in the structural reconfiguration from old to new forms of industrial districts.

Indeed, as Ozawa (2003) illustrates using the sequential catching-up development model, Japanese agglomerations evolved from step to step according to the flying-geese theory, first conceptualised by Akamatsu.[18] Each step is corresponding to agglomeration types (that Ozawa name clusters) such as cottage-industry type, based on labour intensive industries, *konbinato* type, based on heavy industries, company castle towns type (that Ozawa names just-in-time delivery), based on subcontracting. All these types, which are dated even if existing periods are overlapping, are according to Ozawa resource-based clusters while the two types (respectively named: Research clusters/networks and Entrepreneurial clusters) which have emerged since the 80s/90s and which are addressing the globalisation era restructuring, are said to be knowledge-based clusters. The timing of each phase and the characteristics of each type of agglomerations, as described by Ozawa, might be discussed but, following his argument, it seems to us that the present cluster initiatives effectively has to be seen as a new step or phase in the continuous evolution of agglomerations over time. The shift from resource-based clusters to knowledge-based ones or in other terms from former *jibasangyō* to innovating independent SMEs districts or clusters might be interpreted as the necessary qualitative shift that districts have to engage in to survive.

Given that more than firm's closure rate, what is presently at stake is new firm's creation as we have seen in Section 2, and considering the average life time of start-ups, it is still too early to evaluate on the middle or long term results of all the initiatives, especially those taken at the regional or local levels. But whatever they will be, the scope of the gap to be filled by numerous SMEs makes it clear that all *jibasangyō* might not be able to adapt to the new situation. Some redistribution of industrial territories as well as emergence of new configurations might come out from present changes, including around intellectual clusters[19] (Hattori and Lecler, 2008) probably closer to the Western or at least French approach in terms of poles of competitiveness.

---

[18] Akamatsu developed this theory in the 30s. It was then adapted or revised by several authors Shinohara, Kojima, Ozawa, etc.

[19] See Chapter 2, Hattori Akira.

References

AFRIAT, Christine, LECLER, Yveline. (1986). 'L'automatisation des PMI japonaises et son financement (Japanese SMIs automation and its financing),' in *CPE Etude.* 70, juin, p. 75.

Chūshōkigyō sōgōkenkyū kikō ed. (2003). *Sangyōshūseki no aratana Taidō (renaissance of industrial agglomerations)*, Tokyo: Dōyūkan.

Chūshōkigyōchō (2000). *Chūshōkigyō Hakusho 2000* (White Paper on SMEs in Japan 2000), Tokyo: Ōkurashō Insatsukyoku.

Chūshōkigyōchō (2005). *Chūshōkigyō Hakusho 2005* (White Paper on SMEs in Japan 2005), Tokyo: Gyōsei.

Chūshōkigyōchō (2006). *Chūshōkigyō Hakusho 2006* (White Paper on SMEs in Japan 2006), Tokyo: Gyōsei.

Chūshōkigyōkinyōkōko Chōsabu. (2003). 'Sangyōshūseki ni okeru Kōdineitokinō no Kasseika (Activating of Coordinate Functions in Industrial Agglomerations),' online: http://www.c.jfc.go.jp/jpn/result/c2_0205.html (October 2006).

DOERINGER, P. B., TERKLA, D. G. (1995). 'Business Strategy and Cross-industry Clusters' *Economic Development Quarterly*, 9, pp. 225–237.

DORE, P. Ronald. (1986). *Flexible Rigidities, Industrial Policy and Structural Adjustment in the Japanese Economy*, 1970–1980, London: Athlone.

FUJIMOTO, Takahiro, YASUMOTO, Masanori. (2001). *Seikōsuru Seihinkaihatsu (The Successful Product Development)*, Tokyo: Yūhikaku.

FUJIMOTO, Takahiro. (2001). 'Architecture no *Sangyōron* (A Study on Industries with Architecture)' in Fujimoto, T., Takeishi, A., and Aoshima, Y. (eds.), *Business Architecture*, Tokyo: Yūhikaku.

FUJIMOTO, Takahiro. (2003). *Nōryoku Kōchiku Kyōsō: Nihon no Jidōshasangyō wa naze Tsuyoinoka* (The Competition for Ability Developments), Tokyo: Chūkōshinsho.

HATTORI Akira. (2006). 'La revitalisation des territoires japonais à travers les mesures de politiques publiques en faveur des clusters (the revitalization of Japanese territories through public policies measures to foster clusters),' Lyon 2 Lumière University, Master thesis september.

HATTORI, Akira, LECLER, Yveline. (2008). 'Innovation and Clusters: The Japanese Government Policy Framework,' forthcoming in ISS research series, University of Tokyo, Mars.

HAYAKAWA, Yoshio. (1985). 'Yokohama Kogyokan YK Projekuto (The YK Project of Yokohama Industrial Organization),' in NAGASU Kazuji and KIYONARI Tadao dir.: *Haiteku Jidai no Chūshōkigyō* (SMEs of the high tech era), pp. 175–177, edited by Kanagawa prefecture, Tokyo: Kyōsei.

HIRAI, Takumi. (2004). 'Economic Policy Visions by Japanese Local Governments: The Case of Osaka Prefecture,' in *Sangyo Kenkyūron*, March, on line: www.pref. osaka.jp/aid/kisokennkyu/ronsyu16.pdf (October 2006).

Hyogo Chūshōkigyō Shinkōkōsha, Hyogoken Sangyō Jōhō Center. (2002).

Hyogoken no jibasangyō heisei 14 (Jibasangyō in Hyogo 2002), Kobe: Chūshōkigyō Shinkōkōsha, Hyogoken Sangyōjōhō Center.

Hyogo Fukushi Sinsangyō Kenkyūkai, on line: http://www.tokokizai.co.jp/hyogo-fsk/ (Nov. 2006).

Hyogo Prefecture, on line: http://web.pref.hyogo.jp/ (Nov. 2006).

Hyogo Prefecture. (2005). 'Hyogo Keizaikoyō Saiseikasoku Program (Programs for the Acceleration of the Reactivation of Hyogo Ecomony and Employments)', Hyogo Prefecture.

Hyogoken Kenminseisakubu Seisakukyokutōkeika (2006). '2005 nen Kōgyōtōkei-chosa Kekkasokuhō 2005 (News Flash on Preliminary Report on Census of Manufactures 2005),' Hyogoken Kenminseisakubu Seisakukyoku Tōkeika.

Hyogoken Kikakukanribu Kanrikyoku Tōkeika (2006), *Hyogo no Kōgyō* (*Industries in Hyogo*), Hyogoken Kikakukanribu Kanrikyoku Tōkeika.

Industrial Cluster Study Group. (2005). 'Industrial Cluster Study Report,' on line: www.cluster.gr.jp/relation/d.ata/pdf/cluster kenkyu houkoku english.pdf (June 2006).

ISHIKURA, Mitsuo. (1990). *Jibasangyo to chiikikeizai* (Jibasangyō and Local Economies), Kyoto: Mineruvashobō.

ISHIKURA, Yoko, FUJITA, Masahisa, MAEDA, Noboru, KANAI, Kazuhiko, YAMASAKI, Akira. (2003). *Nihon no Sangyōcrastā senryaku* (*Industrial Cluster Strategies in Japan*), Tokyo: Yūhikaku.

ITAKURA, Katsutaka, KITAMURA Yoshiyuki. (1980). *Jibasangyō no chiiki* (District with Jibasangyō), Tokyo: Daimeidō.

ITAMI, Hiroyuki, MATSUSHIMA, Shigeru, KIKKAWA, Takeo. (1998). *Sangyōshūseki no honshitsu* (The Nature of Industrial Agglomeration), Tokyo: Yūhikaku.

JACOBS, Dany, DE JONG, Mark, W. (1992). 'Industrial Clusters and the Competitiveness of the Netherlands,' *De Economist*, **140**, pp. 233–252.

JACOBS, Dany, DE MAN, Ard-Pieter. (1996). 'Clusters, Industrial Policy and Firm Strategy: A Menu Approach,' *Technology Analysis and Strategic Management*, **8**(4), pp. 425–437.

KAMAKURA, Takeshi. (2002). *Sangyōshūseki no Chiikikeizairon* (An Argument about Local Economies based on Industrial Agglomerations), Tokyo: Keisōshobō.

KATO, Hideo. (2003). *Chiiki Chushōkigyō to Sangyōshūseki* (Local SMEs and the Industrial Aggromeration), Tokyo: Shinhyoron.

KAWAI, Hiroki, URATA, Shujiro. (2001). 'Entry of Small and Medium Enterprises and Economic Dynamism in Japan,' *World Bank Institute no 37182*, on line: http//siteresources.worldbank.org/wbi/resources/wbi37182.pdf (July 2006).

Keizaisangyō Kenkyūsho, Nihon Applied Research. (2004). 'Heisei 15 nen no Nihon no Inovēshonsistemu ni kakawaru Sangakurenkeijittaichōsa (A Survey on Industry-university Cooperation for the Innovation in Japan 2003),' Keizaisangyō Kenkyūsho and Nihon Applied Research.

Kikaishinkōkyōkai Keizaikenkyūsho. (2005). 'Chiikisangyō Innovation no Jittaibunseki to Seikōyōin: Kikai Sangyōtou ga Chiikikeizairyoku Kyōka ni hatasu Yakuwari (The Analysis of Actual conditions and the Success Factors of Innovation in Local Industries: The Role of Machine Industries in Regional Economic Reinforcement),' Kikaishinkōkyōkai Keizaikenkyūsho.

KIKKAWA, Takeo, Rengo Sōgōseikatsu Kaihatsu Kenkyūjo (ed.), (2005). 'Chiiki kara no Keizai Saisei, Sangyoshuseki, Innovation, Koyōsōshutsu (Community Based economic Renaissance, Agglomerations, Innovation, Employment),' Yūhikaku.

Kinki Keizai Sangyōkyoku. (2003). 'Clastācoa Jittaichōsa (Investigations into the Actual Conditions of Cluster-core),' Kinki Keizai Sangyō Kyoku.

KODAMA, Toshihiro. (2005). 'An Intermediary and Absorptive Capacity to Facilitate University-Industry Linkage — Based on Empirical Analysis for TAMA in Japan,' revised edition of the paper presented at *The University-Industry Linkages in Metropolitan Areas in Asia, Research Conference* of the World Bank in May 2005 and SSRC, November 17–18, received from the author courtesy.

KURODA, Shozo. (2005). 'Sangyo Kurasutā to Saiensupa-ku no Kankei no Kenkyu (Reserach on the Relation betwenn Industrial clusters and Science parks), in Inovēshon kurasutā Keisei ni muketa Kawasakishi Seisaku he no Teigen (Towards Proposal to Kawasaki City for Measures to address the Formation of Innovative Clusters),' Senshudaigaku Daigakuin Shakaichiseikaihatsu Kenkyusentā, *Toshiseisakukenkyūsentā ronbunshū*, March.

LECLER, Yveline. (1982). 'Les PME japonaises face à l'introduction de biens d'équipement automatisés' (Japanese SMEs and the introduction of electronic capital goods), in *L'électronisation industrielle au Japon* (*electronization of industry in Japan*), Sciences Sociales du Japon Contemporain. 2, EHESS/CDSH, ctobre, pp. 60–77.

ME, Osaka. (2006). 'Clusters de l'Ouest du Japon (West Japan's clusters),' September, *Fiche de synthèse*, online: http://www.missioneco.org/japon/documents_new. asp?V=1_PDF_124330 (Nov. 2006).

METI. (2003). 'Challenges and Directions of Economic and Industrial Policy in Japan,' November. Online: http://www.meti.go.jp/english/information/downloadfiles/ c0310EIPe.pdf (July 2006).

METI. Online: http://www.meti.go.jp/ (Nov. 2006).

MEXT. Online: http://www.mext.go.jp/ (Nov. 2006).

MEXT, MHLW and METI (eds.) (2005). 'Monozukiri Hakusho 2005' (White Paper on Manufacturing), Tokyo: Gyōsei.

NAGASU, Kazuji, KIYONARI, Tadao dir. (1985), *Haitekujidai no Chūshōkigyō* (SMEs of the High Tech Era), edited by Kanagawa prefecture, Tokyo: Gyōsei.

OCDE. (1999). 'Business Incubation, International Case Studies,' online: www.oecd.org/searchResult/0,2665,fr_2649_201185_1_1_1_1_1,00.html, (September 2006).

OKUDA, Shinya. (2006). 'Regional Economic and Industrial Policy Group,' METI, Government of Japan, Conference of 22 April.

Osaka Prefecture. (2005). 'Osaka Keizai-Rōdō hakusho: Osakasangyō no Kyōsōryoku wo takameru Monozukuri Nettowāku (Osaka White Paper on Economics and Labour: Manufacturing Networks to Enhance Competitiveness of Osaka Industry)', Osaka Furitsu Sangyōkaihatsu Kenkyōjo ed.

OZAWA, Terutomo. (2003). 'Structural Transformation, Flying-Geese Style and Industrial Clusters: Theoritical Implications of Japan's Postwar Experience,' Paper presented at the conference on *Clusters, Industrial Districts and Firms: the Challenge of Globalization*, Modena, September, pp. 12–13.

PORTER, Michael. (1990). *The Competitive Advantage of Nations*, London: Macmillan.

PORTER, Michael. (1998). 'Clusters and Competition: New Agendas for Companies, Governments and Institutions,' in *On Competition*, Michael Porter, MA, Boston: Harvard Business Review Books.

PORTER, Michael. (1998). 'Clusters and the New Economics of Competition,' *Harvard Business Review*, 76(6), November–December, pp. 77–90.

PORTER, Michael. (2000). 'Location, Competition and Economic Development: Local Clusters in a Global Economy,' *Economic Development Quarterly*, 14(1), February, 15–34.

ROSENFELD, Stuart. (1995). Industrial Strength Strategies: Regional Business Clusters and Public Policy, Washington DC: Aspen Institute.

ROSENFELD, Stuart. (1997). 'Bringing Business Clusters into the Mainstream of Economic Development,' *European Planning Studies*, 5(1), pp. 3–23.

SAKAMOTO, Koji. (1985). 'Shizuokaken Kaihatsugata Kigyōkenkyukai no Katsudōnaiyō to sono kyōdōkenkyū shisutemu (System of Joint Research and Content of Activities of the Society of Researching-type Firms of Shizuoka Prefecture),' in NAGASU Kazuji and KIYONARI Tadao dir., *Haitekujidai no Chūshōkigyō* (SMEs of the High Tech Era), pp. 64–68, edited by Kanagawa Prefecture, Gyosei.

SEKI,Mitsuhiro, SATO, Hidemi. (2002). 21 *Seikigata Jibasangyō no Hattensenryaku* (The Strategies for the Development of Jibasangyō in the 21st Century), Tokyo: Shinhyōron.

SHIMOHIRAO, Isao. (1985). *Gendai Jibasangyōron* (A Study on Modern Jibasangyō), Tokyo: Shinhyōron.

Shōkōsōgōkenkyūsho. (2004). 'Chūshōkigyō no Takakuteki Renkeisoshiki no Dōkō (Trends in Diversified, Coordinated Organization of SMEs),' Shōkōsōgō Kenkyūsho.

Small and Medium Enterprise Agency, on line: http://www.chusho.meti.go.jp/ (Nov. 2006).

UEDA, Hiroshi. (2000). *Sangyōshūseki to Chūshōkigyō* (Industrial Aggromelations and SMEs), Tokyo: Sōfūsha.

WATANABE, Yukio. (1997). *Nihon Kikaikōgyō no shakaiteki Bungyō kō zoō* (Social Division of Labor in Japanese Machine Industry), Tokyo: Yūhikaku.

WHITTAKER, D. Hugh. (1997). *Small Firms in the Japanese Economy.* Cambridge University Press.

YAMASAKI, Akira. (2002). *Cluster Senryaku* (Cluster Strategies). Tokyo: Yūhikaku.

YAMAWAKI, Hideki. (2001). 'The Evolution and Structure of Industrial Clusters in Japan,' *World Bank Institute no 37183*; online: http//siteresources.world-bank.org/wbi/resources/ wbi37183.pdf (April, 2005).

YAMAZAKI, Mitsuru. (1977). *Nihon no Jibasangyō* (Japanese Jibasangyō). Tokyo: Daiamondsha.

Chapter 6

Competence and Profitability of Small and Medium-Sized Enterprises: The Case of Kawasaki SMEs

Mitsuharu Miyamoto

6.1 Why do Kawasaki SMEs Matter?

This chapter examines the potential of small and medium-sized enterprises (SMEs) in Kawasaki City to develop their business and play the role of actors in the Kawasaki innovation cluster. Generally, SMEs have been called a supporting industry in the sense that they provide the required components to the large-scale manufacturing plants. However, SMEs need to address two challenges; one is how they can become a 'new' supporting industry for the 'new' industrial cluster composed of high-tech innovative firms and research institutions, and the other is how they can evolve their business under the decline of the 'old' industrial district. Both are particularly urgent agendas for Kawasaki SMEs. We start by outlining the current role of SMEs in Kawasaki.

Kawasaki is a typical industrial city in Japan. It is located between Tokyo and Yokohama, has a population of 1.3 million and covers some 144 km². In this small area, large steel and petrochemical plants in the Tokyo Bay area, large electronics and machinery plants in the inland area, and a large number of small and medium-sized enterprise (SMEs) around them have shaped the Kawasaki industrial district. In fact, the value of gross product in manufacturing in Kawasaki City was around 4229 billion yen in 2005, nearly the same as Yokohama, 4416 billion yen, and close to that of Tokyo, 4928 billion yen, while the

163

land area of Kawasaki is far less than both Yokohama, 222 km², and Tokyo, 621 km². Kawasaki is the heartland of Japanese industry.

However, this means that Kawasaki suffered serious hardship from the decline of Japan's manufacturing industries. In fact, almost all the electronics plants of large Japanese companies such as Toshiba, Fujitsu and NEC have moved to other domestic regions or overseas, particularly China. As a result, compared with the 1991 level (=100), the value of gross product and the number of employees in manufacturing in Kawasaki City have decreased respectively to 58.6% and 73.6% level in 2002, while they increased to 128.5% and 116.2% level in non-manufacturing. As shown in Figure 6.1, the decline of manufacturing occurred much faster than the national trend, particularly since the late of 1990s, whereas the growth of non-manufacturing reflects the national trend. Therefore, as a whole, Kawasaki is likely to be stagnant for a long time unless the non-manufacturing sector, particularly information and services, grows much faster than the

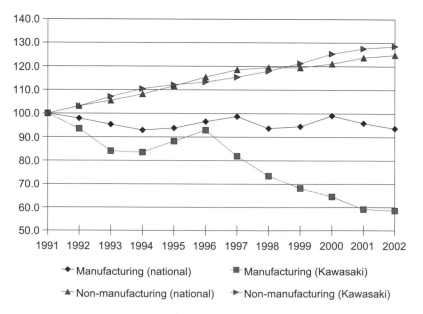

Figure 6.1:   Trend of Gross Product (1991 = 100).

Sources: SNA statistics, Kawasaki municipal indicators.

national trend, or the manufacturing sectors recover to grow at least at the national trend.

Kawasaki City has attempted to rebuild itself as a new industrial city by shaping its innovative cluster. Kawasaki has been the pioneering city for the promotion of municipal industrial policy since the 1980s, for instance, it built the first science park in Japan at the end of the 1980s, and now has three business incubators and one comprehensive public laboratory. The first new business incubator, Kanagawa Science Park, has generated more than 210 firms and succeeded to create four initial public offerings (IPOs). In addition, two or three IPOs are prospected to occur soon. Moreover, some ex-electronics plants have been converted to in-house R&D laboratories or mother plants to develop new technologies and products, where a large number of research engineers are employed. In fact, the number of research engineers working in Kawasaki is the second highest in Japan, 12,267 people in 2005, whereas the highest is in Tokyo, 21,815 people. Although they appear to work solely for their companies, spin-off companies initiated by these research engineers have appeared.

In response to these developments, Senshu University, with one campus located in Kawasaki City, started a five-year research project with a grant from the Ministry of Education and Science and close relationships with Kawasaki municipal officials to make a proposal for the development of the Kawasaki innovative cluster. As part of the second year of research, this study focuses on SMEs in Kawasaki City and conducts a survey and additional interviews.

What conditions will be required for shaping the Kawasaki innovation cluster? How can it be realised? Although a definitive answer cannot be provided yet, it is important to acknowledge that the various innovative participants such as knowledge-based companies, high-tech start-ups, research laboratories, universities, incubators, and active local government are indispensable. However, SMEs should not be ignored as participants in the innovation cluster. Although they seem to play no role in the development of innovations, they are indispensable for innovative activities; for instance, when high-tech plants need highly precise equipment for product development, and high-tech start-ups invent such equipment, it will be the SMEs that provide highly precise components for prototype production. In summary, high-tech innovative activities need support from the various kinds of SMEs with advanced technological potential.

Moreover, Kawasaki SMEs have another important role in the regional economy. It is SMEs that generate jobs and incomes instead of the declining manufacturing industries (Kilby, 1971; Storey, 1994; Gavron *et al.*, 1998). Although high-tech start-ups are expected to generate jobs with high wages and increase the number of jobs within relatively short development periods, it is difficult to imagine a sufficient number of start-ups emerging. It is therefore necessary to rely on the growth of existing SMEs as well as the creation of new businesses for the revival of the Kawasaki regional economy.

How will Kawasaki SMEs be able to develop their business following the decline of large manufacturing plants in the region? This is a particularly important issue because Kawasaki SMEs have conducted business and forged technological competencies through close relations with the large electronics and precision machinery plants. However, as mentioned above, such plants have moved or closed, and these close relations have ended. As a result, a large number of SMEs have closed during the past decade as shown in Table 6.1. About 30% of all SMEs in manufacturing disappeared between 1994 and 2004, although the rate is much larger for firms of over 300 employees. In a sense, it is the surviving SMEs that are the respondent firms for our survey research. How do these SMEs conduct their businesses?

Table 6.1:   Number of SME Plants by Number of Employees (manufacturing).

Number of Employees	1994	2004	Number of Disappeared Plants	Rate of Decrease
4~9	1479	942	537	−36.3
10~49	897	675	222	−24.7
50~299	171	135	36	−21.1
All SMEs	**2547**	**1752**	**795**	**−31.2**
300~999	39	19	20	−51.3
1000~	14	5	9	−64.3

Source: Kawasaki municipal indicators.

From these points of view, this article focuses on the potential of Kawasaki SMEs. Generally, SMEs are employed as subcontractors and SMEs must have technological potential in order to get out of subcontracting status. Do Kawasaki SMEs have the ability to progress from subcontractor status and boost growth in the Kawasaki regional economy through evolutionary development? This chapter proceeds as follows. Section 2 will provide an overview of the business operations of Kawasaki SMEs, and present two conditions for moving beyond subcontractor status, enhancing bargaining power and inventing in-house products. Section 3 examines the competitiveness of Kawasaki SMEs on the basis of four kinds of ability, and presents the concept of development-type SMEs. Section 4 analyses the findings of several regressions for Kawasaki SMEs. This study is not confined solely to Kawasaki SMEs, but rather is intended to shed light on SMEs achieving evolutionary development in general by the investigation of Kawasaki SMEs.

6.2 Overview of Kawasaki SMEs

This section provides an overview of the business operations of Kawasaki SMEs. The questionnaire was sent to 2870 firms by using the company list held by the research company, Teikoku Data Bank, on manufacturing and business/information services in Kawasaki City. These firms include almost all of the main firms established in Kawasaki, while small firms are excluded from the sample. Valid answers were obtained from 570 firms, or around 20% of the firms surveyed. Table 6.2 shows the composition of the respondent firms, which corresponds approximately to the composition of all firms. Therefore, the findings of our analysis will be applicable to the broader group of all Kawasaki SMEs. In particular, the main industrial sectors that this research focuses on, from steel and primary metal products to precision instruments, are adequately represented in our sample.

Table 6.3 shows the distribution of the respondent firms according to employee scale. About 90% of these firms have less than 300 employees and about 70% are small-sized firms with less than

Table 6.2:   Distribution of Respondent Firms by Industrial Sector.

Industrial Sector	Respondent Firms	%	All Firms	%
Food	11 (1)	2.6	114	6.0
Textile	1 (1)	0.2	3	0.2
Wood products	7	1.7	24	1.3
Paper & Allied products	6	1.4	36	1.9
Printing & Publishing	19	4.5	90	4.7
Chemicals	17 (2)	4.0	94	4.9
Rubber products	2	0.5	11	0.6
Non-metallic products	7	1.7	43	2.2
Steel & primary metal products	23 (3)	5.5	74	3.9
Metal products	58	13.7	244	12.7
Machinery	96 (6)	22.7	374	19.5
Electrical equipment	107 (5)	25.4	525	27.4
Transportation equipment	10 (1)	2.4	49	2.6
Precision instruments	27 (1)	6.4	80	4.2
Others	31 (1)	7.3	154	8.0
Manufacturing	422	(100.0)	1915	(100.0)
Information service	53 (8)	35.8	283	29.6
Business service	36 (2)	24.3	300	31.4
Professional service	56 (4)	37.8	348	36.4
Others	3	2.0	24	2.5
(Information/service)	148	(100.0)	955	(100.0)
Total number	**570**		**2870**	

(Parenthesis is the number of firms with more than 300 employees.)

Table 6.3:   Distribution of Respondent Firms.

	Manufacturing		Information/Service	
Number of Employees	Number of Firms	%	Number of Firms	%
1~9	167	39.6	59	39.9
10~49	148	35.1	43	29.1
50~299	66	15.6	25	16.9
300~999	21	5.0	14	9.5
Unknown	20	4.7	7	4.7
Total	422	100.0	148	100.0

50 employees. The definition of SMEs adopted here is firms with less than 300 employees, which is the Japanese criterion, although the EU definition is under 250 employees. Only nine firms are eliminated by using the EU definition.

The first question relates to how the Kawasaki industrial district still remains.

Although SMEs depend their businesses on the industrial district (Porter, 1998), Kawasaki industrial district would have been dissolved as a result of the decline of the manufacturing industries since the early 1990s. If the industrial district itself has disappeared, SEMs are deprived of the foundation of their businesses and the possibility of developing. Then, we asked the geographical location in which Kawasaki SMEs are selling and purchasing. Table 6.4 shows that, currently, only 15% of manufacturing sales and 25% of information/service sales, and only 27% of manufacturing purchases and 20% of information/service purchases of Kawasaki SMEs occur within Kawasaki City. In Kawasaki City, the industrial district seems to have declined in size.

However, it is undesirable to restrict the industrial district area under examination to only those regions in Kawasaki City. Instead, we extend our sample area to include the east area of Yokohama and the west area of Tokyo, because both are adjacent to Kawasaki City and substantially integrated. If these areas are grouped as one region and called 'greater Kawasaki', Kawasaki SMEs realise 44% of manufacturing and 56% of information/service sales, and 52% of manufacturing and 44% of information/service purchases in this region. In this

Table 6.4: Geographical Location of Sales and Purchases.

	Kawasaki	Yokohama/ Tokyo	Metropolitan	Whole Country	Overseas
Selling to					
Manufacturing	15.8	28.4	23.9	24.4	2.8
Info/service	24.6	31.0	21.7	15.6	1.2
Purchasing from					
Manufacturing	27.7	24.1	15.3	15.2	0.2
Info/service	20.3	24.5	17.5	10.1	1.3

Table 6.5:   Percentage of Firms Engaged in Each Type of Production.

	Mass Product	Small-lot Product	Single Product	Proto-type product	Product Development	System Contracting	Software Development
Manufacturing	30.9	68.3	46.9	42.9	19.7	3.0	2.0
Info/service	3.0	11.9	17.2	26.9	22.4	26.1	21.6

sense, the Kawasaki industrial district still operates primarily in 'greater Kawasaki', in which about 50% of their business is generated.

The second question is how Kawasaki SMEs operate as a supporting industry, which includes not only parts and components production but also prototype production and undertaking product development for the large manufacturing plants. Generally, the level of prototype production is a good measure of the technological potential of SMEs. Table 6.5 shows the percentage of Kawasaki SMEs that are engaged in various types of production; 50–70% of them are working in producing small-lot and single-component products, probably as subcontractors, about 40% are producing prototype products, and about 20% are engaged in product development. Although these figures do not reveal the size of each business, Kawasaki SMEs engage in prototype production to a sufficient level to be classified as a high-level supporting industry. In contrast, about 25% of SMEs in the information/service sector are engaged in system contracting and software development.

The third issue relates to the SMEs' status. Generally, SMEs are likely to face the disadvantage of lower profits because their business is conducted on a subcontractor basis. Therefore, it has been important for SMEs to consider how they can operate their business other than on a subcontracting basis. The answer is to produce in-house products and enhance their bargaining position. How are Kawasaki SMEs tackling this challenge?

Table 6.6 shows the bargaining position of Kawasaki SMEs in relation to their largest customer. They are separated into three groups; subcontractor, related company and partner. Subcontractors are necessarily in a weak bargaining position, related companies have no bargaining power by definition, and partners are also divided into three groups in terms of their bargaining position; weak, equal and strong. As shown in Table 6.6, 35–45% of Kawasaki SMEs in both manufacturing and information/service are subcontractors, with very few related companies. Of the remaining SMEs, about 50% are operating as partners, of which about 20% consider their bargaining position to be strong, 15% consider it to be equal and 13% consider it to be weak. Therefore, 35% of SMEs hold bargaining power as the result of either equal or strong positions. Table 6.7 shows the distribution of bargaining positions according to employee size for all sectors. While the ratio of subcontractors increases in the small-sized SMEs with less than 100 employees, they have higher ratio of either equal or strong bargaining positions than those with larger employees.

Table 6.8 shows the percentage of in-house products in total sales. As for manufacturing, about 30% of SMEs have no in-house products, however, about 30% do have in-house products accounting for more than 50% of their total sales. This pattern is similar for information/service SMEs. Table 6.9 shows the distribution of the

Table 6.6: Distribution of Bargaining Positions.

	Sub Contractor	Related Company	Partner but Weak	Partner and Equal	Partner and Strong	Equal and Strong
Manufacturing	44.2	3.2	13.5	14.8	20.8	35.6
Info/service	36.5	6.1	13.9	18.3	17.4	35.7

Table 6.7: Bargaining Position by Employee Size (all sectors).

Employee Size	Sub-cont	Related	Weak	Equal	Strong	Equal + Strong
1~9	49.2	1.4	12.1	15.5	21.7	37.2
10~49	43.0	2.9	14.5	18.0	21.5	39.5
50~99	40.0	2.2	17.8	26.7	13.3	40.0
100~299	30.0	25.0	20.0	2.5	22.5	25.0
300~	25.8	29.0	16.1	22.6	6.5	29.0
Total	43.2	5.7	14.3	16.8	20.0	36.8

Table 6.8:   Distribution of the Ratio of In-House Products.

	0%	0~10%	10~20%	20~30%	30~40%	40~50%	50%
Manufacturing	32.6	14.3	6.7	5.7	5.4	3.0	32.3
Info/service	23.3	18.1	7.8	3.4	1.7	6.0	39.7

Table 6.9:   Ratio of In-House Products by Employee Size (all sectors).

Employee Size	0%	0~10%	10~50%	50%
1~9	29.8	11.6	22.3	36.3
10~49	33.7	19.0	15.8	31.5
50~99	28.3	17.4	21.7	32.6
100~299	21.4	14.3	28.6	35.7
300~	2.9	23.5	26.5	47.1
Total	28.6	15.7	20.7	34.9

ratio according to employee size for all sectors. Even the small-sized SMEs with less than 10 employees have an unexpectedly high ratio of in-house products. Therefore, there is no difference in the ratio of over 50% in-house product firms until employee size is over 300 employees. However, in-house products for SMEs probably include the products provided as OEM (original equipment manufacturer) contracting to their customers.

The last issue is what relations there are between in-house products and bargaining position. Is there a positive relation between them as predicted? Table 6.10 shows very clearly the correlation between in-house products and bargaining position; the higher the ratio of in-house products, the stronger the bargaining position. While 70% of firms with no in-house products are subcontractors, 60% of firms with in-house products representing over 50% of sales have either equal or strong bargaining power. Needless to say, it is necessary to have special abilities to develop in-house products. How do Kawasaki SMEs develop such competencies? This will be examined in the next section.

Finally, as for the performance of Kawasaki SMEs, Table 6.11 shows the change in sales and profit from 2003 to 2005. The figures represent the percentage of firms with an increase (decrease) in sales, and a profit improvement (worsening). For sales, Kawasaki SMEs are

Table 6.10: Bargaining Position by the Ratio of In-House Products (all sectors).

Ratio/In-house Products	Sub-cont.	Related	Weak	Equal	Strong
0%	72.7	4.5	7.6	9.8	5.3
0~10%	46.4	2.9	23.2	15.9	11.6
10~50%	40.2	4.1	14.4	18.6	22.7
50~	19.7	4.6	16.4	21.1	38.2
Total	43.8	4.2	14.4	16.4	21.1

Table 6.11: Change in Sales and Profit.

	Sales from 2003 to 2005		
	Increase	Constant	Decrease
Manufacturing	58.6	7.5	34.0
Info/service	51.2	9.1	39.7

	Final Profit from 2003 to 2005		
	Improved	Constant	Worsen
Manufacturing	37.7	28.6	33.7
Info/service	28.9	37.2	33.9

divided into two groups; increasing and decreasing, and for profit, they are divided nearly evenly into three groups, improved, constant, and worsened. The profit data is given as the final profit after tax, and the profit improved (worsened) group is defined by the difference in the rate of profit per sale between 2003 and 2005; a positive (negative) value indicates profit improvement (worsening) even though both rates are negative values.[1]

---

[1] While it is better to use operating profit to examine business conditions, it is difficult to gather such data on SMEs. Furthermore, there is a critical problem in using the final profit data. That is, SMEs frequently manipulate their final profit to be zero in order to avoid a tax burden. In fact, the ratio of zero-profit firms is remarkably high; about 45% of them are zero-profit, another 45% are positive profit and the remaining 10% are in deficit according to the 2005 data. Given these limitations, we use data on the final profit.

Table 6.12 shows the relation between in-house products and business state and between bargaining position and business state for all SMEs.

The figures represent the percentage of firms that achieved an increase in sales and profit improvement from 2003 to 2005, and positive profit in 2005. There are only two cases that have statistically significant relations, between in-house products and sales increase, between bargaining position and positive profit in 2005. In the two cases, however, the ratio of sales increase is largest in the firms with 10–50% in-house products and the ratio of positive profit is largest in the firms with equal bargaining position. After all, it is difficult to see definite relations between firms' performance and in-house products, and between firms' performance and bargaining position. These findings will be examined in the final section.

From our overview of Kawasaki SMEs up to here, the main points are as follows. While the following points are mainly based on the

Table 6.12:   Relations between In-House Products, Bargaining Position and Firms' Performance.

	Sales Increased	Profit Improved	Positive Profit in 2004
In-house product			
0%	52.4	32.0	40.1
0~10%	50.7	35.2	50.7
10~50%	69.8	33.3	45.8
50%~	57.5	41.9	47.5
	r = 0.031	r = 0.292	r = 0.435
Bargaining position			
Sub-cont.	54.7	32.0	37.4
Related	64.7	41.2	52.9
Weak	64.1	37.5	50.0
Equal	59.5	39.2	54.1
Strong	60.2	39.8	48.4
	r = 0.659	r = 0.636	r = 0.070

manufacturing SMEs, similar patterns exist for the information/ service SMEs.

1) Kawasaki SMEs in both the manufacturing and information/ service sectors have half of their business in the region of 'greater Kawasaki' including eastern Yokohama and western Tokyo, therefore the Kawasaki industrial district seems to be surviving.

2) About 40% of Kawasaki SMEs in manufacturing are engaged in the provision of prototype products and 20% in product development, so they seem to have the role of supporting industries not only for the provision of parts and components to the large manufacturing plants but also for supporting the high tech mother plants and research laboratories.

3) About 40% are operating their business as a subcontractor, and about 50% are operating as a partner with strong (20%), equal (15%), or weak (15%) bargaining positions respectively. By summing up those firms with either equal or strong bargaining power, around 35% of Kawasaki SMEs hold bargaining power.

4) About 30% have no in house products, and about 30% have in-house products constituting over 50% of their total sales. Around 50% of Kawasaki SMEs have in-house products constituting over 10% of total sales.

5) It is clear that there is a positive relation between the ratio of in-house products and bargaining position.

6) Kawasaki SMEs are divided into two groups, increasing and decreasing sales, and into three groups, improving, constant and worsening final profit.

7) However, there is not necessarily a definite relation between firms' outcomes of sales and profit and producing in-house products and enhancing bargaining position.

8) Although it is predicted that SMEs could evolve from subcontractors by producing in-house products and enhancing bargaining positions, such an evolutionary path does not lead directly to profitability. Probably, additional factors other than in-house products will be necessary for SMEs to develop. This is categorised as the development-type SMEs, which is a main

theme investigated in this paper. Prior to this, however, the next question is how Kawasaki SMEs gain the potential to develop their own in-house products.

6.3 Competitiveness of the Kawasaki SMEs

It was confirmed that Kawasaki SMEs require in-house products to move beyond subcontractor status. Needless to say, it is necessary to have abilities to develop in-house products. How do Kawasaki SMEs develop such abilities to achieve competitiveness?

To examine the Kawasaki SMEs' competitiveness, we developed questions about 12 factors related to business advantage, described in the left side column in Table 6.13. The answers were as follows; strong = 5, moderately strong = 4, average = 3, moderately weak = 2, weak = 1, and Table 6.13 shows the percentage of firms that gave the 'strong' or 'moderately strong' answers to each question. As for the manufacturing SMEs, more than 50% replied that they have an advantage in the 'just-in-time supplying', 'variety and small-lot production', 'having good customers' and 'highly precise processing', probably

Table 6.13:   Advantage Factors of Kawasaki SMEs.

Advantage Factors	Manufacturing	Info/Service
Just-in-time supplying	75.8	56.6
Variety and small-lot production	69.6	38.3
Having good customers	61.4	56.8
Highly precise processing	55.5	41.7
Having core technology	50.3	56.9
Proposals/solutions for customers	41.4	63.7
Low price supplying	40.7	43.1
Having good suppliers	39.8	40.0
New products designing development	31.6	45.5
Design of self-equipment	27.3	34.5
Possession of CAD/CAM and fine measure instruments	25.2	15.4
Creation of new customers and markets	14.2	15.5

these factors mean the potentials as subcontractor, and 'having core-technology' was also true for around 50% of firms, whereas an advantage in the 'proposals/solutions for customers' is important for the information/service SMEs. In contrast, the firms that have an advantage in the 'design of self-equipment', 'possession of CAD/CAM and fine measuring instrument' and 'creation of new customers and markets' represent less than 25% of the sample.

Next, these 12 factors are categorised into four abilities by applying factor analysis, as shown in Table 6.14. The four groups are named as follows; 1) 'development ability', ability in new product design and development, to develop proposals and solutions for customers, to possess core technology, and to design self-equipment; 2) 'sales/purchasing ability', having good customers, having good suppliers, and ability to create new customers and markets; 3) 'processing ability', ability to undertake highly precise processing, to possess CAD/CAM and fine measuring instrument, and to produce variety and small-lot components; and 4) 'subcontracting ability', ability to undertake just-in-time supplying, and to undertake low-price supplying.

Table 6.14: Four Categories of Competitiveness.

Development Ability	Sales/Purchasing Ability	Processing Ability	Sub-contracting Ability
New product designing/ development (0.829)	Having goods customers (0.790)	Highly precise processing (0.743)	Just-in-time supplying (0.824)
Proposals/solutions for customers (0.771)	Having goods suppliers (0.762)	CAD/CAM and fine measuring instruments (653)	Low price supplying (0.718)
Having core technology (0.741)	Creation of new customers and markets (0.733)	Variety and small-lot production (0.638)	
Design of self equipment (0.649)			

Table 6.15:   Competitive Scores by Industrial Sector.

	Development Ability	Sales/Purchasing Ability	Processing Ability	Sub-cont. Ability
Machinery	3.26	3.16	3.40	3.43
Electronics	3.31	3.18	3.46	3.51
Automobile	3.00	3.56	3.63	3.78
Precision equip.	3.39	2.93	3.33	3.50
Manufacturing	3.18	3.17	3.38	3.61
Info/service	3.43	3.16	3.03	3.45

Table 6.15 presents the average scores for these four abilities; in general and on average, there is a relatively high score for subcontracting and processing ability in manufacturing SMEs, and a relatively high score for development and subcontracting ability in information/service SMEs. However, the precision instrument and electronic equipment sectors have relatively high scores for development ability, whereas the transportation equipment sector has a relatively high score in sales/purchasing ability. The latter implies a close relationship between customers and suppliers in the automobile industry. In contrast, a high score for development ability in information/service SMEs indicates that they have an ability to develop proposals and solutions for customers as shown in Table 6.13.

Table 6.16 shows the average scores for the four abilities according to employee size for all sectors. This shows that the four abilities, particularly development ability, are unrelated to employee size except sales/purchasing ability. Although the latter score decreases for the small-sized SMEs, the largest score is in the 50–99 employee SMEs. In contrast, small-sized SMEs can achieve the same level of development ability as medium-sized SMEs.

The figures in Table 6.16 also imply that even the small-sized SMEs have levels of processing and subcontracting ability that are sufficient for SMEs to cope with customers' requests. Table 6.17 shows how Kawasaki SMEs cope with customer firms' behaviours and requests, which are described on the left. The first column presents the percentage of firms facing the serious influences from customers'

Table 6.16: Four Abilities by Employee Size (all sectors).

Employee Size	Development Ability	Sales/Purchasing Ability	Processing Ability	Sub-cont. Ability
1~9	3.25	3.03	3.23	3.59
10~49	3.23	3.19	3.41	3.61
50~99	3.24	3.51	3.31	3.58
100~299	3.27	3.38	3.29	3.30
	$p = 0.986$	$p = 0.000$	$p = 0.210$	$p = 0.099$

Table 6.17: Coping with Customers' Behaviours and Requests.

	(1) Facing the Influences from Customers	(2) Able to Cope	(2)/(1) Probability of Coping
Short supply times	58.8	54.3	92.4
Unit price cutting	57.0	43.0	75.6
Improving quality	54.3	48.3	88.9
Improving production technology	33.9	29.7	87.6
Selecting outsourcing	23.1	16.5	71.6
Reduction in orders	21.3	14.7	69.1
Obtaining ISOs	17.6	13.6	77.6
Increasing overseas production	16.8	5.2	31.3
Dealing through internet	15.7	14.2	90.0
Improving designing abilities	15.7	12.9	81.7
Increasing in-house production	12.9	7.3	57.1
Moving domestic plants overseas	11.3	5.2	46.5
Purchasing from overseas	10.5	3.4	32.5
Having the direct line for dealing	7.3	7.3	100.0
Using common components	4.7	3.9	83.3

behaviours and requests, the second column presents the percentage of firms able to cope, and the third column presents the probability of coping, defined as the ratio of the second column over the first. It is difficult for SMEs to cope with customers' behaviour such as 'purchasing from overseas', 'increasing overseas production' and 'moving plants overseas'.

Only one-third can cope with these factors, although there are very few examples of these situations. In contrast, other demands of customers such as 'short supply times', 'unit price cutting', 'improving quality', and 'improving production technology' are managed very well by Kawasaki SMEs. These demands necessitate 'processing ability' and 'subcontracting ability', which are the basic conditions for SMEs to survive as subcontractors, and Kawasaki SMEs possess these abilities as shown in Tables 6.15 and 6.16. In addition, Kawasaki SMEs can cope well with 'selection of outsourcing' and 'reductions in orders' and 'improving designing ability', which also demands 'processing' and 'subcontracting' abilities.

Generally, SMEs are considered to be subcontractors, and desire to change their status. However, SMEs have to achieve minimum conditions to survive as a subcontractor, in particular processing and subcontracting ability, otherwise they will be unable to continue their business even as subcontractors. This research confirms that Kawasaki SMEs are able to achieve these conditions. Adding to these minimum conditions, SMEs need the potential to move beyond being a subcontractor by developing the ability to produce in-house products and sales/purchasing ability to enhance their bargaining position.

Table 6.18 measures the four abilities according to the ratio of in-house products. It is apparent that the higher the ratio of in-house products, the larger the score of both developing and sales/purchasing ability. In contrast, having in-house products contradicts having subcontracting ability. Furthermore, Table 6.19 shows the measures of ability according to bargaining position. It is apparent that strong and equal bargaining positions depend on both development and

Table 6.18: Four Abilities by the Ratio of In-House Products.

Ration of In-house Product	Development Ability	Sales/Purchasing Ability	Processing Ability	Sub-cont. Ability
0%	2.73	2.97	3.25	3.58
0~10%	3.14	3.22	3.46	3.79
10~50%	3.48	3.30	3.28	3.61
50%~	3.63	3.25	3.31	3.43
	$r = 0.000$	$r = 0.004$	$r = 0.368$	$r = 0.005$

Table 6.19: Four Abilities by Bargaining Position.

Bargaining Position	Development Ability	Sales/Purchasing Ability	Processing Ability	Sub-cont. Ability
Sub-contractor	2.90	2.95	3.28	3.63
Related company	2.99	3.02	3.14	3.28
Weak	3.21	3.08	3.29	3.51
Equal	3.62	3.38	3.39	3.57
Strong	3.73	3.52	3.48	3.59
	$r = 0.000$	$r = 0.004$	$r = 0.245$	$r = 0.005$

sales/purchasing ability, and do not depend on processing or subcontracting ability.

Development and sales/purchasing abilities are critically important for SMEs to progress beyond being a subcontractor. Such SMEs are often called 'development-type' SMEs according to two criteria. One is having development ability for inventing new products, the other is having in-house products greater than 10% in their sales. It is possible to set the former criterion as a score over 3.5 on 'development ability', and the latter criterion as a ratio of in-house products over 10%. Then, the percentage of 'development-type' firms among Kawasaki SMEs is shown in Table 6.20. About 30% of SMEs are characterised as development-type in the manufacturing sector, and about 40% in the information/service sector.[2] In particular, these firms are primarily located in the precision instrument and electronics sector, which is consistent with their relatively high score for development ability.

The development-type SMEs are supposed to achieve good business performance. Table 6.21 shows the percentage of both

---

[2] It is reported as for the TAMA cluster that development-type SEMs account for 65% in 164 firms (Kodama, 2003). TAMA cluster, located from Saitama prefecture, via western Tokyo to Kanagawa prefecture, large area as the upper Metropolitan area, is formed by the support of the Ministry of Economy, Trade and Industry and the member firms are selected by the beginning. In addition, this does not necessarily give a definite definition of development ability. In contrast, we define it as score over 3.5 on 'development ability', which is confirmed by its score corresponding with the ratio of in-house products from 10 to 50% in total sales as shown in Table 6.18.

Table 6.20:   Development-Type SMEs.

Development Type	%
Machinery	32.4
Electrical equip.	40.7
Transportation equip.	12.5
Precision instrument	65.2
Manufacturing	32.4
Info/service	39.6

Table 6.21:   Performance of Development-Type SMEs.

	Sales Growth	Profit Growth	Positive Profit in 2005	Strong Position
Manufacturing				
Development-type	65.5	50.0	59.1	39.3
N-dev	56.0	33.6	43.1	12.1
(t-test)	9.4#	16.4**	16.0**	27.2***
Information/service				
Development-type	67.5	30.0	40.0	27.9
N-dev	42.4	28.8	47.0	12.9
(t-test)	25.1*	1.2	−7.0	15.0#

***$p < 0.001$, **$p < 0.01$, *$p < 0.05$, #:$p < 0.1$.

development-type and non-development-type (N-dev) SMEs that achieved sales growth and profit improvement from 2003 to 2005, final positive profit in 2005 and having a strong bargaining position. The 5% statistically significant difference suggests that development-type SMEs in manufacturing achieved better profitability, profit growth and positive profit, and bargaining positions, but not sales growth. This suggests that development-type SMEs, at least in manufacturing, pursue not scale but profit. In contrast, development-type SMEs in the information/service sector achieved higher sales growth but this did not affect profitability.

As previously shown in Table 6.12, there is no clear relation between in-house products and sales growth, or between bargaining position and profit growth. In contrast, such relations can be seen in the development-type SMEs. It is certainly true that SMEs should have in-house products and enhance their bargaining position to progress beyond subcontractor status; however, such conditions themselves do not necessarily assure the SMEs' development in terms of sales growth and profit growth. It seems to be the development-type SMEs that actually achieve sales growth (information/service) and profit growth (manufacturing).

In short, there are three categories of SMEs. The first is the group of subcontractors, who have processing and subcontracting abilities to cope with the requests from their customer firms. The second group has moved beyond subcontractor status by having in-house products and enhanced bargaining positions. The third group is development-type SMEs, who progressed from the second group and achieved good business performance in terms of sales and profit. These conjectures will be confirmed by the formal regression in the final section.

6.4 Technology and Profitability

This study aims to examine how Kawasaki SMEs evolve from sub-contractor status. The findings up to here could presume the path on which Kawasaki SMEs progress; the first step is to have in-house products by inventing new products, the second is to enhance the bargaining position by increasing the number of in-house products, and the third is to improve profit by strengthening bargaining power. While the importance of the first and the second steps is well recognised, it should be stressed that achieving profit is indispensable for the development of SMEs because investment in technology and human resources depends on profit. In other words, as long as SMEs are restricted to low or negligible profit, it is difficult to see SMEs progressing on the development path. Our final investigation is to analyse several key issues on the basis of regression analysis.

The first question is how the potential of Kawasaki SMEs is shaped. Both development and sales/purchasing abilities were recognised to be the most important factors if SMEs were to progress beyond subcontractor status. Then, the question is what elements affect such abilities? Is it possible to find certain elements that promote development and sales/purchasing ability? In this research, it is possible to examine the effects of factors such as whether or not firms have development staff and sales staff. Generally, SMEs cannot afford to employ development staff and sales staff, although such employees are indispensable to the development of new products and new customers. Therefore, we predict that SMEs that have these employees have an advantage in promoting development and sales/purchasing ability. In addition, this research examines the partners that Kawasaki SMEs consult to resolve their business problems and which partners are most useful for problem solving; universities, business organisations, public research institutions, and so on.

By using these variables, we estimate regressions for the four abilities. The results are shown in Table 6.22. Here, the independent variables are the following dummy variables; D1: having development staff, D2: having sales staff, D3: consulting with business organisations, D4: consulting with universities, D5: consulting with public

Table 6.22:   Factors Affecting the Four Abilities (all sectors).

	Development Ability	Sales/Purchasing Ability	Processing Ability	Sub-cont. Ability
Deve-staff	0.618***	0.065	−0.004	−0.120
Sales-staff	0.145#	0.214*	0.127	0.003
Business org.	−0.079	−0.010	−0.188	−0.086
University	0.812*	0.550	0.354	−0.123
Public institution	0.333	0.089	−0.113	0.250
Chamber of Com.	0.474	1.031***	0.423	0.087
Customer	−0.055	0.186	−0.160	0.036
Supplier	−0.012	0.427*	−0.246	−0.024
Bank	0.041	0.361*	−0.008	0.054
Business meeting	0.072	−0.046	−0.154	−0.055
Inemp	−0.063*	0.066	0.037	−0.033
Cons	3.035***	2.655***	3.218***	3.693***
Adj.R2	0.173	0.076	0.004	−0.012
	N = 374	N = 367	N = 360	N = 384

***$p < 0.001$, **$p < 0.01$, *$p < 0.05$, #$p < 0.1$.

research institutions, D6: consulting with chambers of commerce, D6: consulting with customer firms, D7: consulting with suppliers, D8: consulting with banks, and D9: consulting with business meetings. The log-transformed number of employees (lnemp) is introduced as a control variable. Here, the results are shown for SMEs in all sectors. They do not change if the manufacturing and information/service sectors are analysed separately.

It is clearly shown that having development staff positively affects the enhancement of development ability, and having sales staff also positively affects sales/purchasing ability.

Moreover, it is confirmed that consulting with universities is effective in enhancing development ability, and consulting with chambers of commerce, suppliers and banks is also effective in enhancing sales/purchasing ability. In contrast, there is no factor affecting processing and subcontracting ability. It is important to note that consulting with universities on the one hand, and consulting with chambers of commerce, suppliers and banks on the other, is valuable for SMEs. While the effect of universities on development ability is predictable, the effects of chambers of commerce, suppliers and banks on sales/purchasing ability imply that they are useful business partners that will provide SMEs with valuable information for sales and purchases.

The second question is how the evolutionary path of SMEs is confirmed. This was shown as the process of developing in-house products, enhancing bargaining power and achieving profit. As the first step, we confirm the determinants of in-house products. This is achieved by using an ordered logit regression for the ratio of in-house products (0% = 1, 0~10% = 2, 10~20% = 3, 20~30% = 4, 30~40% = 5, 40~50% = 6, over 50% = 7). Independent variables are the four categories of ability, $c1$ (development ability), $c2$ (sales/purchasing ability), $c3$ (processing ability), and $c4$ (subcontracting ability), and employee size (log-transformation of the number of employees) is added as a control variable. The results are shown in Table 6.23.

As for the manufacturing SMEs, it is clearly demonstrated that developing and sales/purchasing abilities positively affect in-house products on the one hand, but negatively affect processing and

Table 6.23:   Determinants of the Rate of In-House Products.

	Manufacturing	Info/Service
c1 (Development)	1.370***	1.558***
c2 (Sales/purchasing)	0.360*	−0.755*
c3 (Processing)	−0.606***	0.312
c4 (Subcontracting)	−0.376*	−0.336
Employee size	0.055	−0.341*
Sample numbers	327	88
Log likelihood	−477.1	−118.2
Pseudo R2	0.103	0.134

***p < 0.001, **p < 0.01, *p < 0.05, #p < 0.1.

subcontracting abilities on the other. While, as shown in Table 6.17, processing and subcontracting abilities are indispensable for SMEs to survive by coping with customers' requests, both abilities do not lead to progression beyond subcontractor status. Instead, both oppose the evolution of SMEs and lock them into subcontractor status. This means that SMEs are divided into two groups; one has development and sales/purchasing abilities, while the other has processing and subcontracting abilities. Table 6.23 shows that there is a large gap in the transition from the latter to the former. Furthermore, as predicted above, employee size has no effect on the ratio of in-house products. In contrast, for the information/service SMEs, development ability has a positive effect as predicted, but sales/purchasing ability has a negative effect, and processing and subcontracting abilities have no effect. While the negative effect of sales/purchasing ability is difficult to explain, the positive effect of development ability is clearly confirmed.

The next step is to confirm the determinants of enhancing the bargaining position. This is conducted by using a logit regression for bargaining position, and the regression is classified according to two categories; the first is strong position = 1, otherwise = 0; the second is strong and equal positions = 1, otherwise = 0. The independent variables are the ratio of in-house products, and the following variables; holding sales staff (yes = 1, no = 0), duration of dealing with

Table 6.24: Determinants of Bargaining Position.

	Manufacturing		Information/Service	
	Strong	Strong + Equal	Strong	Strong + Equal
In-house products	0.342***	0.332***	0.300*	0.230*
Sales-staff	0.679*	0.195	0.582	1.069*
Duration	0.009	0.007	−0.090*	−0.036
Dependance	0.002	0.003	0.064	0.051
Inemp	−0.124	−0.047	0.008	0.075
Cons	−3.131***	−2.027**	−2.183	−1.686
Sample numbers	343	343	107	107
Log likelihood	−153.0	−197.8	−43.0	−61.2
Pseudo R2	0.132	0.121	0.167	0.128

***$p < 0.001$, **$p < 0.01$, *$p < 0.05$, #$p < 0.1$.

the largest customer (spot $= 1$, within one year $= 2$, within five years $= 3$, over five years $= 4$, since foundation $= 5$; these scores are squared), and the degree of dependence on the largest customer (defined as the ratio of the sales to this customer over total sales), and the log-transformed number of employees. As seen above, having sales staff is predicted to positively affect the bargaining position, and the degree of dependence is predicted to negatively affect the bargaining position, whereas the effect of duration is not necessarily predictable. The results are shown in Table 6.25.

It is clearly confirmed that increasing the number of in-house products strengthens the bargaining power. In addition, sales staff effectively work to achieve strong bargaining positions for manufacturing SMEs and to achieve qual bargaining positions for information/service SMEs. For information/service SMEs, as the bargaing duration becomes longer, they tend to lose strong bargaining position. It is also confirmed that employee size has no effect on the bargaining position.

The last step is to examine the determinants of profit. It has been determined that Kawasaki SMEs can progress on the path of development from subcontractor by means of in-house products and bargaining power. Therefore, is it possible to confirm the final path

Table 6.25:   Final Profit Improvement.

	Manufacturing (1)	Manufacturing (2)	Info/ Service (1)	Info/ Service (2)
Bargaining position	−0.023	−0.101	−0.248	−0.322
In-house products	0.100*	0.006	−0.038	−0.024*
Sales growth	2.206*	2.099*	3.358#	3.470#
Sectorial value-added	1.097	1.185	1.099	1.180
Development-type		0.774*		−0.044
Inemp	0.326**	0.339**	0.379*	0.366*
Cons	−1.873***	−1.793***	−2.005**	−1.966**
Sample numbers	354	336	103	100
Log likelihood	−218.9	−205.5	−55.4	−54.5
Pseudo R2	0.057	0.069	0.0814	0.0811

***$p < 0.001$, **$p < 0.01$, *$p < 0.05$, #$p < 0.1$.

on the basis of improving profit? This is conducted by using a logit regression for the change in profit from 2003 to 2005 (improved = 1, otherwise = 0). Independent variables are the ratio of in-house products and bargaining position (strong = 1, otherwise = 0). Related variables are introduced such as the average rate of sales growth from 2003 to 2005, sectoral trend in the national level value-added, and employee size. Then, the presumption is that increasing the ratio of in-house products and holding a strong bargaining position positively affects final profit. Here the regression is classified according to two categories; the first is based on the above independent variables, the second adds a dummy variable for development-type SMEs (development-type = 1, otherwise = 0). The results are shown in Table 6.25.

The first regression shows that both bargaining position and in-house products have no effect on profit for the manufacturing and information/service SMEs except for the positive effect of in-house products for the manufacturing SMEs. The main effects on profit are from sales growth and employee size, in particular sales growth strongly affects profit growth. While employee size has no effect on both in-house products and bargaining position as shown in Tables 6.23 and 6.24, profit is affected by employee size, probably which is related with sales growth. Anyway, supposed development path is interrupted.

In contrast, the second regression shows that development-type SMEs clearly have a positive effect on profit in manufacturing SMEs, although they have no effect in the information/service sector. Here, the effect of in-house products disappears, probably because it is absorbed by the effect of development-type SMEs defined as having in-house products over 10%. These results are important because, given the effects of sales growth and employee size, it is development-type SMEs that serve to improve profit. Although development-type SMEs include the effect of bargaining position as seen in Table 6.21, bargaining position itself does not lead to profit growth. This means that in addition to the bargaining position, which depends on in-house products, there must be another factor for achieving profit, that is, development-type SMEs.

Finally, we examine the factors affecting sales growth. Is sales growth achieved by increasing in-house products? Table 6.26 shows the regression results for the average rate of sales growth from 2003 to 2005.

Table 6.26: Sales Growth.

	Manufacturing (1)	Manufacturing (2)	Info/ Service (1)	Info/ Service (2)
In-house products	0.009	0.008	−0.019	−0.019
Bargaining position	−0.002	−0.002	−0.004	0.000
Sectorial gross prod.	0.053	0.047	0.590**	0.639**
Development-type		0.001		−0.030
Employee size	0.014*	0.014*	−0.006	−0.008
Cons	−0.001	0.000	−0.012	−0.005
Adj.R2	0.01	0.01	0.10	0.12
	N = 354	N = 336	N = 103	N = 100

***$p < 0.001$, **$p < 0.01$, *$p < 0.05$, #$p < 0.1$.

The regressions are classified into two types; the first is composed of independent variables such as the ratio of in-house products, bargaining position, employee size, and the sectoral trends in the national level gross product, while the second regression adds the development-type SMEs.

The first regression shows that sales growth depends only on employee size in manufacturing, and depends only on the sectoral trend in the information/service sector. The latter result is important because it corresponds with the overview of Kawasaki SMEs as shown in Figure 6.1, where SMEs in the information/service sector have grown at the same trend rate as the national level. The second regression also shows that development-type SMEs have no effect on sales growth in both the manufacturing and information/service sectors. While development-type SMEs realise an improvement in profit at least in manufacturing, they do not affect sales growth. In summary, there is no significant factor that achieves sales growth without employee size and sectoral trend. Together with the results for profit, this implies that information/service SMEs in Kawasaki have no advantage in sales and profit. Although old large electronics plants in Kawasaki have converted to in-house research laboratories focused on information technology, information/service SMEs in Kawasaki have no involvement in these activities.

According to these regressions, in-house products and bargaining position are confirmed to be indispensable conditions to progress from subcontractor status. In addition, Kawasaki SMEs have sufficient potential to develop in-house products, and those that have in-house products accounting for over 50% of total sales account for 32% of manufacturing firms, 40% of information/service sector firms, and those that have in-house products accounting for over 10% of total sales account for 53% of manufacturing firms and 59% of information/service sector firms. Similarly, the firms that hold strong bargaining positions account for 21% of manufacturing firms, 17% of information/service sector firms, and those that hold strong or equal bargaining power account for 36% of manufacturing firms and 36% of information/service sector firms. In summary, about 30–40% of Kawasaki SMEs have the potential to progress beyond subcontractor status.

However, this does not necessarily lead to profit growth. Apart from adding to the number of in-house products and enhancing bargaining position, another factor is needed for SMEs to achieve profit growth, that is, development-type SMEs. Although the concept of development-type SMEs is composed of development ability and in-house products, both have to be integrated within development-type SMEs. Then , there are two steps in the evolutionary path for SMEs; the first is to progress from subcontractor by shaping the potential to develop in-house products, while the second step is to progress towards a development-type SME.

It is necessary to examine the development-type SMEs in more detail, but this remains for future research. In particular, the management of development-type SMEs should be investigated because the advantage of development-type SMEs seems to lie in the managerial potential as well as technological potential. For instance, it is often pointed out that managers of SMEs are not necessarily concerned about cost control in their workshop, nor about total cost control of purchasing and selling, so they are likely to face increasing cost and decreasing profit as operations increase in scale. In contrast, successful SMEs often make proposals to their customers that improve operations, so their orders of related components and integrated components will prevent falling prices. In addition, bargaining power depends not only on their technological ability, but also on their ability to use their technological advantage to the benefit of their customers. Finally, the most important ability is to invent a new product suitable to the market conditions; that is, marketing ability. These abilities are based on the personal competence of the SMEs' managers. Such managerial ability will be hired in the large-scale firms, but in SMEs it must be developed by existing managers. In this sense, it is important to support SMEs not only in the advancement of technology but also in the advancement of managerial human resources.

References

GAVRON, R., COWLING, M., HOLTHAM, G. and WESTALL, A. (1998). 'Entrepreneurial Society,' Institute for Public Policy Research (IPPR).

KILBY, P. (1971). 'In Search of the Heffalump', KILBY, P. (ed). *Entrepreneurship and Economic Development*, Free Press, New York.

KODAMA, S. (2003). 'Innovative Technology and Cluster Formation of the Firms in TAMA (TAMA-Kigyo no Gijyuturyoku to Kurasuta Keisei Jyoukyo)', RIETI Policy Discussion Paper Series 03-P-004.

PORTER, M. E. (1998). *On Competition*. Harvard Business School Press.

STOREY, D. J. (1994). *Understanding the Small Business Sector*. London, Loutle.

Part Three: China

The Specificities of Chinese Industrial Clusters: Their Importance and Weaknesses

Chapter 7

New Phenomena and Challenges of Clusters in China in the New Era of Globalisation[1]

Jici Wang

China

R32 P33 F23

P25 L24 L14

7.1 Introduction

In the last two decades China has been industrialising at amazing speed. The contribution of its exports processing trade to the economic growth rate increased from 6% in 1981 to 38% in 1990 and 49% in 2005. Currently the number of export products with the highest share in the world market reached 774 items, among which 1972 items of export products were ranked among the first five of their individual markets in the world. The output value of over 170 items of products shared the largest market in the world exports manufacture.

However, this explosive growth, at least until recently, has been driven primarily by the low wage manufacture of consumer goods for export. Chinese factories have provided OEM (Original Equipment Manufacturer) products for U.S., Japanese and European retailers and manufacturers — 'big buyers' that have shaped economic development throughout East Asia (Hamilton and Feenstra, 2006; Hamilton and Petrovic, 2006; Geneffi, 2006). China has only a manufacturing base and has not yet established a position in international markets for high-value-added products. Even 89.6% of its export of high tech

[1] This research was supported in part by the National Natural Science Foundation of China, under grant No. 40535027.

products comes from the export processing activities with import materials, and this rate keeps increasing.

China's export processing activities began with assembly at the end of the 1970s on the platforms of export processing zones located in the coastal cities, and quickly moved to full-package or OEM production, causing numerous clusters largely in the south-east coast provinces, such as Guangdong, Zhejiang, Jiangsu and Fujian. As the supplier of choice in virtually all labour intensive global value chains, China stands at the centre of the story of offshore production (Geriffi, 2005).

Many reports have commented on the country's export-oriented clusters, e.g.:

'Buyers from New York to Tokyo want to be able to buy 500,000 pairs of socks all at once, or 300,000 neckties, 100,000 children's jackets, or 50,000 size 36B bras. Increasingly, the places that best accommodate orders are China's giant new specialty cities. The niche cities reflect China's ability to form 'lump' economies, where clusters or networks of businesses feed off each other, building technologies and enjoying the benefits of concentrated support centres.' (Barbosa, 2004).

'Drawing on its vast population and mix of free-market and central-command economic policies, China has created giant industrial districts in distinctive entrepreneurial enclaves such as Datang. Each was built to specialize in making just one thing, including some of the most pedestrian of goods: cigarette lighters, badges, neckties, fasteners. The clusters are one reason China's shipments of socks to the U.S. have soared from 6 million pairs in 2000 to 670 million pairs last year. Meanwhile, American producers, pummeled by imports from China and elsewhere, saw their share of the U.S. hosiery market fall from 69% in 2000 to 44% in 2003, according to the latest industry data.' (Lee, 2005).

There is a huge literature on clusters hailed as a universal panacea for regional development. The Chinese literature on clusters is also rich but mostly confusing. Fundamental problems arise for Chinese cities and towns when seeking guidance from the Western literature, which is to believe the external economies within clusters are strong and clusters can facilitate cooperation, trust, and innovation among firms. Then the literature moves to policy. Attempts at cluster development in China have generally taken the form of conventional urban planning approaches, such as localised infrastructure projects, preferential policies and financial assistance. These approaches usually focus on urbanisation via the construction of high cost infrastructure to attract outsiders, rather than emphasising localisation to create learning effects. The Chinese media currently give unprecedented attention to the region-centric view of development (Wang, 2007).

Of course, the location of the existing manufacturing capacities in China refutes the conventional wisdom that low labour costs are the sole source of manufacturing advantage. However, the theoretical underpinning of the deluge of cluster studies in the world is not clear to China. Based on Chinese cluster phenomenon description, this study is beyond traditional or conventional perspectives on clusters. This chapter attempts to make four points.

First, this chapter claims that Chinese clusters are formed in global-local tension. Globalisation and the worldwide increase in contract manufacturing have created new trends toward concentration and dispersal in the international economy. On the one hand, as Guerrieri and Pietrobelli (2004) noticed, a breathtaking speed of geographical dispersion has been combined with spatial concentration, and much of the recent cross-border extension of manufacturing and services has been concentrated on a handful of specialised local clusters. Thus, rapid cross-border dispersion coexists with agglomeration, and agglomeration economies continue to matter, as well as the path-dependent nature of the cluster evolution. On the other hand, both 'race to the bottom' and innovative spirit owe much to the open door policy and liberal attitudes of late 1970s towards entrepreneurship. It is argued that paying more attention to concentrated dispersion caused by offshore outsourcing could provide some insights for cluster formation of China.

The second point is that clusters should be viewed in the perspective of the global value chain and the local supply chain. This is particularly emphasised in the literature on clusters in developing countries which acknowledges the relationships inside the cluster but then stresses the importance of external relationships (Nadvi and Halder, 2005; Schmitz 2006).

The chapter agrees that a value chain could thread through multiple clusters in different localities of a regional economy. Given the rich components of a given cluster, it may either occupy a single segment (e.g. manufacturing of parts and components in a particular industry) or cover multiple segments (R&D, completion of a high-value-added product, marketing) of a value chain anchored to a locality (Chen, 2006). To develop clusters in a country or a region, it is necessary to know which segment(s) a cluster occupies and how it is — high or low value added. Only in this way, can we understand cluster-based initiatives as a highly desirable policy tool for many cities and regions in their efforts to increase growth, productivity, and employment (Cumbers and MacKinnon, 2004). The key task facing China should be to foster innovative clusters instead of building more 'low road' ones. Also, only in this way, can we understand the supply-chain cities characterised by local supply chain activities and centreed by buyer-driven contract manufacturers, and concern about its issues of social responsibility. Those supply-chain cities are the important phenomenon in China which emerged in the demand condition of reducing costs and raising the reaction speed to market.

Thirdly, a theory of the cluster must do more than provide an account for the benefits of co-location. It must also include an explanation for the conditions that may lead to the movement or decline or extinction of the cluster. Over the last two decades, the growing development thinking, based largely on experiences in Western countries, has re-evaluated the significance of agglomeration and co-location. The literature on local production systems stems initially from the analysis of successful industrial districts in developed countries in the 1970s and 1980s. Markusen (1996) argues that the emergence of 'sticky places' in a 'slippery space' — characterised by dramatically improved communications, and increasingly mobile production factors and firms — may be related to numerous variants of industrial districts (clusters). However, the main change in the geography of clusters of China is the dispersal of factories to Middle and

Western China and even to locations outside China. Those clusters are sticky rather than slippery places. In addition, there appears dramatic 'race to the bottom' as firms in clusters compete with one another to offer transnational companies the lowest operating costs (Kaplinsky, 2000).

Fourthly, the clusters of China functioned very well for multinational buyers and contract manufactures, but their roles to build up competitive advantage for the country and the region are limited. In the Western literature, agglomeration may facilitate the 'learning economy' through interaction among actors in a cluster. The cluster has the external economy effect, and is likely to create the opportunity to study mutually. There are many successful examples mainly from the developed countries that can explain that the cluster can promote cooperation based on mutual trust and technology innovation. The growing interest in clusters can be traced back to a number of changes in the competitive environment of firms, e.g. the growth of knowledge-intensity of production and the emergence of innovationbased competition and its globalization. 'The basic unit of analysis for understanding national advantages is the industry. Nations succeed not in isolated industries, however, but in clusters of industries connected through vertical and horizontal relationships. A nation's economy contains a mix of clusters, whose makeup and sources of competitive advantage (or disadvantage) reflect the state of the economy's development (Porter, 1990, p. 73).

However, the massive cluster examples from China and other developing countries show that although the short distance industrial relation can reduce the cost through the external economy, it cannot guarantee the promotion of technology innovation. The foundation of the firms participating in the competition in this category of cluster is the reduced cost, and there is only little cooperation among the firms, even malignant competition. Even if the entrepreneurs live and work together in a very nearby area, they seldom share information and discuss common problems. The developed countries' successful experience has proved that the cluster's competitiveness may be enhanced by suitable public intervention. In regard to the clusters at the low end, if public intervention is not carried out, and the firms don't operate together with a collective efficiency and they don't improve the learning effect, the whole cluster will fall into a difficult situation of 'race to the bottom', and even decline or relocate.

Clusters upgrading is imperative for China's national policies of building an 'innovative nation'. The term 'industrial cluster' has appeared in preliminary research reports for the Eleventh Five-Year Plan in many provinces and cities. Efforts to plan industrial clusters are now under way in China's various regions, especially in underdeveloped regions. This trend is reflected in the speeches and reports of formal government conferences at the provincial and municipal levels. At the beginning of 2006, China's central government outlined several strategic tasks for building an innovation-oriented economy. The strategic importance of region-centric innovation has led China to confront issues of promoting cluster development and upgrading.

In fact, most clusters in China are lacking capability for innovation and are in danger of losing their competitiveness. Appropriate public policies and strategies are needed if China hopes to upgrade the low-cost based clusters in the global value chains. While cluster-based economic policy has a lot of potentials, it is not a panacea (Martin and Sunley, 2003). China needs to learn as quickly as possible how to shape this process in the local arena, not only in adopting lessons from other clusters but also in seeking to position local industries in the global value chain and in strengthening their competitiveness in the global market.

7.2 Global Outsourcing, Township Firms and their Impact on the Forming of China's Clusters

Has the cluster been formed by internal force or external force? Developed countries' research generally believes that the cluster has been bred by internal force, and the building up of clusters is characterised by a bottom-up approach. As the forming of clusters in post-transition economies, such as Hungary, Poland, Slovenia, or Estonia, is based on a great influx of FDI (Foreign Direct Investment), global companies, and global resources (DATER and OECD, 2001), the forming of coastal clusters in China is external driven. But its characteristics lie in the local entrepreneurs' enthusiasm under the reform and open policy, the development of local division of labour and the follow-up impetus of the large domestic markets.

An obvious characteristic of economic globalisation is the general shift toward value chain fragmentation driven by the cost and risk advantages of lead firms' outsourcing. In the 1960s and 1970s, the main outsourcing items were apparel, footwear, toys and low-priced electronic products and so on. In recent years, the daily service industry, such as credit card receipt processing, airline tickets reservation, as well as basic software code writing, is also offshore outsourced. The outsourcing process takes geographical concentration instead of spread around the world. As the value chain actors co-evolve, the clusters of suppliers are created while lead firms increase outsourcing and consolidate their supply-chains. This makes outsourcing more attractive for lead firms which have yet to take the outsourcing plunge.

Since the middle of the 1970s, firms of developed countries have relocated their labour-intensive manufacturing industries to developing countries, and then have developed producer service industry at home, thus controlling the high end link of the global value chain. Meanwhile, with the formation of the clusters of low-grade and average-quality apparel, footwear, consumer electronic products, personal computers and automobiles, for those clusters, the technical standards and training have been provided by the outsourcing firms from abroad and some technical know-how has been provided by the job-hopping or part-time technicians from the state-owned firms.

The inherent tension between localisation and globalisation could be recognised in each cluster's development. Hong-Kong, Macao and Taiwan capital occupies nearly 2/3 of the foreign direct investment in China, and was the initial impetus for the clusters in Guangdong Province and Fujian Province in the early period of the 1980s. At the same time, many clusters in Zhejiang Province originated from the local peasant-entrepreneur's strength, and have developed by consanguinity, affinity and geographic ties with Chinese characteristics, thus inserting into the transnational management network actively. Due to the combined effect of the lead firms' global outsourcing for low-priced land and labour and the local indigenous peasant-entrepreneurs' activities, most of China's clusters thrive from villages and small towns, among which the most obvious symbol is that most of China's over one hundred characteristic textile and apparel clusters covering 45 cities and 59 towns, have been selected as trial regions of the textile industry by the China National Textile and Apparel Council in cooperation with local governments and trade organisations. The clusters are almost unmatched in their scale compared to the rest of the world, yet surprisingly they have gained little international fame.

The formation of the apparel clusters is a typical example reflecting the underlying tension between globalisation and localisation. Dalang wool spinning cluster in Dongguan City, Guangdong Province and Ningbo apparel cluster in Zhejiang Province receive global outsourcing orders from Hong Kong and Shanghai firms respectively, and disperse the orders to Dongguan and Ningbo, thus developing the local division of labour and the short distance transaction, and then they become the low end link of the global value chain.

After the 1980s, the apparel industry in Japan and Asia's Newly Industrialized countries lost the cost advantage gradually and began to relocate overseas. At that time mainland China started the Reform and Open policy, so the Pearl River Delta became Hong Kong-invested apparel clusters because of its unique geographic position. The formation of Dalang apparel cluster benefited from accepting the Hong Kong firms' materials for processing. In 1979, the first Hong Kong-invested woolen factory was established in Dalang Townships, and many farmers started to work there. Some peasant-workers accumulated the capital to start their own business, and then set up varied mills, forming a specialised sweater market. Over 100 button and accoutrement factories thrived and many fabric machinery firms began to open marketing offices.

Now in Dalang there are nearly 2000 woolen firms with over 100,000 workers, producing over 200,000,000 sets of sweaters, which occupy 30% of the domestic market. The local trade volume is over 2 billon yuan, and the volume of export is over 2.4 billion dollars, with the products exported to Europe, America, Russia, East and South Asia and Hong Kong. Dalang is given the title of 'China's Famous Sweater Township' by the China National Textile and Apparel Council.

The Ningbo apparel cluster's appearance mainly relied on the township apparel firms, which mostly have had the experience of processing for the state-owned firms in Shanghai. Different from the Dongguan cluster originating from Hong Kong, the Ningbo apparel cluster originated from Shanghai. At the end of the 1970s and the beginning of the 1980s, there was once a popular saying in the Shanghai apparel field, 'Work depends on the bumpkins'. These firms ran the sales and accepted orders themselves, and let the countryside firms carry out the production. With the local governments' support, many township firms and the local state-owned firms, like Youngor, Shanshan and Romon, had transformed to private firms, and implemented the joint stock system reform in the early 1990s.

Of the 2000 apparel firms in Ningbo, there are only 439 firms with some scale. At present, most firms, with ten to several thousand employees, are doing processing activities only. The small processing firms are unable to receive orders directly from foreign buyers, so they mainly receive processing orders from brand firms, foreign trade companies and the nearby processing firms by personal relationship. But the large-scale processing firms have already founded their own foreign trade companies with export rights. So they may not only directly accept processing orders, but also make trade directly. Around 40 brand firms like Youngor, Shanshan and Romon etc, similarly undertake the massive processing activities. These brand firms with subcontracting system of over 20 factories receive large orders. In order to guarantee the quality, these firms send their own technicians to the processing factories for a long time. For instance, taking the Orient-hongye as the core, in the surrounding area about five kilometres in scope, there are more than 30 embroidery factories, 20 printing and dyeing plants and 10 laundering factories. These bosses and managers are very familiar, so they often need no official contract, making a deal via telephone call or social activity. Therefore, the transaction cost can be reduced and the transaction process can be shortened, thus reducing the information loss and raising the reaction speed to market.

There are many similar examples about the fine local division of labour like those of Ningbo and Dongguan. For instance, in the Datang socks cluster in Zhejiang Province, which has an output of 3 billion pairs of socks, there are 2453 socks firms, 550 raw material firms, 400 raw material dealers, 312 hemstitching factories, 5 printing and dyeing plants, 305 packing factories, 208 mechanical fittings suppliers, 635 sock dealers, and 103 shipment service firms. And there is a Datang Light Fabric and Sock City with 1600 shops. 90% of the residents' occupation in the 120 villages of Datang is related to the sock industry.

7.3 External Linkages in Global and Local Value Chains

Literature on clusters emphasises the importance of local factors in an era of globalisation (Porter, 1990; Markusen, 1996; Scott, 1996). Advantages of masses of firms, especially SMEs, agglomerating locally not only lie in incidental external economies, such as a skilled labour pool, specialist suppliers and knowledge spillover, but also conscious pursuit of joint action between firms and institutions (Schmitz and Nadvi, 1999). But globalisation and technology diffusion make attention to linkages outside clusters more and more necessary, which has been ignored by researchers (Nadvi and Halder, 2005; Schmitz, 2006). External linkages in terms of value chain should be supplementary to recent studies on clusters.

Some pioneers explore the relationship of clusters between developing and developed countries and the effects of global buyer/market on local clusters in developing countries. After comparing production and knowledge linkages in the surgical instrument industry between Tuttlingen (Germany) and Sialkot (Pakistan) (Nadvi and Halder (2005)) stress the importance of external linkages for cluster upgrading. Bair and Gereffi's (2001) study of the Torreon blue jeans industry of Mexico finds arrival of new buyers has resulted in upgrading, but limited to the first tier of full-package firms because of the absence of an institutional environment. In contrast, Rabellotti (2004) reveals the negative impact of external linkages of luxury brands for Brenta shoe clusters (Italy), forcing some local firms to abandon design and material procurement.

Up to now, external linkages are narrowly confined to buyers/clusters in developed countries, rare attention has been paid to the linkages between different districts/clusters in one country, or between different developing countries, because cooperation and learning opportunities also exist in these linkages. In Section Two, analysis of Dalang and Ningbo apparel clusters implies the role of international (Hong Kong, before 1997) and national (Shanghai) linkages to their early development. In the following section, taking Hangji Toothbrush industry as example, external linkages of different levels have been outlined (Figure 7.1).

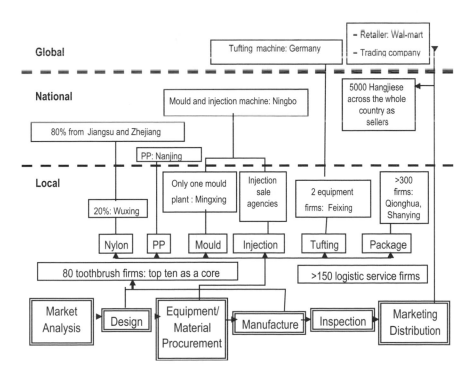

Figure 7.1:   External Linkages of Different Scales in Hangji Toothbrush Cluster.

Hangji, a town of 120 square kilometres and 35 thousand population in Jiangsu Province, occupies 30% of the world's toothbrush market, and 80% of the domestic market. The toothbrush industry in Hangji dates back to the Qing dynasty. Before 1949, family-based toothbrush workshops were scattered in many villages there. After the open and reform policy in 1980s, many technicians and sellers in state-owned and collective enterprises left their jobs and established their own companies. Local big toothbrush firms, such as Sanxiao, Wu'ai, Mingxing and etc, usually share the same story of development. In 2000, global brand Colgate inserted in Hangji through a joint venture with Sanxiao. Sanxiao transferred its capital and brand (Sanxiao Toothbrush) in the joint venture to Colgate in 2003, making Colgate-Sanxiao a wholly foreign-owned enterprise and the world's toothbrush production base for Colgate. Now there are more than 80 toothbrush assemblies in Hangji with Colgate-Sanxiao as a core. Most SMEs focus on design, equipment and material procurement, manufacturing, and producer service providers for market analysis and inspection have not appeared in Hangji.

The two main materials for toothbrushes are nylon filaments and PP (polypropylene) for handles. About 80% of the nylon filaments for the Hangji toothbrush industry come from other areas in Jiangsu and Zhejiang Provinces, and the rest are locally supplied by Wuxing company, etc. Yangtze Petrochemical Co. Ltd in Nanjing, within 200 kilometres, is the only supplier of PP in Hangji. Only one mould plant, Mingxing exists in Hangji, and almost all are from Huangyan and Cixi in Zhejiang Province, which are the two biggest mould clusters in China. More than product linkages between these toothbrush and mould clusters, many toothbrush firms in Hangji establish mould procurement agencies in Huangyan and Cixi to share market and technology information with each other, reflecting division of labour, cooperation and learning opportunities between inter-linked clusters within developing countries, which has not been emphasised by researchers until now.

In Hangji, toothbrush products were made by hand historically. Since the open and reform policy, firms bought tufting machines from Germany which greatly improve the efficiency of toothbrush production.

But now, some local equipment firms, such as Feixing, also offer tufting machines, by adapting German machines to the needs of cheapness and flexibility of local toothbrush assemblies. Some local firms even prefer local tufting machines than imported ones. As for packaging, there are dozens of local firms, among which Qionghua and Shanying are the largest two. Marketing and distribution spread in local, national and global scales. Locally, more than 150 native firms offer logistic services. Nationally, 5000 Hangjiese occupy the whole country as sellers. Globally, some Hangji firms, as Mingxing, indulge in OEM (Original Equipment Manufacturers) production for international buyers, such as Walmart, Carrefour etc.

In short, the Hangji toothbrush cluster is mainly specialised in manufacturing. Materials, equipment and marketing/distribution are offered or controlled by external suppliers or buyers on national or global scales, which means more attention should be paid to external linkages for deeper understanding of the cluster trajectories in China.

7.4 Race to the Bottom and Relocation

Viewed from the conception, cluster has become many countries' policy for economic development. This is because of the common idea that the successful region is a specialised one to a certain degree. Firms' agglomeration, as well as the short distant cooperation with other related organisations, may access the supplier and the specialised supporting services, and obtain the skilled labour market and the invisible knowledge spillover. Not only in the colony can more employment opportunities be created, but also the cluster can foster more clusters.

In China, many clusters are only exporting as foreign procurement bases, but do not necessarily become the innovation centre. During the process of the cluster, the internal force and external force's mutual function is subtle. The primary factors of success are local cooperation, local learning and local absorbency. Otherwise, the cluster is only a weak node of the global production network, and also a production place possibly instantaneous to vanish. Pin factory and supply chain city cannot become the sticky place in the global slippery space, and moreover possibly becomes the position which slides.

In many of China's clusters, the 'race to the bottom' is extremely obvious because they lack the protection of intellectual property rights and professional autonomy. The Zhejiang Province firm investigation team once carried out a special investigation of the below-scale firms. About 39.5% thought 'the race to bottom' was the major problem affecting development. To avoid elimination, some firms do not hesitate to adopt ultra-conventional even illegal methods to reduce the production cost, like lengthening working time willfully, cheating, pirating, tax dodging, etc. The cut-throat competition excessively influences the cluster's following development ability, and even leads to withering away. For example, the Wenzhou lamp cluster once had nearly 2000 firms, more than 10,000 varieties, with the gross output value nearly 3 billion yuan. But now only few survive. As soon as Yongkang's insulated cup factory rushed headlong into mass action, output value once reaching 1.5–1.7 billion yuan disappeared rapidly. Jumping out of 'the besieged city' of excessive competition is also one reason why some firms have moved outside.

Many clusters are at the bottom end of the global value chain, excessively depending on low price competition. For instance, for the exported stained chemical fibre cloth and printed cloth, each metre's average price was only 0.8–0.9 US dollar in 2005; each pair of socks average price was 0.21 US dollar, the tie's average price is 1.6 US dollars, about the cost price. To get the orders, many firms do not hesitate to engage in factional strife, thus bearing the consequences of evil acts. The developed countries' companies have controlled the marketing channel of the cluster's firms, and shared the cost of labour superiority. Many export firms run production by posting the sign, so the profit is meager. For example, the firm only obtains the processing charge of 1–2 US dollar for one dress, which also includes each kind of operation expense, so the firm's average rate of profit is only 3–5%. Because of the big quantity of low-priced goods exportation and the abnormal exportation order, we suffer from more international trade friction. In 2005, Zhejiang Province had each category of overseas trade investigation case, and was involved in costs amounting to 897,000,000 US dollars, occupying the national front row.

In Yongkang, Zhejiang Province, there is cost advantage of electrical bicycle, kart, sand beach vehicle, mini-motorcycle, and golf vehicle, due to the specialised division of labour, occupying 90% of China's exports. But there is unceasing 'race to the bottom'. With the appearance of a new product having market foreground, several hundred, even over a thousand firms imitate quickly, keeps prices down mutually, and compete malignantly.

Since the beginning of this century, a tendency of China's coastal cluster firms is to relocate to the inland and even overseas. The main reason for relocation is the rising price of the coastal labour force, land and the raw materials. The firms must seek a position with cheaper cost. The other reason is to escape from the original cluster's cut-throat competition, environmental protection limit and social responsibility and so on.

The relocation phenomena are very common among the firms in Wenzhou city of Zhejiang Province. An investigation showed that the migration firms out of Wenzhou are more than 1000, also including some large firms. Up to now, there are about 250 firms which moved outside completely. The involved sectors include the low voltage electric appliance, knitting, apparel, and lamps and lanterns and so on. The production activities shifted especially to North and Western areas of the country.

Zhuji's towel firm Jieliya Corporation shifted production to Hubei Province, which is proximate to the cotton habitat, cheap land, water and electricity. Through purchasing 9 factories in the towns of Jiayu, Hanchuan, and Xianning, including the cotton yarn factories, Jieliya can save 1000 yuan per ton production. That is, production of one towel can save 0.1 yuan. In addition, the land cost of the three zones each with a size of 200 mu (about 13.3 hectares) is extraordinary low, while in Zhuji, one mu of land costs 100,000 yuan. Also, the labour cost is very low. Therefore, Jieliya can save 20 million yuan a year compared with production in Zhuji, which occupies 4% of the sales volume of the whole year.

It could infer that the coastal cluster firms moving inland may form new clusters because of agglomeration factors. This kind of phenomenon has already appeared, for example, some Dali aluminum molding firms in Guangdong Province shifted to Linqu county of Shandong Province, and some of Houjie furniture firms in Dongguan of Guangdong Province moved to Jiashan in Zhejiang Province, and some of Jiashan wooden firms shifted to Linyi county of Shandong Province, the Wenzhou nut-and-bolt processing firms shifts to Yongnian county of Hebei Province, and Wenzhou footwear firms shifts to Chongqing city and Shenyang city, Liaoning Province, and so on. In those areas, clusters have appeared.

But, if these places only passively accept the coastal clusters' relocation, and continue the 'race to bottom', they will have no bright future. Therefore, forming clusters can't become the local policy target of economic development. The underdeveloped area needs to learn the lessons of the developed areas' clusters, and learn to upgrade the clusters.

7.5 The Prospect of Upgrading

As mentioned above, China's clusters' underlying global-local tension could both benefit local economy and cost to it. It can provide enormous opportunities but it can also stifle particular types of development (Schmitz, 2006). China's clusters may benefit national and regional innovation system, but may do harm to its industry. As the important bases for China's manufacturing, if the clusters have problems standing out without effective solutions, they will become the hidden problem of the nation's economy.

Since China joined the WTO (World Trade Organisation), a large number of transnational corporations have started to invest and establish factories in China. They have used their superiority of technology and brand to share more and more of the market. The domestic market competition has evolved for the internationalised competition. China's cluster is at a new important crossroad, facing the challenges of rising cost, industrial relocation, superheating local competition, frequent antidumping cases, technical barriers and green barriers, etc.

The prospect of innovation in some clusters of China is really considerable, where the actors have already taken joint actions in technical innovation, social responsibility and environmental protection.

For example, an above-mentioned towel firm, Lijieya Corporation, has established a scientific research base in its Zhuji headquarters, where more than 30 people are doing research on towelling with new materials, new processes and new design appearance. They have developed new products of towel made of hemp, soya, milk albumin fibre, and bamboo fibre. The other example Leqing of Wenzhou, 'China's electrical appliance capital', extends from the low voltage apparatus to the high voltage apparatus, extends from electric appliance parts to complete set of electric appliance, and constructs a whole appliance manufacture system for transmitting, transforming and distribution.

These fast growing clusters have stronger economic vitality, larger employment, and the people's living standard thus rises. In order to enable the cluster to undergo economic undulation, many of China's clusters are making great effort in governing the cluster. At the local level, they should protect intellectual property rights and enhance R&D and technical innovation. The keys for success are to transform the function of government and to exert the industrial association's function, as well as reinforce the firms' social responsibility. It remains to be seen in global perspective how the global linkages affect local relationships and how local clusters manage to upgrade in global value chains. To define the circumstances in which local upgrading strategies can be expected to succeed or fail is necessary.

References

ANDERSSON, T. *et al.* (2004). 'The Cluster Policies Whitebook,' International Organization for Knowledge Economy and Firm Development. 2004: 11–15.

APPELBAUM, R. P., GEREFFI, G., PARKER, R., ONG, R. (2006). 'From Cheap Labour to High-tech Leadership: Will China's Investment in Nanotechnology Pay Off?' Paper available from the Author.

BAIR, J. G., GEREFFI. (2001). 'Local Clusters in Global Chains: the Causes and Consequences of Export Dynamism in Torreon's Blue Jeans Industry,' *World Development*, 29(11), 1885–1903.

CHEN, X. (2006). 'Regionalizing the Global-Local Economic Nexus: A Tale of Two Regions in China,' University of Illinois at Chicago, www.uic.edu/cuppa/gci/publications/working%20paper%20series/pdf/GCIpaper_Chen.pdf.

DATAR-OECD. (2001). 'Proceedings,' World Congress on Local Clusters, Paris, 23 and 24 Jan. 2001.

GEREFFI, G. (2005). 'The New Offshoring of Jobs and Global Development,' ILO Social Policy Lectures, JamaIca, Published by the International Institute for Labour Studies.

GUERRIERI, P., PIETROBELLI, C. (2004). 'Industrial Districts' Evolution and Technological Regimes: Italy and Taiwan?,' *Technovation*, 24(11), 899–914.

HAMILTON, Gary, Misha PETROVIC. (2006). 'Global Retailers and Asian Manufacturers,' in Henry Yeung (ed.), *Handbook of Asian Business*. Northhampton, MA: Edward Elgar.

HAMILTON, Gary, Robert C. FEENSTRA. (2006). *Emergent Economies, Divergent Paths: Economic Organization and International Trade in South Korea and Taiwan*. New York: Cambridge University Press.

HUMPHRY, SCHMITZ. (1995). 'Principles for Promoting Clusters & Networks of SMEs,' by the Small and Medium Firms Branch, UNIDO, p. i.

KAPLINSKY, R. (2000). 'Globalisation and Unequalisation: What can be Learned from Value Chain Analysis?,' *Journal of Development Studies*, 37(2), 117–146.

Los Angeles Times. (2005). 'China's Strategy Gives It the Edge in the Battle of Two Sock Capitals,' (April 10, 2005).

MARKUSEN, A. (1996). 'Sticky Places in Slippery Space: A Typology of Industrial Districts,' *Economic Geography*, 72, 293–313.

MATIN, R., SUNLEY, P. (2003). 'Deconstructing Clusters: Chaotic Concept or Policy Panacea?,' *Journal* of *Economic Geography*, 3–35.

NADVI, K., HALDER, G. (2005). 'Local Clusters in Global Value Chains: Exploring Dynamic Linkages between Germany and Pakistan,' *Enterpreneurship & Regional Development*, 17, 339–363.

OECD: 'Business Cluster: Promoting firm in Central and Eastern Europe,' *LEED Programme*, 2005: 1–2.

ORJAN, S., GORAN, L., CHRISTIAN, K., 'The Cluster Initiative Greenbook,' The 6th Global TCI Conference, 18–19.

PORTER, M. (1990). *The Competitive Advantage of Nations*. London: Macmillan, 73.

RABELLOTTI, R. (2004). 'How Globalization Affects Itatlian Industrial Districts: the Case of Brenta,' In H. Schmitz (ed.), *Local Enterprises in Global Economy: Issues of Governance and Upgrading*. Cheltenham: Edward Elgar.

SCHMITZ, H. (2006). 'Regional Systems and Global Chains,' Paper presented in the Fifth International Conference on Industrial Clusters and Regional Development, Beijing, July 14–15, 2006.

SCHMITZ, H., NADVI, K. (1999). 'Clustering and Industrialization: Introduction,' *World Development*, 27(9), 1503–1514.

SCOTT, A. (1996). 'Regional Motors of the Global Economy,' *Futures*, 28, 391–411.

WU, L., YUE, X., SIM, T. (2006). 'Supply Chain Clusters: A Key to China's Cost Advantage,' *Supply Chain Management Review*, March 1, 2006, http://www.manufacturing.net http//scm.com//article/CA6327542.html.

Chapter 8

The Emergence of Industrial Clusters in Wenzhou, China

Tomoo Marukawa

8.1 Introduction

The peculiar development experiences of Wenzhou since the economic reform, have gathered academic interests inside and outside of China (Yuan, 1987; Nolan and Dong, 1990; Zhang and Li, 1990; Shi *et al.*, 2002; Sonobe, Hu and Otsuka, 2004; Sheng and Zheng, 2004). Early studies on Wenzhou economy, such as Zhang and Li (1990) and Shi *et al.* (2002), paid attention to the dominance of private enterprises in the city, which was exceptional in China during the 1980s, and aimed to insist the effectiveness of 'the Wenzhou Model' — which was virtually a paraphrase of a private-led economy — for rural development. But, as the private sector gains more and more importance in the national economy, the necessity to show the effectiveness of private-led growth becomes less and less. Instead, as the interests in industrial clusters arise in China (Wang, 2001; Zhu, 2003), Wenzhou became known as a case of industrial clustering.

However, one aspect of Wenzhou's economy, which must be evident to whomever that has visited there, has rarely been discussed or analysed in the literature: the diversity of its industrial clusters. Wenzhou has a diverse array of industrial clusters, ranging from leather shoes to electric parts, buttons, apparel, automobile parts, valves, cigarette lighters, and many others. The purpose of this study is to grasp the diversity of Wenzhou's industries and to understand the reason why so many industrial clusters have emerged there. The

213

second section describes the framework and methodology of this paper. The third section shows a comprehensive map of Wenzhou's industrial clusters. The fourth section analyses the emergence of some typical industrial clusters.

8.2 Framework and Methodology

Many authors have argued the economy of agglomeration. Marshall (1920) and Krugman (1991) point out that, by the localisation of a certain industry, the diffusion of technology will be facilitated, intermediate inputs can be supplied economically by gathering a large amount of demand, and a labour market for specialised skills will be created. Itami *et al.* (1998) point out that an urban industrial agglomeration consisted of firms with various skills and technology, such as the metalworking industry at Ohta-ku, Tokyo, can meet various sorts of demand by flexibly organising the division of labour among the firms.

The economy of agglomeration, however, takes place only when an industrial agglomeration already exists. They do not explain why an industrial agglomeration emerges in the first place. If an industrial agglomeration generates external economy which enhances the competitiveness of the enterprises within the agglomeration, then why could the first few enterprises of the agglomeration establish themselves without the help of external economy?

There might be two types of explanations to this question.

The first one is to trace the emergence of the industrial agglomeration back to an era when market economy was not well developed and the domestic market was not integrated. During such a period, enterprises would not face severe competition with other districts, so it would be relatively easy to establish a business. Once an industry emerges, it will grow through technology spillover within the district, and endure the changes of demand by changing the contents of production. Through technology transfer and technology change, the local industry will grow into a cluster which can survive the competition with other districts. For example, in explaining the emergence of the cutlery industry of Tsubame — one of the most famous industrial clusters in Japan — Yoshida (1998) traces its history back to early 17th century, when local craftsmen started producing traditional nails. During the Meiji era, when domestic demand for old-style nails diminished, local firms switched their business to the production of files, copperware, and pipes by applying the nail production technology. Then during early 20th century, local firms began producing cutlery, and later Tsubame developed into a large cutlery industry cluster.

The second type of explanation is to ascribe the emergence of a certain industry to the ampleness of a specific resource. For example, in explaining the emergence of metal working industry of Ohta-ku, Itami *et al.* (1998) point out the proximity of the district to the factories of large automotive and electronics enterprises. In this case, the location nearby the large factories is the key resource. The emergence of Silicon Valley might also be explained by the 'location resource' of having universities and research institutions nearby.

In the case of Wenzhou, which lacks natural resources, land, and 'location resources,' we must, for the most cases, resort to the first type of explanation. Most industrial clusters in Wenzhou, in fact, date back to the prewar period or before 1980s, when the domestic market was not well integrated in China.

In Wenzhou, many industrial clusters emerged in a very short period since 1980s. There seems to be a tendency of Wenzhou's rural society that facilitates the emergence of industrial clusters. Zhu (2001) explains the tendency as follows. In Wenzhou, a certain line of business spreads through the network of relatives, neighbours, and friends. This is because the sources of information on business chances are often limited to relatives and neighbours in a rural society. If someone succeeds in a new business, his relatives and neighbours might imitate him, and the whole village might end up doing the same business.

There are, however, a few innovators in the rural society. Here 'an innovator' means a person who starts a new business for the first time in the rural society. The 'new' business is often simply an imitation of state-owned enterprises or foreign enterprises located outside of Wenzhou, but it certainly is something that no one else in the village has ever tried. The innovators bring a new business in the rural society, and their relatives and friends imitate them, so that in a short period of time an industrial cluster emerges. Because of the existence of a few innovators, the diversity of Wenzhou's industry increases, and because of the existence of a large number of imitators, a business which the innovators started soon develops into an industrial cluster. Many industrial clusters in Wenzhou seem to have emerged through such repetitions of innovation and imitation.

In the following section, we will present a map of industrial clusters in Wenzhou which shows the diversity of industries there. In the forth section, we will describe the emergence of a few industries on the basis of the abovementioned framework. The materials used here are historical studies such as Yu and Yu (1995) and Zhang ed. (1998) and interviews conducted by the author.

The author has conducted field surveys at Wenzhou five times during the period 1998–2007, visiting 31 enterprises and 16 local government offices and social organizations. The interviews lasted for two hours on average, and many aspects of the development process of Wenzhou's industrial clusters which had never been documented were revealed through them. Such interviews, however, have limitations. Because many of the entrepreneurs interviewed joined the business long after the industrial cluster emerged, they rarely know how the cluster emerged and developed before they started business. Even those who experienced the development process of clusters themselves might not remember correctly the early days of the clusters. In some cases it was difficult to cross-check the interviews with historical documents. Even in such cases we cited the interviews in this paper whenever they seemed reliable. Because of the lack of reliable written materials on the development of Wenzhou's industries, the interviews are often the only source of information on the cluster's history.

8.3 Distribution of Industrial Clusters

8.3.1 *Surveys Conducted by Zhejiang Provincial Government*

In this section we will identify the industrial clusters in Wenzhou and draw their locations on a map. Many scholars have reported the existence of various industrial clusters in Wenzhou without being conscious of the criterion of identifying an industrial cluster. The only survey which has a clear definition of industrial clusters is Policy Research Department (2003), which is a thorough survey of industrial clusters in Zhejiang Province. The definition in this survey is that 'more than ten enterprises are producing the same or similar products, and the annual output of the industry exceeds 100 million yuan.' No spatial definition is provided in this survey, but it seems that the basic spatial unit is set at the county (*xian*) level. According to the survey there were 519 industrial clusters in Zhejiang Province in 2001. The same survey was also conducted in 2003 and 2005 by the Provincial Government, and according to them the number of clusters decreased to 430 and 360 in respective years (Project Unit 2006). The decrease was caused by the change of definition and the decline of some clusters.

It is unclear how many among the 360 clusters that existed in 2005 in the Province were located in Wenzhou, but the survey lists six industries as the largest clusters of Wenzhou, namely, leather and shoes, apparel, electric equipments, plastics, automobile and motorcycle parts, and printing. The spatial definition of the 2005 survey seems to be less rigorous than the 2001 survey: while the electric equipment industry's location is identified as Yueqing city, a county (*xian*) level region, the leather and shoes industry's location is identified as Wenzhou, a prefecture (*diqu*) level region.

As the high threshold (output exceeding 100 million yuan) for defining a cluster suggests, the purpose of the abovementioned surveys by the Provincial Government is to identify the leading industries of the Province. Therefore, the surveys do not seem to be interested so much in small clusters in terms of output value, but nevertheless important at the township (*xiang* and *zhen*) level. But the diversity of industries at the township level is a very prominent feature of Wenzhou. Considering the realities of Wenzhou's industries, identifying an industrial cluster at the prefecture or county level is too rough. For example, the 2005 survey identifies the location of automobile and motorcycle parts industry as Wenzhou, a prefecture level city with an area of 11,784 square kilometres. But in fact the industry is highly concentrated in Tangxia, a township with an area of only

15 square kilometres. All the other major clusters in Wenzhou mentioned above are concentrated in just a few townships, so it is necessary to set the level of analysis at the township level. The classification of industries is also too rough in the 2005 survey. The leather and shoes industry, which is listed as the largest cluster in Wenzhou, is actually a generic classification, which includes leather shoes industry, leather processing industry, artificial leather industry, plastic shoes industry, and rubber shoes industry, all located in different townships of Wenzhou. Several industrial clusters with different locations and history are lumped together in the 'leather and shoes industry.' Therefore we need a finer definition of location and a finer classification of industries than the 2005 survey.

8.3.2 *Data Source and the Definition of an Industrial Cluster*

The data source used here to identify industrial clusters in Wenzhou is *The Collection of Information on Wenzhou City's Corporations and Organizations* (*Wenzhoushi jiben danwei ziliao huibian*) published by China Statistics Press in 2003. It is the outcome of the Second National Corporation and Organisation Census held in 2001, and shows the name, address, representative's name, telephone number, zip code, the corporation registration number, and the main product or main activity of each of the 40,686 business corporations in Wenzhou. Though the book is a very useful source of information based on a thorough survey, it has limitations: *The Collection* only has information on firms with legal person status, and hence the cottage industries are largely omitted. But the importance of cottage industries is not negligible especially in those industrial clusters that are still in the primitive stage of development.[1]

---

[1] The author discovered a socks manufacturing cluster in Bishan, Wenzhou, consisted of more than 200 cottage manufacturers. Each manufacturer had around ten employees and thirty to fifty knitting machines. In the *Collection*, however, only 14 socks manufacturing corporations are listed in Bishan, because the cottage subcontractors usually do not have legal person status. Therefore this 'socks cluster' does not appear in our list of Wenzhou's industrial clusters.

The business corporations listed in *the Collection* are classified into 621 industries. Among which, 144 industries belong to the service sector, which are omitted from our analysis. The remaining 477 industries belong to the manufacturing and primary industries. The fine classification of *The Collection* enables us to grasp the realities of Wenzhou's clusters which are concentrated in a narrow line of business, such as leather shoes, valves, and pumps. However, because *The Collection* lumps together some famous industries of Wenzhou into 'other daily necessity production,' we subdivided this group into four groups, namely, 'cigarette lighters and smoking apparatus,' 'buttons,' 'zippers,' and 'the rest.'

Then we classified the location of enterprises into 283 districts. Wenzhou city, which has an area of 11,784 square kilometres and a population of 7.4 million, is subdivided into 11 county-level regions and 299 township-level regions. Among the latter, we grouped together the 17 subdistricts (*jiedao*) which consist the City Centre into one region, so now we have 282 townships (*xiang* and *zhen*) and one City Centre. Figure 8.1 is a map of Wenzhou subdivided into 11 county-level regions, and Figure 8.2 shows the same city subdivided into 283 townships.

Hence Wenzhou's 40,686 business corporations, except for those which belong to the service sector, are subdivided into 480 industries and 283 townships. If a township has more than fifteen corporations which belong to the same industry, and the number of corporations exceeds 5% of the city total, we define the township's industry as 'an industrial cluster.' This definition may seem to be too generous, but fifteen corporations in a single township, which has an area of 43 square kilometres on average, may reveal a severe concentration. For example, the rubber shoes industry consisted of 17 corporations at *Shatou*, a mountainous township located at the north part of Wenzhou, employs 5000 workers in a township with a population of 16,514. Undoubtedly, the rubber shoes manufacturing is the most important industry for the township.

8.3.3 *Distribution of Industrial Clusters*

By the above definition, we identified 153 industrial clusters in Wenzhou as of 2001. Figure 8.2 shows the townships that has more

Figure 8.1:   The County Level Region of Wenzhou.

than one industrial cluster and the size — measured by the number of firms — of the largest industrial cluster in the townships. Table 8.1 shows the clusters with more than 50 firms. Clusters exist in 65 industries (63 of which belong to manufacturing, one to aquaculture, one to pig raising). Among the 283 townships of Wenzhou, 56 have one cluster or more. As can be seen in Figure 8.2, most industrial clusters are located in the coastal and riverside townships. There is no cluster in the mountainous townships with population density less than 400 persons per square kilometre, except for the abovementioned rubber shoe cluster in Shatou, and a stone processing cluster in Shiyang.

Some industries spread over several townships, while some are limited within a single township. The apparel industry, for example, spreads over the City Centre (No. 101 in Figure 8.2) and the

Size of the largest clusters in the township (Number of Firms)
The number in the circle shows the location number in Table 8.1

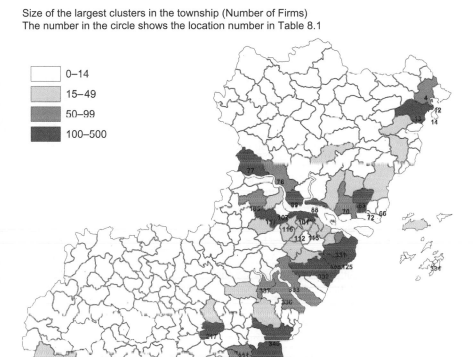

Figure 8.2: Location and Size of Industrial Clusters.

surrounding townships. On the other hand, the button and zipper cluster in Qiaotou and the ballpoint pen cluster in Puzhou are concentrated within the township. Some industries are scattered around several townships which are located far away from each other.

The largest cluster in terms of number of firms located within a single township is the package printing industry of Longgang (No. 341 of Figure 8.2), in which 345 corporations are engaged in printing packages and labels. In other countries, printing industry is

Table 8.1: Industrial Clusters of Wenzhou (with more than 50 firms)

Location No	Township	Industry	No of Firms
4	Daji	Molds	70
12,13,14	Yandang	Electric parts	232
63	Liushi	Switches	321
63	Liushi	Electric parts	241
63	Liushi	Other power control machinery	70
66	Wengyang	Fish cultivation	51
70	Beibaixiang	Switches	93
70	Beibaixiang	Electric parts	87
72	Xiangyang	Electric parts	52
76	Qiaoxia	Stationery	92
77	Qiaotou	Buttons	168
77	Qiaotou	Zippers	117
88,89	Oubei	Valves	221
88,89	Oubei	Leather shoes	120
88,89	Oubei	Pumps	91
88,89	Oubei	Apparel	71
101	City Center	Leather shoes	180
101	City Center	Lamps	116
101	City Center	Cigarette lighters	108
101	City Center	Glasses	98
101	City Center	Package printing	96
101	City Center	Apparel	86
101	City Center	Electric parts	55
105	Tengqiao	Apparel	76
107	Shuangyu	Leather shoes	197
107	Shuangyu	Apparel	61
112	Wuting	Apparel	66
112	Wuting	Glasses	62
113	Sangyang	Non-woven cloth	76
116	Xinqiao	Glasses	52
116	Xinqiao	Plastic shoes	50
117	Guoxi	Leather shoes	155
117	Guoxi	Bolts	66
117	Guoxi	Pig leather	62
125	Shacheng	Valves	146
125	Shacheng	Food machinery	108

(Continued)

Table 8.1: (*Continued*)

Location No	Township	Industry	No of Firms
129	Tianhe	Switches	125
217	Shuitou	Pig leather	145
231	Xiaojiang	Plastic ropes and cloth	99
245	Qianku	Package printing	131
331	Yongzhong	Valves	234
331	Yongzhong	Steel pipes	157
331	Yongzhong	Tiles	57
331	Yongzhong	Artificial leather	55
332	Tangxia	Bolts	313
332	Tangxia	Automobile parts	295
332	Tangxia	Plastic ropes and cloth	111
332	Tangxia	Motorcycle parts	105
332	Tangxia	Water pipes	100
332	Tangxia	Switches	52
333	Anyang	Cotton knitwear	64
333	Anyang	Printing machinery	50
336	Feiyun	Shoes	50
337	Xianjiang	Shoes	66
340	Aojiang	Leather shoes	120
341	Longgang	Package printing	345
343	Lingxi	Plastic ropes and cloth	54

Source: Made by the author from the data of *Wenzhoushi jiben danwei ziliao huibian*

usually located in large cities, but in the case of Wenzhou, its cluster exists at a township far away from the city centre. Longgang used to be called the 'first 'farmer city' in China' during 1980s. This means that the dwellers of the city are ex-farmers who built the city and moved there without changing their household registration status as 'farmers' (Jin, 2002). Longgang farmers made money by the printing business and transformed their village into a city with a population of 270 thousand people.

The second largest cluster in Wenzhou is Liushi's switch industry, in which 321 corporations are engaged in switch production. There are also in Liushi 241 electric parts manufacturers, and the two industries in fact form a huge electric parts industry cluster which produces

Number of firms engaged in electric parts production
The number in the circle shows the location in Table 8.1

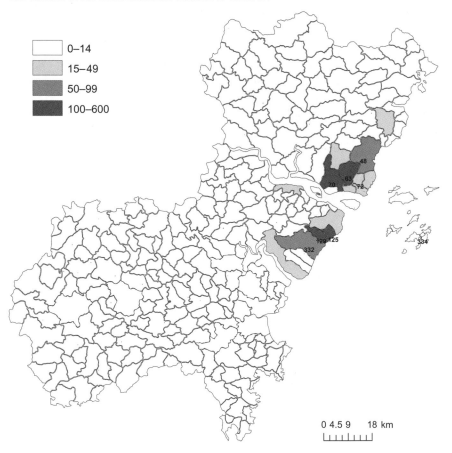

Figure 8.3:   Location of Electric Parts Industry.

switches, circuit breakers, relays, and connectors. The electric parts
industry cluster spreads over Liushi and several neighbouring townships as seen in Figure 8.3, which indicates the townships which have
more than 15 electric parts makers. Previous studies on the electric
parts industry of Wenzhou such as Sonobe, Hu and Otsuka (2004)
and Project Unit (2006) regarded that the industry existed in
Yueqing City, but Figure 8.3 reveals that the electric parts industry
clusters also exist in other countries.

8.4 The Emergence of Industrial Clusters

As discussed in the second section, the emergence of an industrial cluster might be explained by its history that dates back to the era when market economy was underdeveloped, or by the ampleness of a specific resource. Among the various industrial clusters of Wenzhou, only the stone processing industry of Shiyang and the aquaculture industry of Wengyang seem to be able to be explained by the ampleness of local resources. Other industrial clusters do not seem to rely on specific local resources. In the following, we will try to explain the emergence of industries related to leather and shoes, and those related to metal processing.

8.4.1 *Leather*

Zhang (1998, p. 1174) reports that leather (cowhide) production existed in Shuitou during the Jiaqing era (1796–1820) of the Qing dynasty. During the late Qing period, cowhide production also appeared in Huoxi, Guoxi and Xiongxi (which is now a part of Huoxi) as farmers' side business. During the Republican era, leather processing workshops, which used the cowhides produced by suburban farmers, appeared in the Wenzhou city centre. After the outbreak of war with Japan, the leather processing industry in the city centre was stimulated by the increase of demand from the army and developed into a fairly large cluster, having 41 enterprises in the city centre in 1943 (Yu and Yu, 1995, pp. 47–48). Leather production also emerged in the southern townships of Yanshan (which is now a part of Nanyan), Aojiang and Yishan during the Republican era.

Figure 8.4 indicates the townships which have leather processing industry clusters as of 2001 and those which had leather processing industry during the Republican era. It is clear from this figure that the present clusters date back to the Republican era. The clusters, however, have not existed continuously since the Republican era until today. For example, the leather processing workshops of the city centre were integrated and nationalised after the establishment of the

Townships with name tags are where
leather production existed during the
Republican era.
Gray shades indicate the number of leather
processing firms in 2001.

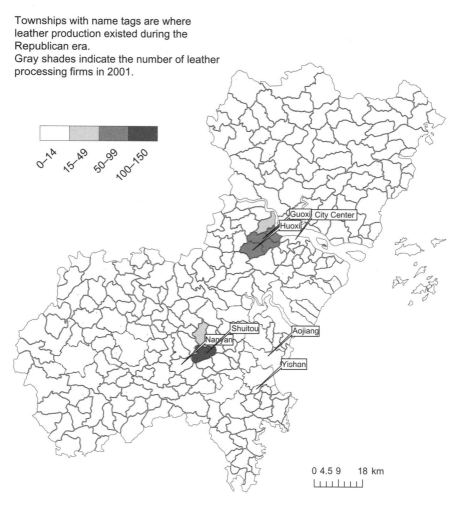

Figure 8.4:   Location of Leather Processing Industry During Republican Era and
the Present Leather Industry Clusters.

People's Republic, and finally there remained only one state-owned
leather factory. The industry was maintained but it was no longer a
'cluster.' After the economic reform started, many workers who
worked at the state-owned leather factory retired or resigned, and
began running leather factories of their own. In 1981, the number of
leather factories in the city centre had reached 210. Hence the once

extinct leather industry cluster revived dramatically. Later, however, the city government decided to move these firms out of the city centre to Yangyi to eliminate the pollution caused by them (Zhang, 1998, p. 1175). Hence leather production in the city centre disappeared, and the neighbouring townships to the west, Yangyi and Shuangyu, emerged as a new leather industry cluster.

The leather industry cluster in Shuitou, which had 145 leather workshops as of 2001, has also experienced extinction and a dramatic recovery (Jin, 2002, p. 149). The private manufacturers which existed before the People's Republic were later integrated with the state owned enterprises in Wenzhou city centre and other cities, and they disappeared from the township. After the reform, workers in state-owned leather enterprises, who had run private leather factories in Shuitou prior to nationalisation, retired or resigned the state owned enterprises, flew back to Shuitou, and established private factories again. Hence the once-extinct leather industry cluster in Shuitou reappeared.

The leather processing clusters of Wenzhou not only revived but also far exceeded the size of the cluster that existed during the Republican era. Shuitou's pig leather production, for example, is said to be the largest in entire China (Yu and Yu, 1995, pp. 197–198). The rise of demand from the leather shoe industry in Wenzhou has stimulated the growth of leather production.

8.4.2 *Leather Shoes*

Leather shoes production started during the 1900s and 1910s in the city centre (Yu and Yu, 1995, p. 35). The supply of leather from the leather industry clusters in suburban townships must have influenced the rise of leather shoes production, but there is no evidence to prove the relationship. Leather shoes workshops in the city centre increased to 70 in 1931, and the demand from army during the war stimulated the growth of the industry. But the industry stagnated after the war, and in 1950 there were only 43 leather shoe manufacturers left, with a total of 130 employees (Zhang, 1998, p. 1175). During the 1950s, the industrial 'cluster' disappeared, because of the collectivisation and nationalisation of private businesses. After the reform, private leather shoes manufacturers started to proliferate in the city centre and in the neighbouring townships of Shuangyu, Guoxi and Oubei. The industrial cluster revived with a scale far exceeding that of the pre-war period. As indicated in Table 8.1, each of these townships has more than 120 corporations that are engaged in leather shoe production. Besides these, there must be hundreds of cottage industries engaged in shoe production. Shoe production has become the most important industry of Wenzhou in terms of number of corporations and output value.

The present leather shoe industry in Wenzhou inherited the shoe production technology that existed before the establishment of the People's Republic. For example, Yu Ashou, the president of Wenzhou Jierda Shoe Company, born in 1936, was apprenticed to a shoemaker in 1948 (Shao, 2000). Because of the collectivisation of his workplace, he became a worker of a collective shoe factory in 1958. Being fired by the factory during the 1960s on the charge of running a side business, he started mending shoes by his own, and in 1981, he established a shoe company. As his career indicates, the technology and craftsmen of the shoe industry before the People's Republic were inherited and preserved in public enterprises during the planned economy period. The workers of public enterprises resigned soon after the reform to establish their own businesses.

Most of the owners of the major shoe companies of Wenzhou, however, were too young to directly experience the pre-reform shoe industry. The owner of Aokang Group — the largest shoemaker in Wenzhou, born in 1965, entered the shoe business in 1986 as a salesman.[2] When he entered the business, the leather shoe cluster already existed in Wenzhou.

8.4.3 *Artificial Leather*

Artificial leather industry cluster is located at Yongzhong and Longwan, having 55 and 22 corporations respectively (Figure 8.5).

---

[2] Interview at Aokang Group (August 29, 2001) and Zhang (1999).

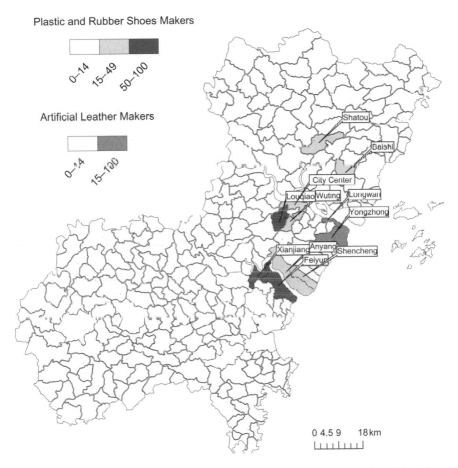

Figure 8.5:   Location of Artificial Leather Industry and Plastic and Rubber Shoe Industry.

Artificial leather production is a very young industry compared to the leather processing industry: the first artificial leather factory was established in 1991.[3] Unlike the leather processing industry, no public enterprise has ever been involved in the industry. Artificial leather industry was a private-led one from the very beginning.

---

[3] The history of the artificial leather industry in Wenzhou is based on the author's interview at Wenzhou Tianniu Artificial Leather Company (November 27, 2007).

The founders of the first artificial leather factories thought that, with a large demand from the local leather shoe industry, the business must be viable. In this sense, Wenzhou's artificial leather industry is an outcome of the backward linkage effect of leather shoe industry. At the same time, however, the founders paid attention to the fact that artificial leather production was becoming more and more costly in Japan, Taiwan, and Korea because of the cost of treating sewage. They thought that in Wenzhou, where the regulations on waste water were not as strict as other countries, artificial leather could be produced at a lower cost. This forecast turned out to be right, and the first artificial leather factory became a great success. The success, however, triggered a conflict between the investors, and the company split into five. Each of the five investors dragged their relatives and friends into the business. In 2001, ten years after the establishment of the first factory, *The Collection* reported that there were 198 artificial leather companies in Yongzhong, Longwan, and neighbouring townships. The production volume of these artificial leather industry clusters accounts for around 40% of the total volume of China.[4]

Though the artificial leather industry in Wenzhou has the same market with the traditional leather processing industry, there is little relationship between the two industries. The owners of the artificial leather industry do not derive from the leather processing industry. Most of them have accumulated the capital for initial investment by working as merchants. The initial investment required to establish an artificial leather plant is at least 30 million yuan, which is too big an amount for a leather dresser to invest.

8.4.4 *Plastic and Rubber Shoes*

The plastic shoe industry in Wenzhou derives from the leather shoe industry, and the rubber shoe industry derives from the plastic shoe

---

[4] According to Ma and Liao (2003), the artificial leather production in Wenzhou was 280 thousand tons, and Feng (2005) reports that the production of entire China was 725 thousand tons in 2002. Ma and Liao (2003) and Qu (2005) write that Wenzhou accounts for 70% of the national production of artificial leather, but we cannot confirm this figure by other sources.

industry. A 'plastic shoe' is a shoe the sole of which is made by injecting polyvinyl chloride (PVC) or polyurethane (PU) into a mold, and 'rubber shoe' is a shoe the sole of which is made from rubber. *The Collection* has four classifications of shoe industry, namely, 'leather shoe manufacturing', 'plastic shoe manufacturing', 'rubber shoe manufacturing', and 'shoe manufacturing'. However, there exist many enterprises which produce both plastic shoes and rubber shoes, or have switched from plastic shoes to rubber shoes in the past. It is often difficult to distinguish a plastic shoe maker from a rubber shoe maker. Besides this, the 'shoe manufacturing' category lumps together plastic shoe makers and rubber shoe makers. Therefore, in our analysis, we will integrate the three categories — 'plastic shoe manufacturing', 'rubber shoe manufacturing', and 'shoe manufacturing', — into one and call it 'plastic and rubber shoe manufacturing'. Figure 8.5 indicates the spatial distribution of the 'plastic and rubber shoe manufacturing'. Several clusters of plastic and rubber shoe industry are scattered around Wenzhou.

The development of plastic and rubber shoe industry in Wenzhou was initiated by a retired worker named Xu Zhaolin. After retiring a local leather shoe factory in 1979, he started making plastic shoes at his home in Xianjiang (Yu and Yu, 1995; Li, 1998). He melted waste plastic and shaped it into soles, and used iron to stick it to leather outer. His plastic shoes sold very well because of their cheapness, so his neighbours started imitating him. Then the whole village and neighbouring villages started imitating him. The number of shoe factories reached 1500, employing more than 8000 people in 1984. The plastic shoes industry of Xianjiang, however, soon faced stagnation of sales, because the quality of its products was bad. The plastic shoe makers jointly invested into injection molding machinery and improved their quality, started producing rubber shoes along with plastic shoes, and hence Xianjiang's shoe industry overcome its bad reputation.

Plastic shoe manufacturing which spread in Xianjiang diffused to other townships during 1980s. In Louqiao, some farmers and merchants, who learned plastic shoe making in Xianjiang, started making polyvinyl chloride shoes in 1982.[5] In Shatou, plastic shoe making was introduced in 1984 from Xianjiang. Shatou's shoemakers later faced the decline of sales, so they switched to rubber shoes manufacturing, and now the township has developed into a rubber shoes cluster, consisted of 17 enterprises employing 5000 workers.[6]

When plastic and rubber shoe clusters emerged in Wenzhou during 1980s, the shoes produced by these clusters were mostly sold in China. Early manufacturers tried to sell their shoes through state-owned consumer goods wholesalers, which were the main distribution channel under planned economy. Later on plastic and rubber shoes manufacturers of Wenzhou expanded their sales to the countryside of inland China and even to Eastern Europe and Africa. Severe competition and the ample supply of cheap immigrant labour have made it possible for plastic and rubber shoes made in Wenzhou to be competitive even in inland China and Africa. Recently, however, Wenzhou's shoemakers are facing the rise of wages and the emergence of competitors in the inland.

8.4.5 *Valves and Pumps*

Most of the industrial clusters in Wenzhou either date back to the Republican era or newly emerged after the economic reform. But the valve industry clusters located in Oubei (No. 88, 89 of Figure 8.1) and Yongzhong (No. 331 of Figure 8.1) emerged during the Cultural Revolution. The first manufacturers of valves which emerged around 1970 were the 'commune and brigade enterprises', the predecessor of township enterprises. 'Commune and brigade enterprise' usually denote public enterprises that are run by people's communes and production brigades, but those which existed in Oubei and Yongzhong resembled private enterprises. The 'commune and brigade enterprises' produced valves without any instruction from the

---

[5] Based on interviews at Wenzhou Yisili Shoes Company (November 27, 2007) and Wenzhou Haibang Manufacturing and Trading Company (November 27, 2007).
[6] Based on an interview at Industry Section, Shatou Township Office (August 29, 2001).

planning apparatus and sold them outside of the planning system. Because there was plenty of demand that was not fulfilled by the planned economy system, valve production in Oubei and Yongzhong grew rapidly during 1970s. In 1976, there were 1069 valve manufacturers in the two townships, producing almost the same amount of valves with Shanghai, the largest valve producing city in China (Yu and Yu, 1995, p. 131).

The central government and provincial government took a hard stance against the valve industry clusters in Oubei and Yongzhong, which disturbed the order of the planning system. The government sent an inspection team and ordered many enterprises to shut down on the charge of producing low quality valves. The number of valve manufacturers decreased to 400. After the reform, however, Wenzhou's valve industry revived by improving quality, and recently it has grown into the largest valve producing district in China, accounting for one third of national production. As of 2001, valve manufacturers were concentrated in Oubei, Yongzhong, and Shacheng (No. 125 of Figure 8.1), with 601 enterprises in total.

Why could the 'commune and brigade enterprises' during the Cultural Revolution start producing valves? Firstly, we must point out the existence of a technological basis of metalworking industry as an initial condition for the development of the valve industry. The history of metalworking industry can be traced back to the Republican era. According to Zhang (1998, p. 1301) and Yu and Yu (1995, pp. 23–24), the first metalworking workshop in Wenzhou was established in 1916 by an entrepreneur named Li Shumeng. In the beginning, he produced a cotton-working machine he had invented. Then during the 1920s the workshop started producing ship engines and moved to city centre. Many other machinery enterprises emerged in the city centre since then, reaching to a total of 47 enterprises with 380 employees in 1947. After the establishment of the People's Republic, these workshops were integrated and nationalised. One of such state-owned enterprises which were established by nationalising private metalworking enterprises was Wenzhou Metalworking Factory, which had 1676 employees in 1958 and produced various machinery for the local market, such as diesel engines, threshing machines, pumps, oil extracting machines, and metallurgy machinery (Yu and Yu, 1995, p. 106). During the Great Leap Forward (1958–1960), several new metalworking enterprises were established. In 1960, the number of metalworking factories in Wenzhou reached 40. Through the establishment of these public enterprises, the technology and equipment of machining, casting, and forging were spread across Wenzhou, forming the technological basis for valve production by commune and brigade enterprises.

It was in 1969 when a commune and brigade enterprise in Oubei started producing valves, and in 1970 an enterprise in Yongzhong started too.[7] The reason why these rural enterprises paid attention to valve production was as follows: In early 1970s, the demand for valves surged because of the increase in investment to the petrochemical industry. There were, of course, state-owned valve manufacturers in China, but these enterprises could not satisfy the domestic demand for valves. Those who wanted a valve had to apply for the supply of valves to the central government one year prior to the actual purchase. After the application was accepted, it took one year to make the supply plan, order production to the valve manufacturer, and distribute the product. Because of the inflexibility of the planning system and state-owned enterprises, there were plenty of business opportunities left for the rural enterprises to cultivate. One of such opportunities was spare valves for imported chemical plants. The repair valves for imported plants would be expensive if imported, but state-owned valve manufacturers would not take the trouble of manufacturing them, so the job was taken up by the manufacturers of Oubei and Yongzhong.

Another reason why the rural enterprises entered the valve business was because they thought that valve production was not difficult. They thought that once they could procure castings, a few lathes would be enough to produce valves. In fact, producing high quality valves was not so easy. Valves made in Wenzhou soon became infamous for

---

[7] The history of the valve industry cluster is based on interviews at Zhejiang Chaoda Valve Corporation (November 28, 2007) and Labour Office of Yongzhong Township (August 30, 2001).

their bad quality. The bad reputation urged Wenzhou entrepreneurs to invite engineers retired from the state-owned valve manufacturers in Shanghai and Shenyang to transfer technology. The transfer of technology and talent from state-owned enterprises to Wenzhou's private valve manufacturers started in 1972 and lasted until 1990s. The state-owned enterprises had been deprived of their technology, talent, and market by private manufacturers, and in the end they were bought by private owners.

The pump manufacturing industry cluster of Oubei, which consists of 91 manufacturers, derived from the valve industry. During mid-1980s, valve manufacturers of Oubei suffered from their bad reputation and lack of distribution channel — because they still had to sell outside of the planning system. Then one entrepreneur in Oubei started producing 'water pipe pumps'. This is an apparatus to raise water pressure at the upper stories of high-rise buildings developed by a company in Dalian. The product could be easily produced by lathe and the demand for it was surging because of the increase of high rises in China. Many valve manufacturers in Oubei switched to pump manufacturing, making Oubei a pump industry cluster.

8.5 Concluding Remarks

During the short period since the reform, as many as 153 industrial clusters emerged in Wenzhou. This paper has provided a thorough list of industrial clusters in Wenzhou, and explored the development process of leather and shoes industry and valve and pump industry through interviews and written materials. The history of most of the industrial clusters in Wenzhou and in China, however, is left unexplored.

We confirmed by our case studies that the industrial clusters emerged and the diversity of industries increased through the repetitions of innovation and imitation. We speculate that the same mechanism generated many of the other industrial clusters in Wenzhou, and even in other places of China. In Wenzhou, the speed of imitation is extremely fast, so the emergence of an industrial cluster can be observed in a short period. In other parts of China, the speed of emergence might be slower, but similar processes might be underway.

References

FENG, Shujun. (2005). 'Renzaoge hechengge hangye fazhan xianzhuang,' (Present Status of Artificial Leather Industry) *Guowai suliao*, 23(10).

ITAMI, Hiroyuki, Shigeru MATSUSHIMA, Takeo KIKKAWA (eds.) (1998). *Sangyo shuseki no honshitsu*, (The Nature of Industrial Agglomerations) Tokyo: Yuhikaku.

JIN, Yongxing. (2002). *Juji yu kuosan: Wenzhou jianzhizhen chengshihua yanjiu* (Agglomeration and Dispersion: A Study on the Urbanization of Townships in Wenzhou), Beijing: Shehuikexue wenxian chubanshe.

KRUGMAN, Paul R. (1991). *Geography and Trade*, MIT Press.

LI, Shihui. (1998). 'Laizi zhenan 'xiedu' de diaocha baogao,' (A Research Report from the 'Shoe Town' in Southern Zhejiang) *Zhongguo gaige*, 2.

Ma, Zhangfeng, Liao, Zhengpin. (2003). 'Pengbo fazhan de zhongguo hechengge gongye,' (The Rising Artificial Leather Industry of China) *Keji qingbao kaifa yu jingji*, 13(3).

MARSHALL, Alfred. (1920). *Principles of Economics, An Introductory Volume*, Eighth Edition, London: Macmillan.

NOLAN, Peter, DONG Fureng (eds.), (1990). *Market Forces in China: Competition and Small Business: The Wenzhou Debate*, London: Zed Books.

Policy Research Department, Zhejiang Committee of Chinese Communist Party. (2003). 'Kuaisu zengzhang de zhejiang quyu kuaizhuang jingji,' (Rapidly Growing Cluster Economies in Zhejiang District), *Nanfang wang* website.

Project Unit, Commission of Economy and Trade of Zhejiang Provincial Government. (2006). 'Fu zhejiang tese quyu jingji: Zhejiang kuaizhuang jingji fazhan baogao,' (Regional Economy with Rich Zhejiang Characteristics: A Report on the Development of Cluster Economy in Zhejiang), Commission of Economy and Trade of Zhejiang Provincial Government website.

QU, Ping. (2005). 'Woguo renzaoge shichang xianzhuang, cunzai de wenti ji cujin cuoshi,' (The Present Status, Existing Problems, and Promotion Measures of China's Artificial Leather Market), *Zhongguo pige*, 6.

SHAO, Zhizhen (ed.), (2000). *Wenzhou qiyejia chuangye fengyunlu*, (The Adventures of Wenzhou Entrepreneurs), Beijing: Zhongyang wenxian chubanshe.

SHENG, Shihao, ZHENG, Yanwei. (2004). *Zhejiang xianxiang: chanye jiqun yu quyu jingji fazhan*, (The Zhejiang Phenomenon: Industrial Clusters and Regional Economic Development), Beijing: Qinghua daxue chubanshe.

SHI, Jinchuan *et al.* (2002). *Zhidu bianqian yu jingji fazhan: wenzhou moshi yanjiu*, (Institutional Change and Economic Development: A Study of Wenzhou Model), Hangzhou: Zhejiang daxue chubanshe.

SONOBE, Tetsushi, HU, Dinghuan, OTSUKA, Keijiro. (2004). 'From Inferior to Superior Products: An Inquiry into the Wenzhou Model of Industrial Development,' *Journal of Comparative Economics*.

WANG, Jici *et al.* (2001). *Chuangxin de kongjian: Qiye jiqun yu quyu fazhan*, (Innovative Spaces: Enterprise Clusters and Regional Development), Beijing: Beijing daxue chubanshe.

YOSHIDA, Keiichi. (1998). 'Kinzoku yoshokki sanchi e no dotei to sanchi kozo henkaku no ayumi,' (The Path to the Cutlery Industry District and the Process of Structural Change) in Seki, Mitsuhiro and Junko Fukuda (eds.). *Henbo suru jiba sangyo: fukugo kinzoku sanchi e mukau Tsubame*, (The Changing Local Industries: Tsubame Heading Towards a Metalworking Complex), Tokyo: Shinhyoron.

YU, Xiong, YU, Guang. (1995). *Wenzhou gongye jianshi*, (A Brief History of Wenzhou's Industries) Shanghai: Shanghai shehui kexue chubanshe.

YUAN, Enzhen (ed.), (1987), *Wenzhou moshi yu fuyu zhi lu*, (Wenzhou Model and the Road to Affluence), Shanghai: Shanghai shehui kexue chubanshe.

ZHANG, Lianjie (ed.), (1999). *Wenzhou laoban*, (Wenzhou Bosses), Beijing: Zhongguo wenxian chubanshe.

ZHANG, Renshou, LI, Hong. (1990). *Wenzhou moshi yanjiu*, (A Study on the Wenzhou Model), Beijing: Zhongguo shehui kexue chubanshe.

ZHANG, Zhicheng (ed.), (1998). *Wenzhou shizhi*, (The History of Wenzhou City) Beijing: Zhonghua shuju.

ZHU, Huacheng. (2003). *Zhejiang chanyequn*, (Industrial Districts of Zhejiang), Hangzhou: Zhejiang daxue chubanshe.

ZHU, Kangdui. (2001). 'Wenzhou chanye qunluo ji qi yanjin,' (The Industrial Colonies and Their Changes) in Shi Jinchuan *et al.* 2002.

Chapter 9

Understanding the Zhejiang Industrial Clusters: Questions and Re-evaluations[1]

Lu Shi and Bernard Ganne

China

R32   L60   P21
P25   P23   L14

9.1 General Introduction

Under the current climate of rapid industrial development in China, the phenomenon of industrial districts or clusters, or concentrations of businesses involved in the same type of industry, are of significant importance in certain regions. Although it may have existed in a more clandestine manner before the reform of the early 1980s, this phenomenon is a relatively recent one, first emerging around a decade ago, and seeing significant growth and taking on a more concrete structure since the turn of the century.

Studies have therefore only been carried out on this phenomenon in China relatively recently. It could be argued — debatably — that this phenomenon was first acknowledged a long time ago, perhaps even before 1949, when Professor Fei Xiaotong carried out his cross-sectional study '块状经济' (similarly to Alfred Marshal's contribution to industrial districts in France). However, it is only since the turn of the 21st century that Chinese researchers have begun to pay close attention to the subject. They include geographers, notably the analytical work of Professor Wang Jici, geographer at the University of

---

[1] Our sincere thanks go to our Chinese colleagues, Professors Wang Jici, Jin Xiangrong, Yu Yingchuan and Sheng Shihao, for their valuable assistance during our field work in Zhejiang in July 2006.

Beijing (Wang, 2001), the economists and sociologists of Sun Yat-sen University, Guangzhou (Wang, 2004), and the economists and management specialists at the University of Zhejiang (Zhang and Jin, 2006) to name but a few. A series of publications on this theme can also be found in other regions of China.

On the whole, it can be argued that the general observations about the phenomenon in China have already been made, such as the geographical location of the clusters and the different types of clusters in place. Even though the various proposals for cluster typologies do not concur precisely, the current Chinese approaches to the phenomenon of clusters suggest 4 principal types of industrial clusters.[2]

1. Clusters of traditional, highly integrated firms, which can be found in several regions of China, more often in small towns and rural zones undergoing urbanisation. These clusters are highly specialised solely in the manufacture of consumer goods, such as those found in Fujian or Zhejiang. Industry has become the main economic activity in these rural areas, favouring companies owned by the State which, prior to the reform, was unable to satisfy market demand. The success of these private, rural companies has attracted many others into the market and created a concentration of businesses.

2. High-tech clusters, more often situated in large cities near university centres. These focus mainly on electronics, such as the Zhongguancun area of Beijing or the fibre optics cluster in Wuhan, etc.

3. Clusters of foreign companies, mainly the result of FDI from Taiwan, Hong Kong and Singapore, etc. They bring together a number of other firms with whom they have working relationships, as seen particularly in Guangdong. Sometimes, investors may bring their own parts suppliers with them, moving an entire

---

[2] Here, we have adopted the typology proposed by Professor Wang Jici in his work '*Chuangxin de kongjian* (Innovative spaces: entreprises clusters and regional development)', 2001.

network into the country. This is especially common among Taiwanese entrepreneurs.

4. SME clusters grouped around large companies, as seen in both the shipbuilding industry in Shanghai and, more recently, the automobile industry in Wuhan, etc.

The problem faced is vast, and there is an immense field for study.

In this study, we have chosen to focus on the first type of business conglomerates, mainly comprising SMEs engaging in the same type of activity — similar to those observed in Europe (and Italy in particular) some thirty years ago. There are numerous zones of highly specialised development in China. However, among these, Zhejiang province is undoubtedly considered the most remarkable, and is seen as a role model in modern evolution towards a market economy.

How have the Zhejiang clusters developed? What are the characteristics of this development? Is it possible to talk about a 'third China' along the same lines as the former '3rd Italy' with regard to industrial districts? Do Chinese clusters in fact have any specific characteristics? These are some of the questions that we will look to address today.

9.2 The Zhejiang Clusters: A Traditional Cluster Model?

9.2.1 *A Small, Rather Neglected Province which has Seen Strong Autonomous Development Over the Last 20 Years*

Zhejiang is, in fact, one of the smallest provinces in China (occupying 1.06% of China's land surface). In 2005, it had 48,980,000 inhabitants (according to the *hukou* register), representing 3.75% of the population of China. With hills and mountains accounting for more than 70.4% of the province, and with few natural resources, Zhejiang has been somewhat neglected by the government. Between 1953 and 1978, the region's inhabitants received an average of just 114 yuan of state aid per person — just over half[3] of the national average. In economic terms, Zhejiang has also received the lowest level of state support. Even in the period between 1982 and 1989, which saw economic reform in both urban and rural areas, state investment in Zhejiang represented just 2.5% of the total investment across the country.[4] However, over the last 20 years, the province has risen from 12th to 4th place in China in terms of gross national product. In 2003, Zhejiang had the third highest average revenue per inhabitant in China.[5]

This development is mainly linked to the rapid industrial expansion that this traditionally agricultural region has experienced — an industry based mainly on the province's large number of small, family companies. Zhejiang was the first province in China to see the development of industrial family workshops in the mid-1980s. Today, the province has the highest proportion of private companies in China: 92%, compared to a national average of 60%. In 2001, the number of SMEs with sales turnovers of less than 5 million yuan was estimated at 682,000. These businesses employ 5,976,400 people, representing 65% of the industrial labour force.[6] One third of these private companies, which mainly manufacture of consumer goods (socks, cigarette lighters, leather, shoes, toys, hardware products, etc.), are involved in the textiles sector (37.2%). A further 8.6% are involved in the clothing industry, and 6.3% in the manufacture of metal goods.[7]

These SMEs are grouped geographically and specialise in a particular manufacturing sector: one product per village and one sector per region (一镇一品, 一乡一业,). This so-called 'compartmentalised economy' (块状经济) can be found in 85 of the 88 towns in the Zhejiang district.[8] In 2001, it was estimated that there were

---

[3] 52.5% of the national average to be more precise.

[4] Sheng and Zheng (2004), *Zhejiang xianxiang*, p. 2.

[5] Sheng and Zheng (2004), *Zhejiang xianxiang*, p. 1.

[6] Sheng and Zheng (2004), *Zhejiang xianxiang*, p. 9.

[7] Sheng and Zheng (2004), *Zhejiang xianxiang*, pp. 10–11.

[8] Sheng and Zheng (2004), *Zhejiang xianxiang*, p. 41.

519 specialised industrial clusters with a production value higher than 100 million yuan.[9]
We will now provide a brief description of these clusters.

9.2.2 The Zhejiang Clusters: A Short Presentation

A number of researchers have proposed 3 distinct zones in the Zhejiang clusters following the endogenous model and spontaneous development.[10]

The first zone (Table 9.1) is located in the north of Zhejiang and comprises 5 administrative areas (towns and districts governed from the provincial capital of Hangzhou). The clusters in the economically developed zone are highly dynamic. The large companies are located in Hangzhou, and the high-tech clusters are also in Hangzhou, as well as in Ningbo. This zone also contains towns of specialised SMEs, such as Chengzhou (ties), Yuyao (plastics) and Xiaoshan (textiles), whose production values are the highest among the Zhejiang clusters.

The second zone (Table 9.2) covers Wenzhou and Taizhou. These clusters are also developed, but there are sometimes significant disparities between levels of development in different districts. Wenzhou represents an economic model upon which the development of Zhejiang is based, and may well be the first town in China where private companies emerged after the reform. Today in Wenzhou, there are around ten different activity sectors in the industrial clusters: shoes, clothing, lighters, glasses, and so on. In 2001, shoes manufactured in Wenzhou represented 20% of the total Chinese market, with lighters at 90% and razors at 60%. Wenzhou is seen as a benchmark for the importance and dynamism of family SMEs.

Zone 3 (Table 9.3) comprises Jinhua, Quzhou and Lishui. Here, the clusters are very young and this is the least developed region of Zhejiang.

The Zhejiang clusters, particularly concentrated in the Wenzhou region, are for the most part developing in rural areas. They focus on

---

[9] Sheng and Zheng (2004), *Zhejiang xianxiang*, p. 41.
[10] Sheng and Zheng (2004), *Zhejiang xianxiang*.

Table 9.1:   Zhejiang Clusters. First zone.

Administrative Areas	Industrial Sectors	Cluster Types
Hangzhou	Machines and equipment, electronic communications, household appliances, medical, high-tech	*Huangzhou*: automobiles *Yan qian/town of Xiao shan*: chemical fibre *Nan yang*: umbrellas *Xin tang*: bird feather products *Xiaoshan*: textiles, automobile parts
Ningbo	Clothing, mechanics, petrochemical industry, etc.	*Yuyao*: industrial moulds, toys, plastics *Hengjie*: watches *Jiangshan*: gas appliances *Xianxiang*: safes
Shaoxing	Textiles, dyes, medicines, chemicals	*Shaoxing*: textiles *Zhuji*: shirts, shoes *Diankou*: hardware *Shangyu*: protective clothing *Yuecheng*: furniture *Chengzhou*: ties *Fengqiao*: shirts *Shanxiahu*: cultured pearls
Jiaxing	Textiles, leather and mechanical equipment	*Haining*: leather *Pinghu*: clothing, bags *Xiuzhouqu*: silk, synthetic fabrics *Haiyan*: machine parts, toys *Tongxiang*: woollen jumpers *Jiashan*: wood
Huzhou	Textiles, children's clothing, construction materials	*Zhili*: children's clothing *Chengau*: textiles *Nanxun*: construction materials *Anji*: bamboo products *Linghu*: farming
Zhoushan	Pisciculture, marine product-based medications, mechanics	*Zhoushan*: piscicultural product distribution market, medicines, toys, hardware

Table 9.2: Zhejiang Clusters. Second zone.

Administrative Areas	Industrial Sectors	Cluster Types
Wenzhou	Mechanics, plastics, printing, electrical appliances, leather	*Pingyang, town of Xiaojiang*: plastics *Cangnan*: signaling manufacture, salty foods *Ruian, town of Tangxia*: automobile and motorcycle parts *Leqing, town of Liushi*: low-voltage electrical appliances *Hongqiao*: electronics *Panshi*: clothing *Beibaixiang*: construction materials *Longgang*: plastic bags *Yongjia*: buttons *Lucheng*: cigarette lighters
Taizhou	Automobile and motorcycle parts, craft products, shoes, plastics	*Shujiang Zhaoqiao*: plastics, *Linhai, family village of Qu*: multicoloured lights *Sanmen gao*: nails

low production cost sectors and are mainly concerned with the manufacture of consumer goods.

How have these clusters developed?

9.2.3 *The Stages in the Development of the Zhejiang Clusters*

9.2.3.1 *From the Planned Economy to the Liberal Economy: the General Framework*

Since the first Five Year Plan in 1955, the Chinese economy has been under the direct control of the state. All private economic interests were dismantled. In the countryside, all farmland was henceforth property of the state. Farmers were organised into cooperatives and communes, and paid in 'work points' according to their participation in work in the fields. At the same time, traditional activities that were

Table 9.3:   Zhejiang Clusters. Third zone.

Administrative Areas	Industrial Sectors	Cluster Types
Jinhua	Mechanics, hardware, agricultural product processing, textiles, clothing	*Jinghua*: measuring instruments *Dongyang*: magnetic materials, suits *Yiwu*: clothes, textiles, decorations, shoes…. *Yiwu*: accessories market *Pujiang*: clothing *Yongkang*: hardware
Quzhou	Chemical fertiliser, cement, mechanical equipment	*Town of Wucun*: shuttlecocks *Shangshan village Shizikou Shangfang, Shangshan Huifu*: heat treatment *Longyouwu village, Miaoxia*: bamboo *Longyou lake; Diyu village*: card paper processing *Jiangshanqing lake*: springs *Xiakou*: steel *Kaihua-Zhangwan*: wood products
Lishui	Wood processing, craft products, agricultural product processing	*Longquan*: umbrellas *Qingtian*: leather, shoes *Yunhe district*: toys

indispensable to farmers' survival[11] (such as crafts and trade) were outlawed in the 1960s, following the 'Great Leap Forward' of 1958, when the Chinese countryside was encouraged to build factories in pursuit of agricultural mechanisation.

These rural factories (社队企业) began to re-emerge in the early 1970s, with the compromise between local collectives and the farmers suffering from poverty. These rural factories were therefore created in the provinces with craft traditions, such as Jiangsu, Guangdong and Zhejiang. This type of semi-public economic structure, within

---

[11] Since the Ming and Qing dynasties, agriculture and craft have been complementary economic activities in the Zhejiang region, as a response to countryside overpopulation and a lack of natural resources.

the framework of the planned economy, achieved political recognition from the central government in 1975.

With the commencement of economic reform in 1978, the 'family responsibility system' (家庭承包责任制) was put in place in the countryside, giving families control over the land. From 1982, land rights were handed back to family units, although the land was not actually owned by the families. Under this system of self-management, it was easier for farming families to organise their agricultural work. This new system of organisation allowed a section of the rural population to adapt to other forms of activity. In order to solve the problem of surplus agricultural population in the countryside, the Chinese government authorised diversification into associated economic activities.

The Chinese countryside was therefore gradually returning to its traditional economic system. Working in the fields became increasingly accompanied by associated activities, which increase the household income. This was the catalyst for the development of specialist agricultural centres and, later, rural companies (乡镇企业) Rural companies, first created in Jiangsu province, are the result of rural factories founded by local communities. From the collective economy, the Sunan model then spread to other regions of China, experiencing significant success in the decade following the economic reform. Across China, between 1979 and 1984, the number and production value of rural companies quadrupled and the work force employed by them doubled.

There was another factor in play, which would help the development of craft and industrial activities. In 1985, the state decided to lower the purchase price for cereals in order to reduce subsidies for urban consumption. As a result, farming the fields gradually became less profitable. An increasing number of farmers were therefore forced to re-evaluate their income generation strategies and look to new economic sectors such as pisciculture, trade and industry. The agricultural sector therefore fell into decline, replaced by industrial and service sectors.

Alongside the flourishing collective rural companies, the birth of private companies[12] constitutes another aspect in the transition of the

---

[12] Private companies are defined as independent trades and businesses employing more than 7 people. See Shi (2006), *Zhongguo minying jingji fazhan baogao*, p. 8.

Chinese economy. Unlike Jiangsu, which is a 'small public model',[13] and Guangdong, whose development was based on foreign investment (mixed capital companies), Zhejiang has adopted another model of development based on the private economy.

9.2.3.2 The Development of the Zhejiang Clusters
— From peddling to family workshops

In the mid-1970s, peddling (crafts, small traders), an ancient tradition that predates the communist regime, began to reappear. Until the mid-1980's, private economic activity was still highly contested in China. The Zhejiang farmers, particularly those from Wenzhou, organised themselves into family units to sell their products: embroidery, scales, cotton mattress covers, etc. Peddlers travelled throughout China and brought back success. During this initial period of the liberal economy, 'black market' family workshops, with a workshop at the front and a shop behind (前厂后店), began to accumulate capital through trade, then moved into manufacturing to satisfy market demand. To avoid 'the capitalist way', they attached themselves to rural companies in the locality or region and local collective companies. This is what is known as 'borrowing the red hat'.[14] These fictitious collective companies, later contested by the government, were stamped out between 1982 and 1984.[15]

From the second half of the 1980s, economic policy became more tolerant towards private companies. Zhejiang moved more towards manufacturing. The activities that developed based mainly on local

---

[13] Li and Pave (1999), '*La Chine actuelle et le marché-L'émergence des PME familiales dans la dynamique de développement économique*' (Modern China and the emerging market of family SMEs in the dynamic of economic development), *Annales des Mines*, mars 1999, pp. 29–42.

[14] Cao Zhenghan in Zhang and Jin (2006), *Zhongguo zhidu bianqian de anli yanjiu* (Case studies in China's institutional change), pp. 95–107.

[15] Eight Wenzhou entrepreneurs were prosecuted for illegal economic activity in 1982. See Cao Zhenghan, in Zhang and Jin (2006), p. 106.

traditional activities or on technically undemanding manufacturing processes, were more effective in generating immediate profits to meet the basic needs of the local population.

In Zhejiang, from the mid-1980s, family workshops were no longer able to deal with market competition on their own. On the one hand, their products were often of poor quality; on the other hand, these isolated family workshops were limited by their access to capital, their technical ability, and their supply and sale networks. When a family workshop was no longer able to meet its demands, it would entrust a proportion of its orders to close relatives. Over time, these workshops collaborated more and more to meet the needs of the market.

A new type of company was therefore born: co-operative capital companies (股份合作企业). In the pursuit of political correctness, local authorities called this new type of business 'collective enterprises'. Although labelled as 'public', these companies were in fact private associations, comprising close relations. In reality, these new family companies represented a movement from the nuclear family to the extended family. At the end of 1997, there were more than 22,000 groupings of this type in the Wenzhou region,[16] giving rise to three types of company: family workshops working together by pooling their capital and equipment; family workshops which remained autonomous and worked together solely for supplies and sales; and family workshops investing in the creation of a new company in which they became shareholders.[17]

— *From craft workshops to industrial districts*

In Zhejiang, these family companies began to group together geo-graphically by specialising in a particular manufacturing sector: shoes, lighters, leather, and so on. This was the beginning of the Zhejiang industrial clusters, characterised by a 'compartmentalised economy'[18]

---

[16] Cao Zhenghan in Zhang and Jin (2006), p. 113.
[17] Cao Zhenghan in Zhang and Jin (2006), pp. 107–116.
[18] This concept is defined by the Zhejiang province Office of Policy Research.

(块状经济), to use the definition given by the Zhejiang authorities.[19] In this region, where there is a high level of geographical mobility (emigration abroad and peddling within China), the trade activities and geographical movements of peddlers, travelling traders and foreign-based Chinese nationals originating from Zhejiang allowed for the spread of information about the region's products. Once this information was disseminated throughout the province, it proved invaluable to the regional economy.[20] If a product had potential in the market, it went into production and was quickly copied by neighbouring businesses. Below is an eyewitness statement about the history of the cigarette lighter sector.

In the early 1990s, foreign-based Wenzhou emigrants returned to their native region and introduced their compatriots to foreign-manufactured lighters. This is how Wenzhou's lighter manufacturing industry began — a product requiring little investment and technical knowledge. The sector peaked in 1993, at a time when 3500 companies were created spontaneously in this promising niche.[21]

This development was therefore a gradual one, based on the high levels of product specialisation and geographical concentration of family companies described earlier: 'one product per village and one sector per region' (一镇一品, 一乡一业) — hardware in Yongkang, specialist markets in Yiwu and circuit breakers in Leqing, etc. (see Section 9.2.1 above).

A significant change in scale was only noticeable in the 1990s and beyond, and more specifically following Deng Xiaoping's visit to Shenzhen in 1992, which was seen as an acknowledgement and encouragement of China's new liberal economy. This economic liberalisation allowed farmers and artisan-entrepreneurs to contemplate commercial and industrial activities on a national (and later international) scale. This was the catalyst for a significant explosion of clusters in Zhejiang.

---

[19] A zone containing a grouping of more than 10 companies manufacturing the same or complementary products, and whose annual production values exceed 100 million yuan. Term taken from Fei Xiaotong.

[20] Li and Pave (1999), pp. 36–37.

[21] Interview carried out at a lighter manufacturing company in Wenzhou, July 2006.

How did this transition happen and what was the basis for these clusters?

— From industrial districts to clusters

The aforementioned phenomenon of the 'compartmentalised economy', comprising groupings of family companies in specialised zones, provided the basis for the development of the Zhejiang industrial clusters. Under the new liberal economy, the movement would be characterised by changes in types of company.

Alongside the existing family companies, the 1990s saw the emergence of new types of businesses: limited responsibility companies or industrial groups. From the beginning of the 1990s, a number of large, market-leading companies began to absorb smaller subcontractors. In 1995, for example, the number of shareholders in the Chint company of Leqing, Wenzhou — a manufacturer of electrical products — rose from 5 (all family members) to 86, following its incorporation of 56 companies into the group.[22] Today, it is the largest low- and high-voltage electrical equipment manufacturing company in China, and sits at the helm of an entire local manufacturing network. With its high presence on the Chinese market and its current attempts to break into the international market, Chint, along with several other similar companies in the Wenzhou zone in southern Zhejiang, represents a model of a complex cluster involving clients and all types of suppliers.

This is, of course, just one example — albeit a remarkable one — of the changes taking place in the Zhejiang clusters. This increased power can also be observed in many other shoe-, lighter-, plastic- and hardware-manufacturing clusters, opening up a vast field of study that remains relatively untouched.

It should be noted that, whilst the situation is changing rapidly, the observed concentration and increasing complexity of the clusters is accompanied by a level of diversification in models, craft forms, family forms and privately financed companies. Along with these, new

---

[22] Interview with the Associate Director of the Chint Company, July 2006.

models of development can be observed, such as those in the field of trade as we will see further on.

Whatever the case may be, the Zhejiang industrial districts seem to have played a major role in the forms of transition between a state-controlled economy and a private economy. In 2000, 89.3% of companies in the province were private companies, representing 78.9% of the province's total production value. The private companies in the clusters, mostly SMEs, form the pillar of Zhejiang's economy. In many respects, the province's development model, and especially that of the Wenzhou zone, is seen by researchers and the authorities as a benchmark, and is presented as a sort of role model for other provinces to follow, rather like the 'third Italy' model in Europe some thirty years ago.

From this point of view, is it possible to see Zhejiang as a sort of 'Third China'?

What can we learn from the Zhejiang clusters and what, if any, are their specific characteristics? This is the second area that we will look to address now.

9.3 The Zhejiang Clusters: A 'Third China'? Similarities, Differences and Theoretical Revisions

The brief retrospective above relating to the development of the Zhejiang clusters presents many strong similarities with the phenomena observed in the development of European clusters. These similarities in terms of observed dynamics must not, however, obscure the significant differences that exist. These differences relate to the development structures of the districts — the very factors that render the clusters highly specific.

We will now look at each of these two points in turn.

9.3.1 *The Zhejiang Districts: Clusters Like any Other?*

In many ways, the Zhejiang districts appear to have many similarities with the development observed in Europe and Italy. In this sense, they support the theory of industrial districts as proposed by Italian researchers such as Beccattini, Bagnasco or Garofoli, etc.

The Zhejiang clusters, like the districts in Italy or France (Ganne, Courlet, etc.), have arisen in unexpected locations — in traditionally rural zones where there was previously very little industry.

These industries developed in zones that had been relatively neglected by the government. It is precisely because they were practically left alone that these zones were forced to develop activities based on the knowledge that they already possessed.

The development of activities to complement agriculture was of paramount importance for these low-resource, neglected zones. Indeed, for many of the villages and small-to-average size towns, it was simply a question of survival.

In order to guarantee their survival, these zones adopted a range of complementary activities, either for processing and selling their agricultural products, or as a supplement to agriculture. Examples include small-scale manufacturing in family workshops and the external sale of processed products outside the agricultural season via peddling. These zones gradually became structured around groups of small craft workshops and family units. Through further development, these in turn gave rise to series of groups of SMEs.

These groupings went on to develop in a highly endogenous manner, taking shape and growing through the mobilisation of internal resources.

They organised themselves around poles of specialised production, compensating for their small manufacturing facilities by concentrating activities of the same type in the same local area.

The implementation of small-scale industrial activities in relatively neglected rural zones; the 'spontaneous' development of family workshops and SMEs in the 'urbanised countryside'; significant specialisation in manufacturing and the strong endogenous growth of activities: these are all the ingredients that characterise and determine the birth and development of industrial districts.

Despite these areas of similarity it must be remembered that, during their rapid expansion, the Zhejiang clusters adopted certain previously unseen measures. It is in this way that they differ significantly and as such demand the updating or revision of certain existing theoretical approaches to this question. We will now attempt to draw up a definitive list of these differences.

9.3.2 Distinguishing Features and Differences of the Zhejiang Clusters

It is our belief that the Zhejiang clusters are unique in five areas:

> The absence of strong links between companies; the importance of trade structures; the role of both national and international endogenous networks; the nature of the labour market; the role of local collectives.

We will look at each of these points in turn.

9.3.2.1 The Apparent Absence of Strong Links Between Companies

One of the central points in the theory of industrial districts is the belief that the accumulation of companies specialising in the same activity in the same location allows these companies to develop innovative systems of cooperation, be they formal or informal. Indeed, it is this very fact that constitutes the competitive advantage of districts. This system of intercompany links compensates for what the companies lack in size through a genuine economy of transaction costs. This close relationship permits more rapid adaptability and flexibility than is the case with isolated companies, and defines the development of new types of synergies, under which districts draw upon their efficiency and create their differential competitive advantages. The key to districts' success lies in these forms of intercompany cooperation.

It would appear, however, that this is not true in the case of the Zhejiang clusters.

Although a high concentration of workshops and SMEs working in the same industrial sector can be observed in each of the province's specialised clusters, the fiercely independent, even secretive culture that exists both between and within these firms is surprising. Besides client-supplier type relationships, few other types of links can be observed, and there is apparently very little mutual assistance and cooperation. There are only a few scattered groupings of entrepreneurs, forming loose information centres or acting as interlocutors with public collectives (see Section 9.3.2.5).

There have been some attempts to analyse this absence of links between companies in more detail. The first studies carried out in this area[23] demonstrate the weakness of intercompany links other than the traditional client-supplier economic relationship. Other forms of business and cultural relationships that, for example, form the very basis of the economic effectiveness of Italian districts and their innovative dynamics, appear to be almost completely absent in this case. It would also appear that family structures — the dominant force in the companies of Zhejiang — contribute to the insular nature of the companies and to their isolation.

This poses a number of questions. If intercompany relationships (other than economic ones) are of such little importance, to what can the dynamism of these zones be attributed? What 'advantage' do these companies gain from being grouped together? Are access to services and the availability of labour sufficient criteria in this case? In the absence of horizontal local relationships, what other types of channels define and galvanise this type of grouping? What other formal or informal links exist? It seems that the Zhejiang model operates in complete opposition to the central features of Italian districts, a fact that causes further problems in our understanding of the phenomenon.

9.3.2.2 *The Importance of the Trade Dimension*

Whilst there are few observable intercompany links in the Zhejiang clusters, these clusters are notable for the innovative role played by

---

[23] See our first studies in Zhejiang and interviews with researchers and entrepreneurs in Hangzhou, Yiwu, Yongkang and Wenzhou in summer 2006, made possible with the help of the the Center For Research of Private Economy of Zhejiang.

trade poles and networks. A number of clusters have implemented their own trade structures for locally manufactured products. In Zhejiang, some towns have formed their own clusters — not for the manufacture of industrial goods, but for the trade of goods produced on a provincial, even national level. A number of similar networks are currently developing in other provinces.

This phenomenon is clearly illustrated by the city of Yiwu, situated at the heart of Zhejiang.

Following the re-opening of the village market in 1979, the 1980s saw the city of Yiwu open an accessory market (tools, small household goods, etc.). Initially, in attempt to retain the local peddling tradition, the market was supplied by the travelling confectionery traders[24] who wandered the regions of China. Providing the village with new items, which were often unavailable in the shops during this time of shortage, these traders' products began to be manufactured locally by family workshops. The products were then sold to the local market at highly competitive prices. This was the beginning of the accessory market, which led to the development of craft workshops and later to small companies. From this consumer goods market, the city developed a specialist clothing market, and later a utensil market. A decade later the city was filled with enormous exhibition centres, open 350 days per year, providing the specialised industries of Zhejiang — as well as those from other parts of China — with a huge collective market. In fact, this market is so large, that major international companies such as Carrefour and Walmart have recently established their Asian distribution facilities in the city. In only a few years, the city of Yiwu has made trade its principal activity, and has become a sort of cluster dedicated to trade.

Although these clusters do not have a highly formal structure, their existence will give rise to a number of specialised activities in districts around a local market, creating future clusters and

---

[24] The history of Yiwu's market dates back to the Qing dynasty and the bartering tradition: sweets for bird feathers (鸡毛换糖). Farmers would produce sweets and sell them wherever they could, especially in Jiangxi, where they would be exchanged for bird feathers.

demonstrating the strength of the specific link between manufacturing and trade.

The importance (and in the case of Yiwu, supremacy) of the trade dimension itself poses a number of questions.

Can the performance of the Zhejiang clusters be attributed to this new link that seems to have been discovered between manufacturing and trade? Are the Zhejiang clusters not simply updating the important link with trade that has always been present in these rural areas, as seen in the peddling and trader traditions, and applying this notion to workshops and small companies? Is it not the case that the Zhejiang clusters are developing, albeit on a different level, and adapting for their own context the re-emerging market structures already noted by some researchers? (See Thireau, 2003.) Can this organised trade dimension not be attributed to international globalisation and the increasing importance of global networks?

It again appears that the traditional theory of clusters cannot provide answers to these phenomena.

It is our belief that the Zhejiang clusters have led to the emergence of a new field of study for theoretical reflection.

The theory of clusters, based on an analysis of European districts, focuses primarily — indeed exclusively — on the organisation and optimisation of production systems,[25] according to the formal and informal models outlined above. The theory makes little mention of trade, and where it does, it is only as a secondary consideration. Yet is it not the case that, alongside companies and production systems, one of the principal defining characteristics observed in the Zhejiang clusters is the presence of markets and systems of trade, organised on a mainly local level?

Is it not true that Chinese clusters are defined not only by their organised forms of production, but also by their local trading systems and their insistence on a strong link between manufacturing and trade?

With its over-emphasis on systems of production, the theory of clusters may only be helpful in this case as an aid to any analysis and

---

[25] Has the term LPS, or 'local production systems' not also been used in France to describe industrial districts?

reflection, which in turn must look much more closely at the impact of the dynamics created by the phenomena of trade and the socio-economic relationships that they engender. These phenomena may also compensate for the structural and production system dynamics found in other types of cluster, particularly those in the west.

9.3.2.3 The Role of National and International Exogenous Networks

Another defining characteristic of the Zhejiang clusters — and one which again sets them apart form traditional types of districts — is undoubtedly the importance of the exogenous networks that have developed in the province, some of which are on an international scale.

It has already been shown, of course, that the Zhejiang industrial districts, like many others around the world, were founded upon a strong local base. However, the way in which they have opened up to the outside world seems to have been much more rapid, and on a much larger scale.

In the late 1980s and early 1990s, these districts implemented a policy of opening up to the north, north-east and north-west of China. They subsequently expanded their networks — especially their trade networks — on a national scale, and almost as quickly onto an international scale.

These networks all have one thing in common: they remain highly local or provincial in nature, and almost exclusively comprise people of Zhejiang origin. In this respect, the Wenzhou zone is unique in its successful development of large system of international branching, reaching as far as major western cities such as Paris — networks consisting mainly of people of Wenzhou origin.

This point does, however, have a counterbalance — namely a tendency to resist external investment. In Wenzhou, there are almost no companies from other provinces of China or foreign companies.[26] The province's social structure is therefore very strong. There is no doubt that this strong, particularly local culture, founded on family

---

[26] Shi (2006), *Zhongguo minying jingji fazhan baogao.*

links and geographical origin ('同乡'), forms the basis for the regulation of important external networks.

In the current context of globalisation, it is clear that the relationship between local organisation and global networks that seems to characterise the Zhejiang clusters goes some way to explaining their performance.

9.3.2.4 *The Labour Market*

Although the strong growth of the Zhejiang clusters was originally supported only by a local, rural workforce, recent trends have seen an increase in the use of external labour. This trend is of course not unique to the Zhejiang clusters, and can be applied to other industrial development zones and clusters in China. However, in this case it should be highlighted that a movement of this size is specific to the development observed in the clusters of this region.

Very few Chinese studies have so far dealt with the labour market and human resources in clusters.[27]

The birth of rural companies in the 1980s gave rise to the emergence of a local rural workforce, both in Zhejiang and elsewhere. At the beginning of this decade, following the implementation of the family responsibility system, many farmers changed to other economic activities in the industrial and service sectors. This agricultural exodus was also accompanied by intraprovincial mobility — 'leaving the land without leaving the countryside' (离土不离乡).

Then, in a climate of increasing liberalisation and economic development, there was a change in the nature of internal migration in China. From 1985 onwards, there was an increase in interprovincial mobility — 'leaving the land and the countryside' (离土又离乡).

---

[27] We are aware of two studies that have been carried out in Zhejiang since 2000. The first looked at 100 private companies in Hangzhou, Wenzhou, Taizhou, Quzhou and Yuyaoporte, focusing on social protection and social advantages for employees is private companies. The second looked at 104 clusters in Zhejiang, and studied the mobility of the rural labour force. Shi (2006), *Zhongguo minying jingji fazhan baogao*, Vol. 2, Chapter 13; Xu and Tang (2004), '*Jiyu chanye jiqun chengzhang de Zhejiangsheng nongcun laodongli zhuanyi shizheng yanjiu*'.

The migratory flow was therefore mainly from rural areas to urban areas.

Today, the Zhejiang labour market mainly comprises migrant farmers from the region and from other provinces. Without exception, the workforces of the companies that we visited in district-level (县级市) or regional-level (地级市) cities comprised between 70% and 80% migrant workers. Xu and Tang's study (2004) on 219 manufacturing units in Zhejiang's 104 clusters confirms that, of 38,010,000 employees, 82.89% are from an agricultural background, and that 34.56% of these do not possess a Zhejiang *hukou*. In this climate of high geographical mobility, especially from one rural area to another or to small and medium-sized cities, a significant rate of professional retraining can be observed, as seen in large cities. When migrants arrive in Zhejiang, the majority enter the industrial sector (manufacturing, construction), with the second largest number entering the service sector (trading, hospitality). Their salary and living and working conditions are at least equal to, if not superior to, those in large conurbations such as Shanghai or in other clusters such as Guangdong. In order to attract its workforce, Zhejiang now allows urban hukou registration for migrant agricultural workers.

Whilst this is common a phenomenon in a number of clusters, its size and distinctiveness in Zhejiang is a distinguishing feature of these clusters. This remains, however, an unexplored area of study.

How does the process of migration to Zhejiang work? Are the patterns of migration largely temporary or more permanent and based on new career paths? How does this migrant population integrate into the strong social structure of the local residents? All these aspects constitute points for analysis via a comparison between the situation in Zhejiang and the labour markets of clusters in other Chinese provinces (Guangdong, Shandong, etc.) or in other types of cities.

9.3.2.5 *The Specific Role of Politics and Local Collectives*

The final area in which the Zhejiang clusters seem distinctive is the form of governmental intervention that can be observed, particularly in terms of local collectives. To varying degrees, local collectives seem always to have played a relatively decisive role, either as interveners, arbitrators or in a complementary role.

As we saw in section 9.2.3.2, although economic reform had already been in progress for a decade, it wasn't until the end of the 1990s that private companies were able to operate without needing the approval of local politicians. These politicians were able to engage in the so-called 'red hat' practice, designed to give a 'collective' label to activities that were actually private.

In due course, under the transitional phase, the economic role of local collectives could be seen on several levels:

— a decision-making role, in terms of resource allocation (authorising sales, approving projects, granting tax incentives to companies, etc.) and decisions about areas of specialisation;
— a motivational role, by putting in place resources and equipment connected with the relevant manufacturing activities (an example being the market halls put in place by the cities of Yiwu, Yongkang, etc.);
— a limited coordination role, without direct intervention on economic actors.

From this point of view, the Zhejiang model appears to represent a highly specific model of interaction between economics and politics. Whilst, as already mentioned, 90% of companies are privatised, there is a significant internal overlap between companies and the government. Many private companies, especially larger ones, have created a Party committee within the company in pursuit of political correctness. Dating back to 1987, this phenomenon was widespread in the 1990's, especially among large companies. The Party's recognition of the private economy, at its 15th Congress in 1997, seems only to have accelerated this movement. In 2004, more than 2000 companies in Wenzhou had a Party committee (党支部), and 28 large companies had a Party commission (党委).[28] At the same time, private entrepreneurs

---

[28] Further up the CCP hierarchy due to the number of company employees.

began to join political bodies and were encouraged to take official posts. In Zhejiang, there were around 20 private entrepreneurs present at the 10th Popular Assembly and at the Political Consultative Conference (政治协商会议). This is evidence of the complex relationship between economics and politics in the different areas of government.

It is clear that the Zhejiang industrial clusters are highly distinctive in the important role played by politics and local collectives.

This is a far cry from the theoretical model seen in Italian districts, as proposed at the time by Beccatini, Garofoli, etc. This theory accords only a secondary or minor role to the interventions of collectives (as opposed to the theory of clusters, which calls for certain forms of regulation and governmental intervention). Instead, an industrial district should be created 'spontaneously' by the principal economic actors (i.e. companies), with no intervention from political actors.

Yet the strength of the Zhejiang clusters appears to lie, as is often the case in China, in the dynamic alliance between private actors and forms of governmental intervention. Is this an example of the occasionally proposed notion of 'State Capitalism'? Their dynamism can be explained to some extent by the support given to specialisation poles by the various public collectives. This support from public collectives has allowed the specialised cities of Zhejiang to create their own markets for specific products (such as in Yongkang, a city specialising in hardware, etc.). Indeed, it was the Yiwu Municipality that had the idea of developing a permanent market fair system, establishing the city as a trade cluster. The role of local collectives is far from marginal, yet neither is it interventionist. In this case, they play an essential complementary role, along the lines of observations made in other Chinese clusters (see Xu, thesis in progress, 2006).

This system of public intervention, in which collectives no longer intervene directly as economic actors, but play a powerful accompanying role to specialised development, represents one of the most original features of the Zhejiang clusters.

9.4 Conclusion

The jewel in the crown of Chinese industrial development, Zhejiang is held up as a benchmark to other provinces in the country, and its industrial districts have developed in a unique and original manner. This therefore offers us a new perspective on, and leads us to reconsider the approaches to districts found in historical models. These are largely dependent on the geographical locations in question, which are mostly European, or more specifically Italian.

It cannot be denied that Zhejiang has experienced a phenomenon of the 'industrial district' type. Taking into account a range of factors, the province owes much of its strong growth to the extraordinary expansion of its highly concentrated zones of small industries. These extremely specialised zones can be found in all areas of the region, and the distribution of activities in the province is characterised by significant differences in the goods manufactured (following the principle of 'one product per village and one sector per region' (一镇一品, 一乡一业)). Another important factor is that Zhejiang, a province that has been relatively neglected by the central government, has developed autonomously, creating its own avenues for expansion. The province has seen the development of a genuine dynamic of industrial districts, a dynamic whose size, importance and intensity clearly single out the Zhejiang clusters as an important benchmark in the range of types of cluster observed around the world.

With this in mind, it is also important to stress the originality and uniqueness of the Zhejiang model, and how it appears to be in conflict with certain central aspects of the theory of industrial districts whilst developing new synergies in new contexts.

It can be seen that the most significant difference relates to the weakness of intercompany co-operation observed in the Zhejiang districts — a central feature of the Italo-European theory of industrial districts. It is precisely because entrepreneurs in a given specialised zone developed both formal and informal, local systems of co-operation that these districts performed well. Yet in Zhejiang, a lack of co-operation between companies seems to prevail. Their success cannot therefore be attributed to this area.

The relationships involved in the development of the Zhejiang clusters are of an entirely new type, and until now little light has been shed upon them. It has been shown that, in the Zhejiang clusters, there is an unusual role accorded to the trade dimension, alongside the manufacturing dimension, the importance of national and international external networks, and the influence of local collectives both within their locality and from a distance.

However, rather than looking at each specific difference in turn, it is important to understand that it is more a question of a shift in these clusters' centre of gravity that has given rise their unique structural and dynamic configuration. The Zhejiang clusters' dynamic lies not so much in how their production is organised, but in the relationship between manufacturing and trade structures, networks and politics, developed as a tool for regulation and stimulation. Could it be argued that the presence of strong trade structures, organised and controlled by local collectives, plays the same regulatory/dynamic role here as the system of co-operation/competition at production level does in western clusters? Rather than relying on direct, formal or informal collaboration between companies, the Zhejiang model constitutes a *third system of regulation*, which allows the circulation of important production and trade information, avoids competition, is open to innovation, etc. This whole system is supplied by external networks, which play a continuing motivational role by guaranteeing market exposure.

This unique organisational model with its own dynamic requires us to reassess the traditional approaches to industrial districts in a new light.

References

BECATTINI, Giacomo. (1991). 'The Industrial District as a Creative Milieu,' in *Industrial Change & Regional Development*, Georges Benko & Mick Dunford, (eds.), Belhaven Press, p. 329.

CHEN, Ling, CAO, Zhenghan. (2006). 'Zhongguo minying qiye chengzhang: zhidu yu nengli'(Développement des entreprises privées:système et capacités), in ZHANG Shuguang, JIN Xinagrong (2006) *Zhongguo zhidu bianqian de anli yanjiu* (Case studies in China's institutional change), pp. 165–203.

GANNE, Bernard. (1990). '*Industrialisation diffuse et systèmes industriels localisés: essai de bibliographie critique du cas français,*' Institut International d'Etudes Sociales, BIT, coll. 'Série Bibliographique', **14**, Genève, p. 124.

GANNE, Bernard. (1991). 'Les approches du local et des systèmes industriels locaux: esquisse de bilan critique du cas français,' in *Sociologie du Travail,* **4**, pp. 545–576.

GANNE, Bernard. (1992). 'Place et évolution des systèmes industriels locaux en France: économie politique d'une transformation,' in *Les régions qui gagnent: districts et réseaux. Les nouveaux paradigmes de la géographie économique,* (G. Benko et A. Lipietz, sous la dir.), Paris, PUF, pp. 315–346.

GANNE, Bernard. (1994). 'Les PME dans le système français: heurts et malheurs et mode de gouvernance', PME et développement économique en Europe, sous la direction de Arnaldo Bagnasco et Charles F. Sabel, La Découverte, p. 201.

GANNE, Bernard. (1995). 'France: Behind Small and Medium Size Enterprises Lies the State,' in *Small and Medium-size enterprises'*, Bagnasco A., Sabel C. (eds.), Pinter, London, pp. 115–133.

GANNE, Bernard. (2000). 'PME, districts et nouvelles territorialités,' in *Les dynamiques de PME: Approches internationales'* (B. Courault, P. Trouve, ss. la dir. de), PUF, pp. 51–74.

GANNE, Bernard. (2001). 'Changes in Policies Support for Industry and SMEs in France Since the 1970s: Towards a New Type of Public Intervention,' *Asian Small Business Review,* **3**(1), 136–154.

GANNE, Bernard. (2004). 'New Development of European Industrial Districts: Changing the Approaches, Symposium 'The development of chinese clusters,' 6–7 décembre 2004, Guangzhou, Zhongshan University (Chine).

JIN, Xiangrong, ZHU, Xiwei. (2001). 'Wenzhou moshi bianqian yu chuangxin' (Evolution et innovation du modèle Wenzhou), *Jingji lilun yu jingji guanli,* **8**.

JIN, Xiangrong, ZHU, Xiwei. (2002). 'Zhuanyehua chanyequ de qiyuan yu yanhua-yige lilun yu lishi shijiao de kaocha,' (Origines et évolution des zones de production spécialisées-Regard théorique et historique), *Jingji Yanjiu,* **8**.

LI, Youmai et PAVE, Francis. (1999). 'La Chine actuelle et le marché. L'émergence des PME familiales dans la dynamique de développement économique', *Annales des Mines,* mars, pp. 29–42.

SHENG, Shihao, ZHENG, Yanwei. (2004). *Zhejiang xianxiang-chanye jiqun yu quyu jingji fazhan* (Phénomène du Zhejiang-clusters industriel et développement économique régionale, éd. Qinghua University, p. 357.

SHI, Jinchuan, JIN, X., ZHAO, W., LUO, W. *et al.* (2002). *Zhidu bianqian yu jingji fazhan-Wenzhou moshi yanjiu,* 'La transformation institutionnelle et le développement économique: la recherche sur le modèle de Wni Zhou,' Université Zhejiang, Hangzhou.

SHI, Jinchuan. (2006). *Zhongguo minying jingji fazhan baogao* (Rapport du développement de l'économie privée en Chine) ed. Jingji kexue, p. 390.

THIREAU, Isabelle. (2002). *Le retour du marchand dans la Chine rurale*, Études rurales No. 161–162 Janvier-Juin, p. 270.

WANG, Jici, TONG, Xin. (2002). 'Industrial Clusters in China: Alternative Pathways to Global Local Perspective,' *Innovation Systems and Innovation Policy in Developing Countries with a Perspective of China*. Edited by Gu, S. and Alcorta, L., Routledge in Association with UNU Press (Forthcoming in 2003).

WANG, Jici, ZHU, Huacheng, TONG, Xin. (2001) 'Districtization in Zhejiang Province of China: With Reference to Datang Sock/Stocking Industrial District,' Paper presented at the residential conference of the IGU Commission on the Organization of Industrial Space, Turin, Italy.

WANG, Jici. (2001). *Chuangxin de kongjian: qiye jiqun yu quyu fazhan* (Innovative spaces: entreprises clusters and regional development), Beijing, Beijing University Press.

WANG, Jici. (2004). *Jiqun yu quyu fazhan La croissance des clusters et le développement régional*, Kexue jingji chubanshe, Beijing.

WANG, Z., QIAN, X. (2003). *Cong xiangcun gongyehua dao chengshihua — Zhejiang xianndaihua de guocheng, tezheng yu dongli*, 'De l'industrialisation des villages à l'urbanisation: le processus, les caractéristiques et la motivation de la modernisation du Zhejiang,' Université Zhejiang, Hangzhou.

XU, Jianniu Hou fatuan zhuyi (2007). Post Local State Corporatism — An Institutional Analysis on the Economic Actions of Township Governments during China's Market Transformation, Thesis, University Sun Yat-sen, China.

XU, Weixiang, TANG, Gennian. (2004). 'Jiyu chanye jiqun chengzhang de Zhejiangsheng nongcun laodongli zhuanyi shizheng yanjiu' (Etude empirique sur la mobilité des mains d'oeuvre rurales dans les clusters du Zhejiang).

ZHANG, Shuguang, JIN, Xinagrong. (2006). *Zhongguo zhidu bianqian de anli yanjiu* (Case studies in China's institutional change), Ed. Economie et finances de Chine, Université du Zhejiang, p. 730.

ZHU, Huacheng. (2003). *Zhejiang chanyequn — chanye wangluo, chengzhang guiji yu fazhan dongli*, 'Agglomération industrielle du Zhejiang: le réseau industriel, la piste de grandissement et la motivation du développement,' Université Zhejiang, Hangzhou.

Chapter 10

Distribution System of China's Industrial Clusters: Case Study of Yiwu China Commodity City[1]

Ke Ding

10.1 Introduction

As for the issue of upgrading developing countries' industrial clusters, the role of global value chains (GVCs) has been extolled for some time. Compared to traditional approaches, which paid much attention to the local relationships between enterprises and institutions, the GVCs approach emphasises the clusters' linkages with the external world even more.[2] Along with the constant advance of economic globalisation, it is almost taken for granted that industrial clusters in developing countries are able to develop only when they are involved in the global production and distribution network controlled by trans-national companies.[3]

However, the rise of some of China's industrial clusters suggests the possibility of building a different theoretical framework. After China gave up its economic policies based on socialistic planning, the domestic market which had been restrained for so long began to

---

[1] This paper is a highly revised version of the 2nd chapter of the author's doctoral thesis (Ding, 2006) and has been originally presented as a Discussion Paper at the Institute of Developing Economies, Japan External Trade Organisation.

[2] Schmitz (2006) has done a lucid survey of the literature on these approaches.

[3] See Global Value Chain Initiative website: http://www.globalvaluechains.org (accessed October 2, 2006).

balloon. The total retail amount of China's social consumer commodities increased nearly 30 times during the period 1978 to 2003 (National Statistics Trading and Foreign Economic Relations Statistic Secretary, ed., 1990–2004). In order to respond to such huge demand, numerous small merchants and small producers began to appear in the clusters and the cities, thus reviving the local tradition of either crafts production or long-distance peddling.[4] In this process, the existing production and distribution networks became increasingly inefficient.

The above-mentioned facts caused an interesting phenomenon. As a platform that gathers numerous small producers and small merchants, the traditional marketplaces made its appearance in most of China's clusters and cities. During the period 1978 to 2003, at the country level, the total number of marketplaces increased from 33,302 to 81,017 (National Statistics Trading and Foreign Economic Relations Statistic Secretary, ed., 2004). In Zhejiang province where marketplaces first appeared and are the most developed, the number increased from 1322 to 4036 (Jin, 2007, p. 35). At the same time, the number of clusters in Zhejiang expanded to more than 1000. Of which the domestic share of 52 clusters amounts to over 30% in 2002 (Jin, 2004, p. 13). Almost every industrial cluster has not less than one marketplace. The relationship between the development of industrial clusters and the expansion of the traditional marketplace must be studied.

This chapter discusses this issue by focusing primarily on the distribution function of these marketplaces. In most developing countries, the difficulty of constructing a distribution system specific to small and medium enterprises (SMEs) and the limitation of the size of the domestic market have usually been the most important factors in constraining the development of industrial clusters. Thus, the reasons why traditional marketplaces are useful to SMEs in marketing in modern China must be clarified first. This work will be the key to understanding the other functions of modern China's marketplaces.

---

[4] For details relating to Zhejiang province where industrial clusters are most highly-developed in China, see Ding (2006, Chapter 1).

This chapter explains these aspects of the marketplaces' distribution function in detail, using Yiwu China Commodity City as a case study, because it is the largest marketplace in China's clusters. In the rest of this paper: Section 10.2 gives a brief introduction of our survey area; Sections 10.3–10.5 explore the features of the distribution system that has Yiwu Market as its hub, and; Section 10.6 concludes this paper.

10.2 Brief Introduction to Yiwu China Commodity City

10.2.1 *Yiwu China Commodity City*

As a *county-level city*, Yiwu is located in Jinhua city, the centre of Zhejiang province, with a total population of over 1.6 million people.[5] By the end of the 1970s, Yiwu was an impoverished rural area. In 1978, the GDP of Yiwu was a mere 128 million yuan, of which agricultural industry accounted for nearly 60%. In the 1980s, Yiwu started growing very rapidly. The GDP of Yiwu exploded to 35,206 million Yuan by 2006, of which the secondary sector accounted for nearly 50% (Yiwu Statistics, ed., 1978–2006). The integrated development level of Yiwu is listed 15th in the top 100 counties and cities of China (Zhejiang China Commodity City Group Co., Ltd., ed., 2006).

This transformation resulted from the rapid development of a huge commodity wholesale market — Yiwu China Commodity City (the Yiwu Market).[6] The local government formally established the Yiwu Market in 1982. Since 1991, this market has been holding the top position as China's largest industrial products market. Currently, the Yiwu Market gathers over 400,000 commodities in 1901 categories from 43 industries. It is even said that this market has become the production and distribution centre of daily necessities in the world.

The commodities of Yiwu Market are currently distributed in not only China's domestic market, but also in 212 countries and regions

---

[5] Of which one million are non-native residents. This fact illustrates that Yiwu had become a typical trading city.

[6] This market had been called the Yiwu Commodity Market until 1992. In this paper, we call both markets the Yiwu Market for brevity.

in the world market (Zhejiang China Commodity City Group Co., Ltd., ed., 2006). At the same time, this market tends to be a main distribution channel for various industrial clusters. In terms of production areas, we can roughly divide the industrial clusters related to Yiwu into three groups. The first group consists of the clusters formed within Yiwu. The second group consists of the clusters located in other areas of the Zhejiang province. The third group includes those clusters in other parts of China. It was estimated by the Yiwu government that the shares of these three groups in the Yiwu Market are 40%, 30%, 30% respectively.[7] How has the Yiwu Market connected these clusters to such broad domestic and overseas demand? The answer must be a key factor in understanding the external linkages of China's industrial clusters.

This paper attempts to answer this question by primarily using the publication known as the '*Specialized Markets and Regional Development — Focusing on Yiwu Markets Radiation Zone*' (SMRD). *Commodities World News* is a newspaper that reports on the Yiwu Market. During 2004 and 2005, this newspaper sent a large number of reporters to China's 25 provinces to investigate the business relationship between Yiwu and these areas. The main result of this investigation was published as the SMRD. Other reports have been published on the website of Yiwu Xinwen Wang (Yiwu News Network).[8] Since the small producers and small merchants related with Yiwu are scattered over an extremely wide area, the SMRD and the website information are the most appropriate material for our work.[9]

Due to the following two reasons, this paper is confined to discussing how the clusters in Zhejiang province became connected to the Yiwu Market and How the Yiwu Market became connected to the domestic market.

The first reason is due to the importance of the domestic market. As stated above, the domestic market is usually the most important

---

[7] According to interviews with some staff of the Yiwu government (September, 2007).

[8] http://www.ywnews.cn/gzywscjj/index.htm (accessed October 2, 2006).

[9] The author has done field work in Yiwu since 2002. However, in order to keep the material consistent, this paper uses field results as complementary material only.

bottleneck in the development of industrial clusters in developing countries. Thus, a study of the Yiwu Market's domestic linkages must be given priority over any others.

The second reason is the lack of reference material. There are two parts in the SMRD. The first part is entitled '*Yiwu Market and Zhejiang's industrial clusters*' and contains many reports on the clusters in Zhejiang's other areas. The second part of the SMRD is entitled '*Yiwu Market and the whole country*.' Though it consists of three reports on the clusters in China's other areas, the main content of this part is about the sales outlets of Yiwu commodities in China. Thus, we have to narrow the focus of this study. But, since the difference in the second and third group of Yiwu related industrial clusters is mainly based on distance, this does not affect our final conclusion.

10.2.2 *Two Important Actors*

To understand how the Yiwu Market has created domestic linkages, two key actors deserve attention. The first actor is the local Yiwu merchant who has a long tradition of peddling. At the beginning of the Ching dynasty, in order to acquire rooster feathers for compost, a few peasants in Yiwu began to move around the neighbouring rural area, selling brown sugar in exchange for feathers. Their trading area gradually expanded to seven provinces and their range of merchandise was also extended to cover many different kinds of daily necessities. Gradually, a peddler's organisation, which is called Qiaotang Bang, was formed. At its peak in the second decade of the twentieth century, Qiaotang Bang had 7000–8000 members (Zhejiang Province Zhengxie Historical Data Committee, ed., 1997, pp. 301–303). After the PRC was established, Qiaotang Bang was dissolved and their peddling activity was discontinued for a while. However, they started peddling again in 1963, at the latest.[10] In the 1970s, these vendors

---

[10] Wu Zhixiong, '*Shichang luodi qian de timing*'. Yiwu Xinwen Wang, http://www.ywnews.cn/20040309/ca777.htm (accessed October 2, 2006).

spontaneously formed two periodic markets in Yiwu (Zhang, ed., 1993, p. 35).[11]

Along with the establishment of the regular market in 1982, the Yiwu peddlers split into two groups. The first group continued to peddle in various places around China. This chapter will mainly pursue their business activity in detail.

The second group became booth-keepers at the Yiwu Market. In order to purchase commodities, they went to various clusters located in Zhejiang, Guangdong and other areas of China in the early days. Some of them gradually took part in the manufacturing process. In the beginning, they primarily organised small-scale family craft production or ran workshops themselves. Since the mid-1990s, as a result of capital accumulation, these merchants began to invest substantially in building modern mass-production factories. Up until 2004, no less than eight large clusters were formed by these merchants in Yiwu, namely socks, shirts, wool, accessories, zippers, toys, key sticks and printing (Ding, 2006, Chapter 4). The changes in the industrial structure of Yiwu City bear out such surprising formation of industrial clusters. As Figure 10.1 indicates, after the rapid expansion of the tertiary sector, Yiwu's secondary sector sustained remarkable growth from the 1990s onwards. This changing pattern in the industrial structure is quite contrary to the well-known Petty-Clark Law.

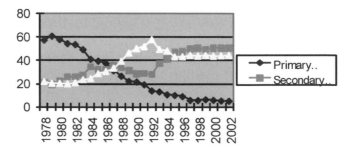

Figure 10.1:   Changes in the Industrial Structure of Yiwu City.

Source: Lu, Bai, Wang (2003). The original source is Yiwu Statistics. ed. (1978–2002).

---

[11] However, their formal organisation never revived.

The second actor that deserves attention is local government. We can derive three features of the Yiwu government's behaviour from Table 10.1.[12]

First, the local government of Yiwu has formulated a few policies for deregulating the private sector. By 1983, Chinese peasants were strictly prohibited from engaging in any commerce. In spite of this, the Yiwu government has partially permitted peddling since 1963. Under the pretext that rooster feathers were still important for compost, they issued many licenses to peddlers. It was confirmed that the number of licenses had been 7000 only in 1980. In 1982, the local government created the well-known policy of '*Sige Xuke*' (Four Permissions). This permitted Yiwu's peasants to engage in four kinds of business, namely: (1) engage in commerce in the city; (2) engage in long-distance logistics; (3) competing with public-owned enterprises, and; (4) opening commodity market. Shortly thereafter, the informal periodic market in Yiwu was altered to become the regular Yiwu Commodity Market.

Second, the local government took measures to manage transactions in the Yiwu Market. Early on, the Yiwu government established a specific managing committee, which consisted of a few local staff in government departments. In 1994, they established a market-managing company called Zhejiang China Commodity City Group (ZCCC Group), which listed its stock on the Shanghai Stock Exchange in 2002. In the meanwhile, the local government departments continued to maintain links with the market in the areas of quality control, forgery exposition and so on.

Third, the Yiwu government provided various infrastructures to the Yiwu Market. The regular market was originally built in 1982. As business expanded and infrastructure and other constraints became felt, a new, second generation market came up in the place of the

---

[12] According to interviews with staff of the Yiwu local government (August, 2002; March and August, 2005; September, 2006). As Ding (2006, see Chapter 4) discusses, the Yiwu government has formulated some policies for fostering the manufacturing sector as well, which are seen in the slogan of the government Yin Shang Zhuan Gong (Exhorting the merchants to from commerce to manufacturing). However, due to paper space is confined, we won't investigate this issue in further detail here.

Table 10.1:   The Profile of Yiwu China Commodity City.

Year	No. of Markets in Yiwu by Generation	Total no. of Booths in Yiwu	Total Transaction Volume of Yiwu Market (Million Yuan)	Policies or Measures for Managing Yiwu Market
1974	Two periodic markets	—	—	Partially deregulation
1982	One first-generation markets, one periodical markets	705	3.92	The Four Permissions
1984	One second-generation markets	1870	23.21	'Xing Shang Jian Xian' (Developing the county by fostering the development of commerce)
1986	One third-generation markets	5500	100.29	—
1992	One fourth-generation markets	16,000	2054	'Yin Shang Zhuan Gong' (Exhorting the merchants to from commerce to manufacturing)
1993	One fourth-generation markets	16,000	4515	The establishment of a market managing company (ZCCC Group)
1995	Two fifth-generation markets	34,000	15,200	
2000	More than three fifth-generation markets	34,500	19,289	The promotion of foreign trade
2002	One sixth-generation market; more than three fifth-generation markets	42,000	22,998	ZCCC Group listed stocks on the Shanghai stock exchange
2006	Two sixth-generation markets; seven fifth-generation markets	58,000	31,500	—

Sources: Lu, Bai, Wang (2003, pp. 38–45); Zhejiang China Commodity City Group Co. Ltd., ed. (2005); Zhejiang Province Zhengxie Historical Data Committee, ed. (1997); Zhang Wenxue and others, ed. (1993, pp. 34–40); the author's fieldwork conducted in August 2002, February 2004, March 2005, August 2005, August 2006 and September 2007.

original. Thus future generations replaced the earlier ones periodically. Now it is the sixth generation market. The number of the booths at all markets reached 58,000 by 2006. In this process, the service sectors which support the market such as logistics and financial systems have been improved accordingly.

10.3 Linkages Between Zhejiang Industrial Clusters and the Yiwu Market

As a starting point for exploring the Yiwu Market's domestic linkages, Section 10.3 explores the linkages between the Yiwu Market and the industrial clusters in Zhejiang province, which sell commodities to Yiwu Market.[13] We find four things worth noting in Table 10.2.

First, the clusters that have linkages with Yiwu are widely distributed in Zhejiang province. Among nine cities of this province, except the cities of Hangzhou and Zhoushan, the rest of the seven cities' clusters are connected with Yiwu. Though data is limited, the share of sales of some industrial clusters in Yiwu as a percentage of the cluster's total sales is considerable. In addition to the features of the clusters in Yiwu, we can infer that Yiwu is becoming a main distribution channel for Zhejiang's clusters.[14]

Second, the Yiwu Market is an important channel for selling commodities to both the domestic market and the overseas market. As Table 10.2 shows, among a total of 36 clusters in Zhejiang, 22

---

[13] Ding (2006, Chapter 4) has already analysed how several clusters were formed within Yiwu. This work illustrates that the owners of Yiwu's factories came mainly from the merchants at the Yiwu Market. Along with their growth, the marketing measures of these factories are becoming diverse. However, even at present, most of the factories still attempt to keep booths in this market. This fact can be easily confirmed by various shopping guides of the Yiwu Market. See Zhejiang China Commodity City Group (2005, 2006).

[14] Indeed, the firms in Zhejiang clusters have various marketing measures. Most of them have made use of local specialised markets or local merchants' networks for a long time. Some have even constructed their own sales network. Even after they got connected to Yiwu, they would never abandon these existing channels. Thus, it is difficult to assert that Yiwu Market has become the only distribution channel for these clusters.

Table 10.2:   Aspects of Some Zhejiang Industrial Clusters' Linkages with the Yiwu Market

City	County	Town	Main Industry	Ultimate Destination*	Ways to Establish Business Relations with Yiwu Market**	Share of Sales***	Leading Firms' Commodities
Ningbo	Various Places	—	Apparel	1	1,2	—	Yes
	Cixi	Various places	Small home appliances	1,2	1,2,3,4	One of the largest domestic sales outlets	Yes
Shaoxing	Zhuji	19 Towns	Socks	1,2	1,2	—	—
	Zhuji	Shaxiahu	Pearls	1,2	2	—	Yes
	Shengzhou	Various places	Neckties	1	2,3	—	Yes

(Continued)

Table 10.2: (*Continued*)

City	County	Town	Main Industry	Ultimate Destination*	Ways to Establish Business Relations with Yiwu Market**	Share of Sales***	Leading Firms' Commodities
Taizou	Xianju	Xiage, other towns	Gifts	1,2	2,4	—	—
	Wenling	Daxi	Water pumps	1	3	—	Yes
	Wenling	Various places	Hats	1,2	—	80% (Nanjian village)	—
	Wenling	Various places	Footwear	1,2	—	Majority	—
	Linhai	Duqiao	Glasses	—	2	—	—
	Luqiao	Various places	Plastic products	1,2 (80%)	2	50%	Yes

(*Continued*)

Table 10.2:   (Continued)

City	County	Town	Main Industry	Ultimate Destination*	Ways to Establish Business Relations with Yiwu Market**	Share of Sales***	Leading Firms' Commodities
Wenzhou	Various places	—	Footwear	1,2	1,2	—	Yes
		—	Glasses	1,2	2	—	—
		—	Lighters	1,2	2	—	—
		—	Shavers	1,2	2	40–50%	—
		—	Zippers	1,2	1,2,3,4	—	—
	Various places in the city	—	Stationery	1,2	2,4	—	Yes
	Pingyang	Zhenglou	Gifts, calendars	1,2	2	50%	Yes
	Yongjia	Qiaotou	Plastic parts of accessories	1	2	80%	—
Quzhou		Wucun	Buttons	1,2	2,3	—	Yes
	Longyou		Bamboo wares (Bird vages, etc.)	2	3	95% or more	—
	Muchen		Mats	1,2	2,3	—	—

(Continued)

Table 10.2: (Continued)

City	County	Town	Main Industry	Ultimate Destination*	Ways to Establish Business Relations with Yiwu Market**	Share of Sales***	Leading Firms' Commodities
Lishui	Various places	—	Stationery	1,2	2,3	Nearly 50%	—
	Longquan	Longyuan	Toy snakes	—	3	80% in Zhangcun village	—
		Various places	Swords	2	2,3	33.3%	—
	Qingyuan	Various places	Bamboo chopsticks	1,2	2	Nearly 50%	Yes
	Yunhe	Various places	Wooden toys	2	3	Majority	—
	Suichang	Various places	Black pottery	—	1 or 3	—	—
Jinhua	Wucheng	Shafan	Chinese knots	—	3	Majority	—
	Pujiang	Various places	Crystal crafts	1,2	2,3	10%	—
		Various places	Handmade sewing commodities	1,2	2,1 or 3	—	—

(Continued)

Table 10.2:   (Continued)

City	County	Town	Main Industry	Ultimate Destination*	Ways to Establish Business Relations with Yiwu Market**	Share of Sales***	Leading Firms' Commodities
	Dongyang	Huashui	Chinese knots	1,2	2	Majority	—
		Qianxiang	Leather commodities	2(1 in early period)	2	Majority	—
		Various places	Apparel	1	2,3	Majority	Yes (in the 1990s)
	Lanxi	Various places	Towels	1,2	1,2,3	50%	Yes
	Panan	Various places	Hair accessories ribbons, etc.	—	2 or 3	Majority	—

Source: SMRD.

Notes: *Ultimate Destination.

1: Domestic Market; 2: Overseas Market.

Ways to establish business relations with the Yiwu Market.

1: Yiwu merchants physically go to clusters to place orders. Some expressions in the SMRD reports are: 'Yiwu Market merchants.' However, as the number of merchants who come from other area is small and they mainly sell their local products in Yiwu, most of the 'Yiwu Market merchants' can be considered to be Yiwu merchants.

2: Local firms directly open booths in the Yiwu Market.

3: Local firms, on their own initiatives, engage Yiwu Market merchants in sales.

4: Other ways.

***Share of Sales of Cluster:** Share of the sale of industrial clusters in Yiwu as a percentage of the cluster's total sales.

*****'—': No description.

clusters are using the Yiwu Market for accessing both markets. But, it is difficult to distinguish which kind of market is more attractive. By checking the reports carefully, we can find a rough trend that the domestic market is definitely crucial in the early stages and in recent years, the overseas market is becoming increasingly important. However, even at present, there are still five clusters which have linkages with the Yiwu Market only for access to the domestic market. Whatever the case may be, what is relevant to our theme is that the development of Zhejiang's industrial clusters is dependent on not just the developed countries' markets.

Third, there are various ways to establish business relations with the Yiwu Market. It has been mentioned in Section 10.2 that since the 1980s, a large number of Yiwu merchants went to clusters outside of Yiwu for purchasing. In Table 10.2, we can observe at least six such cases. However, many linkages with the Yiwu Market are created on these clusters' own initiative. As Table 10.2 indicates, in at least 27 clusters, the local firms themselves opened booths in Yiwu. In 15 clusters, local firms engaged Yiwu Market merchants in sales on their own initiatives.

There are three reasons that explain the initiatives of local firms. First, some clusters have a similar tradition of long-distance peddling. Just like Yiwu merchants, the merchants of these areas attempted to revive and spread their business network as well. For example, the people from Wenzhou are called China's Jews.[15] As the most typical case, there are nine Wenzhou clusters which have opened booths in the Yiwu Market. Second, the local governments of some clusters have played a crucial role in establishing linkages with Yiwu. In some neighbouring areas such as Wucheng, Pujiang, Dongyang, Lanxi and Panan, the local governments not only trained local firms on how to get orders from Yiwu merchants, paying a bonus as an incentive to

---

[15] It is said that whether they are in Whenzhou city, outside of Wenzhou but inside China or outside of China, the number of the people originally from Wenzhou accounted for 1,500,000, most of them engaging in business.

stimulate them to strengthen the linkages with Yiwu, but also set up offices in the Yiwu Market themselves.[16]

To emphasise their strong desire, local governments use the ringing slogan of 'Duijie Yiwu' (Form links with Yiwu). Third, the local government of Yiwu has increased the number of booths at the Yiwu Market several times. The sub-leasing of booths also took place at the Yiwu Market. As a result, even as newcomers, SMEs were able to access this market easily.

Fourth, the leading firm's commodities suggest a considerable presence in the Yiwu Market.[17] A lot of scholars in China asserted that along with growth, most of the leading firms will expand their business scale (and work out brand strategy), then a sales network specific to an individual leading firm will be constructed. As a result, the commodities of these firms must disappear in the marketplace (Zheng, 2003). However, as Table 10.2 suggests, there are 12 clusters' leading firms that do not match this view.

10.4   Linkages Between the Yiwu Market and the Markets of China's Main Cities

By analysing the second part of the SMRD, we can roughly divide the flow of Yiwu Market commodities into two stages. The first stage is from Yiwu Market to China's main cities. The second stage is from those main cities to smaller cities or consumers and so on. Section 10.4 focus on the first stage. From a close examination of Table 10.3, three interesting facts emerge.

First, as its first stage, most of the Yiwu Market commodities are traded at the markets of China's main cities. As Table 10.3 indicates, among a total of 52 sales outlets, there are 41 sales outlets directly named as '*market*' or '*the clustering of a few markets*.' Seven sales

---

[16] Interviews with persons in charge of the Yiwu office of Wucheng (September, 2006) and some reports in SMRD. But, it is difficult to confirm the role of local government in the cases in Table 10.2. Thus, we didn't list it as one of the ways to establish business relations with the Yiwu Market.

[17] This paper defines a leading firm as one that is clearly described in the reference material as being in the top level of an industrial cluster.

Table 10.3:   Yiwu Commodities' Main Sales Outlets in China.

Province/ City	Sales Outlets	Yiwu Commodity	Share in Total Sales of Daily Necessities	Ways to Get Connected with Yiwu Market*	Leading Firm's Commodities
Beijing					
—	Beijing Yiwu commodity wholesale market	Daily necessities	—	1,2,4	—
—	Beijing Tianyi market	Socks, other daily necessities	70% or more (Socks)	1,3	Yes
Shanghai					
—	Chenghuang temple market	Daily necessities	50%	1,2	Yes
Chongqing					
—	Chaotianmen general wholesale market	Socks, shirts, other daily necessities	80% (whole Chongqing) (Socks; 70–80% (Shirts)	1	Yes

(*Continued*)

Table 10.3:   (*Continued*)

Province/ City	Sales Outlets	Yiwu Commodity	Share in Total Sales of Daily Necessities	Ways to Get Connected with Yiwu Market*	Leading Firm's Commodities
Inner Mongolia					
Hohhot	Tongda market	National supplies, other daily necessities	—	1,4	—
	Various shops within the city	Underwear, hardware, cosmetics	—	—	—
Liaoning					
Dalian	Various markets	Daily necessities	Majority	1,5	—
Shenyang	Wuai market	Socks, other daily necessities	70% or more (Socks)	1	Yes
Jilin					
Changchun	Heishui Road wholesale market	Crafts, gifts, clocks, other daily necessities	—	1,4,5	Yes
	Yuandong wholesale market	Socks	Almost all	1,4	Yes

(*Continued*)

Table 10.3:   (*Continued*)

Province/City	Sales Outlets	Yiwu Commodity	Share in Total Sales of Daily Necessities	Ways to Get Connected with Yiwu Market*	Leading Firm's Commodities
Zheijiang					
Ningbo	Yiwu commodity direct sales centre	Daily necessities	100%	5	—
Jiangxi					
Nanchang	Hongcheng market	Daily necessities	Majority	3,4	Yes
Jiangsu					
Xuzhou	Xuanwu market	Socks	90%	1,3,4	Yes
Suqian	Suqian commodity market	Daily necessities	Majority	4	—
Suzhou	Suzhou Yiwu commodity direct sale supermarket	Daily necessities	100%	5	—
Suzhou	Qianwanli bridge commodity market	Daily necessities	—	4	Yes

(*Continued*)

Table 10.3:   (*Continued*)

Province/ City	Sales Outlets	Yiwu Commodity	Share in Total Sales of Daily Necessities	Ways to Get Connected with Yiwu Market*	Leading Firm's Commodities
Anhui					
Hefei	70–80 Wholesale markets in Hefei	Daily necessities	60% or more	1,4	—
Liuan	Huang street	Apparel, textiles, other daily necessities	—	1	—
	Dabie mountain Yiwu commodity market	Daily necessities	90% or more	1,2	—
Shandong					
Jimo	Jimo commodity city	Daily necessities	80%	1,2,4	Yes
Weifang	Weifang commodity market	Apparel, knitwear, watches, crafts, other daily necessities.	—	4	—
Weihai	Weihai international trade city	Daily necessities	—	2,4,5	—
Heze	Huadu market	Daily necessities	80%	5	—

(*Continued*)

Table 10.2: (*Continued*)

Province/ City	Sales Outlets	Yiwu Commodity	Share in Total Sales of Daily Necessities	Ways to Get Connected with Yiwu Market*	Leading Firm's Commodities
Henan					
Zhengzhou	The clustering of a few markets in Zhengzhou city	Daily necessities	Majority	5	—
Luoyang	Guanlin markets	Daily necessities	80% or more	1,3,4	Yes
Kaifeng	Daxiangguo temple market	Socks, hardware, toys, suitcases other daily necessities	50% or more (Of which, Socks: 80%)	3	Yes
Xinxiang	Yiwu commodity general wholesale market	Textiles, toys, crafts, apparel other daily necessities	—	4,5	—
Shanxi					
Taiyan	Jiancaoping market	Daily necessities	—	1	—
	Yiwu commodity wholesale market	Daily necessities	—	2,4	Yes

(*Continued*)

Table 10.3:   (Continued)

Province/City	Sales Outlets	Yiwu Commodity	Share in Total Sales of Daily Necessities	Ways to Get Connected with Yiwu Market*	Leading Firm's Commodities
Hubei					
Wuhan	Hanzheng street market	Cards, accessories, crafts, socks	—	3	Yes
Yichang	Changjiang general wholesale market	Stationary, shirts, socks, crafts, clocks	90% or more	1,3	Yes
Hunan					
Changsha	Gaoqiao Market	Knitwear Stationery, toys Other daily necessities	70% 80% 60%	1,4,5	—
Zhuzhou	The clustering of more than 40 apparel markets	Shirts, underwear, other daily necessities	Majority	1,3	Yes
Guandong					
Guangzhou	Yide fine commodities street	Christmas gifts	50%	—	Yes
	Dejin commodity market	Daily necessities	Majority	5	—

(Continued)

Table 10.3: (*Continued*)

Province/ City	Sales Outlets	Yiwu Commodity	Share in Total Sales of Daily Necessities	Ways to Get Connected with Yiwu Market*	Leading Firm's Commodities
Shenzhen	Laodongmen commodity city	Daily necessities	60%	—	—
	Sungang stationery, toys wholesale market	Daily necessities Of which: lanterns, stationery, artificial flowers	60% 80%	—	—
	Art exhibition centre	Daily necessities	70% (Early period) Nearly 50% (now)	1	—
Guangxi Liuzhou	Feie market	Leather, apparel, footwear	—	1,4	—
Sichuan Chengdu	Hehuachi market	Socks, shirts, accessories, cosmetics	Majority	1	Yes

(*Continued*)

Table 10.3:   (Continued)

Province/ City	Sales Outlets	Yiwu Commodity	Share in Total Sales of Daily Necessities	Ways to Get Connected with Yiwu Market*	Leading Firm's Commodities
Yunnan					
Yunxian	Yunxing commercial street	—	—	1, 2 (Under construction)	—
Dali	Ziyun market	Socks, other daily necessities	60% of dali (Socks)	1,2	Yes
Kunming	Luoshiwan daily necessities wholesale market	Shirts, socks, rainwear, accessories, crafts, other daily necessities	60% (Shirts)	1,3	Yes
Tibet					
Lhasa	Bakuo street	Crafts, buddhism commodities, other commodities	80% or more	1	—
	Chongsaikang general wholesale market	Shirts, socks, other daily necessities	90% or more	1,5	—
Lingzhi	Qingxiang market	Daily necessities	80%	1	—

(Continued)

Table 10.3: (*Continued*)

Province/ City	Sales Outlets	Yiwu Commodity	Share in Total Sales of Daily Necessities	Ways to Get Connected with Yiwu Market*	Leading Firm's Commodities
Shanxi Xi'an	Kangfu road market	Shirts, socks, zippers, buttons, children's wear	—	1	Yes
Gansu Lanzhou	Yiwu commodity city	Daily necessities	—	1,2,4	—
Ningxia Yinchuan	More than 10 markets	Daily necessities	Almost all	1,2,5	
Quinghai Xining	Yiwu commodity city	Daily necessities	Less than 70%	1,2,3,4	Yes

(*Continued*)

Table 10.3: (*Continued*)

Province/ City	Sales Outlets	Yiwu Commodity	Share in Total Sales of Daily Necessities	Ways to Get Connected with Yiwu Market*	Leading Firm's Commodities
Xinjiang Urumqi	Changzheng wholesale market	Daily necessities	90%	1,2,3	—
	The clustering of a few markets around South Station	Of which: shirts, socks socks	100% Nearly 100%	1,3	Yes Yes

Source: SMRD and Yiwu Xinwen Wang (2005).

Notes: **Ways to get connected with Yiwu Market.**

1: Yiwu merchants sell Yiwu commodities in the market.

2: Yiwu merchants open the branch markets of the Yiwu Market.

3: Local merchants or merchants from other region sell Yiwu commodities as agents of Yiwu producers.

4: The managing committee or managing company took the initiative for establishing linkages with Yiwu.

5: Other ways.

Strictly speaking, some of the ways to get connected with Yiwu are not shown clearly in SMRD or Yiwu Xinwen Wang (2005). However, most of these could be judged from the context.

**Some information is derived by studying a few individual cases.

*** '—': No description.

outlets are called '*street*' or '*city.*' In a Chinese context, these can also be considered as a market.[18] Two outlets are named as 'centre.' In the case of 'Art Exhibition Centre' in Shenzhen, it means a market; in the case of 'Yiwu Commodity Direct Sales Centre' in Ningbo, however, it means a retail shop. There are two non-market cases, namely '*various shops in Hohhot, Inner Mongolia*' and a '*supermarket in Suzhou, Jiangsu*'. The former is dispersed wholesale shops in the city and the latter is a retail supermarket. This large dependence on the term '*market*' illustrates that the leading actors who deal with Yiwu commodities in the main cities are small merchants. '*Market*' provided a good platform for them to seek customers and collect information.

Second, Yiwu commodities command an absolute majority in most of the sales outlets. By checking Table 10.3, we find among 52 sales outlets, except 16 sale outlets without description, 28 sales outlets (of which 26 are markets) where no less than half of the daily necessities or some specific commodities are purchased from Yiwu. At ten sales outlets (all of them are markets), though the concrete data are not shown, the share of Yiwu commodities in the total sales of daily necessities or some specific commodities clearly accounted for the majority. Section 10.5 will suggest that the sweep of these sales outlets is very wide as well. Thus, we can conclude that a powerful market network has been formed between the Yiwu Market and the markets in China's main cities. By using this network, the SMEs in Zhejiang's clusters are able to access a huge market.

Third, in these main city markets, the ways to get connected with Yiwu Market are as various as those found in the industrial clusters of Zhejiang.

In most cases, Yiwu merchants can be considered as the biggest contributors to the formation of this market network. In the early stages, they usually gathered together in great numbers at a market for purposes of selling Yiwu commodities. This activity not only caused

---

[18] There are a few markets called wholesale markets. This means its main function is wholesale. However, in reality, usually both retailing and wholesaling take place in the same market in China. The transaction scale is smaller and the share of retail is higher. Their boundaries are not as clear as in most developed countries.

keen competition, but also spread information on the Yiwu Market. Consequently, local merchants began to go to Yiwu. Table 10.3 indicates that there are 34 markets (no other forms of sales outlets exist) where Yiwu merchants sell Yiwu commodities. By checking the details of the SMRD, we find at least 11 markets (no other forms of sales outlets exist) where the number of Yiwu merchants has at some point of time exceeded 100 and at least at 13 markets (no other forms of sales outlets exist) where Yiwu merchants have been the first movers.

However, the mobility of Yiwu merchants was also high. The SMRD and the Yiwu Xinwen Wang website show that in at least at five markets (no other forms of sales outlets exist), the number of Yiwu merchants decreased significantly. For example, in the early stages, among 550 booths at the Beijing Yiwu Commodity Wholesale Market, 80–90% of traders came from Yiwu or a neighbouring area in Zhejiang. But currently, the number of Zhejiang merchants has declined to one-fifth of the total. Inside this, the number of Yiwu merchants fell to below 30. On the other hand, their number increased surprisingly in other markets. As an extreme example, from 1990 to 2005, the number of Yiwu merchants in Chengdu Hehuachi Market increased from 200 to 2800. Such high mobility might be due to their long history of peddling. Based on this tradition, Yiwu merchants have been very sensitive to changes in market conditions, so they constantly move around China and even overseas, in search of better marketing opportunities.[19]

After its incipient stage, some of the Yiwu merchants constructed a steady channel between Yiwu and these markets. With Yiwu local government's strong support,[20] a few Yiwu merchants attempted to

---

[19] Because of the Yiwu Market's remarkable development, it is said that 60–80% of outside Yiwu merchants are going to return to Yiwu (interview with a booth-keeper at Yiwu Market, September, 2006). But as mentioned below, the actors who supported this markets network are not only Yiwu merchants. Their disappearance would not affect this network's strong distribution function.

[20] In most of the cases, Yiwu government helped Yiwu merchants to negotiate with local government in main cities.

At the same time, they have taken the initiative to build up a market information exchange network since 1991, which consists of China's 39 important industrial products wholesale markets. Through this information network, Yiwu Market and its merchants have become more and more famous.

establish branch markets in China's main cities. They applied the management style of the Yiwu Market to these branch markets. They not only invited Yiwu merchants to open booths at the branch, but also told local merchants about Yiwu, helping them to access and purchase from the Yiwu Market. We can observe 12 such cases in Table 10.3.

Likewise, Yiwu's leading hometown factories have also played an important role in strengthening this market network. As these factories grew, some of them intended to build their own sales network. However, the cost of marketing was too high that they had no choice but to make use of the existing market network. As a result, they organised the Yiwu merchants, local merchants or the merchants from other region as their agents.[21] Table 10.3 suggests there are at least 13 markets (no other forms of sales outlets exist) where local merchants or the merchants from other region sell commodities as agents of Yiwu factories. In addition to the commodities dealt with by the agents from Yiwu, we observed Yiwu's leading firm's commodities at 35 markets (no other forms of sales outlets exist).

Lastly, the role of managing committees or managing companies of these main cities' markets is as important as the Yiwu merchants in the formation of this market network. Usually, they (including some Yiwu managers) not only invite Yiwu merchants to open booths, but also send a group of inspectors to Yiwu to learn from its market management experience. Like the local government of the clusters in Zhejiang province, they similarly use the slogan '*Form links with Yiwu*' to emphasise their strong determination to get connected to Yiwu. Table 10.3 presents 19 such kinds of managing committees or managing companies.

10.5 Distribution Network Beyond China's Main Cities

As Section 10.4 suggests, a network which primarily deals with Yiwu Market commodities has been formed between the Yiwu Market and the markets located in China's main cities. After being sold to such a

---

[21] It should be noticed that after several trading at early times, most booths in the Yiwu Market usually send off their commodities to main cities' markets directly without using Yiwu Market.

powerful network, where are Yiwu commodities being dispersed to? In other words, how are Yiwu commodities circulating in the down-stream of this distribution system? In the SMRD, the data related to this stage is not as complete as in the first stage from Yiwu to the main cities. Thus, we have to narrow our focus to some basic features.

First, beyond the market network, Yiwu commodities are still cir-culating with a comparatively wide scope. Five markets and one more sales outlet of different form are circulating the commodities beyond the city but inside the province, 12 markets beyond the province but inside China, and four markets to foreign countries and somewhere of China.

More important to us is that there are at least 13 markets and one more sales outlet which cover some small cities or counties and eight markets with the possibility of covering small cities or coun-ties. These markets and other sales outlets have occupied the big gap between the large low-end demand of consumers in these areas and the poor distribution network, which lasted for a long time. In this sense, China's large domestic low-end market was really exploited.[22]

Second, by checking the buyers who purchase from these mar-kets, the modern distribution organisations such as department stores and supermarkets can be observed in at least 12 markets. In China, prior studies always state that the traditional distribution sys-tem such as wholesale markets must give way to the new system (Zheng, 2003). However, as Table 10.4 suggests, the relationship between the markets and the supermarkets or department stores is not rivalry but complementary.

Third, we try to analyse the way to forge linkages with the mar-kets in the main cities. At this level, Yiwu merchants' efforts are seen again. The Yiwu merchants of three markets tried to open shops directly for the selling of Yiwu commodities. The Yiwu merchants in two markets and one more sales outlet of different form organised local merchants to sell Yiwu commodities. However, all these are just

---

[22] Marukawa (2004) provides an interesting case about how the Yiwu commodities are circulating in the downstream of this distribution system.

Table 10.4: Distribution Network Beyond the Main Cities.

Province/ City	Sales Outlets	Sweep of the Markets in the Main Cities*	Links with Smaller Cities or Counties	Buyers	Ways to Get Linkages with the Markets in the Main Cities**
Beijing					
—	Beijing Yiwu commodity wholesale market	—	—	Wholesale merchants, companies, schools, citizens	3
—	Beijing Tianyi market	3	4	The merchants from other markets, departments, supermarkets	3
Shanghai					
—	Chenghuang temple market	3	—	—	—
Chongqing					
—	Chaotianmen general wholesale market	2	Yes	Wholesale merchants in local county	2
Inner Mongolia					
Hohhot	Tongda market	2	Yes	Wholesale merchants in local city	3
	Various places in the city	2	Yes	Wholesale merchants in local city	2

(*Continued*)

Table 10.4:   (Continued)

Province/City	Sales Outlets	Sweep of the Markets in the Main Cities*	Links with Smaller Cities or Counties	Buyers	Ways to Get Linkages with the Markets in the Main Cities**
Liaoning					
Shenyang	Wuai market	3,4	Δ	Wholesale merchants in local city, supermarkets	3
Jilin					
Changchun	Heishui road market	3	Yes	Wholesale Merchants in big city and local city, Departments	2 or 3
Zhejiang					
Ningbo	Yiwu commodity direct sales centre	—	—	Consumers, local governments, schools	3
Jiangsu					
Xuzhou	Xuanwu market	3	Δ	—	2 or 3
Suzhou	Suzhou Yiwu commodity direct sale supermarket	1	—	Consumers	3
Anhui					
Hefei	70–80 wholesale markets in hefei	2	—	Departments, supermarkets	—

(Continued)

Table 10.4: (*Continued*)

Province/City	Sales Outlets	Sweep of the Markets in the Main Cities*	Links with Smaller Cities or Counties	Buyers	Ways to Get Linkages with the Markets in the Main Cities**
Shandong					
Jimo	Jimo commodity city	3,4	△	—	—
Heze	Huadu market	3	Yes	—	—
Henan					
Zhengzhou	The clustering of several markets	3	Yes	—	—
Luoyang	Guanlin market	2	Yes	The merchants from other markets, departments, supermarkets	1
Hubei					
Wuhan	Hanzheng street market	3,4	△	Wholesale merchants, schools, restaurants	3
Yichang	Changjiang general wholesale market	3	Yes	Supermarkets, departments	1
Hunan					
Changsha	Gaoqiao market	3	Yes	—	—
Zhuzhou	The clustering of more than 40 apparel markets	3	Yes	—	—

(*Continued*)

Table 10.4: (Continued)

Province/ City	Sales Outlets	Sweep of the Markets in the Main Cities*	Links with Smaller Cities or Counties	Buyers	Ways to Get Linkages with the Markets in the Main Cities**
Sichuan					
Chengdu	Hehuachi market	3	Δ	Merchants, departments, supermarkets	1,3
Yunnan					
Dali	Ziyun market	1	Δ	Departments, supermarkets	3
Kunming	Luoshiwan daily necessities wholesale market	3	Δ	Companies, departments, supermarkets	3
Tibet					
Lhasa	Bakuo street	—	—	Tourists	3
	Chongsaikang general wholesale market	2,4	Yes	The merchants from other markets, departments	3
Shanxi					
Xi'an	Kangfu road market	3	Δ	Departments, supermarkets (Shirts)	4

(Continued)

Table 10.4:   (*Continued*)

Province/ City	Sales Outlets	Sweep of the Markets in the Main Cities*	Links with Smaller Cities or Counties	Buyers	Ways to Get Linkages with the Markets in the Main Cities**
Qinghai Xining	Yiwu commodity city	1	Yes	Consumers	4
Xinjiang Urumqi	Changzheng wholesale market	2,4	Yes	The merchants from other markets	3
	The markets cluster around south station	2	Yes	Departments, supermarkets	1,2

Source: SMRD and Yiwu Xinwen Wang (2005).

Notes:

*The Sweep of the Markets in the main cities.

1: Inside the city; 2: Beyond the city but inside the province; 3: Beyond the province but inside China; 4: Foreign countries.

**The sales within smaller cities or rural areas.

Δ: No description about whether or not the commodities are sold to smaller cities and rural areas, but the possibility is large, from the context.

*** Ways to get linkage with the markets in the main cities.

1: Yiwu merchants open shops directly.

2: Yiwu merchants or makers organize local merchants to sell Yiwu commodities.

3: Buyers come to the market for purchasing.

4: Other ways.

****'—': No description.

*****Some information is derived from a few individual cases.

minor cases. Mostly, local merchants go to the market and purchase commodities themselves.

10.6 Conclusion

How to upgrade clusters is a central issue for economic growth in developing countries. There are two lines of work that discuss this issue so far. The first discusses how to forge local linkages between those small firms and institutions within the industrial clusters; the second discusses how to create linkages between small producers and global trans-national companies. It is clear that the role of domestic linkages has been ignored for a long time.[23] The development of Zhejiang's industrial clusters and the Yiwu Market are, in this sense, examples to industrial clusters in developing countries.

First, the case of Yiwu indicates that under some socio-economic conditions, a traditional commercial institution such as a marketplace has a large potential to play a key role in the domestic market, especially its low-end part.

In modern China, while domestic demand expanded quickly, the old distribution system soon collapsed. Consequently, traditional marketplaces appeared. As the most typical case, the Yiwu Market and its related markets in the cities have created a strong domestic distribution system. By checking the flow of commodities, we can generally divide this system into three stages. The first stage is from the clusters to the Yiwu Market. As Sections 10.2 and 10.3 suggest, not only Yiwu,

---

[23] Under this academic circumstance, the argument of Professor Hubert Schmitz deserves attention. According to the case of Brazil and India, he emphasised the role of "*National Value Chain*" many times (Schmitz, 2005, 2006; his presentation in the Fifth International Conference on Industrial Clustering and Regional Development 2006, Beijing). We can derive two points from this concept. The first is that using a national value chain is a good way to weaken the control of a single powerful global buyer. The second is that the national value chains are usually useful to local producers in realising functional upgrading in brand, marketing and so on. However, noteworthy in the cases of Brazil and India, is that national chains are still controlled by some successful leading firms. It seems that no effective distribution system for SMEs has been created as yet.

but also other parts of Zhejiang and even China's other regional industrial clusters' SMEs are making use of this market as one of the most important distribution channels. The second stage is from Yiwu Market to the markets in China's main cities. Section 10.4 indicates that as the core of this distribution system, most of the Yiwu Market commodities command an absolute majority in these markets. In the third stage, we observed that Yiwu commodities are not only spreading across a wide area, but are also trickling down to some smaller cities or counties. Thus, China's huge low-end market is fully exploited.

It is clear that China's numerous SMEs, not only in the industrial clusters, but also in the cities, realised their dynamic growth by just using this powerful distribution system.[24] A noteworthy fact is that this market network-based system is getting upgraded. We found the products of Zhejiang clusters' leading firms in the first stage and the products of Yiwu clusters' leading firms in the second stage. Correspondingly, in the third stage, supermarkets and department stores have appeared that are the nodal points in a modern distribution systems. This trend illustrates a new pattern of industrial clusters' upgrading.

The second implication in the case of the Yiwu Market is that according to domestic circumstances, the expansion of a typical *Gemeinschaft* system, such as the network of Yiwu merchants, might result in the development of a typical *Gesellschaft* system, such as the market network-based Yiwu commodity distribution system.

As indicated throughout this paper, Yiwu peddlers have formed a wide business network in traditional society. This network survived China's socialist planning period. Since the 1980s, a group of Yiwu merchants have gone to various clusters in Zhejiang and other province for purchasing commodities. The other group moved to various markets in the cities for purposes of selling Yiwu commodities, usually playing the role of the first movers in a market. Needless to

---

[24] It must be pointed out that not all the marketplaces in developing countries are as accessible as the marketplaces in China. In order to learn more from Yiwu's experience, a comparative study on the accessibility of marketplaces in developing countries is required.

say, the revival of Yiwu merchants' network is the most important factor in constructing such a powerful distribution system.

However, as suggested in Section 10.4, Yiwu merchants are sensitive to market conditions, so their mobility is high as well. Under this circumstance, the following two factors are indispensable to sustaining and strengthening this distribution system. On the one hand, along with its growth, some of the Yiwu firms intended to construct a business network which transcends the network of people from the same place of origin. As Sections 10.4 and 10.5 suggest, some of them established branch markets or retail shop in the main cities. The others within Yiwu attempted to organise both the Yiwu merchants and the merchants from other region to deal in Yiwu commodities. On the other hand, the efforts of local government, the markets managing committees and managing companies in various places deserve attention. As Sections 10.3 and 10.4 suggest, they have taken several measures to establish and strengthen their linkages with Yiwu, giving rise to the slogan: '*Form links with Yiwu*.' As a result, the network of Yiwu merchants has been gradually transformed into a proper modern business network.

References

DING, Ke. (2006). 'Gendai Chuugoku Niokeru Sanchikeisei Bunseki No Tame No Ichishiron, [A study on the formation of industrial clusters in modern China], Nagoya: Nagoya University, doctoral thesis.

JIN, Xiangrong. (2004). 'Sekkoushou niokeru Sengyouka Sangyouku,' [The industrial districts in Zhejiang province], in *Chuugoku Kougyouka no Nosonteki Kiso: Choukou Karyuuiki wo Chuxin ni* [Rural basis of Chinese industrialization: with particular reference to downstream Yangtze river areas], ed. Takeuchi Johzen, Nagoya University East Asian Study Series I.

JIN, Xiangrong. (2007). 'Zhejiangsheng de Chanyejiqun — Yingdui Chanyeshengji Tiaozhan de Zhongxiaoqiye, [The industrial clusters in Zhejiang — challenge to industrial upgrading and local SMEs], in *Dangqian Zhongguo Chanyeshengji Qushi Yanjiu* [A study on the trend of industrial upgrading in China], ed. The Reach Project on Chinese Enterprises: The Quest for Industrial Upgrading amid Transition, Chiba: IDE-JETRO, JRP Series.

LU, Lijun; Bai, Xiaohu; Wang, Zuqiang. (2003). *Shichang Yiwu — Cong Jimaohuantang Dao Guoji Shangmao* [Market Yiwu — from Jimaohuantang (exchange of the feathers of roosters with sugar) to international business], Hangzhou: Zhejiang People Press.

MARUKAWA, Tomoo. (2004). 'Marketing and Social Network in Inland China,' Paper Presented at the Kobe University. Sichuan Academy of Social Science Conference on the Development of Inland China.

National Statistics Trading and Foreign Economic Relations Statistic Secretary ed. (1990–2004). *Zhongguo Shichang Tongji Nianjian* [Market statistical year-book of China], Beijing: China Statistics Press.

SCHMITZ, Hubert. (2005). 'Understanding and Enhancing the Opportunities of Local Producers in the Global Garment and Footwear Industry: What Does the Value Chain Approach Offer?' Deutsche Gesellschaft für Technische Zusammenarbeit (GTZ) GmbH.

SCHMITZ, Hubert. (2006). 'Regional Systems and Global Chains,' in *Keynote Papers and Session-papers' Abstracts*. Beijing: The fifth international conference on industrial clustering and regional development 2006, pp. 1–18.

Yiwu Forum Secretariat ed. (2005). *Zhuanye Shichang Yu Quyu Fazhan — Guanzhu Yiwu Shichang Fushequan* [Specialized Markets and Regional Development — Focusing on Yiwu Markets' Radiation Zone], Yiwu: published at Yiwu Forum 2005.

Yiwu Statistics ed. 1978–2002. *Yiwu Tongji Nianjian* [Yiwu statistical yearbook].

Yiwu Xinwen Wang (www.yiwunews.cn). (2005). Guanzhu Yiwu Jingji Fushequan [Focusing on Yiwu Markets' Radiation Zone] http://www.ywnews.cn/gzywscjj/index.htm (accessed October 2, 2006).

ZHANG, Wenxue *et al.* ed. (1993). *Yiwu Xiaoshangpin Shichang Yanjiu — Shehuizhuyi Shichangjingji Zai Yiwu De Shijian* [A study on Yiwu commodity market — the practice of the socialist market economy in Yiwu], Beijing: Qunyan Press.

Zhejiang China Commodity City Group Co. Ltd ed. (2005). *Zhongguo Xiaoshangpin Cheng Daogou Zhinan* [China Commodity City shopping guidance manual].

Zhejiang China Commodity City Group Co. Ltd ed. (2006). *2006 Nian Zhongguo Xiaoshangpin Cheng Shangpin Mulu* [Commodities catalogue of China Commodity City in 2006].

Zhejiang Province Zhengxie Historical Data Committee ed. (1997). *Xiaoshangpin, Dashichang — Yiwu Zhongguo XiaoshangpinCheng Chuangyezhe Huiyi* [Small commodities, big market — the memoirs of the founders of Yiwu China commodity city] Hangzhou: Zhejiang People Press.

ZHENG, Yongjun. (2003). *Jiedu 'Shichang Dasheng' — Zhejiang Zhuanyeshichang Xianxiang Yanjiu* [An interpretation on 'the province of market' — a study on the specialized market in Zhejiang], Hangzhou: Zhejiang University Press.

Chapter 11

Post Local State Corporatism: A Case Study of Local Government's Role in the Development of Industrial Clusters after Privatisation

Jianniu Xu

China R32 P31 L67 L33 P25 P23 L33 R58

11.1 Introduction

China has drawn attention for its rapid economic development since the reform and opening-up policy. Many scholars, both native and foreign, strived to explain the secret of this rapid growth. The 'local state corporatism' is one of the keys to unlock the secret of Chinese economic development. Scholars in this kind of approach have brought forward points such as the 'local state corporatism' (Oi, 1992, 1995, 1998, 1999), 'local government industrial firms' (Walder, 1995), 'local market socialism' (Lin, 1995), 'township and village government as industrial corporatism' (Peng, 2001), 'local authoritarianism' (Qiu, 1999), and 'political power's profit-making manager' (Yang & Su, 2002), etc.

'Local state corporatism' stresses the critical role of local government in Chinese economic growth. It argues that the Chinese local government showed the characters of 'corporation', the local government officials played the role of 'entrepreneur', and they participated in the internal activities of enterprises. They made the primary decisions of the enterprises, allocated the scarce resources, provided administrative services and controlled the financial resources. This theory holds that Chinese economic growth is mainly promoted by collective economy in towns and villages. Enabling the local government to benefit from the local economy growth, the fiscal decentralisation provides strong institutional inspiration for local government to promote economic growth. Meanwhile, the local governments with relatively lower administrative rank have less non-fiscal interest and stronger supervision over companies, which makes the officials of local governments play the double roles of both 'official' and 'entrepreneur', and vigorously promote the local economic growth.

Focused on the research of districts where the economic growth is mainly supported by the collective TVEs, previous studies overlook the prerequisite of their theories and the evolution of the local governments' role. 'Local state corporatism' theory is mainly based on the research of those districts where most of the enterprises were publicly-owned before the mid-1990s. It cannot explain the local governments' roles after privatisation in these areas. It cannot explain the economic growth in the region where most of the enterprises are private or foreign, either. Guangdong Province has witnessed rapid economic growth and rural industrialisation since the reform and opening-up policy, whose development is supported by private and foreign enterprises. Through research on the economic development of Guangdong Province, we could find other types of local governments' roles during the Chinese market transition and the different types of government-enterprise relationships.

Choosing Xiqiao — a textile industrial cluster — as a case, this chapter describes how the local government is involved in local economic development after the mid-1990s. It is found that the local governments still actively participated in the economic development, but the measures are obviously different from what has been described by the theory of 'Local state corporatism'. This paper puts forward the concept 'Post local state corporatism' to generalise the new role of the local government in the economic development. This chapter argues that the difference between our observation and previous studies results from the difference of the privatisation and marketisation.

11.2 Survey of Xiqiao Textile Industrial Cluster

Xiqiao, located on the shore of the Xijiang River (in the hinterland of the Pearl River Delta), occupying 177 square kilometres and with 140,000 permanent residents, is a textile industrial cluster. With a long history of more than one thousand years, the textile industry in Xiqiao prospered in the Tang Dynasty (618–907 AD) and reached its peak in the Ming Dynasty (1368–1644 AD). To date, there are 1,286 fabric enterprises in Xiqiao, with more than 30,000 units of fabric machinery. Over 60,000 people are employed by the textile industry in Xiqiao and the annual textile production capacity in the town reaches 1 billion metres. The textile industry in Xiqiao has formed a comprehensive production chain from product R&D, material production, weaving, dyeing and finishing to fashion design.

11.3 The Development of Xiqiao Textile Industrial Cluster and the Government's Role: From 1978 to the Mid-1990s

The first reason is its historical background. There were three state-owned silk weaving factories in Xiqiao before the reform and opening-up policy. Many of the local residents worked in these three factories as managers, technicians and salesmen. In the production team, women weaved on wooden hand-looms, because the government required the production team to fulfill the quotas.

The second reason is the support of the state-owned enterprises. In the 1960s and 1970s, the state-owned silk enterprises were very profitable. Since the reform and opening-up policy, many private enterprises emerged and developed very rapidly with the support of state-owned enterprises. At the beginning, the private mills bought old machines from the state-owned enterprises and the state-owned enterprises also supplied raw materials and sold fabrics for the private mills. Soon after, the private entrepreneurs found it very easy to buy raw materials and sell fabrics by themselves, and it is more profitable than before. The private textile SMEs mushroomed in Xiqiao in the 1980s.

The third reason is the protection and support of the local governments. During this period, the local government focused on running eight public-owned enterprises. But the development of private enterprises depended on the government's protection and support. Firstly, the township government allowed the individuals to set up enterprises in the environment that was not so favourable to the private enterprises. The government also leased the village storehouses to private entrepreneurs as their workshops, and allowed the private enterprises to register as collective enterprises, so that the private enterprises could elude political risks and enjoy preferential policies. Secondly, at that time, it was very difficult for the private entrepreneurs to get loans from the bank. The government helped the private enterprises to get the bank loan and also provided administrative loan to private enterprises. The government borrowed the money from the bank and then lent it to private enterprises. Thirdly, the township government levied less tax from private enterprises than it should be. Regulations stated that if a factory is going through a slow period, the idle looms are not taxed. Government official under-reported the number of looms in operation, and did so even-handedly, across the board, for all of the factories.

11.4 Institutional Change and the Crisis of Xiqiao Textile Industry in the Mid-1990s

In the middle of the 1990s, the political and economic institutional environments greatly changed in China. Firstly, with the rapid rural industrialisation in the 1980s, the seller's market ended and the buyer's market came into being. Secondly, the central government legitimised the private sector and eliminated the preferential policy to the collective enterprises. Thirdly, China had been growing out of the planned economy. Fourthly, the central government promoted the commercialisation of the bank to cut the relation between government and bank.

The crisis of Xiqiao textile was due to the following reasons. Firstly, with the rise of people's living standard, people needed high quality textile products. The market structure had changed. Secondly, the regional competition was rather fierce. With the accomplishment of the property rights reform in Keqiao (the main competitor of Xiqiao's textile industry) public-owned textile enterprises, Xiqiao textile industry faced fierce competition. Thirdly, with the rise of labour, electricity and tax costs, the total production cost was rather high in Xiqiao. Fourthly, the equipments in Xiqiao textile mills were outdated. Finally, most of the enterprises were small and medium-sized, and most of the bosses were peasant entrepreneurs, lacking R&D consciousness and capability. In Xiqiao there were more than 4,000 textile mills at its peak, among which only 300 remained by 1994. How to deal with such a severe crisis?

On the one hand, the town government promoted the property rights reform of the public-owned enterprises. From 1994 to 1998, the main task of the township government was to reform the public owned enterprises (see state owned enterprises). On the other hand, the township government began to support the private textile enterprises.

With privatisation and marketisation, how did the local government participate in the local economic development, and what kind of role did it play? The following section will describe the township government's action.

11.5 Government Action and its Effect After the Mid-1990s

11.5.1 *Setting Up the Xiqiao Light Textile City*

With the development of Xiqiao textile industry, there emerged a textile market along the street nearby the bus station. And in the 1980s, the township government had erected some markets in the downtown for textile manufactures in Xiqiao. The old market contained 800 outlets, some of which exhibited textile from a single enterprise, and some sold textile from two or more small factories that shared shop-front in order to save money. The scene was too backward and untidy to the taste of the township government and impeded the development of tourism because this old market was located nearby the Xiqiao Mountain.

In 1996, the Xiqiao government invested more than 600 million yuan to build the Xiqiao Textile City in a newly-developed urban area.

As the Xiqiao Textile City was nearly completed, the township authority issued a regulation in the name of urban planning that required the
factories to close down their downtown sales outlets and move to the
new textile city. Textile manufactures complained that buying or renting outlets in the new textile city would add their business expense
and only the township government would profit. The township government sold the outlets to textile manufactures and the owners could
sell or rent them out to other people. The city occupies an area of
380,000 square metres and consists of three-storey buildings, each
containing a wholesale outlet downstairs and offices upstairs. Xiqiao
Textile City has more than 3500 shops along the streets. In Xiqiao
Textile City, there are three specialised sections dealing with fabrics,
denim and upholstery. It also has retail, raw materials and clothing
accessories sections. As one of the four largest textile wholesale markets in China (the others being the China Textile City in Keqiao of
Zhejian Province, the Xiliu Fabric Market in Liaoning Province and
the Hehuachi Fabric Market in Sichuan Province), Xiqiao Textile
City's turnover amounted to 17 billion yuan in 2004. Each year,
more than 3 million traders from China, Canada, the US, Italy,
Singapore, Korea and other countries or regions make business transactions in Xiqiao.

In order to manage the textile market and support the development of the textile industry, the township set up the Xiqiao Light
Textile City Management Committee. Two officials of the Economy
Development Office act as the leaders of the committee, other people
are employed from the market, some of whom are former workers of
state-owned enterprises. The affiliated organisation of the committee
included administrative office, financial office, marketing management office, mediating office, private sector office, the information
and publicity office, and the import and export company.

Besides the market management, the main functions of the committee are as follows:

The first is organising the textile manufacturers to attend exhibitions
in Beijing, Zhejiang Province and Guangzhou, and hold exhibitions
in Xiqao. The committee have organised three exhibitions, which are

the 1998 Guangdong International Textile Machine Exhibition, 2000 China (Xiqiao) International Decorative Fabric Exhibition, and 2002 China (Xiqiao) Textile Exhibition.

The second is helping the textile manufacturers to import advanced looms and export products. As all of the textile manufactures are small and medium-sized enterprises, it is difficult for them to get the import and export rights from the government. So the committee set up an import and export company to help the SMEs to import advanced looms with tax free.

The mediating office is in charge of solving the dispute between different textile manufactures and between the manufactures and the machine providers. The committee employed some retired personnel with long work experience in the textile industry to set up the mediating office to solve the dispute between the enterprises.

The third is coordinating the relationship between the factories and the government and acting as the bridge between the township government and the textile industry. Faced with more than one thousand textile factories, it is impossible for the government to deal with each textile manufacturer. Likewise, it is difficult for the SME to influence the government. Therefore, the committee organised an information and publicity office, which also acts as the office of the textile trade association. The main function of the office is to fulfill the government policies and reflect entrepreneurs' advice and opinions to the government officials.

11.5.2 *Promote Equipment Renewing*

The township government also helps the enterprises to renew their weaving machines and promotes technological innovation. The local government used an interest payment subsidy to help the textile-making SMEs to buy high-speed shuttleless automatic weaving machines to replace the older ones. With the support of local government, the private textile enterprises in Xiqiao have invested 4 billion yuan to purchase shuttleless looms and other advanced equipment. Now, the private textile sector in Xiqiao has 13,600 shuttleless looms, accounting for 48% of its total looms, much higher than the 10% nationwide.

11.5.3 *Promoting Technical Innovation*

11.5.3.1 *First Stage: Setting Up a Technical Service Organisation*

In 1998, the Xiqiao township government built the first textile material development centre in China, which is a non-profit public technical service institution. The township government put up 2 million yuan from fees and tax revenues it had collected and imported a computer design system from South Korea, hired a technical team, and provided the office. This design company began operations in 1998, and has produced tens of thousands of new designs. These designs are sold to the local textile SMEs, each for as little as 300 yuan, and each design can be sold to only one buyer. The company is also in charge of fixing the weaving looms for thousands of textile manufactures in Xiqiao.

> 'The textile material development company is subsidised by the government. It is the government which bought the R&D machine and paid the technicians. It is a non-profit technical service institute. The textile material development company sold their products at a low price to the textile manufacturers in Xiqiao. The government has not meant to gain (direct) returns from this company.' (Interview with a government official).

This effect is evident in Xiqiao. Firstly, the company helps enterprises to shorten product development time and lower development costs by providing them with textile materials and technical services. Through the continuing technological transformation, textile manufacturers have been able to greatly improve the quality and amplify the variety of their products. Productivity has risen by 20–30%, and product price has risen by 20%.

Secondly, the company raised the R&D consciousness of the entrepreneurs in Xiqiao. More and more SMEs have grown stronger through the government-subsidised innovation programme, and they are now no longer content with the new designs provided by the design centre. More than 100 of them have set up their own R&D departments to provide different product designs.

The main problem of the textile material development company is that the technicians lacked enough motivation to serve the textile manufacturers.

> 'At that time, the mobility of the technicians was rather high. The technicians felt there is not much difference to do good or not. This cannot raise their motivation to serve the textile manufacturers.' (Interview with the leader of innovation centre).
>
> 'I'm not a civil servant whose salary is guaranteed; nor am I a boss who can make money; nor am I a researcher who can be conferred the title of a technical rank. I'm none of those above. If the problem of identification and incentive problem cannot be solved, it's not reasonable to continue to work only from goodwill ... I did consider leaving at that time.' (Interview with a technician).

11.5.3.2 *Second Stage: Setting Up Building and Lease Office*

In 2000, the Xiqiao township government invested 73 million yuan to build an innovation building. In order to stimulate the technician's enthusiasm to serve the textile manufacturers, the Xiqiao township government privatised the innovation service organisation by selling R&D equipment to the technicians at a low price, and attracted more technical service institutes to move into the Innovation Building. The government leased offices to the technical service institutes and the service institutes provided service to textile factories at market price. Xiqiao Innovation Centre consists of five centres, which are: R&D centre, information centre, E-commerce and logistic centre, training and communication centre, and intellectual property rights protecting centre.

Compared with the former centre, the Innovation Centre has the following characteristics: Firstly, it extended its service scope outside Xiqiao township. It provided service to textile factories outside Xiqiao. Secondly, it broadened its service content, which covered R&D, management, marketing, information collecting and intellectual property rights protecting. Thirdly, the managers of the technical service institutes are much more active in serving the textile factories.

The main problem of the innovation centre is insufficient invest-ment in R&D equipments resulting from the technical service institutes' lack of money. Not only the entrepreneurs but also the gov-ernment officials were not satisfied with the service provided by the technical service institutes of the innovation centre.

11.5.3.3 *Third Stage: Government Buying Equipment and Entering National Textile and Apparel Council*

In 2004, the local government invested more than 20 million yuan to import advanced equipment to set up an innovation platform. The innovation platform was co-built by the local government and China Textile and Apparel Council (CTAC in brief), with the purpose of servicing local small and middle-sized enterprises. Being invested by the local governments and administrated by CTAC, the platform is a nonprofit organisation. In order to stimulate the CTAC to serve the textile factories, the Xiqiao government allowed it to own 51% share. The Textile Industrial Innovation Platform includes five centres, which are: Textiles R&D Centre; Quality Testing Centre; Training Centre; Information Centre and Modern Logistics Centre. The Textile Industrial Innovation Platform mainly helps small and medium-sized enterprises to improve their competitive capability in market.

One of the highlights of the Xiqiao platform is the product testing centre. With an investment of 10 million yuan, it is the most advanced fabric testing facility in China. It will provide fabric quality testing, technology training, quality accreditation and technology consulting services to the textile industry in southern China. In the past, the tex-tile factories have to send their samples to Guangzhou, Hong Kong, or Beijing for quality testing. Now, they can do it in Xiqiao, so that, a lot of time and money are saved. The product testing centre also pro-vides solutions to the textile factory if some quality problem is found.

The R&D centre is a non-profit public service organisation. After paying some fees, the textile factories in Xiqiao can send their technicians to develop the new products for their own factories.

The R&D centre will provide some experts to help the factories in this process. Thus, the R&D centre reduces investment cost for the textile factories.

At the turn of the century, with the coming of the buyers' market, the competition became more and more fierce. The textile manufactures in the clusters are eager to gain support in terms of market information, technological upgrade, introduction of equipment and personnel training, thus creating huge demand for institutional innovation. Because most of the textile manufactures within the industrial clusters are private SMEs and their entrepreneurs are not well-educated, the problems cannot be solved simply by the enterprises themselves. Therefore, it needs the active intervention of the local government. From the establishment and evolution process of innovation centre, we can find that the local government played a critical role in providing public goods for the textile industry.

11.5.4 *Building a Textile Industrial Base*

The township government built a textile industrial base, where there are two companies providing steam and water for the enterprises and deal with the sewerage.

Printing and dyeing is the primary weak link of the Xiqiao textile industrial chain, while the Guangdong Provincial Government carries out moderately tight environmental protection policy. Printing and dyeing and environmental protection become the two bottlenecks of the textile industry development. So the Xiqiao government invested 2.4 billion yuan to build the first 'green' textile industry base in China with centralised water and steam supply and sewage treatment.

In the past, each textile enterprise run its own boiler for steam and water supply system, and had its own chimneys. Such decentralised heat and water supply system led to serious problems, such as high energy consuming, high cost and heavy pollution. Moreover, shortage of professionals resulted in severe hidden danger. So the government introduced the Longguang Corporation to supply steam and water to the enterprises in the base. This corporation running two power plants has a rich supply of steam as a side product of generating power. When the centralised water and steam supply project works, it can supply 360 tons steam per hour and 40,000 cubic metres of water every day to the enterprises, and meanwhile provide water for 15,000 people's daily life. This project has two significant advantages. Firstly, it can provide more steady steam with lower price, which can help the enterprises to cut down investment and production cost. Secondly, it can pollute less air due to the environmental protection fuel and efficient dust removing.

Sewage treatment is a major constraint on the textile industry development. In the textile industry base, the Xinlong Company runs the centralised sewage treatment project, occupying a field of 328 mu (including 228 mu man-made wetland), which can deal with 30,000 tons sewage every day. The sewage from the textile factories is first treated in the workshop, and then receives a deep treatment in the man-made wetland. Finally the output water is treated in the eco-recycle pool and reaches type III standard of surface water. That is to say, the output water flows away without any pollutant.

Xiqiao textile industry base significantly promotes the conglomerating of textile industrial because many large textile and relevant enterprises have moved into it one after another to cut the cost. For example, the vice general manager of South Printing and Dyeing Corporation said, 'After settling in Xiqiao textile industry base, we have cut down our expenses a lot. For the sewage treatment alone, we can save 7 million yuan a year and moreover, we get rid of the bad reputation of "environment killer".' After the settlement of South Printing and Dyeing Corporation — the biggest textile printing and dyeing enterprise in China, a number of textile and apparel enterprises moved to the base one after another. For example, Daphne Co., Ltd, the first bedding brand in Taiwan, moved to Xiqiao on the heels of its upper-stream enterprise South Printing and Dyeing Corporation. Its general manager, Mr Lin Min Chiu, once made a joke, to cut down the cost, 'Where South Printing and Dyeing Corporation goes, there we go'. The world famous textile machinery enterprise Italy SOMET also invested $2,800,000 to set up a textile machinery R&D centre in Xiqiao Base.

Thus, the construction of Xiqiao Textile Industry Base has decreased the enterprises' expense and broken up the environmental bottleneck of the textile industry development. The centralised project of water, steam and sewage treatment has reached a win-win situation. That is, Longguang Corporation has turned waste into asset, the textile and apparel enterprises have cut down operation cost and the local government has broadened its tax base with the enterprises movement to Xiqiao.

11.6 Institutional Analysis on the Action of Local Governments

From the Xiqiao case we can see that the local government still actively engaged in the local economic growth after the end of privatisation process in the mid-1990s. But compared with the local state corporatism, local governments' intentions and actions have changed obviously.

The change of intention includes two aspects. Firstly, local state corporatism argued that the local governments preferred 'collectively owned township and village enterprises and directly involved itself in their management. The private sector has been discriminated against and periodically criticised, received little or no help in securing loans or production inputs (Oi, 1998, p. 36).' But in Xiqiao, the township government declared that they 'don't care about what kinds the enterprises' property rights are, but care where the enterprises are located' (*bu qiou suo you, dan qiu suo zai*). The Xiqiao Township government not only promoted the privatisation of the collectively-owned TVE, but strived to provide all kinds of supports to the private owned enterprises. Secondly, the local government argued that 'the extraction of profits from enterprises is one of the most important mechanisms for allowing local governments to operate as a corporation (Oi, 1992, p. 118).' But in Xiqiao, the township government declared that they benefit from the local economic growth by tax and other fees, not by extracting enterprises' profit directly.

The differences of the measures to promote economic growth are as follows. Firstly, local state corporatism stressed that local government mobilised the resources to set up collectively owned TVE. But the Xiqiao government focused on improving the investing environment to attract enterprises outside to move into Xiqiao to amplify its tax base. Secondly, local state corporatism stressed that the local government was directly involved in the internal management of the public-owned enterprises as the owner. But in Xiqao, the township government did not participate in the internal management of the private sector, but only provide service for them.

These differences are neither predicted nor explained by local state corporatism theory. This paper puts foreword the concept of '*Post Local State Corporatism*' to generalise the local governments' role in the development of private sector after the mid-1990s.

Why did the local governments so actively promote local economic growth? The answer lies in the fiscal contracting system and the change of assessing criterion on the government officials. Under the fiscal contracting system, the local government could retain the residual after handing in a given sum of revenue to the superior government. Since the reform and opening-up policies, the assessing and promotion criterion on the government officials have changed from political faithfulness to economic performance. These two institutional changes stimulated the local officials to throw themselves into local economic development.

Why are the Xiqiao government's actions so different from what has been described by the local state corporatism theory? This paper argues that these differences can be ascribed to the institutional and structural changes in the mid-1990s. Based on the research on the region where economic growth is mainly attained by the development of TVEs, the local state corporatism overlooks its institutional prerequisites. The institutional prerequisites are as follows.

The first institutional prerequisite of local state corporatism is collectively-owned property rights. Under this system, the township governments not only extracts the profit of the enterprises, but also intervenes in the internal management of the enterprise in the name of the owner. But the development of the collectively-owned TVEs has the following prerequisites. Firstly, the central government has not issued clear policies on the development of private sector. In most areas of China, the private enterprises had been discriminated and been criticised frequently. So, it is more secure to develop the collectively-owned TVEs. Secondly, the development of the collectively-owned TVE is also thanks to the seller's market. On the growing market, different kinds of enterprises could sell their products very easily.

The second institutional prerequisite of local state corporatism is the 'dual-track' market. Under this system, the local governments hold some amount of scarce resources which could be used to promote economic growth. The third institutional prerequisite is the localisation of the bank, so the local government has some influence on the bank loan.

But in the mid-1990s, the institutional prerequisites changed and these changes resulted in the evolution of local government's role in the economic development. Firstly, with the coming of the buyer's market, the market competition became more and more fierce. Lots of collectively-owned TVEs failed in the market competition and were closed or sold out by the local government. It was not feasible for the local government to invest and manage the collective TVEs. Then the legitimacy of private sector is rising. Faced with hundreds of or even thousands of private enterprises, the local government could not intervene in the internal management and extract profit directly. Secondly, the end of the 'dual-track' market undermined the capability of the local government to mobilise and distribute scarce resources. Thirdly, the re-centralisation of financial system limited the local governments' ability to get the loans from bank. Thus, the institutional changes in the mid-1990s forced the local government to retreat from the internal management of the enterprises and modify its means and measures to promote local economic growth. Finally, the lack of and immatureness of the intermediary organisations provided the structural space for the local government to participate in local economic activities. Thus, the local government retreated from the internal management and stepped into the social sphere to replace the function of the intermediary organisations.

Therefore, after the mid-1990, institutional changes resulted in the evolution of role and action of the local government. In detail, the privatisation, marketisation, and re-centralisation of the financial system made it impossible for local government to mobilise resources to set up TVEs and involve in their internal management. Lack of intermediary organisations provides structural space for the local government to still play an active role in local economic activities. The local government retreated from the internal economic activities of the enterprises and stepped into the social sphere. They initiated the public service organisations to provide support for the development of private sector.

11.7 Discussion and Conclusion

The Xiqiao case demonstrates that the local government participates in local economic growth in a different way, and it cannot be explained by local state corporatism. According to Jean Oi, local governments not only mobilise resources to set up the collective TVEs, but also intervene in the internal management. In this process, the local government shows the characteristics of corporation and the local officials also play the role of 'entrepreneur'. But in Xiqiao, local government acts in a really different way. It focuses on improving investment environment to attract textile manufacturers or related enterprises to move into Xiqiao, and provide different kinds of support for the private textile manufacturers. The government's main purpose is not to get the profit of the enterprise, but to levy tax. This paper puts forward the concept of '*post local state corporatism*' to generalise the local government's role in Xiqiao, and argues that the local government's role evolved from 'local state corporatism' to 'post local state corporatism' with the end of the privatisation and the coming of marketisation.

The implications of this paper in explaining China's economic growth and the role of local government are: (1) In explaining China's economic growth, the roles of country (local government), market (market system) and society (structure) may not be the case that one is dominant and the other two are subordinate, or either this one or another one has the complete answer to China's economic growth. On the contrary, it is more likely that they promote China's economic growth in the process of interactive evolution, and they play different roles and have different influences in different developmental stages. (2) In the process of market transformation, the actions of local government have gradually evolved in the interaction among country, market and society. The path of the evolution is: from 'local state corporatism' in which government mobilised the resources to set up the collective TVEs and directly intervene in the operation of companies and the government officials played the roles of both officials and entrepreneurs, to the 'post local state corporatism' in which local government vigorously provides all-round service for local economic development instead of directly intervening in the operation of companies.

References

安德鲁 G. 沃尔德. (1996).《作为工业厂商的地方政府:对中国过渡经济的组织分析》, 应星译,《国外社会学》5-6 期。.

安德鲁 G. 沃尔德. (1993).《公司组织与地方国有产权:中国对私有化的抉择》, 《国外社会学》第 6 期。

边燕杰、张文宏. (2001).《经济体制、社会网络与职业流动》,《中国社会科学》第 2 期。.

大卫·斯塔克、维克多·倪.(1996).《走向对社会主义社会的制度分析》,《国外社会学》第 5-6 期。

戴慕珍. (1997).《中国地方政府公司化的制度化基础》, 甘阳 崔之元编《中国改革的 政府经济学》牛津大学出 版社。

洪银兴. (1997).《地方政府行为和中国市场经济的发展》,《经济学家》第 1 期。

洪银兴, 曹勇. (1996).《经济体制转轨时期的地方政府功能》,《经济研究》第 5 期。

林南. (1996). 《地方性市场社会主义:中国农村地方法团主义之实际运行》, 《国外社会学》第 5-6 期。

彭玉生. (2003).《中国村镇工业公司:所有权公司治理与市场监督》,《清华社会学 评论》(2002 卷), 社会科学文 献出版社。

邱泽奇. (1999).《乡镇企业改制与地方威权主义的终结》,《社会学研究》第 3 期

孙立平. (1996).《社会主义研究中的新制度主义理论》,《国外社会学》第 5-6 期。

杨瑞龙. (1998).《我国制度变迁方式转换的三阶段论》,《经济研究》第 1 期。

杨瑞龙、、杨其静. (2000).《阶梯式的渐进制度变迁模型:再论地方,《经济研究》第 3 期。

杨善华、苏红. (2002).《从代理型政权经营者到谋利型政权经营者》,《社会学研究》第1 期。

叶健民. (2000).《迈向共生性的中国农村政企•系》,《香港社会科学学报》第 17 期。

朱虹. (2001). 《中国乡村经济的起飞—— 结构性动因与地方政府法团化》,《二十一世纪》8 月号。

丘海雄、 徐建牛. (2003). 《后地方法团主义》, 中山大学 2003 年 "中国民营经济发展研讨会" 论文 (未发表)。

丘海雄、、徐建牛. (2004).《市场转型过程中地方政府角色研究述评》,《社会学研究》第 4 期。

丘海雄、徐建牛. (2004).《产业集群技术创新中的地方政府行为》,《管理世界》第 10 期。

胡鞍钢、王绍光主编. (2000).《政府与市场》, 中国计划出版社。

张静. (2000).《基层政权——乡村制度诸问题》, 浙江人民出版社。

T.·G. 拉斯基. (1993).《无私有化的进•:中国国有工业的改革》,《国外社会学》第 6 期。

LIN, Nan. (1995). 'Local Market Socialism: Local Corporatism in Action in Rural China.' *Theory and Society* **24**(3).

OI, Jean. (1995). 'The Role of the Local State in China's Transitional Economy.' *China Quarterly* 144.

OI, Jean. (1992). 'Fiscal Reform and the Economic Foundation of Local State Corporatism in China.' *World Politics* **45**(1).

OI, Jean. (1998). 'The Evolution of Local State Corporatism.' in Andrew Walder (eds.), *Zouping in Transition: The Process of Reform in Rural North China*, Cambridge Mass: Harvard University Press.

OI, Jean. (1999). 'Local State Corporatism.' in Jean C. Oi (eds.), *Rural China Takes Off: Institutional Foundations of Economic Reform*, Berkeley: University of California Press.

PENG, Yusheng. (2001). 'Chinese Villages and Townships as Industrial Corporations: Ownership, Governance, and Market Discipline.' *American Journal of Sociology* **106**(5).

WALDER, Andrew. (1995). 'Local Governments as Industrial Firms.' *American Journal of Sociology* **101**(2).

WALDER, Andrew. 'The State as an Ensemble of Economic Actors: Some Inferences from China's Trajectory of Change, http://www.nap.eduPhemlPtransformPch17.html.

Chapter 12

Interaction and Innovation in Cluster Development: Some Experiences from Guangdong Province, China

Jun Wang

China R32 L25
P25 031 L60
R38 L14

12.1 Introduction

In the era of globalisation, industrial clusters are receiving increasing attention in economic research and policy-making. The current literatures can be broadly categorised into two groups. One takes a comparative perspective, seeking to explain the different performance between industrial clusters and non-industrial clusters, particularly, the emergence of competitive firms and regional economies (Porter, 1998). Explanations for the comparative perspectives concerning industrial clusters are: to have a positive externality (Marshall, 1920), externality-based knowledge spillover (Lundvall, 1993), flexible specialisation (Piore and Sabel, 1984), to save transportation costs for the increasing returns to scale in the spatial clustering process (Krugman, 1991), cooperation-based collective efficiency (Schmitz, 1996), and to reduce transaction costs based on the embedded social relation and the trust with each other within clusters (Granovetter, 1985; Pitelis, 1998), as well as to diminish the learning costs for adaptation to increasing internal and external changes (Lundvall and Johnson, 1994). Many empirical studies support the conclusion that performance, innovative ability and competitiveness of firms within the clusters obviously exceeded those in non-clusters firms. 'The Third Italian' industrial districts were prescribed as a successful case of development in the rise of SMEs and the traditional industries (Becattini, 1990; Brusco, 1990). Silicon Valley was also considered as

325

a 'learning region', which displays intensive inter-firm interaction, such as knowledge spillover through labour mobility and strong supporting system (Saxenian, 1994). In fact, in the process of China's transition from a planned economy to a market economy, it is quite evident that regional development is closely related to the quantities and scales of industrial clusters. A good performance in regional development demonstrates a strong positive relationship between the scale and quantities of industrial clusters and the regional development in China (Wang *et al.*, 2003). Regions in the most dynamic provinces such as Zhejiang, Guangdong, are reckoned as 'Hometown of Plastics' or 'Hometown of Metalworking' and so on.

The second perspective takes an evolutional flavour (Nelson and Winter, 1982), which emphasises the dynamic process in clusters. Not all clusters can sustain their earlier growth performance (Amin, 1999; Lyons, 2000). There may be different reasons for the downturn, ranging from local dynamics to external conditions (Kautonen, 1996). With things going, if a cluster cannot make its institutions, the competitive environment will become rigid and lose responsiveness, and a regional force will evolve. However, adjustment is not easy as paths are often historically dependent (Antonelli, 1997). Most of the essays discuss that the evolution of clusters may take many years, often decades. Although the emergence of a cluster could be triggered by chance events, a cluster tends to have a life of its own. The inherent economics of proximity have been enough to attract increasing numbers of firms and other institutions in consequence, leading to a self-reinforcing cycle (Porter, 1990). This is often referred to as the lock-in effect. Consequently, competitive advantages may possibly turn into disadvantage if a deep structural adaptation does not rapidly take place in response to major internal and external changes (Pietrobelli, 2004). To avoid being locked-in, continuous innovation is deemed necessary.

Up to now, a lot of discussions on industrial clusters are concentrated on European countries. Even in these developed economies, 'institution thinness' is often regarded as a constraint for cluster innovation and development, because cluster dynamics cannot occur automatically, but depend on and can be reinforced by purposeful action (Asheim and Isaksen, 2003). Schmitz and Nadvi (1999) stressed the importance of innovative knowledge flowing from outside, while the technological capabilities in industrial clusters remain poor in developing countries. Meanwhile, they propose a strategic question; who are the gatekeepers of knowledge from outside: local technological institutions, large manufacturers or external buyers? As regards the clusters that lack large firms and external resources, the institutional context in which firms operate and learning opportunities are defined as two of the essential factors for local clusters to sustain their competitiveness by learning, adaptation and innovation (Cooke, 2002). There is a strong view in the literature which shows that innovation is important through various institution and measures. However, recently, it became more obvious that not all clusters which carryout formal activities can play an effective role in supporting innovation. In other words, if a local technological institution is regarded as a gatekeeper of knowledge from outside in the clusters that are lacking external resource and large firms, it may not necessarily tend to be productive and efficient. Thus, the question proposed by Schmitz and Nadvi (1999) seems to remain unanswered. Therefore, the question in this chapter is what is the fundamental condition for an institutional context to be necessary and effective for formal innovation. In order to find out these conditions, it is necessary to combine the importance with the effectiveness of the institutional context in the initiation of formal activities.

The aim of this chapter is to present and demonstrate two related assumptions. First, formal innovative activities are more important than informal innovation activities in the initiation of an intentional innovation, according to division of labour and the size of firms. Second, only if there are some reasonable institutions being set up, which include minimum investment and a mechanism of institution for sustainable interaction, the formal activities will be effective to support innovative interaction. The structure of this chapter is as follows. Section 2 gives two variables to determine a classification and evolution of clusters based on the measurement of interaction between different participants. Section 3 describes a dynamic process of formal institutions interacting with small and medium enterprises (SMEs) for innovation. Section 4 discusses a requirement of effective mechanism of formal institution for supporting innovation in the dynamics of interaction. Section 5 examines a successful example from Guangdong province in China, in interaction between firms and formal innovative innovation. Two cases of Guangdong province, such as Xiqiao town that is defined as the Specialisation Town[1] of Textile and Xiaolan town as the Specialisation Town of Metalworking, will be introduced to explain this interaction for innovation. And the final section contains the main conclusions.

12.2 Determinants of Industry-based Interaction

Clusters can be defined as groups of companies and institutions co-located in a specific geographic region and linked by interdependencies in providing a related group of products and/or services (Porter, 1990, 1996). According to this definition, clusters have two defining characteristics, geographical concentration and industrial specialisation. Krugman (1991) emphasises the important impact of the geographical factor on economic activities, while many related literatures focus on industrial specialisation because of the importance in measurement of development types from an evolutionary perspective (Brusco, 1990). For example, industrial specialisation is closely related to the density of inter-firm relationships, which determines the extent of interaction which is as an important resource of innovation because of tacit knowledge, as a main source of knowledge spillover, which is embodied in either individuals, organisations and systems, and ultimately results in the processes of innovative activities (Lundvall, 1988). Feldman (1994) argues that innovation is an interactive process facilitated by face to face contact. In this sense, a cluster is

---

[1] In Guangdong province, Marshall's clusters are located in the administrative region of township, in which one specialised product is being produced in one town, or two different specialised products in one town. Scholars such as Wang *et al.* (1999) in Guangdong called this kind of clustering economy 'specialisation town'.

regarded as an innovative network (Nelson, 1993; Storper 1997; Cooke, 2002), at least as a driver of regional innovation systems (OECD, 2001).

Yet not all clusters are an innovation system. On the one hand, pure agglomeration of firms is no guarantee of interaction between each other in industries. Geographic proximity only creates a potential for interaction, without necessarily leading to dense local interaction. The richness of cluster effects depends on the behaviour of cluster participants. Beaudry and Breschi (2003) find that the innovative performance of companies in Italy and UK depends on the innovation propensity of co-located firms. Cluster externalities seem to exist but can go either way. If other companies in a cluster do not compete on innovation, the other companies are less likely to do so too. In fact, the industrial connection between firms depends mainly on the level of division of labour within the cluster. Clustering and specialisation in a region are regarded as the key elements of growth and competitiveness, due to the reduction of transaction costs, agglomeration economies, and technological and skill advantages (Porter, 1994). The level of division of labour is a measurement to identify the extent of inter-firm interaction in a cluster. The lower the level of division of labour is, the less firms interact with the others. In contrast, the more inter-firm specialisation develops, the more a firm trades, cooperates and interacts with the others (Mcdonald and Vertova, 2002). An empirical study concerning the relationships between level of division of labour and investment in R&D projects provides evidence that more highly specialised sectors seem to lead their firms to higher investment in R&D, whereas lacking of division of labour among firms seems to reduce the incentive to make formal R&D investment (Leoncini and Lotti, 2004).

On the other hand, inter-firm interaction does not necessarily lead to fast-growing innovative activities. A review of cluster studies in the literature indicates a clear link between interaction, research and development, learning and innovation, but it does not confirm that a cluster will necessarily become a dynamic centre for innovation. The key distinction between the cluster in which innovation may occur, and a cluster that becomes an innovative hotspot may be attributed to the existence of competition within clusters (Pauder and St. John, 1996). In fact, leader firms are important determinants to reinforce a linkage between interaction and innovation. There are three reasons for this. First, in contrast to small-medium enterprises (SMEs), relatively large firms may have more continuous and intentional conduct in R&D due to access to finance, control over technology and organisational capabilities. Second, large firms, which take a leading role in growth, can combine two aspects of resources: on the one hand, their linkages with external universities and research organisations, which enable them to generate and transfer knowledge, and on the other hand, their connections with the spin-off firms that have grown under their umbrella (Fraydin, 2005). Third, as organisers of production networks, large firms can play a dominant role in constructing a product production network based on a value chain through outsourcing and sub-contracting within clusters (Yusuf, 2004). Particularly, large firms might integrate local productive resource into global networks (Tödling, 1994).

Researchers have found that the concept of lead firms, as the focal point in cluster and network development is common within the literature (Axelsson and Easton, 1992; Albino, 1998; Scott, 1998). Leader-firms generally have stronger incentive and capabilities than SMEs in investment in R&D projects. They can often bring an intentional investment in R&D, put it into daily budget arrangement, and sign a lot of formal contracts with the others for innovative activities, consequently, leader-firms may become a main source of knowledge spillover (Harrison, 1997). In the case of a lack of leader-firms in a cluster, the content of interaction for innovative activities may be diminished (Camuffo, 2003). In this sense, the difference in the sizeable composition of firms is also regarded as a measurement of cluster classification (Markusen, 1996).

The four-extent interaction for innovation can be identified through combination of level of division of labour and composition of sizable firms in clusters in Table 12.1.

Table 12.1 provides a summary of the principal characteristics of clusters regarding extensiveness of interaction. In type A, the extent of interaction in production chains is so thin that knowledge spillover

Table 12.1: Firm Composition, Division of Labour and Cluster Characteristics.

Dimensions of Classification	Division of Labour	
	Low	High
Composition of sizable firms		
Dominante of SMEs	**A, Thin interaction** Examples Survival cluster (Altenburg and Meyer-Stamer, 1999); Informal cluster (Mytelka and Farinelli, 2000)	**B, Insufficient innovation-led interaction** Examples Marshallian District (Markusen, 1996); Italy districts (Pietrobelli, 2004)
Composition of large–small firms	**C, Impossible Interaction** Examples Industrial Park (Wangjici, 2006); Export processing Zone (Diniz and Borges Santos, 1995)	**D, Relatively innovation-Intensive Interaction** Examples Hub-Spoke District (Markusen, 1996); Cluster of TNCs (Altenburg and Meyer-Stamer, 1999)

derived from tacit knowledge is rather narrow due to low level of division of labour and weakness of lead-firms within cluster. This type which is characterised by simple agglomeration of firms without inter-firm specialisation and leader firms is regarded as a survival cluster (Altenburg and Meyer-Stamer, 1999). Examples are the auto parts clusters, in Kumasi, Ghana and Nnewi, Nigeria which are regarded as informal clusters (Mytelka and Farinelli, 2000), and the shoes cluster in San Mateo Atenco, Mexico, and metal and auto repairs in Gamarra, Lima. The level of inter-firm specialisation is high, while absence of leading firms restrains innovation-led interaction which is regarded as a purposeful action in cooperation with each other in type B. This is a basic reason why researchers take Italian districts as organised clusters rather than innovative clusters. At present, the Italian clusters which are named Marshallian industrial districts are seen as a typical case in traditional industries (Guerrieri and Iammarino, 2001). A comparative study concerning dynamic upgrading of industrial districts between Taiwan and Italy, confirms this evidence that Taiwan's pillar industries transformed successfully into electronics, but Italy did not, which started its economic development from clothing and textiles in 1960s. The difference lies in the size of firms. In two cases, for example, the multinational corporations and leading local firms played a dominant role in dynamic process of leading industries. In contrast, SMEs predominated in Italy (Pietrobelli, 2004). Type C is regarded as the one which is initiated and planned by government with a purposeful action, such as the high-tech-based industrial parks and export processing zones (EPZ). In this type, a number of firms of entrance into EPZ are possibly attributed to different industries, and their vertical and horizontal integration surrounding production chain are not existent. Furthermore, they do not need to build upon intensive linkages network in comparison with outsider networks. Therefore, it is rare to generate an interaction with each other. This type is excluded in this chapter. Comparatively, since the extent of interaction for innovation in type D exceeds other types due to the two advantages, it is defined as a relatively innovation-intensive interaction.

The nature and extensiveness of interaction among different players is an important determinant to identify the opportunity and performance of innovative activities. Innovative activities may be categorised into two aspects: informal and formal innovative activities. Informal innovative activities are a spin-off of interaction between different players, stemming from externalities which include, for example, access to specialised human resources and suppliers, knowledge spillover, pressure for higher performance in head to head competition, and learning from close interaction with specialised customers and suppliers (Vatne and Taylor, 2001), while formal innovative activities are defined as an intentional and purposeful action which is initiated and implemented by formal sectors, such as firms, local governments and technological service centres. Firms are seen as main drivers to make technological progress (Freeman, 1997). However, if they have no capabilities for innovative activities, a number of formal supporting factors may play an important role for innovation. As regards the manner of innovation activities, in type D, since leader firms, as formal sectors, can intentionally bring the investment in R&D into budget plan of activities, and cooperate with other organisations in research and development of products and process, a self-sustained mechanism of industrial-based interaction for innovation activities, generally set up through informal and formal innovation comple ment. Therefore, type D is often regarded as a higher stage of cluster development (Sverrisson, 2004) or innovative clusters (Mytelka and Farinelli, 2000). In type B, informal innovation activ ities are a necessary but not sufficient condition for a sustainable innovation, so the interaction of informal activities with formal activities is emphasised in literature on the competitiveness of Italian districts. Particularly formal innovation may play more important role in innovation for product and processes in comparison with informal innovation activities because codified knowledge is more important for innovation for products and processes than tacit knowledge (Cainelli, and De Liso, 2004). However, the thinness of interaction between firms and institutions in type A is defined as a symbol of the primary stage of cluster in developing countries (Humphrey, 1995; Humphrey and Schmitz, 1996; Nadvi, 1999). In type A, the effect of informal innovation activities, on the importance of innovation as an unintentional form, is rather narrow and small. Furthermore, the effect of externalities presents an advantage to the firm using it as input without cost to that firm, but the source of innovation may be exhausted if every individual firm has this incentive to pin his hope on the effect of externalities instead of their own investment in R&D, in the case of a limited influence from outsiders. In order to overcome the thinness of informal innovation activities, formal innovation activities may play a leading role in the stage of innovative initiation. Most clusters in Guangdong province, China are attributed to this situation. The evolution of this type is examined as the main point of this chapter.

12.3 Processes and Stages of Interaction

The evolution of clusters may be understood as a dynamic process of reinforced interaction through firms and institutions increasing gradually. The emergence of clusters is an uncoordinated and self-interested action of firms responding to historical accidents and geographical conditions (Krugman, 1996; Fujita *et al.*, 1999). However, once a cluster forms, a supporting sector begins to play an important role in its dynamic development. Figure 12.1 displays three features in forming interaction for innovation. First, it is an interactive system composed of six relationships, such as between firms and local government, firms and associations, firms and TICs (Technological Innovation Centre), TICs and local government, local government and associations, TICs and associations. Second, there is a basic sequence in building these interacting networks among different participants. The establishment of TICs financed by local government is the first step because the innovative activities need a special institution for supporting innovation rather than local government due to its multiple responsibilities (Kaufmann, and Tödtling, 2003). And then a part of specific services separated from TICs with multiple functions becomes an independent unit, such as an entrepreneurs association,

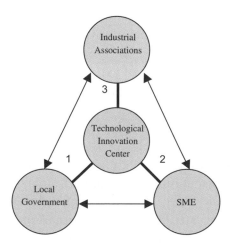

Figure 12.1: Interaction Between TICs and Firms.

training centre and so on. Following is provision of commercial services for innovation, such as financing, accounting, design, advertising, consulting, and legal services. Obviously, the sequence depends on the increase in economic scale based on the level of specialisation. Third, TICs are placed in a central position in interactive networks, which is determined by the importance of formal innovation in supporting a sustainable interaction for innovation. On the one hand, in a cluster defined as in the stage of the survival model, there are different things that obstruct the flow of local knowledge, such as problems arising at the boundary between one speciality and the next and the tendency to safeguard a stock of proprietary knowledge, in other words craft secrets (Sabel, 1996). On the other hand, as the experience of several clusters indicates, agglomeration may be an asset for enterprises, but it can also lead to regional lock-in as a development path, which turns out to be harmful in the long run (Glasmeir, 1994). The main solutions to lock-in problems are related to innovation and innovative networking (Braydin, 2005). Since innovative activities do not occur automatically in the cluster which is characterised by crafts and local small firms (Smallbone, North and Vickers, 2003), a formal supporting sector with a purposeful action is critical for regional innovative activities. Once TICs are established, the interaction between TICs and firms is an important determinant for innovative activities among these six relationships in Figure 12.1.

In order to deeply examine the interaction in innovative activities between SMEs and TICs within a cluster, it is essential to define aims and target of TICs for SMEs innovation. Many empirical studies show that TICs may be given different targets in different countries, for example in the SMEPOL[2] research project (Tödling and Kaufmann, 2001), but the aim of client-oriented services is common (Gil *et al.*, 2003). Since the needs of SMEs for technological innovation are

---

[2] SMEPOL is the abbreviation of 'SME Policy and the Regional Dimension of Innovation,' which is a regional study including Northern Norway, South-Eastern Norway, Upper Austria, Triangle region in Denmark, Lombardy, Apulia (Italy), Limburg (Netherlands), Wallonia (Belgium), Valencia (Spain), London-Lee Valley, the Adjacent-Outer Metropolitan Area (Hertfordshire Essex) in U.K.

changeable in different stages of development, accordingly, supporting functions of TICs are needed to adapt to this change. As regards innovative interaction between SMEs and TICs, to adapt the needs of SMEs for innovation in different stage of development, TICs are often classified into three functions, which include the suppliers of new designs of products and processes; providers of technological facilities, which offer a measurement for standardisation of product quality and provide a service for transformation from a new design into a new sample; and brokers of innovation, who identify the technological need of firms, transfer technological information into firms, and mobilise external research resources for cooperation with internal firms.

The interacting evolution between SMEs and TICs is a dynamic process that TICs have to adapt a changeable need of SMEs for innovative activities. The SMEs needs for innovation services are different when they are in the different stages of development. Thus, it is essential to explicitly define the characteristics of different stages of development based on SMEs needs for innovation. For example, if SMEs lack the awareness of innovation activities because of the limitation in innovative system such as credit, human resource, skill and market (Pake and Senenberger, 1992), it is regarded as a primary stage of innovative activities. If SMEs have few innovative activities in product innovation which is incremental versus radical, such as new designs and styles, but lack the investment in new technological facilities, such as machinery and equipments, it is a second stage for innovative activities in the cluster. If they have a certain capability in both new designs of product and process and intentional investment in R&D projects, but lack accessibility to strategic information, interaction with knowledge providers and adequate human resources, it is a third stage in innovative activities. Some empirical studies on the innovation patterns of SMEs in clusters in European countries indicates that the key of their TICs provides technological information, connection with external institutions and services for training which is mainly attributed to the third stage in innovative activities (Enright, 1996; Asheim *et al.*, 2003), while another study on innovative activities of clusters in developing countries show that it is a precondition for SMEs innovation to raise awareness of SMEs for

Table 12.2: Interaction between Innovative Demands of SMEs and Functional Structure of TICs.

	Three Functions in TICs		
Structure Processes	Intermediate Information & Resource	Technological Facilities	New Designs Products & Processes
Capabilities of firm			
1) Lack of awareness and capabilities for innovation	X	X	X
2) Improvement of design capabilities but lack of facilities	X	X	
3) Enhancement of facilities capabilities but demand for external information and resource	X		

innovation activities which are seen as the first stage of development (Schmitz and Nadvi, 1999). Table 12.2 draws on a dynamic process of interaction between SMEs and TICs which evolves from a primary stage towards an advanced stage.

The first row expresses interaction between SMEs and TICs in the primary stage of innovative activities in Table 12.2. TICs provide almost all supporting functions for SMEs due to their lack of almost all resources of innovative activities. However, it is a dominant part of functional structure for TICs to supply a set of new designs and styles of products and processes for SMEs because it is most important to raise innovative awareness for SMEs. In order to do so, it is necessary to furnish a set of new designs of products at a high price for SMEs. There are three reasons to develop and supply new products from TICs. First, new products are a starting point for SMEs to generate their incentive for innovation despite the lack of innovative awareness because technological support provided by TICs is not as effective as new products supply. The risk of investment in R&D is least for SMEs to get into innovative activities. Second, the price of new products provided by TICs is much lower than those SMEs get from market because the new product developed by TICs is indirectly subsidised by local government. This tends to attract SMEs to buy these new designs of products. Third, SMEs may get technological instruction from TICs if they purchase new designs of products. As a result, although emulation is an important mechanism of technological diffusion in clusters (Carbonara, 2004), for example, SMEs find that once a few of them use these new designs, and make much more profit than before, accordingly, the other firms tend to follow them in the cluster, SMEs are possibly willing to buy new designs of products rather than make an imitation due to the difference in technological instruction from TICs. At the beginning of innovative activities, SMEs behaviour in investment in R&D activities is incidental and unintentional. Along with a stable increase in profit by using new designs of products by SMEs, it makes it possible for SMEs to adopt intentional behaviour for innovation. Obviously, in the evolutional process, SMEs do not only need to get a sustainable support from TICs, but also focus on the functions in designs provided by TICs. In view of supply and demand for new designs of products as a dominant characteristic, this stage of interaction may be defined as a design-oriented interaction.

The second row represents the interaction between SMEs and TICs in the second stage of innovative activities. The emergence of this stage is mainly driven by some firms which become leader ones through their rapid growth. A number of leader firms find that limited designs and styles provided by TICs are relatively bald and slowly variable, and they cannot completely satisfy the needs of SMEs for product diversification, because TICs are not, like SMEs, close to the market (Wang, 2002). However, they have not yet sufficient investment in facilities for new product production designed and developed by them. Furthermore, they are not willing to suffer a high cost from waiting for new designs while more and more SMEs try to buy innovative products from TICs. Thus, some leader firms begin to make new designs of products by themselves instead of purchasing from TICs, and then ask TICs for a process from new designs to prototypes, and finally, make a decision according to the complexity and availability of the prototypes produced by TICs. In evidence, the substitution of making for purchasing new designs of products is a sign by which some leader firms raise their innovative capabilities in a cluster. In order to adapt to the change of these leader firms in innovative needs, the function of TICs needs to be transformed from a supplier of innovative products to a provider of machinery and equipment services which include a measurement to products quality and processing for new designs entrusted by SMEs, since the interaction between these leader firms and TICs concentrates on contracts with technological facilities for services in this stage. Thus, it is referred to be as a facility-focused interaction.

The third row shows the third stage of innovative activities in a cluster. Since this stage is characterised by the interaction between SMEs and TICs concentrated on services for supporting innovative activities, such as technological information, training service, intelligent resource, and connection to external research institution, it is seen as a technological service-intensive interaction. The emergence of this stage still is a consequence of firms interacting with TICs. Along with the enhancement of a number of firms in innovative capabilities, they may worry about the disclosure of specific technological information to competitors, such as new designs and styles which are consigned to TICs for prototypes processing in the environment of imitative-competition in clusters. As a result, through a sizable investment in machines and equipment, they can gradually replace a processing deal outsourced to TICs with one made by themselves. On the other hand, they are gradually strong in the 'hardware' capacities, such as machines and equipment, but weak in the 'software' aspects, such as technological information, expertise resources, connecting to external research institutions (Garofoli and Musyck, 2003). Thus, the change of needs for SMEs requires that TICs take a set of intensive services in 'software' supporting as a main function in functional structure. Eraydin (2005) showed that when local and national R&D institutions proved inefficient to meet the needs of firms, the firms followed two strategies to find R&D based competence, the first was to use foreign R&D institutes and universities in Sweden and Germany and the second to utilise R&D department within the co-operation or to initiate research in co-operation with foreign strategic partners. In the process to find external intelligent resources, TICs play an important role, such as connecting local firms to external research institutions, recommending high quality labour to local firms and stimulating co-operation with outside partners (Schmitz, 2004).

12.4 A Model of Supporting Mechanism

In the innovative interaction between TICs and SMEs, it is not sufficient for TICs to be required to adapt to the changeable needs of firms according to only a functional perspective, it is also very important to consider whether TICs have a sufficient incentive to do it or not in terms of interest because they are not completely regarded as public sectors. Although funds for TICs' establishment are possibly financed completely by local government in the early days of development, once TICs are set up, they are possibly required to become a unit of responsibility for their own profit and loss. There are three reasons for choosing this mechanism. First, local governments are not willing to keep a fixed expense for TICs maintenance as an administrative unit every year, the aim is to stimulate TICs to improve their competition, and reduce pressure on public spending in supporting innovation. The most important target of TICs is to attract a number of outside firms in similar industries to inflow into clusters through TICs' technological services to them (Qiu and Xu, 2004). Second, TICs may feel much more competitive pressure as a unit of responsibility for profit and loss because their survival and development depend mainly on their performance of services for SMEs innovation. Only if TICs provide high quality services and expand the scale of services for SMEs, can they keep their sustainable development. This may lead to improvement in TICs production efficiency and services quality. Third, SMEs may be stimulated to economise the use for TICs resources due to the charge for services although the fee charging is much lower than that of the average level in the market.

Obviously, the functions that TICs should undertake for supporting innovation is not completely consistent with the preference that TICs can choose based on their own benefit. The difference between functions and interest has an important impact on TICs behaviour and performance. Some empirical studies show that TICs' role is considerably different in supporting innovative activities although there are TICs in almost all clusters in European countries (Christensen *et al.*, 2003; Neauwelaers *et al.*, 2003). Therefore, in order to stimulate interaction between TICs and SMEs in clusters, it is very important to identify and to understand this mechanism in special balance between functions and interest. Figure 12.2 shows the specific mechanism of TICs in supporting innovation.

Figure 12.2 is composed of A2 and B2. In A2, as a horizontal axis, OK represents a size of investment in TICs, while OY expresses a return. OM is the line of average earnings, while OF is a functional curve for TICs. There are three parts on OF, which represent three functions of TICs. OF^3 expresses a function in which TICs are mainly regarded as a technological broker, while F^2F^3 shows a function of TICs as a provider of the machinery and equipments for services and F^1F^2 represents a function of TICs as a supplier of new designs and

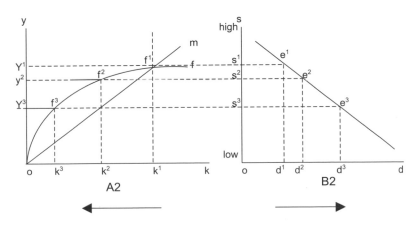

Figure 12.2: Specific Mechanism of TICs in Supporting Innovation.

styles of products and processes. B2 represents a curve of demands of SMEs for technological supplies from TICs. OS represents the extent of technological complexity which is from low to high, while E is a curve of demand for different functions. Since the extent of specific asset is positively related to the transaction cost (Williamson, 1975), and the process of which TICs' functions transform from OF^3 to F^1F^2 is increasing in investment in specific assets, and then along with the increase in specific assets, quantities of demand of SMEs is slowly down in clusters, thus, the curve of demand of SMEs for technological services is negatively related to the technological complexity.

The mechanism in the difference between functions and interest consists of the contracts between local government and TICs, difference between cost and benefit per function and effect of choice in innovation. Three aspects for TICs can be explained in Figure 12.2. First, the contracts between local government and TICs have an important impact on TICs performance in supporting innovative activities in clusters. Generally, the contracts consist mainly of the basic line for funds financed by local government and the incentives that TICs become responsible for their own profit and loss. Basic line for funds means that there is a minimum requirement for TICs in investment in three functions when TICs set up. As shown in A2, OK^1 may be regarded as a minimum requirement in investment at one time. If the investment financed by the public sector is lower than the minimum requirement, the supporting role for TICs to play in innovative activities tends to drop, because an essential demand for SMEs to initiate their innovative activities is some new designs of product but not technological facilities and information in the early days of development. Since the innovation in products and processes as a downward product development is a result of accumulative investment in upward and supporting parts, such as R&D projects, facilities, available intelligence, technological information and connection to external research institutions, thus, insufficiency of public resources is often a significant constraint for TICs in the early days of development but the private sector has capabilities and incentive to make a joint investment with the public sector in these innovative activities (Schimitz and Nadvi, 1999). Therefore, a precondition for TICs to set up is that a public sector in cluster has to reach an amount of accumulation. An empirical study provides some evidence that the existence of a lot of traditional industrial clusters have been more than twenty years in Guangdong province, but TICs were not established in the early days of their development, but at the end of the 20th century and at the beginning of the 21st century. Obviously, the lag of establishment of TICs is closely related to the extent of public accumulation (Wang, 2002).

The incentive for TICs to become responsible for profit and loss is a result of contracts between local government and TICs. TICs are required to further provide technological services, while they get an amount of resources from local government. The question is how to transform a mechanism from an outside requirement to self activation. The incentive contracts play an important role in this evolutional process. At present, two types can be found in the incentive contracts. One is that once TICs set up, it is likely to be a new mechanism of responsibility for profit and loss. For example, the hardware, such as capital goods, productive materials, and specific asset is provided by the public sector, while the software, such as wage and managerial fees depend on their performance. Another is that there is a contractual duration of transformation for TICs from receiving support from local government to self activation. There is a different duration of the transition in different industries, the stage of development and technological complexity, but it is very critical for TICs to deal with the balance between functions and interest in supporting innovative activities.

Second, the difference between cost and benefit in different functions is a key point to understand whether TICs interact successfully with SMEs for innovation. As shown in Figure 12.2, the different functions undertaken by TICs have different proportions between cost and benefit. For example, in the OF^3 phase which is seen as a supplier of general services in sector-related technological information and connection in A2, on the one hand, TICs do not need to spend a great amount of investment in specific machinery and equipments, but only provide the services for connection and information related to the outside knowledge and technological providers. On the other hand, the demand of SMEs for these intensive services provided by TICs is quite extensive because of its commonality for SMEs. As it shows, the demand of SMEs for TICs services is at curve E^3 in B2. This results in $OY^3/OK^3 > 1$. In F^2F^3 stage, the increase of investment in machinery and equipment is much more than that in the OF^3 phase, while the demands of SMEs for machinery and equipments tend to be shrunk to E^2 in B2 because of increase in specific technology. Thus, the proportion between the cost and benefit may be transformed to $Y^2Y^3/K^2K^3 < 1$. F^1F^2 is the most complex in supporting functions undertaken by TICs for innovation. In order to implement this function, TICs not only make a lot of investment in machinery and equipment, as well as information and connection with outside knowledge providers, but also engage directly in product development. Meanwhile, the demand of SMEs for specific technological supply tends to decline because the more specific the new products are provided, the less in the SMEs need. E^1 shows the change in B2. Therefore, the proportion between the cost and benefit tends to be $Y^1Y^2/K^1K^2 < Y^2Y^3/K^2K^3$. The different proportions between the cost and benefit per function are an important reason why there are efficiency gaps in different functions.

Third, the effect of choice on innovation is an unforced consequence of combining a financially independent unit and the difference between the cost and benefit per function. As far as cluster for innovation in the early stage of development is concerned, on the one hand, the proportions between the cost and benefit tend to be $Y^1Y^2/K^1K^2 < Y^2Y^3/K^2K^3 < OY^3/OK^3$ in the three functions. On the other hand, the less firms hold innovative capabilities, the more TICs are required to undertake the three functions for innovation. In contrast, as a financially interdependent unit, the best choice for TICs is to provide technological services in the OY^3/OK^3 phase or Y^2Y^3/K^2K^3 phase but not in Y^1Y^2/K^1K^2, in other words, in order to avoid a loss in supporting innovation, TICs are willing to stay in the services intensive stage or facility oriented stage, but not to enter the designs focused stage. However, the aim and target of TICs set by local government for innovation is to stimulate innovative activities in clusters.

Obviously, the choice which is in favour of TICs may not be completely beneficial to SMEs innovation in clusters. Thus, there is a conflict between the choice of TICs in function and the needs of SMEs for innovation. If this conflict is not effectively solved, the quality of the innovative interacting between TICs and SMEs in cluster is subject to serious influence even though there are TICs in clusters. Some empirical studies provide evidence that the role of TICs to play in supporting innovation is not quite effective for SMEs (Gil *et al.*, 2003). Therefore, the existence of TICs does not necessarily play a role in supporting innovation. The challenge is to deal with the balance between functions undertaken by TICs and their interest.

Apparently, it is necessary for TICs to enter the F^2F^3 phase for new designs of product in supporting innovation, but it is quite important to be shortened in F^1F^2 phase. The feasible and available conditions lie in growing capabilities of leader firms in innovation of products and processes in clusters, because the leader firms may stand in innovation of products for TICs. Thus, the demand of leader firms for TICs tend to slow down, TICs may exit from the function of product development and enter the other functions which have a much higher proportions between benefit and cost. If the leader firms grow rapidly, the duration that TICs are engaged in supporting product development is very short. Consequently, TICs may not generate much loss for supporting innovation of products. In contrast, if the leader firms grow slowly, thus the longer TICs have to remain in F^2F^3 phase, and the more they generate a loss. This is an important reason why TICs cannot afford sustainable maintenance in F^2F^3 phase. Many empirical studies find that the role of leader firms has a complementary relationship to the functions of technological services in supporting innovative activities within clusters (Arthur, 1990; Axelsson and Easton, 1992; Sverrisson, 2004; Eraydin, 2005). When most SMEs within cluster are not strong enough in investment in product innovation, TICs may play an important role in supporting innovation of products. When a number of leader firms are getting strong in product innovation, the adjustment of TICs in their functional structure might possibly occur.

12.5 Evidence from Guangdong Clusters

Guangdong (GD), as a coastal province of China, has played an important role in China's economic development since the 1980s. Some comparative data indicates the difference of development is increasing between GD and the rest of the country. For example, the contribution of GD to national GDP was 11.9%, population 5.9% of gross population in 2005. During the period of 1980–2005, the annual growth rate of GDP in GD was 13.7%, while it was 9.5% in China. The acceleration of GD economic development started from the early days of 1980s. At that time, GDP per capita in GD was US$369, ranking 22 in the whole country which was composed of 27 provinces and 3 municipalities, while average level throughout country was US$389 in 1980 (according to the official exchange rate at that time, which was US$1:2.64 yuan). However, GDP per capita in GD was US$2882, while average level throughout the country was US$1703 in 2005 (the official exchange rate was US$1:8.19 yuan). Looking at GD's development pattern, the industrial clusters have played an important role in the process of rapid economic development in GD since 1980. Particularly, after the 1990s, in some counties with active market economy and better transportation, telecommunication and informative conditions in Guangdong province, in many towns appeared a lot of industries with sales volume of over a billion, several billion up to ten billion yuan. In these towns, relatively concentrated on one industry, reasonable specialised division and business networks have been formed, the key point for economic growth in GD development. In 2003, there were 164 industrial clusters which employed more than 3.25 million workers, and exceeded 426 billion yuan, (approximately US$52 billion) in annual output value, which accounted for 24.3% of total output value of industries in GD province.

According to the different emergence of clusters, GD's industrial clusters can be classified into two types. One is external firms-based clusters with a lot of firms from outside Mainland China concentrated on the eastern side of Pearl River, such as the Shenzhen-Dongguan-Huizhou area. These clusters are mainly overseas Chinese firms and foreign investment driven due to the proximity to Hong Kong and the preferential development policy for coastal regions in the 1980s. Dongguan is regarded as a major base of these clusters with localised concentration (Wang and Tong, 2005). Among these clusters, both famous PC-related companies, including IBM, Compaq, Dell, Acer, and the domestic companies Legend, and Founder have established plants or purchased parts in this area. Over 20,000 firms are engaged in PC parts and component processing. The other is the domestic firms-based cluster which is characterised by SMEs that are engaged in traditional industries, such as shoes, textiles, garments, aluminum alloys, toys, foods and drinks, building material, chapter, auto parts, arts and crafts, leather material, metalwork, plastics, furniture, apparatus manufacturing, non-ferrous metals and so on. Clustering in traditional industries can be found in many regions. These clusters have been anchored to a network of small and medium-sized towns somewhere between the large cities and the deep countryside (Wang, 2005). Among 164 clusters in GD, over 85% belong to this type. Schmitz (2004) found that industrial upgrading depends mainly on the leader firms in the first type such as TNCs, while the supporting schemes and institutions have important effects on upgrading in the second type in a region. In order to examine the evolution of interaction between SMEs and TICs, the second type is a central target of the survey in GD province.

It is clear that there are three features of the endogenous firms-based cluster in the process of their emergence and development in GD. First, almost all endogenous firms-based clusters are mainly composed of SMEs that are often family firms. This confirms the traditional results on the importance of family ties, traditions and a sort of 'path-dependence' in these clusters. Second, the industries penetrated by SMEs are mainly labour intensive and focus on final consumption products, and account for over 80% of clusters in GD province. This reflects the process of their establishment starting with simple products, like food, clothes, shoes, and clustered in neighbourhoods, around a market place for their products. Third, the low price of the products is most important in basic competitiveness due to the low cost of labour. For example, at the beginning of the 1990s, the price of a pair of sport shoes made by stated-owned enterprises in Guangzhou city is nearly double the shoes made by private-enterprises in some rural areas, which is approximately only 50 kilometres away from Guangzhou city. However, low price is often also related to low quality and low technologies of SMEs. With the increase in the cost of labour, the effects of product quality and technological capabilities on their competitiveness become more important.

The establishment of these clusters started in the mid-1980s. After more than 20 years, a number of SMEs broadened their economic scale, refreshed their machinery equipments and created their own brand-name products, while many firms still followed previously traditional mode of production, but profit margins dropped because of the change of the market structure from a seller's market-driven economy into a buyer's market-driven economy in the whole country. Particularly, with the acceleration of technological progress and the the tendency of economic globalisation, the competitive pressure stemming from expanding the domestic and international market faced by SMEs became greater since 1998, when financial crises in South-East Asian countries occurred. In order to support SMEs to improve qualities of products and raise their competitiveness, the provincial government proposed that TICs should be set up in every town with a leading industry, which was defined as an industrial-specialised town,[3] and subsidized 300,000 yuan for the TICs built in these towns, according to the requirement, while the rest was financed by governments at the basic level, including municipalities, counties and town governments. Up to now, among 156 industrial specialised towns, 54% of these towns established TICs with functions of supply technical development, transaction for technology and patents, trainings and consulting for business and management; 66.7% organised industrial associations; 52.5% towns have set up with TI networks;

---

[3] The industry-specific town refers to a town as a basic unit of cluster. This definition is not an administrative classification but a result of a primary stage of clusters development. Meanwhile the cluster with an explicitly administrative boundary is in favour of implement supporting schemes made by local governments (Wang, 2002; 2005).

81.3% have organised trade fairs and so on. The six TICs in Zhongshan and Nanhai cities respectively display the economic environments and conditions TICs were built and endowed with the functions in supporting SMEs innovation in Tables 12.3 and 12.4.

In order to evaluate the effects of TICs on innovation in clusters, we chose two towns as typical cases, which are Xiqiao town in Nanhai city and Xiaolan town in Zhongshan city in Tables 12.3 and 12.4. The common factors are relatively date of the establishment of TICs, more typical in the interacting phases and more significant in the impact on innovation activities and economic development. The difference between them is the approach of TICs to the financially independent units.

As a textile industrial cluster, Xiqiao town is more than 1000 years old, starting from traditional mode of production which is called 'Mulberry Foundation Fish Pond' in a geographical district of transportation pivot.[4] After the 1970s, with the gradual substitution of synthetic fibre products for natural fabric, Xiqiao town began to turn into Dylan textiles mainly with chemical fibre textiles as raw material. Since the 1980s, when China's economic reforms began, Xiqiao entrepreneurs grasped a favourable opportunity for great development of textile industry because of a rapid increase in the domestic demand for textile goods. After the mid-1990s, the growth rate declined in Xiqiao due to the inadaptability of the quality and designs of products produced by SMEs to the change of the demand conditions. TICs set up in 1998 in which Xiqiao town was seen as a turning point of economic development.

Local government at township level imported a set of advanced computer systems for the plate-making of textile goods, such as computer-aided designs (CAD) and computer-aided manufacturing

---

[4] In the Mulberry Foundation Fish Pond production mode, pond mud fertilizes the mulberry trees which produce bigger and healthier leaves for silkworm food. Well fed silkworms produce more silk of enhanced quality and more waste that finally feeds the fishes: mulberry tree culture, sericiculture and fish farming are combined in this old and ecological production system.

Table 12.3:   Economic Indicators in Zhongshan and Nanhai Cities.

Name of Towns / Industries	Xiqiao	Jinsha	Pingzhou	Xiaolan	Dachong	Guzhen
	Textile	Metal Working	Shoes	Metal Working	Furniture	Light and Lantern
Emergence of TICs in	1998	1999	2002	2000	2001	2002
Investment in TICs (10,000 yuan)	836.9	300	1500	700	180	500
Numbers of Patents	188	21(00)	86(01)	13459(02)	130(00)	185
GDP (0.1billion)	45(02)	8.49(02)	29.3(01)	76(03)	6.75(00)	24.6
Total value of Industries and Agriculture (0.1b)	109	16.4(02)			33.62(02)	85.56
Total value of Industry (0.1b)	96.56	13.9	109.73	205	30.2(02)	77.12
Total value of specific Industries (0.1b)	33.5(02)	5.8(00)	60	59(00)	21.30(02)	57.84
Area (sq. km)	176.63	59.6	55.7	75.4	45.5	47.3
Population (10,000)	20	8	23.8	30	6.2	8.5
Number of firms	1380	1198(02)	1804	5100	626(02)	1450(02)

Note: (00), (01), (2) respectively represent the data in 2000–2002, while the others are data from 2003.
Source: Bureau of Science and Technology of GD Province.

Table 12.4: Organisations and Functions of TICs in the Part of Zhongshan and Nanhai Cities.

Regions	Industries	Organisation and Functions
Zhongshan city		
Da Chong Town	Furniture	TICs cooperate with the research institution for energy, Academy of China's Sciences, China's Forestry college and China's Forestry academy and provide furniture designs, R&D, technological training, information services.
Guzhen Town	Lights and lanterns	TICs provide a set of services through investment in machinery equipments for detecting quality of lamps and lanterns, and for designs and in platform for information sectors.
Xiaolan Town	Metal working	TICs hold a set of advanced laser molding and mould fast worked out equipment, provide fast patternmaking for services, and instruct application of Computer-aid Design (CAD), and Computer-aid Manufacturing (CAM) system into operation running.
Nanhai city		
Xiqiao Town	Textiles	TICs hold a set of software for pattern, marking and printing, and provide detecting for product quality, networking, collecting and processing prototypes for services.
Jinsha Town	Metal working	TICs hold an optic trilinear coordinates measuring instrument imported from Germany and data base, as well as laser molding equipment, and provide a set of services for SMEs.
Pingzhou Town	Shoes	TICs hold a set of equipment for detecting the quality of products, provide a self-contained support for the sector, product development, technological and market information.

(CAM), at 2.4 million yuan investment, and established a company for the plate-making of textile goods and technological services (and then renamed TICs). The new designs and styles of textile goods developed by TICs were sold to SMEs in Xiqiao town at a very low price. Many SMEs that bought new designs and styles got technical services from TICs markedly improved their productivity and raised their competitiveness. The two significant differences between before and afterwards of establishment of TICs can be found in Table 12.5. First, the average size of firms has obviously increased large. Quantity of employment per firm increased to 49 persons in 2003 from 32 persons in 1998. Among sizable firms composition, the numbers of large firms which are more than 100 employees increases from 7 to 22, and the share of their output value to total value of product rose from 14.7% to 41.3%. Second, the firms in investment in R&D projects concentrate on the large ones that had more than 100 employees. The amount of investment in R&D per firm was 0.26 million yuan in 1998 while it was 1.34 million yuan in 2003. Meanwhile, the firms whose size were between 50 and 100 employees in investment in R&D projects did not emerge in 1998, while their amount of investment in R&D reached 18.28 million yuan in 2003. The level of investment in R&D was only about 1000 yuan per annum per firm in 1998, while it was up to 35,000 yuan in 2003.

With the increase in investment in R&D projects and enhancement in innovative capabilities, some leader firms began to make their own designs and styles of products rather than buy them from TICs. The replacement of new products developed by firms for these done by TICs forced TICs to adjust their functional structure for services. Starting from the middle of 2003, the functions of TICs in Xiqiao can be decomposed of five parts, including product development, the promotion of technological diffusion, the services for technological information and facilities, the training for technical skill and the protection for intellectual properties such as patents. An empirical survey on change of functional structure of TICs in Xiqian cluster indicates that the share of products development in total amount of investment into TICs went down from 55% to 24%,

Table 12.5:   Some Evolutional Features in Xiqiao Cluster, 1998–2003.

	1998					2003				
	Number of Firm	Employees	Output (0.1b)	R&D (m)	Patents	Number of Firm	Employees	Output (0.1b)	R&D (m)	Patents
<10	795	7055	3.61	No	No	465	3715	2.53	No	No
11–50	583	26235	10.54	No	No	534	25299	7.67	No	No
51–100	205	19475	8.59	No	No	359	33387	26.19	18.28	22
>100	7	1094	4.98	1.85	No	22	6445	27.47	29.55	166
Total	1670	53900	27.72	1.85	No	1380	68800	63.89	47.83	188
Average of firm	32.28		0.017	0.001	No		49.86	0.046	0.035	0.14

although the total amount of investment in TICs financed by local government increased to more than 8.37 million yuan in 2003 (Wang, 2004).

As far as Xiaolan town is concerned, its emergence that was characterised by manufacturing roundness locks was just in the mid of 1980s when an entrepreneur brought a roundness lock like a doorknob from Hong Kong with him, and found it easy to make an imitation while he dissembled it. And then he opened the first plant in the production of locks in Xiaolan. With the expansion of its production, many firms followed to enter the lock-making industry. Until the end of 1990s, there were 356 firms in the lock-making and related metal working industries. Since the increase in needs for high quality products and decrease in low quality of products in market demands, the share of domestic market declined slightly from nearly one fourth at the mid of 1990s to below 20% at the end of 1990s. Facing the supply of low quality lock products, demands for high quality of these products and fierce market competition, local government in Xiaolan town made an investment of nearly 7 million yuan in importing a set of fast laser-modeling technological system from Germany and a whole set of equipment for model-making from Japan, and set up a TIC to provide some new designs of products with a three-dimensional formwork to SMEs in 2000.

Three changes have markedly taken place in Xiaolan cluster since the establishment of TICs. First, the share of output value contributed by leader firms increased in total output value of lock products in Xiaolan town. The sale value that two firms exceeded over 50 million yuan accounted on below 10% of total lock output value in Xiaolan town in 2000, while four firms exceeded over 100 million yuan accounted for over 20% in 2004. Second, the amount in investment in R&D projects made by the leader firms clearly increased. Only two firms that exceeded over 50 million yuan put money into R&D projects before 2000, while eight firms whose output value exceeded over 30 million yuan built their own R&D department within their firms, the average amount in investment in R&D departments was over 0.78 million yuan in 2004. In the same year, the patent application reached 606, which increased 33.6% in comparison to the year before. Among them, 441 pieces got a delegation of authority. Third, the vertical integration between the leader firms and SMEs has been intensified within Xiaolan cluster. There are 110 stages in working process for a roundness lock of production, including model-making, materials supplies, cutting and stamping, electroplating and assembling. Many component parts and a manufacturing process were finished in one firm before 2000, while many parts in the working process were outsourced by the leader firms that exceeded over 30 million yuan to SMEs in 2004. As a result, the division of labour among firms has been refined and the frequency of interaction between suppliers and producers, the leader firms and SMEs grew. In addition, many manufacturers did not directly promote their own products to market, but were bought by specialised traders. The rapid increase in total output value of lock and related metal working industries that increased from 1.1 billion yuan to 3.6 billion yuan is a consequence of this specialisation and interaction.

Obviously, the changes of lock industrial upgrading are closely related to the important role of TICs in Xiaolan cluster. A survey of innovative activities of firms indicates that the present leader firms whose annual output value exceeds over 30 million yuan are those that received technological services early from TICs. Although they make a reduction in the dependence on TICs for new designs of products due to their own investment in R&D, they increase their demand for TICs in provision of facilities and technological information and consulting. Since TICs are parts of the technological infrastructure, their functions and that of the R&D department in firms are complementary but not replaceable, so the establishment and development of TICs do not stimulate the expansion of firms' scale, but also an increment in investment into R&D projects. A fact in Xiaolan town can be found that the investment in R&D projects made by many leader firms was not before the establishment of TICs but after. At present, over 80% of more than 300 SMEs that engage in lock production and related industries have made several contracts with TICs for various services (Wang, 2006).

By comparison between Xiaolan cluster and Xiqiao cluster, the three factors are common, such as the establishment of TICs financed by multi-level governments for interaction with SMEs, the three functions and their dynamic processes in TICs, and mechanism of TICs as financially independent units that are responsible for profit and loss. However, the differences between Xiaolan cluster and Xiqiao cluster have two aspects. First, there is a long phase of the design-oriented interaction between TICs and SMEs in Xiqiao TICs, while it is relatively short in the first phase in Xiaolan cluster but long in the phase of the facilities-focused interaction due to the difference of the two industries. Second, it is unlike in the time of implementing the mechanism that is responsible for profit and loss. As regards TICs in Xiqiao cluster, once it set up, it is required to operate as a financially independent unit, while TICs in Xiaolan cluster get a sustainable subsidy which is 1 million yuan from local government annual according to the contract although it is not sufficient for them to work.

12.6 Conclusion

The purpose of this study is to analyse an innovative interaction between SMEs and TICs in the process of cluster towards regional innovative system, to understand their evolutional mechanism and determinant factors, and to examine some clustering experiences from GD province, in the south of China. Three points of view in this chapter are summarised as follows. First, a formal institutional setting for innovation plays a more important role in the early stage of development in comparison to informal interaction because of the limitation of both level of specialisation and composition of sizable firms. Along with the improvement in the two constraint conditions, the interaction between informal and formal innovative activity makes possible an important source of innovation. Second, although the establishment of TICs is necessary for innovation to interact between TICs and SMEs, it is not sufficient to keep an effective interaction between both sides. The key point depends on both sides. As regards TICs on the supply side, the different functions lead to a different proportion of cost and benefit, thus, it is quite important for TICs to coordinate the balance between functions and profit through an effective institutional arrangement. If the balance is not well solved, the interaction between TICs and SMEs may be not effective. This can explain why TICs have existed but not generated an effective interaction with SMEs in some clusters. On the demand side, firms' demand to the different technological services provided by TICs in different period is also a key factor for sustainable interaction. If expansion of firm size is accelerated in a rapid growing market economy, the substitution of leader firms for TICs may quickly occur along the sequence of functions that is from designs-oriented phase to facilities-focused or services-intensive phase because of the specific nature of technological assets. As a result, along the adjustment that is from relatively higher cost function of services to a lower one for adaptation to the change of firms' demands for innovative services, the financial pressure on TICs may be weakened respectively. This is the reason why the mechanism of TICs is effective but innovative interaction is not considerably successful, such as in the Italian model (Pierrobelli, 2004). Third, Guangdong experiences in clusters innovation provide some evidences about an effective innovation as a result of common action from interaction between supply and demand. However, although TICs are required to use a new mechanism that is responsible for profit and loss, the revenue from their business often cannot cover their costs in many clusters. Therefore, how to attract the private capital inflow into TICs for a sustainable interaction, and eventually institutional reform caused by common actions between public and private sectors still is an issue to be further studied.

References

ALBINO, Vito, CARAVELLI, C., and SCHIUMA, G. (1999). 'Knowledge Transfer and Inter-firms Relationships in Industrial Districts: The Role of the Leader Firms,' *Technovation*, 19: 53–63.

ALVSTAM, Claes G. and SCHAMP, Eike W. eds. (2005). *Linking Industries Across the World: Processes of Global Networking*, Ashgate.

AMIN, A. (1999). 'The Emilian Model: Institutional Challenges', *European Planning Studies*, 7: 389–405.

ANTONELLI, C. (1997). 'The Economics of Path-dependence in Industrial Organization', *International Journal of Industrial Organization*, **15**: 643–675.

ARROW, K. (1962). 'The Economic Implications of Learning by Doing', *Review of Economic Studies*, **29**: 155–173.

ASHEIM, Bjorn T., ISAKSEN, Arne, NAUWELAERS, Claire and TODTLING, Franz, eds. (2003). *Regional Innovation Policy for Small-Medium Enterprises*, Edward Elgar Cheltenham, UK.

AXELSSON, B., and EASTON, G. (1992). *Industrial Networks. A New View of Reality*, Routedge, London.

BEAUDRY, C. and BRESCHI, S. (2003). 'Are Firms in Clusters Really More Innovative?' in *Economics of Innovation and New Technology*, **12**(4): 325–342.

BECATTINI, G. (1989). 'Sectors and/or Districts: Some Remarks on the Conceptual Foundations of Industrial Economics,' in Goodman, E. and Bamford, J. (eds.), *Small Firms and Industrial Districts in Italy*, Boutledge, London.

BECATTINI, G. (1990). 'The Marshallian Industrial Districts as a Socio-economic Notion,' in F. Pyke G, Becattini *et al.* (eds.), *Industrial Districts and Inter-firm Co-operation in Italy*, International Institute for Labour Studies, ILO, Geneva, pp. 37–45.

BRANSCOMB, L. M. and AUERSWALD, P. E. (2001). *Taking Technical Risks: How Innovators, Executives, and Investors Manage High-Tech Risks*, The MIT Press. Cambridge, Massachusetts, USA.

BRENNER, T. (2004). *Local Industrial Clusters: Existence, Emergence and Evolution*, Routledge, Taylor and Francis Group.

BRUSCO, S. (1982). 'The Emilian Model: Productive Decentralization and Social Integration', *Cambridge Journal of Economics*, **6**: 167–184.

BRUSCO, S. (1990). 'The Idea of the Industrial District: Its Genesis', *Industrial Districts and Inter-firm Co-operation in Italy*, in Pyke, F., Becattini, G. and Sengenberger, W. (eds.), International Institute for Labour Studies, Geneva.

CAINELLI Giulio and ZOBOLI Roberto. (2004). *The Evolution of Industrial Districts: Changing Governance, Innovation and Internationalization of Local Capitalism in Italy*, Physica-Verlag, Aspringer-Verlage Company.

CAINELLI, Giulio and DE LISO, Nicola. (2004). 'Can a Marshallian Industrial District be Innovative? The case of Italy', in Cainelli Giulio and Zoboli Roberto (eds.), *The Evolution of Industrial Districts: Changing Governance, Innovation and Internationalisation of Local Capitalism in Italy*, pp. 243–256, Physica-Verlag, A Springer-Verlag Company.

CARBONARA, N. (2004). 'Innovation Processes Within Geographical Clusters. A Cognitive Approach', *Technovation*, **24**: 17–28.

CHOU, Baoxing (1999). *The Small Firms Clustering*, Fudan University Press, Shanghai, China.

COHEN, W., M. and LEVINTHAL, D. A. (1989). 'Innovation and Learning: The Two Faces of R&D', *Economic Journal*, **99**: 569–596.

COOKE, P. (2002). *Knowledge Economies: Clusters. Learning and Cooperative Advantage*, Routledge, London and New York.

ENRIGHT, M. (1996). 'Regional Clusters and Economic Development: A Research Agenda,' in Staber, U. *et al.* (eds.), *Business Networks: Prospects for Regional Development*, Walter de Gruyter, Berlin.

ERAYDIN, A. (2005). 'Global Networks as Open Gates for Regional Innovation System', in Alvstam, C. G. and Schamp, E. W. (eds.), *Linking Industries Across the World: Process of Global Networking*, Ashgate, Aldershot, pp. 53–88.

FELSENSTEIN, D. and TAYLOR, M. (eds.). (2001). *Promoting Local Growth, Process, Practice and Policy*, Ashgate, Aldershot.

FREEMAN, C. and SOETE, Luc. (1997). *The Economics of Industrial Innovation*, third edition, The MIT Press, Cambridge, USA.

FUJITA, M., KRUGMAN, P. and MORI, T. (1999). 'On the Evolution of Hierarchical Urban System', *European Economic Review*, 43(2): 209–251.

GLASMEIR, A. (1994). 'Flexible Districts, Flexible Regions? The Institutional And Cultural Limits to Districts in an Era of Globalisation and Technological Paradigm Shift', in Amin, A. and Thrift, N. (eds.), *Globalisation, Institutions and Regional Development in Europe*, Oxford University Press, Oxford, pp. 118–146.

GRANOVETTER, M. (1985). 'Economic Action and Social Structure: The Problem of Embeddedness', *American Journal of Sociology*, 91(3): 481–510.

GREGERSEN, B. and JOHNSON, B. (1997). 'Learning Economies, Innovation Systems and European Integration', *Regional Studies*, 31: 479–490.

GUERRIERI P. and IAMMARINO, S. (2001). 'The Dynamics of Italian Industrial Districts: Towards a Renewal of Competitiveness?' in Guerrieri, P., Iammarino, S., and Pietrobelli, C. (eds.), *The Global Challenge to Industrial Districts: Small and Medium-sized Enterprises in Italy and Taiwan*, Edward Elgar, MA, USA, pp. 35–62.

HARRISON, B. (1997). *Lean and Mean, The Changing Landscape of Corporate Power in the Age of Flexibility*, Second Edition, New York: Basic Books.

HUMPHREY, J. and SCHMITZ, H. (1996). 'The Triple C Approach to Local Industrial Policy', *World Development*, 24(12): 1859–1877.

HUMPHREY, J. (1995). Industrial Reorganization in Developing Countries: From Models to Trajectories, *World Development*, 23(1): 149–162.

ISAKSEN, A. (2003). 'National and Regional Contexts for Innovation', in Asheim, B. T. *et al.* (eds.), *Regional Innovation Policy for Small-Medium Enterprises*, Edward Elgar, Cheltenham, UK, pp. 49–77.

KAUFMANN, A. and TÖDTLING, F. (2003). 'Innovation Patterns of SMES', in Asheim, B.T. *et al.* (eds.), *Regional Innovation Policy for Small-Medium Enterprises*, Edward Elgar, Cheltenham, UK, pp. 78–119.

KAUTONEN, M. (1996). 'Emerging Innovative Networks and Milieux: The Case of Furniture Industry in the Lahti Region of Finland', *European Panning Studies*, 6(4): 439–456.

KETEL, C. H. M. (2003). 'The Development of the Cluster Concept-Present Experience and the Future Development', Mimeo, Harvard Business School.

KRUGMAN, P. (1991). *Geography and Trade*, Leuven University Press, Leoven & MIT Press, Cambridge, MA.

KRUGMAN, P. (1996). *The Self-Organizing Economy*, Basil Blackwell, Oxford.

LEONCINI, R. and LOTTI, F. (2004). 'Are Industrial Districts More Conductive to Innovative Production? The Case of Emilia Romagna', in Cainelli, G. and Zoboli, R. (eds.), *The Evolution of Industrial Districts: Changing Governance, Innovation and Internationalization of Local Capitalism in Italy*, Phisica-Verlag, A Springer-Verlag Company, Milan, Italy, pp. 257–272.

LUNDVALL, B. A. and JOHNSON, B. (1994). 'The Learning Economy', *Journal of International Studies*, 1(2): 23–42

LUNDVALL, B. A. (1988).'Product Innovation and User-Producer Relations' in Dosi, G. *et al.* (eds), *The Technical Change and Economic Theory*, Pinter, London.

LUNDVALL, B. A. (1993). 'Explaining Interfirm Cooperation and Innovation: Limits of the Transaction-Cost Approach', in Grahher, G. (ed), *The Embedded Firm, On the Socioeconomics of Industrial Networks*, Routledge, London, pp. 52–64.

LYONS, D. (2000). 'Emdeddedness, Milieu, and Innovation Among High Technology Firms: A Richardson, Texas Case Study', *Environment and Planning*, 32: 891–908.

MARSHALL, A. (1920). *Principles of Economics*, Eighth Edition, Macmillan, London, 1979.

MCDONALD, F. and VERTOVA, G. (2002), 'Clusters, Industrial Districts and Competitiveness' in Mcnaughton, R. B. and Green, M. B. (eds.), *Global Competition and Local Networks*, Ashgate, England, pp. 38–37.

MYTELKA, Lynn and FARINELLI, Fulvia (2000). 'Local Clusters, Innovation Systems and Sustained Competitiveness', Working Chapter, United Nations University, Institute for New Technologies, Keizer Kavelplein, 19,6211.TC, Maastricht, The Netherlands, Postmaster@intech.unu.edu, URL: http://www.intech.unu.edu.

NADVI, K. (1999). 'Shifting Ties: Social Networks in the surgical instrument cluster of Sialkot, Pakistan,' *Development and Change*, 30(1): 143–177.

NELSON, R. R. (1993). *National Systems of Innovation*, Oxford University Press, Oxford.

NELSON, R. R. and WINTER, S. (1982). *An Evolutionary Theory of Economic Change*, Harvard University Press, Cambridge.

OECD. (1996). *SMEs: Employment, Innovation and Growth:* The Washington Workshop. OECD, documents.

OECD. (2001). *Innovative Clusters: Drivers of National Innovation Systems*, OECD, Paris.

PAKE, F. and W. SENENBERGER, (eds.). (1992). *Industrial Districts and Local Economic Regeneration*, IILS, Geneva

PARK, Sum Ock. (2001). 'Regional Innovation Strategies for Regional Development in the Knowledge-based Economy', *Geojournal*, **53**: 29–38.

PERROUX, F. (1950). 'Economic Space: Theory and Applications', *Quarterly Journal of Economics*, **64**(1): 89–104.

PIERROBELLI, C. (2004). 'Upgrading and Technological Regimes in Industrial Clusters in Italy and Taiwan', in Pierrobelli, C. and Sverrisson, A. (eds.), *Linking Local and Global Economies: The Ties that Bind*, Routledge, pp. 133–159.

PIORE, M. and SABEL, C. (1984), *The Second Industrial Divide: Possibilities for Prosperity*, Basic Books, New York.

PITELIS, C. (1998). 'Transaction Costs and the Historical Evolution of Capitalist Firm', *Journal of Economic Issues*, **32**(4): 999–1017.

POUDER, R. and ST JOHN, C. H. (1996). 'The Hot Spots and Blind Spots: Geographical Clusters of Firms and Innovation', *Academy of Management Review*, **21**(4): 1192–1225.

QIU, Haixiong and XU, Jianniu. (2004). 'The Behaviour Analyses of Local Government in Regional Innovation', *Management World*, **10**.

SABEL, C. (1996). 'Learning by Monitoring: The Dilemmas of Regional Economic Policy in Europe', *Networks of Enterprises and Local Development: Competing and Cooperating in Local Systems*, OECD, Paris, pp. 23–49.

SAXENIAN, A. L. (1994). 'Regional Advantage: Culture and Competition in Silicon Valley', *California Management Review*, Fall issue, pp. 89–112.

SCHMITZ, H. and NADVI, K. (1999). 'Clustering and Industrialization: Introduction', *World Development*, **27**(9): 1503–1514.

SCHMITZ, H. (ed.). (2004). *Local Enterprises in the Global Economy: Issues of Governance and Upgrading*, Edward, Elgar, Cheltenham, UK.

SCOTT, A. J. (1998). *Regions and the World Economy: The Coming Shape of Global Production*, Competition and Political Order, Oxford University Press, Oxford.

SMALLBONE, D., NORTH, D. and VICKERS I. (2003). 'The Role and Characteristics of SMEs in Innovation' in Asheim, B. T. *et al.* (eds.), *Regional Innovation Policy for Small-Medium Enterprises*, Edward Elgar, Cheltenham, UK pp. 3–20.

TÖDTLING, F. and KAUFMANN, A. (2001). 'The Role of the Region for Innovation Activities in SMEs', *European Planning Studies*, **7**(6): 203–215.

VATNE, E. and TAYLOR, M., (ed.). (2001). *The Networked Firm in a Global World: Small Firms in New Environments, The Organization of Industrial Space*, Ashgate: Aldershot. Burlington, USA.

WANG, Jici and TONG, Xin. (2005). 'Industrial Clusters in China: Embedded or Disembedded,' in Claes G. Alvstam and Eike W. Schamp (eds.), *Linking Industries Across the World*, Ashgate, pp. 223–242.

WANG, Jun, (2002), 'The Innovative Process and Cluster's Development in China', *Management of the World*, **10**.

WANG, Jun, Yao Hailin and Zhao Xiang. (2003). 'The Social Capital and the growth of Private Enterprises in China', *The Economies of Chinese Industries*, **5**.

WANG, Jun. (2004). 'Effect of Social Capital and Production Fashion on the Evolution of Clusters: Discussion and Application of Theoretical frame on the Clusters Forms and Evolution', *Journal of Sociology Research*, **5**.

WANG, Jun. (2005). 'The Emergence and Evolution of Specific Market Based Clusters in Guangdong Province, China', *Management of the World*, **8**.

WANG, Zheng. (2006). 'Technological Innovation and Regional Development: Some Experience from Pearl River Delta, in China,' Undetermined Draft.

WILLIAMSON, O. (1975). *Markets and Hierarchies: Analysis and Antitrust Implications*, Free Press, New York.

YUSUF, S., ALTAF, M. A., and NABESHIMA, K. (eds.). (2004). *Global Production Networking and Technological Change in East Asia?* World Bank.

Part Four: South East Asia

Clusters and the Building of Competitiveness in Emerging Countries: Some Evidence from South East Asia

Chapter 13

From Craft Villages to Clusters in Vietnam: Transition Through Globalisation[1]

Quy Nghi Nguyen

13.1 Craft Villages in Vietnam: A Historical Review

The formation of craft villages in Vietnam can be summarised into 3 stages. In the first stage, craft activities served agricultural activities, and were not yet considered as an independent productive element. It became independent in the 2nd stage, and professional artisans could independently produce and earn a living from these activities. After a long development period, mostly influenced by imitation and emigration processes, artisans gradually concentrated around handicraft centres, or what we now called craft villages.

Alfred Marshall (1890) indicated that although many factors affect the concentration of industry, physical conditions (i.e. raw material resources, transport conditions and Court guarantees) play an important role. Firstly, an industrial concentration develops if the chosen location had easy access to the transport system, and was located near sources of the raw materials. Second, historical development of industries shows that concentration of rich people in a given place often creates special demands, attracting workers

[1] An earlier version of this paper was presented in the international conference 'Asian Industrial Clusters: New and Old Forms' held in Lyon (France), 29–30 November and 1 December 2006. The author would like to express his gratitude to Bernard Ganne, Research Director; Philippe Bernoux, Honored Research Director at MODYS, National Centre for Scientific Research (CNRS, France) for their comments.

nearby, especially skilled workers. According to Marshall, in the feudal period, kings often bring the best artisans with them when moving to a new place.

Marshall's analysis can be interpreted in another way. The development of an industrial concentration not only depends on available physical conditions but also on political, socio-economic environments. This chapter, through the case of a specific craft village, aims at proving that under many different influences, craft villages in Vietnam are gradually reconfiguring for better adaptation to new playing fields. The 'Doi Moi'[2] (reform) policy brought to Bat Trang many remarkable economic changes and social life improvement as well. This new context contributes to a formulation of new social norms/values and actors that are involved in the village development.

13.1.1 *Bat Trang's Development History*

Until today, no official archaeological or historical evidence has been found to clarify the origin of the name 'Bat Trang'. According to many documents, this name might have first appeared in the late 14th or early 15th century (Do, 1989). Regardless of its historical uncertainty, Bat Trang is always considered as the most famous ceramic production centre in Vietnam. The village was a result of migration processes and population concentration.

In the year 1010, King Ly Thai To changed the capital from Hoa Lu to Thang Long, making this location the political and urban centre of Dai Viet. Attracted by its development, many merchants and craftsmen migrated to Thang Long where they resettled and restarted their careers. The development of Thang Long resulted in the formation of a network of specialised villages (including Bat Trang) serving as daily commodity providers for the capital. Bat Trang village possessed a significant clay deposit, an essential

---

[2] This is Vietnamese language which is literally translated as 'reform' in English. It marked an important page in the economic development of Vietnam, changing from planning economy to market-oriented one.

material for ceramic production. Some Bo Bat potters resettled here and together with the Nguyen Ninh Trang family, they built a pottery kiln and formed a potters group called the 'Bach Tho guild'. Followed by a continuous migration, Bat Trang became well known for its transformation from a normal craft village to the most famous ceramic centre that was chosen to produce the offerings to the Chinese Ming Dynasty.

The formation of Bat Trang was both spontaneous and organised with limited government intervention. Initially, Bat Trang was chosen because of its easy accessibility and the availability of raw materials (clay). Although this source of raw material ran out, the village still had other advantages such as easy access, skilled labour and particularly a collective trade mark. The lack of raw materials promoted inter-village relations. Moreover, as mentioned above about the Court's role, the formation of Bat Trang was strongly supported by the Ly dynasty when the King decided to settle in a new capital and got artisans to come to satisfy the Court's needs.

Consisting of Giang Cao and Bat Trang villages, the Bat Trang ward is an administrative unit of Gia Lam district on the periphery of Hanoi. Its total area is 164 ha, with a population of 7300 residents living in 1694 households (Bat Trang People's Committee, 2005). More than 1000 households are directly or indirectly involved in ceramic related activities (production, trade, service). In addition, there are more than 40 enterprises with different forms of legal status ranging from SOE (state-owned enterprise), to limited liability companies and joint stock companies to cooperatives. In its long development history, Bat Trang has experienced important changes in terms of politics, economics and also culture. In the following sections, we would like to give an in-depth analysis of these issues.

13.2 Divergent Transformations in Bat Trang

13.2.1 *From Closed to Open Society*

In this section, we would like to show that there is evidence of the externalisation of Bat Trang compared to its traditional forms.

Certainly, this process did not happen at once, but in a gradual way over the course of history. The issues of marriage, labour training, commercial relations and internalisation will be discussed respectively to show this tendency in Bat Trang.

Like other Vietnamese traditional rural villages, Bat Trang was characterised as a closed society, reflected in marriage relations and knowledge transfer (Phan, 1977). Social norms of marriage were strictly applied to women while it was more open with men. It was very hard for a woman to find her partner outside the village, however a man of Bat Trang might get married with an external woman. During our field trip, participants informed us that the present extension of marriage relations can be viewed as one of the factors that contribute to the diffusion of ceramic production into neighbouring areas.

The reform of Bat Trang can also be explained by the changes in transferring knowledge and skills between generations. In the past, villagers never taught outsiders their skills, not even relatives. Within a family, daughters and sons-in-law could never access such knowledge. Originally Bat Trang villagers kept their family's know-how secret. Yet these norms have significantly changed, primarily because the development and expansion of production caused higher demand for labour. In reality, in Bat Trang, there is a place reserved for those who wish to seek a temporary job. Employers can quickly find people that meet their criteria. Most of these mobile labourers come from the neighbouring province of the Hung Yen.

Bat Trang villagers are now mostly kiln owners or managers. Thus, in daily operation, they have to teach their new employees some skills, keeping secret only crucial family know-how of the job such as glaze making. Other phases are handled by the workers. Accumulating technique and experience in ceramic production, certain workers can build and run their own kiln after working in Bat Trang. At the moment, this industry has spread widely not only to the next village (Giang Cao) but also to other communes such as Da Ton and Kim Lan. This happens more frequently now because knowledge exchange is more open between villagers in Bat Trang and immigrants (who previously were not considered as members of the village, and consequently faced many difficulties in their social integration).

In the traditional society of Bat Trang, commercial relations were one of the links to the exterior. Located favourably, accessible by water or road, Bat Trang constituted a destination for mobile traders who purchased ceramic products in this village and then sold them to outside markets. Apart from this relation, other inter-village linkages tended to be more intensive, notably in terms of raw material, i.e., clay, charcoal, and labour supply. In fact, these relationships dated from traditional society, contributed to a primary form of inter-village division of labour. And now, these relationships undergo a particular transformation towards a more specialised and flexible base.

Other evidence that supports our argument for an open society of Bat Trang is the involvement of other craft villages in new product development and the presence of international customers. In Bat Trang, the market for basic goods is essentially supplied by household workshops while that for fine arts or high quality products is under the control of big enterprises. However, faced with situations in which product designs become boringly similar, producers are trying to integrate other craft villages' products into their own. One important result of this combination is a series of ceramic-rattan/bamboo products that have gradually gained a position in the market.

Regarding international customers, since the 16–17th century,[3] Bat Trang's products have been exported to other countries (Luong, 1998), but the volume has been greatly increasing, especially in recent years. According to the reports of the Bat Trang People's Committee, the last few years annual revenues were 130 billion VND, of which exports account for 40–60%. JICA and MARD (2004) insisted that Bat Trang is among the few ceramic production centres exporting products. Our survey findings revealed that on average, 55.8% of Bat Trang's products are directly or indirectly exported. The on-site

---

[3] According to the archives of the Dutch East India Company, in a period of 20 years from 1663 to 1682, the Dutch exported 1,450,000 pieces of porcelain from Tonkin to other parts of Southeast Asia (Luong, 1998).

export[4] has been promoted at a special Ceramic Market Place, which has been invested in and established by villagers. Bat Trang's products appear in several countries in the world, including Japan, the US, and European countries.

MARD (2005) shows us a more general picture of off-farm activities in rural areas, in which 40% of the products of craft production are exported to more than 100 countries in the world. The export turn-over has continuously increased. In 2003, the export revenue was $367 million, increasing by 56.2% compared to that of 2001. In 2004, it achieved $450 million, 22.6% higher than that of 2003 (this estimation does not include wooden products).

13.2.2 Logic of Production: Toward Commercialisation

In this section, we will argue that ceramic manufacturing in Bat Trang is now reoriented toward commercialisation. Among much evidence of this process, we would like to mention major changes effecting households and enterprises in village: the transformation from agricultural to commercial purpose, technology innovation, product designs, and marketing strategy.

13.2.2.1 From Minor Profession to Main Income Generation Activities

Before the 'Doi Moi' period, all kinds of craft production were considered as side professions that served agricultural cultivation. Nguyen and Bui (1993) show two premises influencing the formation and development of such activities. Firstly, rice cultivation is primarily based on intensive labour and the use of rudimentary farming tools. Its huge demand for farming tools (all kinds of containers; equipment for processing rice) forced peasants to produce them during the slack season. This long period of idle time needed to be occupied by artisan-type and commercial activities. This activity constituted a primary condition for the development of craft production. Secondly, in an

---

[4] This means that retailers sell ceramic products directly to foreign tourists.

independent economy, it seems that income from agriculture cannot cover all farmers' needs. That is why side professions appeared to fill the gap left by agriculture. By selling redundant farming tools, farmers used this income for clothes, housing, and marriage and funeral activities.

The development cycle of Bat Trang is slightly different from that of other villages since agricultural land in Bat Trang is very limited. Few villagers engaged directly in agricultural production even when land was available (Luong, 1998). They would rent out their fields to people in neighbouring villages. It is more evident that the logic of craft production is now changing, with a focus on profit optimisation. MARD (2005) has started up 'one village, one product' project which aims to enhance the capacity of craft villages — a key factor in hunger elimination and poverty reduction. Tran (2004) argued that although craft production first appeared to serve agricultural production, its present division of labour is so specialised that productivity and quality could satisfy not only local demands but also external markets. For many localities including Bat Trang, the role of craft production has switched from a secondary position to the major income generation activity. Income for people working in off-farm sector was three or four times higher than that in agriculture. Therefore, the poverty rate in off-farm sector developed area is only 3.7%, much lower than the national average rate (10.4%).

13.2.2.2 *Technological Innovation*

Technological innovation is a key factor for enterprises in the market-oriented economy. It becomes more significant to Vietnam after becoming an official member of the WTO. In reality, Bat Trang has continuously improved its production techniques in order to produce high-quality products. An example can be seen through the introduction of different types of kilns in Bat Trang: from frog-shaped to liquid petroleum gas (LPG) kilns. The 'Frog-shaped' kiln, the oldest one, which was widely used in the past, has now disappeared. The Dragon kiln appeared at the beginning of the 20th century. This kiln was made up of many trays, usually containing 5 to 7 blocks (sometimes up to 10 blocks). The kiln is about 13 metres long, with a 2-metre-high chimney. The total length is 15 metres. The temperature could reach up to 1300°C. The Box kiln first appeared in 1975. It was normally 5 metres high and 0.9 metre wide, and its interior was made of firebricks like those for house building. The kiln had·two fire doors with a simple structure, small design and low building cost, suitable for household production. As a result, most households had at least one Box kiln, some households even built 2 or 3. Regarding temperature, it could reach up to 1250°C. In recent years, in Bat Trang some modern types of kiln, e.g. the liquid petroleum gas (LPG) kilns have appeared. During the firing process, they use a pyrometre to monitor the temperature which can be adjusted by adding or reducing fuel. Since temperature is under control with the LPG kiln, ceramic firing is easier for artisans.

Change in fuel usage from firewood to charcoal and then LPG improves not only product quality but the environment as well. Now, all registered firms in the village are already using LPG kilns, and household workshops are also following this trend. The local authority reported that of more than 1000 functioning kilns in the village, nearly 300 LPG kilns have been set up. According to our survey findings, 79.4% confirmed that they are using LPG kiln while 17.6% are still running coal-fired kilns and the rest (2.9%) use both LPG and coal-fired kilns. The advantages in using the LPG kiln are evident. By using it, they can minimise an important uncertainty in product quality because workers can control the inside temperature in an exact and scientific way instead of on their subjective feelings based on experience like before.[5] Furthermore, LPG kilns deliver better quality products that permit a higher price.

It is worth noting that LPG kilns require an initial investment that is sometimes too high for household workshops. Most producers who

---

[5] It should be noted that each type of product requires a different level of temperature at different moments in the firing process. Previously, when using charcoal kilns, the main workers relied on their experience to change the temperature. But now with gas kilns, anyone can control the temperature accurately.

have already changed technology are SMEs or household workshops with a significant financial accumulation. The local authorities, in their turn, expressed a very encouraging attitude towards this environment-friendly technology. Many people said that the local government and especially the local banking branch are willing to give them favourable conditions in accessing loans to change production techniques from coal-fired to LPG kiln.

The method of product shaping has now changed to a more standardised mould made from wood or plaster. In the past, product is shaped by hand. Wood or plaster moulds are very convenient for mass production, and ensure the products' homogeneity. However, we must admit that some of the traditional value of handicraft ceramics is likely to disappear when using these kinds of moulds.

13.2.2.3 *New Concept of Product Development*

Another factor that shows commercialisation in Bat Trang resides in the methods of new product development in order to satisfy increasing requirements of customers. In Bat Trang as well as other craft villages, it is difficult to solve the problem of product diversification due to limitations of management capacity. According to MARD's research (1997), only 34.4% of firm managers in craft villages had been enrolled at high school or higher, and a similar rate for heads of household workshops was even lower (24.7%). JICA and MARD (2004) also identified 17 serious problems to overcome in order to develop craft villages, including poor product design. However, we think that this problem is out of the control of single enterprises/ households. These issues necessitate involvement of the local authority and related institutions who enable favourable conditions where household/firms can promote their creativeness. In the current setting, only large firms and artists have enough passion and financial capacity to conduct research on new products. No training exists to develop and/or reinforce this activity.

It is noted that throughout its development history, Bat Trang has always constituted one of leading ceramics centres in Vietnam.

Before 'Doi Moi', unsuitable policies caused terrible economic stagnation and a shortage of consumer goods. As a result, despite low quality, Bat Trang's products were sold easily both in domestic and international markets (almost all in the Eastern Europe market). During our field trip, some manufacturers admitted that they preferred participating in the pre-Doi Moi market conditions to the current ones because of the intensive innovation requests from customers as well as the market.

> 'Before "doi moi", I hadn't set up my company. In the previous time, we didn't pay much attention to the quality of products, we were only concerned with how to produce in a faster cycle and with cheaper production costs. After "Doi Moi", we must be concerned about the quality of products and technology.' (Interview No. 13).

Recognising a new market trend, many enterprises and households are trying to find their own ways, and they have gained significant success. In fact, local producers have two options: producing consumer goods for the domestic market, which does not require much investment either in technology or human resources; or turning to high quality and well-designed products that are mostly reserved for the international market. The domestic market is only important at the end of year, particularly on the occasion of the Tet Holiday. Meanwhile the export market is rather stable. A key factor for a successful firm is the capacity to foresee market trends and other information. Moreover, it is especially important when the present system of finding customers is still based on established or even personal relationships.

In the search for new products, certain changes have happened to the households and enterprises. At first, there is a movement to restore ancient ceramics, in which craftsmen try to recreate works and glaze colours of the feudal period. The advantages of these products are uniqueness, originality and an ancient appearance. However, the market for and productivity in this type is quite limited. Moreover, it is not easy to access the ancient works and kiln owners have to mobilise their personal networks to get understanding

'I had to come to the museum of the College of Fine Arts. I knew the directors and asked them to give advice on the quality and glaze of my product. I would try to improve my products based on their assessment. I also had the experts or antique collectors evaluate the product quality. Or I bought the real antiques to compare with my products. I could have them value the products because I have personal contacts.' (Interview No. 26).

Another group of products is now being developed by combining ceramics and other types of art like sculpture, painting and even statuesque sculpting. Many production units have invested time and capital to adapt some paintings and art works to ceramic materials. However, like the above type, these products have a limited number of customers and are difficult to mass produce

'For example, people never thought that this picture could be made of ceramic. In the old days, pictures were only painted on paper but they now can be carved on wood or made in ceramic. That's the application of fine art. Or no one can imagine there's ceramic jewelry; people only know those made of gold, silver, gem or metal. But now, jewels can be made of ceramic.' (Interview No. 13).

Not only inspired by other kinds of arts, producers in Bat Trang have also strengthened their cooperation with other craft villages to design new products. This leads to inter-village relations as mentioned in the previous section. Obviously, facing internalisation and extensive competition, enterprises tend to cooperate in order to reinforce their competitiveness.

'Demands for ceramic products have become saturated, mostly in the glaze colours, but this year there is a boom in those which combine with rattan or bamboo weaving or lacquer. These products cannot be made by other enterprises outside the village. Ceramic

products have now changed into another development phase.'
(Interview No. 25).

> We cooperate with one or two companies in other fields like rattan
> or bamboo weaving to complete the products.' (Interview No. 10).

Certainly, not all of the local manufacturers can innovate to meet new
demand. Those who can are mostly big enterprises or household
workshops who were already sure of traditional customers in the
export market, and have sufficient financial capacity and human
resources. Furthermore, they are now realising that their competitive
capacity could only be improved by applying new techniques, as well
as the traditional skills and methods.

> 'Now, to be able to do this job a lot of training is needed, unlike in
> the past, when everyone could do it. My friends in this village think
> the same. They said that they have to learn Fine Arts at the College
> of Industrial Fine Arts or Hanoi College of Fine Art on Yet Kieu
> Street. Then they return to Bat Trang to apply what they have
> learned. That's the new way, working with a high level of knowl-
> edge, unlike our parents. That means we follow their way at a higher
> level. We are unlike our ancestors who were based purely on manual
> labour.' (Interview No. 36).

13.2.2.4 New Marketing Strategy

The major changes in marketing strategy of the manufacturers are
those in their promotion and brand name development. Since its
beginning, Bat Trang has always been considered as the country's
most famous ceramic centre. Therefore, 'Bat Trang ceramic' has
become a collective brand for all firms and households in the village.
However, distribution and expansion activities for the collective brand
only started after 'Doi Moi', particularly in flourishing trade fairs and
exhibitions. Many manufacturers participate in these activities to
advertise their products and look for new customers. Besides, other
advertising material like catalogues, web pages or phone directories
can be used as communication channels.

'As I remember, before 'Doi Moi,' launched in the period of 1985 and 1986, there was nothing called a ceramic exhibition or fair. After 'Doi Moi', the market mechanism created more opportunities to strengthen their marketing activities. Exhibition or fairs are a method of marketing, but the booth cost is still a factor, because it is high and many people are not aware of its price. In this market, some guys and I sometimes have to spend our own money to encourage others to join. It's hard to do it but we only care about how to bring profit to the whole village.' (Interview No. 13).

'Promotion and transaction modes by exhibitions and fairs, by our existing partners and customers, by catalogues distributed to visitors in the fairs, or to customers who find us. Or we can send directly to potential partners. We have had our own website since 2004 and we don't think e-commerce is now the trend for Vietnamese enterprises.' (Interview No. 42).

'Nowadays, it's easier to meet customers. In the past, people did not know our craft village, but now they have much more information via the mass media and the Internet. We participate in many fairs... It's effective. In Vietnam, we have local customers, and when my company joined the fairs in Germany or Hong Kong, especially Hong Kong, we gained various potential foreign customers. By participating in the fairs, we can gain contracts.' (Interview No. 25).

The application of information technology in marketing becomes more popular, but it is not the case for the majority of households. They seem unable to catch up with the new production rhythm, being inactive in finding new markets and technical innovations.

— Contact with customers

Obviously, with different advertising campaigns, Bat Trang has become well-known not only at a national level but also worldwide. The number of customers has increased. The producer-customer relations need to be re-determined because of the emergence of international customers. In the past, trading activities of Bat Trang heavily depended on the neighbour village (Giang Cao) due to the fact that it was located near the roads, and external merchants could get there (Giang Cao) to buy goods and sell them elsewhere. We can see now a different perspective. Thanks to the investment of the local authority, a road has been constructed connecting the ancient village of Bat Trang to the exterior. Moreover, an on-site ceramic market has been set up in the centre of village, giving opportunities to household workshop to sell their products directly. With such infrastructure improvement, customers have more choices and they can access their desired manufacturers.

'Now I can work with customers directly, we do not have to wait for long. After a contract is signed, our partner gives us 50% of the contract value, and pays the rest after receiving the goods. We do not like to work with the agents who always try to lower the price. We want to work directly with our customers.' (Interview No. 31).

'It's different nowadays. In the past, customers came here to find us. In fact, the import-export companies came here to order and then took goods to the customer's place. Now those customers do not use the import-export company, they sign directly with the manufacturers here, gradually we have more customers... It's now much easier. Before 'Doi Moi', there was no way to sign contracts directly with customers, but only with intermediary agents. We did not know the customers; we could only take care of the manufacturing process.' (Interview No. 25).

'In comparison with the past, now the modern technologies bring us more efficiency and convenience. Firstly, I don't have to travel, secondly customers receive information faster. Previously, we could only send the photos through the post. Now in a few minutes, they can retrieve them.' (Interview No. 10).

When we received an order from the agents, we might have to use the painters from a customer company like Anh Hong Co., who provided painters that met the agent's requirements. But now, we can find and train painters ourselves, customers only check the quality. (Interview No. 12).

The transformation from intermediary to direct relations (even if it is not with the end-customer) brings many advantages to the manufacturer-customer relationship. Firstly, the delivery and payment are direct in a determined time, independent of the third party. Moreover, the contract value can be negotiated between producer and customer and this can achieve a satisfactory level for both sides. Besides, such direct transaction is useful for manufacturers to know more about the potential market, which encourages them to expand their business and improve production techniques. It also brings about favourable conditions to the expansion of the customer network. In reality, for a long period, new customer development primarily depended on the current customer network. Now, as well as a new marketing strategy, direct transactions will certainly let customers know more about this village.

13.2.2.5 *On-site Market Development*

To commercialise Bat Trang's products, household enterprises and the Craft Village Club successfully established a Ceramic Market Place within the ancient village. The development of the on-site market has been strongly supported by the municipality particularly in that the municipality has established a bus route (No. 47) so that tourists can go from the centre of Hanoi directly to Bat Trang. With more than 100 stalls, the ceramic market place gives household workshops, who before had little opportunity to access local and foreign customers, a good place to display and sell their goods. By joining the ceramic market, many households no longer work for firms as a sub-contractor, they actually focus on commodity goods that have a wider market. Sub-contractor relations due to this new direction also have had to be reconfigured.

'In recent years, Bat Trang has developed much more thanks to the opening of the ceramic market place, where customers can meet the manufacturers directly. Honestly, Bat Trang villagers used not to trade but only manufactured. Now, the ceramic market has come along, and customers can order products from

Bat Trang directly. However, the outcome is still limited in general.' (Interview No. 36).

'Wanting to display our products, we sought to cooperate with a company to build some temporary booths in 3 months to attract customers and tourists. We tried our best to persuade them to build the booths in 3 months and then to build such a market place. After our first success, we persuaded other villagers. Initially we had 27 booths, and then 100. In the construction, other people supported us because it met their needs too. Besides, they considered it inevitable. The special thing is that the market managers received no wages, they spent their own money to maintain the market's operation in the early days.' (Interview No. 13).

This ceramic market is viewed as an example of Bat Trang's success in mobilising its internal strengths. It started with the SEA Games 22 in 2003[6] when they wished to organise a Ceramic Fair. After this event, visitors continued to come to Bat Trang. In this situation, the Craft Village Club and Haprosimex cooperated to build up a market for showing and selling villagers' products.

The success of the ceramic market in Bat Trang also implies that the village's manufacturers will no longer depend on Giang Cao village. Previously, Giang Cao was an exclusively agricultural village, but since January 2006, the agricultural land ran out, giving way to huge extension of ceramic production. Before Doi Moi, people in Giang Cao, with their location advantage (easy access), acted as commercial intermediary between producers in Bat Trang and external customers. They did not produce, but bought the products at the lowest price and sold them on at the highest price possible. In terms of living standards, they are much wealthier than the producers in the ancient village of Bat Trang. Because of this, an internal conflict among villagers of Bat Trang and Giang Cao has emerged and persists today. They are forced to cooperate in selling the product, but Bat Trang villagers always think that it is not fair that Giang Cao's people gain more profit than they do when the craft production is not

---

[6] Like the Olympic Games but only among the countries of South East Asia.

Giang Cao's tradition. Our field trip revealed that the opening of the ceramic market made Bat Trang's people very happy because they were escaping from dependence on Giang Cao.

13.3 Diversification for Development: Emergence of a New System of Actors

In this part, we focus on analysing the changes in actors in the devel opment of Bat Trang, before and after 'Doi Moi' in Vietnam. There are 3 main subjects: (i) the increasing role of the local authority, (ii) the boom of new organisational forms for production and trading and (iii) the appearance of some social-professional organisations.

13.3.1 *From Spontaneous to Organised Development: A Rise in Local Authority Involvement*

Unlike industrial zones formed by government decision, the forma tion and development of craft villages are spontaneous. There is no formal definition of a craft village; each province tries to create its own conception. Only a few years ago, public authorities started to be concerned about craft villages as their products found a place in the market with an increasing export volume. Another reason for this increasing attention is related to environmental pollution caused by unplanned developments. To boost craft production development, at the central level, government released many policies, decisions that primarily deal with (i) regional development; (ii) poverty reduction; (ii) investment and export encouragement; (iv) the promotion of the development of SMEs.[7]

In the case of Bat Trang, the policy to encourage technology update is one of the first steps made by the local authority to balance economic development and environmental sustainability. They created favourable legal conditions (a certification document) for households to get banking loans that could be used to upgrade production techniques. Even the local branch of the Bank for Agriculture

---

[7] For a more detailed discussion: JICA and MARD (2004), pp. 2–19, 2–27.

and Rural Development paid particular attention to households working in this field. According to the communal report, in the period 2001–2005, 280 gas kilns came into operation to replace the coal-fired kilns.

It should be noted that before switching to LPG kilns, most manufacturers burnt coal and firewood. Every 1000 kg of pottery finished product would release 1400 kg of cinders, 800 kg of dust and 140 kg of other waste products. Every day, Bat Trang releases into the environment 1470 kg of dust, 1199 m^3 of CO_2 and a large amount of coal cinders; breakages were thrown into the Red River. With a limited production space and with 1400 coal-fired and LPG kilns continuously firing, the temperature in Bat Trang ranges from 1.5 to 3.5°C, higher than any other places (Tran, 2004).

Beside the encouragement of technology change the matter of infrastructure is also of great concern. In the period 2001–2005, with the city's budget, various projects on building infrastructure were implemented (including a primary school, the civil market, inter-ward roads, street lights). The most remarkable project is the construction of the road connection from the ancient Bat Trang to the Ceramic Market place. After its completion, trading activity between Bat Trang and the outside world has significantly improved.

13.3.2 New Forms of Enterprises

Before the official approval of the 'Doi Moi' policy in 1986 and the acknowledgement of private ownership in the 1992 Constitution, production activities in Bat Trang depended mostly on households, cooperatives and state-owned enterprises (SOEs). Bat Trang's products were exported, but mostly to Eastern Europe in very limited quantities. At that time, only SOEs were permitted to export merchandise. Bat Trang was no exception; its SOEs had an annual exportation value of US$5000. In 1959, the first SOE was established in Bat Trang namely the Bat Trang Ceramic Enterprise, and had been followed by some cooperatives, for example, Hop Thanh (1962), Hung Ha (1977), Hop Luc (1978), Thong Nhat (1982), Anh Hong (1984), and the military firms X51 (1984) and X54 (1988). Obviously in this context of very few established manufacturers, it is hard to find any signs of a private sector, but the public sector and collective units.

Along with the significant institutional changes of the late 1980s and early 1990s, many new forms of enterprises appeared. Cooperatives faced problems due to their low capacity in adapting to market changes. In Bat Trang, as of now, there are only 2 functioning cooperatives that have a reasonably stable customer base due to their reorganisation. New circumstances also forced firms in the public sector to change, delivering new forms of organisation: joint-stock companies. The most remarkable change during the first period of Doi Moi in Bat Trang was the emergence of a private sector with nearly 40 registered firms by 2006.

The development scenario of private enterprises clearly shows a transformation of actors involved in production in order to meet new demands. It can be stated that all current private firms in Bat Trang evolved from the household workshop model. Having accumulated sufficient capital and production capacity, they achieved a higher level of development, a more organised form. Registering as a company, their transactions become easier, especially they are able to have direct contact with foreign customers.

'Previously, I just ran a household workshop, and then I set up a company by myself, without any cooperation. It's necessary to have a company if I want to sell products to foreign customers. Customers do not accept intermediary agents. And we must have legal authority to sign contracts with them.' (Interview No. 47).

'There are some reasons for the establishment of a company. Firstly we can only export our goods to foreign customers as long as we have a company. The State was also encouraging the development of the export of handicrafts, and so we set up the company at that moment. In fact, we did not have many partners. The company was set up to serve the transactions with customers. My wife's uncle set it up, my mother-in-law is the Director, my wife is the Deputy Director, and I am in charge of sales. It's simply a family company, and unlike the other companies, it's small and does not involve people from outside.' (Interview No. 10).

'As I stated at the beginning, it is due to the need for direct transactions with foreign customers, to understand their tastes, not to use agents, to promote our manufacturing, to enhance direct relation with customers. The establishment of a company is inevitable.' (Interview No. 13).

The passage from household workshop to the SME model can also be understood as a strategy of firm managers. This transition, although it is mostly done following customer requests, shows the initial adaptability of Bat Trang's villagers to new business environments.

13.3.3 Inter-firm Relations

13.3.3.1 Interdependent Relations: New Distribution Channels

The emergence of various new factors in Bat Trang led to a new definition of manufacturing relations. One of the manifestations is the relation between raw material suppliers and producers. In the past, a chronic situation of raw material shortage was often reported, especially for households (then private economic forms were not yet legalised). All activities of material trading were concealed, private producers had no choice, they totally depended on the providers' capacity. Luong (1998) completely described the transition in raw material supply from totally forbidden (during the industrial reform in 1959) to partially legalised under sub-contract form between SOEs and household workshops (in 1969) and to total liberation (in the late 1980s and 1990s).

'In the past, we had to hide. It was not easy to buy a cart of clay and bring it here. We had to watch out for the guard. We had to do it at night and as quick as possible, unlike now. Now, if the clay is not good, the seller will take it back. My family used to do clay processing, so, I know. In the past, we had to conceal our purchases of materials ... even if they were low quality, we had to use them.

But now we can say "I asked you for the best quality, why do you bring this kind, take it back".'(Interview No. 13).

The supplier-producer relationship has reached a new level with more specialisation. Based on the characteristics of the product, the division of labour between different units has become based on the production process, including the basic phases: providing input material (clay, mould, glaze, coal, gas) and meeting producers and/or traders.

'Bat Trang does not have any materials, we have to buy raw materials and then process them by ourselves. Our company takes care of the processing of materials on its own. We buy from Quang Ninh, Bac Ninh, Phu Tho. We can produce the glaze or mould by ourselves, but there're things we have to buy from outside, because if the quality is ok, it's better to buy from outside. The machines to make pottery are easy to make, Bat Trang people can do it themselves, I buy them all in Bat Trang.' (Interview No. 42).

'Some households in Bat Trang do not produce pottery but provide clay, glaze and moulds. We come directly to the providers, whoever provides the better and cheaper clay. I do not commit to certain providers. It's cheaper if I pay immediately, and if we delay, the price is higher.' (Interview No. 31).

In Bat Trang nowadays, there are several households/companies who provide only one kind of input material (clay, glaze, etc.), which gives manufacturers more choices. For any new product, people can create a mould (usually made from plaster) for producers. The supplier-producer relation changes are based on the principles of mutual trust and product quality. Moreover, raw material trading is totally open and producers, in their turn, can impose their requirements on suppliers.

13.3.3.2 *Vertical Cooperation: The Satellites Model*

The sub-contract relation between households and firms, which only happened in an underground way in the pre-Doi Moi period

(Luong, 1998),[8] has now flourished, constituting the main relational model between these two entities. Normally, when receiving a big order and to handle it on time, a company may sub-contract to many households within Bat Trang village. With this model, firms can mobilise the capital, techniques, skills and workforce of their partners without needing to make any extra investment in the expansion of their production capacity. Besides, firms also sign sub-contracts with input material providers. Households, in their turn, receive orders within their capacity and a household workshop can be a sub-contractor to different firms at the same time.

'For export products, I only wait for requests from the companies who have gained contracts with international customers. I become their familiar and favoured partner. If they have contracts, they will ask me to get involved. These companies and I are close friends. the companies' leaders are Bat Trang villagers too. I know them very well. I do not have to find orders elsewhere. If these companies have too many contracts, they will hire me as a sub-contractor.' (Interview No. 36).

'They [other companies] request me to follow their designs and I just follow them. I only receive orders based on my manufacturing capacity. Other households can be requested to do the rest of the work. I cannot receive orders beyond my capacity. Sometimes, I receive contracts, which I can work on for the whole month or year.' (Interview No. 29).

'Because I do not sign contracts directly (with customers), I can only receive orders within my capacity. I usually count how many products I can do in one month. If I can finish 3000–4000 products per month, I will receive the order for 3000–4000 only. I dare not

---

[8] Although the private kiln had been abolished, in 1969, SOEs implemented a sub-contract system with 100 private kiln owners (in two specific tasks: molding and trimming). In 1971, this system extended to 302 households and included two additional tasks (painting and glazing). In this period, many manufacturers started up not as sub-contractors for SOEs, but emerged as an underground private sector. (cf. Luong, 1998).

take on more. If my products have flaws, I can ask for help from other kilns.' (Interview No. 38).

Nearly all managers in private firms or households are villagers who know each other very well. This explains why the relations among them mainly rely on mutual trust and oral agreements, which are only sometimes replaced by written contracts. They may have a book to record their monthly exchanges. Due to this pattern, many households have complained of the long delay in payment by firms. It might be one of the reasons why some households are less interested in subcontracting relationships. Household workshops changed their direction of production, notably after the introduction of the Ceramic Market. Having a stall there, small workshops can produce commodity goods and such dynamics bring them more autonomy in term of production and market access as well. They can work no longer as subcontractors of large firms, but as an independent producers.

Further analysis shows that there is a relatively clear differentiation in the ceramic market among producers in Bat Trang. There are producers specialised in export products while others target the domestic market. In general, registered enterprises possess many more relations with the international market than other types of producers. Households primarily rely on the demands of the domestic market through the retail system. For foreign markets, some big companies take a lead role to function as an interface for the village. They receive orders, then subcontract to household partners. This pattern existed in the past, but it depended entirely on SOEs.

13.3.3.3 *International Commercial Transaction: Toward a Formalised Form*

Contrary to the relations among entities inside Bat Trang, relations with international distributors are much more formalised, with the prevalence of the written contract. Oral agreements are no longer accepted. It seems that bilateral exchanges run in a predetermined way. First of all, the customer sends the design by fax or email to the Vietnamese manufacturer. After agreeing on product design and contract value, these two parties sign the contract, a deposit is paid and production starts. With a high use of information technology, cross checks and exchanges between the two parties are maintained throughout the contract implementation.

'We must agree with each other in a contract. With foreign customers, the contract is made in Vietnamese and English versions, everything must be agreed in written records. On financial aspects, there are two types of contract, one is the contract with a new bank account, the other is deposit first — pay later, which means upon contract completion, the full payment will be made." (Interview No. 10).

Before 'Doi Moi', there was no contact with foreigners, in other words, we had no international customers, only the traders who took goods to Bac Qua market. Even when I hadn't finished, they put money into my hands and said 'this is mine', then I handed over the products to them. We did it for long, upon our own prestige. But now, everything should be based on written documents or official contracts. Those who order a large amount will be asked to sign a contract and take an invoice. Those who buy in small amount of several dozen will not have to do so.' (Interview No. 13).

However, most of the current international customers have established a long term relationship with Bat Trang's producers. Within a framework of international commerce and the new playing fields, it is necessary to set up (or redefine) different working norms and standards. To penetrate into very difficult markets like Japan, the EU or the United States, producers must take account of various criteria which are sometimes related to social rather than production matters (e.g., child labour, working conditions).

'I really want to enter the European market, we are now producing some samples to offer to this market; it is easier to serve this market, which is large and has huge demand. In the Asian market, the products tend to be food containers, souvenirs or display things, thus it's more difficult. It's very difficult to produce pottery, sometimes we can only make one product in very limited numbers. We have to introduce new designs regularly, or customers give us their idea for new designs. I design myself, the trend depends on the market, for example there are certain types of design for an area of the market.' (Interview No. 47).

'In reality, some markets are very difficult to penetrate, they have strict requirements for every aspect of the imported products, especially on the workers.' (Interview No. 10).

'They certainly have the right to ask. Foreign customers, especially those from the European market, require a lot of standards to be met. We must promise that our workers are of working age, and abide by our responsibilities toward those workers. Beside the general requirements on quality and techniques, we have to pursue specific standards provided by their country. Firstly, we have to produce products that adapt to a temperate climate, that's their prerequisite. Secondly, we have to prove that the goods do not have germs of certain diseases. In the contract, they provide the standards in detail. Fortunately, pottery is free of any kinds of germs. However, we do have to take care about eliminating mould on the attachments like covers or rattan baskets.' (Interview No. 13).

Apart from social criteria, the products (especially crockery) must meet hygiene requirements. Existing criteria clearly identify the product's whiteness as well as permitted lead concentrations. Normally, if an enterprise meets the requirements of ISO 14000 and SA 8000, their products can be exported. However, since this is craft production, it is very hard to control the manufacturing process, especially for households. On the other hand, in Bat Trang, there is no quality control centre, and companies respond to the need by hiring a foreign quality control firm.

13.3.4 *Emergence of the Professional Association*

Recognising the commercial context, however, some tasks that considerably influence the village operation have been neglected so far.

The latest research results (VNCI, 2004) show why Bat Trang should make more changes, especially on institutions, to enhance its competitive capacity. This study indicated many missing links for development including weak cooperation between producers in Bat Trang and R&D institutions or consultancy firms. The establishment of a Ceramic Association in 2002 by the Hanoi People's Committee is one of the important steps to cope with challenges for industrial development in Bat Trang. Although the role of this association is still under discussion, nearly all participants confirm that such an institution is crucial to long-term development.

> 'All enterprises have agreed with each other some matters after the Association's foundation under the Decision of the Hanoi People's Committee. Firstly, the enterprises have frequent meetings chaired by the Ceramic Association. The most important result is that they get rid of unhealthy competition. Previously, sometimes 3 to 4 enterprises made offers to only one customer, which led to price reductions. Now this has disappeared. Secondly, the Association will control the assignment. Members are bound to their customers and have priority to receive assignments related to their registered customers. For example, regular customers of Red River Handicapped Veteran Company will be assigned to that company. If this company cannot take the whole assignment, the Association will call for support from other companies. Or the Association will do the consultancy, for example with an order of over ten billion dong, the Association will check the legal authority and capacity of that customer and inform its members. The Association confirms to us the reputation of customers to help reduce risks.' (Interview No. 30).

Beside the Association, there are some other unofficial types of cooperation going on under the name Craft Village Club whose members are essentially composed of household workshops. Taking the view that the Bat Trang Ceramic Association is reserved only for registered companies,[9]

---

[9] The Association's regulation stated that companies, cooperatives and households are eligible to become its member. However, in reality, it has very few household members, especially those who do not export their products.

many households within the village have cooperated to set up the Craft Village Club and consider it as a junction linking households and the local authority. This club is the one which tried to get households involved in the construction and development of the Ceramic Market.

'When Bat Trang started its commercial activities, the Association was founded. But then many people said that it was so miscellaneous, some are not Bat Trang enterprises, not Bat Trang villagers. Therefore, some households in Bat Trang left the Association to join the Bat Trang Tourism and Sport Club, or the Club in short. This is the organization which founded the Bat Trang ancient village ceramic market. The Ceramic Village Club consists of 100% Bat Trang villagers.

The Association members are all companies, they do not bring profit to the villagers. For example, the Association stated that they managed the whole area of this craft village. But now when they have contracts, the households cannot join. The Club manages the ceramic market. Any delegates who visit Bat Trang and the ceramic market, they can see the goods at any booth and directly order from the owner. This is fair. The Association receives the order and gives to companies, though they take the name of the village.' (Interview No. 36).

In fact, the establishment of the Craft Village Club and the hostility of households to the Bat Trang ceramic association can be explained through the existing conflict between Giang Cao and Bat Trang villages. While the Association members might be from the whole ward 'Bat Trang' (composed by two villages Bat Trang and Giang Cao), the Club members must be of 100% Bat Trang origin. People think that the Club is important because the Association often hands contracts to its firm members, while households gain no benefit from it. Adhering to the Club and having a stall in market, households may find their own customers.

Therefore, the role of new institutions is not clear and far from confirmed. A brief description of such institutions seems to be useful.

In fact, professional association plays an important role in coordination and boosting the development of many organisational forms of industrial concentration from industrial district to cluster. In a study on business organisation in Silicon Valley, Saxenian (1992) identified two patterns of these organisations: one tries to ensure the competitive position of the cluster by lobbying or influencing federal policy while the other enhances the flexibility of firms by providing collective services. Porter (1998) also confirmed that a business association serves as a forum for exchange and experience sharing among firm managers. Moreover, it is an organ that coordinates all collective actions and develops multiple relationships with R&D institutions, university, local authority, etc. In the case of Vietnam, Dang (2003) said that establishing a business association in craft villages is strongly encouraged with the main purpose of ensuring the homogeneity of a quality product; collective branch development; searching for new markets. It is a fact that most established associations in craft villages do not operate in an effective way due to their limited organisational and human capacity. In the Bat Trang case, although a completed action plan has been developed, covering most key issues of business promotion, its role is still vague. Firms reported the absence of any association role in dealing with the local authority, and they find it difficult themselves to individually submit a collective action. Things depend heavily on the sensitivity of the local authority at ward and district level.

'The proposal must be submitted by an association or group, it can't be from an individual. We can not organise the meeting ourselves, but the commune must do so. The government agency should propose first, and organise meetings in the commune, in the hamlet, and then invite companies to get involved in the meeting. There should be an organising board for meetings, and an association to take the role of preparing proposals. The companies themselves cannot do it, an association has its management board to control it.' (Interview No. 47).

'It's difficult for a company itself, we have many opinions, but in order to gain success from the proposal, many people need to get involved. We have many proposals, but we want to have meetings with other companies in an association to reach an agreement.' (Interview No. 10).

Another problem on which firms need more external support is information on new customer tastes or market trends. Marketing strategy is also rated as poor (VNCI, 2004) and needs to be improved. Even information on new technology is not regularly provided despite being mentioned in the Association's regulations.

> 'It's different, previously customers found us, now we try to find them. In general, it can be stated so. But in detail, it's like this. In the past, we were passive, customers sent us the designs. Now we produce designs by ourselves and offer them on the Internet, and the customer can easily contact us. There should be a promotion and marketing centre to collect data from the market for us. At the same time we provide information about our products. It's better, but it's at a macro level, and over the head of a small company or an individual. We know how it should be, but we can not do it because of our own limited capacity.' (Interview No. 13).

Besides, the association can disseminate information on economic integration and Vietnam's WTO membership. Apparently these issues seem very vague to small and medium firms. It is good to know that the government will shortly publish all bilateral and multilateral agreements made during the negotiation for WTO membership. However, this is the task of professional or business associations to help small and medium-sized enterprises understand those commitments, avoiding uncertainty that might be very costly for firms in international business transactions.

> 'It's like a blind man who gropes his way, because we have not been able to reach the developed countries' level. Besides, we are not as pro-active as they are, thus we can take care of the consumption but cannot meet all demands. Now we are joining WTO, I myself read newspapers a lot but I'm still not clear about the free world trade

market, not to mention others. I'm worried because when Vietnam
joins WTO, of course we have certain preparation, but it's like going
up in smoke without any sense of direction. We only know there is
a fire ahead, because there's smoke, but we don't know whether it's
a big or small fire, hot or warm. It's difficult because our mechanisms of macro environment are weak, we produce while watching
out.' (Interview No. 13).

— Institutional ranking

In order to clarify the changes in the role of organisations in ceramic
production and exportation before and after 'Doi Moi', we asked
our research participants to rank some organisations. The five-scale
questions were introduced with options ranging from 1 (very
important) to 5 (not important at all). After collecting raw data, we
calculated average points for each organisation; so the lower point
it gets, the more important role it plays. Based on primary analysis
on the social configuration of production in Bat Trang, five organisations that represent the main actors involved in village development,
were selected for ranking, including: local authority; SOEs; private
firms; household workshop; Bat Trang ceramic association; and
craft village club. Two areas were addressed: production and
exports. See Figure 13.1.

Concerning the influence on production, the results show an
obvious change among the aforementioned actors. The role of supporting organisations like the association and the craft village club has
remarkably improved with average points in the current period (after
'Doi Moi') correspondingly 2.75 and 3.25 compared with 4.19 and
4.44 in the period before 'Doi Moi'.

Besides, we can see that the role of the private sector and households is more important than that before 1986. In reality, these two
actors had existed before 1986 and have contributed effectively to the
ceramic manufacturing here, but they are not officially recognised.
This is why the private sector and households in the past got only an
average of 2.93 and 2.81 respectively while the points for the current
period are 2.13 and 2.19, respectively.

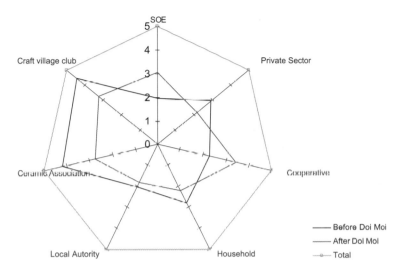

Figure 13.1: The Role of Some Organisations in Production Promotion in Pre and Post 'Doi Moi' Eras.

The role of the local authority has been slightly changed according to respondents' judgments, because its participation is high, especially in providing collective goods such as infrastructure and a favourable business environment. The results also indicate a decline in the role of state-owned enterprises and cooperatives. Average point of SOEs increases from 1.94 (near 'important' level) to 3.06 (close to 'not important' level). Similarly, the cooperatives sector gains the point of 3.44, much higher than that in the period before 1986 (only 2.25). This decline is reasonable because most state-owned enterprises (5) in Bat Trang commune had to transform their ownership into joint-stock companies, instead of being purely SOEs. For the cooperatives, there only remain two that function in an effective way in comparison with five in the pre-'Doi Moi' period.

Data analysis of the organisational role in export promotion show us a similar trend with the decline of the public and collective sectors and an emergence of the private sector (including household workshops) and supporting institutions. In this aspect, the role of SOEs decreased due to the fact that they lost their monopoly advantage in exports while other sectors can now proceed to export directly. The local

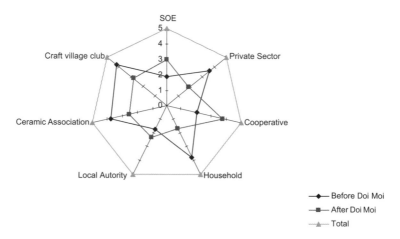

Figure 13.2:   The Role of Organisations in Export Promotion in Bat Trang in Pre and Post 'Doi Moi' Eras.

authority is primarily responsible for creating an equal playing field among firms and they do not intervene deeply in firm operation as prior to the Doi Moi period. The detailed data is illustrated in Figure 13.2.

Regarding the difference in average scores before and after 'Doi Moi', analysis indicates that cooperatives have the largest difference (between average scores in the two period), and second largest is the public sector (SOEs). It means that the role of the two organisations have dramatically decreased in the transition period. Conversely, the roles of households and the private sector have become much more important.

13.4 Discussion

The above analysis aims to prove that entering the transition period has lead Bat Trang to a gradual transformation in terms of economic as well as social structure, reflected in the introduction and emergence of new actors. Ancient institutions become invalid in a new context which confirms the role of new institutional forms. In the following part, we summarise two models of the social configuration of production in Bat Trang prior to and post Doi Moi.

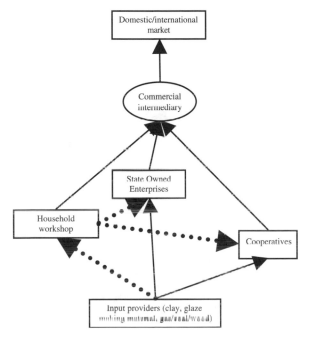

Figure 13.3: Social Configuration of Production in Bat Trang Pre 'Doi Moi' Period.

Figure 13.3 shows simple relations among the actors involved. All transactions with the external market depended on a third party, Bat Trang villagers had almost no direct transactions. The number of involved actors remains limited, mostly cooperatives and SOEs. Most households were members of cooperatives. Subcontractor relations between companies and households went on in an unofficial unrecognised way.

In Figure 13.4, the relations are more complex. Many new factors appear and influence the manufacturing process. The most important changes are the boom of the private sector and the development of household businesses. Moreover, some supporting institutions like the association or club are also created to meet the information and consultancy needs of enterprises. The private sector is officially recognised, leading to the openness of previously implicit relations, notably the raw material supplier-producer relation.

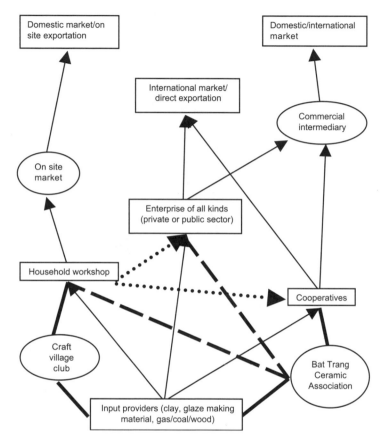

Figure 13.4:   Social Configuration of Production in Bat Trang, Post 'Doi Moi' Period.

Does a typical development model of Vietnam in the transformation period of craft villages exist? What international model can fit such organisational forms in Vietnam? Compared with the development of industrial districts (ID) in Italy in the 1970s and 1980s, we can see some similarities that make these two forms comparable. Pushing further the very first idea of industrial districts developed by Marshall, Beccattini (1992) defined it as 'a socio-territorial entity characterised by the active presence of a human community and enterprises in a given geographical and historical space'. This definition includes all economic, social, historical, cultural aspects of an ID.

Thanks to his important contribution, when studying ID, the units subject to analysis were no longer a single enterprise/organisation, but a cluster of interconnected firms/institutions. Certainly, its development requires updating with the addition of newly arisen features, but its general characteristics remain as follows:

— historical and cultural heritage
— spontaneous development and artisan tradition
— inter connected firms and related organisations
— geographical concentration of production.

As for its Vietnamese counterparts, there are various definitions of craft village that change from study to study. What we attempt to do here is to sum up its main characteristics:

— concentration of production in a given space (village)
— may have long history of development
— artisan character
— vertical cooperation between firms and household workshops
— international and national market.

The similarity in development trajectory between industrial district and craft village encourages us to compare these two industrial organisation forms. Until now, when analysing an ID, sociologists tended to use approaches such as social networks (Chen, 2002; Nakano, 2002) and flexible specialisation (Sabel and Piore, 1987; DiGregorio, 2001). We argue that using these approaches risks omitting an understanding of ID as a whole. Relations within ID or external links tend to be explained in a segmented way. It might mainly focus on the current situation of these relationships, ignoring historical aspects. For these diverse reasons, in this paper, we shall try to conceptualise the term of industrial district in the context of figuration sociology notably developed by Norbert Elias.

In *Time: An Essay*, Elias (1992) argued that all social constructs are culturally and historically determined and we cannot understand them without reviewing how they were formed and evaluated in the past. For Elias, society of any size is comprised of interconnected individuals or groups that he called configurations (Elias, 1991). Configuration is not a static status but changeable when the relationships among actors change, or when new actors appear. Analysing a configuration of a society can help us to understand its transformation, reflected a in a constant change in the system of relations. Forming a configuration means that its components (individuals and groups) all participate in a game, in which each party has its own objective and strategy. If we refer, as earlier, a craft village to an industrial district that is formed by different interdependent actors, we can now consider, in an Elias perspective, industrial district/craft village as a configuration. Using such a working definition, we can analyse craft villages as a whole not only in the current situation, but also in their cultural and historical determination. Bagnasco and Trigilia (1988) made one of the first analyses of the formation and development of IDs from handicraft households to small enterprises, and the participation of the local authority, etc. Returning to Bat Trang's case, we can see that Bat Trang has a long history, which is recognised from at least the late 14th or early 15th century. Its development is marked by the continuous interaction among actors from the macro political environment to the micro intervention of local authority; from the participation of artisans to well-established companies, and the first steps towards the international market. The model of relations between enterprises, local authority, households and so on has continuously changed as explained in the analysis above. Looking at Figures 13.3 and 13.4, we can see a clearer transformation in production structure in Bat Trang, especially when the municipality intends to separate production from the residential area and provide new regulations. The craft village can now be defined as *an industrial district, formed by interconnected actors (firms, households, institution, political power, public etc.) who geographically concentrate and are involved in the production of one or one type of product. Related actors develop not only internal but also external relations that may exceed the geographical boundaries. All these interconnected actors form the social configuration of production of the district.*

Compared to the development process in Italy, where is Bat Trang now? Brusco (1992) has three models for the formation and development of IDs: 'traditional artisan'; 'dependent subcontractor' and 'industrial district-ID (with or without government intervention)'. The first model was popular in the 1950s and 1960s with the characteristics of primitive manufacturing technology and low income. The skills were acquired through apprenticeship and practice. The market was limited to the residential area. The second model, 'dependent subcontractor', developed strongly at the end of the 1960s, in which one enterprise does not take care of all phases but various small and medium ones are involved. The important change in this period was the expansion in domestic and international markets.

The ID model (without government intervention) started in the 1970s and it is now still considered successful. Division of labour within ID became more specified, based on the manufacturing process, accordingly there are enterprises that produce the final product; other enterprises are involved in only one manufacturing phase, and a number of enterprises belonging to different sectors, serving as supporting ones. The interrelation between enterprises includes vertical cooperation and horizontal competition, and accordingly cooperation existed between enterprises which are involved in different phases of the production process. Competition was among enterprises that produced the same products or operated in the same field.

Since the 1980s, important changes in market and technology trends have challenged the IDs development, forcing them to innovate to adapt to new conditions. As a result, the ID model with public intervention emerged. According to this model, collective services such as information on trends in customer taste, new markets and trends in technology are provided by government and some new institutions.

Reviewing the development of Bat Trang and other craft villages, we can see that they do not match completely (due to differences in socio-economic conditions), but their trajectory is quite similar. The present configuration of Bat Trang is a mixture of the models of ID with and without government intervention. We'll take the comparison of Ganne (2005) to make this more obvious. See Table 13.1.

Industrial concentration has become a common trend, and it is now widely spreading in developing countries, especially in Asia.

Table 13.1:   Comparison Between the Configuration of Bat Trang and Others Models of ID.

Classical Characteristics of Industrial Districts	The Bat Trang Situation	Present Development of Industrial Districts in Europe
Groups of independent SMEs	Group of interdependent SMEs and household workshops	Links between big firms and SMEs
Locally concentrated in the country or small towns	Concentrated on the periphery of big cities (Hanoi)	New concentrations also found in centre of big cities, and metropolis
SMEs developing directly informal links of cooperation	Vertical cooperation between SMEs and household workshops	Links more and more organised and formal between all kind of firms in clusters
Accumulating technical and social conditions to produce innovation	Financial resources play an important role in innovation	Innovation through networks can be also disruptive
Spontaneous and continuous development	Transition from spontaneous to organised development	Development endogenous and exogenous
Alternative model to mass production system with big firms	Developing links with big firms (local or international)	Development linked with different types of firms, even with big firms
Few public actions	Increased public intervention	Strong role of governance and public actions

Source: Adapted from Ganne (2004), 'New Development of European Industrial Districts: Changing the Approaches, Paper Presented at Conference 'The Development of Chinese Clusters', 6–7 décembre 2004, Guangzhou, Zhongshan University (China).

More and more branches of the world's biggest corporations are set up in developing countries due to the advantages of low-cost labour and materials. This new order in the international division of labour leads to the probability that industrial concentration will continue in the coming years. According to JETRO-IDE's research in 2002,

Vietnam has 4 types of industrial cluster, including the craft village.[10] Parallel to the development of clusters structured by government or led by a large enterprise/corporation, the craft village or industrial district continues to be developed to meet the demand of rural industrialisation and poverty reduction targets.

References

BAGNASCO, A., TRIGILIA, C. (1988). *La construction sociale du marché*, Editions ENS Cachan.

Battrang People's Committee. (2005). 'Political Report,' submitted to the 19th congress of communal communist party, Hanoi.

BECATTINI, G. (1992). 'Le district industrial marshallien: une notion socio-economique,' in Benko G. et Lipietz A., *Les régions qui gagnent*, PUF, Paris.

BRUSCO, S. (1992). 'The Idea of the Industrial District: Its Generic', in Pyke F., Becattini G., Sengerberger W. (eds.), *Industrial District and Interfirm Cooperation in Italy*, ILO Geneva.

CHEN, M. (2002). 'Industrial District and Social Capital in Taiwan's Economic Development: An Economy Sociological Study on Taiwan's Bicycle industry,' Ph.d. Dissertation, Yale University.

DANG, Thi Lan. (2003). *Vai trò của hiệp hội đối với doanh nghiệp chế biến nông sản thực phẩm nhỏ và vừa ở Việt Nam*, (Role of business associations for SMEs in the agricultural product processing industry), *Questions of International Economy*, 91(11).

DiGREGORIO, M.R. (2001). 'Iron Works: Excavating Alternative Futures in a Northern Vietnamese Craft Village,' Ph.d. Dissertation, University of California, LA.

DO, Thi Hao. (1989). *Quê gốm Bát Tràng* (The home of ceramics: Bat Trang), Hanoi Publishing House, Hanoi.

ELIAS, N. (1981). *Qu'est-ce que la sociologie*, Presses-Pocket, Paris.

ELIAS, N. (1992). *Time: An Essay*. Oxford: Blackwell.

GANNE, B. (2004). 'New Development of European Industrial Districts: Changing the Approaches,' paper presented at conference 'The Development of Chinese Clusters,' 6–7 December 2004, Guangzhou, Zhongshan University (China).

---

[10] These four categories of industrial agglomeration include: (i) District of local specialized product; (ii) Agglomeration of supplier and subcontractor around a large core firm; (iii) Clusters in larges cities; (iv) Industrial parks led by government. For a more detail discussion, see Kuchiki A. (2002).

HY, V. Luong (1998). 'Engendered Entrepreneurship: Ideologies and Political Economic Transformation in a Northern Vietnamese Centre of Ceramics Production,' in Robert W. Hefner (ed.), *Market Cultures: Society and Morality in the New Asian Capitalisms*, Westview Press.

JICA-MARD (2004). 'The Study of Craft Villages Development for Rural Industrialization in Vietnam,' Final report, Almec Corporation.

KUCHIKI, A. (2002). 'Agglomeration of Exporting Firms in Industrial Zones in Northern Vietnam: Players and Institutions,' in Kagami M., Tsuji M. (eds.), *Industrial Agglomeration — Facts and Lessons for Developing Countries*, International Joint Research Project Series 7, IDE, Japan.

MARD. (1997). *Ngành nghẽ nông thôn việt nam* (Rural off-farm activities in Vietnam), Agriculture Publishing House, Hanoi.

MARD. (2005). *Program 'one village, one product'* (draft version), Ministry of Agriculture and Rural Development (Mard), Hanoi.

MARSHALL, A. (1890). *Principles of Economics*, 8th edition, Macmillan and Co., Ltd. 1920. (First edition published 1890.)

NAKANO, T. (2002). 'A Paradox of Embeddedness: Social Network Analysis of a Japanese Industrial District,' Ph.d. Dissertation, University of Columbia.

NEWTON, T. (2001). 'Organization: the Relevance and the Limitations of Elias,' *Organization*, 8(3).

NGUYEN, Khac Tung, Bui, Xuan Dinh (1993), in *The traditional village in Vietnam*, The Gioi Publishing House, Hanoi.

PHAM, Huu Dat (1977). *Vài tài liệu vẽ làng gốm Bát Tràng trước cách mạng tháng Tám*, (Certain documents on the pottery craft village of Bat Trang before the August revolution), in Institute for History Studies, *Rural Vietnam from a Historical Perspective*, Social Sciences Publishing House, Hanoi.

PHAN, Huy Le, Nguyen, Đinh Chien, Nguyen Quang Ngoc (1995). *Gốm Bát Tràng thế kỷ XIV–XIX* (Bat Trang's ceramic in 14–19 century). The Gioi Pulishing House, Hanoi.

PIORE, M.J., SABEL, C.F. (1987). *The Second Industrial Divide: Possibilities for Prosperity*, Basic Book, Inc. Publishers, NY.

PORTER, M. (1998). 'Clusters and the New Economics of Competition,' *Havard Business Review*.

SAXENIAN, A. (1992). 'Divergent Patterns of Business Organization in Silicon Valley,' in Storper M., Scott A.J. (eds.), *Pathways to Industrialization and Regional Development*, Routledge, London.

TRAN, Minh Yen (2004). *'Traditional Craft Village in Industrialisation and Modernization Processes,'* Social Sciences Pulishing House, Hanoi.

Vietnam Competitiveness Initiatives (VNCI, 2003). 'Bat Trang ceramic competitive strategy.'

Chapter 14

The Prevalence of Social Embedding in Vietnamese Industrial Clusters

Stephen J. Appold and Quy Thanh Nguyen

Vietnam   R32 P31 L14   P25 L25 J21   P23

14.1 The Prevalence of Social Embedding in Vietnamese Industrial Clusters

Economic production, whether of goods or services, is spatially concentrated. There are many possible reasons for industrial agglomeration. Concentration may be the result of random factors, the unintended consequence of firm birth and death processes, or the outcome of peculiarities of firm location decisions.

Although there are many possible reasons for industrial agglomeration, one common and very plausible explanation is that the spatial pattern observed is operationally advantageous. Mills (1972, pp. 10–11) identified three possible sources of operational advantage. First, economies of scale in production sufficient to overcome the costs of transportation may be the most basic source of operational advantage. Second, particular regions may be favoured for certain types of production by a comparative advantage based on spatial variation in natural resources. Third, producers may also benefit from proximity to each other.

There are, in turn, three possible sources of proximity benefits. The clustering of producers facilitates the pooling of resources to create efficiency-enhancing infrastructure, such as port and transportation facilities, and it aids in the exploitation of particular markets. Such clustering also allows producers to take advantage of complementary inputs, such as male and female labour, which are linked for family

405

reasons. None of these sources of possible operational advantage requires direct contact between producers and none of these sources of advantage require more than 'arms-length' market relationships among those producing standard products.

There is, however, a third possible basis for proximity benefits. Firms may gain an advantage through various types of information exchange. The information exchange may be about market opportunities, the trustworthiness of particular customers or suppliers, or the intricacies of particular technologies. Much of this information may just be 'in the air' and constitute a non-tradable resource (Marshall, 1892).

The exchange of such information may build up mutual obligations that ensure that business partners carry through on their commitments. The web of mutual obligations, encouraging information exchange and enforcing contracts, may be facilitated when business partners are also social associates. Such non-tradable information exchange embedded in social relationships is frequently held to be at the basis of industrial districts (Becattini, 1992; Pyke, 1992).

Many geographers and economists believe that some form of information exchange lies at the basis of contemporary agglomeration. There is an extensive ongoing discussion of local knowledge spillovers, trust, and cooperation. Unfortunately, there is little empirical evidence — one way or the other — for local information exchange and cooperative relationships. Moreover, the little information that exists is plagued by unbalanced sampling designs and questionable measurement procedures (Markusen, 2003). In this paper, we report on our efforts to document the prevalence and nature of the features of operational advantage that are often simply assumed to exist.

Our research site, detailed below, is Vietnam. If mutual cooperation among firms could be found anywhere, Vietnam is a likely place. The continuing economic growth implies that there is sufficient opportunity to reward efficiency-enhancing behaviours while the state of the public bureaucracy regulating the economy suggests that such action in civil society is needed.

In what follows, we outline relevant aspects of the Vietnamese economy, summarise our dataset, and discuss the findings of our analysis. We conclude by considering the implications of our findings for the theory of industrial agglomeration.

14.2 Private Orderings in Vietnam

With an estimated population of approximately 80 million and an active labour force of approximately 38 million, Vietnam is the world's 40th largest economy, just after Hong Kong (World Bank, 2003). Between 1991 and 2001, Vietnam's economy grew at an impressive average annual rate of 7.7% (World Bank, 2003) making it one of the world's fastest-growing economies even if economic growth possibly has a percentage point recently. Over the past several years, child malnutrition has fallen rapidly, unemployment is low and labour force participation rates have risen, and poverty rates have fallen rapidly (Haughton, 2000), resulting in relatively broad-based improvements in welfare (Glewwe, Gragnolati and Zaman, 2002). Moreover, persistent extreme poverty appears to be relatively rare (Baulch and Masset, 2003). Nevertheless, Vietnam remains one of the poorer countries of the world with approximately half its population living in poverty at any one time and a (constant 1995 dollar) per capita gross domestic product of $390 (World Bank, 2003).

Vietnam has a long history of administrative and legal reform stretching back to at least 1979 which alternately speeds and slows (e.g., Porter, 1993). Property laws have been amended; the credit system revamped; and regulations revised (Tanaka, 1992; World Bank, 1993). Between 1988 and 1991 state-owned enterprises shed nearly 800,000 employees and possibly one million members of the armed forces were demobilised. Beginning in 1989, laws regulating private enterprise were liberalised prompting some (e.g., Fforde and de Velder, 1996) to claim that Vietnam possessed the essential characteristics of a market economy by that time. Few state-owned enterprises have been privatised and despite nominal legal reforms, state capacity to enforce laws is questionable and observers note a continuing need for legal and administrative reform (e.g., Dollar, 1999). However desirable, the high level of government legitimacy necessary make the completion of the recommended legal and administrative reforms are unlikely in the near future.

The combination of lack of state capacity and rapid economic growth suggest that 'private orderings,' such as those implied by the term social capital would be very much in evidence. Property rights appear to be enforced via a system of patron-client relationships (Gainsborough, 2002). Vietnamese small business owners sometimes report a desire to avoid state scrutiny and, as are business owners everywhere, are reluctant to have their activities known to officials, suggesting an expectation of little support from the state.

14.3 Sampling, Data Collection, and the Sample

We have a multi-stage cluster sample of 447 male and female-owned businesses with at least one employee outside the immediate family in rural and urban areas of North and South Vietnam. The heart of the data is detailed rosters of potential and actual employees and the activities undertaken in the enterprise facilities, such as child care, meals, recreation, and homework. Urban and rural sites in Hanoi, Ha Tay Province, Ho Chi Minh City, and Can Tho Province were selected. Hanoi and Ho Chi Minh City are the largest cities in the North and South, respectively. Ha Tay Province borders Hanoi to the southwest and is part of the Northern Delta. Can Tho Province is located approximately 170 km south of Ho Chi Minh City and is part of the Southern Delta. Each area contains urban and rural locations.[1]

---

[1] In Ha Noi, Van Chung and O cho Dua (Hang Bot) wards in Dong Da District (downtown) were chosen as urban sites. Dai Mo Village, Tay Mo Village and Me Tri Village in Tu Liem District (15 km from the centre) were chosen as the rural sites. In adjoining Ha Tay Province, Quang Trung Ward in Ha Dong Town (12 km from Hanoi) was chosen as the urban site. Van Phuc Village (on the outskirts of Ha Dong and 15 km from Hanoi. was the rural site. In Ho Chi Minh City, Wards 1, 2, and 3, in District 4 (downtown) were the urban sites. Tan Thoi Nhi Village and Xuan Thoi Son Village in Hoc Mon District (20 km from the centre) were the rural sites. In Can Tho Province, An Lac, Tan Phu, An Phu, and Xuan Khanh wards in Can Tho Town were the urban sites while Cai Rang Village in Chau Thanh District (7 km from Can Tho Town) was the rural site.

Appendix Table 14.1 provides more detailed information on the location of the sampled firms.

The enterprise owner was our primary informant. In most cases, the enterprise owners were eager to speak to the interviewers. However, 29 business owners refused to be interviewed even after all possible explanation and encouragement. Refusals occurred most frequently among the Chinese-Vietnamese entrepreneurs in the urban areas of Ho Chi Minh City (13) and Can Tho Town (11). In Hanoi and Ha Tay there were five total refusals. In addition, there were five cases in which the interview was not successfully completed. All but 34 of the 481 qualifying businesses contacted completed interviews for a 93% response rate.

We randomly chose one district from a complete list in Hanoi and Ho Chi Minh City for further sampling. (We also randomly chose a district in each city as a reserve in case the administrative procedures, detailed below, were not successfully completed.) In Ha Tay and Can Tho provinces the capital towns was selected. Three wards (two to be held as reserves) were chosen from the wards in each of the urban districts. Three villages in each province were similarly chosen randomly from a list. In each ward or village, the interviewers walked a prescribed path (usually the main business street) interviewing each qualifying business while holding to a prescribed quota of male and female owners. If there was an insufficient number of businesses found along the path in the ward or village, they continued along the prescribed path into the adjoining ward or village.

We requested a letter of introduction from the local authorities in each ward and village. In one case in Ho Chi Minh City, we could receive permission to interview only for a time period that was far later than our planned period of data collection. In that case, we interviewed in one of our reserve wards.

The average interview lasted 40–45 minutes. Our survey instrument included rosters of household and extended family members, of employees, and of business partners so that we can compare potential and actual exchange partners. We provide background information on the sampled businesses and on the owners and their spouses. The bulk of our analysis centres on the external and internal relationships of the businesses.

14.3.1   The Businesses

Table 14.1 shows summary information on the basic characteristics of the sampled businesses. All but one of the 447 sampled businesses were private sector firms; the remaining firm was a state-owned enterprise. Almost all businesses were sole ownerships. Given the history of cooperatives in Vietnam, we had expected to find a higher level of co-ownership but less than 5% of the sampled businesses had a co-owner; more than half of the 20 co-owners were immediate family members (often the spouse).

By design, the businesses were approximately equally distributed among the rural and urban areas of the North and South. The average age of the businesses at the time of interview was approximately ten years. While many businesses were quite new (10% were no more than two years old), over 10% were over 20 years old and several respondents replied that the business had been handed down for generations — in a few cases, since the 18th century. These were mainly craft manufacturers. We coded 1950 as the earliest date of establishment in our analyses.

Our results suggest that small business has a much longer history in Vietnam than official figures would suggest. We did not ask the date of registration nor whether the businesses were, in fact, registered. Although the south of Vietnam is held to have had a longer and uninterrupted tradition of private business, we did not find that reflected in the distribution of business age in our sample.

Most businesses were physically small with a mean floor area of approximately eight metres by eight metres. (The median floor area was 6.3 metres by 6.3.) Many of the businesses were essentially roadside stalls set up in the front room of the family dwelling. In two-thirds of the cases, the business was located entirely within the home. The reason for the choice of location in three-quarters of the cases was that the property was already owned. The most common operational advantage of the locations, cited in approximately one-third of the cases, was that the area was frequented by customers. Our sampling procedure of walking along major business routes may overemphasise the prevalence of that factor for businesses.

Table 14.1: Basic Description of the Sampled Enterprises.

		Count	%	Mean	Min.	Max.
Private enterprise		446	99.8			
Co-owner		20	4.5			
Region	North, Urban	106	23.7			
	North, Rural	117	26.2			
	South, Urban	112	25.1			
	South, Rural	112	25.1			
Year of establishment		447		1992.55	1950	2002
Physical Size (metres-squared)				63.64	2	1600
Place of business	in the home	297	66.6			
	partially in the home	73	16.4			
	separated from home	76	17.0			
	Total	446				
Reason for business location						
input materials are cheaper in this location		22	5.0			
many customers come to this location		150	34.3			
owned the space	332		76.0			
similar businesses were successful in this location		84	19.2			
other	81		18.5			
Number of people who worked in previous week						
full time				3.9	0	43
part time				1.4	0	99
Total				5.3	1	110
% of total sales accounted for the main product				87.2	2.0	100.0
Type of economic activities						
Manufacturer/processor		275	61.8			
Seller (including service)		170	38.2			
Total		445	100.0			

(*Continued*)

Table 14.1: (*Continued*)

	Count	%	Mean	Min.	Max.
Sector					
Food, drink, sugar, fruit, rice	201	45.2			
Daily necessities (gas, footwear, toys, bags etc.)	40	9.0			
Construction related products and service	34	7.6			
Cloth, textile, garment, blanket, etc.	64	14.4			
Furniture, wood, bamboo	25	5.6			
Electric appliances and equipment	15	3.4			
Plastics products (raincoat, etc.)	3	0.7			
Medicines (western and Eastern)	5	1.1			
Metal (iron, aluminum, gold products)	37	8.3			
Paper related 5	1.1				
Other (cosmetic, mash, plastic net, motorcycle)	16	3.6			
Total 445					
Restaurant 70	15.7				

In 75 cases, businesses had changed location. Most of the time the move was near the time of founding and almost half of the moves were of less than 500 metres. Among the businesses that moved, customer traffic was only slightly more important as a consideration than among those who had not. Despite the obvious implication for retail sales, location was not, for most of those sampled, a strategic choice.

The Vietnam Living Standards Surveys are among the few broad-based sources of information about small businesses in Vietnam (Viverberg, 1998).[2] Our sample differs in one important respect. Vijverberg (1998) reported that only 6.9% of Vietnam's businesses hire at least one wage worker. In order to be included in our sample,

---

[2] Other surveys of Vietnamese small businesses include Appold *et al.* (1996) and Ronnas and Ramamurthy (2001).

businesses needed to employ at least one person outside the immediate family. We, therefore, have not included the very large number of businesses that do not employ anyone outside the household.

Still, our businesses were, on the whole, quite small with a mean number of people working full-time of 3.9 (median 3) and a mean number of total people working of 5.3 (median 4). The largest sampled business, an outlier with over twice as many employees as the next largest firm, had 110 people employed. The 33 firms with 10 or more employees were a fairly diverse set differing from the sample as a whole mainly by being almost twice as old on average. The urban businesses had, on average, slightly more employees but we found no North-South differences.

The facts that 93% of small businesses do not hire any employees and that those businesses that do so are, on average, quite small provides evidence in support of the transaction cost arguments for the small size of firms in developing countries. Those facts are also consistent with a range of other explanations for small size ranging from small size of market niches to productive inefficiency, however.

With some 266 different main products offered, the businesses were active in a wide range of branches. Many were quite specialised in narrowly defined products (such as a particular type of noodle dish or a particular type of metal part) and, on average, almost 90% of each business' sales was accounted for by a single product. Over half concentrated on food and other daily necessities. Some businesses specialised in producer products. Some produced or handled goods that required specialised knowledge. All businesses sold at a retail level. Approximately one-fourth counted other businesses among their customers. While almost 40% were simple resellers; 60% also processed the goods to some degree (including cooking). Sixteen percent of the sampled businesses sold ready-to-eat food.

Half of the owners claimed that they were 'satisfied' with their earnings (on a five-point scale) with the most of the remainder being either 'neutral' or 'dissatisfied.' Approximately 60% of the owners thought their businesses were operating at the full capacity of their assets, equipment, and personnel. The businesses generated an average of 620.85 million VN Dong per year in sales, ranging to as much as 129,600 million VN Dong per year and yielded a mean profit of 93.86 million VN Dong per year which went as high as 21,600 million VN Dong per year (median of 24 million VN Dong). The poverty line in Vietnam was approximately 1.8 million VN Dong per year in 1998. The median business generated enough income to support an average-sized family at almost three times the poverty level but approximately one-eighth of the businesses provided insufficient income for an average-sized family. Sales and profits do vary significantly by region, net of business size, with the businesses in the urban north standing out as generating more sales and being more profitable than the other regions while businesses in the urban south generated significantly lower profits, perhaps because of a more competitive environment.

14.3.2   *Owners and Their Spouses*

Table 14.2 shows information about the 447 owners and their (390) spouses, providing additional information about the nature of the sampled firms. Spouses, of course, occupy a special position in many small businesses. By design, ownership was approximately equally divided among males and females. On average, owners and their spouses were in their early 40s and had about ten years of formal schooling with a range from no schooling at all to 18 and 17 years, respectively.

Owner and spouse work experience was approximately equally divided among their own enterprise and other employers — which were largely other private sector employers. Only about one-fifth of the owners (but 40% of those in Hanoi) were employed by state-owned enterprises immediately prior to their setting up their business. Almost two-thirds of the owners (but significantly fewer of the spouses) felt that past work experience benefited the business, so that the businesses often represented an accumulation of human capital. Experience in state-owned enterprises was seen as significantly less beneficial than experience in cooperatives and private enterprise.

Table 14.2: Information about the Enterprise Owners and their Spouses.

	Owner					Spouse				
	Count	%	Mean	Min.	Max.	Count	%	Mean	Min.	Max.
Sex (female)	208	46.6				209	58.9			
Age			42.77	22	77			43.16	20	76
Highest grade completed										
			9.966	0	18			10.06	0	17
Years of experience outside enterprise										
	440		10.11	0	58	385		10.53	0	60
Sector of previous employer										
SOE	86	21.1				105	30.1			
Cooperative	30	7.4				24	6.9			
Private enterprise	257	63.0				175	50.1			
other	35	8.6				45	12.9			
	408					349				
Years of experience with that enterprise										
	202		9.67	0	50	173		10.68	0	50
Past experience contributed to business success										
	272	62.7				139	36.5			
How was the most important skill needed in running this business learned?										
previous job	67	15.9								
schooling	26	6.2								
experience in this business	299	70.9								
other	46	10.9								
Work in enterprise										
	434	97.3				272	70.1			
Total time at enterprise over the past week										
			126.56	0	168			109.07	0	168
Hours worked at the enterprise over the previous week										
			52.3	0	146			34.25	0	168
Paid for work in enterprise in cash?										
Market rate	49	11.5				23	0.3			
Less than market rate	1	0.2								
No	375	88.2				338	93.4			
Earned money elsewhere over previous week										
	36	8.2				94	25.1			

Approximately 70% of those interviewed claimed that experience in their own business was the most important source of skill. Although the technology in these businesses was generally simple, when asked about the most important skill needed in their business, a response indicating technical, rather than social or financial, skill was common. Female-owned businesses were slightly smaller and slightly younger, on average, than male-owned businesses but further differences were slight. Our finding differs from several other studies, including one of our own, perhaps because of the minimum employment requirement.

Seventy percent of the spouses worked in the business as did all but 12 of the owners. For some owners, carrying responsibility, rather than active involvement, was the primary task.

Approximately two-thirds of the 178 husbands worked in their wife's business while three-fourths of the 208 wives worked in their husband's business. Owners who did so spent an average of 53.7 hours working in the business each week while spouses spent an average of 48.2 hours working. Men worked approximately five and a half fewer hours then women, on average, so that the women owners put in an average of 55.6 hours while their husbands who worked in the business did so an average of 42.1 hours per week. Few of the owners or spouses took a salary but since male-owners businesses were more profitable than those owned by women that implies a higher return on men's time. Business sales and profits did not affect decisions to work inside or outside of the firms suggesting that the decision to seek outside employment may have been driven by risk-pooling.

14.4 Choice of Partner and Nature of the Relationship

Although the substantive issues in analysing external (supplier and customer) relationships and internal (employee) relationships are similar, we analyse them separately. We used somewhat different indicators of social embedding because of the likely differences in the frequency and nature of common activities. Our analysis centres on the choice of (external or internal) partner and the extent and nature of social embedding in those relationships.

14.4.1 *Suppliers, Customers, and Collaborators*

External partners, especially suppliers, customers, and collaborators, are critical components of industrial districts and the degree of their embeddedness is a distinguishing feature often discussed in the theory of clusters. The theorised external relationships are sometimes held to result in new organisational forms. Table 14.3 shows information about the basic external relationships of the sampled businesses.

'Horizontal cooperation' forms a central theme in many considerations of industrial districts and of agglomerations of small firms. We found little evidence of such relationships. Less than 3% of the businesses shared equipment with other firms (their competitors) while less than 10% cooperated with other firms (competitors) in filling large orders. There was a slight tendency for businesses with firms as customers and textile manufacturers and those in furniture and electrical equipment sectors to cooperate more frequently than others. Those with a strictly retail orientation and those oriented towards daily needs did so somewhat less frequently. It is noteworthy that the few partners in sharing and cooperating tended not to have a family relationship with the focal (sampled) business owner but they did tend to either buy from or sell to the partner and they tended to be located nearby. One of the key theoretical aspects of network forms of business and of industrial districts was uncommon in our sample and, when it did occur, it had commercial, rather than social, glue.

Over one-fourth of the businesses counted other businesses among their customers; 60% of those had other firms as steady customers. Businesses that counted firms among their steady customers differed only in being slightly larger and slightly older on average than the other sampled businesses. Of the 74 businesses with firms as steady customers, approximately two-thirds (49) had state-owned enterprises as their most important customer, suggesting the integration of small businesses into the state sector as suppliers and support firms. Family members were the point of contact in 23% of the businesses that were steady customers (including the state-owned enterprises), suggesting that their point of contact helped arrange for

Table 14.3:   Critical External Business Relationships.

	Share with Competitors		Cooperate with Competitors		Customers		Material Suppliers		Start-up Capital Source		Working Capital Source	
	count	%	count	%	count	%	count	%	count	%	count	%
Overall total	12	2.7	43	9.6					185	41.4	74	16.6
Has customers that are businesses					121	27.2						
Has regular customers that are businesses							74	60.7				
Nature of creditor												
a person									104	55.9	28	37.8
an informal organisation									7	59.7	16	59.5
a credit organisation									75	100.0	30	100.0
Total									186		74	
Relationship to contact person												
immediate family	3	25.0	10	23.3	12	16.2	21	4.7	57	51.4	9	20.5
relative	2	16.7	3	7.0	5	6.8	20	4.5	29	26.1	7	15.9
friend	1	8.3	11	25.6	14	18.9	51	11.5	15	13.5	8	18.2
other	6	50.0	19	44.2	43	58.1	351	79.2	10	9.0	20	45.5
Total	12		43		74		443		111		44	
Contact person has a business nearby												
	9	75.0	22	51.2	35	49.3	108	24.2	23	20.9	9	20.5
Buy something from that person												
	7	63.6	26	60.5	15	78.9	72	16.9	17	9.2	11	15.3
Sell something to that person												
	7	63.6	24	55.8					23	12.5	16	22.2
Person extends credit												
					27	36.5	231	53.4				
Frequency of contact with that person												
daily	5	45.5	11	25.6	17	23.0	115	26.6	32	17.5	12	16.7
several times per week	3	27.3	4	9.3	21	28.4	105	24.3	20	10.9	6	8.3
several times per month	2	18.2	14	32.6	23	31.1	166	38.4	56	30.6	24	33.3
several times per year	1	9.1	14	32.6	13	17.6	46	10.6	70	38.3	28	38.9
never	0	0.0	0	0.0	0	0.0	0	0.0	5	2.7	2	2.8
Total	11		43		74		432		183		72	

the sale and that having relatives with control over resources can be a benefit for small businesses.

The interviewed owners had family relationships with less than 10% of materials suppliers. That low prevalence didn't hold for the sources of start-up capital. Forty percent of the businesses borrowed funds to start the business. The sources of credit and the materials suppliers tended not to be located nearby (within 500 metres). Individuals were the source of choice but even when funds were borrowed from a formal credit organisation, in three-fourths of the cases, the contact person was an immediate family member or a relative. This suggests that the business owners may receive privileged access to those funds and that there may be a degree of favoritism in the granting of loans. From the point of view of the focal business, socially embedding economic relationships serves to expand access to resources.

The crucial — and still unanswered — question is, however, the degree to which the external points of contact are using their position for their own benefit, gaining respect and resources from the focal business owners, versus for the benefit of their employers, choosing businesses owned by family members because those businesses can be trusted.

Besides having a family tie, we used the frequency of contact with the business partners as a measure of social embedding. Contact was fairly frequent with almost a quarter of the partners interacting on a daily basis; 43% had contact at least several times per week. Contact with business partners who were immediate family members was substantially more frequent than it was with partners who were not — over one half were in daily contact with the business partners who were immediate family members while only 20% were in daily contact with business partners who were relatives, friends, or of no special relation. Contact appears to reinforce, rather than substitute for, family ties.

14.4.2 Household and Employees

The overlay of economic and social relationships is a second major component of the theory of industrial clusters. Trust is a critical concern in selecting internal as well as external partners. Maintaining social ties with workers may help in achieving the maximum possible business efficiency — and therefore in ensuring business survival.

There were a total of 1903 members of the households of the 447 sampled owners. The average household size was 4.26. We collected data on up to eight members of each owner's household. Table 14.4 shows detailed information about the 1855 members of the nuclear family households, including the 447 business owners and their 390 spouses. As would be expected, households were comprised of approximately equal numbers of males and females. Ages ranged from one to 88 with a mean of 33. Almost 60% of the household members worked in the business. Approximately half of the household members aged 60 and older worked in the business. Most children (under 15) did not. One-fourth of the household members attended school. Of the 255 children aged 6 to 15 in the households of the sampled owners, 16% worked in the business. Almost all children also attended school, suggesting that the use of child labour in family businesses did not seriously interfere with the children's education.

Most of those working in the business were not paid a cash salary. Eighteen percent of the household members earned money outside the business (about two-thirds of those did not work in the family business), suggesting a degree of family risk pooling. The low proportion of individuals performing work for someone else on the premises suggests that among the respondents, there is a clear understanding of the concept 'firm'. Adults (15 years or older) tended not to work in the business if they were older and more educated, again, suggesting a degree of risk pooling. The number of employees did not affect their decisions, so business size is not the factor leading to a family orientation, but household adults tended to work in the firm if profits were higher.

Participation is only one measure of embeddedness. Because contact with household members occurs frequently, we used engaging in a series of non-work activities in and away from the enterprise as measures of social embeddedness. These activities were eating meals at the enterprise, resting or sleeping there, socialising, and eating meals with household members away from the enterprise. Most household members socialised and rested at the enterprise and ate

Table 14.4:   Characteristics of Household Members.

	All Immediate Family Members					Not Working in Enterprise			Working in Enterprise	
	count	%	mean	min	max	count	%	mean	count	%
Household size	447		4.26	1	18					
Role: owner	447	24.1				12	1.5		434	41.1
spouse	390	21.0				116	14.6		272	25.8
other	1018	54.9				666	83.9		349	33.1
total	1855					794			1055	
Sex (female)	925	50.6				381	49.4		542	51.5
Age	1854		32.8	1	88	794		26.42	1055	
Highest grade completed	1821		8.98	0	18	772		7.79	1045	
Attend School now?	463	25.5				337	43.2		125	12.2
Total time at enterprise over the past week	1861		109.68	0	168	794		84.61	1064	
Hours worked at the enterprise over the previous week	1849		26.67	0	168				1055	
Work in enterprise	1055	57.1							1055	100
Paid for work in enterprise in cash?										
Market rate	140	13.8							138	13.6
Less than market rate	16	1.6							16	1.6
No	862	84.7							861	84.8
	1018									
Earned money elsewhere over previous week	314	17.7				186	25.2		128	12.4
Non-work activities at the enterprise during the previous week										
Socialise	1481	80.5				488	62.4		991	94.0
Eat meals	1422	77.7				502	64.3		918	87.8
Rest/sleep	1385	75.7				500	64.0		883	84.4
Eat meals with household members outside	1511	83.1				581	75.9		927	88.4
Do school work	303	16.6				198	25.5		105	10.0
Perform paid work for someone else	38	2.1				16	2.1		22	2.1

both at the enterprise and with household members outside the enterprise — but, as the figures in the bottom right of the table indicate, those who worked in the business were significantly more likely to do each, suggesting both that the common activity of maintaining a business helps strengthen family ties and that such common activities are forms of in-kind payment. Children were heavily embedded regardless of their work status.

Our 447 sampled enterprises had a total of 1315 employees who were not immediate family members. The number of employees ranged from one (the minimum required for inclusion in the sample) to 103 with a mean of 3.04. Table 14.5 shows detailed information about a sample of 1077 of those employees. Males outnumbered females. The employees ranged in age from ten years to 65 with an average of 26 years. The number of years of schooling averaged nine — approximately one year less than that of the owners but ranged from no schooling to 16 years. The overwhelming majority of employees was paid a cash wage of the market rate and worked an average of 54 hours per week. Twelve of the employees (all silk weavers) worked in their own homes, rather than in the place of employment. Many of the employees were relatives or came recommended by someone but one-fourth of the employees had no previous relationship with the employer.

Employees were fairly well integrated into the enterprise — often socialising and resting at the place of business and eating in the enterprise or with household members or other employees outside. Interestingly, relatives were by far the most heavily embedded into the business. Those with no previous relationship to the owner were less likely to engage in any of those actions. Some of the employees (288, 27% of those for whom we have detailed data), while not being part of the owner's immediate family, lived in his or her household.[3] This is in and of itself a strong indicator of social embeddedness. Not surprisingly, the live-in employees were also heavily embedded in terms of the four key common shared activities. Although there is

---

[3] We coded someone as living in the household if they spent 120 or more hours per week at the enterprise.

Table 14.5:   Critical Information about Employees.

	Count	%	Mean %	Min %	Max %
Number of employees	432		3.04	1	103
Sex (female)	459	43.5			
Age	1065		25.86	10	65
Highest grade completed	1038		8.94	0	16
Total time at enterprise over the past week	1072		84.11	0	168
Hours worked at the enterprise over the previous week	1072		53.92	0	146
Paid for work in enterprise in cash?					
Market rate	1021	95.5			
Less than market rate	20	1.9			
No	28	2.6			
Total	1069				
Earned money elsewhere over previous week					
	83	8.6			
Previous relationship to business owner					
relative	353	33.4			
recommended by someone	295	27.8			
friend	141	13.2			
no previous relationship	272	25.6			

Non-work activities at the enterprise during the previous week			**by previous relationship to business owner**			
	Count	%	Relative %	Recommended %	Friend %	no previous relationship %
All employees						
Socialise	892	86.8	93.8	89.0	85.7	76.8
Eat meals	599	58.2	75.5	59.9	50.8	40.4
Rest/sleep	458	44.6	65.1	48.5	33.3	22.4
Eat meals with household members outside	385	37.6	55.6	33.8	25.4	26.8

(Continued)

Table 14.5:   (*Continued*)

Non-work Activities at the Enterprise During the Previous Week			By Previous Relationship to Business Owner			
	Count	%	Relative %	Recommended %	Friend %	No Previous Relationship %
Excluding live-in employees	721					
Socialise	605	84.0	88.9	85.8	84.8	78.3
Eat meals	328	45.5	55.6	47.6	45.5	35.8
Rest/sleep	184	25.6	36.1	30.7	25.0	13.3
Eat meals with household members outside	187	26.1	38.6	25.1	19.6	20.6
Homeworker	12	1.1				
Employee task						
Management	5	0.5				
Administration	13	1.2				
Delivery	106	9.8				
Receiving	7	0.7				
Sales	133	12.4				
Cash	11	1.0				
Making	567	52.7				
Skill	14	1.3				
Service	170	15.8				

little variation in the degree of social embeddedness among those living in the household (except for eating out with other employees), the variation in degree of embeddedness among the types of relationship persists among those who do not live in the household. Contrary to the expectations of theory of enforceable trust but consistent with the insurance hypothesis, prior social relationships lead to increased embeddedness in activities.

14.4.3 *Social Embededness and Performance of Work Tasks*

As noted above, the surveyed enterprises operate in a wide variety of fields. Accordingly, those working in those businesses engaged in a very diverse set of tasks. We found a total of 156 separate simplified job descriptions.[4] Table 14.6 shows the simplified job descriptions for family members in the household and for other employees that were held by more than one person in each category. While some of the job descriptions are quite specific, such as loading and unloading rice, several are quite broad with many workers being described simply as 'worker' or 'assistant'. Sales and making something were the most common general functions. Both descriptions mask tremendous differences in the actual work across sectors, however. In some businesses sales work requires little more than being present on the premises. In others, extensive knowledge of production techniques and cost are needed. Despite the several welders, mechanics, and technicians, many of the job descriptions carry little indication of a high level of skill. Some of the job descriptions connote carrying responsibility, such as the supervision of others or the handling of funds. Those job descriptions seem to be more heavily represented among the family members. That appearance is only partially correct.

Table 14.7 shows that the jobs carrying responsibility are concentrated quite heavily among the owners and their spouses. Of course, these brief job descriptions do not capture all the complexities of the tasks performed (only a minority of owners characterised themselves primarily as 'owner' or 'manager' — even if those were crucial aspects of their responsibility) but the job descriptions do show a clear pattern of responsibility being concentrated in the owner and his or her spouse. Nevertheless, most spouses do not carry job descriptions that suggest responsibility. Perhaps 50 of the 272 spouses working in the

---

[4] Our job descriptions modify only minor spelling and phrasing variations in the original responses. They include all denotations and connotations of tasks. The bottom of Table 14.5 contains categorisations of the tasks performed by employees.

Table 14.6:　Most Common Occupations of Workers.

Immediate Family Members	Count	%	Employee	Count	%
Sales	185	20.1	Worker	250	25.6
Management	150	16.3	Sales	112	11.5
Assistant	116	12.6	Manufacture	105	10.8
Owner	73	7.9	Assistant	75	7.7
Making food	62	6.7	Delivery	68	7.0
Making textiles	45	4.9	Making textiles	62	6.4
Manufacture	38	4.1	Making food	56	5.7
Doing business	19	2.1	Waiter	33	3.4
Worker	15	1.6	Carrier	15	1.5
Making food and sales	11	1.2	Operating the machines	15	1.5
Weaving basket	11	1.2	Weaving basket	14	1.4
Accountant	9	1.0	Welder	12	1.2
Manager's assistant	8	0.9	Accountant	9	0.9
Treasurer	8	0.9	Washing dishes	9	0.9
Carrier	7	0.8	Carpenter	8	0.8
Making basket	7	0.8	Repair	8	0.8
Sale and management	7	0.8	Porter	6	0.6
Sale and manufacture	7	0.8	Production assistant	6	0.6
Delivery	6	0.7	Loading/unloading rice	5	0.5
Operating the machines	6	0.7	Worker and selling	5	0.5
Owner-Manager	6	0.7	Making basket	4	0.4
Displaying products	5	0.5	Mechanic	4	0.4
Manufacture and delivery	5	0.5	Pressing raincoat	4	0.4
Cashier	4	0.4	Technician	4	0.4
Supervisor	4	0.4	Auxiliary worker	3	0.3
Housework	3	0.3	Cutting paper	3	0.3
Looking after merchandise	3	0.3	Handling merchandise	3	0.3
Manufacture and sale	3	0.3	Making food and delivery	3	0.3
Production assistant	3	0.3	Management	3	0.3
Waiter	3	0.3	Sale and manufacture	3	0.3
Weaving mat	3	0.3	Splitting rock	3	0.3
Assistant with chores	2	0.2	Classifying paper	2	0.2
Director	2	0.2	Cleaning	2	0.2

(*Continued*)

Table 14.6:   (*Continued*)

Immediate Family Members	Count	%	Employee	Count	%
Getting merchandise	2	0.2	Displaying products	2	0.2
Looking after products	2	0.2	Doing business	2	0.2
Looking after the store	2	0.2	Housework	2	0.2
Making food and delivery	2	0.2	Looking after customers' vehicles	2	0.2
Making textiles and sales	2	0.2	Principal worker	2	0.2
Mechanic	2	0.2	Sale and purchase	2	0.2
Owner and salesperson	2	0.2	Store keeper	2	0.2
Product inspection	2	0.2	Technical personnel	2	0.2
Purchasing waste materials	2	0.2	Transport	2	0.2
Receiving and delivery	2	0.2	Treasurer	2	0.2
Sales and management	2	0.2			
Welder	2	0.2			
Total number with job titles	922			976	

business (13% of all spouses) have job titles that do so. Five other family members were described as managers. This was a small minority of the 282 adult working family members.

On the other hand, a sizable proportion of accountants, those who have extensive knowledge of the business' finances, were not related to the owner. While there is a tendency to keep responsibility close to the owner, responsibility is not the exclusive purview of close family members nor do most family members carry such responsibility. Only a few in the sample did.

We extracted and coded the key attributes from the job descriptions. Examining 'ownership', we see that 99% of such job descriptions are held by the owner and spouse. (Only 16% of the owners characterised themselves primarily as such. Many identified themselves as having the key skill needed in the business.) Slightly fewer (92%) of the job descriptions connoting the management of others were held by owners and spouses. The remainder was in the hands of family

Table 14.7:   Most Common Occupations of Workers by Relationship to the Owner.

Owner	Cnt.	%	Spouse	Cnt.	%	Other Family	Cnt.	%	Live-in Employees	Cnt.	%
Those living in the household											
Management	122	31.0	Sales	56	22.7	Assistant	80	28.4	Worker	65	25.6
Sales	72	18.3	Assistant	34	13.8	Sales	57	20.2	Assistant	37	14.6
Owner	54	13.7	Management	23	9.3	Making food	31	11.0	Manufacture	29	11.4
Making food	16	4.1	Owner	19	7.7	Manufacture	14	5.0	Sales	25	9.8
Making textiles	16	4.1	Making textiles	16	6.5	Making textiles	13	4.6	Waiter	19	7.5
Manufacture	12	3.1	Making food	15	6.1	Worker	11	3.9	Delivery	11	4.3
Doing business	10	2.5	Manufacture	12	4.9	Weaving basket	7	2.5	Making food	10	3.9
Making food and sales	6	1.5	Accountant	6	2.4	Displaying products	5	1.8	Production assistant	6	2.4
Owner-Manager	6	1.5	Doing business	6	2.4	Management	5	1.8	Making textiles	5	2.0
Sale and management	6	1.5	Making food and sales	4	1.6	Carrier	4	1.4	Worker and selling	5	2.0
Cases with occupations	393			247			282			254	
All cases	434			272			349			288	

(Continued)

Table 14.7: (Continued)

Owner	Cnt.	%	Spouse	Cnt.	%	Other Family	Cnt.	%	Live-in Employees	Cnt.	%
Employees who do not live in the household											
Sales	40	21.9	Worker	56	27.6	Worker	20	18.2	Worker	74	34.6
Worker	35	19.1	Delivery	25	12.3	Sales	14	12.7	Manufacture	29	13.6
Manufacture	22	12.0	Making food	22	10.8	Manufacture	12	10.9	Delivery	15	7.0
Making textiles	17	9.3	Sales	19	9.4	Making food	10	9.1	Sales	13	6.1
Delivery	12	6.6	Making textiles	18	8.9	Assistant	9	8.2	Assistant	12	5.6
Assistant	11	6.0	Manufacture	13	6.4	Making textiles	9	8.2	Weaving basket	12	5.6
Waiter	5	2.7	Carrier	10	4.9	Delivery	5	4.6	Making food	11	5.1
Pressing raincoat	4	2.2	Carpenter	8	3.9	Welder	5	4.6	Operating the machines	7	3.3
Washing dishes	4	2.2	Assistant	6	3.0	Making basket	3	2.7	Loading/ unloading rice	5	2.3
Welder	4	2.2	Accountant	4	2.0	Repair	3	2.7	Porter	5	2.3
Cases with occupations	183			203			110			214	
All cases	196			213			127			226	

members but also some with no family ties. Only a few job descriptions indicated a responsibility for administration but owners and spouses accounted for slightly more than half of those. The remaining positions were divided about equally between relatives and non-relatives. Cash is handled primarily by owners and spouses but, beyond that, those with family ties were not well-represented. Service tasks were often performed by family members and live-in employees while unrelated employees were often engaged in making things — particularly when skill is needed. Those with no family relationship to the owners made up the bulk of those few performing jobs that required a measure of skill. Accomplishing complex tasks, such as manufacturing and complex repair, appear to require going beyond the family to employ others. The few employees that performed jobs requiring a high level of skill were more socially embedded in the enterprise than average. Those carrying responsibility were not.

14.4.4 *Help From Extended Family*

Because kinship is a special and powerful form of social embedding, we asked a series of questions about 12 types of extended family members including whether they lived within 2–3 kilometres of the business, the amount of time devoted to internal help (working in or supervising the operations of the business), and whether they had acted as brokers in external relations (helped in negotiations with business partners or the government). Table 14.8 shows information about the help extended by family members. Two-thirds of the business owners reported having relatives nearby. The most common nearby family members were siblings. Seventy percent of the business owners reported that no family members outside the immediate household worked in the business. Eighty five percent of the business owners reported that no family members outside the immediate household helped in the external affairs of the business by helping secure loans, licenses and the like. Almost two-thirds reported receiving no help at all from their relatives. Only about 19% of the businesses received start-up capital from their families (approximately half of those who received loans). Proximity helps

Table 14.8: Availability of Family Help.

Residents reporting that one or more:

	Live Nearby		Worked in the Business		Provided Help in Ext. Relations		Provided Internal or Ext. Help	
	Cnt	%	Cnt	%	Cnt	%	Cnt	%
Parents	192	43.0	51	11.4	27	6.0	69	15.4
Siblings	242	54.1	78	17.5	57	12.8	112	25.1
In-laws	148	33.1	42	9.4	20	4.5	48	10.7
Other relatives	168	37.6	67	15.0	12	2.7	67	15.0
All family members	300	67.1	132	29.5	67	15.0	154	34.5
No family member lives near			2	1.4	0	0.0	2	1.4
At least one family member lives near			130	43.3	67	22.3	152	50.7

n = 447

significantly raise the likelihood of receiving help from relatives but, even when they live nearby, the extended family contributed help in only half the cases. We use a very generous measure of help.

A more stringent cut-off would decrease the measured level of help. While families may be the most common source of help, the degree of family members' willingness and ability to help may often be over-estimated. Institutional arrangements that result in relying on family members for resources may severely limit the possibilities open to business. Aid is forthcoming from family members significantly more often than from random individuals. Yet, at the same time, the level of support is substantially less than what might be expected on the basis of theory which goes so far as to suggest that parents bear children because they are productive assets (Bulatao and Lee, 1983). More broadly, these results suggest that knowing someone apparently does not imply automatic access to their resources. Acquaintance may be necessary but it is not sufficient.

14.5 Conclusion

This paper reports on our empirical explorations of the degree and nature of social embeddedness in small businesses. Vietnam is a particularly appropriate research site because the combination of a state apparatus still in need of reform and rapid economic growth suggest that the use of informal mechanisms of economic regulation, such as social embeddedness, would be widespread.

Our empirical explorations suggest that the theoretical problems of partner choice, performance enforcement, and environmental contingency are real and that social embeddedness is used, to varying degrees, to address all three concerns. We uncovered a more complex situation than is sometimes asserted. Briefly stated, we find the following:

1) The level of embeddedness is substantially higher than that implied by the 'arm's length' relationships of textbooks but less than some descriptions of industrial agglomerations would suggest. We find a moderate level of embedding among the external business relationships, most owners had contact with their partners several times a month or less and that the level of contact was driven by operational need (suppliers are seen most often). Employees are fairly well socially embedded into businesses but still over 40% do not eat meals at the business and approximately 15% do not socialize (the most common social activities). Unfortunately, since ours is the only dataset that we know of that has attempted to systematically measure the level and pattern of social embeddedness in a random sample of small businesses, we are unable to compare our findings to other regions.

2) Important exchanges and activities are undertaken without being socially embedded. A substantial minority of loans are not heavily socially embedded. According to some measures, the sampled business owners have considerably more social capital

than they use. On the other hand, if the business owners were limited to the activities permitted by the social capital they do possess, there would be fewer businesses and less economic activity than there are now.

3) The need for performance monitoring does not appear to affect the level of interaction among business partners (customers and suppliers of material and capital). Family connection, proximity, and operational need each affect the frequency of interaction. Having lent money did not. Personal recommendations and family ties do not reduce the monitoring of employees. Such employees are more, not less, socially embedded than other employees. The low correlation between embedding and the need for trust lead us to conclude that, if embedding is a mechanism for inducing trust, it is not very effective.

4) Families (socially embedded actors) are not especially reliable sources of help. Approximately two-thirds of our respondents received no internal or external help from their relatives. Even when family members were nearby, help was forthcoming in only about half the cases. Family members serve as a source of help more frequently than a baseline expectation of 'no help' but the results suggest that receiving help from family is contingent and an achievement in and of itself. Moreover, family help appears to be expensive help. Compared to other sources of help, they require an extra measure of embedding. Family members may be trustworthy, but we found little evidence that, beyond the spouse, they were trusted.

5) In contrast, business owners often appear to be working to strengthen families. The strength of family relationships appears to be at least partially endogenous to the economic relationships. Even family relationships are partially voluntaristic. Adult household members are more likely to share in the social activities of the business if they work there. Moreover, relatives and those recommended by others are more likely than other employees to be socially embedded, suggesting that business is an instrument of coalition-building to guard against contingencies as much as family is an asset to business. A business provides a focus for family activities and thereby strengthens relationships.

Our results do not necessarily imply a causal linkage from social embeddedness through proximity benefits, leading to financial success. We might very well conclude that the causal linkages were in the opposite direction. The anthropological study of economic action often suggests that those who are able to generate wealth for whatever reason — superior skill, political connections, or luck — are also eager to distribute the proceeds within a community. It is often advantageous to build a political coalition to protect one's economic position in the event the source of income comes under threat or disappears (Polanyi, 1968; Sahlins, 1963). Given the turbulent situation in Vietnam, political protection is as plausible reason for social embedding as operational efficiency. The transfers implied are apparently expensive and inefficient; they may disappear as individuals accumulate savings (North, 1977).

References

APPOLD, Stephen J., NGUYEN Quy Thanh, KASARDA, John D. and LE Ngoc Hung. (1996). 'Small Private Manufacturers in Hanoi: A Pilot Study of Entrepreneurship in a Restructuring Economy,' *Journal of Asian Business*, 12(4): 1–31.

BAULCH, Bob and MASSET, Edoardo. (2003). 'Do Monetary and Nonmonetary Indicators Tell the Same Story about Chronic Poverty? A Study of Vietnam in the 1990s,' *World Development*, 31: 441–453.

BECATTINI, Giaccomo. (1992). 'The Marshallian Industrial District as a Socioeconomic Notion.' Pages 37–51 in Frank Pyke, Giaccomo Becattini and Werner Sengenberger (eds.), *Industrial Districts and Inter-Firm Cooperation in Italy*. Geneva: International Institute for Labour Studies, International Labour Office.

BULATAO, Rodolfo A. and RONALD, D. Lee. (1983). *Determinants of Fertility in Developing Countries*. New York: Academic Press.

DOLLAR, David. (1999). 'The Transformation of Vietnam's Economy: Sustaining Growth in the 21st Century,' Pages 31–46 in Jennie I. Litvack and Dennis A. Rondinelli (eds.), *Market Reform in Vietnam: Building Institutions for Development*. Westport: Quorum.

FFORDE, Adam and DE VYLDER, Stefan. (1996). *From Plan to Market: The Economic Transition in Vietnam*. Boulder: Westview Press.

GAINSBOROUGH, Martin. (2002). 'Understanding Communist Transition: Property Rights in Ho Chi Minh City in the Late 1990s,' *Post-Communist Economies*, 14: 227–243.

GLEWWE, Paul, GRAGNOLATI, Michele and ZAMAN. Hassan. (2002). 'Who Gained from Vietnam's Boom in the 1990s,' *Economic Development and Cultural Change*, 51: 773–792.

HAUGHTON, Jonathan. (2000). 'Ten Puzzles and Surprises: Economic and Social Change in Vietnam, 1993–1998,' *Comparative Economic Studies*, 42: 67–92.

MARKUSEN, Ann. (2003). 'Fuzzy Concepts, Scanty Evidence, Policy Distance: The Case for Rigour and Policy Relevance in Critical Regional Studies,' *Regional Studies*, 37: 701–717.

MARSHALL, Alfred. (1892). *Elements of Economics of Industry*. London: Macmillan and Company.

MILLS, Edwin S. (1972). *Urban Economics*. Glenview: Scott, Foresman.

NORTH, Douglass C. (1977). 'Markets and Other Allocation Systems in History: The Challenge of Karl Polanyi,' *Journal of European Economic History*, 6: 703–716.

POLANYI, Karl. (1968). 'Our Obsolete Market Mentality,' Pages 59–77 in George Dalton (ed.), *Primitive, Archaic, and Modern Economies: Essays of Karl Polanyi*. Garden City: Doubleday.

PORTER, Gareth. (1993). *Vietnam: The Politics of Bureaucratic Socialism*. Ithaca: Cornell University Press.

PYKE, Frank. (1992). *Industrial Development through Small-Firm Cooperation: Theory and Practice*. Geneva: International Labour Office.

RONNAS, Per and BHARGAVI, Ramamurthy. (2001). *Entrepreneurship in Vietnam: Transformation and Dynamics*. Copenhagen: Nordic Institute of Asian Studies.

SAHLINS, Marshall. (1963). 'Poor Man, Rich Man, Big-Man, Chief: Political Types in Melanesia and Polynesia,' *Comparative Studies in Society and History*, 5: 285–303.

TANAKA, Akihiko. (1992). 'Socialism in East Asia: Vietnam, Mongolia, and North Korea,' In Gilbert Rozman (ed.), *Dismantling Communism, Common Causes and Regional Variations*. Washington D.C.: The Woodrow Wilson Center Press.

VIJVERBERG, Wim P. M. (1998). 'Nonfarm Household Enterprises in Vietnam,' Pages 137–176 in David Dollar, Paul Glewwe, and Jennie Litvack (eds.), *Household Welfare and Vietnam's Transition*. Washington D.C.: The World Bank.

World Bank. (1993). The East Asian Miracle: Economic Growth and Public Policy. Washington D.C.: The World Bank.

World Bank. (2003). *World Development Indicators*. Washington D.C.: The World Bank.

Appendix Table 14.1:   Detailed Place Information.

Place	Ward/Village		District/Town		Province	
	cnt	%	cnt	%	cnt	%
Ha Noi					129	29.1
Dong Da District			65	14.6		
Van Chung ward	27	6.1				
O cho Dua ward (Hang Bot)	38	8.6				
Tu Liem District (rural)			64	14.4		
Dai Mo village	11	2.5				
Tay Mo Village	4	0.9				
Me Tri Village	49	11.0				
Ha Tay province					92	20.7
Ha Dong town			92	20.7		
Quang Trung Ward	39	8.8				
Van Phuc village	53	11.9				
Ho Chi Minh City					127	28.6
District # 4 (rban)	1	0.2	64	14.4		
Ward # 1	15	3.4				
Ward # 2	17	3.8				
Ward # 3	31	7.0				
Hoc Mon District (rural)			63	14.2		
Tan Thoi nhi Village	62	14.0				
Xuan Thoi Son village	1	0.2				
Can Tho Province					96	21.6
Can Tho Town			48	10.8		
An Lac ward	45	10.1				
Tan Phu ward	1	0.2				
An Phu ward,	1	0.2				
Xuan Khanh ward	1	0.2				
Chau Thanh district (rural)			48	10.8		
Cai Rang Village	48	10.8				
3 cases are missing detailed place codes			444		444	

Chapter 15

From 'Tradi-cluster' to 'Neo-cluster': First Step for a Typology of Industrial Clusters in Emerging Economies: A Case Study of Thailand

Audrey Baron-Gutty, Catherine Figuière
and Jean-Christophe Simon

Thailand
R32 / O17
O14 L60
L67

15.1 Introduction

Rapid industrialisation in East Asia in the late 20th century was backed by strong agglomeration effects due to the combination of construction of national infrastructure and the increasingly strong connections to the world economy. First Japan and then Asian NICs have developed large industrial estates, world class transport infrastructure facilities with export promotion zones, industrial hubs for globalised industries.

This can be interpreted as a sign of maturation of economic structure in these countries and also a sign that the deepening of competition required sustained public intervention and stewardship of the economy. In most East Asian emerging countries, from Korea to Thailand, public policies have given increasing focus over the past two decades to the regional/spatial dimension of industrial activity: location of new conglomerates, restructuring or grouping of firms, inter-sector linkages and strengthening of local network are viewed as means of improving global competitiveness and enhancing the industrial sectors' performance.

In addition, since the 1997 Asian economic crisis, most first and second generation NICs have faced an increasing challenge from China, resulting in a repositioning of their industrial activities.

In Southeast Asia particularly, public support was required to identify prospects, facilitate private initiatives and support new trends of private industrial organisation. Some inspiration for this thinking came from public policies and economic dynamism observed in more advanced economies: soft intervention, mustering of actors and networks, promotion of technology-based activities, etc. In spite of these policy orientations, research on the local development dimension remained relatively limited. In Southeast Asia, some research was devoted mostly to topics such as industrial estates and export promotion zones activity, provincial development or International Growth Triangles. Very few efforts were focused on clustering phenomena — which attracted comparatively more attention for studies in China.

The aim of this contribution is to provide a bridge between the analytical framework elaborated earlier in advanced economies for interpreting territory and cluster based industrial dynamics and recent trends in policies and industrial organisation phenomena observed through several case studies in emerging Southeast Asia — with another underlying question about the bearing of these trends on national industrial specialisation and competitiveness.

This will be done through a review of several case studies derived from different pieces of research in Thailand concerning both traditional, mature and more advanced industrial activities — with a special focus on two province based systems in Chiang Mai (Northern region, with traditional handicraft industries) and Chayaphum (Northeastern region, with textile and garment industries). It will lead to designing an analytical framework or typology adapted to the local context, taking into account major elements of clustering dynamics: history, local resource, sector pattern, linkages.

This chapter is organised in three parts: firstly a presentation of the economic context and industrial development pattern in Thailand, a second part on cluster analysis and its applicability to an emerging economy, and thirdly, reference to case studies and their contribution to enhancement of the analytical framework.

15.2 Industrial Development and Diversification in Thailand

Thailand is a good example of rapid and sustained industrialisation. It was labelled the 'fifth Tiger' in the late 1980s — concurrently with Malaysia with whom it ranks among the resource rich second generation Southeast Asian NICs. Characteristically, growth took roots in a strong agro based economy, with abundant labour, and diversification sprouted over several decades. Its openness was based on a mix of import protection, mild export facilitation and gentle FDI promotion — rather than a strong liberal attitude though this was frequently advertised. There was actually a step by step opening and liberalisation since the late 1980s. Its production mix diversified steadily — with balanced contribution from local and foreign companies, in a context of regular FDI inflows.

Spatial organisation of activities presented a hyper-centralised pattern over several decades (from the 1930s until the late 1980s) whereas recent trends have shown more dispersion/regional development/relocation of activities — this is related to strategies to access local resource (rural manpower, natural resource, available land) and to a lesser extent public decentralisation policies (such as Eastern Seaboard scheme) or cross-border development projects (such as Greater Mekong Scheme).

This part focuses on some distinctive features of this growth-cum-industrialisation process that determine industrial structure, location pattern, and ultimately international competitiveness. It will then identify current challenges regarding production networks, public support, space and geographic organisation that have bearing on the construction of a new competitive advantage — in the regional as well as world context.

15.2.1 Development in Thailand: Industrialisation and Economic Opening

Thailand's industrialisation is to be understood over a span of five decades (roughly 1955–2005): steady growth was backed by a diversifying economy — with several stages of restructuring of activities well tuned with steady international integration. Beyond the scope of this paper is the fact that the Thai state as an institution contributing to economic and social change achieved consolidation and modernisation, although politics and government instability remained volatile throughout the period considered. The country benefited from consistency of public policy aiming at overall macroeconomic stability together with considerable development of infrastructure and public services (Wonghanchao and Ikemoto, 1988; Chaponnière and Simon, 1988).

In parallel, over the period 1975–95, human development substantial progress, effective made particularly in terms of education and health, facilitated by a vigorous demographic transition. This boosted the supply of educated and trainable manpower — in spite of deficiencies in vocational and professional education. We review here major structural transformations in three major areas: industrialisation through diversification of manufacturing production, opening of the economy to trade and investment, stability of public policies.

15.2.1.1 *Industrial Diversification*

The structure of industrial production over the 1960s and 1970s consisted of both export oriented activities (primary processing and garments) and production for import substitution (light engineering, chemicals and textiles). By the beginning of the 1980s agriculture and industry were on a par in GDP. Thailand experienced strong transformation under stimulus from external markets: the expansion of agro-food, footwear and garment industries, and other light industries (jewelry, toys, decoration items) could rest upon active entrepreneurship and extended trade networks in Japan, North America, the Middle East and Europe (Suehiro, 1992; Tambunlertchai, 1993).

A golden opportunity was snapped up with the relocation of East Asian labour intensive activities following a drop in the US dollar (relative to Yen — or Endaka — and other East Asian NICs currencies from 1985): this led to increasing the import content of manufacturing production as many firms in Thailand became part of a pan-regional network churning out new generations of mechanical and electronic goods ranging from auto parts, home appliances to computer discs or cellular phones with components transferred from several countries (Lecler, 2002; Simon 2001). Maturation of the internal market for intermediary product and consumer goods contributed to strengthening the local manufacturing groups, but very few local conglomerates gained a strong or durable position beyond the national borders.

15.2.1.2 *Growth and Opening of the Economy*

Growth was regular over several decades — it accelerated during the mid 1970s (raw material boom) and late 1980s (post Endaka boom) with two digit growth over several years. Following the 1997 Asian crisis a more gentle rate was sustained — based on both exports and internal market. Steady opening of the economy came hand in hand with overall growth — increasing exports being accompanied with purchase of equipment and intermediary products — the opening rate jumping from 10% to 50% between mid 1960s and mid 1980s (Warr, 1993). This was largely due to trade with advanced industrial nations, although regional trade within ASEAN and East Asian NICs has played an increasingly significant part since the mid 1990s — this being related to stronger integration of manufacturing stages throughout East Asia, particularly in the automobile and electrical/electronics sectors (Horaguchi and Shimokawa, 2002).

Thailand also relaxed its diplomacy leading to renewed ties with neighbours — promoting the idea of a regional area of commerce to foster security and prosperity with former enemies. Regional integration was accelerated through ASEAN enlargement, and particularly the ASEAN Free Trade Area vision implemented since 1992 (but Asean still accounts for about only 20% of total exports).

Although it was more restrictive towards FDI in the 1980s than Malaysia for example, the country benefited fully from the wave of relocations from East Asia following the Endaka. Throughout the early 1990s, Japan and East Asian NICs regularly ranked among the first investors. FDI regulations were relaxed during the 1997–98 crisis, allowing easier full foreign ownership for non export projects and relaxing the promotion of industries in the provinces.

All these elements had bearings on industrial organisation and territorial structuring and to a large extent on cluster dynamics too.

15.2.1.3 *The State and Stability of Economic Institutions and Policies*

A decisive feature for overall growth and transformation was the stability of macro-economic policies — which resulted in a high level of confidence from various actors ranging from farmers to industrial entrepreneurs and foreign investors.

Structural adjustment programme went relatively smoothly in the early 1980s, and further liberalisation was achieved by the early 1990s. In theses circumstances, Thailand's public policies displayed gradual and 'moderate liberalism' — with frequent procrastination or delays in implementing measures such as new fiscal tools (EG; VAT) or lowering import tariffs (Muscat, 1994; Nidhiprabha and Warr, 1996).

On the other hand, sector oriented policies, particularly in the area of industry, were markedly less elaborated and interventionist than what was observed in other Asian NICs: neither a selection of prioritary industries nor a set of adequate tools for proactive policies.

Thailand's government was relatively ineffective in implementing its strategic plans for industrial estates and strategic regional development and growth poles; they did not benefit from efficient government intervention — in contrast to what was observed in Malaysia, for example in the case of the Penang development.

These trends are similar to those observed in other Asian emerging economies, particularly the second generation NICs that were well endowed with natural resource (Perkins, 1994). Compared with other large Southeast Asia NICs, such as Malaysia or Indonesia, Thailand benefited from similar resources and prosperity, derived natural resources for agricultural and manufacturing development but much less proactive 'developmental state' intervention.

It also presents much less integrated industrial structures compared with first East Asian NICs: many fewer industrial oligopolies and spatial concentration than in Korea (Amsden, 1993), and a lack of advanced ventures such as those forming high tech webs in Taiwan (Guerrieri, 2001).

Several publications (see a survey by Van Huffel, 2005) have emphasised the correlation between economic development (measured through per capita income) and geographic concentration of economic activities (with reference to infra national regional disparities — in terms of growth and value added). They suggest roughly three phases of geographic restructuring for industrial production location related to development of emerging economies: the 'pre-industrial' era characterised by dispersion (stage 1), the mass-manufacturing production era where industrial concentration reaches a peak (stage 2), and lastly the technology-based industrial era with a new pattern of dispersion based on more advanced sectors (stage 3; see Feser, 1998 and others). In reference to this pattern, Thailand could be on the verge of reaching stage 3 where concentration and clustering could be both declining and shifting to new forms.

This could be represented by a bell curve representing concentration of industrial activities relative to areas where output is measured. It would show a maximum during phase two — due to the relative decline of dispersed informal activities and regional traditional industries, and correlative strong growth of overall manufacturing production throughout national territory...). In stage 3, relative decongestion would take place, with decline in post mature industries together with new infrastructure networks offering a frame for expansion of new/progressive industrial sectors. See Figure 15.1.

15.2.2 *Challenges for a New Wave of Economic Growth*

Several challenges can be identified behind those sound economic dynamisms — we will consider here four aspect that have a bearing on industrial activity, its location and organisational factors, as well as changes in international competitive advantage.

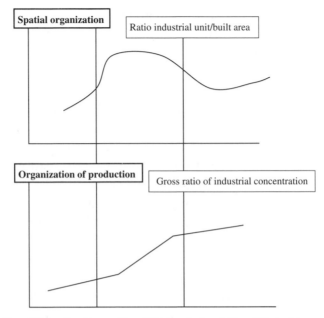

Stage 1/Take off and boom Stage 2/Crisis, adjustment Stage 3/Post-crisis

Figure 15.1:   Three Phases of Geographic Restructuring for Industrial Production Location.

15.2.2.1 *Public-Private Sector Interaction*

This relation improved over the past years: whereas it was chaotic in the 1970s it went on a smoother track in the 1980s, blooming over the 1990s with various institutional improvements related to financial regulations, Build-Operate Transfer schemes, private industrial estates and universities. In the present decade, the Thaksin Shinawatra government period placed a strong emphasis on company private style venture governance: from provincial governors compared to CEOs to local development where each district should be initiator of new economic activity (OTOP Programme). This publicly sponsored programme aimed at encouraging new grassroots activities in rural districts (labelled Tambon in Thai, OTOP meaning One Tambon One Product) to generate more added value from projects based on processing and light manufacturing and trading activities. Another axis was identification and promotion of industrial clusters to strengthen mainstream or high tech manufacturing activities. These new public strategies have taken time to take off and gain substance too: some ideas or 'plans' are little more than catch-words, or advertising for leading politicians, and few analysts would deny that government instability put a load on project design and maturation.

15.2.2.2 *Industrial Diversification and Technological Upgrading*

This is a key element for maintaining a competitive advantage. The expansion of Sino-Thai conglomerates made a decisive contribution to export diversification (several sectors involved such as agro-foods, furniture, jewellery, garments and footwear). Thai companies frequently benefited from intervention (licensing, technology transfer) of foreign firms from major industrial countries Japan, and East Asian NICs at the forefront but North American and European contributing in key activities too over the period 1975–95 (Hoyrup, 2007).

At that time a growing challenge came from China's increasingly strong position as exporter of manufactured products for the world market: consumer electronics, domestic appliances, whereas neighbouring South East Asian countries gained competitiveness for production of labour intensive goods (garments, sportswear, footwear, etc.).

Over the past decade two successful strategies have been pursued by firms. Firstly, taking strong positions in pan-Asian production networks of complex manufactured goods such as automobiles or computer/communication equipment. Secondly, improving technology and the design content of production.

15.2.2.3 *Structure of Manufacturing Sector*

The 'industrial fabric' looks densely established — but actually linkages are lacking: export oriented activities do not maximise local supplies of components as they can access cheap inputs from abroad, local market oriented manufacturing is frequently controlled by oligopolies or cartels. The system was oiled by the dynamism and active networks of the Sino-Thai communities, and their ability to set up ad-hoc bodies or association to liaise with government decision-making bodies and agencies (Laothamatas, 1992).

The structure of the manufacturing sector remained biased towards medium and large scale firms in terms of access to financial and technological resources, but also skilled management and manpower (Simon, 2001).

Thus development of small and medium companies has always been lagging behind, and in addition many have suffered throughout the crisis years — in 1997–98 more than 20% of manufacturing companies went through dire straits largely due to the credit squeeze (Régnier, 2000). Since the beginning of the present decade the double targeting of activities (local and export oriented) is once again put to test, although competitiveness to face neighbouring countries remains a hot issue.

15.2.2.4 *The Territorial Dimension*

The territorial dimension of industrialisation in Thailand has kept a strong Bangkok-based bias, a heritage of the early 20th century. Bangkok being the political, institutional, and economic capital — as well as the largest conurbation — it retained its hub and spoke position for connections between regions. Facing this hyper-centralisation, regional city centres did not gain significant role until the early 1990s (Parnwell, 1990; BOI, 1993). Their secondary position was a handicap for local initiatives although they benefited from the spillover effect from the centre. Active groups of local entrepreneurs snapped up opportunities but were in a subsidiary position to stronger business groups in the metropolis. When local development project and new industrial activities flourished they were to a large extent Bangkok initiated and managed (Kermel and Schar, 1997; Glassmann, 2004) and didn't avoid the overheating and speculative pattern common in the capital city. This intermediation did not generate strong organisation or interactions with local industries!

This explains to a large extent the difficulties encountered to identify or strengthen local clusters.

15.3 Clusters in an Emerging Economy: The Need for a New Typology

The concept of cluster takes its substance from the combining of two dimensions of organisation of industrial activity: territory and production — and it was initially coined as an analytical tool for mature economies with deep industrial history (see Table 15.1 below). Recent literature shows however the relevance of the concept for emerging or developing economies where established or new activities in industry and service sectors display various agglomeration forms. Therefore two aspects will be considered here: theoretical justification for the concept applied to recently developing economies, characterisation leading to a first typology suitable for understanding clustering in reference to concrete cases in Thailand. This approach seems coherent with the perspective offered by Courlet (2001): 'the analysis of territories shows that development stems from a system of inter-linkages and flows of information, production and values related to a specific mode of production ... a territory is therefore a privileged factor of development as it integrates several factors — historical, cultural, social — that form a basis for specific organisation patterns ...' (p. 36; our translation).

Table 15.1: Contemporary View of Cluster Types.

		Inter-firm Linkages Organisation	
		Strong	*Weak*
	Strong	Mode 1. 'Porter type' cluster	Mode 3. Cluster based on local resource or history
Localisation of inter-firms relations	*Weak*	Mode 2. Cluster without deep local base	Mode 4. Scattered activity

Source: Adapted from Torre (2006, p. 21).

15.3.1 *Revisiting the Notion of Cluster: From Developed to Emerging Economies*

When referring here to the idea or notion of cluster we do not mean to discard other ideas frequently put forward in literature and recent research on industrial agglomerations and economic or geographic analysis such as 'local productive system', 'industrial district', 'technological or competitiveness pole', etc. The industrial cluster approach is particularly convenient/useful and relevant for two reasons: firstly it is of widespread use in national industrial and regional development policies and more recently in international organisations (World Bank, Unido, etc.). Secondly we consider the flexible definition — or broad semantic use — of cluster is particularly adequate to qualify agglomeration phenomena presenting heterogeneous forms in rapidly growing or emerging countries.

Torre (2006) suggests that the increasingly frequent use of the idea of cluster — in various contexts, by analysts of various disciplines and traditions — has created imprecision, and he concludes that rather than a strong 'concept' it should be labelled a 'notion': 'the main relevance of this notion is the fact it can be used in an operational way ...' (Torre, 2006, p. 39, our translation). This flexibility is also stressed by Salvador and Chorincas (2006, p. 449) in the case of Portugal, as they consider that cluster analysis is a useful and pragmatic tool to analyse concrete cases.

However several justifications can be put forward to use this notion, and account for the frequent use in several areas of scientific analysis: for identification of territorial dimension of economic activity (Pecqueur, 1996; Colletis-Wahl, 2001; Pecqueur, 2006), for analysing industrial organisation and inter-firms linkage (Tsuji, 2007), to develop new tools for publics policies (Zimmermann, 2002). Additional theoretical development also concerns analysis of innovation systems, identification of elements of social networks (Angeon, 2006; De Bernardy, 2000).

We therefore suggest the following composite notion of a cluster as 'a group of productive units belonging to one or several sectors, either manufacturing or services, settled on a territory'.

Productive units constituting a cluster may be connected though supplier/client relation, share common specific resource (raw material, traditional skill), or infrastructure — these factors having various degrees of intensity. The cluster generally benefits from an image and members share a 'collective reputation'. On top of that institutional support will be given either by collective body or public/state assistance. In addition, the cluster's dynamism will be backed by socio-political networks, leading personalities and entrepreneurs.

Here, we find it useful to refer to the framework designed by Torre (2006) which highlights the two key dimensions to dynamic clustering analysis, namely organisation of linkage between firms and localisation of relations. The Mode 1 type is obviously the most emblematic — and fits Porter's analysis well. We fill focus below on Mode 3. The case of Mode 4 is not to be seen as 'disorganised', referring to Zimmerman (2002, p. 518) 'proximity can accommodate some distance whenever they share common goals or representations that will base their coordination'.

We fully agree with Torre's emphasis on three favourable factors to 'geographic concentration of agents' namely embeddedness of social networks into economic networks, institutions as framework for economic behaviours and finally fundamental conditions for the agglomeration process such as land price, taxation or skilled labour resource.

Although Torre's analysis focuses on mature industrial countries, some key factors he puts forward are evidently relevant for analysing emerging economies. Fundamentals and structures of these economies will have bearing on clustering capacities and patterns — in that respect what has been observed in Thailand is well in line with other works on developing or emerging economies; relevant work was conducted in Taiwan (Paulmier, 2001; Guerrieri, 2001), Tunisia (Ferguène and Hsaini, 1998) India (Schmitz and Nadvi, 1999) and also China (see other sections of this book — we refer to Van Huffel, 2005; Catin and Van Huffel, 2004).

When it comes to the context of our cases studies in Thailand, and in reference to Table 15.1, we will focus on 'Mode 3', showing weak linkage between firms with relatively strong localisation elements — very seldom can we find 'Mode 2 type' in an emerging country (this should lead to further analysis in the case of neo-cluster of Thailand considered in the typology below). Additional research would be needed to take into account another dimension, specific to medium size emerging countries (i.e. non BRICs) — their particular pattern of economic openness and international integration through time. In that respect additional emphasis could be placed on differentiation between 'endogenous opening' or 'exogenous opening' (Catin and Van Huffel, 2004). The former designates the long maturing of industrial clusters over time, as seen in 'old industrial countries' before being subjected to strong international competition, whereas the latter accounts for the external pressure on relatively younger industrial sectors to increase opening and specialisation, as seen in emerging economies. This early confrontation between industrial maturation and international integration is frequently seen as an handicap, and a justification for proactive public policies aiming at reconciling territorial cohesion and enhancement of competitiveness.

Conclusions from all accessible field studies, particularly those mentioned above, seem to agree strongly on the following points:

i.   Clusters in emerging economies show specific dynamisms or creation patterns, and thus present some 'dissimilarities' with those observed in advanced industrial economies. This can be explained by developing economies context where several elements are combined such as a local handicraft tradition, industrial dynamics with imported technologies, public development strategies, constraints of social progress and employment creation (Nadvi and Barrientos, 2004, p. 11).

ii. Many agglomeration that have been identified could be labelled 'embryonic clusters' (Salvador and Chorincas, 2006) or 'potential clusters' due to their incompleteness or immaturity. That will make them heavily dependant on public intervention in terms of building positive externalities, linkages and common institutions to serve groups of activities/enterprises and strengthen their roots.

15.3.2 *Clusters in Thailand: First Step Toward an Analytical Typology*

When it comes to formulating a typology of clusters, the literature presents a variety of sources (cf. an interesting survey done by Nadvi and Barrientos, 2004) but it appears that most works relevant for developing economics do not take into account the institutional dimension in cluster agglomeration. We suggest here that this criterion has particular relevance for countries where promotion of clusters is part and parcel of public industrial policy implemented either through national or local policy packages. In Thailand by the beginning of the present decade, the government focussed on cluster oriented identification and promotion — and two justifications can be put forward for this: on the one hand industrial structure gained considerable complexity over the period 1986–96 (as presented in Section 15.2.2) and new substance and dynamisms going in hand with a larger number of firms led to some agglomeration sprouting in selected sectors. On the other hand public policy considered that backing up 'bunches of firms' could enhance cohesion of activities and improve national competitiveness.

Actually as part of industrial policy, support was targeted towards small and medium (SMEs) companies for several decades — particularly through the Department of industrial Promotion (D.I.P. *Krom Sangseum Outsahakam*, under the Ministry of Industry). Its action was geared mostly towards traditional sectors such as textiles and garments, light engineering, handicrafts, agro-food, etc.

More recently the reference to cluster oriented policy was adopted under influence from international cooperation agencies which explains why the definition of Thai cluster derives directly from Porter (1999) and Unido's (Ceglie and Dini, 1999): 'clusters are concentrations of enterprises — sector or territory based — that produce and sell a range of complementing products and face similar/common constraints and opportunities'.

This matching of industrial dynamics and programme oriented analysis appears thought provoking. Therefore, the typology suggested on the basis of case studies in Thailand will take into account both the clusters' dynamisms and their integration in local public policies and national strategy for industrial competitiveness. Three broad categories of clusters are broadly defined here: tradi-clusters, plani-clusters and neo-clusters. (see Table 15.2).

Table 15.2: Synthesis of Major Clusters Identified in Thailand.

	Tradi-cluster	Neo-cluster	Plani-cluster
Cases from research or accessible documents ⟶	**Bangkok,** urban districts (BoBae, Din Daeng) confection	Automobile Computer parts Hard disk drives	**Chaiyaphum** Textile, Transport vehicles/ coaches Motorcycles (SME 007+)
Criteria for 'clusterisation' ↓	**Chiang Mai** céramics, wood industry, textile		Processed food (Black shrimp) Gemopolis Jewelery
Localisation/ Territorial Dynamics			
Time frame	25–30 years	5–10 years	5–10 years
Spatial dimension	Town + périphery	Several provinces	Town + province
Resource origin	Local	Global	National
Organisation/ Industrial Dynamics			
Sector pattern	Artisan, basic manufacturing	Capital intensive	Manufacturers simple + elaborate
Types of firms	Local SME	Large + MNCs	Local and foreign
Inter firm linkage	Weak	Strong	Weak
Size of firms	SME	Very large	All sizes
Complexity of products	Simple	Standardised/ highly complex	Intermediary/ complex

(Continued)

Table 15.2: (*Continued*)

	Tradi-cluster	Neo-cluster	Plani-cluster
Collective Dynamics			
Shared infrastructure	Not specific	National infrastructures	Specialised or ad-hoc facilities
Common local governance	'Bottom-up' association	'Bottom-up' + global network	'Top-down'
Common tools	Nil or simple	Virtual/ conceptual	Simple standard
Public intervention	Regional promotion	Target promotion	Local territorial

15.3.2.1 *Tradi-cluster*

This is an elementary form of industrial agglomeration — with strong rooting in territory at the city, district or sub-district level (Thai administrative nomenclature: *muang, amphoe, tambon*). It reflects initial conditions of industrialisation of Thailand's economy: tapping of local natural resource and available labour, small and medium scale firms (SMEs) established by local entrepreneurs (on a family basis), with simple technology or traditional know-how (Schmitz and Nadvi, 1999). Sub-contracting appears to be a frequent element in organisation or linkage.

This form of cluster specialises either on handicrafts type products or simple manufacturing — this frequently found with sectors such as woodworks, ceramics, textiles and garments, light enginnering and agricultural equipment.

The cluster's identity, or image, is well recognised, but seldom promoted — as firms tend to be in strong competition they rarely seek a common label or facilities sharing. Usually an 'external' institution would offer a cooperative framework for firms located in the cluster.

15.3.2.2 *Plani-cluster*

This type is more recent in Thailand — and less frequent too — although it gained popularity since the end of the 1990: a plani-cluster is an agglomeration identified by a publicly sponsored project. Several cases can be found in the literature on emerging countries. This could be done either by central government (through ministry or department, specialised body) or local institution, as part of an integrated and focused development plan (Carluer and Samson, 2006).

Clustering strategy is based on existing industries: established firms with potential for local based linkages, private sector partnership that should be enhanced or re-oriented.

Cluster delimitation is thus related to a proposed framework for promotion and improvement of member's competitiveness. It is generally focused on manufacturing only, and frequently geared towards exports. In Thailand activities range from agro-food processing (marine products such as black shrimp, tropical fruits) jewelry and garments. The territory can be extensive, beyond administrative boundaries of municipalities or even provinces.

15.3.2.3 *Neo-cluster*

This type refers to grouping of firms specialised on more advanced/ and internationally competitive products. This is a *de facto* clustering based on a combination of industrial organisation, with internationally reputable leading firms supported by favourable public policy.

On the corporate side can be found both local ventures and well established of more recently rooted foreign partners (the former in the case of automobile assembly and the latter in the production of computer parts and components).

On the public policy side, this is clear evidence of an 'offensive strategy' facilitating foreign direct investment (e.g. relaxing of some restrictive regulations) as well as international transactions and flows (strong infrastructure, low or nil taxation).

The neo-cluster might be the closest to Porter's concept although the territorial dimension remains relatively shallow — with clustering spreading over relatively large space, probably due to the emerging country specificity (see Lecler, 2002, for a case of the automobile assembly and auto parts). Among key shared element are transport infrastructure (both local and export oriented facilities) manpower pools considered both easily trainable and reliable. In the case of the Hard Disk Drive cluster, and based on his experience with National science and Technology Development Administration, Intarakumnerd emphasises the role of public policy together with private firms to promote an environment conducive to highest industrial standards and inter national reputation (see Chapter 16).

15.4 Clusters in Thailand: Contrasting Situations Derived from Case Studies

We present here two case studies that fit into the framework presented above — they derive from a combination of field studies, public research and analysis government sponsored studies reports. They are showcases regarding of the usefulness of typology and bring evidence of specific inter-firm linkage in the context of emerging economies.

15.4.1 *Textile Industries in Chaiyaphum Province: A Case of 'Plani-cluster'?*[1]

This case study of a provincial cluster begins with an overview of the Thai textile industry, paying heed to its structure and challenges. The next section describes a specific case, the textile cluster of Chaiyaphum, located in the North-East of Thailand and focuses on the way it is structured and promoted by public intervention.

15.4.1.1 *The Thai Textile and Garment Industry: Current Challenges*

The Thai textile and garment industry still accounts for a relevant part of the Thai industry with about 20% of manufacturing value added (5% of total GDP, more than 1 million employees, 6% of total

---

[1] This section derives from Baron-Gutty (2006), 'Agglomérations d'entreprises et clusters en Thaïlande.' Théorie et études de cas, Master's degree dissertation. Asie Orientale Contemporaine, Université Lumière-Lyon 2/IAO Lyon.

exports). Although the activity was severely constrained by the expansion of China in the late 1990s and the termination of the Multi Fibre Agreement in 2005, firms based in Thailand remain proactive on many international markets from North America to the Middle East, Russia and Europe.

The industry is organised with many networks, based on hierarchical ties, sub-contracting and spatial agglomerations of activities (Supachalasai, 1992). All stages can be found from spinning to garment making, and production of specialised material/cloth fishnets, etc. A large range of technologies is utilized — from basic/standard to high/advanced (such as those required for colour treatments, special synthetic fibres, fishnets, etc). Bangkok remains a hub — keeping as front window the famous Bobae and Pratunam urban districts. Most of the textile companies are SMEs, family-run and owned by Thai nationals, usually from Sino-Thai background — although many joint-ventures can be found with investors from East Asia and occasionally Europe.

Some manufacturing companies work under license from famous brands — and sell locally with exclusivity, or exports to supply international markets of their contractors (for fashion or sportswear). A few firms have developed their own labels, especially for youth, such as Pena House or Greyhound. These clothes are marketed in Thailand and specially designed for the local population, using popular material and colours.

Today the industry has to cope with many hurdles, and can no longer play on the cheap labour resource. Many segment/firms still lack elements to up-grade activity such as global marketing, design, and R&D input. Some companies have shifted to higher value-added segments of the market such as material for interior decoration, carpeting, man-made fibres. Public policy has tried to give support through international promotion; e.g. government launched the Bangkok City Fashion programme to create an Asian Fashion hub in Bangkok. In addition it has also placed the textile and garment industries within the framework of the cluster initiative.

15.4.1.2 *The Cluster of Chaiyaphum: A Publicly Promoted Initiative*

The Department of Industrial Promotion (DIP) launched the cluster initiative, among other projects targetting up-grading and strengthening of small and medium industries. It mustered support from international agencies and consultants — M. Porter among others — to review local situation and gain knowledge from foreign experience.

The DIP programme was structured in different stages: cluster mapping (where are the clusters located?); promotion and mobilisation of cluster programmes; cluster diagnosis (targeting one specific cluster and assessing its strengths and weaknesses); collaborative strategy (recruitment of members); implementation; monitor and evaluation. Besides, the DIP-cluster based programme was centred around the designation of a CDA (Cluster Development Agent). In the economic literature, it is often referred to as an IFC (Institute for Collaboration). Its aim is to establish connections between the components of the cluster. The CDA can be either private person or civil servant, coming from the DIP itself or from the Federation of Thai industries, or from the local Chamber of Commerce. Very seldom, it will be a direct delegate or emanation from the entrepreneurs themselves.

The cluster of Chaiyaphum targets textile companies located in this province, part of the Northeastern Region. Chaiyaphum belongs to the zone 3 of the BOI (Board of Investment) incentives programme, which means that full benefits and tax allowances are granted to investors setting up plants there, for example, tax exemption on corporate revenues for 8 years.

In 2003, 19 companies took part in the cluster programme launched by the DIP. By the end of 2006, 37 companies were registered as member of the programme. This included companies involved in weaving, knitting, spinning and subcontracting tasks. Companies are mostly Thai-owned but some foreign investors from India and Taiwan are also settled there. They chose Chaiyaphum because of the incentives granted by the BOI but also because they expected to find there skilled and cheap manpower. Recruited members are voluntary and the cluster was supported by DIP funds: in 2003, 3.3 million dollars were awarded to the project. Gradually the DIP decreased its financial support to the cluster, the aim being a self-sufficient basis.

Why did companies agree to join the programme? A study carried out by the DIP for an automotive cluster showed various reasons, including joint use of machine tools, joint purchases of raw materials, order sharing or visiting each other's plants. Surprisingly it was assumed that the motives could be the same for the cluster of Chaiyaphum.

In Chaiyaphum, during the first year the programme was implemented, the DIP did not find a suitable agency to act as a CDA. Therefore, the DIP contacted Chulalongkorn University for business service. They sent a team and set up a structure there to coordinate the programme. The second year, the local agency of the Federation of Thai Industries became involved and acted as the CDA of the Chaiyaphum cluster.

Many activities were offered and coordinated by the CDA such as monthly plant visits and exchange meetings. Meetings involving managers are planned every month, but often only back-up staff is sent to the meeting, managers being too busy. Visiting each other's plant has been a success because most of the managers were interested in doing so but did not dare asking for it. The CDA also organised visit of plants in China as managers wanted to see by themselves how and why China was becoming a threat to the Thai textile industry. Together with cluster members, the CDA organised joint road shows in Bangkok. The aim was to attract new investors in the region. According to the DIP staff, some joint training programmes among members have been implemented in the cluster. In addition some order sharing process was being envisaged too.

Following the implementation over several years, the DIP made an assessment of the cluster programme. A first report suggested that firm managers see the cluster programme more as a threat than an asset, most companies wanting to keep knowledge and activity secret.

It is hard to put together companies that usually make deals on an individual basis.

The definition of a cluster lacks clarity: the administration as a promoter uses the word 'cluster' as a motto, but often underestimates that institution building is a complex, elaborated process, that takes time and energy to succeed. The role of the CDA should not be overlooked, it is central and necessary. Its efficient and adequate action will be the key to the success of the cluster through compromise, conflict solving, and sincerity. At this stage the cluster seemed more the results of a publicy tailored-made programme — thus a 'plani-cluster' — than a fully-developed cluster.

In terms of internal dynamism too, the cluster needs to gain self-sufficiency. Athough some actions in the programme have enabled better cooperation between members, they are not involved in a collective, 'cluster' vision. Managers have not sought links with other financial and technological partners. There is very little relationship between the components, and this does not extend to R&D institutes, trading or financial institutions — whereas this could be useful to find appropriate funding for research programmes to improve products and develop new designs.

15.4.2 *Chiang Mai[2] Province: Looking for Elements of a 'Tradi-cluster'*

Regional economic development in Northern Thailand was vigorous over the past two decades — with pace similar to the national economy as a whole. This is largely due to growth transmitted from Central Region, although the province enjoyed a boom of its own because of its abundant resource, active population and shrewd elites. The capital city Chiang Mai has retained a strong position, inherited from history, placing the city as a regional hub among four provinces (Wongsupbhatsatigul, 1977; TDRI, 1991). Recently connections with neighbouring regions, and even countries like Laos and China have played a more significant role.

---

[2] This was part of a research programme with support from Centre for Education and Labour Studies at Chiang Mai University and IRD/Quesed.

The region has enjoyed prosperity despite its distance from the Bangkok Metropolitan Region, due to a combination of factors: successful agricultural transition and diversification, stability of light manufacturing, expansion of service and particularly tourism on a large scale. Analysis of the diversification pattern shows a sort of paradox: transition from agriculture to services has to some extent 'bypassed industrial activity'. Indeed the manufacturing sector has always retained a limited share of provincial domestic production (always below 20% of provincial value added, a share retained by agriculture until the early 1980s).This is because tourism (both local and international) and real estate development (golf courses, resorts, retirement homes …) have played a considerable part in the economy. Therefore, several systems of production co-exist over the Northern provinces.

In spite of the secondary position, manufacturing remains active and well rooted in the territory and alongside other activities. Traditional sectors such as wood processing, furniture making, ceramics and textile have prospered — and actually offer some cases for analysing clustering dynamics. This clustering relies on local resource (natural resource such as wood bamboo, fine clay) combined with available labour — either young employees or part time off-farm activity — with traditional and artistic skill. The traditional clusters are a good illustration of proto-industrial activity and its evolution.

The industrial activities of the Chiang Mai area are scattered in various urban and rural areas over several districts covering three provinces:

1. Traditional manufacturing areas grouping workshop and small firms, specialised on simple products, or handicraft, such as woodwork and furniture, pottery and crockery, textile and garments. Some groups of firms in this category present some agglomeration that can be labelled clustering — not only do they work connected to close suppliers or customer but also they operate with flexible sub-contracting and order sharing practices. In addition managers frequently belong to associations or clubs forming the base of intense social network intertwined with business.

2. Industrial estates or parks have been in operation for two decades — this is mostly the public operated Norther Industrial Estate in Lamphun province (Chulasai, 1993[3]). Firms located there have seldom input-output relation with their neighbours or local suppliers — many focus on assembling components imported or transferred from the Central Region (plastic parts, electrical and light electronics, leather and textile).
3. Due to lack of regulation and land speculation, some firms sprouted out or dispersed location to the countryside. Most are labour intensive and some tap local agro-forestry resources.

Most workshops or SMEs initially catered for the domestic market but quickly found opportunities for export of manufactured goods. Several manufacturing clusters have become tightly connected to tourism in terms of product design and identification (e.g. 'traditional umbrellas'). The textile based firms have caught the wave of ecology with sustainable raw materials and design to suit the eco-sensitive middle class of Thailand and abroad. In the ceramics industry about 70% of firms can be now labelled 'modern' (registered, with significant equipment and trading capacity). Sales channels range from local emporium to up-market boutique in Bangkok and other Asian and World capital. They are evidence of a well targeted niche market. and they are internationally competitive — which also means they have to face intense competition from Vietnam and China. This call for technological upgrading and product differentiation. As an example there is a specialisation for fine ceramics such as Celadon, Benjarong, tapping on local know how.

Chiang Mai province 'tradi-clusters' show a variety of entrepreneurial forms from self employed craftsmen to modern firm owners. There is indeed a spectrum of business size and production patterns (equipment, production quality, customer market segment). Firms in these clusters do share common territory (such as artisans village, peri-urban factory locations) and identity. However, common facilities are

---

[3] Luechai Chulasai (1993), 'Local economic development core: A case study of northern region industrial estate in Lamphun'. Institute of Developing Economies, Tokyo.

not developed, and linkages kept minimal — mostly under the form of occasional sub-contracting. Cooperation remains at an embryonic stage as tradition of SMEs is not oriented towards sharing information and developing common knowledge. In spite of this a consensus emerge on the promotion of a common image of a region close to nature, even if not eco-friendly — which is an easy way to mark the difference with the capital city. This translates into ranges of products combining local skill and natural or organic products (cosmetics, garments, food). This remains superficial, and so far very few cooperation to develop technologies along these lines has led to cooperation between firms and local educational and university institutions.

Beyond manufacturing, how can we characterise potential for stronger integration of a 'local productive system'? Several issues are at stake: competition for labour is fierce between industry and the tourist service sector (a so called 'tourism cluster' would target some newly created activity parks and even more resorts for senior citizens). Natural resources are being intensively tapped for conflicting use (land for housing estates or golf club versus orchards and 'green hill' landscape).

15.5 Concluding Remarks

At this stage, we would like to stress once again that although 'cluster' remain a very broad notion, it provides a helpful framework in the context of rapidly changing industrial dynamisms. We suggest here several elements that should be scrutinised in further investigations.

Then addressing the analysis of public policies concerning cluster, two elements seem to emerge from our cases:

— The promotion of clusters was part of proactive public policy in Thailand in the first part of the present decade: they were supported in the context of domestic oriented policy with strong fiscal impetus to rejuvenate the domestic market after the post 1997–98 crisis years. Most clustering experiences depend on this contra-cyclical effort and it is unlikely that inter-firm cohesion would remain strong in a more affluent context unless it pre-dated the official clustering period. In addition, public policy to create clusters ex-nihilo from fragmented contexts or for stagnant industries faces (too) many uncertainties. It seems an investment with poor returns.

— Regarding specialisation, our cases show that for a strongly export oriented economy, clusters tend to blur the distinction between offensive and defensive strategies: true to the case both tradi- and plani-clusters tend to be supportive of activities under intense competition or already threatened whereas neo-cluster are identified in more advanced or high tech sectors. However all clusters — and their public support — show the competitiveness challenge of a diversified emerging economy facing globalisation: specialisation and competitiveness are more and more clearly defined within sectors, on niches or segments of production rather than for the sector as a whole. Therefore clustering should also reflect this shift in industrial competition dynamics.

Regarding the improvement of our analytical tool, it would be relevant to revisit our typology with data covering a longer time frame, about two decades of actual activity, regarding both plani- and neo-clusters. Quantitative data is still lacking concerning value derived from clustering for 'members' — registered or de facto — as well as spread effects for the territory.

Beyond this first typology, it would be fruitful to consider the addition of categories or modifications on two aspects. One to take into account connection between manufacturing and other industries, and second to better understand the role of cluster for technological up-grading (densification and up-scaling of production, identification of internationally attractive areas for science parks or technopoles).

We still find it relevant to consider the transfer of this typology to other emerging countries where various forms of cluster can be found — probably relevant contextual situations could be found in Southeast Asia (the Philippines, Indonesia) or in the Mediterranean area (Morocco, Tunisia, Turkey, Egypt, etc.).

References

ANDERSON, T., SCHAAAG SERGER, S., SÖRVICK, J., WISE Hansson, E. (2004). *The Cluster Policies Whitebook*, IKED, Holmbergs, Malmö, Sweden.

ANGEON, V. (2008). 'De l'explicitation du rôle des relations sociales dans les mécanismes de développement territorial,' A paraître in *Revue d'Economie Régionale et Urbaine*, pp. 237–250.

BIGGS *et al.* (1990). TDRI Rural Industry and Employment Study.

BOI (1993). Thailand's Regional Areas An Investor's Guide

CATIN, M., VAN HUFFEL, C. (2004). 'L'impact de l'ouverture économique sur la concentration spatiale dans les pays en développement,' *Région et Développement*, **20**, 123–149.

CEGLIE, G., DINI, M. (1999). 'Mise en route et en réseau des PME dans les pays en développement: expérience de ONUDI en la matière.' Onudi, Vienna.

CHAPONNIÈRE, J.R., SIMON, J-C. (1988). 'Devenir un NPI: les difficultés de la Thaïlande,' *Tiers-Monde*, 1987, t.XXIX, juil–sept, pp. 881–896.

COLLETIS-WAHL, K., PECQUEUR, B. (2001). 'Territories, development and specific resources: What analytical framework?,' *Regional Studies*, **35**(5): 449–459.

COURLET, C., FERGUÈNE, A. (2003). 'Globalisation et territoire: le cas des SPL dans les pays en développement,' *Facef Pesquisa*, **6**(3).

DE BERNARDY, M. (2000) 'Système local d'innovation: Facteurs de cohésion et de perennité,' *Revue d'Economic Rurale et Urbaine*, **2**, 265–280.

FERGUENE, A., HSAINI, H. (1998). 'Développement endogène et articulation entre globalisation et territorialisation: éléments d'analyse à partir du cas de Ksar-Hellal (Tunisie),' *Région et développement*, (7).

FREEL, M. S. (2003). 'Sectoral pattern of small firm innovation, spillover and agglomeration: A review of empirical studies,' *Economics of Innovation and New Technology*, (8).

GLASSMAN, J. (2004). 'Thailand at the Margins. Internationalization of the State and the Transformation of Labour, Oxford Geographical and Environmental Studies,' New York.

GUERRIERI, P. *et al.* (2001). *The Global Challenge to Industrial Districts. SME in Italy and Taiwan.* Edward Elgar. Cheltenham UK.

HORAGUCHI, H., SHIMOKAWA, K. (2002). *Japanese Foreign Direct investment and the East Asia Industrial System.* Tokyo: Springer.

KERMEL, D, SCHAR, P. (1997). 'Croissance industrielle et redéploiement spatial en Thaïlande.' *Autrepart* (3).

LAOTHAMATAS, A. (1992). *Business Associations and the New Political Economy of Thailand.* Westview Press.

LECLER, Y. (2002). 'The cluster role in the development of the Thai car industry.' *International Journal of Urban and Regional Research*, **26**(4).

LEEAHTAM, P. (1991). *Thailand's Adjustment. From Crisis to Double Digit Growth.* Dokya Publ. Bangkok.

MUSCAT, R. J. (1994). *The Fifth Tiger. A Study of Thai Development Policy.* Sharpe.

NADVI, K., BARRIENTOS, S. (2004). 'Systèmes productifs locaux et réduction de la pauvreté. Vers une méthodologie d'évaluation de l'impact des initiatives de développement des SPL sur la pauvreté et la situation sociale,' ONUDI, Vienne, on line.

NIDHIPRABHA, B., WARR, P. G. (1996). *Thailand's Macroeconomic Miracle.* World Bank, OUP.

PARNWELL, M. J. G. (1990) 'Rural industrialisation in Thailand,' Hull Paper in Developing Area Studies no. 1, Centre of Developing Area Studies, University of Hull.

PARNWELL, M. J. G. (1996). *Uneven Development in Thailand.* Avebury Publishing, London, UK.

PAULMIER, T. (2001). 'L'expérience technopolitaine de Hsinchu à Taiwan: un pôle de croissance en transition vers un district industriel?' *Revue d'Economie Régionale et Urbaine* (3).

PERKINS, D. H. (1994). 'There are at least three models of East Asian development', *World Development,* 22(4).

PONGSAPICH, A. (1994). *Entrepreneurship and Socio-economic transformation in Thailand and Southeast Asia,* CUSRI-ORSTOM, Chulalongkorn University Press

PORTER, M. (1999). 'Grappes et concurrence', in Michael Porter (éd), *La concurrence selon Porter,* Editions Village mondial, Paris, chap. 7.

RÉGNIER, P. (2000). *SMEs in Distress. Thailand, the East Asian Crisis and Beyond.* Gower-Ashgate, London.

SALVADOR, R., CHORINCAS, J. (2006). Les clusters régionaux au Portugal, Géographie, Economie, Société, (8).

SCHMITZ, H., NADVI, K. (1999). 'Clustering and industrialisation,' *World Development,* 27(9).

SIMON, J.C. (1996). *The New Pattern of Expansion of the Manufacturing Sector in Thailand;* in Parnwell M. (ed).

SIMON, J.C. (2001). 'Transformations et industrialisation en Thaïlande: croissance et développement économiques à travers cinq décennies,' in Dovert, S. (ed.), *Thailande contemporaine.* L'Harmattan/IRASEC, 'Monographies Nationales', Paris.

SUEHIRO, A. (1992) 'Capital accumulation in Thailand'. CUSRI, Chulalongkorn University Bangkok.

SUPHACHALASAI, S. (1990). 'Export growth of Thai clothing and textiles,' *World Economy,* 13(1).

SUPHACHALASAI, S. (1992). 'Structure of the textile industry and government policy in Thailand'. TDRI Year-End Conference. Jomtien.

TAMBUNLERTCHAI, S. (1993) 'Manufacturing,' in Warr, P. G. (ed.), *The Thai Economy in Transition.* O.U.P.

TORRE, A. (2006). 'Clusters et systèmes locaux d'innovation. Retour critique sur les hypothèses naturalistes de transmission des connaissances à l'aide des catégories de l'économie de la proximité,' *Région et développement,* (24).

TSUJI, M. *et al.* (2007). *Industrial Agglomeration and New Technologies,* E. Elgar.

VAN HUFFEL, C. (2005). 'Développement économique et disparités spatiales,' Thèse, Université du Sud Toulon-Var.

WARR, P. G. (1993). *The Thai Economy in Transition,* D-K Cambridge University Press.

WEBSTER, D. (2006). *Supporting Sustainable Development in Thailand: A Geographic Clusters Approach,* NESDB and World Bank, Geographic Clusters Project, NESDB Bangkok.

WONGHANCHAO, W., IKEMOTO, Y. (1988). *Economic Development Policy in Thailand.* IDE Tokyo.

ZIMMERMANN, J. B. (2002). 'Grappes d'entreprises' et 'petits mondes'. Une affaire de proximité', *Revue économique,* **53**(3).

Chapter 16

Thailand's Cluster Initiatives: Successes, Failures and Impacts on National Innovation System[1]

Patarapong Intarakumnerd

Thailand

R32 038 L14 L86
R38 L62 L66

16.1 Introduction: Concepts and Policy Implementation of Clusters and Innovation Systems

Studies of clusters have a long history. Alfred Marshall's contribution in 1890 in his famous Principle of Economics is a cornerstone in this literature; though he used the label industrial districts. Marshall theorises and emphasises the dynamics of external economies associated with learning, innovation and increased specialisation. In the context of Italy his studies was followed up by a group of Italian scholars where Beccatini was among the most prominent (see Beccatini, 1998). Their research reached a larger audience when Piori and Sabel (1990) published their seminal book *The Second Industrial Divide*. Nonetheless, it was the management guru Michael Porter who recently has made the concept of cluster popular. According to Porter (1998), industrial clusters are geographical concentrations of interconnected companies, specialised suppliers, service providers, firms in related industries, and associated institutions (for example, universities, standard agencies, and trade associations) that combine to create new products and/or services in specific lines of business. Clusters emerge and develop because geographical proximity among firms promotes interactive and collective learning and generates positive

---

[1] Paper presented at International Workshop's Programme, Industrial Clusters in Asia: Old and New Forms. Lyon, November 29–30th and December 1st.

externalities for participating actors. These benefits attract similar and related firms and other actors because they also want to take part in the interactive learning that takes place. Since Porter came out with his definition there has been an intense debate on almost all aspects relating to the cluster concept. Martin and Sunley (2003) have attacked head on and fully dismissed it; they consider it too flawed, elastic and possible contradictory. Benneworth and Henry (2004) acknowledge that the cluster-literature cannot be seen as coherent but reaches the opposite conclusion of Martin and Sunley. They argue that '…From a position of hermeneutic theorizing, "clusters" have the potential to add value by allowing theoretical debate across a wide range of (overlapping and competing) perspectives whose partiality and situatedness are made explicit' (p. 1011). Other studies have questioned whether horizontal or vertical links are most crucial for interactive learning and knowledge spillovers while some studies have even suggested that it is less the traded or untraded interdependencies as the ability to observe competitors activities and/or tap into the local buzz that is behind clusters existence. While it is beyond the scope of the introduction to give a full summary of the positions of findings in the cluster-literature four conclusions can nevertheless be drawn. Firstly, it is an unsettled field and need more studies. Secondly, a few cases (Baden Wuttenberg, Third Italy and Silicon Valley) have received an unjustified hegemonic status in defining what a cluster is and the initial findings concerning these models cannot be said to be valid anymore as the districts are increasing delocating. Delocation refers to outsourcing or offshoring production to other areas (Sabel, 2004). Thirdly, there is an urgent need for empirical studies adapting and discussing the relevancy of clusters for Asian developing economies and how well-functioning Asian clusters can contribute to creating new policy ideas (this is a natural role for Asian clusters as several Asian economies belong to the best performing in today's global economy). Finally, there is a need to explore the relation between clusters and (regional) innovation systems.

Parallel with the development and diffusion of the cluster-literature the so-called innovation system approach has been developed and gained almost equally as much attention. Innovation system is normally associated with the national level, i.e. 'national innovation system'. The basic ideas can be traced back to Friedrich List's National System of Political Economy in 1841. His concept of national systems of production and learning took into account a wide set of national institutions including those engaged in education and training as well as infrastructures such as networks for the transport of people and commodities. However, modern versions of the innovation system concept were first introduced by Freeman in 1982 and Lundvall in 1985. The point of departure for contemporary innovations systems is that innovation is increasingly the source of competitiveness in the globalising economy. Thus for firms, regions and nations to remain or enhance their competitiveness they increasingly have to develop their learning abilities. In contrast to the so-called linear model of innovation an innovation systems approach suggests that interactive learning is the cornerstone in creating innovation. This might be based on interaction between users and producers or between universities and private firms. This has recently been confirmed in quantitative studies (Fagerberg, 2004). How innovative activities are organized is strongly shaped by the institutional setting or context. Johnson (1988, 1992) argues that the uncertainty associated with innovations leads to giving institutions a central position in the innovation systems-literature. Rational choice, he argues, referring to well-defined alternatives cannot explain what comes out of a process where outcomes are by definition unknown. Therefore institutions understood as rules, norms and habits are crucial for the outcome of what individuals decide and do in relation to innovation. By institutions the innovation systems-literature refers to formal (legal regulation) and informal (norms and habits) institutions (see Lundvall, Intarakumnerd and Vang, 2006, for elaborations).

Innovation system is increasingly being applied to the 'region' level (i.e. regional innovation systems (RIS)) (Cooke, 2001), as is also the case in this book. The regional innovation system concept takes explicit account of the central role of local or regional actors and their interaction including their interaction with national government bodies and public and private transnational agents. Traditionally it has regarded firms, universities, R&D laboratories and public agencies at regional level as major elements (Cooke, 2001) but recently attempts have been made in transforming it into a more exogenous-oriented model (see Vang and Asheim in this book).[2] The increased importance of the regional level has been asserted in several recent studies based on qualitative or quantitative data (for a recent paper, see Soon and Storper, 2003).

Policy-wise, different countries pursue different policies regarding promotion of industrial cluster and innovation system. In advanced countries, especially in market economies as the US, well-functioning clusters are mostly a function of 'bottom-up'-initiatives based on the private sector. The governments only play facilitating and supporting roles. On the other hand in some Asian countries governments take a much pro-active roles in stimulating (to some extent, creating) clusters. In Japan, for example, the government is trying to create 'intellectual clusters', i.e., regional-based clusters of universities, public R&D institutions, relevant institutes and knowledge-intensive core companies. The central government provides budgetary support yearly while the cluster plans were initiated by local government together with local universities and local firms. The aim is to foster interaction between the original technological seeds of the public research organisations and universities and business needs of regional companies to create the chain of technological innovations and new industries. To achieve this goal, each cluster is managed and co-ordinated by a Central Project Organisation. Central project organisations can be in various forms depending on local conditions. They can be local/regional RTOs, local/regional scientific foundation, organisations managing science parks or technopolis and industry. These organisations recruited new and experienced executives used to work for private firms. Some of these people have had international experiences (see MEXT, 2002). In less successful Asian countries such as Thailand, Research and Technology Organisations (RTOs), having accumulated knowledge in rather high-technology field, organisational flexibility, and human resources, act as government instruments in the form of bridging intermediaries between transnational corporations, local start-ups,

---

[2] Vang and Asheim (2006). 'Region, Absorptive Capacity and Strategic Coupling with High-Tech TNCs', *Science Technology & Society*, **11**(1), 39–66.

IT service providers, university and government agencies in some clusters (Intarakumnerd, 2005).

This chapter will focus on how a developing country, Thailand, formulated and implemented cluster policies, their impacts on national innovation system. It will examine a few case studies to find success factors and policy lessons. A special attention will be given to the roles of cluster intermediaries in facilitating cluster development process.

16.2 Thailand's STI Policies: Towards More Cluster Specific?

Up to the government of Prime Minister Thaksin Shinawatra (January 2001–September 2006), scope of S&T policy in Thailand was rather narrow. It covered only four conventional functions, namely, research and development, human resource development, technology transfer, and S&T infrastructure development. This narrow scope of S&T was very much based on the perception that private firms were 'users' of S&T knowledge mainly produced by government agencies and universities (see Arnold *et al.*, 2000). There was no articulate national innovation policy. Though the word 'innovation' was mentioned in several national plans, it was not whole-heartedly incorporated into the scope of S&T policies (see Lauridsen, 2002). In addition, unlike Japan, Korea, and Taiwan, S&T elements were not part of broader economic policies namely, industrial policy, investment policy and trade policy and, to the lesser extent, education policies (see Intarakumnerd *et al.*, 2002).

Industrial policy of Thailand did paid enough attention to the development of indigenous technological capability as an integral factor in the process of industrialisation (Sripaipan, Vanichseni and Mukdapitak, 1999, p. 37). Investment policy, especially the promotion of foreign direct investment (FDI), aimed primarily at generating inward capital flow and employment. Unlike Singapore where FDI was specifically used to upgrade local technological capability (see Wong, 1999), there was no explicit and pro-active link between promoting FDI and upgrading of local technological capability in

Thailand. Trade policy, the most important instrument in Thailand being tariff, was used strategically to promote technological learning like in NIEs (see Amsden, 1989; Chang, 1994; Lall, 1996). Instead, trade policy was very much influenced by macro economic policy, for instance, to reduce domestic demand for imports at the time of balance of payment deficit. The Ministry of Finance, the dominant agency which controlled the policy, had little knowledge or experience of industry and industrial restructuring (Lauridsen, 2000, pp. 16–20).

Moreover, industrial policy in Thailand was limited to the so-called 'functional' intervention such as promoting infrastructure building, general education, and export push in general. There were virtually no selective policy measures, such as special credit allocation and special tariff protection, targeting particular industries or clusters. The exception was the local content requirement in automobile industry, which was rather successful in raising local contents of passenger vehicles to 54% in 1986 (see Doner, 1992). Interestingly, with the exception of automotive industry, there was no reciprocal performance-based criteria (such as export and local value added and technological upgrading targets) set for providing state incentives like in Korea or Japan (see Johnson, 1982; Amsden, 1989; Evans, 1989, 1998; Chang, 1994; Lall, 1996). Investment promotion privileges, for example, were given away once approved. The intention to attract foreign direct investment and promote export overshadowed the need to develop local initiatives and indigenous technological capabilities. As a result, linkages between multinational corporations and local firms were also weak. Unlike Taiwan, the governmental protection and promotion, without strengthening absorptive capabilities of Thai suppliers, left a profound impact on the weak technology and suppliers' network of industries (Vongpivat, 2003). The major change in policy came recently under the Thaksin government. Media and academics in Thailand and the Southeast Asia labeled this government distinctive policy as 'Thaksinomics' (Thaksin's Economics). Dual track policy was the main thrust of Thaksinomics. The government tried to enhance international competitiveness of the nation by strengthening 'external' side of the Thai economy, namely, export, foreign direct investment and tourism. At the same time, it attempted to increase capabilities of domestic and grass-root economies by implementing projects like Village Fund (one million baht to increase local capabilities of each village), a three-year debt moratorium on farmers' debt, *One Tambon*,[3] *One Product Project* (supporting each Tambon to have product champion), and People Bank (giving loans to underprivileged people with no requirement of collateral).

The Thaksin government, unlike its predecessors which paid most attention to macro-economic stability, focused more on enhancing meso- and micro-level foundations for international competitiveness. The high priority of 'competitiveness' issue on the government's agenda was illustrated by the establishment of National Competitiveness Committee chaired by the Prime Minister. It was the first time that Thai government had serious 'selective' policies addressing specific sectors and clusters. The government declared five strategic clusters which Thailand should pursue: automotive, food, tourism, fashion, and software. Clear visions have been given to these five clusters. Kitchen of the World (food cluster), Detroit of Asia (automotive cluster), Asia Tropical Fashion, World Graphic Design and Animation Centre (software cluster), and Asia Tourism Capital. Building innovative capabilities of the nation was highly regarded as very important factor increasing and sustaining Thailand's international competitiveness. 'Innovative nation with wisdom and learning base' was one of seven Thailand's dreams projected by the government. To make this dream come true, several strategies were devised. These include continuous investment in R&D and technology, well environment for attracting and stimulating innovation, high accessibility to knowledge and information across the nation, fluent English as a second language, possessing strong learning basis such as passion for reading, better accessibility to cheap but good books, thinking school with innovation movement (see Phasukavanich, 2003).

Equally important, the new ten-year Science and Technology Action Plan (2004–2013) places the concept of national innovation

---

[3] Tambon is a unit of local government administration. One Tambon comprises several villages.

system and industrial cluster at its heart. The scope of the plan is much broader than the aforementioned four functional areas. Measures to stimulate innovations and to strengthen national innovation system and industrial clusters are explicitly highlighted.

National Economic and Social Development Board (NESDB) has been implicitly responsible for overall cluster policy of the country. It has made significant attempts to diffusion the concept to various government and private-sector agencies by organising cluster seminars and workshops in main regions of Thailand. It also commissioned a study to create a 'cluster mapping' of the Thailand, i.e. identifying significant agglomerations of firms that function or have potential to function as clusters in various geographical locations throughout the country. Several implementing government agencies such as Department of Industrial Promotion and sectoral-specific institutes under Ministry of Industry (Thai Automotive Institute, Thailand Textile Institute, National Food Institute, Electrical and Electronics Institute and so forth), National Science and Technology Development Agency under Ministry of Science and Technology, Office of SMEs Promotion and others tried to develop their own cluster projects in their responsible areas (Intellectual Property Institute, 2006).

The Board of Investment (BOI) has substantially changed its policy by paying more attention to issues underlying long-term competitiveness of the country, namely, development of indigenous technological capability and human resources. Special investment package promoting 'Skill, Technology and Innovation or STI' has been initiated. Firms can enjoy one or two years extra tax incentives if they perform the following activities in the first three years: spending on R&D or designing (at least 1–2% of their sales), employing scientists or engineers with at least bachelors degree) at least 5% of their workforce), spending on training of their employees (at least 1% of their total payroll), and spending at least 1% of total payroll on training personnel of their local suppliers. The flourishing of cluster concept also affected investment policy. BOI has initiated in 2004 new investment packages for specific strategic clusters such as hard disk drive and semiconductor. Eligible firms in these sectors are not only final product makers but also suppliers in the value chain. This indicates a transformation of the focus of investment policy measures from giving incentive for individual projects, which might not be related to each other, to using incentives to strengthen cluster as a whole.

Cluster concept was used as a main industrial policy of Thaksin Government for national, regional and local levels. At the national level, it was used to strengthen advanced industries both in service and manufacturing sectors like automotive, textile and garment, software and tourism in order to make them to be coherent and innovative 'industrial clusters'. At the regional level, Thailand was divided into 19 geographical areas. Each area had to plan and implement its own cluster strategy focusing on a few strategic products or services. It was supervised by the so-called 'CEO Governors', who are given authorities by the central government to act like provincial Chief Executive Officers (CEOs). For the local level, the cluster concept was applied to increase the capacity of grass-root economy in the name of 'community-based clusters', especially to help the 'One-Tambon-One Product' succeed.

The private-sector organisations were induced by government policies. They began to acknowledge the importance of cluster and tried to use the cluster concept to formulate and implement their strategies. Thai Chamber of Commerce and Federal of Thai Industries, the two most significant private-sector organisations, started to carry out their activities cluster-wise and reorganise their internal organisations according to clusters (Intellectual Property Institute, 2006).

Nonetheless, the implementation of the aforementioned policies is far from being successful. There are several shortcomings:

A. Confusion of the cluster concept. Different government and private-sector agencies had different understanding of the cluster concept. Some considered a cluster as an industrial sector with no specific geographical concentration in mind. For them, a sector covering the whole country was a cluster. As a result, each agency implemented a cluster strategy according to its understanding.

B. Fragmented implementation. Cross-ministerial policy coordination has been a major problem in Thailand. Though cluster was assigned as a strategic government policy and NESDB oversaw the supposedly integrated national cluster strategy, the implementation was still incoherent.

C. Lack of champions and trust in the private sector. Firms in the same cluster usually see others as competitors; it is quite difficult for them to collaborate. The oversea-Chinese Thais, the dominant group of entrepreneurs in the country, do collaborate more between firms in the same family clans than with outsiders (see Intarakumnerd, 2006).

D. Limited support from the local governments. Unlike other countries, local governments in Thailand have a short development history. Until recently, the local government had very limited roles and budget. Later, even their roles and budgetary authorities expanded, administrators of local government neither have understanding nor pay attention to the cluster concept.

E. Limited linkages between university and public research institutes as knowledge providers, and private firms. The relationship between university and public research institutes, and firms in Thailand is relatively weak. It is based on private relationship rather than organisational ones. Most of them were ad-hoc and concentrating on training and consultancy rather than long-term collaborative R&D. Therefore, universities and government research organisation are not usually agents in clusters. The knowledge flows from them which can help to revitalise firms in clusters are quite limited.

As a result of these shortcomings, the long-lasting positive impacts of the cluster policy on Thailand's national innovation system are still rather limited. However, as mention above, it did somehow shape Thailand's industrial policy to be more focus and sector-or cluster-specific. It induced concomitant changes in several government agencies (at least at the policy formulation level), private-sector organisations, and number of firms, especially those which participated in government projects operated by various government agencies.

The momentum of changes has started and a major transformation might follow in the future.

Though the overall major 'impact' of cluster policy has yet to be seen, there are some relatively successful cases of cluster development in Thailand, which are worth examining.

16.3 From Hard Disk Drive to Bus Assembler to Software and to Chilli Paste: Thai Cluster Experiences

We will discuss at length four cluster development experiences in Thailand: hard disk drive, bus's body cluster, software and chilli paste. These four clusters seem to be different: one appears to be quite modern high-tech manufacturing product, one is in standard manufacturing using mid tech and mature technology, another is knowledge intensive service, and the other look rather primitive. They represent a high-tech and mid-tech manufacturing clusters, a knowledge-intensive service cluster and a community-based cluster respectively.

16.3.1 *Hard disk drive (HDD) Cluster*

National Science and Technology Development Agency (NSTDA) commissioned a study on HDD cluster to Asian Institute of Technology (AIT) and Asia Policy Research (a consulting company) in 2003. They conducted studied the importance of the industry to Thailand's economy, reviewed past studies on the industry, outlined cluster mapping, and evaluate roles, technological capabilities and linkages of key players of the industry.

16.3.1.1 *Importance of HDD Industry*

The hard disk drive is an electronic product playing a significant role in Thailand's electronics exports. Thailand is ranked as the most important global base for hard disk drive manufacturing. In 2005, Thailand stood1st in the world rank of hard disk exporters (with 42% of the world market). The sector employed more than 100,000 people generating an export worth of US$10 billion. This has become possible due to the Thai manufacturing bases of the hard disk giants like Fujitsu, IBM/Hitachi, Western Digital and Seagate. The cluster concentrates around central and northeastern regions, near Bangkok.

Thailand-based operations generally import high technology components from abroad into the country as raw materials and exports the products to markets worldwide. The level of local content is estimated to be quite low, approximately 30–40% of total production cost, due to the lack of suppliers, low quality domestic components and the complicated processes of buying between domestic factories. Since the majority of HDD suppliers receive tax incentives from the Board of Investment (BOI) similar to the HDD assemblers, they are also eligible for raw material import tariff exemption for export products. If the manufactured components are not exported as declared to the BOI, the suppliers must submit papers declaring the value of indirect exports which may be considered as domestic sales for payment of the raw material import duties. Therefore, it is frequently easier for suppliers to directly export to neighbouring countries like Malaysia and Singapore, leaving the assemblers to re-import it as raw materials for use in Thailand.

The industry heavily relies on technology transfer from their foreign affiliates. The foreign affiliates usually provide raw materials, machinery technology and markets. In addition, the TNCs' headquarters play a major role in formulating marketing and production strategies.

16.3.1.2 *The HDD Value-Chain*

The disk drive value chain can be divided into five major activities as follows (see Figure 16.1):

Component fabrication activities: The activities include manufacturing of disk drive components such as substrate, media, head fabrication, wafers, semiconductors and bare PCBs and miscellaneous parts assembly such as base plate, screws, filters, etc. Thailand is relatively

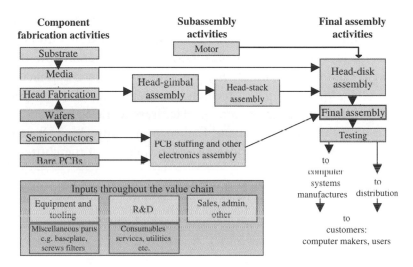

Figure 16.1: Hard-Disk Drive Value Chain.

strong in head fabrication, but doesn't have production capacities for disk media and wafer fabrication. The capacity for tooling support from outside the firm remains virtually non-existent and other service companies are weak.

Subassembly activities: The disk media components are sub-assembled into disk drive head parts, and PCB parts. Motors enter the value chain at this stage. These are areas in which Thailand-based producers are strong.

Final assembly activities: The final assembly of a hard disk drive requires assembling various components into head disks consisting of motor, media and head stacks. The head disk will be finally assembled with finished PCB components to become a unit of a hard disk drive.

Testing: The hard disk drive will be tested in testing lines prior to distribution to customers. Testing activities are major weaknesses in Thailand's HDD industry due to a lack of high-technology laboratory support in the country. Most testing is conducted at the company headquarters in Japan and the United States or in Singapore.

Distribution: The distribution channels for hard disk drive products include computer system manufacturers and HDD distributors who sell the products to computer makers or users. Generally, the distribution of HDDs made in Thailand is controlled by the policies of company headquarters. The products are mainly exported to HDD distributors and computer system anufacturers worldwide.

The HDD cluster in Thailand is shown in Figure 16.2. It can be seen that there are five major private-sector players of the cluster:

1. HGA/HAS/HDD Assembly
2. Motors
3. Suspensions
4. Base plates
5. Flex assembly

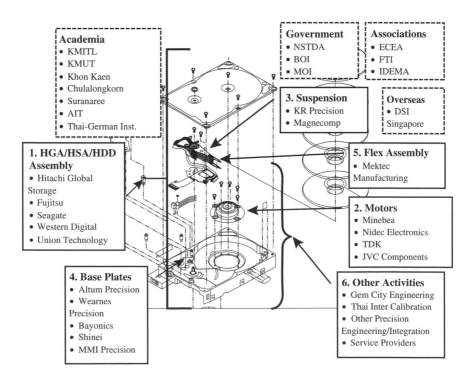

Figure 16.2:   The HDD Cluster in Thailand.

In addition, there are a few other value-added activities carried out by various players such as Gem City Engineering (automation engineering services) and Thai International (calibration). Apart from private-sector players, there are key government agencies important to the industry, namely, BOI, government research institutes like National Science and Technology Development Agency (NSTDA), universities conducting research related to and in cooperation with the industry like Asian Institute of Technology (AIT), Chulalongkorn University, Suranaree University and Khon Kaen University, and training institutes providing courses in automation like Thai German Institute.

16.3.1.3 *Technology Capabilities and Linkages in the HDD Cluster*

Framework for analysing technological capabilities and extent of linkages of firms in the HDD industry (see Table 16.1) was developed based on existing literature (see Lall, 1992; Bell and Pavitt, 1995; Amsden, 2001).

The firm-level interview survey of the HDD industry generated some mixed indications with regard to the technology activities of foreign invested firms in Thailand. Building on detailed interviews with 10 major companies in the HDD sector — all clearly foreign owned with the exception of one firm listed on the Thai stock market, the research exercise measured the technological capabilities in five broad areas and at three different levels — as shown in Figure 16.3.

The basic findings were that:

- The firms exhibited strong capabilities in investment, process development and industrial engineering areas, all areas that are required to support their manufacturing operations in Thailand;
- The firms showed much weaker capabilities in product engineering and innovation, with some indications that American firms had gone much further in building these capabilities in their Thai operations than non-American firms; and

Table 16.1: Technological Capabilities: A Unified Framework for HDD Industry.

		Manufacturing				
	Investment	Process Engineering	Product Engineering	Industrial Engineering	Innovation	Linkage
• Basic	• Feasibility Studies • Site selection • Project preparation	• Scheduling • Maintenance • Quality management	• Understanding basic product design • Adapting minor product changes	• Optimisation based scheduling • Basic skill upgrading programmes	• Process improvement • Local parts development	• Local supplier base development • Subcontracting to technological service providers
• Intermediate	• Technology selection • Contract negotiation • Technology transfer agreements • Recruitment and initial training project execution	• Process optimisation • Process adaptation for product variations • Introduction of TQM/Kanban techniques	• Technology transfer for new products	• Productivity analysis • Bench-marking • Advanced inventory control (JIT, etc.) • Advanced skill development • Logistics management	• Product support improvement (packaging, testing) • R&D transfer • New process design	• Process/product upgrading in collaboration with supplies and R&D institutes • Reverse system engineering in collaboration with external partners

(*Continued*)

Table 16.1:   (*Continued*)

		Manufacturing				
	Investment	Process Engineering	Product Engineering	Industrial Engineering	Innovation	Linkage
• Advanced	• Organisation management using ISO and BS standards • Ability to develop own turn-key projects • Export of project know-how.	• Implementation of MRP ERP systems • Process standardisation using ISO and BS standards	• Tracking global product changes • New product design	• Supply chain management • Long term HR development programmes • Supply chain development (cluster based)	• New product innovation • Organisation set up for innovation	• Industry networking and collaboration for competitive development • Long term linking with R&D institutions and universities • Licensing new technology to partners and suppliers • Strategic alliances with academic and R&D institutes to open new product/service markets

Source: AIT/Asian Policy Research (2003).

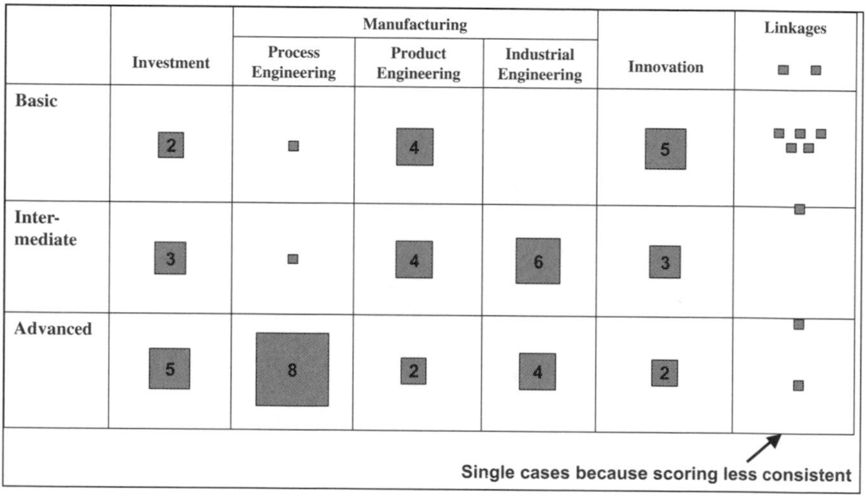

Figure 16.3:   Technological Capabilities in the HDD Industry.
Source: AIT/Asian Policy Research (2003).

- The firms show very weak capabilities in linkage development but showed a strong interest in developing stronger linkages if the support infrastructure is in place, and indicated that it would call for concerted efforts from both industry and the government to build an environment that is conducive to linkage development.

A closer examination of the linkages that were reported, following the basic framework presented in Figure 16.3, indicated that most companies are linked to a certain degree into the vertical supply chain of the Thai HDD cluster and share related information with regard to specific product related issues, especially for new products. But only a few firms co-operate closely with either Thai-based suppliers or customers in broader product, process, or human resource development related activities, indicating rather weak innovation-related vertical links. And even fewer companies have horizontal linkages to universities, R&D institutions, service providers or competitors: indicating weak innovation-related horizontal links.

Most companies are linked to a certain degree into the vertical supply chain of the Thai HDD cluster and share related information with regard to specific product related issues, especially for new products. But it was found that a few firms cooperate closely with either Thai based suppliers or customers in broader product process or human resource development related activities that are marked by weak innovation related links amongst them. Moreover, fewer companies maintain links with universities, R&D institutions and service providers or with the competitors in their field.

16.3.1.4 *The Role of IDEMA*

The success of the HDD cluster in Thailand is partly contributed from the active work of the industrial association, IDEMA Thailand which is the Thai branch of the International Disk Drive Equipment and Materials Association (IDEMA). IDEMA is an international not-for-profit trade association that represents the $22 billion HDD industry and its infrastructure. Founded in 1986, IDEMA provides more than 500 corporate and individual members worldwide with trade shows, technical conferences, symposia, education classes, networking events, and an active international standards programme.

Asia outside Japan produces more than 85% of the world's disk drive output. IDEMA has been very active in Singapore, Malaysia, and the Philippines and extended its activities to Thailand in 1999, raising the awareness of the significant contribution of the industry. IDEMA aims to promote business networking, to facilitate information sharing through education programme and technical symposiums/conferences, and to allow technical issues faced in the industry to be discussed globally. IDEMA activities in Thailand ensure that the country maintains and enhances its competitiveness in the drive industry. It is necessary to make a plan for keeping up with technology development and for providing the training to people at all levels (foundation level, intermediate level, advanced level) involved in the HDD industry.

On July 15, 1999, IDEMA presented a paper on addressing the training needs for the Southeast Asia HDD industry at a workshop organised by the National Science & Technology Development Agency, the National Electronics and Computer Technology Centre (NECTEC), the Federation of Thai Industry, the Thailand Board of Investment, the University of California San Diego and the Brooker Group. Government and industry participants identified HDD industry workforce training as one of their leading issues. IDEMA Asia-Pacific was seen as being able to address this critical educational need. The idea of forming a branch of IDEMA in Thailand was born at this workshop.

On September 15, 1999, the first meeting of the IDEMA Thailand Advisory Committee was held, and IDEMA Asia-Pacific, Thailand was formed. The first Chairman of IDEMA's Thailand Advisory Committee was Senior Vice President Manufacturing, Recording Head Operations of Seagate Technology.

IDEMA Asia Pacific, Thailand's mission statement is as follows:

'Strengthening Thailand's Niche as a Centre of Manufacturing Excellence in the Hard Disk Drive and Related Industries'

The IDEMA Asia Pacific Advisory Committee — Thailand includes the following leading storage technology companies: Seagate, Western Digital, Hitachi, Fujitsu, KR Precision, Magnecomp, and Gem City Engineering. Representatives from BOI, AIT, NECTEC, and Asia Policy Research Co., Ltd. are also on the Advisory Committee.

IDEMA Asia-Pacific, Thailand activities are carried out in close collaboration between industry, academia, and policy makers. It aims to serve the following basic objectives:

- A platform for business networking;
- A platform for information sharing — fundamental education, symposiums, market updates and advance technology seminars; and
- A platform to address issues of relevance to the HDD industry.

Two sub-committees of the IDEMA Asia Pacific Management Committee — Thailand Management Committee have also been formed to focus on critical needs of the industry, namely:

1) Human Resource Development Sub-Committee; and
2) Automation Infrastructure Development Sub-Committee.

In order to kick-off the IDEMA Thailand educational activities, AIT-IDEMA jointly offered a *Certificate of Competence in Storage Technology* (CCST) recognised by both institutions. The first two 'Core Modules' of the CCST were held on November 5 and 6, 1999 — one on Micro-Contamination and one on the Fundamentals of Hard Disk Technology. Subsequent ad-hoc courses have been offered, and a full programme is planned for 2004 with support from the Thailand government.

The IDEMA Thailand Advisory Committee has organised 8 major international disk drive symposiums in Thailand. Each symposium has attracted a world-class set of speakers and around 150–200 industry participants from the industry in Thailand. A number of other networking activities are regularly held by the IDEMA Thailand Advisory Committee.

An early symposium was the platform for the launch of IDEMA's Thailand Storage Industry White Paper. The White Paper aimed to strengthen relationships between all key partners in the storage industry arena — industry/academe/government — and to map out critical directions for human resource development, automation infrastructure development, and supplier industry development in the disk drive and related industries.

In January 2004, IDEMA worked closely with the BOI to make the HDD industry a 'prioritised' industry with a special investment privileges. One extra year of tax exemption will be given to HDD assemblers and components workers if they perform the following activities:

A) invest in R&D in the first three year for on average not less than 1–2% of sales or not less than 50 million baht for assemblers and not less than 15 million baht for component makers,

B) employ personnel educated in sciences, technology and engineering or disciplines concerning with R&D and design not less than 5% of their workforce for the first three years,

C) spend not less than 1% of their payroll on training of their Thai personnel in the first three years,

D) spend not less than 1% of their payroll or not less than 150 million baht for assemblers and not less than 15 million baht for component makers to develop capabilities of Thai suppliers or to support related education institutes,

E) establish R&D centres within three years of their operation.

This is a remarkable change in the Thai industrial policies, since the country did not have serious selective industrial policies promoting specific sectors or cluster in the past 50 years of its industrialisation.

In August 2004, IDEMA worked with NSTDA to set up a cluster management organisation headed by a technopreneur-cum-university professor who used to work for the industry and understand the industry's needs. This organisation is acting as a coordinator between all main actors, and push forward future projects aiming to upgrade capabilities of the whole industry in Thailand such as joint training programmes and collaborative R&D projects.

16.3.2 *The Bus's Body Cluster*

16.3.2.1 *Importance of the Automotive Industry*

The automotive sector has been an important industrial sector for Thailand for the past 30 years. In 2005, the production volume (excluding motorcycle) reached 1.1 million cars, exceeding 1 million threshold for the first time. More than 400,000 cars were exported. Together with automotive parts, Thailand's automotive export was above US$10 billion (Thai Automotive Institute, 2006).

The government has an aspiration to make Thailand the Detroit of Asia, i.e. to be a global centre for producing car, motorcycle and automotive part. It sets a clear target for the country to produce 10 million cars by 2010. To realise this mission, the ten-year National Science and Technology Strategic Plan (2004–2013) aims to produce 1000 researchers, and 4000 specialised engineers in automotive industry (National Science and Technology Policy Committee, 2004).

16.3.2.2 *The Roles of Automotive Institute in General*

Implementation of the aforementioned government plans by concerned agencies is still far from being coherent and synergistic (Institute of Intellectual Property, 2006, p. 29). However, there is a specific organisation responsible for development of the country's automotive industry. The Thai Automotive Institute was set up as an independent public organisation under the Ministry of Industry in 1988. It aims to operate like a private-sector organisation with high level of flexibility and efficiency. The main objective is to be the centre for supporting development of the Thai automotive sector to be a main exporting base in the world. The institute has broad functions. It plays an important role in formulating policies for the industry, coordinating to implement those policies, setting and enforcing industrial standards, providing technical services such as testing, calibrating and quality assurance, and market information, applying results from research to up grade technological capabilities and quality control system to the global standard, and finally developing high-caliber human resources for the industry.

Importantly, the institute is trying to act as an intermediary bringing in external technology and knowledge to upgrade technological capabilities of local suppliers. One of the important programmes of the institute was Automotive Experts Dispatching Programme (2003–2005) to bring Japanese experts to transfer key production technologies and skills, including those for mold and die design, and plant management to engineers and technicians of 200 Thai OEMs and REMs[4] which joined the programme. The programme was a collaborative programme between Thai and Japanese governments. Japanese experts were dispatched from Japan, including those who used to work for Japanese TNCs before (Thai Automotive Institute, 2006).

16.3.2.3   Background of Banpong Bus's Body Cluster

Interestingly, this is a cluster of agglomerated small Thai-owned firms, located in the country side of a developing country, and competing in a global industry that is considered to be fiercely competitive and dominated by giant TNCs. The cluster is located at Banpong District of Rachaburi Province, around 100 km from Bangkok. It has a long history dating back for more than 50 years. At present, there are around 40 companies with the total production of 1500 buses per year. Unlike many firms in the industry, they are not part of the supplier networks of TNCs. However, since they have accumulated 'tacit' craftsman-type skill for quite a long time, they have a capability in designing and assembling passenger buses tailored to diverse demands of customers. Before the engagement with the Automotive Institute, the cluster had several weaknesses, namely, inability to satisfy large order volume, limited knowledge in designing and production that require high precision, limited marketing and management skills, higher material costs as compared to those of suppliers of TNCs, limited information, knowledge linkages and joint activities among firms in the cluster and virtually no linkages with non-firm agents in the geographical area. Though, there was the 'Association of Banpong Bus's Body Assemblers'. Its roles was limited to political bargain with the government in terms of tax reduction and relaxing regulations such as

---

[4] Original Equipment Manufacturers (OEMs), produces a finished product to the precise specification of its customers. Replacement Equipment Manufacturers (REMs), instead, focus on selling parts in replacement markets locally and abroad.

those concerned with city planning. It did not play roles in building trust and facilitating knowledge exchange among association's members (Pongsakornpreutikool, 2006a).

16.3.2.4 *The Roles of the Thai Automotive Institute (TAI) as an Intermediary in the Cluster*

Since, the year 2004, TAI started to provide support to the cluster. It began with finding and sending a German expert to help firms in the cluster in automotive body design. The consultancy lasted 10 months. This helps to strengthen firms' design capability which was relied on unverified 'tacit' skills. After that, TAI played the roles of cluster's intermediary in the following aspects:

A) Facilitating the changing of roles of the 'Association of Banpong Bus's Body Assemblers' from a mere political lobbying group to an organisation promoting mutual trust, joint activities and collective learning of members such as taking larger order from customers, dividing the order, and assigning smaller tasks to each member. TAI provided budget and encouraged the association to generate more communication between members through seminars and informal meetings.
B) Facilitating linkages between firms and non-firms agent in the area. For example, facilitating linkages with local technical college, Rachaburi Technical College 2, to have a specific vocational programme on body assembling technology. It encouraged the provincial authority (CEO, governor) to recognise the cluster as a 'strategic' cluster of the province, entitled to receive budgetary support. TAI also assist firms to link with a local public training institute, Labour Skill Development Institute Region 4, which subsequently provided training on critical assembling skills (please see the cluster map in Figure 16.4).

As a result, the technological capabilities of firms in the cluster has increased. They are now able to assemble with higher precision. They are able to combine their existing tacit craftsman skills with external

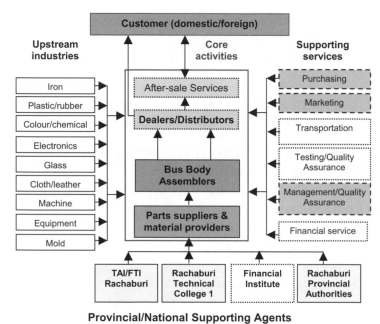

Figure 16.4:   Cluster Map of Banpong Bus's Body.
Source: TAI.

scientific knowledge such as knowledge on selecting suitable material inputs. Importantly, division of labour and joint activities among firms enabled them to receive larger order volume from customers (Pongsakornpreutikool, 2006b).

16.3.3 *Software Cluster*

16.3.3.1 *NSTDA: The Largest Research Technology Organisation in Thailand*

NSTDA is a leading research technology organisation in Thailand. It undertakes a broad-based, systematic approach towards enhancing the entire science and technology system of Thailand in support of national economic and social development. Four specialised centres — Genetic Engineering and Biotechnology (BIOTEC), Metal and Materials Technology (MTEC), Electronics and Computer

Technology (NECTEC), and Nanotechnology — come under the NSTDA umbrella. Three centres, except Nanotechnology Centre, have been established in the 1980s in line with the global trend at the time and perceived local needs for strong research capability in these areas. Though it is not an official policy, NSTDA, therefore, has strong path dependency of focusing on R&D with a smaller interest in supporting advancement of technological capability development of private firms through several financial and technical supporting schemes such as technical consultancy services, IP services, training services, quality control services. Nonetheless, NSTDA is trying to change its orientation from a 'mere' R&D institute to an intermediary in selected clusters. Software cluster is one of NSTDA's targeted clusters.

16.3.3.2 *An Overview of Software Industry in Thailand*

The performance of software industry in Thailand is not quite impressive. Going by the Board of Investment statistics, the number of promoted software companies increased from just 2 in 1996 to 49 in 2001 and declined to 13 in 2003. Since 1996, the cumulative number of promoted companies stands at 170. Out of these, 75 were fully owned by Thai companies, 34 were foreign companies and the others were joint ventures. Of these, 33 licenses were issued during 2002 and 2003 and hence most of them have not started operations. The total investment commitment by 137 companies promoted prior to 2002 amounted to 1632 million baht with a mean investment of 11.9 million baht. But the actual investment made amounted to only 52% (846.5 million baht) with an average investment of 9.7 million baht.

In the case of fully Thai owned companies the investment commitments amounted to 532 million baht and actual investment was of the order of 389 million baht (73%). When it comes to fully-owned foreign companies, total investment commitments were of the order of 113 million baht and the actual investment was about 90.8 million baht (80%). This tends to suggest that, in contrast to electronics, the foreign firms have been less enthusiastic to invest in the ICT software and service sector of Thailand. In the case of 55 joint ventures (1996–2002) total investment commitment was of the order of 986 million Baht with an actual investment of 365.9 million baht (35.7%).

Total employment commitment by the 170 promoted companies has been of the order of 4207, whereas the actual employment generated was only of the order of only 1969 — a fraction of the total employment one of the leading IT firm in India. Out of the realised employment, 1184 (60%) was accounted by Thai firms, 165 (8%) by foreign firms and 620 (32%) by joint ventures. From discussion with industry sources it was discerned that the export base of Thailand is rather limited.[5]

16.3.3.3 A New Initiative: Thailand Software Park

To strengthen the industry, NSTDA in 1997 received an approval by the cabinet to set up the Software Park Thailand (SPT) in order to induce the first local cluster of software industries. The SPT has been successfully run, occupying 13,000 square metres of a high-rise building, for nearly five years. It received strong supports from well-known transnational corporations like IBM, HP, SUN, Oracle, etc. Around 50 companies, mostly Thai nationals, have fully occupied the available space. Among various facilities, NSTDA together with the Carnegie-Mellon University has consistently offered training and certifying the Capability Maturity Model (CMM) to raise the standard of software production of the tenants. Many of them now have customers and business links with their foreign counterparts such as US, EU, Australia, New Zealand, Malaysia and so on. Local universities are also participating with some companies in the SPT to produce the local e-learning services. The establishment of SPT has facilitated technology transfer within and outside the Park and encouraged a first step toward the clustering concept that the tenants will be able to learn from each other, NSTDA, participating universities, and firms located outside the park, especially transnational corporations.

---

[5] One estimate claimed exports in 2000 at $11 million.

16.3.4 *Chilli Paste Cluster*

As mentioned above, cluster development is a major industrial policy of this government. At the local or community level, the government initiated 'One Tambon, One Product' by encouraging each Tambon to select its product champion based on their comparative advantage. A 'product' can be anything such as handicraft, herbal medicine, food-stuff, manufacturing items, and tourism. Cluster concept is applied at the community level to support these products and the government called them community-based clusters. Here we will examine a community-based cluster in the making. This cluster grew rather successfully before the government cluster policy initiative and, to larger extent, with little government intentional supports. The study was done by Rajaphat Phetchaburi Wittiyalongkorn under joint funding of the Office of Rajabhat Institutes and National Science and Technology Development Agency in 2002.

16.3.4.1 *History of the Community*

Wat Tuptimdang Community is located at Tambon Klong Song, Klong Luang District, Pathumtani province. This community is an old community dating back to the reign of King Rama V or more than 100 years ago. The community was named after a Temple, Wat Tuptimdang Dharmadaram, which was highly respected and used for religious ceremony by local people. At present, there are 1031 inhabitants living in 171 households. Most inhabitants are farmers with their own land. Their economic status is fair and quite sufficient. Most of them are Buddhists and had only primary and/or secondary level of education. Relatives live together closely and rely on each other. These rural people live simply and close to nature.

16.3.4.2 *Local Wisdom*

The Taptimdang Community has been rather stable. Ways of life have been maintained. The community has wisdom in the areas of agriculture (e.g. farming, breeding, mixed animal and plant farming), handicraft, food and food processing. These areas of knowledge are mostly tacit as it is embodied in certain individuals of the community. The most striking local wisdom of this community is, of course, knowledge in making grilled fish chilli paste. Fish has been very abundant and can be consumed all year round. Fish is cooked, processed and preserved in many forms. Chilli paste is an every-day food of people in the central region. Grilled fish has been used as important ingredient in a certain types of chilli paste and is considered as local wisdom passed on from one generation to another.

16.3.4.3 *Cluster Mapping of Grilled Fish Chilli Paste*

There are several concerned actors in the chilli paste cluster.

1. Producer of grilled fish chilli paste are local people who live in the community. They grouped together as Klong Song Housewives Association. At present, there are 70 members. The association acquires all necessary ingredients, grind and fry them, put them into small plastic packages ready to market.
2. Raw material and packaging suppliers. These include farmers producing general raw materials and growing vegetable, and producers of can and other types of packaging.
3. Specialised suppliers. These are suppliers of specific ingredients like fish, garlic, fish sauce, dried chilli, tamarind, salt. These suppliers are mostly located in a local wholesale market called 'Rangsit Market' (or Talad Thai).
4. Customers. The chilli paste is sold both to local customers and ordinary customers in Thailand.
5. Knowledge institutes. Several local tertiary education institutes and knowledge-diffusion organisations of government helped the association by the means of knowledge transfer. For example, Rajabhat Phetchaburi Wittiyalongkorn, a local university, help the association by introducing canning technology, so that the chilli paste would have a long shelf live and being able to market with higher price.

6. Government promoting and regulating agencies. They are several government agencies both at the district and provincial levels concerning agriculture, development, cooperative, and health issues, which directly and indirectly promote and regulate activities of the Housewives' Association. For example, Agriculture District Authority provided the association with agriculture knowledge, especially in food processing. Livestock District Authority provided knowledge in animal farming, animal disease prevention, Cooperative District Authority helped the association with fertiliser and pesticide, Commerce Provincial authority gave soft loan for the association's investment in setting up booth for selling the chilli paste in a nearby department store, and Health Provincial Authority certified the quality and standard of the chilli paste and helped to assure the public in this respect.

7. Community networks. The Housewives' Association has linkages with several existing community networks like Women Cooperative Group, Agriculture Saving Group, Community Shop and so on. They exchanges agriculture knowledge and experiences regularly.

8. Service and specialised infrastructure providers. Marketing channels are provided by a few private organisations such as the Future Park Rangsit Department Store, with the financial support from Commerce Provincial Authority provided a booth for the association to sell chilli paste. Several organisations both private and public also invited the association to their trade and exhibition fairs (see the cluster map in Figure 16.5).

16.3.4.4 *The Significant Roles of Klong Song Housewives Association*

The driving force of the cluster is the Klong Song Housewives Association. The association was established in 1992 with 19 founding members. These people observed the development of an association in a neighbouring area and decided to set up their own association. The objectives of the associations are: a) to promote career advancement and increase incomes of its members, and b) to

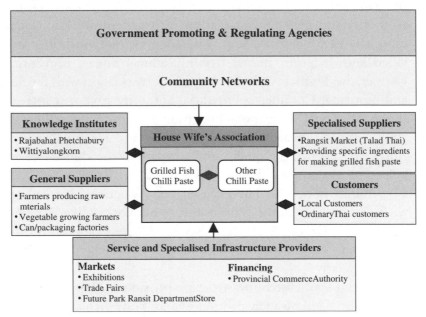

- Live Stock District Authority
- Agriculture District Authority
- Cooperative District Authority

- Commerce Provincial Authority
- Cooperative Provincial Authority
- Development Provincial Authority

- Development Provincial Authority
- Health District Authority
- Food and Drug Authority

- Klong Luang Women Coop. Group
- Klong Luang Coop. Group
- Cooperative District Authority

- Community Shop
- Klong Luan Women Coop. Agriculture Group

Government Promoting & Regulating Agencies

Community Networks

Knowledge Institutes
- Rajabahat Phetchabury
- Wittiyalongkorn

General Suppliers
- Farmers producing raw mterials
- Vegetable growing farmers
- Can/packaging factories

House Wife's Association
Grilled Fish Chilli Paste   Other Chilli Paste

Specialised Suppliers
- Rangsit Market (Talad Thai)
- Providing specific ingredients for making grilled fish paste

Customers
- Local Customers
- OrdinaryThai customers

Service and Specialised Infrastructure Providers

Markets
- Exhibitions
- Trade Fairs
- Future Park Ransit DepartmentStore

Financing
- Provincial CommerceAuthority

Figure 16.5:   Cluster Map of the Production of Chilli Paste with Grilled Fish.
Source: Derived from Rajabhat (2002).

create solidarity among members and enhance the strength of Klong Song community. In the setting-up process, the Agriculture District Authority sent its official to act as an assistant. The chairperson of the group is a charismatic and well-respected person. He later became the head of the village. After the association was established, the association has allowed its members to hold its shares (valued 50 baht or 1.25 dollar per share) at the maximum of 100 shares. Apart from making chilli paste the association also engage in making preserved gargle, growing vegetable, making natural fertiliser and growing flowers.

16.4 Conclusion

Today, the word 'cluster' has become a buzz word. It has been used by policy makers, business people and general public. Though, the concept of cluster should not be theorised rigidly, for developing countries, the concept should be well placed in the development context. It can and should be seen as a 'development' tool bringing people to work together, facilitating trust building process, and encouraging them to share their knowledge. Many developing countries face two different sets of development problems. On the one hand, many countries want to be well integrated in the global production network of TNCs. These countries want to be internationally competitive, attractive to foreign investment especially in higher technologically sophisticated activities such as R&D, design and engineering, and being able to export high-value added products. On the other hand, a large part of developing countries' economies are still economically backward. Here, the problem is not to about how to be well integrated to the global economy but on how to improve welfare of local people, enhance grass-root economy and, to a certain extent, being able to be self-sufficient.

The case of Thailand demonstrates how the cluster concept can be used as a 'development' tool addressing these two sets of problems. As illustrated above, it works both for technologically sophisticated manufacturing and service clusters mainly dominated by TNCs' investment and knowledge, and community-based clusters relying mainly on local knowledge and wisdom. The long-lasting and substantial positive impacts of the cluster policy on Thailand's national innovation system are still rather limited. Implementation of the concept faces several problems such as lack of understanding of concept, policy coherence among different government agencies, trust and champions in the private sector, enough support from the local governments and knowledge flows between firms and universities and public research institutes. However, it did somehow shape Thailand's industrial policy to be more focus and sector- or cluster-specific. It induced concomitant changes in several government agencies (at least at the policy formulation level), private-sector organisations, and number of firms, especially those which participated in government projects operated by various government agencies. The momentum of changes has started and a major transformation might follow in the future.

One significant policy-relevant issue is the roles of 'intermediaries' in clusters. The four case studies clearly points out the significant roles such intermediaries can play. In the hard disk drive cluster where the industry's direction is mostly in the hand of transnational corporations, technological capabilities of actors are relative not so high and their linkages among each other are still reasonably weak. Nonetheless, there is a possibility that industrial associations like IDEMA can stimulate the 'clustering' process leading to more interaction and knowledge sharing among actors. In a mid-tech industry like bus's body assembling, a cluster mainly composed of small local firms originally relying on tacit assembling skills can technologically progress with the external support from a government 'sector-specific' authority which behaves like an intermediary. They stimulate the formation of knowledge linkages between local firms and local non-firm agents. In knowledge-intensive services like software, Research and Technology Organisations, having accumulated knowledge in rather high-technology fields, organisational flexibility, and human resources, can be well placed to act as bridging intermediaries between transnational corporations, local start-ups, IT service providers, university and government agencies. For the community-based clusters like chilli paste cluster, their main sources of knowledge are very much tacit and localised. They are embedded in individuals and their relationship. The success of the clusters depends very much on a community-based intermediary that have local knowledge and trust of community members.

To summarise, the roles of an industrial association, a sector-specific authority, an RTO and a community-based organisation are quite striking here. IDEMA, TAI, NSTDA and the Housewives' Association have played significant roles in building trust between actors of the cluster, encouraging knowledge flows, and envisaging shared cluster vision. Government should work with these types of intermediary organisations, try to enhance their capability, and implement its policies through them.

References

AIT/Asia Policy Research. (2003). 'Strengthening the Hard Disk Drive Cluster in Thailand,' An Interim Report submitted to National Science and Technology Development Agency.

AMSDEN, A. (2001). *The Rise of the Rest: Challenges to the West from Late-industrialising Economies*, New York: Oxford University Press.

AMSDEN, A., HIKINO, T. (1993). 'Borrowing Technology or Innovating: An Exploration of the Two Paths to Industrial Development,' in Thomson R. (ed.), *Learning and Technological Change*, New York: St. Martin's Press.

ARNOLD, E. *et al.* (2000). 'Enhancing Policy and Institutional Support for Industrial Technology Development in Thailand,' Volume 1: The Overall Policy Framwork and the Development of the Industrial Innovation System, December 2000, World Bank.

ARROW, K. (1962). 'The Economic Implications of Learning by Doing,' AER.

BECATTINI, G. (1998). 'Distretti industriali e made in Italy. Le basi socioculturali del nostro sviluppo economico,' Torino, Bollati Boringhieri.

BELL, M. (1984). 'Learning and Accumulation of Technological Capacity of Developing Countries' in Fransman, M., King K. (eds.), *Technological Capability in the Third World*, London: Macmillan

BELL, M. (2002). 'Knowledge-Capabilities, Innovation and Competitiveness in Thailand: Transforming the Policy Process,' A report for National Science and Technology Development Agency (Thailand) sponsored by the World Bank.

BELL, M., PAVITT, K. (1995). 'The Development of Technological Capabilities,' in Haque, I. (ed.), *Trade, Technology and International Competitiveness*, Washington D.C.: The World Bank.

BELL, M., SCOTT-KEMMIS, D. (1985). 'Technological Capacity and Technical Change,' Draft Working Paper No. 1, 2, 4 and 6, Report on Technology Transfer in Manufacturing Industry in Thailand, Science Policy Research Unit, University of Sussex.

BESSANT, J. (2003). *High-Involvement Innovation: Building and Sustaining Competitive Advantage Through Continuous Change*, John Wiley and Sons, West Sussex, England.

BRIMBLE, P. *et al.* (1999). 'The Broader Impacts of Foreign Direct Investment on Economic Development in Thailand: Corporate Responses,' An unpublished paper prepared for the high-level roundtable on *Foreign Direct Investment and its Impact on Poverty Alleviation*, Singapore, 14–15 December 1998; Revised April 1999.

Brooker Group Public Company Limited. (2003). 'Final Report. Thailand's 2nd R&D/Innovation Survey in Manufacturing and Service Sectors and Database Development,' May 2003.

CHANG, H. (1994). *The Political Economic of Industrial Policy*, London: Macmillan.

CHANG, H. (1997). 'Institutional Structure and Economic Performance: Some Theoretical and Policy Lessons from the Experience of the Republic of Korea,' *Asia Pacific Development Journal*, **4**(1), 39–56.

CHANG, P.L., Hsu, C.W (1998). 'The Development Strategies for Taiwan's Semiconductor Industry,' *IEEE Transactions on Engineering Management*, **45**(4), 349–356.

CHANTRAMONKLASRI, N. (1985). 'Technological Responses to Rising Energy Prices: A Study of Technological Capability and Technological Change Efforts in Energy-Intensive Manufacturing Industries in Thailand,' Unpublished D.Phil. Thesis. Science Policy Research Unit, University of Sussex, Brighton.

CHURSTENSEN, S. *et al.* (1992). 'Institutional and Political Bases of Growth-inducing Policies in Thailand,' (mimeo) Bangkok, TDRI.

COHEN, W., Levinthal, D. (1990). 'Absorptive Capacity: A New Perspective on Learning and Innovation,' *Administrative Science Quarterly*, **35**, 128–152.

College of Management. (2003). 'Draft Final Report of S&T Needs and Production of Manpower in the Manufacturing Sector,' Mahildol University, June 2003 (in Thai).

COOKE, P. (2001). 'Regional Innovation Systems, Clusters, and the Knowledge Economy,' *Industrial and Corporate Change*, **10**(4), 945–974.

DAHLMAN, C., BRIMBLE, P. (1990). 'Technology Strategy and Policy for Industrial Competitiveness: A Case Study of Thailand,' paper prepared for the World Bank, April, 1990.

DAHLMAN, C. *et al.* (1991). 'Technology Strategy and Policy for Industrial Competitiveness: A Case Study of Thailand,' in World Bank, *Decision and Change in Thailand: Three Studies in Support of the Seventh Plan*, Washington, D.C.

DAVENPORT, T.H., PRUSAK, L. (2003). *What's the Big IDEA? Creating and Capitalizing on the Best Management Thinking*, HBS Press.

DODGSON, M. and BESSANT, J. (1996). *Effective Innovation Policy: A New Approach*, London: International Thomson Business Press.

DONER, R. (1992). 'Politics and the Growth of Local Capital in Southeast Asia: Auto Industries in the Philippines and Thailand,' in McVey, R. (ed.), *Southeast Asian Capitalists, Southeast Asia Programme (SEAP)*, New York: Cornell University Press.

EVANS, P. (1989). 'The Future of the Developmental State,' *The Korean Journal of Policy Studies*, **4**, 129–146.

EVANS, P. (1998). 'Transferable Lessons?: Re-examining the Institutional Prerequisites of East Asian Economic Policies,' *Development Studies*, **34**(6), 66–86.

FAGERBERG, J. (2004). 'What Do We Know About Innovation? Lessons from the TEARI Project,' paper presented at the TEARI final conference 'Research, innovation and economic performance. What do we know and where are we heading?', Brussels.

GOTO, A. (1997). 'Cooperative Research in Japanese Manufacturing Industries,' in A. Goto, H. Odagiri, (eds.), *Innovation in Japan*, Oxford: Oxford University Press.

HOBDAY, M. (1995). *Innovation in East Asia: The Challenge to Japan*, Aldershot: Edward Elgar.

HOBDAY, M. (1996). 'Taiwan-Incubating High-Technology Industries,' in Rush, H. *et al.* (eds.), *Technology Institutes: Strategies for Best Practice*, Suffolk: St Edmundsbury Press.

HOU, C., GEE, S. (1993). 'National Systems Supporting Technical Advance in Industry: The Case of Taiwan,' in Nelson R. (ed.), *National Innovation System*, Oxford: Oxford University Press.

INTARAKUMNERD, P. (2006). 'Thailand's National Innovation System in Transition,' in Lundvall, B., Intarakumnerd, P., Vang, J. (eds.), *Asia's Innovation Systems in Transition*, Cheltenham, UK and Northampton, USA: Edward Elgar.

INTARAKUMNERD, P., CHAIRATANA, P., TANGCHITPIBOON, T. (2002). 'National Innovation System in Less Successful Developing Countries: The Case Study of Thailand,' *Research Policy*, 8–9, 1445–1457.

INTARAKUMNERD, P., VIRASA, T. (2002). 'Broader Roles of RTOs in Developing Countries: From KnowledgeCreators to Strengtheners of National Innovation System', Paper presented at Science, Technology and Innovation Conference, JFK School of government, Harvard University, 23–24 September.

Intellectual Property Institute. (2006). 'Evaluation of Technological and Innovative Capabilities of Motorcycles and Parts Cluster,' A Progress Report submitted to National Science and Technology Agency, 12 September.

JOHNSON, B., LUNDVALL B.-Å. (2000). 'Promoting Innovation Systems as a Response to the Globalizing Learning Economy,' second draft of contribution to the Project Local Productive Clusters and Innovations Systems in Brazil: New industrial and technological policies.

JOHNSON, C. (1982). *MITI and the Japanese Miracle: The Growth of Industrial Policy, 1925–1975*, CA: Stanford University Press.

KATRAK, H. (1990). 'Imports of Technology, Enterprise Size, and R&D Based Production in a Newly Industrializing Country: The Evidence from Indian Enterprises,' *World Development*, **23**(3), 459–68.

KIM, L. (1993). 'National System of Industrial Innovation: Dynamics of Capability Building in Korea,' in Nelson R. (ed.), *National Innovation System*, Oxford: Oxford University Press.

KIM, L. (1997). *Imitation to Innovation: The Dynamics of Korea's Technological Learning*, Harvard Business School Press, Boston.

KIM. L., NELSON, R. (eds.) (2000). *Technology, Learning, and Innovation: Experiences of Newly Industrializing Economies*, Cambridge University Press.

LALL, S. (1992). 'Technological Capability and Industrialization,' *World Development*, **20**(2), 165–186.

LALL, S. (1996). *Learning from the Asian Tigers: Studies in Technology and Industrial Policy*, Macmillan Press.

LAURIDSEN, L. (1999). 'Policies and Institutions of Industrial Deepening and Upgrading in Taiwan III-technological upgrading,' Working Paper no. 13, International Development Studies: Roskilde University, Roskilde.

LAURIDSEN, L. (2001). 'Coping with Globalization: The Recent Thai Experience with Openness and Increased World Market Integration,' International Development Studies, Roskilde University, Denmark.

LAURIDSEN, L. (2002). 'Coping with the Triple Challenge of Globalization, Liberalization and Crisis: The Role of Industrial Technology Policies and Technology Institutions in Thailand,' *The European Journal of Development Research*, **14**(1), 101–125.

LEONARD-BARTON, D. (1995). *Wellsprings of Knowledge: Building and Sustaining the Sources of Innovation*, Boston: Harvard Business School Press.

LIND, M. and PERSBORN, M. (2000). 'Possibilities and Risks with a Knowledge Broker in the Knowledge Transfer Process,' paper presented at the 42nd Annual Conference of the Operational Research Society, 12–14 September 2000, University of Wales, Swansea, UK.

LUNDVALL, B.-Å. (2002). *Innovation, Growth and Social Cohesion: The Danish Model*, London: Elgar Publishers.

LUNDVALL, B.-Å. (ed.) (1992). *National Innovation Systems: Towards a Theory of Innovation and Interactive Learning*, London: Pinter Publishers.

LUNDVALL, B.-Å., JOHNSON, SLOT ANDERSEN E., DALUM, B. (2001). 'National Systems of Production, Innovation and Competence Building,' paper presented at the Nelson and Winter DRUID Summer Conference, Aalborg Congress Centre, Alborg, Denmark, 12–15 June, 2000.

MARTIN, R., SUNDLEY P. (2003). 'Deconstructing Clusters: Chaotic Concept or Policy Panacea?, *Journal of Economic Geography*, **3**(1), 5–35.

Ministry of Education, Culture, Sports, Science and Technology (MEXT). (2002). 'Cluster: Cooperative Link of Unique Science and Technology for Economy Revitalisation,' A published paper prepared by Ministry of Education, Culture, Sports, Science and Technology, Japan.

MUKDAPITAK, Y. (1994). 'The Technology Strategies of Thai Firms,' Unpublished D.Phil. Thesis. Science Policy Research Unit, University of Sussex, Brighton.

National Science and Technology Policy Committee. (2004). 'Science and Technology Strategic Plan 2004–2013,' National Science and Technology Development Agency (NSTDA), Bangkok.

NIOSI, J. *et al.* (1993). 'National Systems of Innovation: In Search of A Workable Concept,' *Technology in Society*, **15**, 207–227.

ODAGIRI, H., GOTO, A. (1993). 'The Japanese System of Innovation: Past, Present and Future,' in Nelson, R. (ed.), *National Innovation System*, Oxford: Oxford University Press.

OECD. (1999). 'Boosting Innovation: The Cluster Approach,' Paris.

OECD. (2000). 'Knowledge Management in the Learning Society,' Paris.

PHASUKAVANICH, C. (2003). 'The Pace of Thailand through the Year 2020,' power point presentation by Chakramon Phasukavanich, 20 May 2003.

PIORE, M.J., SABEL, C.F. (1990). *Second Industrial Divide: Possibilities for Prosperity*, Basic Books.

PONGSAKORNPREUTIKOOL, R. (2006a). 'Banpong Bus's Body Cluster,' Presentation at the First Annual Cluster Development Agent Workshop, National Economics and Social Development Board, Novotel Hotel, 6–7 July.

PONGSAKORNPREUTIKOOL, R. (2006b.). personal conversation, 21 September.

PORTER, M.E. (1998). 'Cluster and the New Economics of Competition', *Harvard Business Review*, November–December, 77–90.

PRUSAK, L., COHEN, D. (1998). 'Knowledge Buyers, Sellers, and Brokers: The Political Economy of Knowledge' in *The Economy Impact of Knowledge*, Neef, D., Siesfeld A., Cefola, J. (eds.), Butterworth Heinemann.

RAJABHAT Phetchaburi Wittiyalongkorn. (2002). 'The Study of Strategic Methods for Upgrading Local Wisdom: A Case Study of the Production of Chilli Paste by Klong Song House's Wife Association,' A report submitted to the Office of Rajabhat Institutes and National Science and Technology Development Agency.

RUSH, *et al.* (1996). 'Overview,' in Rush, H. *et al.* (eds.), *Technology Institutes: Strategies for Best Practice*, Suffolk: St Edmundsbury Press.

SABEL, C.F. (2004) 'Districts on the Move: Note on the Tedis Survey of the Industrialization of District Firms,' preliminary draft, August 2004, presented at Local Governance and Production conference in Turin, December 2004. Available on http://www2.law.columbia.edu/sabel/papers.htm.

SOON, J.W., STORPER, M. (2003). 'The Increasing Importance of Geographical Proximity in Technological Innovation: An Analysis of US Patent Citations, 1975–1997', paper prepared for the Conference: What Do We Know About Innovation? In Honour of Keith Pavitt, Sussex, 13–15 November 2003. Downloadable on http://www.lse.ac.uk/collections/geographyAndEnvironment/whosWho/profiles/storper/pdf/Sonn_Storper.pdf.

SRIPAIPAN, C., VANICHSENI, S., MUKDAPITAK, Y. (1999). '*Technological Innovation Policy of Thailand*', (Thai version), Bangkok: National Science and Technology Development Agency.

STEINER, M. (1998). *Cluster and Regional Specialization*, Pion Limited, London.

TDRI. (1989). 'The Development of Thailand's Technology Capability in Industry,' 2–5, TDRI: Bangkok.

TDRI. (1994). 'Final Report of S&T Manpower Production,' Thailand Development Research Institute Foundation (in Thai).

TDRI. (1998). 'Effective Mechanisms for Supporting Private Sector Technology Development and Needs for Establishing Technology Development Financing Corporation,' A report submitted to National Science and Technology Development Agency.

TDRI. (2002). 'Final Report S&T Manpower Production Framework,' (in Thai).

TEECE D.J. (1981). 'The Market for Know-How and the Efficient International Transfer of Technology,' *The Annuals of the Academy of Political and Social Science*, **458**, 81–96.

TEECE, D.J. (2000). *Managing Intellectual Capital*, Oxford University Press.

TEECE, D.J., PISANO, G., SHUEN, A. (1997). 'Dynamic Capabilities and Strategic Management,' *Strategic Management Journal*, **18**(7), 509–533.

TEUBAL, M. (1996). 'R&D and Technology Policy in NICs as Learning Processes,' *World Development*, **24**(3), 449–460.

Thai Automotive Institute. (2006). Retrieved 4 July 2006, from http://www.thaiauto.or.th.

TIRALAP, A. (1990). 'The Economics of the Process of Technological Change of the Firm: The Case of the Electronics Industry in Thailand,' Unpublished D.Phil. Thesis. Science Policy Research Unit, University of Sussex, Brighton.

TUNZELMAN, N. Von (1995). *Technology and Industrial Progress: The Foundations of Economic Growth*, Edward Elgar, Aldershot.

VANG and ASHEIM (2006). 'Region, Absorptive Capacity and Strategic Coupling with High-Tech TNCs', *Science Technology & Society*, **11**(1), 39–66.

VONGPIVAT, P. (2003). 'A National Innovation System Model: An Industrial Development in Thailand,' Unpublished D.Phil. Thesis, The Fletcher School of Law and Diplomacy, Tufts University.

WINTER, S. (2002). 'Understanding Dynamic Capabilities,' A working paper of the Reginald H. Jones Center, The Wharton School, University of Pennsylvania.

WONG, P. (1996). *National Systems of Innovation: The Case of Singapore*, Korea: Science and Technology Policy Institute.

WONG, P. (1999). 'National Innovation Systems for Rapid Technological Catch-up: An Analytical Framework and a Comparative Analysts of Korea, Taiwan, and Singapore,' paper presented at the DRUID's summer conference, Rebild, Denmark.

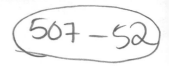

Chapter 17

'Penang's Illustrious Story' Revisited: Local Authorities, Labour Force and the Multinationals

Elsa Lafaye de Micheaux

17.1 Introduction

The old free port of the British Empire, a part of the *Straits Settlement* (from 1786) with Singapore and Malacca, Penang is a small state (1000 km[2] and 1.5 million inhabitants) of today's Malaysia. A majority of its inhabitants are urban[1] and of Chinese ethnicity in a country of Malay and muslim tradition and politically dominated by the Malay UMNO party in a coalition government since Independence (1957). Regularly won by opposition parties, Penang has always been governed by the Chinese. The main city of the state of Penang, Georgetown (250,000 inhabitants approximately) is the old capital, which regrouped most commercial activity of the island with the Chinese lifestyle of the country (the Chinese population there is five times greater than the Malay population). Between 1970 and 1990, the 'Pearl of the Orient' as Penang Island was called in the past, became the Silicon Valley of South-East Asia. During this period, Penang was turned into the most industrialised state as well as the second most important port and airport of the country[2].

---

[1] In 2005, Penang Island's urbanisation rate is 80% and Malaysia's 63%.

[2] In 2000, Penang was also the second Malaysian state for motorcycles or cars and telephones per 1000 population, for the population provided with piped water, for the number of doctors per 10,000, etc. (it was the first in 1995) (Economic Planning Unit, *8th Malaysian Plan*, p. 145). In 2005 it ranked second for economic activity and quality of life measured by the Development Composite Index (Malaysia, Economic Planning Unit, *9th Malaysian Plan*, p. 356).

Table 17.1   Penang: GNP.

Penang	1970	1990	1997p	Malaysia 1997p
Agriculture, mines	266	213	372	26,480
Manufacture	172	3107	6386	49,577
Construction	78	176	374	6879
Services	835	2720	4970	57,701
Total	1351	6216	12102	140,637

Source: PDC, 1997. (p: forecast)

At the time of the New Economic Policy (NEP, 1970–1990) which led the Malaysian nation towards head-long development, the local development of Penang has contributed to the extraordinary growth of the Malaysian economy.

During 1970–1980, Penang, having become the regional capital of the electronics industry, led Malaysia to become one of the main global producers and exporters. Penang's contribution to national GNP more than doubled, going from 4.6% in 1970 to 9.6% in 1997 (see Table 17.1). Income per head was on average higher in Penang than in the rest of the country and this difference grew during the 1990s: in 1990, the GDP per head in Penang was 19% higher than the national average; in 1995 GDP per head had passed above 34%. The mean monthly household income's growth for 1995–1999 has been the highest in Penang, with an average annual growth rate of 8.9% (+5.2% for Malaysia).

Like Singapore and Thailand, Penang's growth experienced contraction in 1998 (–8.5%), but has quickly recovered from the Asian Crisis, as the whole country did. Malaysia's annual GDP growth accounted for 4.5% (2001–2005), and Penang for 5% (see Table 17.2). It is expected to rise to 6% (Malaysia) and 6.1% (Penang) in the coming years.[3] However, the gap between Penang and the rest of Malaysia reduced after the 2001 recession in the electronics sector: the income gap of 26% in 1999 has reduced to 8% in 2004.

During the 1960s, the state of Penang was economically stagnant because of the eroding role of the port. It was a period of high

---

[3] Malaysia, Economic Planning Unit, *9th Malaysian Plan*, p. 357.

Table 17.2:   Penang's GDP annual growth rates.

	1970–80*	1980–90*	(1990–97)□	1990–2000□	2000–2005□
Penang	+9.7%	+5.6%	+10.8%	+8.1%	+5%

Source: Penang Strategic Development Plan, 1991–2000 (*1978 and □1987 prices); 9th MP 2006–2010.

unemployment, much higher than in the rest of the country. In 1969, the local government of Penang (of the opposition party *Gerakan*) advocated an active policy of opening up trade and welcoming foreign investment[4] in order to set-up free trade zones and industrial parks. The decision to receive FDI (Foreign Direct Investments) coming in order to attract the best foreign investors (in terms of infrastructure such as aid to expatriates) turned out well. Local unemployment was quickly reduced and the standard of living continued to increase at a level higher than that of Malaysia from the 1970s onwards. These investments were followed by the Penang Development Corporation (PDC), the development agency of the State, formed in November 1969. Headed by Penang's Chief Minister, Tun Dr. Lim, its principal role was land management and regional development. Until today, PDC has been in charge of:

— *promotion and industrial development:* the setting-up of the institutional and physical structure of the first free-trade zone (Bayan Lepas, 1972), then others; management of the business parks;
— *urban re-development and development of new communities:* the conception development of new urban communities and amenities (college further education, hospitals);
— *promotion and development of tourism:* this activity was particularly developed with the construction of hotels, luxury tourist parks, etc. Today tourism is the second most important sector of economic activity of the island. The last few years have led to an

---

[4] Before becoming Chief Minister of Penang in May 1969, Tun Dr. Lim Chong Eu, as opposition leader, proposed such an orientation for Penang in 1965. It has been contained in the later *Penang Master Plan*.

attachment and recognition of the value of historical heritage, relative to the local and colonial culture;
— *land development:* PDC controls, amongst other things, the value of land and protects it against speculation, even though real estate speculation was helpful during the 1990s. The development of land has played a role of arbiter between the orders of the NEP concerning agricultural reform (land clearance and land redistribution in favour of Malaysians) and the industrialisation strategy based on the relocation of factories (land reserved for industrial zones).

The industrial park set up by the PDC has been largely dominated by foreign subsidiaries since 1969. In a quarter of a century the industrial areas run by the PDC, went from, counting all industrial sectors, 31 established companies in 1970 to 731 companies in 2002.[5] See Table 17.3.

It is important to notice that in Penang's cluster, there are other firms than those run by the PDC: Penang is for instance home to 126 Japanese companies which employ some 20,000 people.[6] See Table 17.4.

Table 17.3: Investment According to Country (December 2002).

Country	Number of Factories	Employment
Local	342	35,050
Taiwan	61	12,770
Japan	58	19,887
USA	40	35,025
Germany	12	9237
Singapore	27	4151
Hong Kong	4	2870
United Kingdom	4	3608
Other Countries	24	18,554

Source: Survey, PDC, 2006.

---

[5] Source: PDC, 2006, www.pdc.gouv.my, see p. 5 in this article for details.
[6] *Business Times*, 29 June 2006.

Table 17.4:   Type of Industry (December 2002).

Industry	Number of Factories	Employment
Electronics/Electrical	164	84,642
Fabricated Metal	158	11,735
Plastics/Plastic Products	84	7112
Chemical/Fertiliser	53	4535
Paper/Printing	68	5332
Textiles/Garments	24	11,204
Others	195	25,520

Source: Survey, PDC, 2006.

The electronics specialisation was made possible largely thanks to this foreign capital and expertise once a number of multinationals, firstly American,[7] then Japanese[8] and Taiwanese,[9] out-sourced their production workshops to Malaysia, particularly in Penang. The electrical and electronics (E&E) industry, the leading contributor to Malaysia's industrial development, is now projected to grow at an average 7.2% a year, during the Third Industrial Master Plan (IMP3) period (2006–2020) to reach RM82.4 billion by 2020.[10] Malaysia continues to attract substantial investments in the E&E industry: from 1980 to this year, investments in E&E projects totalled RM116.9 billion. For the period from January to August 2006, investments amounting to RM4 billion were approved for the electronic components sub-sector; RM716.9 million for industrial electronics; RM158 million for consumer electronics; and RM142.7 million for electrical products. The average annual growth of exports is expected to be at 7.1%, with exports at the end of the IMP3 period projected to reach RM738.9 billion. Penang is part of the fully-developed

---

[7] Intel, Hewlett Packard, AMD, Texas Instrument, Motorola, Omron, Seagate, Fairchild, etc.
[8] Japanese companies operating in Penang include Sony, Sanyo, Toray, Renesas, Kobe Precision, Nikko Electronics, Hitachi etc.
[9] Like ACER.
[10] *News Straits Times*, 13 September 2006.

semiconductor cluster which is expected to strengthen in the future (cluster covering the north-western corridor including Perak, Penang, Kulim Hi-Tech Park and the neighbouring industrial areas in Kedah).

In Penang today, the electronics industry is predominant both in number of factories and by employment. Can it be rigorously explained? (Hempel, 1942).

We will now look back at the history of this cluster, starting from the theoretical canvas of economic geography which deals with the relationship of initial land assets, factors influencing companies choices, accidents that can tip the balance in one way or another and economies of agglomeration which reinforce the process of the con-centration of companies in this particular area.[11] In doing so we will underline the importance of labour as a factor in this process, which is often forgotten in par contempary studies of industrial develop-ment. We will then look at its current situation through the official rhetorics is the local authorities.

17.2 A Model for Economic Geography: The History of the Relocation of Companies to Penang

At the end of the 1960s, poverty and under-employment were the principal problems of Malaysia, as they were for the major part of Asia as a whole.[12] In 1970, 65% of Malaysia's rural population lived below the poverty line and in the cities unemployment was 10% of the working

---

[11] We refer mainly to W.B. Arthur, 'Urban Systems and Historical Path Dependance' in Ansubel J. and Herman R. (eds.), *Cities and their Vital Systems,* NAP, Washington, 1988, and 'Silicon Valley Locational Clusters: When Do Increasing Returns Imply Monopoly?' *Mathematical Social Sciences,* 1990, **19**, pp. 235–251. For P. Krugman, 'Space: the Final Frontier' *Journal of Economic Perspectives,* 1988 Spring, **12**(2), pp. 161–174; 'First Nature, Second Nature and Metropolitan Location' *Journal of Regional Science,* 1993, **33**(2), pp. 129–144; 'History versus Expectation' *Quaterly Journal of Economics,* 1991, **106**, pp. 651–667; 'Increasing Returns and Economic Geography', *Journal of Political Economy,* 1991, **99**(3), pp. 483–499.

[12] G. Myrdal, *Asian Drama: Enquiry into the Poverty of Nations,* 1968.

population (and 12.5% on average for urban Malaysians).[13] Penang was no different with an unemployment rate of 16% in the same year. Following the increasing dissatisfaction with the programme of substituting imports put in place by the first industrialisation policy, the strategy of the promotion of exports appeared to be the only way to break the impasse. The government therefore passed a law on encouraging investment in net exporters and the electronics sector (work intensive) as a priority: this was the *Investment Incentives Act* of 1968. This attempt by the government to develop a new and promising industrialisation strategy with regards to work was intensified following the race riots of 1969 which were attributed to the inequalities of the division of wealth and jobs between ethnic groups.

It is notable that a great part of the success of the site was for reasons that were generally admitted by everyone in order to explain the growth in the number of off-shore industrial sites: the first aim of the multinational companies that located at the time was to take advantage of, other than the tax breaks, the low labour costs and labour laws that worked in favour of the employer when they were set up in the free-trade zone: the electronics industry that was set up in Penang was from the start a labour intensive industry.

But the willingness of the Malay state must be highlighted in the creation of the advantages for Penang: during the state of emergency that followed the race riots of 13 May 1969, the government decided, in order to give its New Economic Policy some substance, to open up its territory to foreign industrial exporters, to create free trade zones and envisage that it would be the electronics industry that would come.[14]

---

[13] S. Narayanan and R. Rasiah, 'Malaysian Electronics: The Changing Prospects for Employment and Restructuring,' *Development and Change*, **23**(4), 1992, p. 76. Note: the poverty line that is made reference to in the majority of texts on Malaysia is based on an approximate definition given by the Malaysian government: 'those who can cover the minimum basic needs of food, clothing, housing, durable goods and transport in order to maintain a decent standard of living ', without precise measurement (Jomo, 1987, p. 277).

[14] Free trade zones were developped in Asia in the 1960s. The first relocation of electronic firms in a free trade zone was in 1962, in Hong Kong.

This change of policy, which we have interpreted as a compromise, led the Malay government to have recourse to foreign investments to finance its industrialisation policy. If we hold that the creation of the free trade zone in 1970 was an element of a political compromise (a serious strain on nationalist principles that had prevailed until this time), Penang, as an urban and trade-based island with a large Chinese population (60% of the population) traditionally independent from Kuala Lumpur — appeared as the ideal place to put it into action politically. In 1969 the status of free port was removed from Penang, the new Chief Minister, supported by the Federal State, created the *Penang Development Corporation* PDC to transform this island from a trade post to an industrial site. The PDC was then charged with creating and managing, from the land belonging to the state of Penang, the conditions and infrastructure necessary for the creation of an industrialised zone. This industrialisation depended upon a Free Trade Zone.[15] Before this free trade zone was set up, not a single foreign nor electronics company operated in Malaysia.

17.2.1 *Penang's Territorial Advantages*

Retrospectively and considering the extent to which relocations throughout the world took from this period onwards, the assets of Penang at the start of the 1970s appear rather unoriginal and summary. But they have been the decisive in the eyes of the heads of multinationals. It is perhaps important to look at these advantages again as contempary problems linked to the globalisation of capital have a tendency to distance us from the detail.

---

[15] The free trade zone of Penang was created following the Singaporean institutional model (which played a pioneering role in its industrialisation by means of using foreign capital from relocated foreign companies): in 1967, *The Economic Expansion Incentives Act* provided the structure of tax incentives for foreign investors, whose absence of tax revenue for pioneering industry lasted 10 years.

17.2.1.1 *Tax Breaks in the Free Trade Area*

The principal condition for companies to set up inside the free trade zone (created in 1972) was to invest foreign capital and to export at least 80% of their production.[16] In this case imports destined for re-export benefited from exemption from custom duties and the companies themselves benefited from a status of 'pioneer': over a period of 10 years, only 30% of revenues were taxed at normal rates (30%).[17]

The first electronics factories were established at the end of 1971 at Bayan Lepas where the free trade zone extended to on the first of January 1972. The subsidiaries of multinationals specialising in semi-conductors were all situated within the free trade zone; their sale on the domestic market was prohibited without the authorisation of the government and were counted as imports. But many exported the totality of their production.

17.2.1.2 *Unions Strictly Limited*

Government brochures calling for investment in the country mentioned the fact that workers were rarely members of trade unions and that trade unions were uncommon.[18]

In fact, the law, under the *Trade Union Act* and the *Trade Union Regulations* of 1959, largely restricted trade union rights in the country: the unions were not allowed to have any links to political parties,[19]

---

[16] N.D. Karunaratna and M.B. Adbullah, 'Incentive Schemes and Foreign Investment in the Industrialization of Malaysia', *Asian Survey*, **18**(3), 1978, pp. 261–264.

[17] The *Far Eastern Economic Review* titled 'Electronics: Malaysia's Jackpot', 1 April 1972.

[18] In *Malaysia, the 'Solid State' for Electronics: an Invitation to Invest*, Federal Industrial Development Authority (FIDA), Malaysia, 1970–1971.

[19] Generally communist and socialist parties are banned in Malaysia, as is reading authors judged dangerous for public order (Marx to Mao): the sale of such work is illegal, packages sent by post are checked and the recipient placed under surveillence. The ban has also been used for a long time against authors from populist democracies (Vietnam for example).

could not be national (they are restricted to the Peninsula, at Sabah and Sarawak), nor general unions (they must be strictly limited to a branch of industry, a profession or trade). The largest trade union originated during the period of British administration of the mines and plantations during the 1920s,[20] the National Union of Plantation Workers, considered by many to be complicit with the authorities and officials (K.S. Jomo observed that salaries have not increased since the rise in power of the organisation which took place in the 1940s with the merging of different local branches at a national level[21]).

The right to strike is limited to members of an officially recognised union who must follow a very strict procedure for it to be legal: in order to reduce tension (the principle of cooling off), the government service in charge of the general management of unions has seven days to determine the validity of a strike as soon as it has been announced, whilst the Employment Minister checks for procedural irregularity and can declare the industrial action illegal, after having made a referral to the court that has jurisdiction over the affair (an Industrial Court).[22]

Sympathy strikes or political strikes are prohibited, as are general strikes. The legislation of 1971 imposed further limits the right to strike (in restricting, by decree, the valid reasons for industrial action and the terms of recognising a union). There is no minimum wage. Finally in the free trade zone even if trade unions are not explicitly prohibited by law (contrary to what is said sometimes), the State, through the MIDA (Malaysian Industrial Development Authority) guarantees investors protection from all 'unreasonable demands' made by unions for a period of five years or more.[23] As a matter of fact, unions are non-existent in the electronics industry. G. Benko

---

[20] The right to strike in Great Britain dates from 1915.

[21] K.S. Jomo, *A Question of Class, Capitalism, the State and Uneven Development in Malaysia*, Oxford University Press, Singapore, 1987.

[22] This data comes from *Malaysian Industrial Relations*, Marilyn Aminuddin, 1990.

[23] 'Protection of pioneer industries during their establishment against any unreasonable demands from a trade union. Trade unions cannot demand better terms of employment than those stipulated under the *Employment Act 1955*.' *Industrial Relations Act* 1967.

observed that in general all the major industrial poles of activity in South-East Asia are very repressive concerning trade unions.[24]

17.2.1.3 *Low Labour Costs*

We know that in general, as in Asia at the time, labour costs are but a small fraction of those in the West. The interviews conducted with CEOs bring out the importance of the first argument concerning how low labour costs led to Malaysia being chosen. Some available data allows to precisely quantify Malaysia's advantage in this area (see Table 17.5).

Singapore is the offshore site with the highest salaries (Malaysia comes second). An unskilled worker earns an eleventh of the wage for equivalent work in the USA; in other words, one day's work (11 hours) of a Singaporean worker earns the equivalent of one hour's work of an American worker. Equally qualified and in the same sector, the Malaysian average wage is between half to two thirds of that of Singapore. Indonesia (the cheapest) has a wage that is only one quarter of the Singaporean wage.

In Malaysia we also see that average earnings are inferior in the export sectors than in the rest of the manufacturing sector, it was even

Table 17.5:   Asian Wage Levels Expressed as a Fraction of American Wage Levels. Unqualified Labourers (Comparable Industries) 1969.

Country	Fraction of American Salary (electronics)
USA	1
Singapore	1/11 (around 9%)
Malaysia	$1/22 < w < 2/33$ (between 4.5–6%)
Indonesia	1/44 (2.2%)

Source: UNCTAD, 1975.[25]

---

[24] G. Benko, *Géographie des Technopôles*, Masson, Paris, 1991. We will come back to this point with the debate about the feminisation of the work in workshops.

[25] UNCTAD: 'International subcontracting arrangements in electronics between developed market-economy countries and developing countries' NY, ONU, 1975, p. 20.

lower at the start of the transitional period between import economy and export economy: in 1973 the monthly earnings in the electronics industry (which only accounts for 12,000 workers) represents only 87% of average industrial earnings.[26] In addition wages differ according to the area in which multinationals are established: in 1976 in the electronics industry, the daily wage was US$1.60 in Kuala Lumpur but it is even lower in Penang (where the unemployment rate is higher) and drops to $1.20 in Malacca and rural areas.

Data allowing us to make a comparison of the electronics sectors of different countries is scarce, and the data that we have managed to get to have an idea of certain Asian countries where relocations took place dates from 1980 (10 years after the period that we would like to look at here). See Table 17.6.

Although only indicative, the data seem good and indeed promising because we can imagine that a certain amount of catching-up has taken place after 10 years. Thus the difference between Malaysia and the NPIs of Asia remains very high: in 1980 the average Malaysian wage in the electronics industry was half that (or even less) of wages in Singapore, Hong Kong and Korea. It was 14.2 times lower than in Japan and 16.5 times lower than in the USA: at this level we note that

Table 17.6: Average Earnings per Hour in the Electronics Industry in Asia, 1980.

Country	Hourly Earnings (US$)
USA	6.96
Singapore	0.90
Malaysia	0.42
Philippines	0.30 (1978)
South Korea	0.91
HongKong	0.97
Japan	5.97

Source: K.S. Jomo, 1987, p. 231.

---

[26] Even in sectors that did not export the same revenue was 108% of the industrial average. Source: Jomo, *A Question of Class,* 1987, p. 230.

the gap between the NPIs and the USA has already closed. Therefore the low Malaysian labour costs are a major advantage vis à vis the USA, Europe and Japan but it is also an advantage compared to the countries that are relocated to: Malaysian wages are lower than those of the NPIs.[27]

Therefore we can conclude with certainty that in 1970 in Penang the labour market having spent many years with a worrying level of unemployment (much higher than the national average) a large pool of cheap workers was immediately available for employers. Operators were mainly females (80–90%): young (16–24 years old), little educated (6 years of schooling) and not yet married. These women from the countryside constituted the most abundant and the less paid labour force in Penang: they had no professional experience, they did not have to support their family, as not married they might not be pregnant, and as young, they were supposed to ignore labour conflicts.[28] 'Who therefore could be better qualified by nature and inheritance to contribute to the efficiency of a bench assembly production line than oriental girls?' (FIDA, 1975) [29]

17.2.1.4 *Low Political Risk*

Since its Independence (1957), the same coalition of national parties dominated by UMNO has been in power. But after the riots of 1969, the country lived through a state of emergency and controls on political and social movements were reinforced: this *quasi-democratic* country according to the definition given by H. A. Zakaria,[30] could

---

[27] Cf. again the evocative title of an article in the *Wall Street Journal*, 'So long, Taiwan-Electronics Firms Rush to Malaysia as Labour Gets Costly and Scarce Elsewhere in Asia', 20 September 1973.

[28] M. Blake, *Participation of Female Factory Workers in Voluntary Associations: Electronics Factory Workers in Malaysia and Thailand*, Ph.D Thesis, Universiti Sains Malaysia, Penang, 1984.

[29] Quoted by A. Ong: 'Japanese Factories, Malay Workers: Class, and Sexual Metaphors in West Malaysia', in J. Monning Atkinson, S. Errington (eds.), *Power and Difference: Gender in Island Southeast Asia*, Stanford U. Press, 1990, p. 396.

[30] H.A. Zakaria, 'Malaysia: Quasi Democracy in a Divided Society' in L. Diamond *et al.* (eds.) *Democracy and Developing Countries*, 3 Asia.

be considered at the time to be semi-authoritarian.[31] During the period of the Cold War political stability meant that the country belonged to the non-aligned movement and did not seek to join the communist camp[32] and that property rights were guaranteed as a result. It is an argument in favour of capital investment in the country (an idea drawn from the notion of 'risk country' today used by rating agencies), and which distinguishes both Malaysia and Indonesia notably.

17.2.1.5 Untrained Workforce

However in 1970 the work force was far from being trained in sufficient numbers above the primary sector: the literacy rate of the adult population was only 60% at the time which was one of the lowest in the region (see Table 17.7). The level of training of local workers was even lower, the industrial site set-up was developed to combat unemployment, create immediate jobs. It aimed therefore to develop an industry of labourers geared towards exportation.

Table 17.7: Comparison of Literacy Levels in Different Countries of Asia, 1970.

Malaysia	60%
Indonesia	54%
Thailand	79%
Singapore	69%
Korea	88%
Philippines	82%

Source: Mingat Tan, 1992.

---

[31] H. Crouch, *Government and Society in Malaysia*. Cornell U. Press, London, 1996.
[32] In 1948, a state of emergency was declared and the army under the orders of a civil authority fought against guerillas supported by Peking/Beijing for a number of years (end of the emergency: 1960; end of the rebellion: 1989). Cf. D. Camroux, 'The Asia-Pacific Policy Community in Malaysia.' *The Pacific Review*, 7(4), 1994, pp. 421–433. This struggle against communist insurrection, even though it was not proof that the country might not one day join that camp, does demonstrate the political orientation of the authorities at the very least.

Table 17.8: Level of Schooling in Primary and Secondary Education, 1970.

	Primary, 1970 (%)	Secondary, 1970(%)
Malaysia	87	34
Indonesia	80	16
Thaïland	83	17
Singapore	105	46
Korea	103	42
Philippines	108	46

Source: Mingat Tan, 1992.

As for the schooling of children in 1970, it was almost full at the primary level (87% for the school age range), it was rather weak at the secondary level, 34%, and remained negligible for further education: 2,6% between the ages of 19–24, much lower than the average for Asia which stood at 4,6% (see Table 17.8).

Finally on the eve of the 1970s further education was very small (there were centres for technical training created by the state, but they did not fulfil the needs of companies and did little training in industrial skills). Furthermore up until 1993 no financial incentives led to companies really investing in the training of their workers. In Singapore on the other hand, from 1979 onwards development funding for further education was put in place.

17.2.2 *Factors Influencing Firm's Preference for Location*

The types of companies concerned in this chapter are foreign multinationals in the electronics industry. The factors that form the companies' preferences for relocation can be logically deduced from the conditions for the massive relocation of production by American multinationals of Silicon Valley in the 1970s (then Japanese companies in the 1980s), from the nature of the production of electronics, and knowing the circumstances surrounding these relocations. In fact when electronic technologies matured it allowed for a new logic of industrial production, although the market evolved in parallel and imposed — with the arrival of new Japanese and European competitors on the international market — research into new ways of gaining in productivity, a new form of spatial distribution of the functions of a company became technically possible.

It was the Californian electronics industry that first reached, under the auspices of competition, the limits of its working methods that had presided over its success and led to the search for better organisational innovation that would allow it to displace the assembly lines involving components and products. Additionally the assembly lines, work intensive, could be separated from the other steps of the production process and thus relocated. The preferences of companies, concerning location, are dependent on a series of different parametres that have not really been formulated in an extensive manner nor quantified, but which can give us certain elements:

A. The cost of labour must be low because it is a labour intensive industry that is established. In fact one of the principal reasons for the relocation of companies from Silicon Valley in the 1970s were serious problems linked to the lack of work because of the cost of labour;

B. For the same reason (it is a labour intensive industry) a weak trade union membership or even a strict limitation of social movements would be preferred.[33] More specifically the electronics sector was originally (in Silicon Valley from the 1950s) considered 'unorganisable' by American unions, whilst local employers judged that the sectors survival required the prolongation of this tendency.[34] But at the start of the 1970s in Silicon Valley, the sector suffered its first labour problems and its first successes in organising the

---

[33] G. Benko underlines, following A.L. Saxeinian (1981) the weak politicisation and lack of organisation and discontent from the employees in the electronics industry of the Californian Silicon Valley.

[34] For example the positions held by William Shockley, co-inventer of the transistor (Nobel Prize 1956) and at the origin of Silicon Valley, or Robert Noyce, co-founder of Intel: they both consider that this point is a determining question for the industry which would not be able to accept the conditions imposed by unions in other sectors (D. Bacon, 1999).

workforce (this primarily concerns semi-conductors: National Semiconductor, Fairchild, Siliconix, Siltec, Semimetals and others);

C. The training of the labour force is a secondary priority because assembly factories are being set-up above all;

D. Land prices have to be taken into account: the lack of available space made itself felt in the county of Santa Clara (Silicon Valley, California) and the price of land which had considerably risen in only a few years;

E. Taxes and excise duties must be low, firstly because the local market is not the target of the finished products, secondly many of the parts produced are components of other products, finally the production of these elements (semi conductors for example) require materials that are not available locally (silicium plaques in particular). Recalling the fact that the companies that chose to set up in Penang export the quasi-totality of their production: USA, Singapore, Japan, Taiwan and Hong Kong are the main destinations for these exports;

F. Transport costs are not a determining factor in the choice of location because the products are not difficult to transport (it is not uncommon for certain electronic components to be produced in Malaysia and then sent by plane to the workshops of the parent company where they undergo one or more delicate alterations before being sent back to Penang where they are assembled and then exported again);

G. Airport and seaport infrastructure are on the other hand essential.

In the following example the rationality of their behaviour is a substantive rationality that consists of adopting a maximising behaviour in a situation of complete information. 'Every company is kindly informed of the profits and returns — the actual net value of the establishment in each of the localizations — at the moment of their choosing, making the latter decision according to the maximum return of the location then going there.' (Arthur, 1990, p. 299). It is all about making the choice of location that maximises the return of the location being aware that the information that the individual has about his local environment is not only complete and perfect but remains so in the future: 'we put forward the hypothesis that the rhythm of entry of new companies is slow and that takes into account that the future is such that it is impossible to ignore questions of expectations and to assume that new companies decide to locate on sites that provide a maximisation of their current return.' (*ibid.*, p. 300). W.B. Arthur decides to remain vague over this rather confused issue, one cannot really talk about expectations[35] nor the failure of taking the future into account: in truth the model that was kept is a sequential model where the past locations are integrated into the decisions of companies to come (they have perfect knowledge), and where all the present and future intrinsic advantages of the different sites are known with absolute certitude.

Concerning the preferences, we can add that hypothetically, these are never saturated, as in neo-classical consumer theory of which it is a transposition: whatever the present interest of a place, if another offers more it will be preferred (for example if the tax rate is lower, then all things remaining equal, the advantages offered have increased).

However, the choices made are not undoable, we must reason in a sequential manner (companies arrive one after another, taking into account all the available information) on a potentially infinite number of companies. Yet having made their choice these companies then stick to it.

17.2.3 *Agglomeration Effect in Penang*

Here we will put forward the hypothesis that agglomeration effects are to be found in Penang, which can be defined simply as 'the benefits of being close to other firms.'[36] More exactly, the net advantage

---

[35] In 1991, P. Krugman proposed a model integrating expectations with the schemes of locating in 'History versus Expectation', *Quaterly Journal of Economics*, **106**.

[36] W.B. Arthur, 1988, 'Urban Systems and Historical Path Dependence,' p. 85. In this article, Arthur places the different case studies according to hazard or determination guiding the location and pushes the reasoning to its ends: a configuration of the spatial repartitioning of companies. These different possibilities were integrated into a single model in an article of 1990 that we will treat as central to the current reflections on this subject.

gained by a relocated company increases with the number of companies present in the area. We could think that the advantage has limits and that beyond a certain number of companies all present in a limited amount of space, saturation would soon be felt: the disadvantages of being close are therefore greater than advantages. In Penang during the period that we are concerned with (now passed), the agglomeration effects are limitless in the sense that the advantage of being there, increased by the arrival of a new company, will always be positive. The space occupied by the companies is not saturated particularly because the PDC responsible for the development of Penang controls land prices.

17.2.3.1 *The Sources of Agglomeration Effects in Penang*

There are numerous sources of these agglomeration effects: infrastructure, an increased labour market, the appearance of specialised financial and legal services, the presence of suppliers or local subcontractors (provision facilities, specific and generic), in social networks (where information, expertise, and contracts are easily available). Among these advantages to be concentrated in Penang we can already highlight some important achievements, gradually made over a period of time, with the aim of the construction or development of public goods that are beneficial to all: accompanying the successive arrival of companies, infrastructure, training and producing information have all developed on Penang site.

Notice the progressive improvement in infrastructure: since 1972, the date of the establishment of the first electronics companies in the Penang free zone, hundreds of hectares of land was cleared and assured by the PDC, the authority in charge for the development of Penang, a bridge linking the island and the Peninsula and in particular the industrial park which was built just opposite (September 1985): thus the points of access between companies, between residential areas and factories on the island have multiplied. Telephone lines and networks developed slowly followed by cable communication. For organising further education and training on the scale of the industrial site, the Penang Skill Development Centre (PSDC) was founded in 1989 on the initiative of electronics companies — above all American — and the help of the authorities. The pooling of materials and resources to make up for the insufficiencies of the workforce makes Penang a qualified success: the institution that was created developed and improved with the arrival of new members. The new members had new needs and thus introduced new training programmes. This achievement seems emblematic of agglomeration effects.

The information about the site itself goes through institutional channels with the publication of a monthly review by the PDC called the *Penang Development News*, and an annual publication of statistics on the local labour market, by sector and by zone (industrial or commercial). The powerful Malaysian entrepreneurial organisation, the Federation of Malaysian Manufacturers, set up in Penang and further developed the demand of training schemes and regularly publishes data and statistics for its members. Finally Penang very often hosts conferences and organises international trade fairs for the electronics industry.

17.2.4 *The Dynamics of Locating in Penang*

17.2.4.1 *Intrinsic Advantages and Chance Events Explaining the Choice of Malaysia at the Dawn of the 1970s*

Given the tastes of electronics companies those that have been already mentioned in the initial circumstances relative to the types of company, Penang had objective advantages at the end of the 1960s for this type of company and must have been preferred over lots of others on the simple basis of its intrinsic assets (its assets of *first nature*). However the problem posed by the application of B. Arthur's model goes much further, on the determination of the hierarchy of preferences concerning location for a given firm: what weight should be given to the different arguments over tastes? Undeniably it is more advantageous to locate to Penang than in the Western country (the countries of the OECD) in terms of labour costs, tax, and legal and social restrictions.

However, we have also said, certain essential elements like the cost of labour and the training of the workforce are not totally satisfactory on the site (in comparison to Thailand or Singapore). Therefore, among the elements that, for any given electronics firm, make Malaysia more advantageous, it is difficult to draw a clear line. The first relocations did not, in any case, affect Malaysia: they went to the NPI that had already made the conversion of an industry adapted to exportation. Singapore in particular created a free zone in 1967 and mainly attracted factories for assembly.

Table 17.9 shows that, in 1974 the advantages (both geographical and agglomerative) of Malaysia — concerning American companies at least — prevailed over other countries for 11 factories, in other words the biggest number of factories (the proportion is thus one quarter)

In 1985, the proportion (the geographical share in the words of B. Arthur) has (very) slightly dropped (because it is around 23%), but Malaysia remains the country that attracts American electronics facto ries more than the others. Our interpretation, in the light of the laws laid out by Arthur is that what happened in the first sequences (the arrival of factories in the industry before 1964) was insufficient to be able to determine what might happen in the future. On the other hand, the evolution from 1964 to 1974 leads to what follows: the country that dominated in 1974 continues to dominate in 1985. Thus,

Table 17.9:   American Assembly Lines in South East Asia.

Number of Factories	1964	1974	1985
HongKong	1	8	8
Indonesia	0	2	2
South Korea	1	9	5
Malaysia	0	11	14
Philippines	0	1	11
Singapore	0	9	11
Taiwan	0	3	8
Thaïland	0	1	4
	2	44	63

Source: Scott, 1987.

according to Arthur, one or more historical accidents took place during 1964 and 1974 to explain this deviation from the pattern of localisations from its original trajectory: 'When does history matter in the determination of industry location patterns? We can now answer this question, at least for the broad class of models that fits our general framework. History — that is, the small elements outside our economic model that we must treat as random — becomes the determining factor when there are multiple solutions or multiple fixed points in the proportions-to-probabilities mapping. Most intuitively, history counts when expected motions of region's shares do not always lead the location process toward the same share.' (p. 95).[37]

We will now explain what could be interpreted as historical accidents in the relocation of electronics industry in South-East Asia, defined as events that — at different stages of localisation — changed the course of events. We have conducted researched into Malaysian history as well as the world history of the electronics sector.

Chance event 1: Singapore which welcomed factories into its free zone in 1967 saw its unemployment rate reduced. A period of technological enrichment began: the government of Lee Kuan Yew decided to promote a technological and capital intensive industrialisation strategy, this forced (by imposing big salary increases) the factories to change their production processes or leave Singapore. The factories established in Singapore looked to relocate and neighbouring Malaysia seemed a good compromise.

Another risk of history, because it is based on the social evolution of a very specific sector, with no relation to Malaysian historical development, we can consider *Chance event 2*: At the end of the 1960s, American factories started to unionise, as we have already mentioned, and up until then the electronics sector had been sheltered from social movements. National Semiconductor and Fairchild[38] were amongst

---

[37] Arthur, 1988, *op. cit.*

[38] The Fairchild factory at Shiprock (New Mexico) was occupied by Indian militants during the 1960s: this event is often used as an example of the extreme difficulties encountered which justifies moving production centres to regions that are considered to be stable.

the first to be affected by the movement. Inconvenienced by the labour problems that they were confronted by in their own country, the argument of the social stability of a country — and its repression of trade unions whilst being encouraged by government in Singapore — plays a major role. They were amongst the first to decide to relocate to Penang.

17.2.4.2. Locating in Penang Rather than Somewhere Else: The Role of Chance and Path Dependency in Agglomeration Effects' Dynamic

'Yet in a way this is another definition of the presence of agglomeration economies: if above a certain density of settlement a region tends to attract further density, and if below it, it tends to lose density, there must be some agglomeration mechanism present. The underlying system will then be nonconvex and history will count.' (Arthur, 1998, p. 95).

It was in Penang that companies initially concentrated, by accident too, and that this area became the main attractor of new entrants to the industry over the years that followed, illustrating a process of path dependency. The companies that chose to go to Malaysia were actually established in a geographically concentrated manner within the country, in order to benefit from economies of agglomeration, without which the actual assets of the country would perhaps not have been sufficient to make it so attractive.

This is exactly what is illustrated by the Director General of Integrated Device Technology (Idt): this company, a producer of semi-conductors was created in the United States in 1980, and 'our first overseas subsidiary was established in Penang (in 1988), because it was a well-established place (the Penang Cluster). So we took no risks. And of course because of the labour force.'[39]

It was in Penang that this concentration took place. The first year clearly attracted more factories than Kuala Lumpur and amongst these establishments those of the most famous companies of Silicon Valley, no doubt more likely to be imitated and followed than others.

---

[39] Idt, Bayan Lepas interview (personal fieldwork, 1998).

Why then did they choose Penang and not the capital — with little difference in intrinsic assets? S. Lall admits that Penangs success was thanks to the necessary legitimate elements for industrialisation but 'in addition, there was a strong element of luck,'[40] this opportunity is what Brian Arthur calls chance. For us it is the fruit of historical *chance events* 3 and 4, which, from the outset, 'tipped the balance' in favour of Penang:

Chance event 3: The application of the NEP through the creation of free zones benfited from a local political willingness for economic reforms that seem circumstantial but totally deteminant. In 1969 a new Governor was elected (of Chinese origin, like almost all the Governors of Penang since its independence) who, faced with the economic ruin of the island, created the PDC, which was charged with running the land reforms and promoting Penang to investors. For this promotion, delegates of the Ministry for Industry and Trade (MITI where the Federal Industrial Development Authority comes from) and the Secretary of the PDC were sent to the United States to Santa Clara in Silicon Valley to visit the companies in the electronics sector and invite them to relocate to Penang. This local political willingness which reinforced the tax breaks already offered by the federal government was remarked upon by authors interested in the origins of the Penang site: one says that the representatives of the state in 1971 went 'knocking on the doors' of Californian companies.[41]

Finally there is the anecdote that those involved cannot help but recount and which has entered into local mythology as an element of pure chance that determined what followed. This we will call *Chance event* 4: It is said that the visitors to Penang, were very impressed when, at the end of a meal, Mr. Hewlett (of Hewlett-Packard)

---

[40] S. Lall, 1999, p. 30. This opportunity is to be found in the colonial inheritance of physical and legislative infrastructure, the geographical proximity of Singapore and the beginning of the industry coinciding with the boom in the assembly of semi-conductors.

[41] [Hill, 1988] quoted by Narayanan and Rasiah, 1992.

asked for the bill. A young waitress who was standing there pulled out a calculator from her pocket and announced the total. Hewlett, very surprised that calculators were used in that part of the world, asked her how she knew how to use the product so easily. She replied simply that even though the tool was relatively new, it was not very difficult to use if you knew how to work it. This facility of adapting to modern technology was taken as a good sign by the investors present who decided to establish their factories in Penang.

This well-known anecdote is attributed to Tun Dr. Lim Chong Eu, the Governor of Penang at the time. It is a classic in the sense that, according to Jean Saglio, the make believe of industrial districts always support myths about their origins.[42] This was told to us during interviews in the company and features in a special edition of the Penang Development News (1992) celebrating the 20th anniversary of the industrial site of Penang.

The following years (1973–1974) saw certain choices taken and put into effect before the first establishment of companies materialised and chose a distribution that was roughly equal between the two sites. A second wave of companies wanting to setup in the area arrived in the 1980s, all centred on Penang, all the more so as Japanese and Taiwanese factories chose this moment to relocate to Penang and they too had a number of important achievements. The electronics companies, inexistent in the 1970s, were more than a hundred strong in Penang from the 1990s. 'It seems that an attractive localisation will benefit at the start of the process from favours given by a number of companies, which reinforces the likelihood that they will occupy a dominant position. The initial attractiveness and the way historical accidents interact with the order of company choice determine the result.'[43]

During this 25 year period production at Penang has almost multiplied by a factor of 10, surpassing (at stable rates) US$1350 million in 1970 to US$12,100 million in 1997 and the industrial sector accounts for the majority of this, from 13% to 53% over the same

---

[42] Saglio, 1997.
[43] Arthur, 1990, *op.cit.*, p. 307.

Table 17.10: Factory Statistics at PDC Areas 1970–2002 (All Industries).

Year	Factories	Employment
1970	31	2,784
1980	216	56,012
1990	430	100,953
1996	736	196,774
1998	725	188,591
1999	715	191,565
2000	693	192,241
2001	746	172,596
2002	731	150,080

Source: Survey, PDC, 2006.

period. The earnings per head in Penang have been multiplied by 6 in 20 years, going from RM1747 in 1970 (around US$700) to RM248 in 1991 (US$3700).

17.3 Penang, Malaysia: Your Dynamic Partner

The very term of cluster is used by the Malaysian Minister for Industry as meaning an 'agglomeration of inter-related activities, including principal industrial production, suppliers, company services, the infrastructure and necessary accompanying institutions and the undertaking of the principal activity'.[44]

Many sectors are identified by the Minister as being the groups of activity that are likely to create clusters in the next few years,[45] but only electronics is considered as already being one. A geographical

---

[44] The definition used in the Second Industrial Malaysian Plan, 1996–2005 *(IMP2)* which aims to orientate the efforts of industrialsation to come along less sectorial lines and instead on traversal lines, synergising complementary activities by using exisiting geographical opportunities (IMP2, Chapter 2).

[45] There are eight regroupings of industrial sectors: E&E, transport, chemistry, textiles, industry based on natural resources, base materials, agrarian, machine-tools and supplies.

Table 17.11:   Examples of Established Electronics Companies.

Source of Agglomeration Effects		Examples of Established Electronics Companies	N*
PDC founded	1969	Clarion (Japan, 20 workers, audio systems)	0
USM founded	1970		
(Universiti Sains Malaysia)		National	2
First building of the electronics factory at Bayan Lepas, first factories established		Semiconductor (USA, 120 workers, integrated circuit)	
		Litronix (USA, diodes, Then Siemens Penang)	
Creation of the first Frre Trade Zone (FTZ) of the country: Bayan Lepas	1972	Robert Bosch (RFA, 29 workers, cameras)	7
		Intel (USA, 2 ha, 100 wrokers, live memory)	
		AMD Advanced Micro Devices (USA, 150 workers)	
		Hewlett Packard (USA, 60 workers, central memory)	0
		Fairchild (USA)	
	1973	Robert Bosch integrates a design department	8
Construction of the Penang International Airport		Motorola (USA, telecommunications:	
	1975	products and electronic components)	
		ENG (local company)	
Modernisation of Port Butterworth	1975		17
	1980		23
Penang Bridge between the island and Wellesley province	1985		38
	1988	Applied Magnetics (USA, all types of head and magnetic components)	
		Integrated Device Technology (USA, integrated circuits)	

(Continued)

Table 17.11:   (*Continued*)

Source of Agglomeration Effects		Examples of Established Electronics Companies	N*
		Seagate Industries (USA, production, assembly and testing of thin films)	
		Thomson CSF (France, varistors)	
	1989	Acer (Taiwain, keybords)	
PSDC (training centre)		Sony (Japan, audio)	
		Canon (Japan, printers)	
	1990	Sammatech, local subcontractor of Intel	91
HRDF (Human Resource	1991	ASE (Taiwan)	
Dept Funds)	1992	Alcatel (France, circuits breakers)	129
	1993	Siantronics, local subcontractor of HP	
	1994	Readrite (hard disks)	
	1995	Dell Asia Pacific	
	1996		
	1997		160
	Asian Crisis		
	1999		157
	2001		
	(Dot-com bubble)		
	2002		164

*Run by the PCD.

presentation of this new element structuring local development looks at the regional repartition of industrial activity and highlights Penang as welcoming the largest concentration of companies and jobs in the sector electronics and electrics.

The production in Penang is concentrated essentially on basic electronic components and the assembly of household electrical products: this destined for re-export to production sites and the distribution centres of the parent companies. Therefore the Malaysian's transition in the direction of high technology through industrial exports is clearly more noticeable. The gross electronics production of Malaysia (assembly of semi-conductors, household goods and telecommunication systems) amounts to RM26 billion — 56% of exported manufactured goods in 1990 (Bank Negara Malaysia, 1991). At the beginning of the 21st century Malaysia is still one of the largest producers and exporters of electronics in the world. The labour force employs a majority of women on the production lines: the theoretical debates continue whether the predominance of women being employed by multinationals in the Third World is due to their manual dexterity or the docile natures because in fact women are less political and less involved in union movements than men, which goes back to the factors affecting companies preferences.

The official message in brochures published by the Penang Development Centre allows us to re-examine the reasons, thirty years later, that explain the presence of multinationals still operating there and the arrival of new companies. This presentation (self promoting but sometimes nuanced) confirms the arguments that were given during our interviews,[46] and those that another study conducted in 91 companies relocated in the region also highlighted.[47]

17.3.1 *A Peaceful and Stable Political Climate that Ensures Coherent Long-term Policies*

The argument of political stability put forward by the Malaysian authorities seems somewhat cynical when one recalls the arrest of the Deputy Prime Minister, Anwar Ibrahim, the Finance Minister of Mahathir and the Interim Prime Minister during the absence of the

---

[46] Personal fieldwork.

[47] S. Natarajan and T.J. Miang, *Impact of MNCs Investment in Malaysia, Singapore and Thailand*, ASEAN Economic Research Unit, Institute of Southeast Asian Studies, 1992. This last work, led by Natarajan and Miang without any theoretical pretensions, only allows investors to have an overview of the advantages and dis-advantages of the three countries that were studied: Malaysia, Singpore and Thaïland.

latter in 1998. Mahathir's disciple was sent to prison without trial by the Prime Minister — who also has the powers of Minister for the Interior. The trials for corruption and immorality that finished in this imprisonment do not bear witness to the impartiality of Malaysian justice.[48] During his incarceration the ex-deputy Prime Minister completed his 6-year sentence for contempt of court and then had to stay for another 9 years for sodomy.[49] Finally acquitted of this charge in July 2004, he left prison, but remained ineligible for re-election for 5 years. Malaysian law allows for imprisonment without trial under the *Internal Security Act* (ISA).

This 'political stability' is also part of social stability, implied in words and proven in reality. This we can consider is assured in Penang by the mass employment of female workers in assembly factories (80% to 100% of operators are women).[50] The idea of a clear preference for female workers due to their docile nature and reduced propensity for complaining or even rebelling is one debate amongst authors concerned with gender studies and questions of development.[51]

---

[48] The bribing of witnesses is the least of the problems of this trial, regardless of attempts to modernise and the political maturity of Malaysian society as a whole, according to the opinions of local observers and foreign journalists.

[49] Judgement, 8 August 2000.

[50] Type of occupational rank and salary scale are clearly not the same for men and women. In Japanese companies in Penang, on 1030 workers, 806 are unskilled operators. Among them, the 5 men are paid 3.75–4.80 RM/day while the normal salary scale for women is 3.50–4.00 RM/day. But 224 of them are 'temporary operators' at 3.10/day according to A. Ong, 'Japanese Factories, Malay workers: Class, and Sexual Metaphors in West Malaysia', in J. Monning Atkinson and S. Errington (eds.), *Power and Difference: Gender in Island Southeast Asia*, Stanford University Press, 1990, pp. 385–425.

[51] See for instance: Elson, Person: 'The Subordination of Labour and the Internationalisation of Factory Production', in K. Young, C. Wolkowitz and R. McCullagh (eds.), *Of Marriage and the Market*, Routledge, London, 1984; C. Enloe. 'Women Textile Workers in the Militarization of Southeast Asia' in J. Nash and M.P. Fernández Kelly, *Women, Men, and the International Division of Labour*, SUNY Press, New York, 1983; L. O'Brien, 'Four Paces behind: Women Works in Peninsular Malaysia', in L. Manderson (ed.), *Women's Work and Women's Roles: Economics and Everyday Life in Indonesia, Malaysia, and Singapore*, ANU Press, Canberra, 1983.

17.3.2 *An Active and Responsible Government that Involves the Private Sector in the Formulation of Economic Policies*

This argument is founded because no one can deny that political willingness, from which large companies have greatly benefited, and which led to the development of Penang.[52] This argument was developed in the preceding section on the system of national innovation and the role of public institutions, in concertation with the private sector (within the Malaysian Business Council), on the technological development strategy.

17.3.3 *Attractive Tax Incentives for Urgent Project*

Penang is still qualified today as a *tax free heaven*.[53] Since 1970, the tax breaks have been increased in terms of the activities that are favoured and in the Penang area. For example the status of pioneer covering the first five years of activity is then prolonged by the status of 'post-pioneer'. Prioritised projects include 54 activities and products of the Electronics and Electrics industry covered by the law of 1986 on encouraging investment (Pioneer Status and Investment Tax Allowance). Then there are the zones in the Penang State area, which were partly set up as part of the Free Zone for trade (FTZ, from 1972), which became free industrial zones in 1990 (FIT). There are therefore three free trade zones and four industrial zones. These zones are covered by companies in the stage of successive phases of development, as long as the available land in the zone is not

---

[52] Cf. the preamble of Roger Bertelson, president of the Malaysian American Electronics Industry (MAEI), in the annual report 1994–1995.

[53] Which an American company located in Penang today says with enthusiasm at the top of its web site. It is the number one argument mentioned by companies according to all recent inquiries (whether it is ours or someone elses. Cf. D. Eiteman, 'Multinational Firms and the Development of Penang, Malaysia', *International Trade Journal*, 11(2), 1997, pp. 169–170; S. Natarajan and T.J. Miang, *Impact of MNCs Investment in Malaysia, Singapore and Thailand*. ASEAN Economic Research Unit, Institute of Southeast Asian Studies, 1992.

exhausted: the free trade zones concern Bayan Lepas, Prai, Mankin, Seberan Jaya, Bukit Minyat. However concerning importations of raw materials, since 1990, the companies having been in Penang for more than three years have to use local materials for 50% of their intermediary consumption in order to keep certain tax breaks.

17.3.4 *An Efficient Distribution Network, in Fact the Point of Entry to the Markets of the ASEAN*

Since 1992, ASEAN (of which Malaysia is a member) envisaged creating a regional free trade zone. AFTA (Asean Free Trade Area), created on 1 January 1993 is the first step towards economic integration within ASEAN with the aim of reinforcing the choice of establishing foreign companies in the region. The forecasted date for the application of free trade agreements is 2003. The country has the aim of the reinforcement of regional economic (and political) cooperation which includes the 'growth triangle: Indonesia-Malaysia-Thailand' within which Penang occupies a special role.[54] Therefore, it should be more advantageous for multinationals today as, in a few years time being located in Penang for exports and imports the perspectives of new markets being opened will continue to increase. This will also become easier due to the improvements in infrastructure.

17.3.5 *A High Quality Personalised Service for Companies Offered by the Penang Development Corporation (PDC), Internationally Recognised*

Little by little it is the interface between the industrial site of Penang and foreign investors, which imposes its own logic and demands. Today the PDC is orientated towards a consultancy service for investors. It received its ISO 9001 certificate for design and development of industrial commercial and residential properties in 1999.

---

[54] On the multiplication of regional commercial relationships of Malaysia and on the political policy in which this strategy is grounded, see D.Camroux: 'The Asia-Pacific Policy Community in Malaysia', *Pacific Review*, 7(4), 1994, pp. 421–433.

However, despite a more rationalised economic activity, the annual *PDC 1999* report continues to attribute its projects in favour of the Malay community for entirely political reasons. It has also developed an ITC service for companies.

17.3.6 *A Local Network of Suppliers for Hi-Tech Multinationals*

In fact, at the end of the 1990s local small and medium sized businesses auxiliary to multinationals in all domains (subcontracting, packaging, repairs, metallurgy) are innumerable: the institutions in charge of local development have barely started to include them in their own development projects and to index them via the PDC.[55] According to the numbers given for the 2000 small and medium sized businesses in Penang, we estimate that 90% of them are in auxiliary sectors of plastics and metallurgy.[56] This local network of local subcontractors and suppliers of multinationals was created, from the particular case of old metallurgy workshops and constitutes the examples of the creation of local subcontracting companies.[57]

Typically this network was inexistant in 1970 when the first foreign companies arrived; this is an argument that results in the local concentration of multinationals. Finally we note that this grouping of small local companies has not been helped at all by the local authority nor by the PDC, quite the opposite in fact.

17.3.7 *A Disciplined, Well-Trained English-Speaking Workforce*

We will examine three successive arguments concerning labour in Penang. Firstly, the workforce is disciplined. It is remarkably true; we

---

[55] The company listing in Penang published by the PDC in 1997 records exactly 686 companies but the authors recognise that the list is far from exhaustive.

[56] Source: interview with Mr. Rivzal Fauzi, director of the PME and PDC, July 1998.

[57] D. Borsutzky, 'The Transformation of the Informal Sector in Penang, Malaysia: The Case of Small Scale Metal-Working Enterprises', *Internationales Asienforum*, **23**(3–4), 1992, pp. 245–259.

need not go back over the restrictions on union freedoms that exist in the country, those that we described in 1970. More than 20 years later, the countryside has remained unchanged, more so than any form of dissent which seems to have foundered during the years of the state of emergency and the restrictions on the freedom of speech. Regarding the subject that concerns us, unions are still absent from the free trade zone and, unlike Thailand, in 1997 there was still no minimum wage. The point reference for union-employer relations is still the law of 1967 relative to industrial relations that limits the demands from unions to the labour law of 1955.[58] The last twenty-five years of industrialisation have not changed anything in this respect.

Only the number of registered unions in the country has slowly increased (see Table 17.12), but this evolution does not affect the electronics industry.[59] The engagement of the government via the MIDA to contain trade union movements can legitimately appear credible to foreign investors. For companies constant efforts are maintained to diffuse any problems and in particular to offer non-salary advantages. If multinationals get by relatively easily,[60] it is far more difficult on the other hand for small local subcontractors to do so.

Table 17.12:   Number of Registered Unions in Malaysia.

1965	1970	1980	1985	1992	1996
286	237	369	369	489	516

Source: Aminuddin, 1990; Labour & HR Statistics, 1992–1996.

---

[58] M. Aminuddin, *Malaysian Industrial Relations*, MacGraw Hill, London, 1990.

[59] Many believe that unions are illegal in this sector which is not true.

[60] Beyond the creation of concrete advantages that can be offered by companies employing a large number of workers (crèches, bus services, medical insurance...), the directors of human resources have been inspired by american multinationals particularly by motivational training and group activities developped in the United States during the 1980s, in order to cater for the psychological needs of workers while strictly avoiding any dimension of ecomonic and political opinion.

Additionally this workforce will be well trained: at the levels of initial training, schooling, professional training or university education it should be noted that Malaysia is not in an advantageous position compared with its Asian neighbours. In fact even if the population of the education system has increased, secondary education has not been generalised as only 57% of children in the age range are schooled.[61] Finally further and higher education has remained strictly and narrowly limited in its expansion by law and the system of ethnic quotas. Despite the development of oversea education (1/3 of Malaysian students go abroad to foreign universities or colleges) which clearly distinguishes the higher education of Malaysians from other students in Asia, the country remains far behind its neighbours from this point of view (see Table 17.13).

In 2004, the enrolment rate at tertiary level is 7.9%.[62] That said, compared to 1970, we can affirm that globally the average level of education is much higher if we measure the proportion of adults

Table 17.13: Level of Schooling in Tertiary Education.

	Level of Schooling in Tertiary Education			Professional Teaching
	Tertiary Education (Total Enrolment)	Science and Applied Science	Engineering	
	(Enrolment Rate)	% of Total Population		
Malaysia	7% (10% with overseas)	0.15	0.07	0.017
Thaïland	16	0.16	0.09	0.80
Taiwan	37	0.92	0.60	2.12
South Korea	40	0.96	0.58	1.93
Japan	31	0.43	0.37	1.17

Source: UNESCO, 1994.

---

[61] Source: World Bank, *World Development Indicators*, 1997.
[62] Economic Planning Unit, 'Selected Social Indicators' in *Economic Indicators*, www.epu.jpm.my, p. 8.

Table 17.14: Literacy Level.

Country	Literacy Level (1996) (%)	GNP/Head (US$, 1995)
Japan	99	39,640
Singapore	91	26,730
HongKong	92	22,990
South Korea	99	9700
Malaysia	83	3890
Thaïland	94	2740
Philippines	95	1050
Indonesia	84	980
China	81	620

Source: World Bank 1997.

being able to read and write (literate) in Malaysia in 1996, even though the country does not keep the same level with regards to its GNP/inhabitant (see Table 17.14).

The training of the workforce has therefore greatly improved in Malaysia, with the creation of the HRDF (the Human Resources Development Fund), in 1993 and obligatory company funding for further education and training. The principle is that of the levy-grant which is a constraint and an incentive: the funding is fixed at 1% of pay-roll and pays for an increased percentage of the costs of further training and education that the company requires — up to 1% of the total pay-roll. This training takes place in centres that must be financed by the funding so that the reimbursement can take place. The improvement of further education and training and the extent to which this phenomenon is taken are even more significant for Penang where the PSDC — which was immediately approved by the HRDC in 1993 — has trained an increasing number of workers in techniques and skills that are particularly useful in the Penang basin since 1993, moreover, because the companies themselves define what should be taught.[63]

---

[63] If, originally, the central aim was to train electronics workers in multinationals, the training has started to be opened little by little to other sectors and to local subcontractors. This was not really the case until 1993 with the help of further education funding.

The workforce's familiarity with English is however not quite so good: in fact the old capital gave Malaysia a certain advantage from this point of view in comparison to Thailand where the majority of production line workers have no knowledge of English. However measures taken in the 1970s to unite the nation via Malay has led English to be removed from the school and university syllabus.

So, company heads complain of the low level of English among the Malaysian workers. The research conducted by S. Natarajan and Tan Juay Miang in 1991 covering around a hundred CEOs of multi-nationals in Malaysia, Thailand and Singapore shows that concerning workers the problem that was most often cited in Malaysia was the lack of English amongst Malay graduates: 'Because local institutions use Bahasa Malaysia as the medium of instruction, local graduates lack proficiency in English. This hampers their ability to absorb new technology fully and slows down the process of technology transfer from the MNCs.'[64] Thus this advantage — if it really exists in comparison to Thailand or even more with less developed countries like China, Vietnam or Burma — is very limited compared to the population of Singapore, which has kept English as an official language. The authors of the study added that multinationals had to sometimes ask for technical assistance from Singapore or their own countries because of the weakness of Malaysian graduates.

Finally we should underline the role of this argument concerning the initial training of the workforce in Penang is relative, even in the opinion of entrepreneurs themselves, to the choice of where to establish. We must remember that the electronics industry at Penang is above all a labour intensive industry even in 2000.

17.3.8 *Excellent Infrastructure, Amenities and Telecommunication for Present and Future Demand*

This is the result of a serious effort made by the PDC over the last 30 years. The question of infrastructure is typical to geography, above

---

[64] S. Natarajan and T.J. Miang, *Impact of MNCs Investment in Malaysia*, 1992, p. 31.

all in economic geography: the existence of a port is often considered a condition for the establishment and development of industries founded on trade. In Penang the traditional trading port has become the modern site for the loading and unloading of containers (16 piers, 9 derricks and 16.7 million tons of waste in 1995): the industrial port of Penang, situated at Butterworth (Wellesley Province) is the second largest seaport of the country today. A container terminal was constructed which saw the volume of transport more than double during the 1990s (from 222.4 tons in 1990 to 566.4 tons in 1999). Infrastructure also includes roads (more than 3000 km, of which only 3% are not tarmac in comparison to the national average of 43%). Since 1985, the state of Penang was linked up by a 13.5 km long bridge (Penang Bridge) which links the island — from the north of the FTZ Bayan Lepas — to the Peninsula at the Free Zone of Prai which has greatly developed.

The Penang international airport was built to the south of Bayan Lepas. Since then it has become the second major airport in the country (after Kuala Lumpur) and transports 2.5 million passengers per year and 14,451 million tons of goods, 93% of which are destined for overseas (Source: PSDC, 1999).

Finally the provision of running water and electricity, which for so long has not worked in the rest of the country, is fully functional in Penang. Since 1995 running water provision covers 100% of the entire territory of the state of Penang (i.e., rural and urban areas: national average 89%) Nevertheless companies complain about its quality (a little too acid for the production of semi-conductors). That said, it is the supply of electricity that is a recurrent source of discontent for multinationals: they have had to depend largely on individual generators, due to bad quality and irregular current.

17.3.9 *A Good Standard of Living, Facilities for Housing, Health, Education and Leisure Activities*

Penang, called the 'Pearl of the Orient' for its charm as attested to by oldest luxury hotel of the country, the Eastern and Oriental Hotel, has attracted Westerners for a long time. Today it offers the best hospital cover[65] and supports a number of educational institutions for expatriate children: the Dalat School (American course), St Christopher Primary School (English), Penang Japanese School, Penang Taiwanese School, international college Upland Scholl and three secondary schools English or Australian: Penang International College, Disted College and the Adorna College (run by the Royal Melbourne Institute of Technology).[66]

Finally, the last praise must go to the facilities available for someone to stay; it should be known that in Penang as in Kuala Lumpur luxurious and pretentious building called condominiums were constructed for expatriate workers, complete with swimming pools and shopping centres,[67] tennis and badminton courts. The rent, incomparable to normal rents, makes these apartments a sign of wealth to which the new Malay bourgeois businessmen aspire.

17.4 Conclusion

Even today Penang remains an attractive and extremely dynamic industrial site. The local political willingness to support companies continues (via services to companies in particular in the area of ICT). Recognising the importance of biotechnology, the Penang government has also launched a biotechnology initiative to attract investment and research activities to the state in anticipation of the world market for biotech industries hitting US$1.76 trillion by 2010. The state is adopting a three-pronged strategy encompassing marine biotech research works, bio-ICT development and biotech education.[68]

---

[65] If we add together the number of beds in public hospitals and private clinics, the state of Penang has 3374 beds, the biggest number of beds for a state after Kuala Lumpur (4328). Therefore, although the population Penang only accounts for a fifth of the total population, this state has 10% public hospital beds and 18% of beds in private clinics.

[66] In this area, Penang is the only state to have one *L'Alliance Française* except Kuala Lumpur.

[67] 'Modern and convenient shopping complexes with a wide range of imported foodstuff are readily available' (PDC, 1997, p. 17).

[68] PDC, 2006.

Table 17.15:   Approved Manufacturing Projects.

Year	Approved Projects	Employment	Capital Invest./ RM Million
1990	132	24,952	1867
1995	89	13,779	1525
1997	90	9736	1606
2000	132	15,327	1449
2001	124	14,630	3837
2002	110	13,487	2398
2003	137	9890	1923
2004	144	9235	2030
2005	148	21,904	4808

Source: SERI 2006.

Penang's attractiveness has been sustained during the 8th Malaysian Plan (2001–2005): Penang (after Selangor and Johor) remained as the major choice of location of both domestic and foreign investment; A total of 4807 manufacturing projects was approved (663 in Penang) with a proposed capital investment of RM132.4 billion of which RM15 billion (US$4.3 billion) or 11% for Penang with a potential employment of 70,000 people (16% of total potential employment).[69] (See Table 17.15.)

As a Malaysian laboratory of growth, Penang has also had a modernising influence in Malaysia:

— From the point of view of links between universities and companies.
— In terms of training personnel and labour law.
— In terms of society, with rural Malaysian women working in industry, and through the distribution of income.[70]

---

[69] Source: MIDA, in *9th Malaysian Plan* (2006–2010), pp. 17–18.

[70] Ong, 'The Production of Possession: Spirits and the Multinational Corporation in Malaysia', *American Ethnologist*, 15(1), 1988, pp. 28–42.

— In terms of lifestyle and spending habits of expatriate and local workers (condominiums, etc.) who have progressively joined the heart of the more or less wealthy, emerging middle-class in the 1990s–2000.[71]

But what about salaries?

The principal reason attracting companies to Penang in 1970 is no longer discussed today. In reality the advantage of the wage differential has all but disappeared. Local salaries have risen over the years, whilst numerous countries in the region under communist regimes in the 1970s have started to open their economies to foreign capital and are offering even lower wages. (See Table 17.16).

According to G. Rajasekaran, Secretary General of the Malaysian Trade Union Congress, Malaysian wages are today one third of Singapore's and Indonesian are one third of Malaysian's.[72] If we try

Table **17.16:** Wages Levels. Comparison Between South East Asian Countries.

Country	Average Monthly Earnings (US$, 1992)
Malaysia	137
Philippines	118
China	45
Indonesia	25
Vietnam	20

Source: S. Lall, 1999.

---

[71] R. Robison and David S.G. Goodman (eds), *The New Rich in Asia: Mobile Phones, McDonald's and Middle-Class Revolution*, Routledge London, 1996; Peter Searle: *The Riddle of Malaysian Capitalism: Rent-Seekers or Real Capitalists?* Allen & Unwin, St Leonards, 1999 or the more recent Abdul Rahman Embong, *State-Led Modernization and the New Middle Class in Malaysia*, Palgrave, New York, 2002.

[72] 'Tripartite Forum on the Tripartite Declaration of Principles concerning Multinational Enterprises and Social Policy (MNE Declaration)', ILO, Geneva, 2002.

Table 17.17:   Education, Literacy Rate, R&D/GDP and RSE. Comparison Between South East Asian Countries.

	Education Index	Literacy Rate (%)	R&D/GDP (%)	RSE
Malaysia	0.76	83.50	0.40	1
Penang	0.88	93.10		
Singapore	0.83	91.10	1.50	60
Philippines	0.9	94.60	0.10	1
Thailand	0.81	93.80	0.20	2
China	0.76	81.50	0.60	5
Korea	0.93	98.00	2.80	26

Sources: UNPD, 1999; Lall, 1999 (mid 90s data).

to compare it with other Southeast Asian emerging countries, the wages in industry in Malaysia remain weaker than elsewhere, but in Penang or Kuala Lumpur, the pressure created by turn-over and the progressive saturation of the labour market have led to an increase in salaries despite the recourse to immigrant labourers (only multinationals have the right to recruit them). The low wage levels that have encouraged relocations are however found in countries that were previously communist; the labour market of Malaysia has saturated progressively concerning unskilled workers.

Its technological trajectory remains limited by institutional and national restraints: the limits that have been encountered concerning the labour force, either in terms of quantity or training, limited the prospect of further industrial progress at the end of the 1990s. In fact Malaysia has made itself prisoner of a perverse education policy and a mediocre national system of innovation,[73] and it would appear that Penang has not managed to free itself at all from these restraints.

Therefore Penang, the laboratory of Malaysian growth, seems stuck on a technological trajectory that will not enable it to progress

[73] E. Lafaye de Micheaux, *Education et croissance en Malaisie, étude d'un lien fragile,* Dijon, unpublished PhD thesis, 2000; K.S. Jomo and G. Felker, *Technology, Competitiveness and the State: Malaysia's Industrial Technology Policies,* Routledge, New York, 1999.

to the next level where Singapore preceded it a long time ago.[74] The assembly and testing of semi-conductors must progressively be replaced by the production of components, especially when taking into account the increase in wages and the value of local real estate, the increased regional competition following the opening of Vietnamese markets and the accelerated development of China. The initial advantages that have been enjoyed have now largely changed, even been lost. The effects of agglomerations, evident at Penang, will they be enough to maintain the interest of foreign investors for relocation? The industrial, technological and social importance of the cluster for Malaysia as a whole is such that we can but hope so.

References

AMINUDDIN, M. (1990). *Malaysian Industrial Relations,* (London: MacGraw Hill).

ARTHUR, W.B. (1990). Silicon Valley locational clusters: when do increasing returns imply monopoly?, *Mathematical Social Sciences,* 19, pp. 235–251.

ARTHUR, W.B. (1988). Urban systems and historical path dependence in ANSUBEL, J. and ATKINSON, J., ERRINGTON, S. (eds). (1990). *Power and Difference: Gender in Island Southeast Asia,* (Stanford U. Press).

HERMAN, R. (cds), *Cities and their Vital Systems,* (NAP, Washington).

BENKO, G. (1991). *Géographie des Technopôles,* (Paris, Masson).

BLAKE, M. (1984). *Participation of Female Factory Workers in Voluntary Associations: Electronics Factory Workers in Malaysia and Thailand.* Ph.D Thesis, Universiti Sains Malaysia, Penang.

BORSUTZKY, D. (1992). The transformation of the informal sector in Penang, Malaysia: The case of small scale metal-working enterprises, *Internationales Asienforum,* 23(3–4), pp. 245–259.

CAMROUX, D. (1994). The Asia-Pacific policy community in Malaysia, *The Pacific Review,* 7(4), pp. 421–433.

---

[74] This diagnostic is shared by many researchers since the end of 1990s. A. Ong Cheng Imm, 'Penang's Manufacturing Competitiveness', *Briefing to the Penang State Governement,* 2000; R. Rasiah, 'Human Resources and FDI with a Focus on Electronics and Garment Industries (Malaysia)', *WB Report,* 2005, p. 45.

CROUCH, H. (1996). *Government and Society in Malaysia*, (London: Cornell U. Press).

EITEMAN, D. (1997). Multinational firms and the development of Penang, Malaysia, *International Trade Journal*, 11(2), pp. 169–170.

EMBONG, A.R. (2002). *State-led Modernization and the New Middle Class in Malaysia*, (New York: Palgrave).

ENLOE, C. (1983). Women textile workers in the militarization of Southeast Asia in NASH, J., KELLY, M. P. Fernández. *Women, Men, and the International Division of Labor*, (New York: SUNY Press).

HEMPEL, C.G. (1942). The function of general laws in history, *Journal of Philosophy*, 39, pp. 231–243.

JOMO, K.S. (1987). *A Question of Class, Capitalism, the State and Uneven Development in Malaysia*, (Singapour: Oxford University Press).

JOMO, K.S., FELKER G. (1999). *Technology, Competitiveness and the State: Malaysia's Industrial Technology Policies*, (New York: Routledge).

KARUNARATNA N.D., ADBULLAH, M.B. (1978). Incentive Schemes and Foreign Investment in the Industrialization of Malaysia, *Asian Surve*, 18(3), pp. 261–264.

KRUGMAN, P. (1993). First nature, second nature and metropolitan location, *Journal of Regional Science*, 33(2), pp. 129–144.

KRUGMAN, P. (1991). History versus expectation, *Quarterly Journal of Economic*, 106, pp. 651–667.

KRUGMAN, P. (1991). Increasing Returns and Economic Geography, *Journal of Political Economy*, 99(3), pp. 483–499.

KRUGMAN, P. (1988). Space: the final frontier, *Journal of Economic Perspectives*, 12 (2), pp. 161–174.

DE MICHEAUX E, Lafaye. (2000). *Education et croissance en Malaisie, étude d'un lien fragile*, unpublished PhD thesis (Dijon).

DE MICHEAUX E, Lafaye, Mulot, E., Ould-Ahmed P. (2007). *Institutions et développement*, (Rennes: Presses Universitaires de Rennes).

LALL, S. (1999). Technology policy and competitiveness in Malaysia, in JOMO, K.S., FELKER, G., *Technology, Competitiveness and the State: Malaysia's Industrial Technology Policies*, (New York: Routledge).

Malaysia. (1991–2000). *Penang Strategic Development Plan*.

Malaysia. (2001–2005). Economic Planning Unit (EPU), *8th Malaysian Plan*.

Malaysia. (2006–2010). Economic Planning Unit (EPU), *9th Malaysian Plan*.

Malaysia. (2006). Economic Planning Unit (EPU), Economic Indicators.

Malaysia. (1970–1971). Federal Industrial Development Authority (FIDA), *Malaysia, the 'Solid State' for Electronics: an Invitation to Invest*.

Malaysia. (1996–2005). *Second Industrial Malaysian Plan*.

MINGAT, A., TAN, J.P. (1992). *Education in Asia: A Comparative Study of Cost and Financing*, World Bank, Regional and Sectoral Studies.

MYRDAL, G. (1968). *Asian Drama: Enquiry into the Poverty of Nations* (Harmondswork: Penguin Books).

NARAYANAN, S., RASIAH, R. (1992). Malaysian electronics: the changing prospects for employment and restructuring, *Development and Change*, **23**(4), pp. 75–99.

NARAYANAN, S.,WAH, L.Y. (1995). Human resource constraints on technology transfer: the electronics and electrical sector in Penang, Malaysia, *Singapore Economic Review*, **38**(2), pp. 155–165.

NARAYANAN, S., WAH, T.Y. (1999). Sources of technology inflow to Malaysia: U.S. firms versus Japanese firms in Jomo and Felker, *Technology, Competitiveness and the State.*

NATARAJAN, S., MIANG, T.J. (1992). *Impact of MNCs Investment in Malaysia, Singapore and Thailand*, ASEAN Economic Research Unit, Institute of Southeast Asian Studies.

O'BRIEN, L. (1983). Four paces behind: women works in peninsular Malaysia in MANDERSON, L. (ed.), *Women's Work and Women's Roles: Economics and Everyday Life in Indonesia, Malaysia, and Singapore*, (Canberra: ANU Press).

ONG, A. Japanese factories, Malay workers: class, and sexual metaphors in West Malaysia in MONNING, J., ATKINSON, S.

ONG, A. (1988). The production of possession: spirits and the multinational corporation in Malaysia, *American Ethnologist*, **15**(1), pp. 28–42.

ONG, Cheng Imm (2000) *Penang's manufacturing competitiveness, Briefing to the Penang State Government.*

PERSON, E. (1984). The subordination of labour and the internationalisation of factory production in YOUNG, K , WOLKOWITZ, C., MCCULLAGH, R. (eds), *Of Marriage and the Market*, (London: Routledge).

RASIAH, R. (2005). Human resources and FDI with a focus on electronics and garment industries (Malaysia), *WB Report*, p. 45.

ROBISON, R., DAVID, S., GOODMAN, G. (eds). (1996). *The New Rich in Asia: Mobile Phones, McDonald's and Middle-class Revolution*, (London: Routledge).

SAGLIO, J. (1997). Local industry and actor's strategies: form combs to plastics in Oyonnax in SABEL, C., ZEITLIN, J. (eds), *World of Possibilities: Flexibility and Mass production in Western Industrialisation*, (Cambridge: Cambridge U. Press), pp. 419–160.

SAXENIAN, A.L. (1996). Beyond boundaries: open labor markets and learning in Silicon Valley in ARTHUR, W.B. (dir.), *Beyond Boundaries*, pp. 23–39.

SEARLE, P. (1999). *The Riddle of Malaysian Capitalism: Rent-seekers or Real Capitalists?* (St Leonards: Allen & Unwin).

Southeast Asia. (1990). (Stanford U. Press), pp. 385–425.

SCOTT, A.J. (1987). The semiconductor industry in South-East Asia organization, location and the international division of labour, *Regional Studies*, **21**, pp. 143–160.

UNCTAD. (1975). International subcontracting arrangements in electronics between developed market-economy countries and developing countries, *UNCTAD Report,* (New York: ONU).

ZAKARIA H.A. (1989). Malaysia: quasi democracy in a divided society in DIAMOND, L. *et al.* (eds), *Democracy and Developing Countries,* 3 *Asia.*

Index